SURVEY
OF
SOCIAL
SCIENCE

SURVEY
OF
SOCIAL
SCIENCE

PSYCHOLOGY SERIES

Volume 5
1905-2328

Psychoanalytic Psychology—Social Psychological Models

Edited by
FRANK N. MAGILL

Consulting Editor
JACLYN RODRIGUEZ
OCCIDENTAL COLLEGE

SALEM PRESS
Pasadena, California   Englewood Cliffs, New Jersey

Library of Congress Cataloging-in-Publication Data
Survey of social science. Psychology series/edited by
Frank N. Magill; consulting editor, Jaclyn Rodriguez.
   p. cm.
   Includes bibliographical references and index.
   1. Psychology—Encyclopedias. I. Magill, Frank Nor-
then, 1907-   . II. Rodriguez, Jaclyn.
BF31.S79   1993   93-34708
150'.3—dc20   CIP
ISBN 0-89356-732-9 (set)
ISBN 0-89356-737-x (volume 5)

Second Printing

PRINTED IN THE UNITED STATES OF AMERICA

CONTENTS

PSYCHOLOGY

PSYCHOANALYTIC PSYCHOLOGY: AN OVERVIEW

Type of psychology: Origin and definition of psychology
Fields of study: Psychodynamic and neoanalytic models; psychodynamic therapies

Psychoanalytic and neoanalytic schools of thought provide explanations of human and neurotic behavior. Each of these models contributes to the understanding of personality development and psychological conflict by presenting unique theoretical conceptualizations, assessment techniques, research methodologies, and psychotherapeutic strategies for personality change.

Principal terms
ANALYTIC PSYCHOLOGY: a school of psychology founded by Carl Jung which views the human mind as the result of prior experiences and the preparation of future goals; deemphasizes the role of sexuality in psychological disorders
DYNAMIC CULTURAL SCHOOLS OF PSYCHOANALYSIS: two branches of psychoanalysis, represented in the schools of Karen Horney and Harry Stack Sullivan, both emphasizing cultural, environmental, and social factors
INDIVIDUAL PSYCHOLOGY: a school of psychology founded by Alfred Adler which stresses the unity of the person and his or her striving for superiority in order to compensate for feelings of inferiority
NEOANALYTIC PSYCHOLOGY: schools of psychology that extended and revised the ideas proposed by Freud; included are the theories of Adler, Jung, Horney, Sullivan, and Erikson
PSYCHOANALYTIC PSYCHOLOGY: a school of psychology founded by Sigmund Freud, which provides a theory concerning mental disorders, a procedure for examining mental processes, and the therapeutic technique of psychoanalysis
PSYCHOSOCIAL THEORY: an eight-stage model of human growth and psychosocial development proposed by Erik Erikson, emphasizing the role played by social and cultural forces

Overview

One grand theory in psychology that dramatically revolutionized the way in which personality and its formation were viewed is psychoanalysis. Orthodox psychoanalysis and later versions of this model offer several unique perspectives of personality development, assessment, and change.

The genius of Sigmund Freud (1856-1939), the founder of psychoanalysis, is revealed in the magnitude of his achievements and the monumental scope of his works. Over the course of his lifetime, Freud developed a theory of personality and psychopathology, a method for probing the realm of the unconscious mind, and a therapy for dealing with personality disorders. He posited that an individual is motivated by unconscious forces that are instinctual in nature. The two major instinctual forces are the life instincts, or Eros, and the death instinct, or Thanatos. Their source is biological tension whose aim is tension reduction through a variety of objects. Freud viewed personality as a closed system composed of three structures: the id, ego, and superego. The irrational id consists of the biological drives and libido, or psychic energy. It operates according to the pleasure principle, which seeks the immediate gratification of needs. The rational ego serves as the executive component of personality and the mediator between the demands of the id, superego, and environment. Governed by the reality principle, it seeks to postpone the gratification of needs. The superego, or moral arm of personality, consists of the conscience (internalized values) and ego ideal (that which the person aspires to be).

According to Freud, the origins of personality are embedded in the first seven years of life. Personality develops through a sequence of psychosexual stages which focus upon an area of the body (erogenous zone) that gives pleasure to the individual; these are the oral, anal, phallic, latency, and genital stages. The frustration or overindulgence of needs contributes to a fixation, or arrest in development at a particular stage.

Clinically speaking, Freud also developed a therapy for treating individuals experiencing personality disturbances. Psychoanalysis has shown how physical disorders have psychological roots, how unbearable anxiety generates conflict, and how problems in adulthood result from early childhood experiences. In therapy, Freud surmounted his challenge to reveal the hidden nature of the unconscious by exposing the resistances and transferences of his patients. His method for probing a patient's unconscious thoughts, motives, and feelings was based upon the use of many clinical techniques. Free association, dream interpretation, analyses of slips of the tongue, misplaced objects, and humor enabled him to discover the contents of an individual's unconscious mind and open the doors to a new and grand psychology of personality.

Erik Erikson's (1902-   ) theory of psychosocial development occupies a position between orthodox psychoanalysis and neoanalytic schools of thought. His theory builds upon the basic concepts and tenets of Freudian psychology by illustrating the influential role of social and cultural forces in personality development. Erikson's observations of infants and investigations of the parent-child relationship in various societies contributed to his development of the model of the eight stages of human development. He proposes that personality unfolds over the entire life cycle according to a predetermined plan. As an individual moves through this series of stages, he or she encounters periods of vulnerability that require him or her to resolve crises of a social nature and develop new abilities and patterns of behavior. Erikson's eight psychosocial stages not only parallel Freud's psychosexual ones but, more important, have contributed immensely to contemporary thought in developmental psychology.

Several other schools of thought arose in opposition to Freudian orthodoxy. Among the proponents of these new psychoanalytic models were Carl Gustav Jung (1875-1961), Alfred Adler (1870-1937), Karen Horney (1885-1952), and Harry Stack Sullivan (1892-1949). These theorists advocated revised versions of Freud's psychoanalytic model and became known as the neo-analysts.

Jung's analytical psychology stresses the complex interaction of opposing forces within the total personality (psyche) and the manner in which these inner conflicts influence development. Personality is driven by general life process energy, called libido. It operates according to the principle of opposites, for example, a contrast between conscious and unconscious. An individual's behavior is seen as a means to some end, whose goal is to create a balance between these polar opposites through a process of self-realization. Personality is composed of several regions, including the ego (a unifying force at the center of consciousness), the personal unconscious (experiences blocked from consciousness), and the collective unconscious (inherited predispositions of ancestral experiences). The major focus of Jung's theory is the collective unconscious, with its archetypes (primordial thoughts and images), persona (public self), anima/animus (feminine and masculine components), shadow (repulsive side of the personality), and self (an archetype reflecting a person's striving for personality integration). Jung further proposed two psychological attitudes the personality could use in relating to the world: introversion and extroversion. He also identified four functions of thought: sensing, thinking, feeling, and intuiting. Eight different personality types emerge when one combines these attitudes and functions. Like Freud, Jung proposed developmental stages: childhood, young adulthood, and middle age. Through the process of individuation, a person seeks to create an inner harmony that results in self-realization. In conjunction with dream analysis, Jung used painting therapy and a word association test to disclose underlying conflicts in patients. Therapy helped patients to reconcile the conflicting sides of their personalities and experience self-realization.

The individual psychology of Adler illustrates the significance of social variables in personality development and the uniqueness of the individual. Adler proposed that an individual seeks to compensate for inborn feelings of inferiority by striving for superiority. It is a person's life-style that helps a person achieve future goals, ideals, and superiority. Adler extended this theme of perfection to society by using the concept of social interest to depict the human tendency to create a productive society. He maintained that early childhood experiences play a crucial role in the development of a person's unique life-style. An individual lacking in social interest develops a mistaken life-style (for example, an inferiority complex). Physical inferiority as well as spoiling or pampering and neglecting children contributes to the development of faulty life-styles. Adler examined dreams, birth order, and first memories to trace the origins of life-style and goals. These data were used in psychotherapy to help the person create a new social-interest-oriented life-style.

Horney's social and cultural psychoanalysis considers the influence of social and cultural forces upon the development and maintenance of neurosis. Her theory focuses upon disturbed human relationships, especially between parents and children.

She discussed several negative factors, such as parental indifference, erratic behavior, and unkept promises, which contributed to basic anxiety in children. This basic anxiety led to certain defenses or neurotic needs. Horney proposed ten neurotic needs that are used to reestablish safety. She further summarized these needs into three categories that depicted the individual's adjustment to others: moving toward people (compliant person), moving against people (aggressive person), and moving away from people (detached person). Horney believed that neurosis occurs when an individual lives according to his or her ideal rather than real self. She also wrote a number of articles on feminine psychology that stressed the importance of cultural rather than biological factors in personality formation. Like Freud, she used the techniques of transference, dream analysis, and free association in her psychotherapy; however, the goal of therapy was to help an individual overcome his or her idealized neurotic self and become more real as he or she experienced self-realization.

Sullivan's interpersonal theory examines personality from the perspective of the interpersonal relationships that have influenced it, especially the mother-infant relationship. Sullivan believed that this relationship contributed to an individual's development of a "good me," "bad me," or "not me" personification of self. He also proposed six stages of development: infancy, childhood, juvenile epoch, preadolescence, early adolescence, and late adolescence. These stages illustrate an individual's experiences and need for intimacy with significant others. Overall, his theory emphasizes the importance of interpersonal relations, the appraisals of others toward an individual, and the need to achieve interpersonal security and avoid anxiety.

Applications

Psychoanalytic psychology and its later versions have been used to explain normal and abnormal personality development. Regardless of their perspectives, psychologists in all these schools have relied upon the case study method to communicate their theoretical insights and discoveries.

The theoretical roots of orthodox psychoanalysis may be traced to the famous case of "Anna O.," a patient under the care of Josef Breuer, Freud's friend and colleague. Fascinated with the hysterical symptoms of this young girl and with Breuer's success in using catharsis (the talking cure) with her, Freud asked Breuer to collaborate on a work entitled *Studien über Hysterie* (1895; *Studies in Hysteria*, 1950) and discuss his findings. It was the world's first book on psychoanalysis, containing information on the unconscious, defenses, sexual cause of neurosis, resistance, and transference. Freud's own self-analysis and analyses of family members and other patients further contributed to the changing nature of his theory. Among his great case histories are "Dora" (hysteria), "Little Hans" (phobia), the "Rat Man" (obsessional neurosis), the "Schreiber" case (paranoia), and the "Wolf Man" (infantile neurosis). His method of treatment, psychoanalysis, is also well documented in contemporary cases such as the one described in the book *Sybil* (1974).

In his classic work *Childhood and Society* (1950), Erikson discussed the applicability of the clinical method of psychoanalysis and the case-history technique to normal development in children. His case analyses of the Sioux and Yurok Indians and his observations of children led to the creation of a psychosocial theory of development that emphasized the significant role played by one's culture. Moreover, Erikson's psychohistorical accounts, *Young Man Luther: A Study in Psychoanalysis and History* (1958) and *Gandhi's Truth on the Origins of Militant Nonviolence* (1969), illustrated the applications of clinical analyses to historical and biographical research so prominent today.

The founders of other psychoanalytic schools of thought have similarly shown that their theories can best be understood in the context of the therapeutic situations and in the writings of case histories. Harold Greenwald's *Great Cases in Psychoanalysis* (1959) is an excellent source of original case histories written by Freud, Jung, Adler, Horney, and Sullivan. Jung's case of "The Anxious Young Woman and the Retired Business Man" clarifies the differences and similarities between his theory and Freud's psychoanalytic model. In "The Drive for Superiority," Adler uses material from several cases to illustrate the themes of life-style, feelings of inferiority, and striving for superiority. Horney's case of "The Ever Tired Editor" portrays her use of the character analysis method; that is, she concentrates upon the way in which a patient characteristically functions. Sullivan's case of "The Inefficient Wife" sheds some light on the manner in which professional advice may be given to another (student) practitioner. In retrospect, all these prominent theorists have exposed their independent schools of thought through case histories. Even today, this method continues to be used to explain human behavior and to enhance understanding of personality functioning.

Context

Historically, the evolution of psychoanalytic psychology originated with Freud's clinical observations of the work conducted by the famous French neurologist Jean Martin Charcot and his collaborations on the treatment of hysteria neurosis with Breuer. The publication of *Studies in Hysteria* marked the birth of psychoanalysis since it illustrated a theory of hysteria, a therapy of catharsis, and an analysis of unconscious motivation. Between 1900 and 1920, Freud made innumerable contributions to the field. His major clinical discoveries were contained in the publications *Die Traumdeutung* (1900; *The Interpretation of Dreams*, 1913) and *Drei Abhandlungen zur Sexualtheorie* (1905; *Three Contributions to the Sexual Theory*, 1910; also translated as *Three Essays on the Theory of Sexuality* in 1949) as well as in various papers on therapy, case histories, and applications to everyday life. During this time, Freud began his international correspondence with people such as Jung. He also invited a select group of individuals to his home for evening discussions; these meetings were known as the psychological Wednesday society. Eventually, these meetings led to the establishment of the Vienna Psychoanalytical Society, with Adler as its president, and the First International Psychoanalytical Congress, with Jung as its president. In 1909, Freud, Jung, and others were invited by President G. Stanley Hall of Clark University to come to the United States to deliver a series of introductory lectures on psychoanalysis. This momentous occasion acknowledged Freud's achievements and gave him international recognition. In subsequent years, Freud reformulated his theory and demonstrated how psychoanalysis could be applied to larger social issues.

Trained in psychoanalysis by Anna Freud, Erikson followed in Freud's footsteps by supporting and extending his psychosexual theory of development with eight stages of psychosocial identity. Among the members of the original psychoanalytic group, Adler was the first to defect from the Freudian school, in 1911. Protesting Freud's Oedipus complex, Adler founded his own individual psychology. Two years later (in 1913), Jung parted company with Freud to establish his analytical psychology; he objected to Freud's belief that all human behavior stems from sex. With Horney's publications *New Ways in Psychoanalysis* (1939) and *Our Inner Conflicts: A Constructive Theory of Neurosis* (1945), it became quite clear that her ideas remotely resembled Freud's. Objecting to a number of Freud's major tenets, she attributed the development of neurosis and the psychology of being feminine to social, cultural, and interpersonal influences. Similarly, Sullivan extended psychoanalytic psychology to interpersonal phenomena, arguing that the foundations of human nature and development are not biological but rather cultural and social.

The accomplishments of Freud and his followers are truly remarkable. The creative genius of each theorist spans a lifetime of effort and work. The magnitude of their achievements is shown in their efforts to provide new perspectives on personality development and psychopathology, theories of motivation, psychotherapeutic methods of treatment, and methods for describing the nature of human behavior. Clearly, these independent schools of thought have had a profound influence not only upon the field of psychology, but also upon art, religion, anthropology, sociology, and literature. Undoubtedly, they will continue to serve as the cornerstone of personality theory and provide the foundation for new and challenging theories of tomorrow—theories that seek to discover the true nature of what it means to be human.

Bibliography

Adler, Alfred. *Social Interest, a Challenge to Mankind.* New York: Capricorn Books, 1964. An excellent summary of Adler's theories of human nature and social education, incorporating his ideas on life-style, inferiority/superiority complex, neurosis, childhood memories, and social feelings. Also contains a chapter on the consultant and patient relationship, and a questionnaire for understanding and treating difficult children.
Erikson, Erik Homburger. *Identity, Youth, and Crisis.* New York: W. W. Norton, 1968. An impressive summation of Erikson's theories of human nature and development and the importance of societal forces. Erikson discusses his clinical observations, the life cycle and the formation of identity, and case histories to illustrate identity confusion and other relevant issues. This book carries forward concepts expressed in *Childhood and Society* (1963).

Freud, Sigmund. *A General Introduction to Psychoanalysis.* New York: W. W. Norton, 1977. An easy-to-read account of Freud's complete theory of psychoanalysis. Freud presents twenty-eight lectures to reveal major aspects of his theory, essential details in his method of psychoanalysis, and the results of his work. He also examines the psychology of errors, dream analysis technique, and general theory of neurosis.

Greenwald, Harold, ed. *Great Cases in Psychoanalysis.* New York: Ballantine, 1959. An outstanding source of case histories written by the theorists themselves. Greenwald uses these case histories to portray the historical context of the psychoanalytic movement. These original case studies provide insight into therapeutic methods used by these great analysts as well as their assessments. Included are Freud, Adler, Jung, Horney, and Sullivan.

Horney, Karen. *The Neurotic Personality of Our Time.* New York: W. W. Norton, 1937. This classic work contains Horney's portrayal of the neurotic personality and the relevance of cultural forces in the etiology of psychological disturbances. This post-Freudian document examines Horney's theoretical conceptualizations, including basic anxiety, neurotic trends, methods of adjustment, and the role played by culture.

Sullivan, Harry Stack. *The Interpersonal Theory of Psychiatry.* New York: W. W. Norton, 1953. A classic work on human development from an interpersonal perspective. Sullivan provides a comprehensive overview of his theory by describing his key concepts and developmental stages. He further illustrates the application of his theory by focusing upon inappropriate interpersonal relationships.

Joan Bartczak Cannon

Cross-References

Analytical Psychology: Carl G. Jung, 240; Case-Study Methodologies, 481; Dream Analysis, 830; Ego Defense Mechanisms, 860; Ego Psychology: Erik Erikson, 867; Individual Psychology: Alfred Adler, 1275; Psychoanalysis: Classical versus Modern, 1898; Psychoanalytic Psychology and Personality: Sigmund Freud, 1912; Psychology of Women: Karen Horney, 1950; Psychosexual Development, 1969; Psychotherapeutic Effectiveness, 1989; Social Psychological Models: Erich Fromm, 2318; Social Psychological Models: Karen Horney, 2324.

PSYCHOANALYTIC PSYCHOLOGY AND
PERSONALITY: SIGMUND FREUD

Type of psychology: Personality
Fields of study: Classic analytic themes and issues; personality theory;
psychodynamic and neoanalytic models

Sigmund Freud's theory of personality, emphasizing unconscious motivation, sexual instincts, and psychological conflict, is one of the most profound and unique contributions in psychology. Freud described both the normal and abnormal personality, and he proposed a therapy for the treatment of mental problems.

Principal terms

ANAL STAGE: the second psychosexual stage of development, approximately from ages two to four; sexual energy is focused on the anus, and conflicts center on toilet training

EGO: the part of the personality responsible for perceiving reality and thinking; mediates between the demands of the id, superego, and reality

GENITAL STAGE: the fourth psychosexual stage, beginning at adolescence; sexual excitation from the oral and anal zones is integrated into mature, genital sexuality

ID: the most primitive part of the personality, composed of the instincts

INSTINCTS: psychological representations of biological needs, they are the source of all psychological energy; the sexual instincts are the most important in Freudian theory

LATENCY: the period between approximately age six and adolescence, when sexual instincts are not strongly manifested; strictly speaking, not a psychosexual stage

OEDIPAL CONFLICT: sexual attraction for the parent of the opposite sex, and jealousy of and fear of retribution from the parent of the same sex; first manifested in phallic stage (in girls, sometimes called the "Electra complex")

ORAL STAGE: the first stage of psychosexual development, from birth to approximately age two; sexual energy focuses on the mouth, and conflicts may arise over feeding

PHALLIC STAGE: the third stage of psychosexual development, from approximately age four to six; sexual energy focuses on the genitals

SUPEREGO: the part of the personality internally representing the ideals and punishments of society, as transmitted by one's caregivers; it strives for moral perfection

Overview

Sigmund Freud saw people as engaged in a personal struggle between their instinctual urges and the requirements of society. This conflict often takes place outside one's awareness, in the unconscious, and affects all aspects of people's lives. The instinctual energy which fuels the mind has its source in the unconscious. It is highly mobile, and once engaged must achieve expression, however disguised the expression might be.

Freud likened the mind to an iceberg in that most of the mind is below the level of awareness—in the unconscious—as most of the mass of an iceberg is below the surface of the water. The id, the most primitive structure in the mind, is in the unconscious. The id is composed of the instincts, including the sexual and other life instincts and the aggressive and other death instincts. For Freud, the sexual instincts were particularly important. They take a long time to develop, and society has a large investment in their regulation.

The instincts press for gratification, but the id itself cannot satisfy them, because it has no contact with reality. Therefore, the ego, which contacts the id in the unconscious, but also is partly conscious, develops. The ego can perceive reality and direct behavior to satisfy the id's urges. To the extent that the ego can satisfy the id's instincts, it gains strength, which it can then use to energize its own processes, perceiving and thinking. It is important that the ego can also use its energy to restrict or delay the expression of the id. The ego uses psychological defense mechanisms to protect the individual from awareness of threatening events and to regulate the expression of the instincts. For example, a strong ego can use the defense mechanism of sublimation to direct some sexual energy into productive work rather than sexual activity itself.

In the course of development, the superego develops from the ego. The ego attaches energy to the significant people in the child's world—the caregivers—and their values are then adopted as the child's own ideal and conscience. This process becomes particularly significant during the phallic stage, between the ages of four and six. At that time, the child becomes sexually attracted to the opposite-sex parent. In giving up that passion, the child adopts the characteristics of the same-sex parent; this process shapes the child's superego. The superego is mostly unconscious, and it strives for perfection. Throughout life, the id will strive for instinctual gratification, and the superego will strive for perfection. It is the task of the ego to mediate between the two, when necessary, and to chart a realistic life course.

Freud considered the childhood years particularly significant, not only because during these years the ego and superego develop from energy captured from the id, but also because during this time the sexual instincts manifest themselves in a variety of forms. The sexual instincts become focused on particular erogenous zones of the child's body in a set order. This produces a series of psychosexual stages, each characterized by instinctual urges, societal response, conflict, and resolution. During the course of this process, lasting personality traits and defenses develop. At first, the sexual energy is focused on the mouth. In this, the oral stage, conflicts may surround feeding. At approximately age two, the anal stage begins. The sexual instincts focus on the anus, and conflicts may occur around toilet training. The phallic stage, in which the child is attracted to the opposite-sex parent, follows. According to Freud, for boys this Oedipal conflict can be severe, as they fear castration from their father in retribution for their attraction to their mother. For girls, the conflict is somewhat less severe; in Freudian psychology, this less-severe conflict means that in adulthood women will have less mature personalities than men. At approximately age six, the sexual instincts go into abeyance, and the child enters a period of latency. In adolescence, the sexual instincts again come to the fore, in the genital stage, and the adolescent has the task of integrating the impulses from all the erogenous zones into mature genital sexuality.

Psychological problems occur when the psychosexual stages have left the instinctual urges strongly overgratified or undergratified, when the instincts are overly strong, when the superego is overly tyrannical, or when the ego has dealt with childhood traumas by severe repression of its experiences into the unconscious. Undergratification or overgratification of the instincts during childhood can result in fixations, incomplete resolutions of childhood conflicts. For example, a person who is severely toilet trained can develop an "anal character," becoming either excessively neat, miserly, or otherwise "holding things inside." If the id urges are too strong, they may overwhelm the ego, resulting in psychosis. An overly strong superego can lead to excessive guilt. If the ego represses childhood trauma, relegating it to the unconscious, that trauma will persist, outside awareness, in affecting a person's thoughts and behaviors.

Freud believed that no one could escape the conflicts inherent in the mind but that one could gain greater familiarity with one's unconscious and learn to direct instinctual energies in socially appropriate ways. This was the task of psychoanalysis, a form of therapy in which a client's unconscious conflicts are explored to allow the individual to develop better ways of coping.

Applications

Freud's theory has had a dramatic impact on Western society, strongly influencing the ways people view themselves and their interactions with others. Terms such as "Freudian slip," "Oedipal complex," and "unconscious" are a part of everyday language. Emotions may be seen as "buried deep," and emotional expression may be called therapeutic. Assumptions about the unconscious influence both popular and professional conceptions of mental life.

The assumption that the expression of emotion is healthy and the repression of emotion is unhealthy may be traced to Freud. To some extent, this idea has received support from research which suggests that unresolved anger may contribute to physical health problems. Unfortunately, the release of anger in verbal or physical aggression may cause those aggressive behaviors to increase rather than decrease. The vicarious experience of aggression via watching television or films may also teach aggression rather than reduce the urge to aggress.

Freud believed that dreams were one vehicle of unconscious expression. He viewed dreams as expressing the fulfillment of a wish, generally of a sexual nature. During sleep, the ego relaxes its restrictions on the id; instinctual wishes from the id, or repressed material from the unconscious, may be manifested in a dream. The bizarre sense of time and the confusing combinations of people and odd incidents in dreams reflect that the unconscious is without a sense of time, logic, or morality.

In dreams, the ego transforms material from the id to make it less threatening. Once one awakens, the ego disguises the true meaning of the dream further. Important points will be repressed and forgotten, and distortions will occur as the dream is remembered or told. For this reason, it is virtually impossible, according to Freud, to interpret one's own dreams accurately. A psychoanalyst interprets dreams by asking a patient to free associate—to say whatever comes to mind—about the dream content. In this fashion, the censoring of the ego may be relaxed, and the true meaning will be revealed to the therapist.

Revealing unconscious material is at the center of Freudian psychotherapy. Since Freud, many have viewed psychological problems as the result of childhood conflicts or traumas. Once the source is revealed, the patient is expected to improve. The nature of treatment is considerably more complicated than this might suggest, because the patient's ego may actively defend against acknowledging painful unconscious material. One of the few cases that Freud reported in detail was that of "Dora." Dora was referred to Freud because of a persistent cough that was assumed to be of psychological origin. According to Freud, such physical symptoms often are the result of childhood sexual conflict. Dora's cough and other psychosomatic complaints were found to be rooted in her sexual attraction to her father and to other men who were seen as resembling him—including a family friend, and even Freud himself. Her attraction was accompanied by jealousy of her mother and the family friend's wife. The situation was complicated, because Dora's father was having an affair with the family friend's wife, to whom Dora was also attracted, and the family friend had expressed his attraction for Dora.

All this and more is revealed in two dreams of Dora's that Freud analyzes in detail. The first is a dream of being awakened by her father, dressing quickly, and escaping a house that is on fire. The dream does its work by equating her father with the family friend, who once really was beside her bed as she awoke from a nap. This caused her to decide to "dress quickly" in the mornings, lest the friend come upon her unclothed. Her unconscious attraction for the friend, however, is belied by the symbol of fire, which might be likened to consuming passion. In her second dream, Dora dreamed that her father was dead and that a man said "Two and a half hours more." The dream symbolizes both Dora's turning away from her father as an object of her sexual interest and her intention (not evident to Freud at the time) of leaving therapy after two more sessions.

If Dora had not stopped therapy prematurely, Freud would have continued to bring his interpretation of her unconscious conflicts to the fore. In particular, he would have used her transference of childhood emotions to Freud himself as a vehicle for making the material revealed by her dreams, free associations, and behaviors evident to consciousness. The use of such transference is a key element of psychoanalysis. While this would not have completely resolved Dora's strong instinctual urges, it would have allowed her to come to terms with them in more mature ways, perhaps by choosing an appropriate marriage partner. Indeed, Freud reveals at the end of his report of this case that Dora married a young man she mentioned near the end of her time in therapy.

Context

Freud was a unique, seminal thinker. His theory was controversial from its inception; at the same time, however, it is such a powerful theory that, while many have criticized it, no subsequent personality theorist has been able to ignore the ideas Freud advanced. Psychoanalytic theory has also provided an interpretive framework for literary critics, historians, philosophers, and others.

Freud's theory was a product of his personal history, his training in science and medicine, and the Viennese culture in which he lived. Freud's early training was as a neurologist. As he turned from neurology to psychology, he continued to apply the skills of careful observation to this new discipline and to assume that the human mind followed natural laws that could be discovered. Viennese society at the time of Freud was one of restrictive social attitudes, particularly for women, and of covert practices that fell far short of public ideals. Thus it was relatively easy to see the psychological problems of the middle-class Viennese women who often were Freud's patients as being attributable to sexual conflicts.

Although Freud himself was dedicated to developing a science of mental life, his methods are open to criticism on scientific grounds. His theory is based upon his experiences as a therapist and his own self-analysis. His conclusions may therefore be restricted to the particular people or time his work encompassed. He did not seek to corroborate what his patients told him by checking with others outside the therapy room. Freud was not interested in the external "truth" of a report as much as its inner psychological meaning. He did not make details of his cases available to scrutiny, perhaps because of confidentiality. Although he wrote extensively about his theory, only five case histories were published. In all, these difficulties make the assessment of Freudian theory in terms of traditional scientific criteria problematic.

Freud's theory has had strong adherents as well as critics. Although theorists such as Alfred Adler and Carl Jung eventually broke with Freud, arguing against the primacy of the sexual instincts, his influence can be seen in their theories. Similarly, the important work of Erik Erikson describing human development through the life span has its roots in psychoanalytic theory. Many contemporary psychoanalytic theorists place a greater emphasis on the ego than did Freud, seeing it as commanding its own source of energy, independent of and equal to the id. Much contemporary literature and social criticism also possess a Freudian flavor.

Bibliography

Freud, Sigmund. *An Outline of Psychoanalysis.* Translated by James Strachey. New York: W. W. Norton, 1949. A brief introduction to Freudian theory. Beginning students of Freud may find the tone too didactic and the treatment too abbreviated; however, it is valuable when read in conjunction with a good summary of Freud from a secondary source.

Gay, Peter. *Freud: A Life for Our Time.* New York: W. W. Norton, 1988. A very well-written biography of Freud. Places Freud's work in historical and psychological context. Accessible to the reader who may only have a passing familiarity with Freudian theory.

_____, ed. *The Freud Reader.* New York: W. W. Norton, 1989. A well-edited volume of selections of Freud's work. *The Interpretation of Dreams, Fragment of an Analysis of a Case of Hysteria ("Dora")*, and *Three Essays on the Theory of Sexuality* are particularly important in defining the basics of Freud's theory.

Hall, Calvin Springer, and Gardner Lindzey. "Freud's Classical Psychoanalytical Theory." In *Theories of Personality.* 3d ed. New York: John Wiley & Sons, 1978. This chapter is the classic textbook summary of Freud's theory. Very readable, thorough, and accurate. Also presents a brief discussion of psychoanalytic research methods and criticisms of the theory.

Jones, Ernest. *The Life and Work of Sigmund Freud.* Edited and abridged by Lionel Trilling and Steven Marcus. New York: Basic Books, 1961. This is an abridged edition of Jones's three-volume biography of Freud. Jones was a confidant of Freud, and his official biographer. Interesting as an "insider's" account of Freud's life.

Kardiner, Abram. *My Analysis with Freud.* New York: W. W. Norton, 1977. Kardiner is a well-known analyst. This brief volume is a personal account of his own analysis, with Freud as the therapist. A fascinating "insider's" account of Freudian analysis and the forces that shaped the psychoanalytic movement.

Susan E. Beers

Cross-References

Abnormality: Psychodynamic Models, 74; Dream Analysis, 830; Ego Defense Mechanisms, 860; Psychoanalysis: Classical versus Modern, 1898; Psychoanalytic Psychology: An Overview, 1905; Psychology of Women: Karen Horney, 1950; Psychology of Women: Sigmund Freud, 1956; Psychosexual Development, 1969; Psychotherapeutic Effectiveness, 1989; Psychotherapeutic Goals and Techniques, 1996; Psychotherapy: Historical Approaches to Treatment, 2002; Psychotherapy with Children, 2009.

PSYCHOLINGUISTICS

Type of psychology: Language
Fields of study: Cognitive processes; thought

Psycholinguistics, or the psychology of language, examines one of the most important questions of cognition: how people use language to communicate. It investigates the mental processes involved in the production and comprehension of language (spoken, written, or signed), the mental representation of linguistic knowledge, and how language is acquired.

Principal terms
DISAMBIGUATION: the process of determining which meaning is intended from among the possible alternatives
DISCOURSE: generally refers to language units larger than the sentence or utterance—paragraphs, stories, conversations, novels, speeches
LEXICAL ACCESS: the process by which listeners and readers understand word meanings or by which speakers or writers select words, presumably by accessing some mental dictionary
LINGUISTICS: a field of inquiry that focuses on the underlying structure of language; linguists study phonology (the sound system), syntax (sentence structure), and semantics (meaning), among other topics
MODELING: the enterprise of constructing a simulation of a psychological process, using either traditional computers or computer-simulated networks of neuronlike units
MODULARITY: the assumption that processing stages in production and comprehension are independent and follow a strict sequence; by strict modularity, phonological processing happens independently of semantic processing
PSYCHOLOGICAL REALITY: the proposal that linguists' theoretical constructs, created from analysis of linguistic structure, correspond to actual psychological processes
REPRESENTATION: the format or code in which information is embodied in the mind

Overview

Broadly defined, psycholinguistics is the study of language use. Psycholinguists study the mental processes involved in the production and comprehension of language, as well as the mental representation of linguistic information. Psycholinguists ask a wide variety of questions about language and cognition. They are concerned with how words are organized in people's mental dictionaries so that they can be retrieved quickly and conveniently and with what people remember from what they hear and read. People may understand what they hear or read word by word, for example, or they may "chunk" the information. Do such chunks correspond to grammatical structure? Psycholinguists ask how intentions are translated into grammatical sequences so that people can produce coherent strings of words and sentences. How do people then organize their thoughts into larger structures so that longer sequences of utterances make sense? How do hearers or readers, in turn, understand such longer sequences? Yet another question is how, in a conversation, people know whether they have been understood. How does a person tailor what is said to particular addresses? How do children acquire so much language so quickly? How do speakers of more than one language process language?

Psycholinguistics began as psychology's response to strong psychological claims made in the field of theoretical linguistics. Linguist Noam Chomsky, for example, made claims about language processing based on his structural analyses of language, but no one had yet tested whether these claims were "psychologically real." Much of the early research in psycholinguistics focused on the psychological reality of grammatical (syntactic) structures, but as the field evolved, more and more processes were found to be relevant to answering such questions. Psycholinguists now study production processes such as how people conceive of messages, how they plan them, and how they produce them. Psycholinguistics also involves comprehension processes such as how people analyze and parse the incoming stream of language, how they access words, how they figure out the grammar of the message, how they distinguish among multiple possible meanings, how they determine word and sentence meaning, and how they determine speakers' or writers' intentions. Psycholinguists study the knowledge required to engage in interactive communication and look at how speaking and understanding vary among different media of communication (face-to-face conversation, telephone conversation, letter-writing, electronic mail, and so on). Many psycholinguists study how children acquire language in all its complexity.

Defining the limits of the field of psycholinguistics is difficult, since language pervades so many psychological phenomena and since it is studied in a number of fields besides psychology (for example, linguistics, literature, sociology, anthropology, computer science, and neuroscience). Psycholinguists inform and are informed by language research in these fields. For example, much of the cognitive psychology research on memory and representation has to do with the memory and representation of linguistic expressions (syllables, words, sentences, stories), and most psycholinguists consider this research to be part of the domain of psycholinguistics.

Psycholinguists use a number of different methods of experimentation to test their hypotheses. The vast majority of studies involve human subjects in controlled laboratory situations. Psycholinguists study production processes by observing aspects of speech or writing that they elicit from subjects. These aspects vary depending on the research question, but they might include speech errors, pausing time, formulation time, word choice, changes in word choice over time, speech rate, sentence type, discourse structure, and story organization. Subjects are induced to speak or write in a number of ways, from simply being asked to respond verbally to stimuli, to participating in some task or game that happens to require speech, conversation, or writing.

Psycholinguists study comprehension processes in the laboratory using a number of measures and by engaging subjects in a variety of tasks. The most common measures include reaction time and reading time, accuracy of comprehension, accuracy of performance on a task, and memory accuracy (as measured by recognition or recall). Like the tasks used in experiments on production, the tasks used in comprehension studies vary widely depending on the research question. Subjects whose phonological processes are being studied might listen to sequences of sounds in stereo headphones and make judgments about them. Subjects whose syntactic processes are being investigated might read sentences presented on a computer screen, perhaps phrase by phrase, and press a bar when they have understood the sentences. Other subjects might be required to make a quick judgment about a word flashed on a computer screen as they listen to a stream of speech. Others might play a game that requires them to have understood their conversational partners in order to succeed.

One alternative method in psycholinguistics is modeling. In this approach, researchers devise computer simulations of already studied psychological processes, with the purpose of exploring computationally how the actual psychological process might work. Connectionist modelers devise computer-simulated networks of neuronlike units that share some properties with actual mechanisms of the human brain. For these modelers, the behavior of neural networks provides insights into how language processes might arise from human neuronal activity.

Applications

Since psycholinguists study such a broad range of topics, the kinds of applications within the field vary substantially. Studies on children's acquisition of grammatical form, for example, look quite different from studies of how adults access word meanings. Studies on how readers integrate the logical structure of a text look different from studies on what leads to speakers' slips of the tongue.

One of the enduring questions in psycholinguistics has been how the different aspects of language processing interact with one another. Researchers have isolated a number of processes required to comprehend a sentence. For example, comprehension requires both phonological processes (whereby sounds are distinguished from one another) and morphological processes (whereby words and their grammatical markers, like the English *s*, indicating the plural, are identified). It also requires syntactic processes, whereby the grammatical structure of the sentence is identified; for example, the grammatical subject is distinguished from the grammatical object, although usually not consciously. Comprehension also requires semantic processes, which identify the meanings of individual words and put them together to create sentence or utterance meaning. In addition, other processes must coordinate utterance meanings to generate discourse meaning, and to make more complex judgments about speakers' intentions, based on knowledge about speakers in general and the current speaker in particular.

The question is whether these different aspects of processing proceed simultaneously or in a strict ordering from the lowest level (phonology) to the highest (discourse). In other words, how modular are the different processes? One cannot understand the meaning of an utterance if one has not yet deciphered its phonology, but just as certainly one's expectations can influence one's perceptions of phonology. Which processes operate simultaneously? How does the context in which people perceive an utterance affect their perceptions?

One influential approach to answering this question appeared in a 1979 study by David Swinney. Swinney was concerned with how the linguistic context in which a word appeared would affect people's interpretations of the word. People actually encounter ambiguous words all the time; careful analysis of most sentences English-speaking people use shows that many common words have multiple possible interpretations. People do not, however, feel confused by these ambiguities most of the time. Swinney looked at how people resolve the ambiguities and at the extent to which the context in which the word appears reduces the ambiguity before one even starts to process the word.

He devised a clever method for answering these questions. He had subjects listen to sentences that contained an ambiguous word. The sentences also had information that would (correctly) bias a listener to pick only one of the possible meanings. For example, one such sentence had the ambiguous word "bugs":

> Rumor had it that, for years, the government building had been plagued with problems. The man was not surprised when he found several spiders, roaches, and other bugs in the corner of the room.

The word "bugs" could refer to an insect or a spying device, but in this sentence, the correct interpretation is clearly "insect." As soon as the subjects heard the ambiguous word (in this case, "bugs"), they were required to make a judgment about a string of letters that flashed onto a screen in front of them: They had to judge whether the string of letters formed a word or not. For example, the string "sew" would require a judgment of "yes" and the string "siw" would require a judgment of "no."

Among the strings of letters that were actually words (and would thus require a "yes" response), Swinney included words that fit in with the correct interpretation (such as "ant," which fits in with the "insect" interpretation of "bugs") and words that fit in with the incorrect interpretation (such as "spy," which goes with the "spying device" interpretation). He also included words that fit in with neither interpretation, such as "sew." What Swinney found was quite surprising: If he presented the to-be-judged word within 400 milliseconds of the subjects' hearing the ambiguous word, they were quicker to make their judgments for "spy" and "ant" than for "sew." After 700 milliseconds, however, subjects were quicker to make their judgments only for "ant," and slower for "spy" or "sew."

Swinney interpreted these results as follows. Immediately after people hear an ambiguous word, both (or all) possible interpretations are active in their minds. (This is why judgments of words related to both interpretations were facilitated in Swinney's study.) Within a short time, however, the correct interpretation wins out, and the incorrect one fades away. (This is why judgments after 700 milliseconds only showed availability for the correct interpretation.) Thus, while the linguistic context of an ambiguous word does help in disambiguation, this occurs only after all possible meanings have been accessed. The sentence context does not help one narrow down the search *before* one reaches the ambiguous word. This implies that lexical access starts out as a modular process, but that very quickly other processes intervene to rule out alternatives.

This is only one example of one kind of psycholinguistics experiment. The kinds of experimental studies in psycholinguistics vary substantially, and the practical implications of these studies lead in a number of different directions—most notably into therapeutic, educational, and technological areas. For example, work on the nature of phonological difficulties and speech errors has implications for how professionals treat language disorders of various sorts: speech impediments, dyslexia, aphasia (language deficits attributable to brain damage), and so on. It also has implications for how people with learning disabilities should be educated and for how computer systems that generate and recognize speech could be designed. Much of the work on comprehension has implications not only for how people can understand other people better, but also for how writers of textbooks and designers of educational software should design their materials and for how technologists might design computers that use language as people ordinarily do. Work on understanding in dyadic (two-way) conversation not only has implications for the design of human-computer interfaces, but also has therapeutic implications for people in dyadic interactions in which misunderstandings can arise, such as marital, medical, legal, and parental situations.

Context

Psycholinguistics emerged as a distinct field in psychology during the 1960's and early 1970's, but its roots can be seen in earlier changes in psychology. In the early 1960's, many psychologists—embarrassed by the telling criticisms of Noam Chomsky's works—had become aware that behaviorist explanations of language use could not account for the facts of language acquisition and use. A new approach, which has since been called the "cognitive revolution," made the study of mental processes fashionable again. Cognitive psychologists saw the explanation of language use as a central concern in understanding the mind, and they began to look for potential answers in the work of linguists such as Chomsky, who studied language's structure.

Changes in other fields also led to the advent of psycholinguistics. Advancing computer technology and psychology's awareness of information theory provided psychologists with new metaphors for the human mind and its processes—metaphors which could be applied to questions of language use. Researchers intent on getting machines to translate sentences from one language to another began to find that language use was far more complex than they had imagined. Chomsky himself added fuel to the fire with his distinction between competence (stored information about how language works) and performance (the actual processes involved in producing and understanding language). By articulating this distinction, Chomsky made it clear that the study of linguistic performance and its relations to competence was worthy of attention.

Language use is a significant part of many different areas of psychology. Clinicians and their clients use language as the medium for therapy. Researchers who deal with human subjects use language in giving instructions and in creating experimental manipulations. In many areas of psychological research, the primary data come from subjects' language use, such as oral or written answers to questions, reading time, speak-aloud protocols, and conversation. Through their language use, experimenters sometimes can influence their subjects' behavior or thinking in unintended ways (for example, by presenting presuppositions in their instructions that bias their subjects). Since language is so central to psychology, psychology cannot help but advance as further understanding of psycholinguistic processes is gained.

On a larger scale, language use is central to most human social and intellectual endeavors. Language is the medium in which a large proportion of human activity occurs: Most interchanges with other people are based at least partly on language. Even one's private thoughts may be linguistic, or may be influenced by language. As can be seen in Elizabeth Loftus' work on eyewitness testimony, the wording of an interrogator's question can influence witnesses' answers—and even witnesses' memories of what they saw. The structure of the language people use might have some influence on the kinds of thoughts they can have, which may in turn have ramifications for cross-cultural communication. A strong version of this proposal can be found in Benjamin Lee Whorf's *Language, Thought, and Reality: Selected Writings* (1956). Insights gained from psycholinguistics have implications for people's conceptions of themselves as thinking and social beings.

Bibliography

Akmajian, Adrian, Richard A. Demers, Ann K. Farmer, and Robert M. Harnish. *Linguistics: An Introduction to Language and Communication.* 3d ed. Cambridge, Mass.: MIT Press, 1990. Chapter 10 of this introductory linguistics text, "Psychology of Language: Speech Production and Comprehension," offers a clear overview of questions and ideas in psycholinguistics. The chapter is very understandable in the context of the book's preceding chapters, which constitute an excellent introduction to the ways linguists study language. Also relevant is chapter 9, "Pragmatics: The Study of Language Use and Communication."

Chomsky, Noam. *Language and Mind.* Enl. ed. New York: Harcourt Brace Jovanovich, 1972. Classic series of lectures Chomsky gave at University of California, Berkeley, in 1967, along with further chapters elaborating his views. This work, though very technical in parts, is probably the most readable of Chomsky's writings, and it exemplifies the thinking of one of the grand originators of psycholinguistics.

Clark, Herbert H. "Language Use and Language Users." In *The Handbook of Social Psychology*, edited by Gardner Lindzey and Elliot Aronson. 3d ed. New York:

Lawrence Erlbaum, 1985. This very readable chapter gives an excellent basic outline of language use in social settings. It provides a vocabulary and makes critical distinctions that inform the research of psycholinguists interested in higher-level language processes, including very clear discussions on reference, turn taking, and repair of misunderstandings.

Clark, Herbert H., and Eve V. Clark. *Psychology and Language: An Introduction to Psycholinguistics.* New York: Harcourt Brace Jovanovich, 1977. In its nearly 600 pages, this book summarizes an amazing amount of research. Clark and Clark detail complicated theories, principles, and data in clear and elegant prose, illustrated with excellent examples. A classic in the field of psycholinguistics, and an extremely comprehensive work.

Foss, Donald J., and David T. Hakes. *Psycholinguistics.* Englewood Cliffs, N.J.: Prentice-Hall, 1978. This introduction and summary of the field provides an interesting contrast to Clark and Clark's approach, as it focuses more explicitly on questions of modularity. Foss and Hakes are sympathetic to the proposals that the processing stages in both comprehension and production are independent and occur in a strict sequence, and they direct their reviews of the literature to these issues.

Just, Marcel Adam, and Patricia A. Carpenter. *The Psychology of Reading and Language Comprehension.* Boston: Allyn & Bacon, 1987. A review of the literature on language comprehension that focuses especially on reading. A good summary that will expose the reader to the details of scientific techniques for studying reading.

Levelt, Willem J. M. *Speaking: From Intention to Articulation.* Cambridge, Mass.: MIT Press, 1989. An excellent comprehensive summary of research on speech planning, production, and articulation. The book's organization reflects actual speech production, moving from the high-level principles of dyadic interaction and message planning to low-level motor control and error-repair principles. Very well written, but in its length and complexity not for the beginner.

Miller, George Armitage. *Language and Speech.* San Francisco: W. H. Freeman, 1981. Miller's short book is a good introduction to the data and theories of psycholinguistics, with interesting discussions of language evolution and development in humankind and in the individual. Miller brings up issues of biology and issues of society at large that affect language use. A very good source for the beginner.

Michael F. Schober

Cross-References

PSYCHOLOGICAL DIAGNOSIS AND CLASSIFICATION: DSM-III-R

Type of psychology: Psychopathology
Fields of study: Personality assessment; schizophrenias; stress and illness

The standard system of diagnosis and classification of psychological and emotional disorders utilizes the DSM-III-R, the revised, third edition of the Diagnostic and Statistical Manual of Mental Disorders *of the American Psychiatric Association. Mental health workers in the United States use this system of communication for insurance purposes, treatment recommendations, and overall assessment.*

Principal terms
CLUSTER ANALYSIS: analysis that involves the grouping of variables that explain the same event
FACTOR ANALYSIS: the statistical procedure of determining the key factors that describe a given event
NEUROLOGICAL PROBLEMS: problems that are the result of brain or central-nervous-system damage
PSYCHOANALYSIS: the theory and treatment of psychological disorders devised by Sigmund Freud
SUICIDAL IDEATION: thoughts and ideas that revolve around the act of suicide
VALIDITY: a statistical value that tells the degree to which a test measures what it is intended to measure; the test is usually compared to external criteria

Overview

Nearly all mental health workers in the United States employ the same system for making psychological and psychiatric diagnoses. This system, which was established by the American Psychiatric Association, is called the *Diagnostic and Statistical Manual of Mental Disorders* (rev. 3d ed., 1987, DSM-III-R). This manual was coordinated with an international diagnostic system that was established by the World Health Organization and published in the *Manual of the International Statistical Classification of Diseases, Injuries, and Causes of Death* (9th ed., 1977). This coordination of diagnoses permits researchers to investigate whether some disorders are more prevalent in certain areas and whether some disorders are virtually nonexistent in certain countries or ethnic groups.

DSM-III-R is a multiaxial classification system; that is, a patient is diagnosed on a series of relevant axes that examine various aspects of the patient's functioning. This classification system consists of five axes. Axis 1 requires the diagnostician to indicate the major disorder of the patient. This refers to the set of symptoms that best describes the patient's problems. There are fourteen categories of disorders listed under axis 1. There is one category that is not attributed to mental disorders but for which people may seek help, such as marital problems, parent-child problems, and academic or vocational problems. Generally, however, axis 1 reflects serious disorders that require treatment, such as anxiety disorders, sexual disorders, mood disorders, substance-abuse disorders, schizophrenia, dissociative disorders, organic and mental disorders, and disorders usually first evident in infancy, childhood, or adolescence. In order for a person to be diagnosed under axis 1, the patient must exhibit a required number of symptoms. The presence of a minimum number of symptoms for each disorder ensures that all diagnosticians rate the same disorder in the same way.

Axis 2 includes personality disorders or developmental disorders. Personality disorders refer to long-standing maladaptive behaviors that lead to difficulty in social or occupational functioning. Often, individuals who suffer from personality disorders exhibit antisocial behavior or paranoid or schizoid behavior, which makes it difficult for them to function effectively under ordinary circumstances. Such persons tend to resist treatment, and their pattern of adjustment tends to become progressively worse. Developmental disorders are those that occur very early in life, such as mental retardation, autistic disorders, and specific disorders of language or of motor or social skills.

Axis 3 requires the clinician to indicate any physical disorders that the patient may have or conditions that may be relevant to the management or treatment of the case, such as neurological problems or diabetes or any physical condition that could affect the patient's treatment.

Axis 4 refers to the severity of any psychosocial stress that the patient has experienced in the year preceding the evaluation that might have started the disorder, made an existing disorder worse, or caused a past mental disorder to recur. The clinician is asked to rank the severity of stresses that the person is experiencing on a scale from 1 to 6, on which 1 refers to the least amount of stress and 6 refers to catastrophic stress. Examples of moderate stress are marital separation and the loss of a job; the death of a spouse or a child is an example of severe stress.

With children or adolescents, psychosocial stressors take on a different perspective. For example, severe stress might involve the divorce of parents or an arrest by the police, while extreme stress might involve sexual or physical abuse or the death of a parent. The death of both parents or the development of a life-threatening illness such as leukemia would be considered catastrophic stress for children and adolescents.

Axis 5 is called "Global Assessment of Functioning" (GAF). This axis allows the clinician to indicate an overall judgment of the patient's psychological, social, and occupational functioning during the past year. The GAF scale is viewed as a hypothetical scale of mental health and illness. It ranges from 1 to 90. A ranking at the end of the scale near the value of 1 reflects the presence of a serious psychological disorder as a result of which the person is dangerous either to himself or herself or to others. The high end of the scale reflects the absence of symptoms or the presence of very minimal symptoms; in other words, it indicates a person who is functioning well in daily life.

This classification system is a noticeable improvement over those of previous diagnostic manuals. The format of five axes allows clinicians to describe more accurately the symptoms and syndromes the patient is expressing. It also allows the clinician to indicate several diagnoses for the same patient if they happen to coexist. For example, while the patient may be principally exhibiting a depressed mode, he or she may also be experiencing a personality disorder. This system allows for a broader perspective on the patient's functioning, since multiple diagnoses may be made.

Characteristically, the clinician will assess the patient on the first three axes. These are viewed as the important clinical axes. The last two are often used for research purposes. These axes, which provide for background information on the patient, are useful as a means of collecting information about situations and stresses that may contribute to and sustain some disorders.

Users of this system have indicated its advantages and disadvantages. Those who see its advantages point out that such a system is important in facilitating communication between professional persons. They also note that it is useful for statistical purposes, since it tracks the incidence of disorders nationally and internationally. Such a system can contribute to the planning for a patient's treatment if what the patient is experiencing is known. In addition, using specific diagnostic criteria that match a clear list of symptoms with a client's behavior increases the accuracy and reliability of the diagnosis.

Critics of the system point out that this is basically a medical approach to classification and diagnosis rather than a psychological approach. They point out that the medical model that looks for symptoms leading to treatment may not be accurate or applicable to psychological disorders. Many emotional problems show the same symptoms but emerge from different causes, often requiring very different forms of treatment.

A second criticism involves the question of the reliability and validity of the diagnosis. Reliability refers to whether clinicians viewing the same patient would arrive at the same diagnosis. While the reliability of this system is substantially better than the reliability of systems described in prior manuals, there is still some question about the reliability of the diagnosis when judging axis 2. A third criticism of this system is that it depends too much on internalized processes and ignores external events in a person's life, such as family functioning, societal pressures, and ethnic or racial differences.

Finally, some view this system as having an insufficient theoretical basis. The system simply lists symptoms and behaviors without attempting to explain the cause or the reasons for their existence. These critics believe that the system is much too descriptive, providing little explanation for the existence of the disorder itself.

Applications

Since it was first devised in 1952, the *Diagnostic and Statistical Manual of Mental*

Disorders has become an important part of the diagnostic process for most mental health workers. This is partly because almost all insurance companies require the diagnosis of a patient's illness before payment is made for services, and the DSM-III-R system has been widely accepted. The following example will illustrate the way in which clinicians translate a case study into the multiaxial system.

This is the case of a twenty-five-year-old male who came to the clinic complaining about depression, sadness, suicidal thoughts, and a general sense of hopelessness. He was born and reared in a large city on the East Coast. His mother was a caring, affectionate woman who nurtured her four children, but his father was a chronic alcoholic who verbally and physically abused his wife and children. The patient, the oldest boy in the family, was made to feel responsible for everything that went wrong.

At age seventeen, he left home and moved to California, where he had hoped the stress of life would be diminished. He found himself drinking heavily, using drugs excessively, and slowly drifting into a life of homelessness. He tried several times to obtain a job but was refused because of his disheveled appearance. In his wandering, he met a girl who shared his life of alcohol and drugs. This relationship, while superficial, was the only meaningful adult relationship that the patient had. They had traveled together for several years when, without much explanation, his girlfriend committed suicide. At this time, the patient's depression and despair became more severe, and his alcohol abuse increased significantly. Two weeks after this event, he was admitted to a mental health clinic for attempting to slash his wrists after being arrested for alcohol intoxication. The mental health worker who conducted the initial interview produced the following diagnoses.

On axis 1, the clinician diagnosed "Major Depression, severe, without psychotic features" and "Alcohol Abuse and Dependence." The clinician observed some significant symptoms that are characteristic of major depression: a depressed mood most of the day nearly every day; a marked diminished interest in any activities during the day; a significant weight loss and decrease in appetite; feelings of worthlessness and guilt, particularly over the death of the girlfriend; and recurrent thoughts of death, as well as a suicide attempt. Since this patient also had a long-standing alcohol problem, he was also diagnosed on axis 1 with a second disorder—alcohol abuse and dependence.

No diagnosis was made on axis 2 or on axis 3. On axis 4, the clinician found "Psychological Stressors." The death of the man's girlfriend by suicide was judged to have a value of 6, implying that it was catastrophic for this individual.

On axis 5, the current "Global Assessment of Functioning" was rated 10 because of the persistent danger of the patient committing suicide. The clinician was also asked to estimate the highest global assessment of functioning during the past year. Prior to the suicide attempt of his girlfriend, the patient was judged to be functioning at 50. This reflected the fact that there was suicidal ideation and that it was difficult for this young man to find and keep a job for any long period of time.

This illustrates the manner in which clinicians report information after taking a thorough history and often doing considerable psychological testing to determine the assets and liabilities of the patient's functioning at the moment.

Context

The first *Diagnostic and Statistical Manual of Mental Disorders* was published in 1952. Prior to that time, there was no systematic procedure for establishing diagnosis and classification. Clinics and hospitals devised systems that were unique to their own settings and often to their own communities. It was difficult for professionals to communicate with one another when a patient went from one setting to another or from one therapist to another.

It was not until 1952 that the American Psychiatric Association published its first manual, which attempted to define all the known psychological and psychiatric disorders. It encouraged all mental health workers to use the same terminology and the same description of disorders so that statistical data could be accumulated on the incidence of mental health disorders in various communities and states. That early manual achieved the purpose of standardizing diagnostic terms, but it had shortcomings; for example, it had no section for children or adolescents. The manual assumed that only adult disorders were diagnosable. Additionally, the manual made assumptions about the origins of disorders on the basis of only one theory: psychoanalytic theory. Since most psychiatrists at that time were psychoanalytically oriented, the manual reflected their theoretical bias in its description of some of the major disorders.

In 1968, the second revision of the *Diagnostic and Statistical Manual of Mental Disorders* was published. In this version, many disorders that had been omitted from the first volume were added. A new section—"Behavior Disorders of Childhood and Adolescence," which listed six disorders—was added. While this was a notable improvement on the prior volume, it certainly did not reflect a comprehensive understanding of disorders in children or adolescents.

In 1980, the third version of the diagnostic manual was published; a complete revision was made. This manual was more complete than the previous one; it added many more disorders that were not present in the previous volume and omitted those disorders that were duplicated or extremely rare. This volume also altered its theoretical perspective by attempting to describe behaviors rather than to explain them. No theoretical assumptions were made regarding the cause of the disorders. The clinician was to match the list of symptoms with the disorder. This volume used more precise language, increased its coverage, and introduced the multiaxial classification system that was described above. It also made a significant attempt to coordinate the manual with the International Classification of Diseases, a system adopted by the World Health Assembly of the World Health Organization, thus allowing statistical comparisons to be made between different countries and different parts of the world.

Clinical psychology has taken the view that it, too, should play a role in the establishment of the diagnosis and classification of psychological disorders. This perspective would be based on a psychological rather than a medical model. Its starting point is the assumption that measured behavior should determine the description of a syndrome. Such measured characteristics may be obtained by means of rating scales or tests. Using a statistical procedure called cluster analysis or factor analysis, one can reduce the largest number of variables into the smallest number of categories that are distinctly different from one another. These categories can be viewed as different diagnostic states. This procedure would increase the reliability of the measurement and the validity of the diagnosis; it would establish a direct relationship between the diagnosis of the clinician and the data from which that diagnosis is obtained. The American Psychological Association has discussed ways of proceeding with the establishment of such a system of classification.

Bibliography

American Psychiatric Association. *Diagnostic and Statistical Manual of Mental Disorders.* Rev. 3d ed. Washington, D.C.: Author, 1987. This manual summarizes all the psychological and psychiatric disorders and gives the criteria for each classification. Almost all mental health workers are familiar with this volume and use it when diagnoses must be made for insurance companies.

_____. *DSM-IV Options Book.* Washington, D.C.: Author, 1991. Presents the diagnostic dilemmas and debates involved in the development of the fourth diagnostic manual of the American Psychiatric Association. It was prepared by a group of recognized experts on each disorder. DSM-IV promises to be more objective and reliable than its predecessors.

Spitzer, Robert L., M. Gibbon, A. E. Skodol, J. B. W. Williams, and Michael First. *DSM-III-R Casebook: A Learning Companion to the Diagnostic and Statistical Manual of Mental Disorders.* 3d rev. ed. Washington, D.C.: American Psychiatric Press, 1989. This excellent paperback provides many case histories with accompanying diagnoses according to the DSM-III-R. The book, which also includes mental disorders of children and adolescents, discusses fascinating historical cases that were treated by such great therapists as Sigmund Freud, Emil Kraepelin, and Alois Alzheimer. In addition, presents a number of cases from Africa, India, Polynesia, and Russia.

Spitzer, Robert L., J. B. Williams, and A. E. Skodol, eds. *International Perspectives on DSM-III.* Washington, D.C.: American Psychiatric Press, 1983. Highlights the American diagnostic system from the perspective of different countries. It notes the role that ethnic and cultural differences play in the development of psychological disorders and the problems involved in making a diagnosis in another country.

World Health Organization. *Manual of the International Statistical Classification of Diseases, Injuries, and Causes of Death.* 9th rev. ed. Geneva, Switzerland: Author, 1977. An internationally recognized diagnostic system established under the auspices of the United Nations. It allows the diagnostician to record and compare disorders from around the world. The mental health section permits nations to compare the incidence of specific psychological disorders in different countries.

Gerald Sperrazzo

Cross-References

Abnormality: Behavioral Models, 33; Abnormality: Biomedical Models, 39; Abnormality: Psychodynamic Models, 74; Anxiety Disorders: Theoretical Explanations, 272; Bipolar Disorder, 422; Clinical Depression, 521; Clinical Interviewing, Testing, and Observation, 527; Schizophrenia: Theoretical Explanations, 2141.

PSYCHOLOGICAL EXPERIMENTATION: INDEPENDENT, DEPENDENT, AND CONTROL VARIABLES

Type of psychology: Psychological methodologies
Fields of study: Experimental methodologies; methodological issues

The scientific method involves the testing of hypotheses through the objective collection of data. The experiment is an important method of data collection in which the researcher systematically controls multiple factors in order to determine the extent to which changes in one variable cause changes in another variable. Only the experimental method can reveal cause-effect relationships between the variables of interest.

Principal terms

CONTROL GROUP: a group of subjects that are like subjects of the experimental groups in all ways except that they do not experience the independent variable

CONTROL VARIABLES: extraneous factors that might influence the dependent variable, making it difficult to evaluate the effect of the independent variable

DEPENDENT VARIABLE: the behavior of interest to the experimenter; it is measured to determine the effect of changes in the independent variable

ECOLOGICAL VALIDITY: the extent to which the results of a study reveal something about "real-life" phenomena

EXPERIMENT: one of several data collection methods; requires systematically manipulating the levels of an independent variable under controlled conditions in order to measure its impact on a dependent variable

FIELD EXPERIMENT: an experiment conducted outside the laboratory in a naturalistic setting

HYPOTHESIS: an educated guess or prediction that is to be tested by research

INDEPENDENT VARIABLE: the fact manipulated by the experimenter in order to assess its impact on the dependent variable

RANDOM ASSIGNMENT: a technique for creating groups of subjects across which individual differences will be evenly dispersed

Overview

Psychology is typically defined as the science of behavior and cognition and is considered a research-oriented discipline not unlike biology, chemistry, and physics. To appreciate the role of experimentation in psychology, it is useful to view it in the context of the general scientific method employed by psychologists in conducting their research. This scientific method may be described as a four-step sequence start-ing with identifying a problem and forming a hypothesis. The problem must be one suitable for scientific inquiry—that is, questions concerning values, such as whether rural life is "better" than city life, are more appropriate for philosophical debate than scientific investigation. Questions better suited to the scientific method are those that can be answered through the objective collection of facts—for example, "Are children who are neglected by their parents more likely to do poorly in school than children who are well treated?" The hypothesis is the tentative guess, or the prediction regarding the question's answer, and is based upon other relevant research and existing theory. The second step, and the one with which this article is primarily concerned, is the collection of data (facts) in order to test the accuracy of the hy-pothesis. Any one of a number of methods might be employed, including simple observation, survey, or experimentation. The third step is to make sense of the facts that have been accumulated by subjecting them to careful analysis; the fourth step is to share any significant findings with the scientific community.

In considering step two, the collection of data, it seems that people often mistak-enly use the words "research" and "experiment" interchangeably. A student might ask whether an experiment has been done on a particular topic when, in fact, the student really wants to know if *any* kind of research has been conducted in that area. All experiments are examples of research, but not all research is experimental. Re-search that is nonexperimental in nature might be either descriptive or correlational.

Descriptive research is nearly self-explanatory; it occurs when the researcher wants merely to characterize the behaviors of an individual or, more likely, a group. For example, one might want to survey the students of a high school to ascertain the level of alcohol use (alcohol use might be described in terms of average ounces consumed per student per week). One might also spend considerable time observing individuals suffering from, for example, infantile autism. A thorough description of the typical behaviors could be useful for someone investigating the cause of this dis-order. Descriptive research can be extremely valuable, but it is not useful when re-searchers want to investigate the relationship between two or more variables (things that vary, or quantities that may have different values).

In a correlational study, the researcher measures how strongly the variables are related, or the degree to which one variable predicts another variable. Suppose a researcher is interested in the relationship between exposure to violence on televi-sion (variable one) and aggressive behavior (variable two) in a group of elementary school children. She could administer a survey asking the children how much vio-lent television they view and then rank the subjects from high to low levels of this variable. The researcher could similarly interview the school staff and rank the chil-dren according to their aggressive behavior. A statistic called a correlation coeffi-cient might then be computed, revealing how the two variables are related and the strength of that relationship.

Correlational studies are not uncommon in psychological research. Often, how-ever, a researcher wants even more specific information about the relationships among variables—in particular, about whether one variable *causes* a change in another variable. In such a situation, experimental research is warranted. This drawback of the correlational approach—its inability to establish causal relationships—is worth considering for a moment. In the hypothetical study described above, the researcher may find that viewing considerable television violence predicts high levels of aggressive behavior, yet she cannot conclude that these viewing habits cause the aggressiveness. After all, it is entirely possible that aggressiveness, caused by some unknown factor, prompts a preference for violent television. That is, the causal direction is unknown; viewing television violence may cause aggressiveness, but the inverse (that aggressiveness causes the watching of violent television programs) is also feasible. As this is a crucial point, one final illustration is warranted. What if, at a certain Rocky Mountain university, a correlational study has established that high levels of snowfall predict low examination scores? One should not conclude that something about the chemical composition of snow impairs the learning process. The correlation may be real and highly predictive, but the causal culprit may be some other factor. Perhaps, as snowfall increases, so does the incidence of illness, and it is this variable that is causally related to exam scores. Maybe, as snowfall increases, the likelihood of students using their study time for skiing also increases.

Experimentation is a powerful research method because it alone can reveal cause-effect relationships. In an experiment, the researcher does not merely measure the naturally occurring relationships between variables for the purpose of predicting one from the other; rather, he or she systematically manipulates the values of one variable and measures the effect, if any, that is produced in a second variable. The variable that is manipulated is known as the independent variable; the other variable, the behavior in question, is called the dependent variable (any change in it depends upon the manipulation of the independent variable). Experimental research is characterized by a desire for control on the part of the researcher. Control of the independent variable and control over extraneous variables are both wanted. That is, there is a desire to eliminate or hold constant the factors (control variables) other than the independent variable that might influence the dependent variable. If adequate control is achieved, the researcher may be confident that it was, in fact, the manipulation of the independent variable that produced the change in the dependent variable.

Applications

Returning to the relationship between television viewing habits and aggressive behavior in children, suppose that correlational evidence indicates that high levels of the former variable predict high levels of the latter. Now the researcher wants to test the hypothesis that there is a cause-effect relationship between the two variables. She decides to manipulate exposure to television violence (the independent variable) to see what effect might be produced in the aggressiveness of her subjects (the dependent variable). She might choose two levels of the independent variable and have twenty children watch fifteen minutes of a violent detective show while another twenty children are subjected to thirty minutes of the same show. If an objective rating of playground aggressiveness later reveals more hostility in the thirty-minute group than in the fifteen-minute group, she still cannot be confident that higher levels of television violence cause higher levels of aggressive behavior. More information is needed, especially with regard to issues of control. To begin with, how does the researcher know that it is the violent content of the program that is promoting aggressiveness? Perhaps it is the case that the more time they spend watching television, regardless of subject matter, the more aggressive children become. This study needs a control group: a group of subjects identical to the experimental subjects with the exception that they do not experience the independent variable. In fact, two control groups might be employed, one that watches fifteen minutes and another that watches thirty minutes of nonviolent programming. The control groups serve as a basis against which the behavior of the experimental groups can be compared. If it is found that the two control groups aggress to the same extent, and to a lesser extent than the experimental groups, the researcher can be more confident that violent programming promotes relatively higher levels of aggressiveness.

The experimenter also needs to be sure that the children in the thirty-minute experimental group were not naturally more aggressive to begin with. One need not be too concerned with this possibility if one randomly assigns subjects to the experimental and control groups. There are certainly individual differences among subjects in factors such as personality and intelligence, but with random assignment one can be reasonably sure that those individual differences are evenly dispersed among the experimental and control groups.

The experimenter might want to control or hold constant other variables. Perhaps she suspects that age, social class, ethnicity, and gender could also influence the children's aggressiveness. She might want to make sure that these subject variables are eliminated by either choosing subjects who are alike in these ways or by making sure that the groups are balanced for these factors (for example, equal numbers of boys and girls in each group). There are numerous other extraneous variables that might concern the researcher, including the time of day when the children participate, the length of time between television viewing and the assessment of aggressiveness, the children's diets, the children's family structures (single versus dual parent, siblings versus only child), and the disciplinary styles used in the homes. Resource limitations prevent every extraneous variable from being controlled, yet the more control, the more confident the experimenter can be of the cause-effect relationship between the independent and dependent variables.

One more example of experimental research, this one nonhypothetical, will further illustrate the application of this methodology. In 1973, Mark Lepper, David Greene, and Richard Nisbett tested the hypothesis that when people are offered external rewards for performing activities that are naturally enjoyable, their interest in these activities declines. The participants in the study were nursery school children who had already demonstrated a fondness for coloring with marking pens; this was their preferred activity when given an opportunity for free play. The children were randomly assigned to one of three groups. The first group was told previously that they would receive a "good player award" if they would play with the pens when later given the opportunity. Group two received the same reward but without advance notice; they were surprised by the reward. The last group of children was the control group; they were neither rewarded nor told to expect a reward.

The researchers reasoned that the group one children, having played with the pens in order to receive a reward, would now perceive their natural interest in this activity as lower than before the study. Indeed, when all groups were later allowed a free play opportunity, it was observed that the "expected reward" group spent significantly less time than the other groups in this previously enjoyable activity. Lepper and his colleagues, then, experimentally supported their hypothesis and reported evidence that reward causes interest to decline in a previously pleasurable behavior. This research has implications for instructors; they should carefully consider the kinds of behavior they reward (with gold stars, lavish praise, high grades, and so on) as they may, ironically, be producing less of the desired behavior. An academic activity that is enjoyable play for a child may become tedious work when a reward system is attached to it.

Context

While most would agree that the birth of psychology as a science took place in Leipzig, Germany, in 1879, when Wilhelm Wundt established the first laboratory for studying psychological phenomena, there is no clear record of the first use of experimentation. Regardless, there is no disputing the attraction that many psychologists have had for this method of research in the twentieth century. Psychologists clearly recognize the usefulness of the experiment in investigating potential causal relationships between variables. Hence, experimentation is employed widely across the subfields of psychology, including developmental, cognitive, physiological, clinical, industrial, and social psychology.

This is not to say that all psychologists are completely satisfied with experimental research. It has been argued that an insidious "Catch-22" exists in some experimental research that limits the usefulness of that research. The argument goes like this: Experimenters are motivated to control rigorously the conditions of their studies and the relevant extraneous variables. To gain such control, they often conduct experiments in a laboratory setting. Therefore, subjects are often observed in an artificial environment, engaged in behaviors that are so controlled as to be unnatural, and they clearly know they are being observed—which may further alter their behavior. Such research is said to be lacking in ecological validity or applicability to "real-life" behavior. It may show how subjects behave in a unique laboratory procedure, but it tells little about psychological phenomena as displayed in everyday life. The Catch-22, then, is that experimenters desire control in order to establish that the independent variable is producing a change in the dependent variable, and the more such control, the better; however, the more control, the more risk that the research may be ecologically invalid.

Most psychologists are sensitive to issues of ecological validity and take pains to make their laboratory procedures as naturalistic as possible. Additionally, much research is conducted outside the laboratory in what are known as field experiments. In such studies, the subjects are unobtrusively observed (perhaps by a confederate of the researcher who would not attract their notice) in natural settings such as classroom, playground, or workplace. Field experiments, then, represent a compromise in that there is bound to be less control than is obtainable in a laboratory, yet the behaviors observed are likely to be natural. Such naturalistic experimentation is likely to continue to increase in the future.

Although experimentation is only one of many methods available to psychologists, it fills a particular need and that need is not likely to decline in the foreseeable future. In trying to understand the complex relationships among the many variables that affect the way people think and act, experimentation makes a valuable contribution: It is the one methodology available that can reveal unambiguous cause-effect relationships.

Bibliography

Barber, Theodore Xenophon. *Pitfalls in Human Research.* New York: Pergamon Press, 1976. It is useful to learn from the mistakes of others, and Barber provides the opportunity by describing ten categories of likely errors in designing and conducting research. This is not a long book (117 pages), and it is enjoyable reading, especially the specific accounts of flawed research.

Carlson, Neil R. *Psychology: The Science of Behavior.* 3d ed. Boston: Allyn & Bacon, 1990. The second chapter of this introductory psychology text may be the most reader-friendly reference in this bibliography. Entitled "The Ways and Means of Psychology," it provides a brief introductory overview of the scientific method, experimental and correlational research, and basic statistics; it is well suited for the novice. Colorful graphics, a concluding summary, and a list of key terms are all helpful.

Hearst, Eliot, ed. *The First Century of Experimental Psychology.* Hillsdale, N.J.: Lawrence Erlbaum, 1979. Primarily for the student interested in the history of experimental psychology. This is a 693-page book; while most of the fourteen chapters are devoted to specific topics in psychology such as emotion, development, and psychopathology, the final chapter by William Estes provides an excellent overview of experimental psychology and considers some broad, profound issues.

Shaughnessy, John J., and Eugene B. Zechmeister. *Research Methods in Psychology.* 2d ed. New York: McGraw-Hill, 1990. This is one of a number of textbooks that discusses psychological research in the light of the scientific method. It is fairly accessible, has a thorough and competent description of experimentation, and, as a bonus, considers some ethical issues. Glossary, index, and references are all provided.

Stern, Paul C. *Evaluating Social Science Research.* New York: Oxford University

Press, 1979. This is a clearly written, nonthreatening book for the early to middle-level college student. The focus of the author is on encouraging the critical analysis of research; to this end, case-research examples are presented for examination. End-of-chapter exercises are included to aid the student in integrating information.

Mark B. Alcorn

Cross-References

Animal Experimentation, 252; Complex Experimental Designs: Interactions, 625; Sources of Experimental Bias, 1006; Quasi-Experimental Designs, 2024; Sampling, 2122; The Scientific Method in Psychology, 2148; Within-Subject Experimental Designs, 2647.

PSYCHOLOGY: FIELDS OF SPECIALIZATION

Type of psychology: Origin and definition of psychology
Fields of study: Behavioral therapies; cognitive development; experimental
  methodologies; psychodynamic and neoanalytic models

*Psychology and its various fields of specialization play a growing and vital role in
everyone's lives; as basic needs are thwarted and as technology becomes more sophisticated, people increasingly rely on professionals in these fields to help them find
solutions to their problems.*

  Principal terms
    BEHAVIORISM: a subfield of psychology devoted to the study of
      observable behavior and learned responses
    COGNITIVE PSYCHOLOGY: a subfield of psychology that attempts to
      understand human behavior through studying mental processes
    GESTALT PSYCHOLOGY: a subfield of psychology which holds that the
      whole of perceived information is greater than the sum of its
      individual parts
    SOCIAL PSYCHOLOGY: a subfield of psychology that studies how
      individuals are affected by environmental factors, and particularly
      by other people
    STRUCTURALISM: an early school of psychology that studied how the
      mind is composed of basic units of consciousness

Overview

  Because the fields of specialization within psychology are so numerous, one must
first examine the science as an entity unto itself. This involves defining psychology,
exploring the reasons for its existence, reviewing its history, and surveying the diverse specialists who assist various populations. Although the semantics of defining
psychology differ from text to text, the actual explanation remains constant: It is the
science of human behavior as it relates to the functions of the mind. More specifically, it provides evidence for why people experience a gamut of emotions, think
rationally or irrationally, and act either predictably or unpredictably.
  Its very existence justifies humankind's need to plumb the depths of its interior to
search for the self, to process conflict, to solve problems, and to think critically as
well as act pragmatically. Its challenge is to assist people in understanding themselves. Humans have a natural curiosity; it moves them to try to determine their
relationship to the world in which they live. With this comes the inclination to observe and compare other people: their ideas, behavior patterns, and abilities. These
analyses and comparisons, which people cannot help but make, involve the self as
well as others. People may be either overly harsh or selectively blind when examin-

ing themselves; both these situations can handicap a person, and both can be helped by psychology.

At times, one's anxiety level may peak uncontrollably. Through the science of the mind, one seeks to temper one's agitation by becoming familiar with and acknowledging vague fears and uncomfortable feelings. Thus, one learns about the source of one's tension. From this, experts learn how behavior originates. They assist an individual in learning to cope with change; the person discovers how to make adequate adjustments in daily living. The fast pace that humans keep requires them now, more than ever before, to have a working knowledge of people—their thought processes and behavior patterns. From all of this, experts are able to arrive at reasonable predictions and logical conclusions about humankind's future behavior.

Psychology did not become accepted as a formal discipline until the late nineteenth century. Prior to that time, even back to antiquity, questions were directed to philosophers, the wise men of the time. Though they were versed in reasoning, logic, and academia, only a few of these scholars could deal with the complexities of the human mind. Their answers were profound and lengthy, but these scholars frequently left their audiences bewildered and without the solutions they sought. Some of these logicians used the Socratic method of reasoning; they often frustrated those who questioned them and expected realistic replies. Inquires were redirected to the questioner, whose burden it was to arrive at his or her own solutions.

One of these savants was Gustav Fechner, a nineteenth century philosopher and physicist. He postulated that the scientific method should be applied to the study of mental processes. It was his contention that experimentation and mathematical procedures should be used to study the human mind. From the mid-nineteenth century onward, many disciplines contributed to what was to become the science of psychology. Wilhelm Wundt and Edward Titchener were the leaders of the structuralist school, which identified the elements and principles of consciousness.

Other early giants of the field included William James and John Dewey. They inaugurated the study of functionalism, which taught that psychological knowledge should be applied to practical knowledge in fields such as education, business law, and daily living. A champion of behaviorism, John B. Watson, advocated that the study of psychology should concentrate on observable behavior; he urged that objective methods should be adopted. The Gestalt movement was originated by Max Wertheimer. In concert with Kurt Koffka and Wolfgang Köhler, he embraced the premise that the whole may be different from its parts studied in isolation.

Psychoanalysis was introduced by Sigmund Freud. He studied the unconscious using techniques of free association, hypnosis, and body language. The neobehaviorist model defended the behaviorist position that complicated phenomena such as mental and emotional activities cannot be observed. Love, stress, empathy, trust, and personality cannot be observed in and of themselves. Their effects, however, are readily apparent.

The cognitive school of thought focuses on mental activities. Eclectic in nature, it espouses the philosophy that precise knowledge of mental activities should be applied to everyday life. It supports the theory that informal introspection should be used to develop hunches; the use of objective methods to confirm hunches is then advocated. Carl Rogers and Abraham Maslow pioneered the area known as humanism. Its goals are to expand and to enrich human lives through service to humankind.

Applications

As well as their theoretical and experimental aspects, various fields of psychology are involved with helping people in their daily lives. In the area of education, for example, educational psychologists develop and analyze materials and strategies for effective educational curricula. The academic psychologist focuses on grades and academic achievement; issues such as truancy and drop-out rates are central to this work. School psychologists design instructive programs, consult with teachers, and assist students with problems.

Children who are abused or neglected, or who suffer as a result of being members of dysfunctional families, require the services of a child psychologist. He or she evaluates, diagnoses, and treats youngsters; this usually occurs in a clinical setting. Thus, the child psychologist is considered a clinical practitioner.

The genetic psychologist studies the activities of the human organism in relation to the hereditary and evolutionary factors involved; functions and origin play a central role. The physiological psychologist examines the biological bases of behavior. He or she is often interested in the biochemical reactions underlying memory and learning. The engineering psychologist designs and evaluates equipment, training devices, and systems. The goal is to facilitate the relationship between people and their environment. The industrial and organizational (IO) psychologist researches and develops programs that promote on-the-job efficiency, effectiveness, challenge, and positive disposition. He studies ability and personality factors, special training and experience, and work and environment variables, as well as organizational changes.

Personality psychologists study the many ways in which people differ from one another; they are instrumental in analyzing how those differences may be assessed and what their impact is. Criminal psychologists study the complexities of a perpetrator's thought process. They are keenly interested in a criminal's habits, idiosyncrasies, and possible motives. Developmental psychologists study changes in people as they age and mature. Their work may be protracted over the span of an individual's life; their theories may be advanced several years after they were first conceived.

Social psychologists study how people influence one another. They may be interested, for example, in the concept of leaders and followers. Environmental psychologists monitor the physical and social effects of the environment on behavior. They are interested in how elements such as heat, noise, health, and activity affect the human condition. Their contributions are in the areas of urban planning, architecture, and transportation.

Consumer psychologists determine factors that influence consumer decisions, exploring such issues as the effect of advertising on purchasing decisions, brand loyalty, and the rejection or acceptance of new products. Experimental psychologists design and conduct research in specific areas. Learning, sensation, motivation, language, and physiological bases of behavior are disciplines that would be investigated by these professionals.

The scope of psychology's fields of specialization is great. The professionals who work in these areas strive to help humans to know, understand, and help themselves. To accomplish this, they use numerous tests to help them ascertain specific information about an individual, a group of people, or a particular population. The categories of tests include ability tests that measure multiple aptitudes, creativity, achievement, and intelligence levels, as well as occupational and clinical assessment. Also included in the area of assessment are personality tests, which encompass self-report inventories, measures of interests, attitudes and values, projective techniques, and performance and situational evaluations.

An example of a multiple-aptitude test would be the Differential Aptitude Test (DAT), first published in 1947, then revised in 1963, 1973, and 1991. Its primary purpose is to counsel students in grades eight through twelve in educational and vocational matters. Creativity tests have received much attention from researchers and practitioners alike. The Aptitudes Research Project (ARP) was developed by the University of Southern California. It is a structure-of-intellect (SI) model, which encompasses all intellectual functions. Though its initial platform was reasoning, creativity, and problem solving, its base was expanded to divergent production. Until the ARP, research resources in this area were very limited.

Achievement tests, which differ from aptitude tests, measure the effects of specific instruction or training. Some of the most respected tests are the California Achievement Tests, the Iowa Tests of Basic Skills, the Metropolitan Achievement Test, and the Stanford Achievement Test. Their significance lies in reporting what the individual can do at the time of test administration. Aptitude instruments, on the other hand, make recommendations about future skills. Intelligence tests speak their own language; it is unfortunate, though, that so much importance is placed upon the results they yield. One should always remember that the scores identified in the Stanford-Binet Intelligence Scale and in the various Wechsler intelligence scales are but part of a big picture about any given human being and should be evaluated accordingly.

Personality tests measure the emotional, motivational, interpersonal, and attitudinal characteristics of an individual. The Kuder Interest Inventories list occupations according to a person's interest area. The Rorschach Inkblot Projective Technique investigates the personality as a whole. The Thematic Apperception Test (TAT) researches personality and attitude.

Context

Psychology as a formal discipline is still relatively new; of its many specializations, therefore, some have found their way to maturity, while others are still in their early stages. The development of diverse fields has been justified by the changing nature of social and psychological problems as well as by changing perceptions as to how best to approach those problems. For example, because more people live closer together than ever before, they must interact with one another to a greater degree; finding ways to deal with issues such as aggression, racism, and prejudice therefore becomes crucial.

Economic conditions require parents to work—whether they are single parents or parents in a two-parent family—thus depriving children of time with their parents. This has created a need for day-care centers; the care and nurturing of young people is being transferred, to a significant degree, to external agents. Moreover, older children may be expected to assume adult responsibilities before they are ready. All these issues point to an increasing need for family counseling. Educational institutions demand achievement from students; this can daunt students who have emotional or family problems that interfere with their ability to learn. The availability of school counselors or psychologists can make a difference in whether such children succeed or fail. Businesses and organizations use psychologists and psychological testing to avoid hiring employees who would be ineffective or incompatible with the organization's approach and to maximize employee productivity on the job.

The specialized fields of psychology have played both a facilitative and a reflective role. Therapists and counselors, for example, have enabled individuals to look at what they have previously accomplished, to assess the present, and to come to terms with themselves and the realities of the future. The future of psychology itself will hold further developments both in the refining of specializations that already exist and in the development of new ones as inevitable societal changes require them.

Bibliography

Anastasi, Anne. *Psychological Testing.* 4th ed. New York: Macmillan, 1976. Anastasi clearly evaluates psychological tests and accurately interprets and uses their results; she demonstrates a balanced sensitivity to social and ethical implications of test use. Presents a comprehensive picture (in 750 pages) of the nature of testing. Offers significant details about the various tests discussed. A very thorough examination of the scope of testing.

Groth-Marnat, Gary. *Handbook of Psychological Assessment.* New York: Van Nostrand Reinhold, 1984. This book is a digest of psychological tests. It explains the nature of certain tests and candidly weighs their pros and cons; it also offers interpretation procedures in assessing the meanings of IQ scores. Advances the history and development of several of the tests presented. An in-depth work, it is a must for anyone who seriously studies the different specializations of psychology.

Kennedy, Eugene C. *On Becoming a Counselor.* New York: Seabury Press, 1977. A reference source for paraprofessionals and professionals alike. Provides insight into the many problems experienced by human beings. This work causes the reader to deal with his or her own issues prior to attempting to help others confront theirs. It is logically progressive in moving from the interview process to the different types of people one will encounter in counseling situations.

McCormick, Ernest James, and Daniel R. Ilgen. *Industrial and Organizational Psychology.* 8th ed. Englewood Cliffs, N.J.: Prentice-Hall, 1985. The text critically investigates a broad field of industrial-organizational psychology. It treats the human condition and the problems generated by the sophistication of a complex technological society. It realistically brings together the concepts of organizational dynamics as they relate to industry, the contributions of industry to organizations, and the policies initiated by personnel which affect both of these areas.

Mathis, Robert L., and John H. Jackson. *Personnel.* 3d ed. St. Paul: West, 1982. Details components of successful and effective organizational behavior. Equal employment opportunity issues and staffing dynamics challenge the reader to compare text information with on-the-job situations. Chapters entitled "Training and Development" and "Appraising and Compensating Human Resources" motivate the reader to search for the most applicable and feasible methods of compensation, incentives, and benefits. Clearly identifies critical areas of organizational behavior.

Denise S. St. Cyr

Cross-References

Behaviorism: An Overview, 401; Cognitive Psychology: An Overview, 572; Development: Theoretical Issues, 804; Educational Psychology, 855; Humanism: An Overview, 1203; Industrial and Organizational Psychology, 1283; Mental Health Practitioners, 1569; Neuropsychology, 1667; Psychoanalytic Psychology: An Overview, 1905; Psychology Defined, 1945.

PSYCHOLOGY DEFINED

Type of psychology: Origin and definition of psychology
Fields of study: Classic analytic themes and issues; methodological issues

The term "psychology" first appeared in written form during the early sixteenth century and meant the systematic study of the soul and mind. The meaning of the concept changed gradually during the next three centuries, until psychology emerged in the 1880's as a separate field of study. Defined as the scientific study of mind and consciousness, the discipline was by the 1920's redefined as the scientific study of behavior and mental processes, creating some significant problems. In spite of definitional ambiguities, contemporary psychology is a vigorous and broad field of study.

Principal terms

ACT PSYCHOLOGY: an approach to psychology that emphasizes mental processes such as perceiving and thinking

BEHAVIORISM: an approach to psychology that views the discipline as the study of the relationships between behavioral and environmental events

FUNCTIONALISM: an approach to psychology that emphasized the functions served by psychological processes

PSYCHOLOGICAL DOMAIN: the information each person has available that allows him or her to move with direction and control; subsumes the concepts mind and consciousness

STRUCTURALISM: an approach to psychology that focused on the structural features of mind and consciousness

Overview

The term "psyche," while personified by the ancient Greeks as a goddess, essentially means "breath," which was equated with soul or mind. The suffix "-ology" means "science" or "study of." Psychology, as originally defined, then, means the scientific study of soul or mind. The term "scientific," as used here, means systematic; scientific fields of study did not emerge until the seventeenth century.

Apparently, the concept of psychology was not formulated until the early to middle sixteenth century, appearing first in 1530 as part of the title of a series of academic lectures given by Philipp Melanchthon, a German scholar. The first book with the Latin word *psychologia* (psychological) as part of the title was published in 1594. When used by philosophers and theologians during the next three centuries, the term had a gradually changing meaning, with the focus being much more on the study of mind and consciousness than soul.

Psychology, as a separate field of study, came into being in Germany in 1879 and, during the 1880's, in many other European countries and the United States. The field was defined as the scientific or systematic study of mind and consciousness and was largely modeled after physics and chemistry. Wilhelm Wundt (1832-1920), the acknowledged founder of the new discipline, believed that psychologists should be concerned primarily with investigating the structure of mind and consciousness using rigorous introspective techniques. Psychology was, according to Wundt, to focus on identifying the properties of simple mental elements and the laws by which these elements combined to form the more complex structures of mind and consciousness, for example, percepts and ideas. This approach, and a derivative of it developed in the United States by Edward Titchener, became known as structuralism. Animal research, the study of infants and children, the study of people with psychological problems, and concern with individual differences were not seen as central to psychology.

Some of Wundt's European contemporaries, however, such as Franz Brentano and Oswald Külpe, argued that psychology should focus on processes associated with mind and consciousness, such as perceiving, thinking, and intending, rather than attempting to divide the mental domain into simple elements. Brentano's approach became known as act psychology, in contrast to Wundt's mental-content psychology, and the two perspectives generated some interesting controversies. They did agree, though, that psychology should be concerned primarily with the study of mind and consciousness in normal adult human beings; animals, children, and people with mental and emotional problems were not of particular interest to them as subjects of research.

Also emphasizing conceptions of mind and consciousness as process rather than content were prominent early American psychologists such as William James, John Dewey, James Rowland Angell, and Harvey Carr. In contrast to Brentano and Külpe, however, these psychologists were primarily interested in the functions served by the processes. It was generally assumed that each of these capabilities evolved to help humans survive, and that it was the job of psychologists to determine how seeing, hearing, feeling, thinking, willing, planning, and so forth contributed to individuals' survival. Since not everyone adapts equally well to the challenges of life, this approach to psychology, which became known as functionalism, emphasized the study of individual differences in intelligence, personality, social skills, and so forth, as well as applied psychology and animal research. Psychology, however, was still defined as the systematic study of mind and consciousness. Functionalism has its foundations in Charles Darwin's theory of evolution and in late nineteenth century British psychology and applied statistics.

With the introduction of animal research into psychology and continuing controversies over the meanings of the concepts of mind, consciousness, and terms referring to the varying aspects of private experience, some psychologists increasingly believed that a scientific psychology could only be created if research centered on behavior (responses) and environmental features (stimuli), both of which are observable. Therefore, when American psychologist John B. Watson proclaimed, in 1913, that psychology should abandon attempts to study mind and consciousness introspectively and redefine itself as the scientific study of behavior, many of his peers were ready to follow his call; behaviorism had its formal beginning.

The behavioral orientation had its greatest influence on American psychology from about the 1920's until the early 1970's, undergoing a number of transformations. During that time, most textbooks defined psychology as the scientific study of behavior, or of behavior and mental and affective processes. Even as the limits of behavioral psychology, in its various forms, became apparent by the late 1960's, definitions of psychology changed very little. According to most contemporary psychologists in the United States and in many other countries, psychology is primarily the study of behavior, and only secondarily—and sometimes grudgingly—the study of such difficult-to-define mental and affective states and processes as thoughts, percepts, images, and feelings. Nevertheless, even the concepts of mind and consciousness, the original concerns of psychology, have somewhat reluctantly been readmitted to the field as necessary research concerns.

Applications

There are a number of serious problems associated with defining psychology as the scientific study of behavior and mental and affective states. Not only is the definition imprecise, but also it has apparently made it very difficult to generate an integrated body of psychological knowledge. While impressive research on the behavior of animals and humans has been conducted, and some progress has been made in understanding mental and affective processes and states, the knowledge generated is fragmented and therefore of limited value.

One could argue, in fact, that psychology is not the study of behavior at all but is rather the study of the information each person or animal has available that makes behavior—that is, directed and controlled actions—possible. While this information has traditionally been referred to as mind and consciousness, there might be some virtue in calling it "the psychological domain" in order to avoid long-standing arguments. Behavior is a methodological concept because it refers to something researchers must study in order to make inferences about the psychological domain. On the other hand, researchers can also investigate the products of human actions, such as the languages people develop, the buildings they construct, and the art and music they share, to the same end. Some psychologists perform research on the physiological processes associated with seeing, hearing, feeling, and thinking. Definitions of psychology should include the terms "culture" and "physiological and biochemical correlates" as well as the concept of behavior.

A better approach might be to define psychology as the systematic study of the psychological domain, this domain being the personal information that makes it possible for individual human beings and other life-forms to move with direction and control. To go beyond this definition is to describe how psychologists do research rather than what the field is about.

Another problem associated with standard definitions of psychology is the assumption that there is general agreement concerning the meaning of the concept of behavior. As has been pointed out by many analysts, that is not the case. The term has been used to refer to sensory responses, cognitive and affective processes, muscle movements, glandular secretions, activity taking place in various parts of the nervous system, and the outcomes or consequences of particular complex actions. Behavior, in other words, is an ambiguous concept. In a strict sense, the only actions or changes relevant to the psychological level of analysis are those that are self-initiated and unique to the total-life-form level of organization in nature, because it is these changes that depend on the psychological domain. Changes in the individual cells or subsystems of life-forms, on the other hand, do not constitute behavior in the psychological sense.

Context

Even though a clear and generally agreed-upon definition of psychology has not emerged, psychology today is a vigorous and broad scholarly field and profession, extending from biological subdisciplines and animal research laboratories to the study of humans in social, political, economic, industrial, educational, clinical, and religious contexts. It is not surprising, therefore, that psychologists have made contributions in a wide variety of areas; among the most notable are those having to do with cognitive and emotional development, child rearing, formulating new ways to view and treat psychological problems, devising ways to deal with the crises of life associated with each stage of human experience from infancy to old age, consumer research and marketing, group dynamics, and the development of tests and educational procedures.

Psychology is one of the most popular majors in American colleges, and the discipline has experienced dramatic growth since the 1940's. There were about four thousand psychologists in the United States during the 1940's; by the early 1990's, there were approximately 100,000. Since the mid-1970's, the number of women majoring in psychology has held steady, while the number of men has decreased significantly; as a consequence, by the late 1980's, more women than men were earning Ph.D.'s in psychology.

One of the most challenging new areas of study is health psychology, which emerged during the 1980's in response to the health care crisis, a crisis brought about by increasing costs associated with an aging population, expensive high-technology medical techniques, the acquired immune deficiency syndrome (AIDS) epidemic, economic restructuring and stagnation, and a variety of other factors. Pressures have also been emerging for people to reexamine their values and roles and, in a sense, their personal and national identities; these pressures derive from such powerful forces and dynamics as the feminist and multicultural movements, the emergence of nontraditional social and child-rearing arrangements, the change from a production to a service society, the loss of American economic dominance in the world, and the collapse of communist societies. A mass identity crisis may, in fact, provide the psychologists of the twenty-first century with their major challenge.

Bibliography

Carr, Harvey A. *Psychology: A Study of Mental Activity.* New York: Longmans, Green, 1925. Presents a clear picture of the functionalist view of psychology. Carr was one of the Americican psychologists who formalized functionalism.

Gilgen, Albert R. *American Psychology Since World War II: A Profile of the Discipline.* Westport, Conn.: Greenwood Press, 1982. Presents an overview of the major developments and trends in American psychology during World War II, which ended in 1945, and from the postwar period through the 1970's.

—————. "The Psychological Level of Organization in Nature and Interdependencies Among Major Psychological Concepts." In *Annals of Theoretical Psychology.* Vol. 5, edited by Arthur W. Staats and Leendert P. Mos. New York: Plenum Press, 1987. Presents a detailed rationale for defining psychology as the systematic study of the information available to each person that allows each individual to move with direction and control.

Lapointe, François H. "Who Originated the Term 'Psychology'?" *Journal of the History of the Behavioral Sciences* 8, no. 3 (1972): 328-335. The most thorough analysis of the origination of the term "psychology." An essential reference for anyone interested in the history of the concept.

Murray, David J. *A History of Western Psychology.* 2d ed. Englewood Cliffs, N.J.: Prentice-Hall, 1988. Includes clear discussions of the origins of the term "psychology" and the meaning of the concept for the act psychologists, the structuralists, the functionalists, and the behaviorists.

Titchener, Edward Bradford. *A Primer of Psychology.* Rev. ed. New York: Macmillan, 1913. Presents a clear and detailed analysis of psychology from the structuralist perspective, and in the process identifies many of the challenges involved in attempting to decipher the structure of mind and consciousness.

Albert R. Gilgen

Cross-References

Behaviorism: An Overview, 401; Cognitive Psychology: An Overview, 572; Functionalism, 1055; Humanism: An Overview, 1203; Psychoanalytic Psychology: An Overview, 1905; Psychology: Fields of Specialization, 1939; The Scientific Method in Psychology, 2148; Structuralism, 2477.

PSYCHOLOGY OF WOMEN: KAREN HORNEY

Type of psychology: Personality
Fields of study: Classic analytic themes and issues; personality theory

Karen Horney's theories emphasize the effects of cultural influences on women's personality development. Her theories modified classical psychoanalytic views and provided new insights into women's interpersonal relationships.

Principal terms

BIOLOGICAL INFLUENCES: the effects of organic or anatomical factors on human behavior

CLASSICAL PSYCHOANALYSIS: a system of psychology based on Freudian doctrine and procedure; seeks the root of human behavior in unconscious motivation and conflict, particularly sexual conflict

CULTURAL INFLUENCES: the effects of interpersonal relations and social attitudes on human behavior

INSTINCT: an innate or inherited tendency that motivates a person to act without reasoning, instruction, or experience

NEO-FREUDIANS: those psychoanalysts who place more emphasis on security and interpersonal relations as determining human behavior than on the exclusively biological theories of Freud

REPRESSION: the forceful ejection from consciousness of shameful or painful experiences, impulses, or memories which generate a high level of anxiety

SEXUAL INSTINCT: the tendency toward pleasure seeking, particularly through achieving sexual aims and objects

UNCONSCIOUS: a region of the mind that is the seat of repressed impulses and experiences of which the conscious mind is unaware

Overview

Karen Horney (1885-1952) considered people to be products of their environment as well as of biology. She stressed the ways in which cultural influences affect women's personality development. These cultural influences include interpersonal relationships and society's attitudes about women.

Cultural influences are overlooked by classical psychoanalysis, according to Horney, but play an important role in women's development. She viewed women as living in a male-oriented world in which they are judged by men according to male standards. Women have come to believe that these male-based standards represent their true nature. As a result, according to Horney, women live with the dilemma of having to choose between fulfilling their ambitions or meeting their needs for love by adhering to the passive role that society expects of them. These circumstances contribute to depression and low self-esteem.

Horney described three basic patterns of behavior by which people relate to others: moving toward (or self-effacing), moving away from (or distancing), and moving against (or expansive). The moving-toward behavior involves dependency and taking care of others as well as self-effacement. Women have been conditioned since birth to relate to others in this manner, according to Horney.

Horney's theories were modifications of classical psychoanalytic beliefs. Her theories are best understood when viewed in relation to the Freudian concepts that were prevalent during her lifetime. According to Sigmund Freud, who founded classical psychoanalysis during the late nineteenth century, biological influences determine human behavior. Of these biological factors, sexual instincts are the strongest motivators of human behavior. Neurosis, or mental disorder, was considered by Freud to be the result of unconscious sexual conflicts which began in early childhood.

Horney was grounded in psychoanalytic thinking and agreed with many of Freud's concepts. She disagreed radically, however, with the heavy sexual content of Freudian theory. A major point of departure was the Freudian concept of penis envy. Freud essentially viewed all psychological problems in women to be the result of the woman's inherent wish to be a man. Freud maintained that girls are not born with a natural sense of their femininity and regard themselves as inferior, castrated boys. As a result of penis envy, the female rebels against her biological inferiority. The consequences, according to Freud, are resentment, devaluation of her "negative sexual endowments," envy of the opposite sex, and a constant search for compensation.

Horney considered penis envy to be contrary to biological thinking. She maintained that little girls are instinctively feminine and aware of their femaleness in early childhood. Thus, girls are not programmed to feel inferior. Women may envy men the power and freedom they have in their private and professional lives, but women do not envy men's genitals. The behaviors which Freud associated with penis envy—greed, envy, ambition, and others—Horney attributed to the restrictions society places on females.

Horney also disagreed with the Freudian theory that viewed frigidity and masochism as biologically determined parts of woman's nature. Frigidity, or the inability of a woman to experience sexual desire, is neither a normal condition for a woman nor an illness, according to Horney. She considered frigidity to be a symptom of an underlying psychological disturbance, such as chronic anxiety. Frequently, it is caused by tensions between marital partners. Powerful forces in society restrict a woman in the free expression of her sexuality. Custom and education promote female inhibitions. Men's tendency to view their wives as spiritual partners and to look for sexual excitement with prostitutes or others whom they do not respect may also cause frigidity in wives.

Masochistic tendencies, wherein a woman seeks and enjoys pain and suffering, particularly in her sexual life, result from special social circumstances, Horney maintained. Freudian theory, holding that women are biologically programmed for masochism, is associated with Freudian concepts of the female having been rendered less powerful than the male through castration. Horney, on the other hand, believed that society encourages women to be masochistic. Women are stereotyped as weak and emotional, as enjoying dependence, and these qualities are rewarded by men. Masochistic tendencies, according to Horney, are a way of relating by which a woman tries to obtain security and satisfaction through self-effacement and submission.

Horney's theories stressed the positive aspects of femininity. As her ideas developed, she became more influenced by social scientists of her period. Her theories placed increasing emphasis on interpersonal and social attitudes in determining women's feelings, relations, and roles. Her ideas about the development of women's sexuality were focused on adolescent girls, rather than on young children, as in Freudian theory. According to Horney, adolescents develop attitudes to cope with sexual conflict, and these attitudes carry over into adulthood.

Applications

Karen Horney's theories opened the door for new ways of understanding women's personalities and relationships. In a 1984 study of women's reaction to separation and loss, psychotherapist Alexandra Symonds found Horney's theories to be relevant to what she encountered in her female patients. Writing in the *American Journal of Psychoanalysis*, Symonds reported female reaction to separation and loss to be a frequent motivation for women to enter therapy. In contrast, she found that men come into therapy in these circumstances mainly because of pressure from a wife or girlfriend. According to Symonds, women are more eager than men to create relationships, and women express more feeling when the relationships end.

Symonds considered these behaviors from the viewpoint of the three basic patterns of behavior described by Horney: moving toward, moving away from, and moving against. Symonds viewed the moving-toward, self-effacing type of behavior as love oriented, or dependent; the moving-away-from, detached type as freedom oriented; and the moving-against, expansive type as power oriented. According to Symonds' views, society assigns the love-oriented, dependent pattern to women, while men are encouraged to develop power- and/or freedom-oriented patterns. She described a frequent combination in a couple to be a detached, expansive, power-oriented male married to a dependent, self-effacing, love-oriented female. Relationships often develop between the silent, strong, withdrawn, noncommunicative male and the loving, dependent woman who always wants to talk about feelings.

As people develop character patterns, such as love oriented and dependent, they suppress feelings that cause inner conflicts, such as aggressiveness, according to Symonds. By contrast, power-oriented people suppress dependent feelings. People idealize their self-values and feel contempt for what is suppressed; thus, the power-oriented person views dependency and need as contemptible weaknesses. This contempt is conveyed to those who are aware of their dependency needs. Women then add self-hate for needing others to the anxiety they feel when a relationship ends.

Extremely dependent, self-effacing women often stay in poor and even abusive relationships rather than separate, according to Symonds. They are victims of a culture that considers a woman nothing unless attached to a man. Symonds found these women to be coming from two different backgrounds: either having been held close by mother and/or father during childhood and adolescence, thus having no opportunity for healthy growth; or having separated prematurely from parents in childhood in an effort to become self-sufficient at an early age, often having developed a façade of self-sufficiency with deep, unresolved dependency needs.

Horney's theories predicted the anxiety women feel about their own ambition and the ways in which women sabotage their competence and success. In the book *Women in Therapy* (1988), psychotherapist Harriet Goldhor Lerner discusses female work inhibition in the light of Horney's theories. Lerner views work inhibition as an unconscious attempt to preserve harmony within a relationship as well as to allay fears of being unfeminine. Women often fear success because they fear they will pay dearly for their accomplishments. Women frequently equate success, or the wish for it, with the loss of femininity and attractiveness, loss of significant relationships, loss of health, or even loss of life. Feelings of depression and anxiety are ways women either apologize for their competence and success on the one hand or ensure the lack of success on the other hand, according to Lerner. She views self-sacrifice or self-sabotage to be other common ways women react to their feelings of guilt and anxiety about becoming successful.

When faced with the choice (real or imagined) of sacrificing the self to preserve a relationship or strengthening the self at the risk of threatening a relationship, women often choose the former, according to Lerner. She applies Horney's views to the situation of a thirty-year-old married woman who entered therapy because of personal distress and marital tension over her desire to enroll in graduate school and embark on a career. Lerner found that multigenerational guilt on the part of the woman was involved, as well as fears of destroying her marriage. The woman's husband was opposed to his wife's enrolling in graduate school. In addition, the woman was the first female in her family to aspire to graduate school. In the face of these circumstances, she put aside her ambitions in order to preserve harmony in her relationships. The woman's work inhibition involved profound anxiety and guilt over striving for things previous generations of women in her family could not have. Work inhibition also may result when a woman perceives her strivings as "too masculine," a perception Lerner sees as reinforced by society. Being labeled "masculine" triggers deep guilt and anxiety in women.

Context

Horney's theories on female psychology developed from a series of papers she wrote over a thirteen-year period in response to Freud's views on female sexuality. The last paper was published after Horney emigrated to America from Germany at a highly productive point in her career.

One of the first women admitted to medical school in Berlin, she had completed her psychiatric and psychoanalytic training there by 1913. By that time, Freud had passed the peak of his greatest creative years. Horney was thirty years younger than Freud and a product of the twentieth century. Her views were more in tune with the relatively open structure of twentieth century science than with the more closed science of Freud's period. Horney was influenced greatly by sociologists of her time. She and other neo-Freudians, such as Harry Stack Sullivan, Alfred Adler, and Erich Fromm, were the first psychoanalysts to emphasize cultural influences on personality development.

Horney's theories grew out of a need for a feminine psychology different from male psychology. She believed that women were being analyzed and treated according to a male-oriented psychology that considered women to be biologically inferior to males. She did not find these male theories supported by what she observed in her female patients or in her own life experience.

Horney was the first female doctor to challenge male theory and went on to take a position in the foreground of the psychoanalytic movement. In so doing, she became a role model for women in general and professional women in particular. She was a controversial figure, and her career involved many disputes with the established psychoanalytic world. She and her followers eventually were ostracized by the establishment, and for a time her name disappeared from the psychoanalytic literature. Her biographers attribute this to a fear on the part of some Freudians of being contaminated by association with her ideas.

A growing interest in her work occurred during the women's liberation movement in the 1970's. The feminist movement brought her name back into the literature as a pioneer in upgrading women's status. Her name began appearing more frequently in literature associated with women's therapy. The series of important books which she had written throughout her career remain popular and continue to be used as textbooks.

An independent thinker, Horney is considered an individual who was always ahead of her time. Her work anticipated a revival of interest in the narcissistic personality. Her theories predicted popular trends in psychology, although she often is not credited for her ideas. One of these trends is the increasing emphasis on social and cultural factors as causes of emotional illness. Systems theory is another popular trend related to Horney's concepts. Systems theory, which includes a type of psychology called family therapy, emphasizes the continuous interaction between cultural conditions, interpersonal relations, and inner emotional experience.

Bibliography

Horney, Karen. *Feminine Psychology.* New York: W. W. Norton, 1967. A collection of all of Horney's writings on feminine psychology. Gives a flavor of Horney's personality and force as a psychoanalyst and educator. Includes an informative introduction by Harold Kelman, one of Horney's colleagues. Available through college libraries.

Lerner, Harriet Goldhor. *Women in Therapy.* Northvale, N.J.: Jason Aronson, 1988. Discusses women and their psychotherapists from a psychoanalytic perspective, with references to Horney's theories. Illustrates how Horney's theories apply to many themes and issues in women's psychology.

Quinn, Susan. *A Mind of Her Own: The Life of Karen Horney.* Reading, Mass.: Addison-Wesley, 1988. This biography is an excellent source of information about Horney's personal and professional life. Much of it is devoted to her female psychology. Easy to read; contains photographs, biographical essays, extensive source notes, and a complete list of Horney's work.

Rubins, Jack L. *Karen Horney: Gentle Rebel of Psychoanalysis.* New York: Dial Press, 1978. The first biography of Karen Horney. Thorough and well documented; includes detailed discussions of Horney's theories on women. Lengthy but well organized. Can be read by the college or high school student.

Symonds, Alexandra. "Separation and Loss: Significance for Women." *American Journal of Psychoanalysis* 45, no. 1 (1985): 53-58. Discusses women's feelings about separation and loss. Important illustration of how Horney's theories help explain women's role in interpersonal relationships. Available in college libraries.

Margaret M. Frailey

Cross-References

Abnormality: Psychodynamic Models, 74; Abnormality: Sociocultural Models, 82; Feminist Psychotherapy, 1025; Psychoanalysis: Classical versus Modern, 1898; Psychoanalytic Psychology: An Overview, 1905; Psychology of Women: Sigmund Freud, 1956; Social Psychological Models: Karen Horney, 2324.

PSYCHOLOGY OF WOMEN: SIGMUND FREUD

Type of psychology: Personality
Fields of study: Classic analytic themes and issues; personality theory

Sigmund Freud, the first person to develop a comprehensive theory of personality, thought that women undergo distinct experiences in the development of their person- alities. He believed that traumatic events during the phallic stage (from approx- imately three to five years of age) were likely to hinder normal female development, the results being a failure of same-sex identification and a diminished superego or moral capacity.

Principal terms
FREE ASSOCIATION: a process whereby the therapist has the patient report what comes to mind without editing; the result is said to reveal the contents of the unconscious
ID: the subconscious part of the mind that fuels the ego and superego; it operates on the basis of the pleasure principle, constantly seeking immediate gratification in a childlike fashion
IDENTIFICATION: the process whereby the ego defends itself from incestuous feelings by taking on the characteristics of the same-sex parent; necessary for development of the superego
INSTINCTS: biological sources of excitation that direct the development of personality into adulthood; Freud proposed the existence of life instincts (Eros) and death instincts (Thanatos)
OEDIPUS COMPLEX: the complex that occurs when a male child unconsciously desires his mother, competes with his father for her affection, fears castration by his father, and gives up his mother as love object
PENIS ENVY: a condition theorized by Freud to exist in females in which they subconsciously believe they have been castrated and therefore have a chronic wish for the male organ
PSYCHOSEXUAL STAGES OF DEVELOPMENT: the stages of personality development from birth; the oral stage lasts from birth to one year, the anal stage from two to three, the phallic stage from three to five, the latency period from six to twelve, and the genital stage from twelve through adulthood
REPRESSION: a type of motivated forgetting, repression is an unconscious process that keeps unacceptable material from conscious awareness; it is an ego defense mechanism
SUPEREGO: the internalization of society's values and ideals as interpreted by one's parents; the superego acts as a conscience, emphasizing what one should do

Overview

Two central concepts underlie Sigmund Freud's theory of personality development. The first is the notion of the unconscious; the second concept has to do with the role of infantile sexuality.

Freud believed that consciousness could be viewed as a continuum of experience, with one pole being the familiar one of acute awareness of one's thoughts, feelings, and behaviors and the other pole being a state of profound unconsciousness in which one's feelings, thoughts, and wishes are completely beyond one's awareness. Midway between these poles is the preconscious, which Freud believed contained material or mental life from both the conscious and the unconscious and could, with effort, be made totally conscious. Freud believed that the bulk of mental life is represented in the unconscious, with only a small portion, "the tip of the iceberg," being conscious awareness.

Operating from the depths of the unconscious, a structure of personality known as the id operates to seek pleasure, to avoid pain at all costs, and to accomplish solely selfish aims. The id is the source of all psychic energy, including both sexual and aggressive instincts.

Freud proposed that the sexual instincts are critical and that personality develops over time as the individual responds to these instincts. He believed that a number of component instincts arise from various regions of the body. These instincts strive for satisfaction in what he calls organ pleasure. Each of these organs is the focus of a phase or stage of development, the first of which is the oral stage. The oral stage begins at birth and continues through the first year, as the infant seeks pleasure through the mouth and the mouth becomes the source of all gratification. Milk from the mother's breast or a bottle is devoured, just as, later, any object that the child can reach will be manipulated and explored orally. The child takes in physical nourishment in the same way that he or she takes in, in a very rudimentary way, the behaviors, values, and beliefs of others, beginning the basis for later identification with others.

The second psychosexual stage of development is the anal stage, which Freud believed revolved around the pleasure associated with elimination. During the second year of life, the child begins taking control of urination and defecation, trying to do so within parental and societal limits.

Freud believed that both boys and girls proceed through the oral stage in essentially the same manner. For both, the mother is the primary love object. Sometime after the third year, however, Freud believed that the sexes diverge. In the third, or phallic, stage of development, both boys and girls discover the pleasurable nature of the genitals. For boys, the stage is centered on the Oedipus complex, in which they develop strong sexual feelings toward their mothers. These feelings are accompanied by others, such as anger and jealousy, as fathers are perceived as competitors for mothers' affection and attention. As sexual desires heighten, the boy begins to perceive competition and hostility from the father. The sense of peril becomes located in the physical source of the boy's feelings for his mother, the penis, and the result is a phenomenon that Freud called castration anxiety—the fear that the father will retaliate. Over time, fear of castration motivates the boy to give up the mother as a love object and turn toward the father in same-sex identification. According to Freud, this strengthening identification with the father is essential for the development of a solid superego, which, in turn, empowers the male, making possible major contributions to culture and society.

Unlike the male's experience, the onset of the phallic stage for females entails a major trauma: the realization that she does not have a penis. Often, the realization is accompanied by the notion that the mother is responsible for her own and her daughter's castrated state. Here the little girl turns away from her mother as the primary love object and turns toward her father, limiting her future chances for same-sex identification. Feelings of inferiority pervade, and she falls victim to penis envy, a chronic wish for the superior male organ. Freud believed that, as a result of this trauma, the remaining course of female development would be difficult at best and that the accomplishment of same-sex identification was questionable. The girl's life is thus spent in search of a substitute penis, which Freud thought might be a husband or a child, particularly a male child. Indeed, Freud believed that the single most rewarding relationship in a woman's life would be her relationship with her son, regarding which her feelings would be totally unambivalent. Freud believed that the foundations of personality were in place by the end of the phallic stage. He described the post-Oedipal period, beginning with the latency stage, as a period when children repress, or make unconscious, the sexual conflicts of the Oedipal period. Females during this time are said to be more passive and less aggressive than boys, but, like boys, they tend to seek out same-sex play groups.

The final psychosexual stage of development is the genital stage. Unlike the previous, more self-centered periods of stimulation and gratification, the genital stage marks a period of sexual attraction to others and a time during which social activities and career goals become important before marriage. The child is thus transformed into an adult. Freud believed that, in some cases, failure to resolve the female Oedipus complex results in neurosis, which he often observed in his practice with female patients. He believed that in other cases the lack of resolution caused a masculinity complex in which women attempt to succeed in traditionally male endeavors (he offered this explanation to his contemporary female analysts for their behavior). Freud believed that the female's failure to unite with her mother in post-Oedipal identification, and her subsequent diminished superego capacity, caused her to have a tendency toward negative personality traits and an inability to apply objective standards of justice.

Several of Freud's contemporaries, including some female analysts, were critical of Freud's views on the psychology of women. Among his critics was Karen Horney, who rejected the idea that penis envy is central to normal female development. She acknowledged, however, that from a cultural point of view, envy of the male role might explain some of Freud's clinical observations better than the biological notion of penis envy. In addition, after many years of analyzing female patients, Horney began analyzing males; from her observations, she concluded that males often exhibit an intense envy of pregnancy, childbirth, and motherhood, as well as of the breasts and of the act of suckling.

Applications

Historically, psychoanalysis has represented a method of psychological observation, a set of theoretical constructs or ideas, and an approach to psychotherapy. When Freud began psychoanalysis, it was a method of observation intended to broaden the knowledge of human behavior. Believing that the unconscious is the major clue to solving problems of human behavior, Freud used two processes to understand it: free association and dream interpretation. Free association, the reporting of what comes to mind in an unedited fashion, was an important tool used to discover the contents of the unconscious. Freud believed that all thoughts are connected in some fashion and that therefore the spontaneous utterances of the patient are always meaningful clues to what has been repressed or buried in the unconscious. Freud also believed that the unconscious can be clarified by means of dream interpretation. Those thoughts and impulses that are unacceptable to the conscious mind are given symbols in dreams.

An interesting study conducted by Calvin Hall (1964) illustrates how the interpretation of dreams has been used in research—in this case, to test Freud's observation that the female superego is not as strong as it appears to be in males. Hall reasoned that a person with a strong internalized superego would be independent of external agents, whereas a person who has a less internalized superego would tend to disown his or her own guilt and blame external authority figures. Hall further made the assumption that dreams in which the dreamer was the victim of aggression were expressions of an externalized superego, whereas dreams in which the dreamer was the victim of misfortune (accident, circumstance) were expressions of an internalized superego. It was hypothesized that females would be more likely to dream of themselves as victims of aggression and males would be more likely to dream of themselves as victims of misfortune. Careful content analysis of more than three thousand dreams of young adults was performed. Results supported the hypotheses, although Hall cautions that additional hypotheses should be tested and more diverse data collected to support thoroughly Freud's theory of the differences between the male and the female superego.

Freud was also the first to understand and describe the concept of transference, the patient's positive or negative feelings that develop toward the therapist during the long, intimate process of analysis. These feeling often relate to earlier ones that the patient has had for significant others: namely, mother, father, or sibling. The analysis of transference has become extremely important to neo-Freudian analysts, particularly as it relates to the treatment of borderline and other personality disturbances.

Another aspect of Freud's legacy involves the many theoretical constructs that psychoanalysis has generated. Among these is the concept of the unconscious. Freud provided many everyday examples of the operation of the unconscious as he described slips of the tongue and other phenomena. He was convinced that such slips, now known as "Freudian slips," were not accidental at all, but somehow expressed unconscious wishes, thoughts, or desires. For example, the woman who loses her wedding ring wishes she had never had it.

Finally, psychoanalysis also represents a method of therapy that Freud and later analysts used to treat the symptoms of mental illness. Practicing for many years, Freud refined his technique, using free association and dream interpretation to help patients gain insight into themselves by recognizing their unconscious patterns and to help them work through the unconscious conflicts that affect everyday life. Many of Freud's patients were women, and it was from these women's recollections in analysis that Freud built his theory of female development. Some of Freud's critics argue that building a theory of normal development from the observation of pathology or abnormality represents an inappropriate conceptual leap.

During years of analysis, Freud became convinced of the sexual basis of neurosis. He believed that sexual experiences occurring prior to puberty and stored in the unconscious as memories produced conflict that later caused certain neurotic conditions. These ideas, often referred to as Freud's seduction theory, were used to explain hysterical symptoms such as paralysis, blindness, inability to understand the spoken word (receptive aphasia), and sexual dysfunction as the result of sexual abuse probably occurring before ages six to eight. It is important to note, however, that Freud later revised his thinking on infantile sexuality and concluded that it is the thought or psychic reality of the individual that counts more than the physical reality of events. In other words, a person might fantasize a seduction, store the fantasy in unconscious memory (repress it), and have that conflictual memory cause neurosis just as readily as the memory of an actual seduction. Some recent critics have suggested that Freud's reformulation represented a form of denial in his inability to recognize the prevalence of sexual abuse at that time.

Context

Born in 1856 to Jewish parents, Freud lived and practiced most of his life in Vienna. He was graduated from medical school in 1881 and practiced as a clinical neurologist for several years before becoming interested in the "talking cure" that his colleague, Josef Breuer, had developed as a means of dealing with his patients' emotional symptoms. Freud's writings and lectures on the subject of hysteria and its sexual roots led him to be ostracized by most of his medical colleagues. His medical training and the work of Charles Darwin were largely responsible for his emphasis on sexual and aggressive instincts as the basis for behavior.

Freud's theory was important because it was the first of its kind and because it was controversial, generating further research into and theorizing about the female personality.

Over the years, many aspects of Freudian theory have been challenged. Freud's notion that penis envy is a primary motivator in the female personality was challenged by Karen Horney, who believed that, if it existed, a woman's envy was related to the male's privileged role in society. Freud's idea that the clitoral orgasm is immature and must be surrendered for the vaginal orgasm at puberty spurred work by William Masters and Virginia Johnson, who concluded, after much rigorous research, that orgasm is a reaction of the entire pelvic area.

Freud's theory has forced critics to determine what is uniquely female about personality. In *Toward a New Psychology of Women* (1976), Jean Baker Miller has attempted to show how traditional theories of female behavior have failed to acknowledge the essence of the female personality. Miller suggests that affiliation is the cornerstone of the female experience and that it is in response to her relationships with others that a woman's personality grows and develops.

In her book *In a Different Voice* (1982), Carol Gilligan disputes Freud's notion that females show less of a sense of justice than males and have weak superegos. She argues that morality involves respect for the needs of self balanced with respect for the needs of others; thus, it is not that females lack the justice principle, but rather that they have different expressions of justice and different internal and external demands.

Heavily influenced by Freud, many object relations theorists continue to make contributions in the area of psychotherapy with clients whose early relationships have been disturbed or disrupted. This work will continue to constitute the basis for decisions made by courts, adoption agencies, and social-service agencies regarding the placement of children.

Freud's views on the origins of neurosis may continue to play a role in the understanding of multiple personality disorder and its roots in early sexual abuse. The concept of body memory, the physical memory that abuse has occurred, may well bridge the gap between Freud's concepts of repressed psychic memory and repressed actual memory of early sexual abuse; it may streamline the treatment of this condition. Finally, Freud's theory will no doubt continue to generate controversy, motivating both theory and research in the area of women's personality development.

Bibliography

Freud, Sigmund. *New Introductory Lectures on Psychoanalysis.* New York: W. W. Norton, 1933. This volume contains seven lectures or papers that Freud wrote toward the end of his career. Among them is "The Psychology of Women," in which Freud attempts to explain some fundamental differences between the sexes. Freud describes female behavior and the Oedipus complex for males and females, and he elaborates on the role of penis envy in female development. The volume also contains lectures on dreams, on the structure of personality, and on anxiety and the instincts.

_____. *The Standard Edition of the Complete Psychological Works of Sigmund Freud.* Edited by James Strachey. London: Hogarth Press, 1953-1974. Volume 7 in this collection of Freud's works contains a detailed case history of a woman named Dora, whom Freud treated over a period of years. This case history illustrates Freud's ideas about the causes of neurosis and hysterical symptoms. The work also contains three essays on sexuality, including sexual aberrations, infantile sexuality, and puberty.

Gilligan, Carol. *In a Different Voice.* Cambridge, Mass.: Harvard University Press, 1982. Traditional theories of development have tried to impose male thinking and values on female psychology. Gilligan discusses the importance of relationship as well as female conceptions of morality, challenging Freud's views on female superego development.

Horney, Karen. *Feminine Psychology.* Edited by Harold Kelman. New York: W. W. Norton, 1967. A collection of some of Karen Horney's early works in which she describes Freudian ideas on the psychology of women and offers her own observations and conclusions. Horney disputes Freud's notion of penis envy and in later essays explores such topics as distrust between the sexes, premenstrual tension, and female masochism.

Miller, Jean Baker. *Toward a New Psychology of Women.* Boston: Beacon Press, 1976. Miller proposes that traditional theories of female development have overlooked a critical ingredient in female behavior—affiliation—which she believes is a cornerstone of female psychology.

Miller, Jonathan, ed. *Freud: The Man, His World, His Influence.* Boston: Little, Brown, 1972. Miller has edited a series of essays that put Freud's work in historical, social, and cultural perspective. One essay, by Friedrich Heer, describes the impact of Freud's Jewish background on his life and work in Vienna. Another, by Martin Esslin, describes Vienna, the exciting and culturally rich background for Freud's work.

Rychlak, Joseph F. *Introduction to Personality and Psychotherapy.* 2d ed. Boston: Houghton Mifflin, 1981. This introductory personality text carefully reviews the work of several leading psychologists and psychotherapists, including Sigmund Freud. Rychlak describes the gradual development of Freud's structural hypothesis, and he reviews Freud's ideas about the instincts, dynamic concepts such as defense mechanisms, and the development of the Oedipus complex for males and females, noting the concerns of modern feminists who have found Freud's work offensive.

Ruth T. Hannon

Cross-References

Abnormality: Psychodynamic Models, 74; Levels of Consciousness, 663; Dream Analysis, 830; Feminist Psychotherapy, 1025; Instinct Theory, 1309; Psychoanalysis: Classical versus Modern, 1898; Psychoanalytic Psychology: An Overview, 1905; Psychoanalytic Psychology and Personality: Sigmund Freud, 1912; Psychology of Women: Karen Horney, 1950; Psychosexual Development, 1969.

PSYCHOPHYSICAL SCALING

Type of psychology: Sensation and perception
Fields of study: Experimental methodologies; general constructs and issues

Psychophysical scaling is concerned with measuring how perception of a stimulus changes as some physical aspect of the stimulus (for example, its intensity) changes. Experiments using magnitude estimation have shown that a single "power law" describes this relationship for a wide variety of sensory experience.

Principal terms
 CROSS-MODALITY MATCHING: a technique for measuring perceptual experience by having a person indicate the magnitude of one stimulus by adjusting the intensity of a stimulus in another sensory modality
 INTENSITY: a measure of a physical aspect of a stimulus, such as the frequency of a sound or its sound pressure
 MAGNITUDE ESTIMATION: a technique for measuring perceptual experience by having persons assign numbers to indicate the "magnitude" of an experience
 POWER LAW: a statement of the lawful relationship between two variables that expresses one of them as the other raised to some exponent
 PSYCHOPHYSICS: a set of techniques for measuring the relationship between a physical stimulus and the perception of that stimulus

Overview

One of the earliest issues addressed by the science of psychology was the relationship between a physical stimulus (something actually out there in the world) and human perception of it. For example, if one light bulb emits a light twice as intense as another, will it look twice as bright? "Psychophysics" is the general term for techniques designed to study this relationship between the psychological and the physical.

Psychologist Stanley S. Stevens, beginning in the 1930's, developed the method of psychophysical scaling, which has become a standard tool for studying psychophysical relationships. One method of psychophysical scaling, called magnitude estimation, involves presenting a stimulus (for example, a light of a known physical intensity) to a human experimental subject and telling him or her that this particular light has an intensity of 100 (or some other arbitrary number). The subject is then shown another light of some different intensity and asked to assign a number to it: If it looks twice as bright, the subject would call it 200; if it is one-third as bright, the subject would call it 33; and so on. By having a person make many such judgments, the relationship between the brightness of a light (its psychological aspect) and the intensity of the light (its physical aspect) can be measured. The same technique could be used for the loudness of a sound or the sweetness of various concentrations of sugar in water.

Stevens and others discovered, using this technique, that after a little initial practice subjects could make quite reliable estimates. That is, they were highly consistent in the numbers they assigned from one occasion to another. Further, he discovered that while people differ somewhat in the numbers they assign, they all perceive highly similar relationships between the actual intensities of the stimuli and the numbers they assign. For most magnitude estimations (including the brightness of a light, loudness of a sound, smell of coffee, and vibration), the intensity of the stimulus had to be double or more before the perceived magnitude (brightness, loudness, smell, and so on) also doubled. The exact amount of change that is perceived as twice as much differs from one sensory modality to another. A sound, for example, must be almost four times as loud as another before it sounds twice as loud, while a light must be ten times as intense before it is perceived as twice as bright.

Some sensory modalities show a more nearly one-to-one correspondence between the physical intensity and perceptual magnitude. For example, if subjects are shown a line of some given length and told that this line has a magnitude of 100, then shown other lines and asked to make judgments of their magnitudes, they will come quite close to assigning 200 to a line twice as long, or 50 to a line half as long. Estimates of the duration of a time interval (for example the time between two beeps) also show a nearly one-to-one correspondence, as do estimates of the pressure of a weight on the palm of the hand.

A few of the stimuli studied have shown yet another type of relationship: If the stimulus intensity is doubled, the perceived magnitude is more than doubled. This type of relationship holds for such modalities as the taste of salt or sugar in water and the roughness of emery cloths. Perhaps the most striking of all the stimuli that have been studied is the response to changes in intensity of an electric shock. Doubling the intensity of an electric shock led to a more than tenfold increase in the magnitude reported. Thus, if a given shock was assigned a magnitude of 100, doubling the intensity would result in the subject reporting a number greater than 1,000.

Despite the appearance that these are different sorts of psychophysical relationships, Stevens found that a very simple formula could describe all the relationships; that formula has become known as Stevens' power law. A "law" in the sciences is a known relationship—here, the relationship between the physical intensity of a stimulus and its psychological magnitude. It is a "power law" because the formula involves raising the physical intensity of the stimulus to a "power." Almost every sensory modality studied (and the list is very long) shows a clear adherence to Stevens' power law. Despite the very real difference between human response to light, taste, electric shock, roughness, and pressure, they can all be described using the same basic formula.

The use of numbers in this fashion does sometimes seem arbitrary to the subjects, and Stevens has found that allowing subjects to assign a number completely independently—that is, with no "standard" that they are told is 100—yields the same results. (The actual number assigned will differ with this technique, but the relationship between the numbers assigned and the physical measure of the stimulus remains the same.)

Applications

Stevens' method of magnitude estimation has provided a useful device for measuring many aspects of human experience, and such measurements have proven especially useful in human factors work, which is concerned with adapting tools, controls (such as those in a power plant or airplane), and other equipment to the needs of the humans who must use them. An understanding of the basic relationship between a physical stimulus and the perception of it is required in order to solve many everyday problems.

Studies of hearing, as already noted, show that the intensity of a sound must be increased fourfold to double the perceived magnitude, and this has implications for the design of sound systems for both home and the concert hall. For example, if one wants a new stereo that will sound twice as loud as the stereo one now has, an amplifier with twice the output in watts would not be enough. One would actually need an amplifier four times as powerful. In fact, the "sone" scale of loudness constructed by Stevens on the basis of magnitude estimation studies is endorsed by the International Organization for Standardization, and it provides a direct measure of loudness that is used by acoustical engineers, who can easily convert physical instrument readings into reliable measures of loudness. This is of practical benefit because it means that instead of having a human observer make periodic reports of noise levels (say, near an airport), recordings can be used. The physical information about intensity and frequency of sound can then be translated into a measure of loudness, as it would have been perceived had a human observer been present.

Other aspects of sound can be revealed by magnitude estimation. Studies have been conducted in which subjects gave magnitude estimates of the loudness of a sound as the frequency (pitch) of the sound was varied. As the frequency of the sound is increased, it takes on a higher and higher pitch, but the sound also seems softer and softer. Thus, a higher-pitched instrument in an orchestra must produce a higher intensity of sound in order to sound as loud as a lower-pitched instrument. Even the design of a simple siren must take this fact into account and balance the pitch of the sound and the physical intensity that the siren can produce in order to make the sound as easily heard as possible.

Just as psychophysical scaling has implications for the design of sound systems, it also affects the design of visual displays. If one wants an electric sign to be twice as bright as others around it, one will need to increase the intensity about tenfold. Since the intensity of the light is basically proportional to the amount of current used, one's electric bill will increase much faster than the brightness of the sign.

Psychophysical scaling goes beyond judgments about perceptions: It has also been applied to judgments about social variables. For example, subjects asked to make magnitude estimates of the social status of people with varying numbers of years of schooling will produce results very like those for perceptions: In one study, the status of persons with a college degree was ranked about twice as high as that of those with a high school diploma, while a Ph.D. degree led to a ranking more than four times as high as that for a high school graduate.

Subjects have also been asked to assign numbers (magnitude estimates) to indicate how common various words are. The words were chosen to cover an objective range from very common ("the") to very uncommon ("grout"). When those estimates are compared to the actual frequencies in the language, they follow quite well the power law proposed by Stevens.

Perhaps the most important aspect of psychophysical scaling is that it makes it clear that perceptions can be measured. This had long been in dispute, with most early psychologists holding that no such measurement could be made. The now-voluminous literature on psychophysical scaling has provided a practical method for doing just that.

Context

In 1859, the philosopher Gustav Fechner published his book *Elemente der Psychophysik* (translated as *Elements of Psychophysics* in 1966), which provided a methodological basis for the study of the relationship between the physical world and human perception of it. Fechner's principal concern was with the measurement of absolute and difference thresholds. The absolute threshold is the smallest intensity of a stimulus that can reliably be detected, while the difference threshold is the smallest difference between two stimuli that can be detected. The methods he outlined are still in use today, both in the scientific laboratory and in real-world applications. Indeed, a visit to the optometrist or a standard hearing test makes use of exactly those same methods to measure visual or auditory acuteness. The optometrist is concerned with measuring the smallest letter someone can read, and the audiologist is concerned with the faintest sound the person can detect. Psychophysics also made up a large part of the advance of psychology as a science in the late nineteenth century. At that time, psychophysics and trained introspection were the principal methods used by psychologists to study the mind. During the early part of the twentieth century, however, trained introspection was gradually abandoned as it became clear that the method did not produce reliable results. Psychophysics, on the other hand, continues to be a mainstay in the measurement of perception.

While this article has focused on magnitude estimation, that is not the only approach to psychophysical scaling, or even the only one pursued by Stanley S. Stevens. Another approach that he has used, which nicely complements magnitude estimation, is called cross-modality matching. Using this approach, one might have a subject squeeze a hand dynamometer (a device for measuring the strength of one's grip) repeatedly as lights of varying intensities are presented. Subjects are to match the perceived brightness of the light with their grip—if one light is twice as bright as the last, they are to squeeze twice as hard. Stevens found that this approach works as well as magnitude estimation. Other approaches have subjects draw lines to indicate the magnitude of a sensation, drawing a line twice as long for a stimulus perceived to be twice the magnitude of another.

The techniques of psychophysical scaling have proved to be applicable to the measurement of a wide range of situations, going beyond perception to include social judgments as well. The contributions to understanding of how perception functions have been enormous and are likely to continue to be for some time to come.

Bibliography

Geldard, Frank Arthur. *The Human Senses.* 2d ed. New York: John Wiley & Sons, 1972. In this excellent general review of what is known about the human senses, Geldard discusses psychophysical scaling (and psychophysics generally) in an introductory chapter. In various chapters, he describes scales derived by Stevens' method of magnitude estimation, including the "gust" scale of taste, the "dol" scale of pain, and psychophysical scaling of estimates of lifted weights and loudness of tones of varying frequencies. Discussion also includes the anatomy and physiology of the senses.

Geschieder, George A. *Psychophysics: Method and Theory.* Hillsdale, N.J.: Lawrence Erlbaum, 1976. Geschieder presents a balanced view of the whole of psychophysics, including signal detection theory. This is an excellent source for the reader seeking more advanced information.

Stevens, Stanley Smith. *Psychophysics.* New York: John Wiley & Sons, 1975. This is Stevens' last, and likely best, exposition of his views on psychophysics in general, with a major emphasis on magnitude estimation and cross-modality matching. One especially appealing aspect of the book is that it presents many anecdotes about the development of the ideas, and thus illustrates the scientist at work rather than simply presenting the results of that work.

Stevens, Stanley Smith, Fred Warshofsky, and the editors of *Life. Sound and Hearing.* New York: Time, 1965. This presents a nontechnical and highly readable discussion of psychophysics in general and Stevens' power law in particular, with emphasis on studies using magnitude estimation. The impact of psychophysical scaling on the practice of acoustical engineering is also discussed. There is an entertaining look at the early psychophysics of Fechner.

Wickens, Christopher D. *Engineering Psychology and Human Performance.* Columbus, Ohio: Charles E. Merrill, 1984. Wickens provides a general survey of engineering psychology, or the application of knowledge from experimental psychology to engineering objects and systems for human use. Treats perception extensively and illustrates the impact of psychophysics and perceptual measurement on practical problems.

James D. St. James

Cross-References

The Auditory System, 344; Hearing: Loudness, Pitch, and Frequency, 1146; Sensation and Perception Defined, 2207; Sensory Modalities and Stimuli, 2214; Signal Detection Theory, 2271; Smell and Taste, 2290; Touch and Pressure, 2578; Vision: Brightness and Contrast, 2610.

PSYCHOSEXUAL DEVELOPMENT

Type of psychology: Personality
Field of study: Classic analytic themes and issues

Psychosexual development proceeds along five distinct stages, named for the primary body parts from which individuals derive pleasure during a given period of their lives; they are the oral, anal, phallic, latency, and genital stages. According to Sigmund Freud, passing through these stages successfully is critical to the healthy development of human beings.

Principal terms

EGO: the part of the human psyche that mediates between pleasure-seeking behavior and rule-directed behavior; it defines who a person is and what a person wants

FIXATION: the failure to master the tasks of one stage of development that results in failure to move to the next stage; a potential cause of psychopathology

GRATIFICATION: the satisfying of a desire or need, either through a behavior or through other means

ID: the part of the psyche that is directed solely by pleasure seeking; present at birth, it is the most primitive part of a person's psyche

LIBIDO: the energy used to direct behavior that is pleasurable either for the self or others; directed toward the self, it results in self-gratification, follows the pleasure principle, and is immature

PLEASURE PRINCIPLE: the idea that all human beings are driven to behave in certain ways by their desire to have pleasurable experiences

PSYCHOPATHOLOGY: emotional or mental illnesses or problems of sufficient severity to warrant treatment by a psychologist or psychotherapist

REGRESSION: the process of reverting to behavior appropriate to a prior stage of development, resulting from conflict

STAGES: the distinct periods in a person's life that are important to some aspect of development; they can vary in length from a few months to several years

SUPEREGO: the part of the psyche directed by rules, regulations, and morals; the last part of the psyche to develop, this is its most mature part

Overview

Psychosexual development is a major developmental theory proposed by Sigmund Freud which suggests that humans behave as they do because they are constantly seeking pleasure. During different periods, or stages, of life, the types of pleasure a person seeks will change. Each change in body location from which the person finds pleasure represents one stage in the psychosexual development. There are a total of five stages; four of them are named for the primary body part from which a person derives pleasure during a given time in life.

The first stage is the oral stage, which begins at birth and ends around one year of age. Pleasure is gained from activities of the mouth, such as sucking at a mother's nipple to obtain nourishment. The purpose of this behavior is to secure physical survival, as the infant depends upon parents for food. The infant is entirely dependent, seeks immediate gratification of needs, and does not consider other people's needs or wishes, or even recognize others as separate human beings. The selfish energy that drives the infant at this age is called libido and is attributed to the child's id, the pleasure-seeking part of a person.

The second stage is the anal stage, named for the child's preoccupation with feces and urine, as this is generally the time of toilet training. This stage begins around age one and ends around age three. The child now sees herself or himself as separate from other people and begins to assert wishes. The child becomes more demanding and controlling and often refuses parents' wishes, but also learns to delay gratification and put up with frustration. For example, the child will learn to hold in a bowel movement until a time convenient for the caregiver, rather than eliminate it as soon as pressure is felt on the sphincter. Learning to be assertive and autonomous, as well as to delay gratification, are the two most important advances for the child that occur during this stage of development. They make up an important part of a child's ego, the part of the psyche that defines who a person is and what a person wants from life.

Between age three and age six, the child passes through the phallic stage of psychosexual development. The child now knows who she or he is and who her or his parents are, and begins to have a sense of rules and regulations. Behavior becomes more moral, and the opinions of others begin to gain importance. The child begins to love others and wants to be loved by them. To ascertain that others will continue to love and cherish her or him, the child learns to suppress pleasure derived from the genitalia because of social pressures against behaviors such as masturbation. Children at this age are believed to fall in love with their parent of the opposite sex and to envy their same-sex parent. This pattern is called the Oedipus complex in boys and the Electra complex in girls. The Oedipus complex results in the fear that the boy may be hated by his father for loving his mother. To prevent being punished (the feared punishment being castration), the boy begins to identify and behave like his father and slowly learns to distance himself from his mother. Through this process of modeling and imitating the father, the boy learns rules and becomes a moral being. In the Electra complex, the girl feels that, because she has no penis, she has already received the ultimate punishment of castration. To compensate for the resultant feelings of envy of the male's penis, she decides that pregnancy will be important one day, as this is something not obtainable by the male. The girl's desire to bear a child begins. As she knows that only women bear children, she begins to identify and model after her mother and begins to distance herself from her father. The most important change in this stage of development is the child's acquisition of a super-ego, an internal sense of what is right and what is wrong that guides behavior and inhibits illegal or immoral acts.

The distancing from the same-sex parent in the phallic stage of development, which occurs around age five or six, is seen as ushering in the latency stage. At this time, children withdraw from the opposite sex and no longer seek pleasure from their body. Instead, they reorient their behavior toward skill acquisition and learning, as well as peer interaction. This makes them ready for school and play with their peer group. Not until approximately age thirteen will the desire for pleasure reawaken.

At around age thirteen, the adolescent enters the final stage of psychosexual development, the genital stage. At this time, the person has matured enough to be able to love others in an unselfish and altruistic manner and should be willing to put the welfare of others ahead of her or his own. Empathy and caring for humans begins, and the libido, which was selfishly directed in infancy, is now directed toward giving pleasure to others. The desire awakens to be intimately involved with a person of the opposite sex. This desire, however, is aim-inhibited, is complemented by feelings of affection, and does not find expression until the person has matured beyond adolescence. Mature sexuality develops as an activity that is pleasuring for both people involved, is the result of mature love, and serves procreation. Such maturity is the final goal of this stage of development.

Applications

The two most important outcomes of psychosexual development are the development of the ego and superego, and the development of psychopathology if the stages are not successfully mastered. The anal and phallic stages are particularly critical in the development of the ego and superego. During the anal stage, ego development progresses rapidly as the child learns what he or she likes and what distinguishes him or her from other people. In the phallic stage, the development of the superego occurs as a result of the Oedipus and Electra complexes.

Only if the child accepts the rules of society—that is, falls out of love with the opposite-sex parent and identifies with the same-sex parent—is she or he able to feel free of fear of punishment. Thus, the child learns to live by rules and regulations out of fear of punishment. The internalized sense of rules is represented by the child's superego. The superego serves to counteract the selfish and pleasure-seeking actions of the id, which is present at birth and remains with all human beings throughout the lifespan. Often, the superego and id will come into conflict because a selfish desire expressed by the id is being opposed by the superego. The ego will then mediate between the two, and will attempt to come up with a compromise solution. For example, a college student who has to study for an exam sometimes is overcome by the desire to party. The desire to party is driven by the id. The superego then admonishes the student to stay home and continue to study without any breaks. The ego may finally step in and mediate, and the student may decide to stay two more hours, then take a break for pleasure for an hour, and return to study some more.

The development of psychopathology is closely related to psychosexual development. First, pathology is seen as a possible consequence of fixation—that is, the child's failure to resolve a given stage and advance beyond it. Second, psychopathology may be caused by regression—the return to an earlier stage of development because of conflicts or problems. Adults with oral pathology, those who either did not move beyond or regressed to the oral stage, are said to be dependent and afraid to be alone, or else very hostile, evidencing verbal biting sarcasm to prevent getting too close to people. People with anal pathology can be either very retentive—that is, miserly, tense, orderly, and constricted—or expulsive—impulsive, disorganized, free-spending, and venting. Both types of pathology are severe and were considered by Freud to be not treatable through psychoanalysis. Only pathology arising from the phallic stage lends itself well to treatment. It is referred to as neurosis and implies that the person has significant conflicts between id wishes and superego restrictions that cannot be successfully mediated by the ego.

The neurotic pathology is seen as a result of a boy's failure to pass through the Oedipus complex or a girl's failure to pass through the Electra complex. In both cases, the child may fail to withdraw attachment to the same-sex parent and/or may fail to identify with the same-sex parent. Thus, healthy development is hampered and stopped. The child will live with the conflict of having a superego that is not completely developed and being aware that the id's wish to possess the opposite-sex parent is inappropriate. The superego chastises the person yet is unable to stop the ego. Conflict is ever-present in the person, as the wishes of the id cannot be controlled by the incomplete superego but certainly can be recognized by the superego as inappropriate. This pathology sometimes leads the person to regress to earlier stages of development and develop an oral or anal personality. If there is no regression, only fixation at the phallic stage, the person will show traits of neurosis, such as being focused on gaining pleasure for the self in general, being centered on seduction, developing symptoms of hysteria, or developing physical complaints.

Pathology does not arise from the latency or genital stages, as progression to the latency stage implies successful resolution of the Oedipus and Electra complexes: The person has matured psychosexually beyond a point of development at which neurotic pathology develops. This is true because the child is considered to have developed all necessary structures of the self, or psyche, by the end of the phallic phase. The personality structure and characteristics evidenced by the child at that time are deemed lifelong traits and are not prone to significant future change.

Psychosexual development is critical from Freud's perspective primarily because it is responsible for the development of a healthy self-structure that consists of an id, an ego, and a superego. Further, it is the most important factor in the development of the psychopathology of human beings. Mastery or failure in the realm of psychosexual development has extremely important implications for a person's functioning and mental health.

Context

The Freudian stages through which psychosexual development progresses must be considered within the historical framework present at the time that Sigmund Freud conceptualized them—that is, from the perspective of the late 1800's and early 1900's. The spirit of the times was much different from that of today, particularly with regard to how freely people were allowed to express themselves in general and with regard to sexuality in particular. It was a time in which morals and ethics forbade many normal human urges and resulted in people having to deny large parts or aspects of themselves.

This atmosphere of self-denial resulted in many different symptoms, especially among women, who were expected to follow even stricter codes of behavior than men. For example, sometimes people were observed to have paralysis of a hand that could not be explained by any actual neurological damage. Freud was one of the first physicians to recognize that this paralysis had psychological rather than physical causes. He hypothesized that the strong moral restrictions placed upon the individual were directly contrary to what the person wanted to do (perhaps masturbate, a definite transgression of permissible behavior). He believed that this person had a very strong id without a sufficiently strong superego to control it. The person's unconscious mind had to devise some other strategy to keep the id controlled: hence the paralysis of the hand. The idea that the individual has an unconscious mind was a crucial development in psychology and has been maintained to date by many types of psychologists, though not by all. It is directly related to the theory of psychosexual development.

Psychosexual development was proposed by Freud strictly to explain why certain symptoms developed in individuals. His ideas had an extremely strong impact on the future of psychology, as they were complex and explained human behavior in an understandable manner (given the spirit of the times in which they were formulated). Many followers applied Freud's theories to the treatment of psychopathology, and the profession of psychoanalysis was born. Psychoanalysts specialized in the treatment of persons with neuroses; they did so through daily sessions that lasted fifty minutes. Treatment often continued for many years. Only through this approach, psychoanalysts believed, could they effect changes in a person's psychic structure—that is, in the person's ego and the relationship between the id and superego. The profession of psychoanalysis is still a prominent one, but many changes have been made. Few psychoanalysts today follow a strictly Freudian approach to the development of a person's psyche; new ways of understanding human development and behavior have been developed. Psychoanalysis and psychosexual development, however, remain important features of psychology's history. They were important milestones in the discipline of clinical psychology, the branch of psychology concerned with the treatment of mental illness.

Bibliography

Freud, Sigmund. *Civilization and Its Discontents.* New York: W. W. Norton, 1961.

Provides a good, brief overview of the psychosexual stages and places them in the larger context of general living. Written only ten years before Freud's death, this book contains his later ideas. The writing style is excellent.

_____. *Dora: An Analysis of a Case of Hysteria.* New York: Collier Books, 1963. Provides the case history of a woman who suffered from a neurosis. The treatment description of this case provides an excellent practical application of the theory of psychosexual development and its implications for psychopathology and personality development. Very readable; targets the layperson.

_____. *A General Introduction to Psychoanalysis.* New York: Garden City Books, 1952. Provides a thorough but very readable overview of the theories and thoughts Freud developed that support his notion of psychosexual development. A good and relatively brief primer for the layperson.

_____. *Three Case Histories.* New York: Collier Books, 1963. Provides three applied examples of psychopathology as an outgrowth of fixation at or regression to early psychosexual stages. Written for the layperson; presented in an interesting manner.

Rychlak, Joseph F. "The Beginnings of Psychoanalysis: Sigmund Freud." In *Introduction to Personality and Psychotherapy.* 2d ed. Boston: Houghton Mifflin, 1981. This chapter is part of a textbook and therefore somewhat technical, but it is an outstanding account of psychosexual development. It deals with the topic thoroughly, places it in a historical context, and discusses its implications for more recent psychology. An excellent overview that can be read by the layperson who is willing to spend some time rereading the material to understand it thoroughly.

Christiane Brems

Cross-References

Abnormality: Psychodynamic Models, 74; Analytical Psychotherapy, 246; Dream Analysis, 830; Ego Defense Mechanisms, 860; Psychoanalysis: Classical versus Modern, 1898; Psychoanalytic Psychology: An Overview, 1905; Psychoanalytic Psychology and Personality: Sigmund Freud, 1912; Psychotherapy with Children, 2009; Social Psychological Models: Karen Horney, 2324.

PSYCHOSOMATIC DISORDERS

Type of psychology: Psychopathology
Fields of study: Cognitive processes; organic disorders; stress and illness

Psychosomatic disorders are physical disorders produced by psychological factors such as stress, mental states, or personality characteristics. A variety of psychological or psychotherapeutic interventions have been developed to alter the individual's ability to cope with stressful situations and to change the personality or behavior of the individual.

Principal terms

BEHAVIOR MODIFICATION: therapeutic techniques based on operant conditioning methods employing rewards for desirable behaviors and nonreinforcement or punishment for undesirable behaviors

BIOGENIC: of biological or physical origin

BIOPSYCHOSOCIAL: combining biological, psychological, and social factors

COGNITIVE: having to do with thought processes, such as images, memories, thinking, and problem solving

PSYCHOGENIC: of psychological origin

PSYCHOLOGICAL FACTORS AFFECTING PHYSICAL CONDITION: DSM-III-R terminology that refers to psychosomatic or psychophysiological disorders

PSYCHOSOMATIC DISORDERS: physical disorders that are the result of psychological factors; synonymous with psychophysiological disorders

TYPE A BEHAVIOR PATTERN: a pattern of personality characteristics which leads to behavior that is thought to contribute to coronary heart disease

TYPE C BEHAVIOR PATTERN: a pattern of personality characteristics thought to contribute to development of cancer

Overview

Psychosomatic disorders are physical disorders which are caused by, or exacerbated by, psychological factors. These psychological factors fall into three major groups: stress resulting from encounters with the environment, personality characteristics, and psychological states. It should be noted that psychosomatic disorders are different from two other conditions with which they are often confused. Psychosomatic disorders are real—that is, they are actual physical illnesses that have underlying psychological causes or that are made worse by psychological factors. In somatoform disorders (such as hypochondriasis), by contrast there is no physiological cause; another condition, malingering, is the faking of an illness.

Psychosomatic disorders can affect any of the organ systems of the body. Certainly, not all physical disorders or illnesses are psychosomatic disorders; in many cases, an illness or physical disorder is caused entirely by biogenic factors. In many other cases, however, there is no question about the importance of psychogenic factors. The American College of Family Physicians has estimated that 90 percent of the workload of doctors is the result of psychogenic factors.

There are many familiar and common psychosomatic disorders that can affect the body's various organ systems. Included among them are skin disorders, such as acne, hives, and rashes; musculoskeletal disorders, such as backaches, rheumatoid arthritis, and tension headaches; respiratory disorders, such as asthma and hiccups; and cardiovascular disorders, such as hypertension, heart attacks, strokes, and migraine headaches. Other disorders have also been related to psychological factors, including anemia, weakening of the immune system, ulcers, and constipation. Genitourinary disorders such as menstrual problems, vaginismus, male erectile disorder, and premature ejaculation are included among psychosomatic disorders, as are certain endocrine and neurological problems.

The relationship between the mind and the body has long been the subject of debate. Early societies saw a clear link between the mind and the body. Early Greek and Roman physicians believed that body fluids determined personality types and that people with certain personality types were prone to certain types of diseases. Beginning during the Renaissance period and continuing almost to today, the dominant line of thought held that there was little or no connection between the mind and the body. Illness was seen as the result of organic, cellular pathology. Destruction of body tissue and invasion by "germs," rather than personality type, were seen as the causes of illness.

Sigmund Freud's work with patients suffering from conversion hysteria began to demonstrate both the importance of psychological factors in the production of physical symptoms of illness and the value of psychological therapy in changing the functioning of the body. Research conducted in the 1930's and 1940's suggested that personality factors play a role in the production of a variety of specific illnesses, including ulcers, hypertension, and asthma.

Today, the ascending line of thought can be described as a biopsychosocial view of illness, which begins with the basic assumption that health and illness result from an interplay of biological, psychological, and social factors. A man who suffers a heart attack at age thirty-five is not conceptualized simply as a person who is experiencing the effects of cellular damage caused by purely biological processes that are best treated by surgery or the administration of drugs. The victim, instead, is viewed as a person who also has engaged in practices that adversely affected his health. In addition to drugs and surgery, therefore, treatment for this man might include changing his views on the relative value of work and family as well as emphasizing the importance of daily exercise and diet. If he smokes, he will be encouraged to quit smoking. He might receive training in stress management and relaxation techniques.

Few people today would argue with the proposition that stress is a fact of life. Most have far more experience with stressors—those events that humans find stressful—than they would willingly choose for themselves. Stress is one of the major causes of psychosomatic disorders. Stressors are often assumed to be external events, probably because stressful external events are so easily identified and recognized. Many stressors, however, come from within oneself. For example, one is often the only person who demands that one meet the strict standards that one has set for oneself, and frequently judges oneself more harshly than anyone else for failing to meet those standards. Especially since the late 1970's and early 1980's, cognitive psychologists have focused attention on the internal thinking processes, thoughts, values, beliefs, and expectations that lead people to put unnecessary pressure on themselves that results in the subjective sense of stress.

Another contribution made by cognitive psychologists was the realization that a situation can be a stressor only if the individual interprets it as stressful. Any event that people perceive as something with which they can cope will be perceived as less stressful than an event that taxes or exceeds their resources, regardless of the objective seriousness of the two events. In other words, it is the cognitive appraisal of the event, coupled with one's cognitive appraisal of one's ability to deal with the event, rather than the objective reality of the event, that determines the degree to which one subjectively experiences stress.

Continuing the tradition of the early Greek and Roman physicians, modern personality theorists have often noted that certain personality characteristics seem to be associated with a propensity to develop illness, or even specific illnesses. Other personality characteristics appear to reduce vulnerability to illness. One of the best-known examples of a case in which personality characteristics affect health is that of the Type A behavior pattern (or Type A personality). The person identified as a Type A personality typically displays a pattern of behaviors which include easily aroused hostility, excessive competitiveness, and a pronounced sense of time urgency. Research suggests that hostility is the most damaging of these behaviors. Type A personalities typically display hyperreactivity to stressful situations, with a corresponding slow return to the baseline of arousal. The hostile Type A personality is particularly prone to coronary heart disease. By contrast, the less driven Type B personality does not display the hostility, competitiveness, and time urgency of the Type A personality, and is about half as likely to develop coronary heart disease.

Studies conducted in the 1970's, and especially in the 1980's, have led to the suggestion that there is a Type C, or cancer-prone, personality. It is well known that many natural and artificial substances produce cancer, but many researchers have also noted that people with certain personality characteristics are more likely to develop cancer, are more likely to develop fast-growing cancers, and are less likely to survive their cancers. These personality characteristics include repression of strong negative emotions, acquiescence in the face of stressful life situations, inhibition, depression, and hopelessness. Encounters with uncontrollable stressful events appear to be particularly related to the development of cancer. In addition, some research suggests that not having strong social support systems contributes to the likelihood of developing cancer.

Recent research has begun to focus on the possible interaction between risk factors for cancer. For example, depressed smokers are many more times likely to develop smoking-related cancers than are either nondepressed smokers or depressed nonsmokers. One theory suggests that the smoking provides exposure to the carcinogenic substance that initiates the cancer, and depression promotes its development.

It has been suggested that hardiness is a broad, positive personality variable that affects one's propensity for developing stress related illness. Hardiness is made up of three more specific characteristics: commitment (to become involved in things that are going on around oneself), challenge (accepting the need for change and seeing new opportunities for growth in what others see as problems), and control (a belief that one's actions determine what happens in life and that one can have an effect on the environment). It has been hypothesized that people who possess these characteristics are less likely to develop stress-related disorders because they view stressful situations more favorably than do other people. Commitment and control seem to be more influential in promoting health. Locus of control is a related concept which has received much attention.

Locus of control refers to the location where one believes control over life events originates. An external locus of control is outside oneself; an internal locus of control is within oneself. The individual who perceives that life events are the result of luck, or are determined by others, is assuming an external locus of control. The belief that one's efforts and actions control one's own destiny reflects an internal locus of control. Internalizers are thought to be more likely to assume responsibility for initiating necessary life-style changes, to employ more direct coping mechanisms when confronted with stressful situations, and to be more optimistic about the possibility of successfully instituting changes that are needed. This last characteristic is sometimes called self-efficacy. Self-efficacy refers to the belief that one is able to do what is needed and attain the intended effect.

Martin E. P. Seligman began to investigate the phenomenon of learned helplessness in 1964. In part, his interest was fueled by his observations of the life and fate of his father, who suffered a series of devastating strokes. Seligman found that when faced with a situation in which they can do nothing to prevent or escape from what is happening to them, both dogs and people often simply lie down and take it (literally or figuratively). They learn the attitude of helplessness. He also found that helplessness can be unlearned, but that it is usually difficult to do so because the individual has quit trying to escape or avoid the situation. A decade later, Seligman and his colleagues began to investigate the question of why some people (and dogs) did *not* become helpless. They concluded that people (and, presumably dogs) who adopt a pessimistic explanatory style become helpless when adversity is encountered, but that an optimistic explanatory style prevents the development of learned helplessness.

Applications

Martin E. P. Seligman has described the chain of events by which the pessimistic explanatory style may lead to illness. Beginning with unfortunate experiences such as a serious loss, defeat, or failure, the person with a pessimistic explanatory style becomes depressed. The depression leads to depletion of a neurotransmitter substance called catecholamine, and the body increases the secretion of endorphins— the body's own naturally produced form of morphine. When receptors in the immune system detect the increased presence of the endorphins, the immune system begins to turn itself down. Any disease agents that are encountered while the immune system is weakened have a much greater likelihood of overwhelming the remaining defenses of the immune system. This process is very similar to the situation faced by the individual who contracts the human immunodeficiency virus (HIV) and develops acquired immune deficiency syndrome (AIDS). When the immune system of the person with AIDS is unable to function effectively, opportunistic infections against which the body could normally defend itself are able to take over. It is those opportunistic infections that kill, rather than the HIV or AIDS itself.

Since the hyperreactivity of the Type A behavior pattern is thought to be at least partially genetically based, there are probably some limits on what can be done to reduce the incidence of coronary heart disease resulting from physiological hyperreactivity. There is, however, much that can be done in other areas. Persons who are prone to such disorders can be taught to exercise properly, eliminate unhealthy dietary practices, and reduce or quit smoking. Of particular interest to psychologists is the opportunity to help these individuals by teaching effective coping strategies, stress management, values training, behavior modification to control Type A behaviors, and cognitive control of depression and other negative emotions.

Studies by psychologists have demonstrated a wide range of interventions that can be helpful in reducing the danger of cardiovascular disease in Type A personalities. Exercise produces positive effects on physiological functioning, appears to improve general psychological functioning, and reduces Type A behaviors. Cognitive behavioral stress management techniques have been shown to reduce behavioral reactivity. Values training focusing on changing the person's perceptions of the importance of occupational success and competitiveness has enabled them to concentrate on more beneficial behaviors. Behavior modification techniques have been used to alter the kinds of behavior that appear to be most dangerous for the Type A person, substituting other behavioral responses in place of explosive speech and hostility. Cognitive control of emotions produces more rapid physiological recovery after stress.

Efforts by psychologists to help the Type C personality might focus on assertiveness training and altering the person's belief that it is not appropriate to display strong negative emotions, such as anger or frustration. Teaching the Type C person to fight back against stressful life situations, rather that acquiescing to them, might also be of benefit. Imagery therapy appears to be beneficial to some cancer patients, perhaps for that reason, but also because it promotes the development of learned optimism in place of learned pessimism. Promoting the development of effective social support systems is another means for psychologists to have a positive impact on the fight against cancer.

Context

It is important that a distinction be made between psychosomatic disorders and three other conditions listed in the *Diagnostic and Statistical Manual of Mental Disorders* (rev. 3d ed., DSM-III-R), which is the official classification system for mental disorders that was published by the American Psychiatric Association in 1987. Psychosomatic disorders, which are covered by the category Psychological Factors Affecting Physical Conditions, are not themselves considered mental disorders. While the psychological factors that cause the physical illness are unhealthy or abnormal from a psychiatric or psychological perspective, the psychosomatic disorder is a real, physical illness or condition controlled by real, physical processes.

Somatoform disorders, on the other hand, are mental disorders which manifest themselves through real or imagined physical symptoms for which no physical cause exists. These symptoms are not intentionally produced by the client. Conversion disorder is one of the somatoform disorders that laypeople often confuse with psychosomatic disorders. Unlike the case with psychosomatic disorders, there is no organic or physiological pathology that would account for the presence of the physical symptoms displayed by the person suffering from a conversion disorder. Hypochondriasis is the second somatoform disorder that is often confusing for laypeople. The person suffering from hypochondriasis fears or believes that he or she has the symptoms of a serious disease, but the imagined "symptoms" are actually normal sensations or body reactions which are misinterpreted as symptoms of disease.

Malingering is the third condition which is sometimes confused with psychosomatic disorders. The person who is malingering is faking illness, and is either reporting symptoms that do not exist at all or which are grossly exaggerated. The malingering is motivated by external goals or incentives.

By eliminating many of the diseases that used to be epidemic, especially those which killed people early in life, medical science has increased the average life expectancy of Americans by about thirty years since the beginning of the twentieth century. Eliminating the psychological factors that cause psychosomatic disorders holds promise for another increase in average life expectancy in the next few decades. Heart disease, cancer, and strokes are the top three killer diseases in the United States, and each has a powerful psychosomatic component. The reduction in human suffering and the economic benefits that can be gained by controlling nonfatal psychosomatic disorders is equally promising.

Cognitive and health psychologists have, particularly since the 1970's, tried to determine the degree to which cognitive psychotherapy interventions can boost immune system functioning in cancer patients. They have also used behavioral and cognitive therapy approaches to alter the attitudes and behaviors of people who are prone to heart disease and strokes with considerable success. In the near future, they can be expected to focus their efforts on two major fronts. The first will involve further attempts to identify the psychological factors which might increase people's propensity to develop psychosomatic disorders. The second will involve continuing efforts to develop and refine the therapeutic interventions intended to reduce the damage done by psychosomatic disorders, and possibly to prevent them entirely.

Bibliography

Chopra, Deepak. *Creating Health.* Boston: Houghton Mifflin, 1987. Chopra is a proponent of meditation, an approach that many American psychologists do not necessarily feel comfortable advocating. Nevertheless, this book is written by a practicing physician for the layperson. He covers a wide variety of psychosomatic disorders, suggests a variety of healthy habits, and presents the viewpoint that "health is our natural state."

Reisner, Morton F., ed. *Organic Disorders and Psychosomatic Disorders.* Vol. 3 in *American Handbook of Psychiatry.* 2d ed., edited by Silvano Arieti. New York: Basic Books, 1975. Do not let the name of the publisher fool you; this is heavy reading. It is, however, an authoritative source of information on the subject of psychosomatic disorders. Chapters 1, 21, 25, and 36 are particularly pertinent overviews of the topic, and several chapters in part 2 focus on specific psychosomatic disorders.

Seligman, Martin E. P. *Learned Optimism.* New York: Alfred A. Knopf, 1991. Chapter 2 provides an especially interesting account of how two young upstart graduate students can blow a hole in one of the most basic assumptions of a well-entrenched viewpoint and promote the development of a new way of looking at things. Chapter 10 describes how explanatory styles might affect health and the mechanism by which this is thought to occur. A test developed to measure explanatory styles is included in chapter 3, and the last chapters focus on how to develop an optimistic orientation. A very readable book which examines a most interesting concept.

Simonton, O. Carl, Stephanie Matthews-Simonton, and James L. Creighton. *Getting Well Again.* New York: Bantam Books, 1980. Cancer researchers and therapists examine the mind-body connection, effects of beliefs, causes of cancer, effects of stress and personality, and effects of expectations on the development and progress of cancer. They describe a holistic approach to treatment, emphasizing relaxation and visual imagery, that is reported to produce cancer survival rates that are twice the national norm. A very readable book which is readily available in paperback.

Taylor, Shelley E. *Health Psychology.* 2d ed. New York: McGraw-Hill, 1991. A moderately high-level college textbook that comprehensively covers the general field of health psychology. As could be expected, many research studies are presented, and not all of them corroborate one another. The general reader should have no particular difficulty handling this material; the writing is reader-friendly.

John W. Nichols

Cross-References

PSYCHOSURGERY

Type of psychology: Psychotherapy
Field of study: Biological treatments

Psychosurgery is a method for treating certain mental disorders by performing surgical operations on the brain, either by severing the connections between different parts of the brain or by destroying brain tissue in specific areas. Psychosurgery was popular from about 1935 to 1960; it has now largely been replaced by drugs. It remains a highly controversial procedure.

Principal terms

BIOETHICS: includes the study of the moral, ethical, and social issues posed by treating mental disorders by biological means, especially psychosurgery

BIOLOGICAL DETERMINISM: the belief that behavior is determined or caused by a corresponding set of conditions within the brain

BIOMEDICAL MODEL: the belief, similar to biological determinism, that mental illness is the result of dysfunction in certain areas of the brain

BIOMEDICAL TREATMENT: a therapy for mental disorders that is based on altering brain function; includes drugs, electroconvulsive shock, and psychosurgery

LOBOTOMY: the archetypical psychosurgical technique for destroying brain tissue; although it is but one of several methods, it was the first and most commonly performed and remains the most notorious

Overview

Psychosurgery, also referred to as psychiatric surgery, psychiatric neurosurgery, or functional neurosurgery, is a medical procedure intended to alleviate certain mental illnesses by destroying brain tissue in selected areas of the brain. Psychosurgery is based on the biomedical model of mental illness, which posits that mental states and ensuing behavior are the result of activity in the nervous system. That is, at the most fundamental level, human thoughts and actions are biologically determined by the functioning nervous system. Therefore, mental illness and abnormal behavior are caused by abnormalities in the nervous system: by the release of certain neurotransmitters and/or by abnormalities in brain structure. If it is assumed that the basis of a mental illness is an abnormality of the nervous system, the appropriate therapy is biomedical: The nervous system is treated directly to alleviate the problem. Biomedical treatments include psychosurgery, electroconvulsive shock, and drugs.

Contemporary psychosurgery was founded in 1935 by the Portuguese neurosurgeon António Egas Moniz. Egas Moniz attended a symposium in August, 1935, at which Carlyle Jacobsen reported anecdotally a marked change in the level of emotionality of a chimpanzee following destruction of a large part of the frontal lobe of the cerebral cortex. Formerly, the chimpanzee had been highly emotional and obstinate; following the operation, the chimpanzee appeared calm and cooperative. Egas Moniz inquired of Jacobsen whether the technique could be used to relieve anxiety states in humans; less than three months later, in November, 1935, Egas Moniz performed his first operation.

In these operations, two holes were drilled into the skull of mental patients. Initially, alcohol was injected through the holes directly into the frontal lobes. Commencing with the eighth operation, however, a scalpel-like instrument was inserted through the hole into the frontal lobes, and a wire loop was then extended from the scalpel and rotated, destroying whatever nerve tissues it contacted. Egas Moniz coined the term "psychosurgery" to describe this kind of treatment. He referred to his particular technique as prefrontal leucotomy (from the Greek *leuco*, meaning "white matter," or nerve fibers, and *tome*, meaning "knife"). The instrument he used was called a leucotome.

Egas Moniz's claims of success in alleviating extreme states of emotionality with this procedure stimulated worldwide interest, excitement, and practice. About thirty-five thousand operations were performed in the United States from 1936 through 1978, with perhaps double that number worldwide. Psychosurgery was seen as a quick and effective method for alleviating certain commonly occurring mental illnesses which could not be treated rapidly and effectively by any other means, as well as providing a partial solution to the problem of overcrowding in mental hospitals.

As other psychosurgeons began performing psychosurgery, new techniques were developed that were believed to be improvements. Egas Moniz's prefrontal leucotomy, which did not permit precise location of the area to be cut, was superseded by the prefrontal lobotomy, developed by the Americans Walter Freeman and James Watts in 1937. Larger holes were drilled into both sides of the skull, and a leucotome was inserted and precisely moved in a sweeping motion through the frontal lobe. In 1948, Freeman introduced the transorbital lobotomy. This procedure involved inserting an ice-picklike knife through the top of the eye socket into the brain and then swinging it back and forth. This procedure was quick and efficient and could be performed as an office procedure. Freeman said that he could perform fifty operations in a day.

The lobotomy was handicapped, however, by two important limitations. Destruction of the frontal lobe usually produced a number of serious side effects. Although the lobotomy was perhaps more precise than the leucotomy, the psychosurgeon still could not know with certainty exactly what part of the brain was being excised. A considerable risk of damaging other areas of the brain or of inducing hemorrhaging was present.

Later technological innovations and increased understanding of the structure of the nervous system permitted more precise and less invasive surgical procedures. An apparatus called the stereotaxis allowed precise mapping of the brain. Using this instrument, Ernest Spiegel and Henry Wycis inserted electrodes into previously inaccessible parts of the brain and destroyed a small area of tissue with electricity.

This procedure initiated surgery on small and precisely located areas of the brain other than the frontal lobes, thus minimizing side effects. Nevertheless, over its more than fifty-year history, the vast majority of psychosurgical operations have been lobotomies.

Applications

As John Kleinig observes in *Ethical Issues in Psychosurgery* (1985), nearly every brain structure has at some point been subject to a psychosurgical procedure. Psychosurgery involving various brain structures has been performed in the belief that specific abnormal mental states and behaviors that are unaffected by other treatments can be alleviated through psychosurgery. According to Kleinig, psychosurgery has been used to treat many disorders.

Psychosurgery has not in general produced favorable results with schizophrenia. Drugs are the preferred biomedical procedure. Schizophrenia is still occasionally treated by psychosurgery, but only in those cases with a high emotional component—that is, with affective behaviors or mood states. Psychosurgery has been most commonly used with cases characterized by severe and disabling depression, obsessive-compulsive disorders, and acute tension and anxiety. The purpose is to even or level out the patient's feelings and emotions. As with schizophrenia, drugs are the preferred mode of treatment for these disorders; however, psychosurgery may be a consideration for those patients who do not respond appropriately to drugs and whose dysfunction is extremely severe.

Anorexia nervosa is the chronic refusal to eat sufficient food to maintain normal health. It has been viewed by some as an extreme compulsion which may be related to a disorder of the limbic system. Psychosurgery has been performed in extreme cases. Hyperactive syndrome, or attention-deficit hyperactivity disorder, in children has been viewed by some as a disorder that is a genetically based brain dysfunction, and psychosurgery has been performed when other treatments have failed. Uncontrollable rage and/or aggression is believed to be regulated by the amygdaloid body in the limbic system. Moderately favorable results have been reported with amygdalectomies performed on both adults and children.

Substance abuse and addictions can be viewed as analogues to compulsions. The purpose of psychosurgery is to reduce the strength of the desire of the addiction's object. Data indicate favorable outcomes for certain groups of alcoholics and drug addicts, but the efficacy of the procedure with obesity and compulsive gambling is lacking.

Psychosurgery has been performed on pedophiliacs (child molesters) and others who have engaged in violent sexual offenses, in order to remove the desire to perform such acts. The operation has focused on the hypothalamus, a structure in the limbic system. In some cases, the operation has succeeded, probably by producing a reduction of sexual desire in general.

The anterior angulate region of the limbic system, which is believed to be involved with the perception of pain, has been subjected to psychosurgery. Some favorable results have been obtained, which some believe are the result of the alleviation of depression or obsessive behaviors associated with intractable pain. Some pain specialists believe that psychosurgery is not appropriate in any instance.

It is apparent from this survey that psychosurgery has been employed for a wide variety of disorders and performed upon a wide variety of patient populations. With its introduction by Egas Moniz in the 1930's, and its vigorous advocacy by Egas Moniz in Europe and by Freeman and Watts in the United States, psychosurgery was received with great hope and expectation. It was seen as providing a fast, easy, and inexpensive way of treating certain mental illnesses that were unresponsive to any alternative treatments available at the time. In addition, if institutionalized patients could be successfully treated by psychosurgery, they could be released, thus simultaneously alleviating the abysmal overcrowding and intolerable conditions of mental institutions and returning the patients to a productive life in society. In fact, Egas Moniz won the Nobel Prize in Physiology or Medicine in 1949 in recognition of his work. The citation states: "Frontal leucotomy, despite certain limitations of the operative method, must be considered one of the most important discoveries ever made in psychiatric therapy, because through its use a great number of suffering people and total invalids have recovered and have been socially rehabilitated."

Context

Egas Moniz's Nobel citation may be contrasted with David L. Rosenhan and Martin E. P. Seligman's assessment of lobotomy in the second edition of their book *Abnormal Psychology* (1989): "There is the danger that physicians and patients may become overzealous in their search for a quick neurological cure. . . . [T]he disastrous history of frontal lobotomies . . . should serve as a warning."

Although the biomedical model is a sound theory, and biological treatments have proved to be valuable and worthwhile, in retrospect, Rosenhan and Seligman were correct. Lobotomies were, in general, "disastrous," and their sorry history provides a textbook example of how not to bring a new medical procedure on line. Irreversible destruction of brain tissue and side effects were produced by procedures of highly questionable effectiveness.

The goals and desires of the early psychosurgeons may have been laudable, but their methods were not. Within three months of hearing Jacobsen's anecdotal account, Egas Moniz was performing lobotomies, despite the lack of clear evidence from prior animal experimentation that might at least support the irreversible destruction of the brain tissue. Egas Moniz performed no animal experimentation himself. He declared the frontal lobes to be the area of the brain responsible for the mental disorders to be treated by psychosurgery. His reading of the scientific literature to support his beliefs, however, was spotty and selective, and contradictory evidence was ignored. Furthermore, there was present a large animal and human literature clearly demonstrating a range of serious side effects and deficits produced by lesions of the frontal lobes, such as apathy, retarded movement, loss of initiative, and mutism. Yet, with no supporting evidence, Egas Moniz insisted these side effects were only temporary. In fact, they could be permanent. Egas Moniz's initial report on twenty patients claimed a cure for seven, lessening of symptoms in six, and no effect on six. An impartial review of these cases by Stanley Cobb, however, concluded that only one of the twenty cases provided enough information to allow a judgment.

Mercifully, the introduction of psychoactive drugs and growing criticism of lobotomies effectively brought them to an end by the late 1950's. Psychosurgery is still occasionally performed; its advocates argue that newer techniques are used that avoid the frontal lobes, that the procedure is based upon a good understanding of how the nervous system functions, that side effects are minimal, that its use is much more strictly monitored and regulated, and that it is viewed only as a treatment of last resort. Nevertheless, psychosurgery still remains highly controversial. Many practitioners and scientists are skeptical about its effectiveness, arguing that destruction of any brain tissue can produce unavoidable side effects; psychosurgery is believed by these individuals to be an ethically and morally unacceptable procedure of dubious value.

Bibliography

Kleinig, John. *Ethical Issues in Psychosurgery.* London: Allen & Unwin, 1985. This informative book focuses on the bioethical problems raised by psychosurgery. Discusses psychiatric diagnosis, the use of experimental therapies, criteria for success, informed consent, medical priorities, safeguards, and the relation between personality and the brain.

Marsh, Frank H., and Janet Katz, eds. *Biology, Crime, and Ethics.* Cincinnati: Anderson, 1984. Explores the relationship between biological factors (genetics, physiology) and criminal and aggressive behavior. Contains a section on psychosurgery and its appropriateness in treating violent and aggressive behavior.

Shuman, Samuel I. *Psychosurgery and the Medical Control of Violence.* Detroit: Wayne State University Press, 1977. This wide-ranging book focuses on the public concern over psychosurgery, its legitimacy as a scientific technique, and possible erosion of legal rights. Individual chapters examine landmark legal cases, the difficulties involved in deciding when psychosurgery is a viable option, and constitutional threats posed by psychosurgery.

Smith, J. Sydney, and L. G. Kiloh, eds. *Psychosurgery and Society.* New York: Pergamon Press, 1977. Presents a number of articles on various aspects of psychosurgery. Based upon a symposium held in Australia in 1974. Presentations include discussions of traditional psychosurgery, social apprehensions concerning psychosurgery, and potential safeguards to protect patients.

Valenstein, Elliot S. *Great and Desperate Cures.* New York: Basic Books, 1986. Highly recommended. A very interesting and readable treatment of psychosurgery and other extreme treatments for mental illness. Concentrates on psychosurgery and presents a thorough consideration of its history from its inception to the 1980's. Filled with many interesting photographs and anecdotes that collectively provide an intimate, insider's view on psychosurgery.

_____, ed. *The Psychosurgery Debate.* San Francisco: W. H. Freeman, 1980. A wide-ranging discussion of various aspects of psychosurgery. Presentations include the rationale for psychosurgery, selection of patients, postoperative evaluation, techniques, evaluation, legal issues, and ethical issues.

Laurence Miller

Cross-References

Abnormality: Biomedical Models, 39; Brain Specialization, 455; The Cerebral Cortex, 500; Lobotomy, 1464; Madness: Historical Contexts, 1492; Neuropsychology, 1667; Psychoactive Drug Therapy, 1891.

PSYCHOTHERAPEUTIC EFFECTIVENESS

Type of psychology: Psychotherapy
Field of study: Evaluating psychotherapy

Psychotherapy is a rapidly expanding field; it has been estimated that there are more than four hundred psychotherapeutic approaches. Research evaluating the effectiveness of psychotherapy serves a primary role in the development and validation of therapeutic approaches. Studies have examined the effectiveness of psychotherapy on thousands of patients. Although such studies often produce contradictory and perhaps even disappointing findings, there is clear evidence that psychotherapy is effective.

Principal terms

CASE STUDY: an unsystematic report of treatment which is typically based on a therapist's opinions about the results

EMPATHY: the ability to convey an understanding of the client's emotional experiences

META-ANALYSIS: a set of quantitative (statistical) procedures used to evaluate a body of empirical literature

NEUROTIC DISORDERS: an array of difficulties associated with anxiety or distress with which an individual feels unable to cope (the term is no longer used to describe specific psychological problems)

PLACEBO: a procedure designed to be inert or inactive; used frequently in research designs as a method of controlling certain variables

RANDOMIZATION: a procedure in which patients or treatments are selected without regard for particular variables; for example, flipping a coin to decide who goes first

RELAPSE: reexperiencing an earlier problem or returning to a previous level of functioning

SPONTANEOUS REMISSION: recovery from an illness; improvement without treatment

Overview

Although the roots of psychotherapy can be traced back to ancient times, the birth of modern psychotherapy is frequently targeted with the famous case of "Anna O." in 1882. Physician Josef Breuer, who was a colleague of Sigmund Freud, described Anna O. as a twenty-one-year-old patient with multiple symptoms including paralysis and loss of sensitivity in her limbs, lapses in awareness, problems in vision and speech, headaches, and dual personality. During treatment, Breuer found that if Anna discussed every occurrence of a symptom until she described its origin and vividly recalled its first appearance, the symptom would disappear. Hypnosis was also employed to help Anna O. eliminate the symptoms more rapidly. (Eventually,

Breuer stopped working with this patient because of numerous difficulties, including his jealous wife and his patient's tendency to become hysterical.) Anna O., whose real name was Bertha Pappenheim, later became well known throughout Germany for her work with children, prostitutes, and Jewish relief organizations.

The case of Anna O. is not only important as perhaps representing the birth of modern psychotherapy but also characteristic of a method of investigation referred to as the case study or case report. A case report attempts to highlight descriptions of a specific patient and treatment approach, typically as reported by the therapist. Given the fact that most patients treated in psychotherapy are seen individually by a single therapist, it is not surprising that some of the most influential literature in the history of psychotherapy is based on case reports. Unfortunately, the vast majority of case reports are inherently problematic in terms of scientific merit and methodological rigor. Moreover, it is very difficult to determine which factors are most effective in the treatment of any particular patient. Thus, whereas case reports are common in the history of psychotherapy research, their value is generally limited.

The earliest psychotherapy outcome studies were conducted from the 1930's to the 1960's. These initial investigations were concerned with one primary question: "Does psychotherapy demonstrate positive effects?" Unfortunately, the research methodology employed in these studies was typically flawed, and interpretations proved ambiguous. The most common area of disagreement in the early investigations was the concept of "spontaneous remission." That is, psychotherapy was evaluated in comparison to the rates of improvement seen among patients who were not currently receiving treatment.

For example, British psychologist Hans Eysenck created a furor in the early 1950's, one which continued to trouble psychologists and mental health workers for several decades. Eysenck concluded, on the basis of his review of twenty-four studies, that psychotherapy produced no greater changes in individuals than did naturally occurring life events. Specifically, he argued that two-thirds of people with neurotic disorders improve over a two-year period with or without psychotherapy. Two particular problems with his review warrant comment, however; first, the studies that were included in his review rarely employed randomization, which raises significant concerns about subsequent interpretations. Second, later analyses of the same data set demonstrated that Eysenck's original estimates of improvements in the absence of treatment were inflated.

The manner in which research investigations were conducted (the research methodology) became more sophisticated in the 1970's. In particular, research designs included appropriate control groups to account for spontaneous improvements, randomly assigned experimental conditions, well-specified treatment protocols administered by well-trained therapists, and improved instruments and procedures to measure effectiveness. As a result, it became increasingly clear that many psychotherapies demonstrate statistically significant and clinically meaningful effects on patients. Not all patients reveal improvement, however, and many patients relapse following successful treatment.

In 1977, researchers Mary Smith and Gene Glass presented a review of 375 psychotherapy outcome studies via a newly devised methodology called "meta-analysis." Meta-analysis literally means "analysis of analyses" and represents a statistical procedure used to summarize collections of research data. Meta-analysis is frequently regarded as more objective and more sophisticated than traditional review procedures such as those employed by Eysenck. Smith and Glass revealed that most patients who entered outpatient psychotherapy showed noticeable improvement. In addition, the average therapy patient improved more than did 75 percent of comparable control patients.

The results reported by Smith and Glass were controversial, and they stimulated much productive debate. In particular, the authors were criticized for certain procedural steps (for example, excluding particular studies and including others). In response to such criticism, many researchers conducted additional meta-analytic investigations to examine the empirical effectiveness of psychotherapy. Of particular importance is the large follow-up investigation that was conducted by Smith, Glass, and Thomas Miller in 1980. The authors presented many detailed analyses of their results and expanded the data set from 375 studies to 475 studies involving approximately twenty-five thousand patients treated by seventy-eight therapies over an average of sixteen sessions. Smith, Glass, and Miller revealed that the average therapy patient was better off than 80 percent of the control group.

To date, numerous studies have provided evidence for the general effectiveness of psychotherapy to produce positive changes in targeted problem areas; however, psychotherapy is not a unitary procedure applied to a unitary problem. Moreover, many of the nearly four hundred psychotherapeutic approaches have yet to be systematically evaluated. Thus, it is important to understand the empirical evidence for specific treatment approaches with specific patient populations. It is similarly important to note that each therapist is a unique individual who provides his or her own unique perspective and experience to the psychotherapeutic process. Fortunately, positive effects are generally common among psychotherapy patients, and negative (deterioration) effects, which are also observed regularly, often appear related to a poor match of therapist, technique, and patient factors.

Applications

Recent research has focused on some of the factors associated with patient improvement, and several specific methods have been used to evaluate different treatments. Common research designs include contrasting an established treatment with a new treatment approach (for example, systematic desensitization versus eye-movement desensitization for anxiety) or therapeutic format (group depression treatment versus individual depression treatment), separating the components of an effective treatment package (such as cognitive behavioral treatment of anxiety) to examine the relative effectiveness of the modules, and analyzing the interactions between therapist and patient during psychotherapy (process research).

The results from studies employing these designs are generally mixed and reveal limited differences between specific therapeutic approaches. For example, in the largest meta-analytic studies, some analyses revealed that behavioral and cognitive therapies were found to have larger positive changes when compared to other types of psychotherapy (psychodynamic and humanistic), while other analyses did not. Similarly, several large comparative studies revealed considerable patient improvement regardless of treatment approach. Such results must be carefully evaluated, however, because there are numerous reasons for failing to find differences between treatments.

All psychotherapy research is flawed; there are no "perfect studies." Thus, studies should be evaluated along several dimensions, including rigor of methodology and adequacy of statistical procedures. Psychotherapy is both an art and a science, and it involves the complex interaction between a socially sanctioned helper (a therapist) and a distressed patient or client. The complexity of this interaction raises some significant obstacles to designing psychotherapy research. Thus, methodological problems can be diverse and extensive, and they may account for the failure to find significant differences between alternative psychotherapeutic approaches. Moreover, some researchers have argued that the combination of methodological problems and statistical limitations (such as research samples that are too small to detect differences between groups or inconsistency with regard to patient characteristics) plagued many of the comparative studies completed in the 1980's.

Still, the search for effective components of psychotherapy remains a primary research question focused on several key areas, including patient characteristics, therapist characteristics, treatment techniques, common factors across different psychotherapies, and the various interactions among these variables. As highlighted in Sol Garfield and Allen Bergin's edited book entitled *Handbook of Psychotherapy and Behavior Change* (1986), some evidence reveals that patient characteristics (such as amount of self-exploration and ability to solve problems and express emotions constructively) are of primary importance in positive outcomes. Therapist characteristics such as empathy, interpersonal warmth, acceptance toward patients, and genuineness also appear to play a major role in successful therapy. Treatment techniques seem generally less important than the ability of the therapist and patient to form a therapeutic relationship.

Additional studies have asked patients at the conclusion of psychotherapy to identify the most important factors in their successful treatment. Patients have generally described such factors as gradually facing their problems in a supportive setting, talking to an understanding person, and the personality of their therapist as helpful factors. Moreover, patients frequently conclude that their success in treatment is related to their therapist's support, encouragement, sensitivity, honesty, sense of humor, and ability to share insights. In contrast, other research has examined negative outcomes of psychotherapy in order to illuminate factors predictive of poor outcomes. These factors include the failure of the therapist to structure sessions and address primary concerns presented by the patient, poorly timed interventions, and negative therapist attitudes toward the patient.

Taken as a whole, psychotherapy research reveals some consistent results about many patient and therapist characteristics associated with positive and negative outcomes. Yet remarkably few differences have been found among the different types of treatment. This pattern of evidence has led many researchers to conclude that factors which are common across different forms of psychotherapy may account for the apparent equality among many treatment approaches. At the forefront of this position is psychiatrist and psychologist Jerome D. Frank.

In various books and journal articles, Frank has argued that all psychotherapeutic approaches share common ingredients that are simply variations of age-old procedures of psychological healing such as confession, encouragement, modeling, positive reinforcement, and punishment. Because patients seeking treatment are typically demoralized, distressed, and feeling helpless, all psychotherapies aim to restore morale by offering support, reassurance, feedback, guidance, hope, and mutual understanding of the problems and proposed solutions. Among the common factors most frequently studied since the 1960's, the key ingredients outlined by the client-centered school are most widely regarded as central to the development of a successful therapeutic relationship. These ingredients are empathy, positive regard, warmth, and genuineness.

Various factors should be considered when one chooses a therapist. To begin with, it may be wise to consider first one's objectives and motivations for entering treatment. A thoughtful appraisal of one's own goals can serve as a map through the maze of alternative treatments, therapy agencies, and diverse professionals providing psychotherapeutic services. In addition, one should learn about the professionals in one's area by speaking with a family physician, a religious adviser, or friends who have previously sought psychotherapeutic services. It is also important to locate a licensed professional with whom one feels comfortable, because the primary ingredients for success are patient and therapist characteristics. All therapists and patients are unique individuals who provide their own distinctive perspectives and contributions to the therapy process. Therefore, the most important factor in psychotherapeutic outcome may be the match between patient and therapist.

Context

Although the roots of psychotherapy can be traced back to antiquity, psychotherapy research is a recent development in the field of psychology. Early evidence for the effectiveness of psychotherapy was limited and consisted of case studies and investigations with significant methodological flaws. Considerable furor among therapists followed psychologist Hans Eysenck's claims that psychotherapy is no more effective than naturally occurring life events are. Other disagreements followed the rapid development of many alternative and competing forms of psychotherapy in the 1960's and 1970's. Claims that one particular approach was better than another were rarely confirmed by empirical research. Still, psychotherapy research is a primary method in the development, refinement, and validation of treatments for diverse patient groups. Advancements in research methodology and statistical applications have provided answers to many important questions in psychotherapy research.

Rather than examining the question of whether psychotherapy works, researchers are designing sophisticated research programs to evaluate the effectiveness of specific treatment components on particular groups of patients with carefully diagnosed mental disorders. Researchers continue to identify specific variables and processes among patients and therapists that shape positive outcomes. The quality of interactions between patient and therapist appear to hold particular promise in understanding psychotherapy outcome.

To address the complexity of psychotherapy, research must aim to address at least two important dimensions: process ("how and why does this form of therapy work?") and outcome ("to what degree is this specific treatment effective for this particular client in this setting at this time?"). In addition, empirical comparisons between psychotherapy and medications in terms of effectiveness, side effects, compliance, and long-term outcome will continue to shape clinical practice for many years to come. As one example, the National Institute of Mental Health (NIMH) sponsored a large comparative psychotherapy and drug treatment study of depression. In that investigation, the effectiveness of individual interpersonal psychotherapy, individual cognitive therapy, antidepressant medication, and placebo conditions were tested. While findings from initial analyses revealed no significant differences between any of the treatment conditions, secondary analyses suggested that severity of depression was an important variable. For the less severely depressed, there was no evidence for the specific effectiveness of active-versus-placebo treatment conditions. The more severely depressed patients, however, responded best to antidepressant medications and interpersonal therapy. Future reports from the NIMH team of researchers may reveal additional results which could further shape the ways in which depressed patients are treated.

Bibliography

Beutler, Larry E., and Marjorie Crago, eds. *Psychotherapy Research: An International Review of Programmatic Studies.* Washington, D.C.: American Psychological Association, 1991. Reviews a variety of large-scale and small-scale research programs in North America and Europe. Presents a summary of research findings from studies investigating various aspects of psychotherapy including prevention of marital distress, process variables in psychotherapy, treatment of difficult patients, and inpatient hospitalization approaches.

Frank, Jerome David. *Persuasion and Healing.* Rev. ed. Baltimore: The Johns Hopkins University Press, 1973. Provides an overview of Frank's position on psychotherapy. The significance of common treatment components shared by all forms of healing, including psychotherapy, continues to be an important consideration in treatment outcome work.

Garfield, Sol L., and Allen E. Bergin, eds. *Handbook of Psychotherapy and Behavior Change.* 3d ed. New York: John Wiley & Sons, 1986. Provides a historical overview and synopsis of research studies concerned with the evaluation of psychotherapy.

Patient and therapist variables are highlighted in terms of their importance in successful intervention. Additional topics include training therapeutic skills, medications and psychotherapy, and the effectiveness of treatment approaches with children, couples, families, and groups.

Kazdin, Alan E. *Single-Case Research Designs: Methods for Clinical and Applied Settings.* New York: Oxford University Press, 1982. Provides an overview of various research methods used in psychotherapy research. In particular, this book presents information about case studies and single-case research designs. Single-case research has become increasingly common in psychotherapy research as an alternative approach to group designs.

Smith, Mary Lee, and Gene V. Glass. "Meta-Analysis of Psychotherapy Outcome Studies." *American Psychologist* 32, no. 9 (1977): 752-760. A classic in the field of psychotherapy research, this journal article represents a significant step in the manner in which knowledge is distilled from the scientific literature. This controversial article concluded that psychotherapy was effective.

Smith, Mary Lee, Gene V. Glass, and Thomas I. Miller. *Benefits of Psychotherapy.* Baltimore: The Johns Hopkins University Press, 1980. Presents many detailed analyses from 475 psychotherapy research studies that were systematically analyzed via meta-analysis. Provides a follow-up to many of the criticisms that were expressed about Smith and Glass's initial psychotherapy meta-analysis.

Gregory L. Wilson

Cross-References

Adlerian Psychotherapy, 110; Behavioral Family Therapy, 394; Clinical Depression, 521; Cognitive Behavior Therapy, 546; Gestalt Therapy, 1088; Group Therapy, 1120; Obsessions and Compulsions, 1707; Phobias, 1816; Psychoanalytic Psychology and Personality: Sigmund Freud, 1912; Psychotherapeutic Goals and Techniques, 1996; Psychotherapy: Historical Approaches to Treatment, 2002.

PSYCHOTHERAPEUTIC GOALS AND TECHNIQUES

Type of psychology: Psychotherapy
Field of study: Evaluating psychotherapy

The goals to be reached in the meetings between a psychotherapist and a client, or patient, and the techniques employed to accomplish them vary according to the needs of the client and the theoretical orientation of the therapist.

Principal terms

BEHAVIORAL THERAPY: an approach emphasizing how behaviors are controlled by stimuli that precede or follow them

CORRECTIVE EMOTIONAL EXPERIENCE: a feeling a client may get, as a result of unexpected interactions with the psychotherapist, that changes established patterns of relating

DESENSITIZATION: a behavioral technique of gradually removing anxiety associated with certain situations by associating a relaxed state with these situations

ECLECTIC THERAPY: a therapy in which a combination of models and techniques is employed, rather than a single approach

HUMANISTIC THERAPY: an approach that emphasizes the innate capacity of people for positive change and ways of relating that encourage this change

INTERPRETATION: a psychodynamic technique in which the psychotherapist points out to a client patterns in behavior or the origin of these patterns

PSYCHODYNAMIC THERAPY: an approach emphasizing the influences of different parts of the mind on one another and the origins of these influences in childhood experience

RESISTANCE: the tendency of clients to avoid revealing themselves or attempting to change

SHAPING: a behavioral technique in which the psychotherapist rewards, usually through praise and attention, a client's gradual changes toward meeting psychotherapeutic goals

THERAPEUTIC ALLIANCE: a relationship between psychotherapist and client characterized by collaboration and trust, for the purpose of producing change in the client

Overview

Psychotherapy is an interpersonal relationship in which clients present themselves to a psychotherapist in order to gain some relief from distress in their lives. It should be noted that although people who seek psychological help are referred to as "clients" by a wide range of psychotherapists, this term is used interchangeably with the term "patients," which is traditionally used more often by psychodynamically and medically trained practitioners. In all forms of psychotherapy, patients or clients must tell the psychotherapist about their distress and reveal intimate information in order for the psychotherapist to be helpful. The psychotherapist must aid clients in the difficult task of admitting difficulties and revealing themselves, since a client's desire to be liked and to be seen as competent can stand in the way of this work. The client also wants to find relief from distress at the least possible cost in terms of the effort and personal changes to be made, and, therefore, clients often prevent themselves from making the very changes in which they are interested. This is termed resistance, and much of the work of the psychotherapist involves dealing with such resistance.

The goals of the client are determined by the type of life problems that are being experienced. Traditionally, psychotherapists make a diagnosis of the psychiatric disorder from which the client suffers, with different disorders presenting certain symptoms to be removed in order for the client to gain relief. The vast majority of clients suffer from some form of anxiety or depression, or from certain failures in personality development, which produce deviant behaviors and rigid patterns of relating to others called personality disorders. Relatively few clients suffer from severe disorders, called psychoses, which are characterized by some degree of loss of contact with reality. Depending on the particular symptoms involved in the client's disorder, psychotherapeutic goals will be set, although the client may not be aware of the necessity of these changes at first. In addition, the diagnosis allows the psychotherapist to anticipate the kinds of goals that would be difficult for the client to attain. Psychotherapists also consider the length of time they will likely work with the client. Therefore, psychotherapeutic goals depend on the client's wishes, the type of psychiatric disorder from which the client suffers, and the limitations of time under which the psychotherapy proceeds.

Another factor that plays a major role in determining psychotherapeutic goals is the psychotherapist's theoretical model for treatment. This model is based on a personality theory that explains people's motivations, how people develop psychologically, and how people differ from one another. It suggests what occurred in life to create the person's problems and what must be achieved to correct these problems. Associated with each theory is a group of techniques that can be applied to accomplish the goals considered to be crucial within the theory utilized. There are three main models of personality and treatment: psychodynamic therapies, behavioral therapies, and humanistic therapies. Psychodynamic therapists seek to make clients aware of motives for their actions of which they were previously unconscious or unaware. By becoming aware of their motives, clients can better control the balance between desires for pleasure and the need to obey one's conscience. Behavioral therapists attempt to increase the frequency of certain behaviors and decrease the frequency of others by reducing anxiety associated with certain behavior, teaching new behavior, and rewarding and punishing certain behaviors. Humanistic therapists try to free clients to use their innate abilities by developing relationships with clients in which clients can be assured of acceptance, making the clients more accepting of themselves and more confident in making decisions and expressing themselves.

Most psychotherapists use a combination of theories, and therefore of goals and techniques, in their practice. These "eclectic" therapists base their decisions about goals and techniques upon the combined theory they have evolved or upon a choice among other theories given what applies best to a client or diagnosis. It also appears that this eclectic approach has become popular because virtually all psychotherapy cases demand attention to certain common goals associated with the various stages of treatment, and different types of therapy are well suited to certain goals and related techniques at particular stages.

Applications

When clients first come to a psychotherapist, they have in mind some things about their lives that need to be changed. The psychotherapist recognizes that before this can be accomplished, a trusting relationship must be established with clients. This has been termed the "therapeutic alliance" or a "collaborative relationship." Establishing this relationship becomes the first goal of therapy. Clients must learn that the therapist understands them and can be trusted with the secrets of their lives. They must also learn about the limits of the therapeutic relationship: that the psychotherapist is to be paid for the service, that the relationship will focus on the clients' concerns and life experiences rather than the psychotherapist's, that the psychotherapist is available to clients during the scheduled sessions and emergencies only, and that this relationship will end when the psychotherapeutic goals are met.

The therapist looks early for certain recurring patterns in what the client thinks, feels, and does. These patterns may occur in the therapy sessions, and the client reports about the way these patterns have occurred in the past and how they continue. These patterns become the focal theme for the therapy and are seen as a basic reason for the client's troubles. For example, some clients may complain that they have never had the confidence to think for themselves. They report that their parents always told them what to do without explanation. In their current marriage, they find themselves unable to feel comfortable with any decisions, and they always look to their spouse for the final say. This pattern of dependence may not be as clear to the clients as to psychotherapists, who look specifically for similarities across past and present relationships. Furthermore, clients will probably approach the psychotherapist in a similar fashion. For example, clients might ask for the psychotherapist's advice, stating that they do not know what to do. When the psychotherapist points out the pattern in the clients' behavior, or suggests that it may have developed from the way their parents interacted with them, the psychotherapist is using the technique of interpretation. This technique originated in the psychodynamic models of psychotherapy.

When clients are confronted with having such patterns or focal themes, they may protest that they are not doing this, find it difficult to do anything different, or cannot imagine that there may be a different way of living. These tendencies to protest and to find change to be difficult are called "resistance." Much of the work of psychotherapy involves overcoming this resistance and achieving the understanding of self called "insight."

One of the techniques the psychotherapist uses to deal with resistance is the continued development of the therapeutic relationship in order to demonstrate that the psychotherapist understands and accepts the client's point of view and that these interpretations of patterns of living are done in the interest of the achievement of therapeutic goals by the client. Humanistic psychotherapists have emphasized this aspect of psychotherapeutic technique. The psychotherapist also responds differently to the client from the way others have in the past, so that when the client demonstrates the focal theme in the psychotherapy session, this different outcome to the pattern encourages a new approach to the difficulty. This is called the "corrective emotional experience," a psychotherapeutic technique that originated in psychodynamic psychotherapy and is emphasized in humanistic therapies as well. For example, when the client asks the psychotherapist for advice, the psychotherapist might respond that they could work together on a solution, building on valuable information and ideas that both may have. In this way, the psychotherapist has avoided keeping the client dependent in the relationship with the psychotherapist as the client has been in relationships with parents, a spouse, or others. This is experienced by the client emotionally, in that it may produce an increase in self-confidence or trust rather than resentment, since the psychotherapist did not dominate. With the repetition of these responses by the psychotherapist, the client's ways of relating are corrected. Such a repetition is often called "working through," another term originating in psychodynamic models of therapy.

Psychotherapists have recognized that many clients have difficulty with changing their patterns of living because of anxiety or lack of skill and experience in behaving differently. Behavioral therapy techniques are especially useful in such cases. In cases of anxiety, the client can be taught to relax through "relaxation training" exercises. The client gradually imagines performing new, difficult behaviors while relaxing. Eventually, the client learns to stay relaxed while performing these behaviors with the psychotherapist and other people. This process is called "desensitization," and it was originally developed to treat persons with extreme fears of particular objects or situations, termed phobias. New behavior is sometimes taught through modeling techniques in which examples of the behavior are first demonstrated by others. Behavioral psychotherapists have also shown the importance of rewarding small approximations to the new behavior that is the goal. This shaping technique might be used with the dependent client by praising confident, assertive, or independent behavior reported by the client or shown in the psychotherapy session, no matter how minor it may be initially.

Context

The goals and techniques of psychotherapy were first discussed by the psychodynamic theorists who originated the modern practice of psychotherapy. Sigmund

Freud and Josef Breuer are generally credited with describing the first modern case treated with psychotherapy, and Freud went on to develop the basis for psychodynamic psychotherapy in his writings between 1895 and his death in 1939. Freud sat behind his clients while they lay upon a couch so that they could concentrate on saying anything that came to mind in order to reveal themselves to the psychotherapist. This also prevented the clients from seeing the psychotherapist's reaction, in case they expected the psychotherapist to react to them as their parents had reacted. This transference relationship provided Freud with information about the client's relationship with parents, which Freud considered to be the root of the problems that his clients had. Later psychodynamic psychotherapists sat facing their clients and conversing with them in a more conventional fashion, but they still attended to the transference.

Carl Rogers is usually described as the first humanistic psychotherapist, and he published descriptions of his techniques in 1942 and 1951. Rogers concentrated on establishing a warm, accepting, honest relationship with his clients. Rogers established this relationship by attempting to understand the client from the client's point of view. By communicating this "accurate empathy," clients would feel accepted and therefore would accept themselves and be more confident in living according to their wishes without fear.

Behavioral psychotherapists began to play a major role in this field after Joseph Wolpe developed systematic desensitization in the 1950's. In the 1960's and 1970's, Albert Bandura applied his findings on how children learn to be aggressive through observation to the development of modeling techniques for reducing fears and teaching new behaviors. Bandura focused on how people attend to, remember, and decide to perform behavior they observe in others. These thought processes, or "cognitions," came to be addressed in cognitive psychotherapy by Aaron T. Beck and others in the 1970's and 1980's. Cognitive behavioral therapy became a popular hybrid that included emphasis on how thinking and behavior influence each other.

In surveys of practicing psychotherapists beginning in the late 1970's, Sol Garfield showed that the majority of therapists practice some hybrid therapy or eclectic approach. As it became apparent that no one model produced the desired effects in a variety of clients, psychotherapists utilized techniques from various approaches. An example is Arnold Lazarus' multimodal behavior therapy, introduced in 1971. It appears that such trends will continue and that, in addition to combining existing psychotherapeutic techniques, new eclectic models will produce additional ways of understanding psychotherapy as well as different techniques for practice.

Bibliography

Garfield, Sol L. *Psychotherapy: An Eclectic Approach.* New York: John Wiley & Sons, 1980. Focuses on the client, the therapist, and their interaction within an eclectic framework. Written for the beginning student of psychotherapy and relatively free of jargon.

Goldfried, Marvin R., and Gerald C. Davison. *Clinical Behavior Therapy.* New York:

Holt, Rinehart and Winston, 1976. An elementary, concise description of basic behavioral techniques. Includes clear examples of how these techniques are implemented.

Goldman, George D., and Donald S. Milman, eds. *Psychoanalytic Psychotherapy.* Reading, Mass.: Addison-Wesley, 1978. A very clear, concise treatment of complicated psychodynamic techniques. Explains difficult concepts in language accessible to the layperson.

Phares, E. Jerry. *Clinical Psychology: Concepts, Methods, and Profession.* 3d ed. Chicago: Dorsey Press, 1988. An overview of clinical psychology that includes excellent chapters summarizing psychodynamic, behavioral, humanistic, and other models of psychotherapy. Written as a college-level text.

Rogers, Carl Ransom. *Client-Centered Therapy.* Boston: Houghton Mifflin, 1951. A classic description of the author's humanistic psychotherapy that is still useful as a strong statement of the value of the therapeutic relationship. Written for a professional audience, though quite readable.

Teyber, Edward. *Interpersonal Process in Psychotherapy: A Guide to Clinical Training.* Chicago: Dorsey Press, 1988. An extremely clear and readable guide to modern eclectic therapy. Full of practical examples and written as a training manual for beginning psychotherapy students.

Wolpe, Joseph. *The Practice of Behavior Therapy.* 4th ed. Elmsford, N.Y.: Pergamon Press, 1990. Written by the originator of behavioral psychotherapy. Introduces basic principles, examples of behavioral interventions, and many references to research. Initial chapters are elementary, but later ones tend to be complicated.

Richard G. Tedeschi

Cross-References

Aversion, Implosion, and Systematic Desensitization Therapies, 368; Behavioral Family Therapy, 394; Cognitive Therapy, 586; Existential Analysis and Therapy, 999; Feminist Psychotherapy, 1025; Group Therapy, 1120; Music, Dance, and Theater Therapy, 1629; Psychoactive Drug Therapy, 1891; Psychoanalysis: Classical versus Modern, 1898; Psychoanalytic Psychology: An Overview, 1905; Psychotherapeutic Effectiveness, 1989.

PSYCHOTHERAPY: HISTORICAL APPROACHES TO TREATMENT

Type of psychology: Psychotherapy
Fields of study: Classic analytic themes and issues; psychodynamic and neoanalytic models

Psychotherapy as a socially recognized process and profession emerged in Europe during the late nineteenth century. Although discussions of psychological or "mental healing" can be found dating back to antiquity, a cultural role for the secular psychological healer has become established only in modern times.

Principal terms

CATHARSIS: the discharge of emotional tension, yielding relief from symptoms

FUNCTIONAL DISORDERS: signs and symptoms for which no organic or physiological basis can be found

MENTAL HEALING: the healing of a disorder, functional or physical, through suggestion or persuasion

MESMERISM: hypnotic states induced and explained by "animal magnetism"

NONSPECIFIC TREATMENT FACTORS: those factors that can be attributed to the relationship between the patient and therapist and to suggestion and placebo effects

SUGGESTION: the induction of actions or beliefs in a person through subtle means

TRANSFERENCE: the transferring of emotions from childhood onto adult figures in one's life, including a psychotherapist

Overview

The term "psychotherapy" (originally "psycho-therapy") came into use during the late nineteenth century to describe various treatments that were believed to act on the psychic or mental aspects of a patient rather than on physical conditions. It was contrasted with physical therapies such as medications, baths, surgery, diets, rest, or mild electrical currents, which, while producing some mental relief, did so through physical means. The origins of psychotherapy have been variously traced. Some authors call attention to the practices of primitive witch doctors, to the exorcism rites of the Catholic church, to the rhetorical methods of Greco-Roman speakers, to the naturalistic healing practices of Hippocrates, and to the Christian practice of public (and later, private) confession.

One of the best argued and supported views claims a direct line of development from the practice of casting out demons all the way to psychoanalysis, the most widely recognized form of psychotherapy. The casting out of demons may be seen as leading to exorcism, which in turn led to the eighteenth century mesmeric technique (named for Franz Mesmer) based on the alleged phenomenon of "animal magnetism." This led to the practice of hypnosis as a psychological rather than a physiological phenomenon and finally to the work of Sigmund Freud, a late-nineteenth century Viennese neurologist who, in his treatment of functional disorders, slowly moved from the practice of hypnosis to the development of psychoanalysis.

There are two histories to be sought in the early forms of treatment by psychotherapy: One is an account of the relationship between a patient and a psychological healer; the other is the story of the specific techniques that the healer employs and the reasons that he or she gives to rationalize them. The latter began as religious or spiritual techniques and became naturalized as psychological or physiological methods. The prominence of spiritual revival during the mid- to late nineteenth century in the United States led to the rise of spiritual or mental healing movements, as demonstrated by the Christian Science movement. Religious healing, mental healing, and psychotherapy were often intertwined in the 1890's, especially in Boston, where many of the leading spokespersons for each perspective resided.

The distinction among these viewpoints was the explanation of the cure—naturalistic versus spiritualistic—and to a lesser degree, the role or relationship between the practitioner and the patient. A psychotherapist in the United States or Europe, whether spiritualistic or naturalistic in orientation, was an authority (of whatever special techniques) who could offer the suffering patient relief through a relationship in which the patient shared his or her deepest feelings and most secret thoughts on a regular basis. The relationship bore a resemblance to that which a priest, rabbi, or minister might have with a member of the congregation. The psychotherapeutic relationship was also a commercial one, however, since private payment for services was usually the case. Freud came to believe that transference, the projection of emotional reactions from childhood onto the therapist, was a critical aspect of the relationship.

Initially, and well into the early part of the twentieth century, psychotherapists treated patients with physical as well as functional (mental) disorders, but by the 1920's, psychotherapy had largely become a procedure addressed to mental or psychological problems. In the United States, its use rested almost exclusively with the medical profession. Psychiatrists would provide therapy, clinical psychologists would provide testing and assessment of the patient, and social workers would provide ancillary services related to the patient's family or societal and governmental programs. Following World War II, all three of these professions began to offer psychotherapy as one of their services.

One could chart the development of psychotherapy in a simplified, time-line approach, beginning with the early use of the term by Daniel H. Tuke in *Illustrations of the Influence of the Mind upon the Body in Health and Disease* in 1872, followed by the first use of the term at an international conference in 1889 and the publication of Sigmund Freud and Josef Breuer's cathartic method in *Studien über Hysterie* (1895; *Studies in Hysteria*, 1950). Pierre Janet lectured on "The Chief Methods of Psychotherapeutics" in St. Louis in 1904, and psychotherapy was introduced as a heading in the index to medical literature (the *Index Medicus*) in 1906; at about the same time, private schools of psychotherapy began to be established. In 1909, Freud lectured on psychoanalysis at Clark University. That same year, Hugo Münsterberg published *Psychotherapy.* James T. Walsh published his *Psychotherapy* in 1912. During the 1920's, the widespread introduction and medicalization of psychoanalysis in the United States occurred. Client-centered therapy was introduced by Carl Rogers in 1942, and behavior-oriented therapy was developed by Joseph Wolpe and B. F. Skinner in the early 1950's.

Whatever form psychotherapy may take, it nearly always is applied to the least severe forms of maladjustment and abnormal behavior—to those behaviors and feelings that are least disturbing to others. When the patient has suffered a break with reality and experiences hallucinations, delusions, paranoia, or other behaviors that are socially disruptive, physical forms of treatment are often utilized. The earliest examples include "trephining," a Stone Age practice in which a circular hole was cut into the brain cavity, perhaps to allow the escape of evil spirits. The best-known of the Greek theories of abnormal behavior were naturalistic and physicalistic, based on the belief that deviations in levels of bile caused mental derangement. The solution was bleeding, a practice that continued until the early nineteenth century. Rest, special diets, exercise, and other undertakings that would increase or decrease the relevant bile level were also practiced.

Banishment from public places was recommended by Plato. Initially, people were restricted to their own homes. Later, religious sanctuaries took in the mentally ill, and finally private for-profit and public asylums were developed. Institutions that specialized in the housing of the mentally ill began opening during the sixteenth century. Among the best-known institutions were Bethlehem in London, (which came to be known as "Bedlam"), Salpetriere in Paris, and later St. Elizabeth's in Washington, D.C. Beyond confinement, "treatments" at these institutions included "whirling" chairs in which the patient would be strapped; the "tranquilizing" chair for restraining difficult patients; the straitjacket, which constrained only the arms; rest and diet therapies; and hot and cold water treatments.

By the 1930's, electroconvulsive therapy ("shock therapy") was invented; it used an electric charge that induced a grand mal seizure. During the same period, the earliest lobotomy procedures were performed. These surgeries severed the connections between the brain's frontal lobes and lower centers of emotional functioning. What separates all these and other procedures from psychotherapy is the employment of physical and chemical means for changing behavior and emotions, rather than persuasion and social influence processes.

Periodic reforms were undertaken to improve the care of patients. Philippe Pinel, in the late eighteenth century, freed many mental patients in Paris from being chained in their rooms. He provided daily exercise and frequent cleaning of their quarters. In the United States, Dorothea Lynde Dix in the mid-1800's led a campaign of reform that resulted in vast improvement in state mental hospitals. In the 1960's and 1970's, some states placed restrictions on the use of electroconvulsive therapy and lobotomies, and the federal government funded many community mental health centers in an attempt to provide treatment that would keep the patient in his or her community. Since the 1950's, many effective medications have been developed for treating depressions, anxieties, compulsions, panic attacks, and a wide variety of other disorders.

Applications

Modern textbooks of psychotherapy may describe dozens of approaches and hundreds of specific psychotherapeutic techniques. What they have in common is the attempt of a person in the role of healer or teacher to assist another person in the role of patient or client with emotionally disturbing feelings, awkward behavior, or troubling thoughts. Many contemporary therapies are derivative of Sigmund Freud's psychoanalysis. When Freud opened his practice for the treatment of functional disorders in Vienna in the spring of 1886, he initially employed the physical therapies common to his day. These included hydrotherapy, electrotherapy, a mild form of electrical stimulation, massage, rest, and a limited set of pharmaceutical agents. He was disappointed with the results, however, and reported feeling helpless.

He turned to the newly emerging procedure of hypnosis that was being developed by French physicians. Soon he was merely urging his patients to recall traumatic episodes from childhood rather than expecting them to recall such memories under hypnosis. In what he called his "pressure technique," Freud would place his hand firmly on a patient's forehead, apply pressure, and say, "you will recall." Shortly, this became the famous method of free association, wherein the patient would recline on a couch with the instruction to say whatever came to mind. The psychoanalytic situation that Freud invented, with its feature of one person speaking freely to a passive but attentive audience about the most private and intimate aspects of his or her life, was unique in the history of Western civilization.

Psychoanalysis was not the only method of psychotherapy to emerge near the end of the nineteenth century, as an examination of a textbook published shortly after the turn of the century reveals. James J. Walsh, then Dean and Professor of Functional Disorders at Fordham University, published his eight-hundred-page textbook on psychotherapy in 1912. Only two pages were devoted to the new practice of psychoanalysis. For Walsh, psychotherapy was the use of mental influence to treat disease. His formulation, and that of many practitioners of his time, would encompass what today would be termed behavioral medicine. Thus, the chapters in his book are devoted to the different bodily systems, the digestive tract, cardiotherapy, gynecological psychotherapy, and skin diseases, as well as to the functional disorders.

The techniques that Walsh describes are wide ranging. They include physical recommendations for rest and exercise, the value of hobbies as diversion, the need for regimentation, and varied baths, but it is the suggestion and treatment of the patient rather than the disease (that is, the establishment of a relationship with detailed knowledge of the patient's life and situation) that are the principal means for the cure and relief of symptoms. A concluding chapter in Walsh's book compares psychotherapy with religion, with the view that considering religion simply as a curative agent lessens its meaning and worth.

Context

In the mid-twentieth century, two new psychotherapies appeared that significantly altered the field, although one of them rejected the term, preferring to call itself behavior therapy in order to distinguish its method from the merely verbal or "talk therapies." The first was found in the work of psychologist Carl Rogers. Rogers made three significant contributions to the development of psychotherapy. He originated nondirective or client-centered therapy, he phonographically recorded and transcribed therapy sessions, and he studied the process of therapy based upon the transcripts. The development of an alternative to psychoanalysis was perhaps his most significant contribution. In the United States, psychoanalysis had become a medical specialty, practiced only by psychiatrists with advanced training. Rogers, a psychologist, created a role for psychologists and social workers as therapists. Thus, he expanded the range of professionals who could legitimately undertake the treatment of disorders through psychotherapy. The title of his most important work, *Counseling and Psychotherapy: Newer Concepts in Practice* (1942), suggests how other professions were to be included. In the preface to his book, Rogers indicated that he regarded these terms as synonymous. If psychologists and social workers could not practice therapy, they could counsel.

Behavior therapy describes a set of specific procedures, such as systematic desensitization and contingency management, that began to appear in the early 1950's, based on the work of Joseph Wolpe, a South African psychiatrist, Hans J. Eysenck, a British psychologist, and the American experimental psychologist and radical behaviorist B. F. Skinner. Wolpe's *Psychotherapy by Reciprocal Inhibition* appeared in 1958 and argued that states of relaxation and self-assertion would inhibit anxiety, since the patient could not be relaxed and anxious at the same time. It was argued that these were specific techniques based upon the principles of learning and behavior; hence, therapeutic benefits did not depend upon the nonspecific effects of mere suggestion or placebo. Behavior therapy was regarded by its developers as the first scientific therapy.

In all of its forms, the rise of psychotherapy may be explained in a variety of ways. The cultural role hypothesis argues that psychotherapists are essentially a controlling agency for the state and society. Their function is to help maintain the cultural norms and values by directly influencing persons at the individual level. This view holds that whatever psychotherapists might say, they occupy a position in the culture similar to that of authorities in educational and religious institutions. A related view argues that psychotherapy arose in Western culture to meet a deficiency in the culture itself. Such a view holds that if the culture were truly meeting the needs of its members, no therapeutic procedures would be required.

Psychotherapy has been explained as a scientific discovery, although exactly what was discovered depends on one's viewpoint. For example, behavior therapists might hold that the fundamental principles of behavior and learning were discovered, as was their applicability to emotional and mental problems. Others might hold that nonspecific or placebo effects were discovered, or at least placed in a naturalistic context. Another explanation follows the historical work of Henri Ellenberger and views psychotherapy as a naturalization of early religious practices: exorcism transformed to hypnotism, transformed to psychoanalysis. The religious demons became mental demons and, with the rise of modern psychopharmacology in the 1950's, molecular demons.

More cynical explanations view psychotherapy as a mistaken metaphor. Recalling that the word was originally written with a hyphen, they argue that it is not possible to perform therapy, a physical practice, on a mental or spiritual object. Thus, psychotherapy is a kind of hoax perpetuated by its practitioners because of a mistaken formulation. Others suggest that the correct metaphor is that of healing and hold that psychotherapy is the history of mental healing, or healing through faith, suggestion, persuasion, and other rhetorical means. Whatever one's opinion of psychotherapy, it is both a cultural phenomenon and a specific set of practices that did not exist prior to the nineteenth century and that have had enormous influence on all aspects of American culture.

Bibliography

Corsini, Raymond J., comp. *Current Psychotherapies.* 3d ed. Itasca, Ill.: Peacock, 1984. An excellent survey of more than a dozen approaches to psychotherapy, with a brief historical description of the origin of each.

Ehrenwald, Jan. *The History of Psychotherapy: From Healing Magic to Encounter.* New York: Jason Aronson, 1976. A survey introduction to the history of psychotherapy. Contains excerpts from many original sources.

Ellenberger, Henri F. *The Discovery of the Unconscious: The History and Evolution of Dynamic Psychiatry.* New York: Basic Books, 1970. A comprehensive and scholarly history of nonmedical psychiatry. Traces the development of psychotherapy from exorcism to hypnosis to suggestion to the methods of Sigmund Freud and Carl G. Jung.

Janet, Pierre. *Psychological Healing: A Historical and Clinical Study.* 2 vols. New York: Macmillan, 1925. Reflects the biases of its author but provides detailed descriptions of nonmedical treatments from the middle of the nineteenth century to the early part of the twentieth century. Contains material that can be found nowhere else.

Masson, Jeffrey Moussaieff. *Against Therapy: Emotional Tyranny and the Myth of Psychological Healing.* New York: Atheneum, 1988. Attacks the very idea of psychotherapy by examining selected historical instances from the nineteenth century onward.

Pande, Sashi K. "The Mystique of 'Western' Psychotherapy: An Eastern Interpretation." In *About Human Nature: Journeys in Psychological Thought*, edited by Terry J. Knapp and Charles T. Rasmussen. Dubuque, Iowa: Kendall/Hunt, 1989.

Argues that psychotherapy appears only in Western cultures and that it serves as an illustration of what these cultures lack.

Rogers, Carl. *Counseling and Psychotherapy: Newer Concepts in Practice.* Boston: Houghton Mifflin, 1942. Introduces nondirective or client-centered therapy, and provides the first verbatim transcripts of all the therapy sessions for a single patient.

Torrey, Edwin Fuller. *The Mind Game: Witchdoctors and Psychiatrists.* New York: Bantam Books, 1973. A leading American psychiatrist argues that the cultural and social role of the psychological healer has its origins in the primitive practices of the witch doctor.

Valenstein, Elliot S. *Great and Desperate Cures: The Rise and Decline of Psychosurgery and Other Radical Treatments.* New York: Basic Books, 1986. This is a scholarly and readable account of the history of physical therapies for mental disorders. While it focuses on lobotomy, many other forms of treatment are also described.

Wolpe, Joseph. *Psychotherapy by Reciprocal Inhibition.* Stanford, Calif.: Stanford University Press, 1958. Introduces the techniques of behavior therapy; Wolpe argues for specific therapeutic techniques to reduce anxiety.

Terry Knapp

Cross-References

Abnormality: Behavioral Models, 33; Abnormality: Psychodynamic Models, 74; Analytic Psychotherapy, 246; Cognitive Therapy, 586; Madness: Historical Concepts, 1492; Operant Conditioning Therapies, 1714; Psychoanalysis: Classical versus Modern, 1898; Psychosurgery, 1983.

PSYCHOTHERAPY WITH CHILDREN

Type of psychology: Psychotherapy
Fields of study: Behavioral therapies; group and family therapies; psychodynamic
therapies

Psychotherapy with children involves the use of psychological techniques in the treatment of children with behavioral, cognitive, or emotional disorders. The specific focus of treatment varies and may involve children only, parents only, or a combination of these individuals.

Principal terms

BEHAVIOR THERAPY: therapy based on the principles of learning theory; may be administered directly to children or by instructing parents in these principles

BEHAVIORAL PARENT TRAINING: the training of parents in learning-theory principles so that they may modify their children's maladaptive behavior

EXTERNALIZING DISORDERS: children's psychiatric disorders that are likely to disrupt the lives of individuals with whom they come in contact

FAMILY THERAPY: a type of psychotherapy that focuses on correcting the faulty interactions among family members that maintain children's psychological problems

INTERNALIZING DISORDERS: children's psychiatric disorders that are likely to cause greater internal distress to the children affected than to others

INTERPRETATION: therapists' comments regarding some aspect of children's behavior designed to promote insight into the causes of their psychological disorders

LEARNING THEORY: principles derived from extensive experimentation that explain the production and modification of behavior

PLAY THERAPY: a system of individual psychotherapy in which children's play is utilized to explain and reduce symptoms of their psychological disorders

WORKING THROUGH: a psychoanalytical term that describes the process by which children develop more adaptive behavior once they have gained insight into the causes of their psychological disorders

Overview

Various psychological techniques designed to treat children's behavioral, cognitive, or emotional problems are used in psychotherapy with children. The number of children with psychological disorders underscores the need for effective child psychotherapy: It is estimated that between 7 and 14 million, or between 5 and 15 percent, of America's children suffer from psychological disorders. It is believed that only one-fourth to one-third of all children who have psychological problems receive psychotherapeutic services.

Children, like adults, may experience many different kinds of psychological disorders. For example, in the *Diagnostic and Statistical Manual of Mental Disorders* (rev. 3d ed., 1987, DSM-III-R), published by the American Psychiatric Association, forty-seven separate disorders are listed which primarily affect children. This number does not include many disorders, such as major depressive disorder, which primarily affect adults but may also affect children. In general terms, children's disorders can be divided into two major categories: externalizing and internalizing disorders.

Externalizing disorders are those in which children engage in activities that are physically disruptive or are harmful to themselves or others. An example of this type of disorder is conduct disorder. Conduct disorder is characterized by children's involvement in a continued pattern of behavior that demonstrates a fundamental disregard for the safety or property of others. In contrast to externalizing disorders, internalizing disorders create greater emotional distress for the children themselves than for others around them. An example of an internalizing disorder is overanxious disorder. In overanxious disorder, the child experiences persistent, unrealistic anxiety regarding numerous situations and events such as being liked or school grades.

In response to the prevalence and variety of childhood disorders, many different treatments have been developed to address children's psychological problems. Historically, the earliest interventions for addressing these problems were based on psychoanalytic theory, developed by Sigmund Freud. Psychoanalysis is a type of psychotherapy based on the idea that individuals' unconscious processes, derived from early childhood experiences, are responsible for the psychological problems they experience as adults. One of the first therapists to adapt Freud's psychoanalysis to the treatment of children was Anna Freud, his daughter.

Psychoanalysis had to be modified for the treatment of children because of its heavy reliance on individuals' verbalizing their unconscious thoughts and feelings. Anna Freud realized that children would not be able to verbalize regarding their experiences to the extent necessary for effective treatment. Therefore, beginning in the 1920's, she created play therapy, a system of psychotherapy in which children's responses during play provided information regarding their hidden thoughts and feelings. Although play therapy had its roots in Sigmund Freud's psychoanalysis, this type of therapy came to be associated with other systems of psychotherapy. For example, Virginia Axline demonstrates her version of play therapy in the 1964 book *Dibs: In Search of Self*; her approach is based on Carl Rogers' person-centered therapy.

Also in the 1920's, Mary Cover Jones was applying the principles of behavior therapy developed by John B. Watson and others to the treatment of children's fears. Behavior therapy rests on the notion that all behavior, whether adaptive or maladaptive, is learned and thus can be unlearned. Jones's treatment involved reconditioning, a procedure in which the object of which the child is afraid is gradually associated with a pleasurable activity. By regularly associating the feared object with a pleasurable activity, Jones was able to eliminate children's fears.

Although early child analysts and behaviorally oriented psychologists attributed many children's problems to difficulties within their family environments, these treatment providers' primary focus was on treating the children, not their parents. In the early 1940's, however, Nathan Ackerman, a psychiatrist trained in the psychoanalytic tradition, began to treat children in conjunction with their families. His justification for seeing all family members in treatment was that families, like individuals, possess hidden conflicts that prevent them from engaging in healthy psychological functioning. Therefore, the role of the family therapist was to uncover these family conflicts, thus creating the possibility that the conflicts could be addressed in more adaptive ways. Once these family conflicts were properly handled, the causes of the child's psychological problems were removed. Ackerman's approach marked the beginning of the use of family therapy for the treatment of children's problems.

Another historical movement within child psychotherapy is behavioral parent training (BPT). BPT evolved from the recognition that parents are important in shaping their children's behavior and that they can be trained to eliminate many of their children's problems. Beginning in the late 1960's, researchers such as Gerald Patterson and Rex Forehand began to develop programs designed to target parents as the principal persons responsible for change in their children's maladaptive behavior. In this system of psychotherapy, parents were taught ways to assess and to intervene in order to correct their children's misbehavior. The role of the child was deemphasized to the point that the child might not even be seen by the therapist during the treatment process.

It is estimated that more than two hundred different types of child psychotherapy exist; however, these specific types of therapy can be roughly divided into three larger categories of treatment based on the primary focus of their interventions. These three categories are children only, parents only, or children and parents combined.

Applications

Individual child psychotherapy, the first category of psychotherapy with children, focuses on the child alone because of the belief that the greatest amount of improvement can result when the child is given primary attention in treatment. An example of individual child treatment is psychodynamic play therapy. Originating from the work of Anna Freud, the basic goal of psychodynamic play therapy is to provide the child with insight into the internal conflicts that have caused his or her psychological disorder. Once the child has gained sufficient insight, he or she is guided in handling these conflicts in more adaptive ways. Play therapy can be divided into three basic phases: initial, interpretative, and working-through phases.

In the initial phase of play therapy, the major goal is to establish a cooperative relationship between the child and the therapist. The attainment of this goal may require considerable time for several potential reasons. These reasons include a child's unwillingness to participate in therapy, lack of understanding regarding the therapy process, and lack of a previous trusting relationship with an adult. The participation in play activities provides an opportunity for the therapist to interact with the child in a relaxed and interesting manner. The specific kinds of play utilized differ from therapist to therapist but may include competitive games (such as checkers), imaginative games involving different figures (hand puppets, for example), or cooperative games (playing catch).

Once a sufficient level of cooperation is established, the therapist can begin to make interpretations to the child regarding the play. These interpretations consist of the therapist identifying themes in the content or style of a child's play that may relate to a psychological problem. For example, in playing with hand puppets, a child referred because of aggressive behavior may regularly enact stories in which a larger puppet "beats up" a smaller puppet. The child's therapist may interpret this story as meaning that the child aggresses against others because he or she feels inadequate.

Once the child gains insight into the internal conflict that has caused his or her problematic behavior, the child is guided by the therapist to develop a more adaptive way of handling this conflict. This final process of therapy is called working through. The working-through phase may be the most difficult part of treatment, because it involves the child abandoning a repetitive and maladaptive manner of handling a conflict in favor of a new approach. In comparison to most other psychotherapies, this treatment process is lengthy, ranging from months to years.

The second category of child psychotherapy, parent training, focuses intervention on the parents, because they are viewed as potentially the most effective persons available to alleviate the child's problems. This assumption is based on several factors, including the great amount of time parents spend with their children, the parents' control over the child's access to desired reinforcers, and the parents' understanding of the child's behavior because of their past relationship with the child. Behavioral parent training (BPT) is the most common type of parent training program. In BPT, parents are taught ways to modify their children's environment in order to improve their behavior.

The initial phase of this treatment process involves instructing parents in the basics of learning theory. They are taught that all behavior, adaptive or maladaptive, is maintained because it is reinforced. The application of learning theory to the correction of children's misbehavior involves three principles. First, positive reinforcement should be withdrawn from children's maladaptive behavior. For example, a parent who meets the demands of his screaming preschooler, who throws a temper tantrum in the checkout line of the grocery store because she wants a piece of candy, is unwittingly reinforcing the child's screaming behavior. Second, appropriate behavior that is incompatible with the maladaptive behavior should be positively reinforced. In the case of the screaming preschooler, this would involve rewarding her for acting correctly. Third, aversive consequences should be applied when the problem behavior recurs. That is, when the child engages in the misbehavior, he or she should consistently experience negative costs. For example, the preschooler who has a temper tantrum in the checkout line should not be allowed money to purchase gum, which she had previously selected as a potential reward for good store behavior, as the cost for her tantrum. In order to produce the greatest effect, positive reinforcement and negative consequences should be administered as close as possible to the occurrence of the appropriate or inappropriate behavior.

The final category of child psychotherapy, family therapy, focuses intervention on both the child and the child's family. Family therapy rests on the assumption that the child's psychological problems were created and are maintained by interactions among different family members. In this model, attention is shifted away from the individual child's problems toward the functioning of the entire family. For example, in structural family therapy, a widely practiced type of family therapy, the boundaries between different family members are closely examined. Family boundaries represent the degree of separation between different family members or subsets of members (for example, the parent-versus-child subset). According to Salvador Minuchin, the originator of structural family therapy, families in which there is little separation between parents and children may cause certain children to misbehave as a way to gain increased emotional distance from their parents. On the other hand, families characterized by too much separation between parents and children may cause certain children to become depressed because of the lack of a confiding relationship with a parental figure. Regardless of the child's specific disorder, all family members, not the child or parents alone, are the focus of treatment.

Context

The two large questions that can be asked regarding psychotherapy for children are whether it is effective and whether one type of treatment is more effective than others. The answer to the first question is very clear; psychotherapy is effective in treating the majority of children's psychological disorders. Two major studies in the 1980's reviewed the existing research examining the effects of child psychotherapy. The first of these studies was conducted by Rita Casey and Jeffrey Berman (1985), and the second was conducted by John Weisz, Bahr Weiss, Mark Alicke, and M. L. Klotz (1987). Both these studies found that children who received psychotherapy were better off than approximately 75 percent of the children who did not receive psychotherapy. Interestingly, Weisz et al. found that younger children (ages four to twelve) appeared to obtain more benefit from psychotherapy than older children (ages thirteen to eighteen). In addition, Casey and Berman found that girls tend to receive more benefit from psychotherapy than boys.

As one might expect, some controversy exists in attempting to answer the second question, regarding which treatment is the most effective. Casey and Berman concluded that all treatments were equally effective; however, Weisz et al. found that behavioral treatments were more effective than nonbehavioral treatments. Disagreement regarding which type of psychotherapy is most effective should not be allowed

to obscure the general conclusion that psychotherapy for children is clearly beneficial. Many investigators would suggest that the common characteristics shared by all
types of child psychotherapy are responsible for the relatively equivalent improvement produced by different treatments. For example, one of these common characteristics may be the therapist's and child's expectations that therapy will result in a
reduction in the child's psychological problems. In spite of the treatments' apparent
differences in rationale and method, it may be that this component, as well as other
common elements, accounts for much of the similarity in treatment outcomes.

The number of psychotherapeutic approaches available to treat children's psychological disorders has exploded since their introduction in the 1920's. Recent research
has clearly demonstrated the effectiveness of psychotherapy for children. Controversy still remains, however, regarding which treatment approach is the most effective; continued research is needed to address this issue. Of greater urgency is the
need to provide psychotherapy to the approximately 5 to 10 million children with
psychological disorders who are not being served. Perhaps even more cost effective,
in terms of both alleviating human suffering and reducing costs, would be the development of programs to prevent children's psychological disorders.

Bibliography

Axline, Virginia. *Dibs: In Search of Self.* New York: Ballantine Books, 1964. This
book, written for a general audience, presents Axline's play therapy, illustrated by
the presentation of a clinical case. The two-year treatment process with Dibs, a
seriously disturbed child, is described in detail. The book provides an excellent
example of child-centered play therapy.

Gordon, Thomas. *Parent Effectiveness Training.* New York: Peter H. Wyden, 1970.
Written primarily for parents interested in successfully handling parent-child interactions. The author utilizes behavioral parent training principles to address various topics which primarily relate to improving communication between parents
and children as well as handling children's misbehavior.

Minuchin, Salvador. *Families and Family Therapy.* Cambridge, Mass.: Harvard University Press, 1974. This book, largely intended for professionals, is widely cited
by family therapy experts as one of the most pivotal works in the field. Minuchin
outlines his views regarding the functioning of healthy and unhealthy families.
Specifically, he addresses the maladaptive interactions among family members
that create psychological disorders such as anorexia nervosa in children.

Monte, Christopher. "Anna Freud: The Psychoanalytic Heritage and Developments
in Ego Psychology." In *Beneath the Mask: An Introduction to Theories of Personality.* 4th ed. Fort Worth, Tex.: Holt, Rinehart and Winston, 1991. In this textbook
chapter, Monte describes Anna Freud's contributions to the field of child psychotherapy. The chapter traces Anna Freud's adaptation of her father's psychoanalytic
therapy to her work with children. This is a valuable work because it describes
Anna Freud's therapy in understandable terms—which is difficult, given the complexity of child psychoanalysis.

Nemiroff, Marc A., and Jane Annunziata. *A Child's First Book About Play Therapy.* Washington, D.C.: American Psychological Association, 1990. Children ages four to seven who are entering play therapy are the intended audience of this book. The book uses frequent illustrations and simple words to communicate to children the purpose and process of children's play therapy. An excellent resource for parents whose children are about to enter play therapy.

Schaefer, Charles E., and Steven E. Reid, eds. *Game Play: Therapeutic Use of Childhood Games.* New York: John Wiley & Sons, 1986. An edited book in which numerous types of games and activities that may be used in play therapy are described. Discusses games which have been specifically designed for play therapy as well as familiar games, such as checkers, whose use may be modified for therapeutic work. The book is largely intended for child therapy professionals of various treatment orientations.

R. Christopher Qualls

Cross-References

Abnormality: Behavioral Models, 33; Abnormality: Family Models, 53; Abnormality: Psychodynamic Models, 74; Behavioral Family Therapy, 394; Operant Conditioning Therapies, 1714; Play Therapy, 1835; Psychotherapeutic Effectiveness, 1989; Strategic Family Therapy, 2382.

PUNISHMENT

Type of psychology: Learning
Fields of study: Aversive conditioning; behavioral therapies; instrumental
  conditioning

Punishment involves employing a noxious or painful stimulus to stop an undesirable behavior. While punishment can be a very effective means of controlling behavior if certain rules for its use are followed, those rules can be difficult to follow; in addition, punishment generates a variety of problems and negative side effects.

  Principal terms
    AVERSIVE CONDITIONING: a behavior modification technique that employs
      punishment or aversive stimulation to control behavior
    BEHAVIORAL PSYCHOLOGISTS: psychologists who are oriented toward
      explanations and procedures involving learning theory
    EXTINCTION (CLASSICAL or PAVLOVIAN): a process in which the temporal
      contiguity of the conditioned stimulus and the unconditioned
      stimulus is disrupted and the learned association is lost
    EXTINCTION (OPERANT or INSTRUMENTAL): a process in which undesirable
      behavior is not followed by reinforcement
    PUNISHER: may refer either to the noxious or painful stimulus used as a
      punishment for undesirable behavior or to the punishing agent who
      inflicts the punishment
    PUNISHMENT: a process in which undesirable behavior is followed by a
      noxious or painful stimulus; may also refer to the noxious or painful
      stimulus itself
    REINFORCEMENT: an operation or process that increases the probability
      that a learned behavior will be repeated
    REINFORCER: a stimulus or event that increases the probability that a
      learned behavior will be repeated; a reward
    TEMPORAL CONTIGUITY: the closeness of two events or objects in time

Overview

  Parents and other agents of society have long operated on the assumption that undesirable behavior can best be eliminated by punishment. John Wesley, the founder of Methodism, wrote in 1760 that he had used electrical shock to cure a wide range of "nervous" problems. In the late eighteenth century, the British physician John Birch used electric shocks applied to the head of a patient to eliminate depression, and the American physician Benjamin Rush, one of the signers of the Declaration of Independence, used tartar to stop an alcoholic from drinking. Camphor oil, another nauseant, has been used by doctors since at least the eleventh century to treat a variety of mental disorders and aberrant behaviors, including schizophrenia. Russian psychologists used aversive classical conditioning techniques on alcoholics in the 1920's.

Today, many psychologists employ aversive conditioning techniques to control such undesirable behaviors as excessive drinking, overeating, smoking, bed-wetting, compulsive gambling, and fetishism. Proponents of aversion therapies report success in treating these and many other problem behaviors. Other psychologists have been less convinced of the value and effectiveness of using punishment to control behavior. While recognizing that under some circumstances punishment can at least cause temporary suppression of the punished behavior, psychologists have found many reasons to be wary of using punishment as the principal means of control.

In the late 1800's and early 1900's, educational and experimental psychologist Edward L. Thorndike was interested in understanding how the consequences (effects) of behaviors shaped and fixated those behaviors. After years of research involving both humans and animals, he formulated his law of effect. According to Thorndike, satisfying states of affairs (now generally called reinforcers) increase the frequency or probability of the response they follow. He originally proposed the reciprocal negative law of effect, which held that annoying states of affairs (now generally called punishers) decrease the frequency or probability of the response they follow. He later repealed the negative law of effect after concluding that it was not simply the converse of the law of effect and that punishment did not, in fact, eliminate the punished behavior by causing it to be "unlearned" but rather simply caused it to be suppressed.

Today psychologists use the term "punishment" to refer both to the administration of an aversive stimulus contingent upon a particular behavior and to the aversive stimulus itself. They also, in some cases, use the term "punisher" when referring to the aversive stimulus. An aversive stimulus is one which causes pain or discomfort to the recipient.

In actuality, the punishment can involve the presentation of an unpleasant stimulus such as a spanking or an electrical shock, or it can involve the removal of something that is pleasant and desirable such as money or affection. In addition, punishment might be administered because an undesirable behavior such as a criminal act or disobedience has occurred or because a desirable behavior such as studying for a test has not occurred. The threat of punishment is also sometimes considered to be punishment.

In recent years, researchers have focused on a variety of aspects of punishment. Certainty of punishment has received considerable attention. In general, if punishment is certain, it is more likely to be effective than if there is a chance of avoiding it. Severity of punishment and reactions to punishment have also been a focus of recent research. The effects of severity of punishment are somewhat more complicated than the effects of certainty of punishment. In order for punishment to be effective, it must be noxious enough to offset any reinforcement the punished behavior produces.

On the other hand, punishment that is too severe may interfere with the desired learning or with future learning. It might also generate resentment, anger, the desire to aggress, avoidance, or an unintended sense of hopelessness or helplessness. In extreme cases, excessively severe punishment has the potential for producing unintended suffering, injury, or even death. In order to be effective, then, punishment must be severe enough to accomplish the task but not so severe as to produce unwanted negative effects. Even if the punishment is not excessively severe, if it is presented too frequently it can produce many of the same negative effects as excessively severe punishment. Moreover, determining beforehand how severe the punishment must be is usually extremely difficult.

In general, animal studies usually show a clearer indication of the effectiveness of punishment in controlling behavior than do human studies. While the effects of punishment on animals and on humans are similar in many ways, humans and animals are different in at least one important way: Humans have cognitive capacities far beyond those of any other animals. Humans can therefore rationalize and justify their undesirable behavior and can use problem-solving strategies to discover ways to avoid or escape the punishment. Humans can also analyze the probability of being caught and punished. They are capable of concluding that the probability is sufficiently low, and the rewards for the behavior are great enough, that the risk of punishment is justified. Consequently, research using human subjects usually shows greater variability of effects when punishment is used to control behavior.

Applications

Psychologists do not debate whether punishment can be used to control behavior effectively. There is no doubt that when punishment is used properly, it will control behavior very effectively. The debate concerns how punishment should be used properly in order to control behavior effectively, and whether it is worth the inherent risks and trouble when behavior can be controlled equally effectively by using rewards for desirable behavior coupled with extinction to eliminate undesirable behavior. There is virtually no disagreement with the contention that it is imperative to include positive control measures in any punishment program.

Using punishment to control behavior entails a variety of risks and problems. Punishment often increases, rather than decreases, the probability of the behavior occurring again. Since attention is a very powerful reinforcer for most people and many species of animals, and because punishment cannot be administered without first paying attention to the learner, attempting to punish undesirable behavior can constitute unintended reward for that same behavior. Although punishment conveys information about what the learner should not do again, it does little to help the learner determine what should be done the next time. Punishment of undesirable behavior is not sufficient—specific additional training of desirable behavior is also necessary.

Punishment arouses strong emotional responses which may generalize in unintended ways. Once negative feelings or impulses are generated because of the painful or unpleasant stimulus, neither the form nor the direction of the feelings or impulses is controllable. The recipient of the noxious stimulus may develop negative feelings about self or the punishing agent which are stronger than intended. Feelings of worthlessness, helplessness, or hopelessness, as well as a desire to avoid the punishing agent can result even though they are not among the intended outcomes.

Using punishment models aggression as a means of controlling behavior. In the event that punishment accomplishes the intended purpose, it also provides the learner with both an illustration of its effectiveness and an example of how to employ punishment to reach goals. The meaning of "social power" is exemplified. Punishment does not teach the internal control of behavior. Although punishment may teach the offender to inhibit the punished response while under surveillance in order to avoid further punishment, once surveillance ends there is no internal control mechanism which can serve to continue inhibiting the behavior.

Punishment can easily become abuse. Loss of control by the punishing agent because of anger or frustration can result in unintended damage and injury. Most parents who abuse children do not intend to do the damage they inflict. They are usually simply intending to teach the child a lesson. The lesson may well be one that most of society agrees should be taught, but when the parent loses control and goes beyond the bounds of reasonable behavior, unintended damage and injury occur.

Pain is strongly associated with aggression. By definition, pain is produced by the administration of the noxious stimulus that constitutes the punishment. That pain often leads to a display of aggression against the source of the pain, the self, or an innocent scapegoat. Punishment works best when it follows every occurrence of the undesired behavior. While reward works best when given on an intermittent basis, punishment works best when given on a continuous basis. The degree of vigilance required to monitor behavior constantly so that every occurrence of the undesired behavior can be punished is rarely possible. The undesired behavior is, therefore, intermittently reinforced whenever it is not punished, and the behavior may continue.

Considering these problems and negative side effects, most behavioral psychologists have concluded that there are relatively few cases in which the use of punishment is justified. Since rewarding desirable behavior does not generate such problems and can be used in conjunction with normal extinction procedures to control behavior effectively, reward is usually considered a more attractive alternative than is punishment.

There are some cases, however, in which the dangers of allowing the behavior to continue are greater than the dangers posed by the use of punishment. In those cases in which rational analysis determines that the use of punishment is justified as a means of temporarily stopping the undesirable behavior while a more desirable behavior is taught, it should be obvious that the punishment should be administered in such a way as to maximize its effectiveness. In order to maximize the effectiveness of punishment so that its use can be minimized, behavioral psychologists have suggested several rules for the effective use of punishment.

First, an alternative response, which will lead to reinforcement, must be provided. Since most behavior, including undesirable behavior, is goal-directed, there should be a permissible behavior that will result in the attainment of a legitimate goal. Specific discrimination training is almost always necessary, since punishment will not by itself direct the learner toward the desirable behavior.

The punishment should be response- and situation-specific. One form of punishment for all types of offenses should not be expected to work well. Ideally, a different punishment would be available for each possible offense. The punishment should be given immediately and consistently. The only exception to immediate punishment should be for those cases in which an immediate response might be based on anger or frustration untempered by rational consideration. If more than a minimal amount of time transpires between the commission of the offense and receipt of the punishment, other behavior and stimuli will occur in closer temporal contiguity to the punishment than to the punished offense and might therefore become associated with the punishment as a result of classical conditioning.

There must be no escape from the punishment once the punishable offense occurs. Escape or avoidance of the punishment would constitute a reward for whatever behavior led to escaping or avoiding the punishment, increasing the probability of that behavior occurring again (it would have no effect on the probability of the punishable offense occurring again).

The pain produced by the punishment should be intense. A small amount of pain is not likely to be effective in stopping undesirable behavior. Since the idea underlying the use of punishment is to inflict pain, enough pain to accomplish the goal of stopping the punished behavior is necessary. Because the pain should be intense, it should also be of short duration. Specifically in the case of physical pain, the pain is an indication of damage or potential damage. Pain resulting from actual physical damage tends to last longest. Long-lasting pain is, therefore, usually an indication that physical damage has occurred. While punishment implicitly involves the intentional infliction of pain, the purpose is not usually to inflict damage. Therefore, pain that does not last long is generally desirable, because it indicates that no serious damage is being inflicted.

No sympathy or affection should be connected to the punishment. If sympathy or affection is tied to the punishment, the learner may learn to accept the punishment in order to receive them. This condition might describe the masochistic individual—one who has come to equate pain with love. Since punishment is being used to control the behavior of the individual, rather than to encourage the development of masochism, there should be a clear separation between the punishment and any sympathy or affection the individual is to receive. Affection should be withheld until after some desirable behavior occurs. That way, the affection can serve as a reward for desirable behavior. Sympathy is probably an inappropriate response for the punishing agent to display, since it might actually encourage the undesirable behavior inadvertently. One should never generalize from the act to the disposition. There is a significant and important difference between "Johnny did a bad thing" and "Johnny is a bad boy." Johnny should be convinced that he is a good boy, and that is why he should not do bad things.

One should allow, even encourage, constructive expression of anger. It is important to remember that pain is strongly associated with aggression. Anger, and the desire to aggress, is therefore a natural by-product of the use of punishment. It is unreasonable to expect the punished learner to not be angered by the punishment; the learner will need to be able to release that anger in a manner that will not lead to further punishment. This is probably the most difficult rule with which to comply fully, because it is difficult to find a way to encourage a totally constructive expression of anger. Most expressions of anger are at least partially or symbolically destructive. For example, working off the anger that the pain of the punishment produces by hitting a punching bag or "Bobo" doll may be preferable to hitting another person or kicking a cat, but it is still encouraging the learner to strike out at something when angered. While striking inanimate objects may be better than striking a living thing, it still might not be a desirable coping mechanism. Performing a constructive physical activity such as weeding the garden is generally recognized as a good way to work off the anger. It is incumbent upon the punishing agent to ensure, however, that the work is a means of releasing the anger rather than a continuation of the punishment.

It is difficult to follow even this short list of rules for the effective use of punishment. Consequently, most behavioral psychologists try to avoid relying on punishment to control behavior whenever possible, relying instead on rewarding desirable behavior and extinguishing undesirable behavior.

Context

Pavlovian (or classical) conditioning and instrumental (or operant) conditioning are both relatively old concepts in the field of psychology. Ivan Pavlov and Edward L. Thorndike were working on their conditioning theories in the late nineteenth and early twentieth centuries. B. F. Skinner began studying the principles underlying operant conditioning shortly before World War II, and he continued to be one of the most influential psychologists of all time until his death in late 1990, serving as the catalyst and leader of the modern behaviorist movement for more than fifty years. None of these giants in the history of learning theory enthusiastically embraced punishment as a desirable means of controlling behavior.

Pavlov occasionally employed aversive stimuli in his work with classical conditioning, but since the aversive stimulus always preceded the response, it is difficult to justify calling the aversive stimulus a punisher or punishment. It does not seem logical to talk about punishing a response that has not yet occurred.

Thorndike found that he could dispense with the negative law of effect because it did not add to the understanding of learning of behavior. Skinner concluded that rewarding desirable behavior would produce any behavior he desired, and to stop behavior that was undesirable only required that the reward or reinforcement for that behavior be stopped. Failure to receive reinforcement was all that was necessary to produce extinction of the behavior.

Other psychologists, however, found they could use aversive stimuli in classical conditioning situations, and punishment in instrumental or operant conditioning situations, to eliminate undesirable behaviors. Effective aversive conditioning techniques were added to the behaviorist's repertoire of therapeutic techniques.

Electric shocks were administered to people with drinking problems, for example, as they sat in a barlike setting. The objective was to condition them to experience an unpleasant feeling in the kind of place that could tempt them to drink. The expectation was that if they no longer enjoyed being in the bar, they could more easily avoid the temptation to drink. Homosexuals were shocked while becoming sexually aroused as they viewed pictures of same-sex people or talked about homosexual lovemaking. Again, the objective was to make something that had once been pleasurable into an unpleasant activity. Approaches such as these were based on Pavlovian (classical) conditioning.

Other approaches focused on making the consequences of the behavior unpleasant or painful, rather than changing the emotional connotations of places and activities. They were based on instrumental or operant conditioning principles. Alcoholics were administered a drug such as Antabuse, which by itself produced no particular effects. If, however, alcohol was ingested while the Antabuse was present, the person would become violently ill because of the ingestion of the alcohol. The sickness was a punishment for drinking. The intent was that the threat of further violent illness would help the individual avoid drinking.

Ethical concerns and legal constraints instituted in the 1970's and 1980's, however, have led to fewer efforts to control behavior through the administration of punishment, at least in therapeutic situations. Society still feels free to use imprisonment and fines to punish some forms of undesirable behaviors. Many, perhaps most, parents still feel free to use spankings, verbal haranguing, grounding, and punitive assignment of chores as a means of punishing their children's misconduct. Fewer schools use spanking as a means of controlling students, but detention, suspension, expulsion, and extra assignments remain common forms of punishing misconduct by students.

Bibliography

Bandura, Albert. *Principles of Behavior Modification.* New York: Holt, Rinehart and Winston, 1969. An older, college-level textbook with a strong empirical orientation that is surprisingly easy to read. Especially interesting from a historical perspective, because Bandura presents some of the studies that moved him from the ranks of traditional learning theorists to become one of the major innovators in the field of social learning theory. Observational or vicarious learning and vicarious reinforcement and punishment are discussed in detail.

Bergin, Allen E., and Sol R. Garfield, eds. *Handbook of Psychotherapy and Behavior Change: An Empirical Analysis.* New York: John Wiley & Sons, 1971. Heavy reading, but an excellent source of detailed information. The four chapters in part 3 cover behavioral therapies.

Burgess, Anthony. *A Clockwork Orange.* London: Heinemann, 1962. A fictional account of an antisocial personality whose behavior is modified through the use of aversive conditioning techniques. Burgess opposes the use of such aversive conditioning techniques, and the book is an indictment of behavior modification. The behavior modifiers are described in the least favorable possible light, the techniques (although described fairly accurately) are the most shocking ones available, and the treatment is carried to an unreasonable extreme and executed for the wrong reasons. It is, however, an interesting, entertaining, and informative novel.

Matson, Johnny L., and Thomas M. DiLorenzo. *Punishment and Its Alternatives: A New Perspective for Behavior Modification.* New York: Springer, 1984. An excellent and realistic description of the ranges of the punishment techniques available and the conditions under which it might be reasonable to employ them. The criteria for employing punishment when it is deemed to be the best available treatment, its limitations when used exclusively, and the need to employ positive reinforcement in punishment programs are covered. Legal and ethical concerns, empirical analysis, and predictions of future trends are also discussed.

Sansweet, Stephen J. *The Punishment Cure.* New York: Mason/Charter, 1975. An older but very readable book, authored by a professional writer who avoids using professional jargon yet accurately describes what occurs in aversive therapy situations. A historical perspective of the use of punishment as a means of controlling behavior is offered. Sansweet describes how aversive therapy techniques have been applied to alcoholism, smoking, homosexuality, fetishism, compulsions and phobias, gambling, and bed-wetting in considerable detail.

John W. Nichols

Cross-References

Avoidance Learning, 375; Conditioning: Pavlovian versus Instrumental, 649; Escape Conditioning, 985; Instrumental Conditioning: Acquisition and Extinction, 1315; Learned Helplessness, 1425; Misbehavior and Learning, 1581; Pavlovian Conditioning: Acquisition, Extinction, and Inhibition, 1757; Reinforcers and Reinforcement, 2084.

QUASI-EXPERIMENTAL DESIGNS

Type of psychology: Psychological methodologies
Fields of study: Experimental methodologies; methodological issues

The ideal psychological study is a true experiment that allows unequivocal causal judgments to be made about the variables being investigated; the goal is to have confidence in the validity of judgments made from the experimental data. Quasi-experimental designs are ways of collecting data that maximize confidence in causal conclusions when a true experiment cannot be done.

Principal terms

CONTROL GROUP: a group assembled to provide a comparison to the treatment group results

DEPENDENT VARIABLE: the outcome measure in a study; the effect of the independent variable is measured by changes in the dependent variable

EXTERNAL VALIDITY: the extent to which the results of any particular study can be generalized to other settings, people, and times

HYPOTHESIS: a proposed causal link between the independent and dependent variable; the experimental hypothesis is the experimenter's belief about the causal link

INDEPENDENT VARIABLE: the causal factor in a study; if an experimenter suspects that violent television shows cause aggression, a violent television show would be the independent variable

INTERNAL VALIDITY: the extent to which the dependent variable is caused by the independent variable; if relevant plausible rival alternative hypotheses can be ruled out, the study has strong internal validity

PLAUSIBLE RIVAL ALTERNATIVE HYPOTHESIS: a hypothesis, different from the experimenter's preferred hypothesis, that offers another reasonable explanation for experimental results

POST-TEST: a measure of the dependent variable or other relevant variable after the treatment

PRETEST: a measure of the dependent variable or other relevant variable before the treatment

TRUE EXPERIMENT: a study that requires randomly assigning people, called subjects or respondents, to treatment and control groups

Overview

The feature that separates psychology from areas such as philosophy is its reliance on the empirical method for its truths. Instead of arguing deductively from premises to conclusions, psychology progresses by using inductive reasoning in which psychological propositions are formulated as experimental hypotheses that can be tested by experiments. The outcome of the experiment determines whether the hypothesis is accepted or rejected. Therefore, the best test of a hypothesis is one that can be interpreted unambiguously. True experiments are considered the best way to test hypotheses, because they are the best way to rule out plausible alternative explanations (confounds) to the experimental hypothesis. True experiments are studies in which the variable whose effect the experimenter wants to understand, the independent variable, is randomly assigned to the experimental unit (usually a person); the researcher observes the effect of the independent variable by responses on the outcome measure, the dependent variable.

For example, if one wanted to study the effects of sugar on hyperactivity in children, the experimenter might ask: "Does sugar cause hyperactive behavior?" Using a true experiment, one would randomly assign half the children in a group to be given a soft drink sweetened with sugar and the other half a soft drink sweetened with a sugar substitute. One could then measure each child's activity level; if the children who were assigned the sugar-sweetened drinks showed hyperactivity as compared to the children who received the other drinks, one could confidently conclude that sugar caused the children to show hyperactivity. A second type of study, called a correlational study, could be done if one had investigated this hypothesis by simply asking or observing which children selected sugar-sweetened drinks and then comparing their behavior to the children who selected nonsugar-sweetened drinks. The correlational study, however, would not have been able to show whether sugar actually caused hyperactivity. It would be equally plausible that children who are hyperactive simply prefer sugar-sweetened drinks. Such correlational studies have a major validity weakness in not controlling for plausible rival alternative hypotheses. Quasi-experimental designs stand between true experiments and correlational studies in that they control for as many threats to validity as possible.

Experimental and Quasi-Experimental Designs for Research, by Donald T. Campbell and Julian Stanley (1966), describes the major threats to validity that need to be controlled for so that the independent variable can be correctly tested. Major plausible alternative explanations may need to be controlled when considering internal validity. ("Controlled" does not mean that the threat is not a problem; it means only that the investigator can judge how probable it is that the threat actually influenced the results.)

An external environmental event may occur between the beginning and end of the study, and this historical factor, rather than the treatment, may be the cause of any observed difference. For example, highway fatalities decreased in 1973 after an oil embargo led to the establishment of a speed limit of 55 miles per hour. Some people believed that the cause of the decreased fatalities was the 55-mile-per-hour limit. If the oil embargo caused people to drive less because they could not get gasoline or because it was higher priced, however, either of those events could be a plausible alternative explanation. The number of fatalities may have declined simply because people were driving less, not because of the speed-limit change.

Maturation occurs when natural changes within people cause differences between the beginning and end of the study. Even over short periods of time, for example, people become tired, hungry, or bored. It may be these changes rather than the treatment which causes observed changes. Suppose an investigation of a treatment for sprained ankles measured the amount of pain people had when they first arrived for treatment, and then measured their pain again four weeks after treatment. Finding a reduction in reported pain, the investigator concluded that the treatment was effective. Since a sprained ankle will probably improve naturally within four weeks, however, maturation (in this case, the natural healing process) is a plausible alternative explanation.

Testing is a problem when the process of measurement itself leads to systematic changes in measured performance. Suppose a study was done on the effects of a preparatory course on performance on the American College Test (ACT)—a college entrance exam. Students were given the ACT, then given a course on improving their scores, then tested again; they achieved higher scores, on the average, the second time they took the test. The investigator may attribute the improvement to the prep course, when actually it may have been simply the practice of taking the first test which led to improvement. This plausible alternative explanation suggests that even if the students had not taken the course they would have improved their scores on the average upon retaking the ACT. A control group would help improve this study.

A change in the instruments used to measure the dependent variable will also cause problems. This is a problem particularly when human observers are rating behaviors directly. The observers may tire, or their standards may shift over the course of the study. For example, if observers are rating children's "hyperactivity," they may see later behavior as more hyperactive than earlier behavior not because the children's behavior has changed but because, through observing the children play, the observers' own standards have shifted. Objective measurement is crucial for controlling this threat.

Selection presents a problem when the results are caused by a bias in the choice of subjects for each group. For example, suppose a study of two programs designed to stop cigarette smoking assigned smokers who had been addicted for ten years to program A and smokers who had been addicted for two years to program B. It was found that 50 percent of the program B people quit and 30 percent of the program A people quit. The investigators concluded that program B is more effective; however, it may be that people in program B were more successful simply because they were not as addicted to their habit as the program A participants.

Mortality, or attrition, is a problem when a differential drop-out rate influences the results. For example, in the preceding cigarette study, suppose that of one hundred participants in program A, ninety of them sent back their post-test form at the end of the study; for program B, only sixty of the participants sent their forms back. It may be that people who did not send their forms back were more likely to have continued smoking; that may have caused the apparent difference in results between programs A and B.

When subjects become aware that they are in a study, and awareness of being observed influences their reactions, reactivity has occurred. The famous Hawthorne studies on a wiring room at a Western Electric plant were influenced by this phenomenon. The investigators intended to do a study on the effects of lighting on work productivity, but they were puzzled by the fact that *any* change they made in lighting—increasing it or decreasing it—led to improved productivity. They finally decided it was the workers' awareness of being in an experiment that caused their reactions, not the lighting level.

Statistical regression is a problem that occurs when subjects are selected to be in a group on the basis of their extreme scores (either high or low) on a test. Their group can be predicted to move toward the average the next time they take the test, even if the treatment has had no effect. For example, if low-scoring students are assigned to tutoring because of the low scores they achieved on a pretest, they will score higher on the second test (a post-test), even if the tutoring is ineffective.

External threats to validity are the other major validity issue. Generally speaking, true experiments control for the internal threats to validity listed above by experimental design, but external threats may be a problem for true experiments as well as quasi-experiments. Since a scientific finding is one that should hold true in different circumstances, external validity is a very important issue.

An interaction between selection and treatment can cause an external validity problem. For example, since much of the medical research on the treatment of diseases has been performed by selecting only men as subjects, one might question whether those results can be generalized to women. The interaction between setting and treatment can be a problem when settings differ greatly. For example, can results obtained on a college campus be generalized to a factory? Can results from a factory be generalized to an office? The interaction of history and treatment can be a problem when the specific time the experiment is carried out influences people's reaction to the treatment. The effectiveness of an advertisement for gun control might be judged differently if measured shortly after an assassination or mass murder received extensive media coverage.

Applications

Quasi-experimental designs have been most frequently used to examine the effects of social phenomena and social programs that cannot be or have not been investigated by experiments. For example, the effects of the public television show *Sesame Street* have been the subject of several quasi-experimental evaluations. One initial evaluation of *Sesame Street* concluded that it was ineffective in raising the academic abilities of poor children, but a reanalysis of the data suggested that statistical regression artifacts had contaminated the original evaluation and that *Sesame Street* had a more positive effect than was initially believed. This research showed the potential harm that can be done by reaching conclusions while not controlling for all the threats to validity. It also showed the value of doing true experiments whenever possible.

Many of the field-research studies carried out on the effects of violent television programming on children's aggressiveness have used quasi-experimental designs to estimate the effects of violent television. Other social-policy studies have included the effects of no-fault divorce laws on divorce rates, of crackdowns on drunken driving on the frequency of drunken driving, and of strict speed-law enforcement on speeding behavior and accidents. The study of the effects of speed-law enforcement represents excellent use of the "interrupted time series" quasi-experimental design. This design can be used when a series of pretest and post-test data points are available. In this case, the governor of Connecticut abruptly announced that people convicted of speeding would have their licenses suspended for a thirty-day period on the first offense, sixty days on a second offense, and longer for any further offenses. By comparing the number of motorists speeding, the number of accidents, and the number of fatalities during the period before the crackdown with the period after the crackdown, the investigators could judge how effective the crackdown actually was. The interrupted time series design provides control over many of the plausible rival alternative hypotheses and is thus a strong quasi-experimental design. The investigators concluded that it was probable that the crackdown did have a somewhat positive effect in reducing fatalities but that a regression artifact may also have influenced the results. The regression artifact in this study would be a decrease in fatalities simply because there was such a high rate of fatalities before the crackdown.

Organizational psychology has used quasi-experimental designs to study such issues as the effects of strategies to reduce absenteeism in businesses, union-labor cooperation on grievance rates, and the effects of different forms of employee ownership on job attitudes and organizational performance. The latter study compared three different conversions to employee ownership and found that employee ownership had positive effects on a company to the extent that it enhanced participative decision making and led to group work norms supportive of higher productivity. Quasi-experimental studies are particularly useful in those circumstances where it is impossible to carry out true experiments but policymakers still want to reach causal conclusions. A strong knowledge of quasi-experimental design principles helps prevent incorrect causal conclusions.

Context

Psychology has progressed through the use of experiments to establish a base of facts that support psychological theories; however, there are many issues about which psychologists need to have expert knowledge that cannot be investigated by performing experiments. There are not too many social situations, outside a university laboratory, where a psychologist can randomly assign individuals to different treatments. For example, psychologists cannot dictate to parents what type of television programs they must assign their children to watch, they cannot tell the managers of a group of companies how to implement an employee stock option plan, and they cannot make a school superintendent randomly assign different classes to different instructional approaches. All these factors in the social environment vary, and quasi-experimental designs can be used to get the most available knowledge from the natural environment.

The philosophy of science associated with traditional experimental psychology argues that unless a true experiment is done it is impossible to reach any causal conclusion. The quasi-experimental view argues that a study is valid unless and until it is shown to be invalid. What is important in a study is the extent to which plausible alternative explanations can be ruled out. If there are no plausible alternative explanations to the results except for the experimenter's research hypothesis, then the experimenter's research hypothesis can be regarded as true. The first generally circulated book that argued for a quasi-experimental approach to social decision making was William A. McCall's *How to Experiment in Education*, published in 1923. Education has been one of the areas where there has been an interest in and willingness to carry out quasi-experimental studies. Psychology was more influenced by the strictly experimental work of Ronald A. Fisher that was being published at around that time, and Fisher's ideas on true experiments dominated psychological methods through the mid-1950's.

The quasi-experimental view gained increasing popularity during the 1960's as psychology was challenged to become more socially relevant and make a contribution to understanding the larger society. At that time, the federal government was also engaged in many social programs, sometimes collectively called the War on Poverty, which included housing programs, welfare programs, and compensatory educational programs; they needed to be evaluated. Evaluation was needed so that what worked could be retained and what failed could be discontinued. There was an initial burst of enthusiasm for quasi-experimental studies, but the ambiguous results that they produced were discouraging, and this has led many leading methodologists to reemphasize the value of true experiments.

Rather than hold up the university-based laboratory true experiment as a model, however, they called for implementing social programs and other evaluations using random assignment to treatments in such a way that stronger causal conclusions could be reached. The usefulness of true experiments and quasi-experiments was also seen to be much more dependent on psychological theory: The pattern of results obtained by many different types of studies became a key factor in the progress of psychological knowledge. The traditional laboratory experiment, upon which many psychological theories are based, was recognized as being very limited in external validity, and the value of true experiments—carried out in different settings, with different types of people, and replicated many times over—was emphasized. Since politicians, business managers, and other social policymakers have not yet appreciated the advantages in knowledge to be gained by adopting a true experiment approach to social innovation, quasi-experimental designs are still an important and valuable tool in understanding human behavior.

Bibliography

Campbell, Donald Thomas, and Julian C. Stanley. *Experimental and Quasi-Experimental Designs for Research*. Chicago: Rand McNally, 1966. The clearest and most accessible presentation of the principles of quasi-experimental design.

Includes many excellent examples and a description of sixteen experimental and quasi-experimental designs, each evaluated for twelve threats to validity. Many examples are from educational research. Includes illustrations of designs.

Cook, Thomas D., and Donald T. Campbell. "The Design and Conduct of Quasi-Experiments and True Experiments in Field Settings." In *Handbook of Industrial and Organizational Psychology*, edited by Marvin D. Dunnette. Chicago: Rand McNally, 1976. An excellent overview of the principles of quasi-experimentation as applied in industrial and organizational settings. Written for the educated non-professional, this article includes the revamped validity scheme developed completely in Cook and Campbell's 1979 book.

_____. *Quasi-Experimentation: Design and Analysis Issues for Field Settings.* Chicago: Rand McNally, 1979. A large book built on the foundations of Campbell and Stanley (1966). It has a much more complete consideration of the philosophical analysis of cause and effect, a reorganized conception of validity issues, detailed statistical analysis methods for quasi-experiments, and a discussion on the conduct of randomized experiments in field settings. By recasting validity into statistical conclusion validity, construct validity, internal validity, and external validity, a more comprehensive view is presented. The complex statistical information may make parts of the book incomprehensible to the nonprofessional, but it is worth reading for the parts one can understand. Illustrations of designs and statistical analyses.

Cronbach, Lee Joseph. *Designing Evaluations of Educational and Social Programs.* San Francisco: Jossey-Bass, 1982. Cronbach disagrees with the Campbell, Stanley, and Cook approach to quasi-experimentation in that he thinks they overemphasize internal validity and the importance of unequivocal causal conclusions. Cronbach argues that the major issue shaping any quasi-experimentation should be the application that the study is designed to inform. He develops a different typology of issues based on this criterion of value.

Trochim, William M. K., ed. *Advances in Quasi-Experimental Design and Analysis.* San Francisco: Jossey-Bass, 1986. A series of articles by various experts on quasi-experimental design. Some of the issues are rather technical, but most of the articles are understandable. Chapter 3, "Validity Typologies and the Logic and Practice of Quasi-Experimentation," by Melvin M. Mark, is an excellent overview, review, and discussion of different approaches to quasi-experimentation.

Don R. Osborn

Cross-References

Archival Data, 293; Sources of Experimental Bias, 1006; Field Experimentation, 1031; Hypothesis Development and Testing, 1248; Psychological Experimentation: Independent, Dependent, and Control Variables, 1932; Psychotherapeutic Effectiveness, 1989; The Scientific Method in Psychology, 2148; Violence and Sexuality in the Mass Media, 2603.

RACE AND INTELLIGENCE

Type of psychology: Intelligence and intelligence testing
Fields of study: General issues in intelligence; intelligence assessment

The relationship between race and intelligence has long been the subject of heated debate among social scientists. At issue is whether intelligence is an inherited trait or is primarily attributable to environmental influences.

Principal terms

CORRELATION: the situation that results when changes in one factor are associated with changes in another factor

CULTURE: the shared attitudes, values, customs, symbols, art, experiences, and rules of a given people

ENVIRONMENT: all the conditions, circumstances, and influences surrounding and affecting a person or group of individuals; may be physical, social, political, and/or psychological in nature

HEREDITY: the transmission of characteristics from parent to offspring through genes in the chromosomes

HERITABILITY: the extent to which a given characteristic, such as intelligence, is inherited

INTELLIGENCE: the ability to learn, solve problems, and direct conduct effectively; mental ability

INTELLIGENCE QUOTIENT (IQ): a score received on an intelligence test

NATURE VERSUS NURTURE: the controversy over whether intelligence is solely or primarily inherited (nature) or is attributable to environmental factors (nurture)

RACE: commonly defined as a group of people distinguishable from another group of people on the basis of physical characteristics or inherited features

Overview

In 1969, educational psychologist Arthur Jensen published an article in the *Harvard Educational Review* entitled "How Much Can We Boost I.Q. and Scholastic Achievement?" He attempted to explain the consistent finding that whites, on the average, outperform blacks by about 15 points on intelligence quotient (IQ) tests. His major conclusion was that racial differences in intelligence are primarily attributable to heredity and that whites, as a racial group, are born with abilities superior to those of blacks.

Jensen, as well as William Shockley, presents the hereditarian hypothesis of intelligence. It argues that some people are born smarter than others and that this fact cannot be changed with training, education, or any alteration in the environment. Because they believe that African Americans as a group are not as smart as Caucasians, they suggest that special programs, such as Head Start, which are designed to help disadvantaged children improve in school achievement, are doomed to fail.

In contrast to the hereditarians, Urie Bronfenbrenner and Ashley Montagu can be described as environmentalists. They believe that although intelligence has some genetic component, as do all human characteristics, the expression of intelligent behavior is defined, determined, and developed within a specific cultural context. Therefore, what people choose to call intelligence is primarily caused by the interaction of genetics with environmental influences. Environmentalists believe that a person can improve in his or her intellectual functioning with sufficient changes in environment.

Much of the hereditarian argument is based on two types of studies: those comparing IQ test performance of twins, and studies of adopted children. Because identical twins have the same genetic endowment, it is thought that any differences observed between them should be attributable to the effects of the environment. Hereditarians also suggest that one should observe more similarities in the IQs of parents and their biological children (because they share genes) than between parents and adopted children (who are biologically unrelated, and therefore, share no genes).

Statistical formulas are applied to comparisons between family members' IQs to determine the relative contributions of heredity and environment. Using this method, Sir Cyril Burt in 1958 reported a heritability estimate of .93. This means that 93 percent of the variability in intelligence could be explained genetically. People have also interpreted this to mean that 93 percent of the intelligence level is inherited. Jensen has more recently reported heritability estimates of .80 and .67, depending on what formula is used. Hereditarians have also pointed out that when they compare African Americans and Caucasians from similar environments (the same educational level, income level, or occupation), the reported IQ differences remain. This, they argue, supports their view that heredity is more important in determining intelligence.

For environmentalists, it is not so much the reported IQ differences between different racial groups that are in question. Of more concern are the basic assumptions made by the hereditarians and the reasons they give for the reported differences. Not surprisingly, environmentalists challenge the hereditarian arguments on several levels. First, they point out that there is no evidence of the existence of an "intelligence" gene or set of genes. They say that scientists have been unsuccessful in distinguishing the genetic from the environmental contributions to intelligence.

Environmentalists also refute the assumption that IQ tests adequately measure intelligence. Although IQ has been noted to be a good predictor of success in school, it turns out to have little relationship to economic success in life. S. E. Luria reports an analysis that shows that the son of a Caucasian businessman with an IQ of 90 has a greater chance of success than an African-American boy with an IQ of 120. This example calls into question what actually is being assessed. It is not at all clear that "intelligence" is being measured—especially since there is no generally accepted definition among social scientists about what intelligence is.

The definition of race is also problematic. Although most people may identify several racial groups (such as African, or black; Caucasian, or white; and so on), Ashley Montagu and many other social scientists agree that race is a pseudoscientific concept, used as a social or political category to assign social status and to subordinate nonwhite populations. Because of the intermingling among different cultural groups, it is also difficult to identify strict biological boundaries for race, which in turn makes genetic interpretations of racial comparisons of IQ differences much less meaningful.

In addition to questioning what IQ tests measure, many psychologists have criticized IQ tests as being biased against individuals who are culturally different from the mainstream group (Caucasians) and who have not assimilated the white middle-class norms upon which the tests were based. Tests developed in one culture may not adequately measure the abilities and aptitude of people from another culture, especially if the two cultures emphasize different skills, ways of solving problems, and ways of understanding the world.

Environmentalists have also criticized the research and statistical techniques used by the hereditarians. It is now widely acknowledged that the data reported by Burt, upon which Jensen heavily relied, were false. In many different studies, he came up with the same figures (to the third decimal point) for the similarities between IQ scores for twins. This is statistically impossible. He also did not take into account how other variables, such as age and gender, might have produced higher IQ values in the twins he studied. Rather, he assumed that they shared genes for intelligence.

It is also charged that the concept of heritability is misunderstood by the hereditarians. This is a statistic that applies to groups, not to individuals. If one states that the heritability estimate of a group of IQ scores is .80, that does not mean that 80 percent of each IQ score is attributable to genetics, but that 80 percent of the difference in the group of scores can be attributed to genetic variation. Therefore, according to the enviromentalists, it is incorrect for hereditarians to establish heritability within one group (such as Caucasian children) and then apply that figure to a different racial group (such as African-American children).

Applications

Several examples may help clarify the relationships between heredity, environment, and characteristics such as IQ. The first example involves a highly heritable characteristic, height. Suppose a farmer had two fields, one rich in nutrients (field A) and the other barren (field B). The farmer takes seed from a bag that has considerable genetic variety and plants them in the two fields. She cares for the two fields of crops equally well. After several weeks, the plants are measured. The farmer would find that within field A, some plants would be taller than others in the same field. Since all these plants had the same growing environment, the variation could be attributed to the genetic differences in the seeds planted. The same would be the case with the plants in field B.

The farmer would also find differences between the two fields. The plants in field A would be taller than the plants in field B, because of the richer soil in which they grew. The difference in the average heights of the plants would be attributable to the quality of the growing environment, even though the genetic variation (heritability) within field A may be the same as that within field B. This same principle applies to IQ scores of different human groups.

Taking the example further, the farmer might call a chemist to test the soil. If the chemist was able to determine all the essential missing nutrients, the farmer could add them to the soil in field B for the next season. She would find that the second batch of plants would grow larger, with the average height being similar to the average height of plants in field A. Similarly, if one is comparing African Americans and Caucasians, or any number of racial groups, on a characteristic such as IQ test scores, it is important to understand that unless the groups have equivalent growing environments (social, political, economic, educational, and so on), differences between the groups cannot be easily traced to heredity.

As another example, suppose one took a set of identical twins who were born in Chicago, separated them at birth, and placed one of the twins in the Kung! desert community in Africa. The life experiences of the twin in Africa would differ significantly from those of his Chicago counterpart because of the differences in diet, climate, and other relevant factors required for existence and survival in the two environments. The twin in Africa would have a different language and number system; drawing and writing would likely not be an important part of daily life. Therefore, if one were to use existing IQ tests, one would have to translate them from English to the Kung! language so that they could be understood. The translation might not truly capture the meaning of all the questions and tasks, which might interfere with the Kung! twin's understanding of what was being asked of him. More problems would arise when the Kung! twin is asked to interpret drawings or to copy figures, since he would not be very familiar with these activities.

It is likely that the Kung! twin would perform poorly on the translated IQ test, because it does not reflect what is emphasized and valued in his society. Rather, it is based on the schooling in society in which the Chicago twin lives. This does not mean that the Kung! twin is less intelligent than his Chicago twin. Similarly, the Chicago twin would do poorly on a test developed from the experience of Kung! culture, because the Kung! test would emphasize skills such as building shelter, finding water, and other activities that are not important for survival in Chicago. In this case, the Kung! test would not adequately measure the ability of the Chicago twin.

Studies done by psychologist Sandra Scarr show that evidence for a genetic basis for racial differences in IQ is far from clear. She looked at the IQ scores of African-American children who were born into working-class families but were adopted and reared by white middle-class families. The IQ scores of these children were close to the national average and were almost 10 to 20 points higher than would have been expected had they remained in their birth homes.

Change in children's environments seems to be a critical factor in enhancing their ability to perform on the IQ tests, as seen in the research done by Scarr. Bron-fenbrenner found similar results. He examined a dozen studies that looked at early intervention in children's lives; he found that whenever it was possible to change the environment positively, children's scores on IQ tests increased.

Context

The notion of inherited differences is an ancient one; however, the concept of racial classifications is more recent. According to psychologist Wade Nobles, the Western idea of race emerged during the sixteenth century as Europeans began to colonize other parts of the world. As they came into contact with people who looked different from them, many Europeans developed the notion that some races were superior to others. This belief often was given as a justification for slavery and other oppressive activities.

Charles Darwin's theory of evolution was critical in promoting the belief that human differences were a result of heredity and genetics. His notion of "the survival of the fittest" led psychologists to research racial differences in intelligence in order to understand the successes and failures of different human groups. Francis Galton, Darwin's cousin, was instrumental in furthering the hereditarian perspective in psychology. In his book *Hereditary Genius: An Inquiry into Its Laws and Consequences* (1869), he attempted to illustrate that genius and prominence follow family lines. He also began the eugenics movement, which supported the use of selective mating and forced sterilization to improve racial stock.

Following Galton's lead, many psychologists embraced the notions of inherited racial differences in intelligence. G. Stanley Hall, the founder of the American Psychological Association, believed that African people were at a lower evolutionary stage than Caucasians. By the beginning of the 1900's, psychological testing was widely being used to support the view that intelligence was hereditary and was little influenced by the environment. More recently, Burt, R. J. Herrnstein, and Jensen have argued in favor of an overriding genetic factor in intelligence.

There were also early efforts to challenge the hereditarian perspective in psychology. During the 1920's and 1930's, Herman Canady and Howard Long, two of the first African Americans to receive graduate degrees in psychology, produced evidence showing the importance of environmental influences on IQ test performance. They were concerned about the increasing scientific justifications for the inequality and injustice experienced by African Americans, Native Americans, and other groups. Fighting racism was a major reason Leon Kamin became involved in the debate about race and intelligence. He gathered the original information that had been reported by scientists and reexamined it; Kamin was responsible for discovering that Burt had reported false information. He also noted that many hereditarians misused and misinterpreted their statistics.

Hereditarians maintain that racial differences in IQ test scores are primarily caused by genetics and that these scores do reflect differences in intelligence; environmentalists say no. It has not been proved definitively that IQ tests measure intelligence;

however, the evidence does suggest that performance on IQ tests is determined by the interaction between genetic and environmental influences. The quality of the environment will determine how well people will reach their potential. In a society where the history of certain groups includes oppression, discrimination, and exclusion from opportunity, it is difficult to explain differences in achievement as being primarily inherited. Instead, it would seem to be a more important goal to eliminate injustices and to change the conditions of life so that all people could do well.

Bibliography

Fancher, Raymond E. *The Intelligence Men: Makers of the IQ Controversy.* New York: W. W. Norton, 1985. Examines the historical contexts of the IQ controversy. The life experiences of the major hereditarians and environmentalists and how these experiences influenced their perspectives are emphasized. This book is easy to read and does an excellent job of making complex statistics understandable.

Goldsby, Richard. *Race and Races.* New York: Macmillan, 1971. Provides straightforward and accurate information about issues of race, racial differences, and racism. There is a balanced discussion of both the hereditarian and environmentalist perspectives of the IQ controversy. Enjoyable and easy to read for high school and college students alike.

Guthrie, Robert V. *Even the Rat Was White.* New York: Harper & Row, 1976. Provides an excellent historical view of how psychology has dealt with race as an issue. The first section of the book focuses on methods of study, early psychological testing, and the development of racism in the profession of psychology.

Jensen, Arthur R. *Bias in Mental Testing.* New York: Free Press, 1980. An attempt to deal comprehensively with the issues of IQ testing and bias. Jensen challenges the criticisms against IQ tests and offers research to support his view that group differences in IQ test scores are not attributable to bias.

Kamin, Leon J. *The Science and Politics of IQ.* New York: Halstead Press, 1974. Discusses the political nature of the role psychologists have played in support of IQ testing. The role of psychologists in the eugenics movement and in education is discussed. Includes strong critiques of the work done by Burt and Jensen.

Montagu, Ashley, ed. *Race and IQ.* New York: Oxford University Press, 1975. Written to challenge the interpretations offered by the hereditarians. Most of the articles were previously published in professional journals or popular magazines. Some of the chapters contain very technical material; however, the authors generally do an effective job translating this into more understandable language.

Derise E. Tolliver

Cross-References

RACISM

Type of psychology: Social psychology
Field of study: Prejudice and discrimination

Students of racism examine the phenomenon of negative attitudes and behavior by members of the majority toward those who belong to racial and ethnic minorities. The topic of racism, which straddles the boundaries between social psychology and sociology, is connected with the study of intergroup relations, cognition, and attitudes in general.

Principal terms

AMBIVALENCE: a state of wavering between two sharply opposed attitudes toward a particular racial group

ATTRIBUTION ERROR: the wrongful ascription of someone else's behavior to personality characteristics, rather than to situational effects, and vice versa

AVERSIVE RACISM: the desire to avoid members of a different racial group

DISCRIMINATION: the behavioral acceptance or rejection of a person based on his or her belonging to a particular racial or ethnic group

INSTITUTIONAL RACISM: the behavior patterns followed in organizations and in society at large that produce discrimination against members of racial minorities regardless of the prejudice or lack thereof of individuals

OUT-GROUP HOMOGENEITY HYPOTHESIS: the failure to notice differences within a racial or ethnic group to which one does not belong

PREJUDICE: a strong preconceived dislike directed against members of a different racial or ethnic group

STEREOTYPE: a set of beliefs, often rigidly held, about the characteristics of an entire racial or ethnic group

Overview

The social and psychological study of prejudice and discrimination, including prejudice and discrimination against African Americans, has a long history; the term "racism," however, did not enter the language of social psychology until the publication of the Kerner Commission Report of 1968, which blamed all-pervasive "white racism" for widespread black rioting in American cities. While usually applied to black-white relations in the United States, the term is also sometimes used with regard to white Americans' relations with other minority groups such as Asians or Latinos, or to black-white relations outside the United States, for example, in Britain, Canada, or South Africa. Most of the studies and research on racism have focused on white racism against blacks in the United States.

Racism is seen by many social psychologists not as mere hatred but as a deep-rooted habit that is hard to change; hence, subvarieties of racism are distinguished. Psychoanalyst Joel Kovel, in his book *White Racism: A Psychohistory* (1970), distinguishes between dominative racism, the desire to oppress blacks, and aversive racism, the desire to avoid contact with blacks. Aversive racism, Samuel L. Gaertner and John Dovidio find, exists among those whites who pride themselves on being unprejudiced. David O. Sears, looking at whites' voting behavior and their political opinions as expressed in survey responses, finds what he calls symbolic racism: a resentment of African Americans for making demands in the political realm that supposedly violate traditional American values. Social psychologist James M. Jones distinguishes three types of racism: individual racism, the prejudice and anti-black behavior deliberately manifested by individual whites; institutional racism, the social, economic, and political patterns that impersonally oppress blacks regardless of the prejudice or lack thereof of individuals; and cultural racism, the tendency of whites to ignore or denigrate the special characteristics of black culture.

Where Dovidio and Gaertner find aversive racism, Irwin Katz finds ambivalence. Many whites, he argues, simultaneously see African Americans as disadvantaged (which creates sympathy) and as deviating from mainstream social norms (which creates antipathy). Such ambivalence, Katz contends, leads to exaggeratedly negative reactions to negative behaviors by an African American, but also to exaggeratedly positive reactions to positive behaviors by an African American. He calls this phenomenon ambivalence-induced behavior amplification.

The reasons suggested for individual racism are many. John Dollard and others, in *Frustration and Aggression* (1939), see prejudice as the scapegoating of minorities in order to provide a release for aggression in the face of frustration; in this view, outbursts of bigotry are a natural response to hard economic times. Muzafer and Carolyn Sherif, in *Groups in Harmony and Tension* (1953) and later works, see prejudice of all sorts as the result of competition between groups. Theodor Adorno and others, in *The Authoritarian Personality* (1950), view prejudice, whether directed against blacks or against Jews, as reflective of a supposedly fascist type of personality produced by authoritarian child-rearing practices. In *Racially Separate or Together?* (1971), Thomas F. Pettigrew shows that discriminatory behavior toward blacks, and the verbal expression of prejudices against them, can sometimes flow simply from a white's desire to fit in with his or her social group. Finally, both prejudice and discrimination, many psychologists argue, are rooted in those human cognitive processes involved in the formation of stereotypes.

Stereotypes are ideas, often rigidly held, concerning members of a group to which one does not belong. Social psychologists who follow the cognitive approach to the study of racism, such as David L. Hamilton, Walter G. Stephan, and Myron Rothbart, argue that racial stereotyping (the tendency of whites to see blacks in some roles and not in others) arises, like any other kind of stereotyping, from the need of every human being to create some sort of order out of his or her perceptions of the world. Although stereotypes are not entirely impervious to revision or even shattering in the face of disconfirming instances, information related to a stereotype is more efficiently retained than information unrelated to it. Whites, it has been found, tend to judge blacks to be more homogeneous than they really are, while being more aware of differences within their own group: This is called the out-group homogeneity hypothesis. Whites who are guided by stereotypes may act in such a way as to bring out worse behavior in blacks than would otherwise occur, thus creating a self-fulfilling prophecy.

Why is stereotypical thinking on the part of whites about African Americans so hard to eliminate? The history of race relations in the United States deserves some of the blame. Some mistakes in reasoning common to the tolerant and the intolerant alike—such as the tendency to remember spectacular events and to think of them as occurring more frequently than is really the case (the availability heuristic)—also occur in whites' judgments about members of minority groups. In addition, the social and occupational roles one fills may reinforce stereotypical thinking.

Thomas F. Pettigrew contends that attribution errors—mistakes in explaining the behavior of others—may have an important role to play in reinforcing racial stereotypes. The same behavioral act, Pettigrew argues, is interpreted differently by whites depending on the race of the actor. A positive act by a black might be ascribed to situational characteristics (for example, luck, affirmative action programs, or other circumstances beyond one's control) and thus discounted; a positive act by a white might be ascribed to personality characteristics. Similarly, a negative act might be ascribed to situational characteristics in the case of a white, but to personality characteristics in the case of a black. The tendency of whites to view the greater extent of poverty among blacks as solely the result of lack of motivation can be seen as a form of attribution error.

Applications

Institutional racism occurs when policies that are nonracial on their face have differential results for the two races. For example, a stiff educational requirement for a relatively unskilled job may effectively exclude blacks, whose educational preparation may be weaker, in part at least because of past racial discrimination. The policy of hiring friends and relatives of existing employees may also exclude blacks, if blacks have not historically worked in a particular business. In both cases, the effect is discriminatory even if the intent is not.

Somewhat connected with the concept of institutional racism is Pettigrew's notion of conformity-induced prejudice and discrimination. A classic example is that of the pre-Civil Rights era southern United States, where urban restaurant owners, regardless of their personal feelings about blacks, refused them service out of deference to local norms. Another example is the case of the white factory worker who cooperates with black fellow workers on the job and in union activities but strenuously opposes blacks moving into his neighborhood; norms of tolerance are followed in one context, norms of discrimination in the other.

The concept of symbolic (sometimes called "modern") racism, a form of covert prejudice said to be characteristic of political conservatives, arose from a series of questions designed to predict whether white Californians would vote against black political candidates. It has been used to explain opposition to school busing to achieve integration and support for the 1978 California referendum proposition for limiting taxes. John B. McConahay shows that white experimental subjects who score high on the modern racism scale, when faced with hypothetical black and white job candidates with identical credentials, are more likely than low scorers to give a much poorer rating to the black candidate's resume.

Aversive racism cannot be detected by surveys. Since aversive racists wish to maintain a nonprejudiced self-image, they neither admit to being prejudiced nor discriminate against blacks when social norms clearly forbid it; when the norms are ambiguous, however, they do discriminate. In a New York City experiment, professed liberals and professed conservatives both got telephone calls from individuals identifiable from their speech patterns as either black or white. At first, the caller said he had the wrong number; if the recipient of the call did not hang up, the caller then asked for help regarding a disabled car. Conservatives were less likely to offer help to the black, but liberals were more likely to hang up when they were told by the black that a wrong number had been called. In another experiment, white college students proved just as willing to accept help from a black partner as from a white one when the help was offered. When the subjects had to take the initiative, however, discomfort with the reversal of traditional roles showed up: More asked for help from the white partner than from the black one.

Both symbolic and aversive, but not dominative, racists manifest ambivalence in their attitudes toward blacks. Katz's concept of ambivalence-induced behavior amplification has been tested in several experiments. In one experiment, white college student subjects were told to insult two individuals, one black and one white. After they had done so, they proved, when asked for assistance in a task later on, more willing to help the black they had insulted than the white person.

The effect of the availability heuristic in reinforcing stereotypes is seen in the case of a white who is mugged by a black criminal. If the victim knows no other blacks, he or she may well remember this one spectacular incident and forget the many blacks who are law-abiding. The effect of occupational roles in reinforcing stereotypes can be seen in the example of a white policeman who patrols a black slum neighborhood and jumps to the conclusion that all blacks are criminals.

Experiments on stereotyping indicate that white subjects remember the words or actions of a solo black in an otherwise all-white group better than they do the words or actions of one black in a group of several blacks. With a mixed group of speakers, some white and some black, white experimental subjects proved later to be more likely to confuse the identities of the black speakers than those of the white speakers, while remembering the race of the former. The self-fulfilling prophecy concept has been tested in experiments with white subjects interviewing supposed job candidates. The white subjects were more ill at ease and inarticulate interviewing a black candidate than in interviewing a white one; in turn, the black candidate was more ill at ease than the white one, and made more errors.

Since most such experiments use college students as subjects, there is inevitably some doubt about their generalizability to the outside world. Nevertheless, it seems likely that the evidence from social psychology experiments of just how deeply rooted racial bias is among white Americans has played at least some role in leading governments to adopt affirmative action policies to secure fairer treatment of blacks and other minorities in hiring procedures.

Context

Although the study of racism per se began with the racial crisis of the 1960's, the study of prejudice in general goes back much further; as early as the 1920's, Emory Bogardus constructed a social distance scale measuring the degree of intimacy members of different racial and ethnic groups were willing to tolerate with one another. At first, psychologists tended to seek the roots of prejudice in the emotional makeup of the prejudiced individual rather than in the structure of society or the general patterns of human cognition. For many years, the study of antiblack prejudice was subsumed under the study of prejudice in general; those biased against blacks were thought to be biased against other groups such as Jews, as well.

In the years immediately following World War II, American social psychologists were optimistic about the possibilities for reducing or even eliminating racial and ethnic prejudices. Adorno's *The Authoritarian Personality* and *The Nature of Prejudice*, by Gordon Allport, reflect the climate of opinion of the time. Allport, whose view of prejudice represented a mixture of the psychoanalytic and cognitive approaches, used the term "racism" to signify the doctrines preached by negrophobe political demagogues; he did not see it as a deeply ingrained bad habit pervading the entire society. Thomas F. Pettigrew, who wrote about anti-black prejudice from the late 1950's on, cast doubt on the notion that there was a specific type of personality or pattern of child rearing associated with prejudice. Nevertheless, he long remained in the optimistic tradition, arguing that changing white people's discriminatory behavior through the enactment of civil rights laws would ultimately change their prejudiced attitudes.

The more frequent use by social psychologists of the term "racism" from the late 1960's onward indicates a growing awareness that bias against blacks, a visible minority, might be harder to uproot than that directed against religious and ethnic minorities. Social psychologists studying racial prejudice shifted their research interest from the open and noisy bigotry most often found among political extremists (for example, the Ku Klux Klan) to the quiet, everyday prejudices of the average apolitical individual. Racial bias against blacks came to be seen as a central, rather than a peripheral, feature of American life.

Responses to surveys taken from the 1940's to the end of the 1970's indicated a steady decline in the percentage of white Americans willing to admit holding racist views. Yet in the 1970's, the sometimes violent white hostility to school busing for integration, and the continuing social and economic gap between black and white America, gave social psychologists reason to temper their earlier optimism. The contact hypothesis, the notion that contact between different racial groups would reduce prejudice, was subjected to greater skepticism and ever more careful qualification. Janet Ward Schofield, in her field study of a desegregated junior high school, detected a persistence of racial divisions among the pupils; reviewing a number of such studies, Walter Stephan similarly discerned a tendency toward increased interracial tension in schools following desegregation. The pessimism suggested by field studies among younger teenagers was confirmed by experiments conducted in the 1970's and 1980's on college students and adults; such studies demonstrated the existence even among supposedly nonprejudiced people of subtle racism and racial stereotyping.

Yet while social psychological experiments contribute to an understanding of the reasons for negative attitudes toward blacks by whites, and for discriminatory behavior toward blacks even by those whites who believe themselves to be tolerant, they do not by any means provide the complete answer to the riddle of racial prejudice and discrimination. Unlike many other topics in social psychology, racism has also been investigated by journalists, historians, economists, sociologists, political scientists, legal scholars, and even literary critics. The techniques of social psychology—surveys, controlled experiments, and field studies—provide only one window on this phenomenon.

Bibliography

Allport, Gordon W. *The Nature of Prejudice.* Cambridge, Mass.: Addison-Wesley, 1954. This detailed (510-page), beautifully written, and influential book, accessible to both the general reader and the scholar, devotes equal space to anti-Jewish and antiblack prejudice, with passing references to other types of prejudice. Contains one of the earliest expositions of the contact hypothesis, and one of the earliest treatments of the relationship between prejudice and stereotyping. Somewhat dated by both its optimistic meliorism and its references to extremist political movements of the 1940's. Includes chapter endnotes, name index, and subject index.

Dovidio, John F., and Samuel L. Gaertner, eds. *Prejudice, Discrimination, and Racism.* Orlando, Fla.: Academic Press, 1986. This rich collection includes one essay apiece on aversive racism and racial ambivalence; three essays on racial stereotyping; a difficult but rewarding chapter by John D. McConahay on the formulation and testing of the symbolic racism concept; an essay by Janet Schofield on the persistence of aversive racism in a recently desegregated school; and a piece by James L. Jones on cultural racism. Most are suitable for upper-level undergraduate psychology majors and graduate students; the introductory and concluding general essays, however, are accessible to the general reader. Includes chapter references, tables, graphs, and subject index.

Hamilton, David L., ed. *Cognitive Processes in Stereotyping and Intergroup Behavior.* Hillsdale, N.J.: Lawrence Erlbaum, 1981. A rich harvest of the fruits of research. All essays except that of Richard Ashmore (dealing solely with sexual stereotyping) discuss, to a greater or lesser extent, racial stereotyping. The contributions by Shelley E. Taylor (on the salience of the solo black), Myron Rothbart, Mark Snyder, and Terrence E. Rose are especially worth reading. Hamilton provides a summary of the other contributors' work, placing it in the context of earlier research. Includes chapter references and author and subject indexes.

Katz, Irwin. *Stigma: A Social Psychological Analysis.* Hillsdale, N.J.: Lawrence Erlbaum, 1981. A slim but path-breaking study which reports on subjects' reactions to both blacks and the physically handicapped, and develops the notion of ambivalence-induced behavior amplification. A convenient summary of research results is found in the final chapter. Includes tables, references, and author and subject indexes. For upper-level undergraduates on up.

Katz, Phyllis A., ed. *Towards the Elimination of Racism.* New York: Pergamon Press, 1976. Particularly good essays in this collection include one by the editor on racism in small children; a survey by Richard D. Ashmore and Frances K. Delboca of psychological approaches to intergroup conflict; one of Samuel L. Gaertner's early essays on aversive racism experiments; and an incisive and readable discussion by Myron Rothbart of the reasons of self-interest behind some whites' opposition to racial reform. Includes chapter references and a subject index. For the general reader.

Katz, Phyllis A., and Dalmas A. Taylor, eds. *Eliminating Racism: Profiles in Controversy.* New York: Plenum Press, 1988. Contains an essay by Marilynn Brewer and Norman Miller on the contact hypothesis; several essays on school desegregation; an essay by James L. Jones on three types of racism and possible remedies for each; and a piece by David O. Sears on symbolic racism. Several essays compare and contrast anti-black racism with sexism and with bigotry against Mexican Americans, Japanese Americans, and American Indians. Includes introductory and concluding essays by the editors, chapter references, and author and subject indexes. For the general reader.

Kovel, Joel. *White Racism: A Psychohistory.* New York: Vintage Books, 1970. Reprint. New York: Columbia University Press, 1984. As the title implies, Kovel's approach to antiblack prejudice is psychoanalytic rather than cognitive: No attempt is made to examine stereotyping as a normal human activity. This somewhat turgidly written book is shaped by a left-wing political sensibility that was in vogue in the late 1960's. Nevertheless, the work remains valuable for its paradigmatic distinction between different types of racism. Includes a bibliographical essay, and an index of authors and subjects. For the general reader.

Pettigrew, Thomas F. "Prejudice." In *Prejudice*, by Thomas F. Pettigrew, George M. Frederickson, Dale T. Knobel, Nathan Glazer, and Reed Ueda. Cambridge, Mass.: The Belknap Press of Harvard University Press, 1982. Presents a concise and clearly written review of the social psychological literature on prejudice and racism up to 1980. For the high school student and the lower-level undergraduate. Includes a bibliographical essay and an index.

_____. *Racially Separate or Together?* New York: McGraw-Hill, 1971. A collection of reprinted essays, originally written between 1961 and 1969, interspersed with brief summaries of the contents of essays dealing with the same subtopic. Two essays dealing with late-1960's politics are somewhat dated; the essay on social psychology and research on desegregation, however, is useful to the beginning student. Includes chapter endnotes, author index, subject index, tables, and figures. For lower-level undergraduates and the general reader.

Stephan, Walter G., and David Rosenfield. "Racial and Ethnic Stereotypes." In *In the Eye of the Beholder: Contemporary Issues in Stereotyping*, edited by Arthur G. Miller. New York: Praeger, 1982. A good critical review of the social psychological literature on whites' and blacks' stereotyping of each other. All technical terms are carefully explained and, when necessary, illustrated by examples. Especially informative on the issue of racism in children, and on the mixed record of school desegregation as a means of breaking down racial stereotypes. Includes figures, chapter references, annotated list of additional readings, author index, subject index, and contributor information at end of book.

Paul D. Mageli

Cross-References

Attitude Formation and Change, 326; The Contact Hypothesis, 675; Theories of Intergroup Relations, 1356; Effects of Prejudice, 1848; Reduction of Prejudice, 1855; Race and Intelligence, 2031; Social Identity Theory, 2297.

RADICAL BEHAVIORISM: B. F. SKINNER

Type of psychology: Personality
Fields of study: Behavioral and cognitive models; instrumental conditioning

Radical behaviorism describes the views of B. F. Skinner, an influential figure in American psychology since the 1930's. Skinner argued that most behavior is controlled by its consequences; he invented an apparatus for observing the effects of consequences, advocated a technology of behavior control, and believed that everyday views about the causes of behavior were an obstacle to a true understanding of it.

Principal terms

CONTINGENCY OF REINFORCEMENT: the dependent relationship between a response and a reinforcer

DISCRIMINATIVE STIMULUS: any stimulus in the presence of which a response is reinforced

EXPERIMENTAL ANALYSIS OF BEHAVIOR: a demonstration of the causes of behavior by controlling the behavior of an individual organism

MENTALISM: the view that an organism's actions are caused by ideas or feelings that arise in the mind

OPERANT: a class of responses defined by their common effect

PRIVATE EVENTS: events to which only the individual has access; for example, the pain of a toothache

RULE-GOVERNED BEHAVIOR: behavior under the discriminative control of formulized contingencies

SHAPING: the inducing of a response by reinforcing successive approximations

Overview

According to B. F. Skinner (1904-1990), the behavior of an organism is a product of current and past environmental consequences and genetic endowment. Since little can be done, at least by psychology, about genetic endowment, Skinner focused on those things that could be changed or controlled: the immediate consequences of behavior. By consequences, Skinner meant the results or effects that a particular behavior (a class of responses, or "operant") produce. There are many ways to open a door, for example, but since each one allows a person to walk to the next room, one would speak of a "door-opening" operant. The consequences not only define the class of responses but also determine how often members of the class are likely to occur in the future. This was termed the law of effect by early twentieth century American psychologist Edward L. Thorndike, whose work Skinner refined.

There are several kinds of consequences, or effects. Events that follow behavior and produce an increase in the rate or frequency of the behavior are termed reinforcers. In ordinary language, they might be called rewards, but Skinner avoided this expression because he defined reinforcing events in terms of the effects they produced (an increased rate) rather than the alleged feelings they induced (for example, pleasure). To attribute the increase in rate of response produced by reinforcement to feelings of pleasure would be regarded by Skinner as an instance of mentalism—the attribution of behavior to a feeling rather than an event occurring in the environment. Other consequences which follow a behavior produce a decrease in the rate of behavior. These are termed punishers. Skinner strongly objected to the use of punishment as a means to control behavior because it elicited aggression and produced dysfunctional emotional responses such as striking back and crying in a small child. Notice that consequences (reinforcers and punishers) may be presented following a behavior (twenty dollars for building a doghouse, for example, or an electric shock for touching an exposed wire) or taken away (a fine for speeding, the ending of a headache by the taking of an aspirin). Consequences may be natural (tomatoes to eat after a season of careful planting and watering) or contrived (receiving a dollar for earning an A on a test).

Reinforcing and punishing consequences are one example of controlling variables. Events that precede behaviors are also controlling variables and determine under what circumstances certain behaviors are likely to appear. Events occurring before a response occurs are called discriminative stimuli because they come to discriminate in favor of a particular piece of behavior. They set the occasion for the behavior and make it more likely to occur. For example, persons trying to control their eating are told to keep away from the kitchen except at meal times. Being in the kitchen makes it more likely that the person will eat something, not simply because that is where the food is kept but also because being in the kitchen is one of the events which has preceded previous eating and therefore makes eating more likely to occur. This is true even when the person does not intend to eat but goes to the kitchen for other reasons. Being in the kitchen raises the probability of eating. It is a discriminative stimulus for eating, as are the table, the refrigerator, or a candy bar on the counter. Any event or stimulus which occurs immediately before a response is reinforced gets reinforced with the response and makes the response more likely to occur again if the discriminative stimulus occurs again. The discriminative stimulus comes to gain some control over the behavior.

Discriminative stimuli and reinforcing stimuli are the controlling variables Skinner used to analyze behavior. These events constitute a chain of behavior called a contingency of reinforcement. It is a contingency because reinforcement does not occur unless the response is made in the presence of the discriminative stimuli. Contingencies of reinforcement are encountered every day. For example, a soda drink is purchased from a machine. The machine is brightly colored to act as a discriminative stimulus for dropping coins in a slot, which in turn yields a can or bottle of soft drink. The machine comes to control a small portion of a person's behavior. If the machine malfunctions, a person may push the selector button several times repeatedly, perhaps even putting in more coins, and still later, strike the machine. By carefully scheduling how many times an organism must respond before reinforcement occurs, the rate of response can be controlled as is done in slot or video machines, or gambling devices in general. Responses are made several hundred or thousand times for very little reinforcement—a near win or a small payoff. Schedules of reinforcement are another important set of controlling variables which Skinner explored.

Contingencies are relationships among controlling variables. Some of the relationships become abstracted and formulized, that is, put in the form of rules. When behavior is under the control of a rule, it is termed rule-governed behavior, as opposed to contingency-shaped behavior. As a person first learns any skill, much of his or her behavior is rule governed, either through written instructions or by the person's repeating the rule to him- or herself. For example, a novice golfer might review the rules for a good swing, even repeating them aloud. Eventually, though, swing becomes automatic; it seems to become "natural." The verbal discriminative stimuli have shifted to the very subtle and covert stimuli associated with swing without the golfer's thinking about it, and the natural consequences of a successful swing take over.

Skinner analyzed behavior by examining the antecedents and consequences which control any specific class of responses in the individual organism. From this view, he elaborated a psychology that encompassed all aspects of animal and human behavior, including language. By the late 1970's, historians of psychology ranked Skinner's work as the second most significant development in psychology since World War II; the general growth of the field was ranked first. Three journals arose to publish work in the Skinnerian tradition: *Journal of the Experimental Analysis of Behavior, Journal of Applied Behavior Analysis*, and *Behaviorism*. Moreover, an international organization, the Association for Behavior Analysis, was formed, with its own journal.

Applications

The operant chamber is a small experimental space or cage that Skinner invented to observe the effects that consequences have on behavior. A food-deprived organism (Skinner first used rats and later switched to pigeons) is placed in the chamber containing a lever that, when depressed, releases a small piece of food into a cup from which the organism eats. The first bar-press response is produced through the process of shaping, or reinforcing approximations to bar pressing (for example, being near the bar, having a paw above the bar, resting a paw on the bar, nearly depressing the bar) until bar pressing is regularly occurring. Once the operant of bar pressing is established, an experimental analysis of the variables which influence it can be done. The schedule of reinforcement can be changed, for example, from one reinforcer for each response to five responses required for each reinforcer. Changes in the rate of response can be observed on a device Skinner invented, a cumulative record, which automatically displays the rate at which the operant is occurring. A discriminative stimulus can be introduced in the form of a small light mounted on the wall of the chamber. If bar presses are reinforced only when the light is turned on, the light will come to have some control over the operant. Turning the light on and off will literally turn bar pressing on and off in a food-deprived rat.

Skinner controlled his own behavior in the same fashion that he had learned to control the behavior of laboratory organisms. He arranged a "writing environment," a desk used only for that purpose; wrote at a set time each day; and would keep careful records of time spent writing. Other examples of self-management may be found in Skinner's book *Walden Two* (1948). In this fictionalized account, children learn self-control through a set of exercises that teach ways to tolerate increasing delays of reinforcement.

Skinner also performed a behavior analysis of language (see his *Verbal Behavior*, 1957). For example, a behavioral analysis of the word "want," "believe," or "love," an operational definition in Skinner's sense, would be all those circumstances and situations which control the use of the word, that is, the discriminative stimuli for the verbal response. Skinner tried to show in *Verbal Behavior* that speaking and writing could be explained with the same principle he had used to explain animal behavior. Many of Skinner's works, and much of his private notebooks, are taken up with the recording of how words are used. His purpose was to de-mentalize them, to show that what controls their use is some aspect of the environment, or some behavioral practice on the part of the verbal community, rather than some internal or mental event. The earliest uses of the word "to know," for example, referred to action, something the individual could do, rather than something he or she possessed or had stored inside the mind.

Context

So much has been written about Skinner, some of it misleading or false, that it is important to clarify what he did not do. He did not rear either of his daughters in a "Skinner box." His youngest daughter was reared during her infancy with the aid of an "aircrib," a special enclosed crib Skinner built that allowed control of air temperature and humidity, and in which the infant could sleep and play without the burden of clothes. "Aircribs" were later available commercially. Skinner did not limit his analysis of behavior only to publicly observable events, as did the methodological behaviorists. Part of what made Skinner's behaviorism radical was his insistence that a science of behavior should be able to account for those private events to which only the individual has access. He described how the community teaches its members to describe covert events such as toothaches and headaches. He did not regard such events as anything other than behavior. That is, he did not give them a special status by calling them "mental events."

Skinner did not argue that reinforcement explains everything. He allowed, especially in his later works, that genetic endowment plays a role in the determination of behavior, as do rules and antecedent events. He did not reject physiological explanations of behavior, when actual physiology was involved. He did object to the use of physiological terms in psychological accounts, unless the physiological mechanisms were known. For Skinner, physiology was one subject matter, and behavior was another. Finally, he did not ignore complex behavior. Many of his works, particularly *Verbal Behavior* and *The Technology of Teaching* (1968), offered behaviorist analyses of what in other psychologies would be termed cognitive phenomena, such as talking, reading, thinking, problem solving, and remembering.

Skinner made many contributions to twentieth century psychology. Among them was his invention of the operant chamber and its associated methodology. Operant equipment and procedures are employed by animal and human experimental psychologists in laboratories around the world. Most of these psychologists do not adhere to Skinner's radical behaviorism, or to all the features of his science of behavior. They have, however, found the techniques that he developed to be productive in exploring a wide variety of problems, ranging from the fields of psychopharmacology to learning in children and adults to experimental economics. Skinner and his followers developed a technology of behavior that included techniques for working with the developmentally disabled, children in elementary classrooms, and persons with rehabilitation or health care problems; they also considered approaches to public safety, employee motivation and production, and any other field which involved the management of behavior. Although the technology developments never reached the vision described in *Walden Two*, the efforts are ongoing.

Skinner may have exhausted the law of effect. The idea that consequences influence behavior can be found in many forms in the literature of psychology and philosophy, especially since the middle of the nineteenth century, but it is only in the work of B. F. Skinner that one sees how much of human and animal behavior can be brought within its purview. Because Skinner took behavior as his subject matter, he greatly expanded what could be regarded as of interest to psychologists. Behavior was everywhere, in the classroom, at the office, in the factory. Nearly any aspect of human activity could become the legitimate object of study by a Skinnerian psychologist, a point well illustrated in Skinner's description of a utopian community which takes an experimental attitude toward its cultural practices and designs a culture based on a science of behavior (*Walden Two*). Finally, Skinner conceptualized an epistemology, a way of understanding what it means for humans to know something, that may be a lasting contribution to twentieth century philosophy.

In placing the radical behaviorism of B. F. Skinner in historical context, two nineteenth century doctrines are often called on. One view, shared by Skinner, is that operant psychology represents an extension of the principle of natural selection which Charles Darwin described at the level of the species. Natural selection explained the origin of species; contingencies of reinforcement and punishment explain the origin of classes of responses. The environment selects in both cases. In operant psychology, the role of the environment is to reinforce differentially and thereby select from among a pool of responses which the organism is making. The final effect is some one particular operant which has survival or adaptive value for the individual organism. Skinner has suggested that cultural evolution occurs in a similar fashion.

It is also observed that Skinner's psychology resembles nineteenth century pragmatism. The pragmatists held that beliefs are formed by their outcome, or practical effect. To explain why someone does something by reference to a belief would be regarded as mentalism by Skinner; he would substitute behavior for beliefs. Yet he comes to the same doctrine: one in which environmental consequences act in a Darwinian fashion. Finally, Skinner's philosophy shows the influence of the nineteenth century positivism of physicist Ernst Mach. Skinner desired a description of behavior and its causes, while avoiding mental states or other cognitive or personality entities that intervene between behavior and the environment.

Bibliography

Modgil, Sohan, and Celia Modgil, eds. *B. F. Skinner: Consensus and Controversy.* New York: Falmer Press, 1987. A collection of essays by psychologists and philosophers. Each topic has a pro and contrary opinion, with replies and rebuttals. Although written at a professional level, this is an excellent volume for a global view of Skinner's ideas and for the clearest understanding of what is "radical" about Skinner's behaviorism.

Nye, Robert D. *What Is B. F. Skinner Really Saying?* Englewood Cliffs, N.J.: Prentice-Hall, 1979. The best introductory-level secondary account of Skinner's psychology and philosophy.

Reynolds, George Stanley. *A Primer of Operant Conditioning.* Rev. ed. Glenview, Ill.: Scott, Foresman, 1975. This introductory-level book describes the basic processes and methods of operant psychology, explaining shaping, reinforcers and punishers, discrimination, and schedules of reinforcement.

Skinner, B. F. *About Behaviorism.* New York: Alfred A. Knopf, 1974. In this work, Skinner argues for his radical behaviorism by contrasting it with methodological behaviorism and by illustrating how it treats topics such as perception, memory, verbal behavior, private events, and thinking.

_____. *Particulars of My Life.* New York: Alfred A. Knopf, 1976.

_____. *The Shaping of a Behaviorist.* New York: Alfred A. Knopf, 1979.

_____. *A Matter of Consequences.* New York: Alfred A. Knopf, 1983. Skinner published his autobiography in these three separate volumes. The first describes his life from birth, through his college years as an English major, to his entering Harvard University for graduate study in psychology. *The Shaping of a Behaviorist* presents his years at Harvard and his rise to national prominence. *A Matter of Consequences* begins with his return to Harvard as a professor in the late 1940's.

_____. *Science and Human Behavior.* New York: Macmillan, 1953. A fine introduction to Skinner's thought. The principles of operant psychology are described, with numerous examples of the applicability to an individual's life and the major institutions of society. The chapter on private events illustrates one important way in which Skinner's radical behaviorism differs from methodological behaviorism.

_____. *Walden Two.* New York: Macmillan, 1948. A description of a fictional community based upon experimental practices and behavioral principles.

The book was the source of inspiration for several communes and illustrates how all aspects of culture can be submitted to a behavioral analysis. Contains a lengthy criticism of democracy as a form of government.

Vargas, Julie S. "B. F. Skinner, Father, Grandfather, Behavior Modifier." In *About Human Nature: Journeys in Psychological Thought*, edited by Terry J. Knapp and Charles T. Rasmussen. Dubuque, Iowa: Kendall/Hunt, 1987. An intimate description of Skinner by his eldest daughter, who is herself a psychologist. Skinner's home, study, and the activities occurring over a Thanksgiving weekend are described.

Terry J. Knapp

Cross-References

RATIONAL-EMOTIVE THERAPY

Type of psychology: Psychotherapy
Field of study: Cognitive therapies

Developed by psychologist Albert Ellis, rational-emotive therapy aims to minimize the client's self-defeating style by helping the client acquire a more rational and logical philosophy of life. It has been successfully applied to marital couples, family members, individual patients, and group clients across a host of psychological difficulties, including alcoholism, depression, anxiety disorders, and sexual dissatisfaction.

Principal terms

A-B-C THEORY OF PERSONALITY: a theory in which activating events (A) are evaluated in light of a person's beliefs (B), which directly influence and shape consequential emotional (behavioral and cognitive) reactions (C)

IRRATIONAL BELIEFS: unreasonable evaluations that sabotage an individual's goals and lead to increased likelihood of experiencing needless pain, suffering, and displeasure

LONG-RANGE HEDONISM: the idea that well-adjusted people seek happiness and avoid pain today, tomorrow, and in the future

RATIONAL-EMOTIVE TREATMENT: a method of personality change that incorporates cognitive, emotional, and behavioral strategies; designed to help resist tendencies to be irrational, suggestible, and conforming

SCIENTIFIC THINKING: the idea that individuals intend to be reasonably objective, rational, and logical; via scientific thinking, attempts are made to construct hypotheses, collect data, and evaluate the validity of these personal hypotheses

Overview

Rational-emotive therapy (RET) was founded in 1955 by Albert Ellis following his disappointment with traditional methods of psychoanalysis. From 1947 to 1953, Ellis had practiced classical analysis and analytically oriented psychotherapy, but he came to the conclusion that psychoanalysis was a superficial and unscientific form of treatment. Specifically, rational-emotive therapy was developed as a combined humanistic, cognitive, and behavioral form of therapy. Although Ellis initially used RET primarily in individual formats, group and workshop formats followed quickly. Ellis would publish approximately fifty books and more than five hundred articles on RET, and he would present more than fifteen hundred public workshops.

According to Ellis (in 1989), the philosophical origins of rational-emotive therapy include the Stoic philosophers Epictetus and Marcus Aurelius. In particular, Epictetus wrote that "people are disturbed not by things, but by the view which they take of them" during the first century A.D. in *The Encheiridion*. Ellis also gives much credit to the theory of human disturbance highlighted by psychotherapist Alfred Adler in the development of rational-emotive therapy. Specifically, Ellis was persuaded by Adler's conviction that a person's behavior originates from his or her ideas. As Ellis began writing about and describing RET in the 1950's and 1960's, clinical behavior therapy was conceptually distinct and distant from Ellis' ideas. The primary similarity was that Ellis employed a host of behavioral techniques in his approach. As time passed, however, behavior therapy engaged in a controversial yet productive broadening of what was meant by "behavior" and started to include cognitions as a form of behavior that could be learned, modified, and studied. Ellis' RET approach shares many similarities with other common cognitive behavioral approaches to treatment. These include Donald Meichenbaum's cognitive behavioral modification (focusing on self-instructional processes and adaptive coping statements), Maxie C. Maultsby, Jr.'s, rational behavior therapy (which is essentially RET with some adaptations, including written self-analysis techniques and rational-emotive imagery), and Aaron T. Beck's cognitive therapy. Cognitive therapy has many similarities to RET but was developed independently; it uses fewer "hard-headed approaches." For example, Beck advocates the use of collaborative empiricism and a focus on automatic thoughts and underlying cognitive schemas. RET strongly emphasizes irrational beliefs, especially "unconditional shoulds" and "absolutistic musts," as the root of emotional and behavioral disturbances.

There are six principal propositions of rational-emotive therapy as Ellis described them in 1989. First, people are born with rational and irrational tendencies. That is, individuals may be either self-helping or self-defeating, short-range hedonists or long-range hedonists; they may learn by mistakes or repeat the same mistakes, and they may actualize or avoid actualizing their potentials for growth. Second, cultural and family experiences may exacerbate irrational thinking. Third, individuals may seem to think, act, and feel simultaneously. Thinking, however, appears actually to precede actions and feelings. For example, the process of "appraising" a situation usually triggers feelings. Fourth, RET therapists differ from person-centered therapists in that RET practitioners do not believe that a warm interpersonal relationship between therapist and patient is a sufficient or even necessary condition for effective change. RET therapists also do not believe that personal warmth is necessary in order to accept clients fully. In fact, it is important in RET treatment to criticize and point out the deficiencies in a person's behavior and thinking style. Moreover, Ellis argues that RET therapists often need to use "hard-headed methods" to convince clients to employ more self-discipline.

Fifth, rational-emotive therapists use a variety of strategies, including assertiveness training, desensitization, operant conditioning, support, and role playing. The usual goal of RET is to help rid clients of symptoms and modify underlying thinking styles that create symptoms. Ellis further identifies two basic forms of RET: general RET, which is similar to other forms of cognitive behavior therapy; and preferential

RET, which includes general RET but also emphasizes philosophic restructuring and teaches clients how to dispute irrational thoughts and inappropriate behaviors via rules of logic and the scientific method. Sixth, all emotional problems are caused by people's tendencies to interpret events unrealistically and are maintained by irrational beliefs about them.

Thus, the basic underlying tenet of RET is that emotional disturbances are primarily the result of irrational thinking. Specifically, RET argues that people upset themselves with "evaluative irrational beliefs" (rather than with "non-evaluative" irrational beliefs). For example, Ellis (1987) describes the following scenario:

> If you devoutly believe that your fairy godmother looks out for you and is always ready to help you, you may live happily and undisturbedly with this highly questionable and unrealistic Belief. But if you evaluate your fairy godmother's help as extremely desirable and go even further to insist that *because* it is desirable, you absolutely *must* at all times have her help, you will almost certainly make yourself anxious (whenever you realize that her magical help that you *must* have may actually be absent) and you will tend to make yourself extremely depressed (when you see that in your hour of need this help does not actually materialize).

Although many forms of irrationality exist, rational-emotive therapy focuses on a client's strong "desires" and "commands." Ellis has developed various lists of irrational beliefs that highlight the most common thinking difficulties of patients. These include such beliefs as "I must do well or very well"; "I am a bad or worthless person when I act weakly or stupidly"; "I need to be loved by someone who matters to me a lot"; "People must treat me fairly and give me what I need"; "People must live up to my expectations or it is terrible"; "My life must have few major hassles"; and "I can't stand it when life is unfair."

Ellis has refined his ideas about irrational thoughts to three primary beliefs. These are: "I *must* do well and be approved by *significant* others, and if I don't do as well as I *should* or *must*, there is something really rotten about me. It is terrible that I am this way and I am a pretty worthless, rotten person"; "You (other humans with whom I relate, my original family, my later family that I may have, my friends, relatives, and people with whom I work) *must*, *ought*, and *should* treat me considerately and fairly and even *specially* (considering what a doll I am)!"; and "Conditions under which I live—my environment, social conditions, economic conditions, political conditions—must be arranged so that I easily and immediately, with no real effort, have a free lunch and get what I command." In summary, Ellis defines the three primary irrationalities as "I *must* do well; you *must* treat me beautifully; the world *must* be easy."

Psychological disturbances are based on irrational thinking and behaving. The origin of irrational beliefs and actions stems from childhood. Irrational beliefs are shaped in part by significant others (parents, relatives, and teachers), as well as from misperceptions on the part of children (such as superstitions and over-interpretation). Rational-emotive therapy also maintains that individuals have tendencies, which are both biologically and environmentally determined, for growth and actualization of one's potential. On the other hand, Ellis argues that people also have powerful innate tendencies to condemn themselves, others, and the world when they do not get what they "childishly need." This pattern of self-sabotage is argued by Ellis to be both inborn and acquired during childhood. Moreover, via repetitive self-talk and self-evaluative tendencies, false beliefs are continually re-indoctrinated by the individual. From the RET perspective, self-blame and self-condemnation are the cornerstones of most emotional disturbances. By challenging self-blame and self-condemnation, via an analysis and refutation of irrational beliefs, a client can be helped.

Ellis (1987) defines mental health as incorporating self-interest, social interests, self-direction, tolerance, acceptance of ambiguity and uncertainty, scientific thinking, commitment, risk taking, self-acceptance, long-range hedonism, non-perfectionism, and self-responsibility for one's emotional disturbances. Three primary processes seem to be associated with mental functioning and mental disorders: self-talking, self-evaluating, and self-condemning. That is, individuals are constantly engaged in an internal dialogue (self-talk) with themselves, appraising and commenting upon events that occur in their lives. Individuals also are self-evaluating in that humans seek meaning and constantly evaluate events and themselves, frequently placing blame on themselves for events. Self-evaluating is thus often associated with self-condemnation. For example, this condemnation may start in response to evaluating oneself as doing poorly at work or in school, which in turn leads to feeling guilty. This vicious cycle then leads to condemning oneself for condemning oneself, condemning oneself for not being able to stop condemning oneself, and finally condemning oneself for entering psychotherapy and not getting better (Ellis, 1989).

Emotional and behavioral difficulties often occur when simple preferences are chosen above thoughtful decisions. Ellis believes that individuals have inborn growth and actualization tendencies, although they may become sabotaged through self-defeating and self-condemning patterns. Based on the RET model, clients benefit from exposure to three primary insights. Insight number one is that a person's self-defeating behavior is related to antecedent and understandable causes. Specifically, an individual's beliefs are more important in understanding emotional upset than are past or present activating events. Insight two is that individuals actually make themselves emotionally disturbed by re-indoctrinating themselves with irrational and unproductive kinds of beliefs. Insight three is that through hard work and practice, irrational beliefs can be corrected.

Applications

As detailed by Gerald Corey in 1986, practitioners of rational-emotive therapy actively teach, persuade, and direct clients to alter irrational styles of thinking and behaving. RET can be defined as a process of re-education in which clients learn to think differently and solve problems. The first step in treatment often focuses on distinguishing rational (or reasonable) thoughts from irrational (or unreasonable) beliefs. Educational approaches are employed to highlight for the client that he or she has acquired many irrational "shoulds, oughts, and musts." The second step in treatment emphasizes an awareness of how psychological disturbances are maintained through a client's repeated re-indoctrination of illogical and unreasonable beliefs. During the third phase of treatment, therapists assist clients in modifying maladaptive thinking styles and abandoning irrational beliefs. Via a variety of cognitive, emotive, and behavioral approaches, self-condemnation and self-blame are replaced with more rational and logical views. Finally, the fourth step in RET involves developing a rational life-style and philosophy. Specifically, from internalizing rules of logic and scientific thinking, individuals may prevent future psychological disturbances and live more productive lives.

The A-B-C theory of personality and the A-B-C (D-E) theory of emotional change are also central to RET approaches. "A" refers to an activating event. Activating events can include facts, events, behaviors, or perceived stimuli. "B" refers to beliefs triggered by the event or beliefs about the event. "C" refers to the consequential emotional (behavioral or cognitive) outcomes that proceed directly from beliefs. "D" is the application of methods to dispute or challenge irrational beliefs, and "E" refers to the effect of disputing beliefs on the emotional (behavioral or cognitive) reaction of the client.

Activating events are generally regarded as inherently neutral, and they have no particular emotional meaning in and of themselves. Thus, activating events do not directly cause emotions. Instead, beliefs about events primarily cause emotional reactions. For example, a woman who had been depressed for more than twelve months following the death of her husband from terminal cancer was participating in a hospice therapy group and had demonstrated little or no improvement over the last year. She reasoned that because her husband was dead, she would never feel happy again (nor "should" she feel happy again, since he was dead and she was "not entitled" to experience pleasure without him). She added, "He was the center of my life and I can never expect to feel happiness without him." Her resulting emotional reaction was severe depression, which accompanied her complicated grief and underlying anger.

In an effort to uncover and dispute her unreasonable beliefs, a variety of strategies were employed. First, group members provided feedback about her reasonable and unreasonable ideas following (and during) her husband's death. In particular, group members pointed out that she could expect to experience happiness again in her life since she had experienced pleasure on many occasions before she met her husband, while her husband was away during military service, and while they were married and she enjoyed activities in which he did not share. Next, her emotional reaction was examined and viewed as being caused not by her husband's death, but instead by the manner in which she interpreted his death (as awful), her own ability to cope and change (as limited), and her future (as hopeless). A variety of behavioral and cognitive strategies were employed to challenge her irrational and self-condemning assumptions. Behavioral homework assignments included increasing activity levels and engaging in pleasurable activities to challenge the notion that she could never experience happiness again. Self-confidence and hope were fostered via strategies which highlighted her ability to cope with stress. This client also found cognitive homework assignments, wherein she listed her irrational beliefs on a daily log and then disputed those beliefs or replaced or modified them with more reasonable statements, to be helpful.

Rational-emotive therapy and its various techniques have been evaluated in at least two hundred studies. Although many of these studies have been associated with various methodological flaws, the effectiveness of RET with a broad range of psychological disturbances is impressive. At the Evolution of Psychotherapy Conference in Phoenix, Arizona, in 1985, Ellis himself identified several limitations of RET (and other therapies). These included several key "irrationalities." Because individuals falsely believe that they are unchangeable, they fail to work to change themselves. Because individuals falsely believe that activating events cause emotional reactions, they blame the activating events and fail to change their beliefs about them. Individuals falsely believe that unpleasant emotional reactions must be good or useful and should be cherished instead of minimized. Individuals are often confused about emotional reactions (for example, concern and caution versus anxiety and panic) and experience difficulty surrendering the inappropriate negative feelings. Because some RET techniques require subtle and discriminative styles of thinking by clients, some clients are not capable of succeeding in therapy. RET is not particularly useful for young children or developmentally delayed individuals (typically RET requires a chronological age of at least eight years and average intelligence).

Context

Albert Ellis is regarded by many psychologists as the most prominent theorist in the cognitive behavioral school of psychotherapy. His insights and conceptualizations are evident in many of the various cognitive behavioral psychotherapeutic approaches. Specifically, the A-B-C theory of personality is well regarded among cognitive behavioral therapists, and many of Ellis' treatment strategies are frequently used by clinicians across other schools of psychotherapy. On the other hand, Ellis' interpersonal style in treatment has been criticized by many authors. Specifically, a warm, confiding relationship between therapist and client is often de-emphasized in Ellis' writings, and confrontational interactions may be commonly observed in videotapes of rational-emotive therapy. It also appears, however, that more attention is being paid to the quality of the interpersonal relationship between RET practitioner and client. Moreover, the strengths of the RET approach are not based on the style of any particular therapist, but instead are evident in its underlying theory and therapeutic strategies.

Undoubtedly, the influence of rational-emotive therapy in the field of psychotherapy will continue to be prominent. Ellis has written extensively on the application of RET principles to diverse psychological disturbances. The Institute for Rational-Emotive Therapy in New York continues to train hundreds of therapists and serves as a distribution center for most of the books and pamphlets developed by RET therapists.

Bibliography

Corey, Gerald. *Theory and Practice of Counseling and Psychotherapy.* 3d ed. Pacific Grove, Calif.: Brooks/Cole, 1991. Corey reviews many of the primary schools of psychotherapy and specifically highlights the key concepts, therapeutic techniques, and research associated with RET. Also provides a brief critique of RET.

Ellis, Albert. "The Evolution of Rational-Emotive Therapy (RET) and Cognitive Behavior Therapy (CBT)." In *The Evolution of Psychotherapy*, edited by Jeffrey K. Zeig. New York: Brunner/Mazel, 1987. This edited book provides an interesting blend of dialogue, debate, and scholarly review of various schools of psychotherapy. Ellis presents thoughtful answers to questions concerning the future of RET, the primary treatment processes, and training procedures.

_____. "Rational-Emotive Therapy." In *Current Psychotherapies*, edited by Raymond J. Corsini and Danny Wedding. 4th ed. Itasca, Ill.: F. E. Peacock, 1989. Provides a review of the basic concepts, history, theory, and treatment approach of RET. Written by Ellis, this chapter provides much insight into his views of RET and presents a transcript of a treatment session that highlights many of the therapeutic processes involved in RET.

Ellis, Albert, and Russell Grieger. *Handbook of Rational-Emotive Therapy.* New York: Springer, 1977. Presents an overview of RET with emphasis on the conceptual foundations and fundamental treatment components. Also highlights procedures for conducting RET with children.

Ellis, Albert, and Robert A. Harper. *A New Guide to Rational Living.* Englewood Cliffs, N.J.: Prentice-Hall, 1975. A self-help book emphasizing RET approaches. A classic RET book in that therapists have suggested this book for their clients for many years. Presents a clear, straightforward approach to RET.

Gregory L. Wilson

Cross-References

REALITY THERAPY

Type of psychology: Psychotherapy
Field of study: Cognitive therapies

Reality therapy is a system of counseling or psychotherapy which attempts to help clients accept responsibility for their behavior. Its aim is to teach clients more appropriate patterns of behavior. Its significance is that it helps clients meet their basic needs more effectively.

Principal terms
> FREEDOM: basic to reality therapy; emphasizes that people are free to choose how they act
> MORALITY: standards of behaving; the "rightness" or "wrongness" of behavior
> RESPONSIBILITY: basic to reality therapy; stresses that people are responsible for their behavior
> SUCCESS IDENTITY: what reality therapy strives for; describes people who are able to give and receive love, feel worthwhile, and meet their needs appropriately
> VALUE JUDGMENTS: making decisions about one's behavior as to its merit or value

Overview

William Glasser, the founder of reality therapy, believes that people are motivated to fulfill five basic needs: belonging, power, freedom, fun, and survival. When these needs are not met, problems begin. Individuals lose touch with the objective reality of life (what is appropriate behavior and what is not) and often stray into patterns of behavior that are self-defeating or destructive. The reality therapist attempts to help such people by teaching them more appropriate patterns of behavior. This, in turn, will enable individuals to meet their basic needs more effectively.

Reality therapy differs from conventional theories of counseling or psychotherapy in six ways. Reality therapy rejects the concept of mental illness and the use of diagnostic labels; it works in the present, not the past; it rejects the concept of transference (the idea that clients relate to the therapist as an authority figure from their past). Reality therapy does not consider the unconscious to be the basis of present behavior. The morality of behavior is emphasized. Finally, reality therapy teaches individuals better ways to fulfill their needs and more appropriate (and more successful) ways to deal with the world.

In practice, reality therapy involves eight steps. First the therapist makes friends, or gains rapport and asks clients what they want. Then the client is asked to focus on his or her current behavior. The client is helped to make a realistic evaluation of his or her behavior. Therapist and client make a plan for the client to do better, which consists of finding more appropriate (realistic) ways of behaving. The therapist gets a commitment from the client to follow the plan that has been worked out. The therapist accepts no excuses from the client if the plan is not followed. No form of punishment is utilized, however, if the client fails to follow through. Finally, the therapist must never give up on the client.

Paramount to the success of reality therapy is the planning stage, consisting of discovering ways to change the destructive or self-defeating behavior of the client into behavior oriented toward success. Success-oriented behavior leads to a success identity: the feeling that one is able to give and receive love, feel worthwhile, and meet one's needs appropriately. Glasser states that putting the plan into writing, in the form of a contract, is one way to help ensure that the client will follow through. The client, not the therapist, is then held accountable for the success or failure of follow through. Commitment is, in many ways, the keystone of reality therapy. Resolutions and plans of action become meaningless unless there is a decision (and a commitment) to carry them out.

Like behavior therapists, reality therapists are basically active, directive, instructive, and oriented toward action. Reality therapists use a variety of techniques, including role-play, humor, question-and-answer sessions, and confrontation. They do not employ some commonly accepted therapeutic techniques, such as interpretation, insight, free association, analysis of transference and resistance, and dream analysis. In addition, reality therapists rarely recommend or promote the use of drugs or medications in treatment.

Confrontation is one technique of special consideration to reality therapy. Through confrontation, therapists force clients to evaluate their present behavior and to decide whether they will change it. Reality therapy maintains that the key to finding happiness and success is accepting responsibility. Thus the therapist neither accepts any excuses from the client for his or her self-defeating or destructive behavior nor ignores the reality of the situation (the consequences of the client's present behavior). The client is solely responsible for his or her behavior. Conventional psychotherapy often avoids the issue of responsibility; the client (or "patient") is thought to be "sick" and thus not responsible for his or her behavior.

Throughout reality therapy, the criterion of what is "right" plays an important role in determining the appropriateness of behavior; however, the therapist does not attempt to state the morality of behavior. This is the task and responsibility of the client. Clients are to make these value judgments based on the reality of their situation. Is their current behavior getting them what they want? Does their current behavior lead to success or to failure? The basic philosophy of reality therapy is that people are ultimately self-determining and in charge of their lives. People are, in other words, free to choose how they act and what they will become.

The strengths of reality therapy are that it is relatively short-term therapy (not lasting for years, as classical psychoanalysis does), consists of simple and clear concepts that can be used by all types of helpers, focuses on present behavioral problems, consists of a plan of action, seeks a commitment from the client to follow through, stresses personal responsibility, can be applied to a diverse population of clients (including people in prison, people addicted to drugs and alcohol, and juvenile offenders), and accepts no excuses, blame, or rationalizations.

The weaknesses of reality therapy are that it fails to recognize the significance of the unconscious or of intrapsychic conflict, minimizes the importance of one's past in present behavior, appears overly simplistic (problems are rarely simplistic in nature), may give the therapist an inappropriate feeling of power or control, minimizes the existence of biological or biochemical factors in mental illness, and fails to recognize the significance of psychiatric drugs in the treatment of mental illness.

Applications

Reality therapy can be applied to individuals with many sorts of psychological problems, from mild to severe emotional disorders. It has been used in a variety of counseling situations, including individual and group counseling, marriage and family counseling, rehabilitation counseling, and crisis intervention. The principles of reality therapy have been applied to teaching, social work, business management, and community development. Reality therapy is a popular method of treatment in mental hospitals, correctional institutions, substance abuse centers, and facilities for delinquent youth.

Reality therapists usually see their clients once weekly, for between forty-five minutes and one hour per visit. Therapists come from a variety of disciplines, including psychiatry, psychology, counseling, and social work. Important in applying reality therapy is that the therapist adopt no rigid rules. The therapist has a framework to follow, but within that framework he or she should be as free and creative as possible.

Reality therapy begins with the establishment of a working relationship. Once rapport is established, the process proceeds through an exploration of the client's needs and wants and then to an exploration of the client's present behavior.

Reality therapists stress current behavior. The past is used only as a means of enlightening the present. The focus is on what a client is doing now. Through skillful questioning, clients are encouraged to evaluate current behavior and to consider its present consequences. Is their current behavior getting them what they want or need? If not, why? As this process of questioning and reflecting continues, clients begin to acknowledge the negative and detrimental aspects of their current behavior. Slowly, they begin to accept responsibility for these actions.

Once responsibility is accepted, much of the remaining work consists of helping clients identify specific and appropriate ways to fulfill their needs and wants. This is often considered the teaching stage, since the therapist may model or teach the client more effective behavioral patterns.

Marriage therapy is often practiced by reality therapists; the number of sessions ranges from two to ten. Initially, it is important to clarify the couple's goals for marriage counseling: Are they seeking help in order to preserve the marriage, or have they already made the decision to end the relationship? In marriage counseling, Glasser recommends that the therapist be quite active, asking many questions while trying to understand the overall patterns of the marriage and of the interrelationship.

It is difficult to discuss the application of reality therapy to specific problems, since reality therapists do not look at people as objects to be classified according to diagnostic categories. Reality therapists, like others in the holistic health movement, believe that most ailments—whether physical or psychological—are manifestations of the way people choose to live their lives. William Glasser has stated:

> It makes little difference to a reality therapist what the presenting complaint of the client is; that complaint is a part of the way the client is choosing now to deal with the world. . . . When the client begins to realize that instead of being the victim of some disease or diagnostic category he is a victim of his own ineffective behavior, then therapy begins and diagnosis becomes irrelevant.

The following example shows how the eight steps of reality therapy can be applied to a real-life situation. The client's name is Jim; he is thirty-five years old. For years, Jim has been unable to hold a job. He is twice divorced and is subject to angry outbursts. He has been arrested three times for disorderly conduct. Recently Jim has lost his driver's license because of alcohol intoxication; he has been referred by the court for counseling.

In step one, the therapist makes friends and asks the client what he or she wants. Here the reality therapist, David, will make himself available to Jim as a caring, warm individual but not as someone whom Jim can control or dominate. David will ask, "What is it that you want?" Jim says, "Well, what I want is a job." Once the client states what he or she wants, the therapist can move to step two, asking the client to focus on his or her current behavior. Together David and Jim talk about Jim's behavior—his tendency for angry outbursts, his arrests, and his problems with alcohol.

The third step attempts to get clients to evaluate their present behavior and to see whether what they are now doing is getting them what they want. David asks Jim whether getting in fights is helping him find a job. As this step unfolds, Jim begins to understand that what he is doing is not helping him to become employable. Paramount at this step is that the clients see that their current behavior is within their control: They "choose" to act this way.

Once clients begin to see that what they are doing is not working (not getting them what they want), then the next step (step four) is to help them make a plan to do better. Once Jim realizes that getting in fights and drinking is ineffective and self-defeating, then David will begin to talk with him about a plan to change his behavior and find more appropriate ways of behaving. They plan a course of action. To "cement" this plan, a contract is made. The contract might state that Jim will not get in fights, Jim will control his anger, and Jim will stay out of bars and refrain from alcohol. David may also advise Jim on how to get a job: where to look for work, whom to contact, even what to wear and say during a job interview. Throughout this job search, which may be long and frustrating, David needs to be encouraging and supportive.

Step five involves getting a commitment from the client to follow through. David now asks Jim, "Are you going to live up to the contract? Are you going to change your behavior?" David needs to stress that commitment is the key to making this plan a success. David also must accept only a yes or no answer from Jim. Reality therapy does not accept excuses or reasons why plans are not carried through; this is step six. David's response to excuses should be that he is not interested in why Jim cannot do it; he is interested in when Jim will do it.

Step seven holds that David needs to be "tough" with Jim, but must not punish him if he does not follow through. Instead of finding ways to punish Jim, David may ask instead, "What is it that will get you to follow through?" Reality therapy recognizes that punishment is, in the long run, rarely effective. Step eight is simply never giving up. For most people, change does not come naturally, nor is it easy. A good therapist, like a good friend, does not give up easily. David needs to persevere with Jim. Through perseverance, Jim's life can change.

Context

The tenets of reality therapy were formed in the 1950's and 1960's as a reaction to the dominant psychotherapeutic approaches of the times, which were closely based on Freudian psychoanalysis. William Glasser, the founder of reality therapy, was trained as a physician and psychoanalyst, but during his psychiatric training in the early 1950's, he became more and more dissatisfied with the psychoanalytic approach. What disturbed him was the insistence of psychoanalysis on viewing the patient as a victim of forces beyond his or her control. In other words, the person was not considered responsible for his or her current behavior.

In 1956, Glasser became a consultant to a school for delinquent female adolescents in Ventura, California, developing a new therapeutic approach that was in sharp opposition to classical psychoanalysis. In 1962, he spoke at a meeting of the National Association of Youth Training Schools and presented his new ideas. The response was phenomenal; evidently many people were frustrated with the current mode of treatment.

Initially Glasser was hesitant to state his dissatisfaction with the conventional approach to treatment, psychoanalysis; however, his faculty supervisor, G. L. Harrington, was supportive. This started a long relationship in which Harrington helped Glasser formulate many of the ideas that became reality therapy.

In 1965, Glasser put his principles of counseling into a book entitled *Reality Therapy: A New Approach to Psychiatry*. Since then, he has written extensively, including *Schools Without Failure* (1968), *The Identity Society* (1972), *Positive Addiction* (1976), *Stations of the Mind: New Directions for Reality Therapy* (1981), *Control Theory: A New Exploration of How We Control Our Lives* (1985), and *The Quality School* (1990). The Institute for Reality Therapy, in Canoga Park, California, offers programs designed to teach the concepts and practice of reality therapy. A journal, the *Journal of Reality Therapy*, publishes articles concerning the research, theory, and application of reality therapy. Reality therapy has seen remarkable success since its conception, and many consider it one of the important approaches to counseling and psychotherapy.

Bibliography

Corey, Gerald. *Theory and Practice of Counseling and Psychotherapy.* 4th ed. Monterey, Calif.: Brooks/Cole, 1991. An excellent source of information on the major theories of counseling and psychotherapy. In one chapter, Corey states the essentials of reality therapy. Also gives a detailed evaluation of the strengths and weaknesses of reality therapy.

Glasser, Naomi, ed. *What Are You Doing? How People Are Helped Through Reality Therapy.* New York: Harper & Row, 1980. Presents twenty-five successful cases of reality therapy. Each case, described in detail, shows how reality therapy is put into practice. The cases range from a patient in a mental hospital to teenage delinquents to problems of aging. An excellent teaching aid in the training of counselors.

Glasser, William. *Control Theory: A New Exploration of How We Control Our Lives.* New York: Harper & Row, 1985. Control theory explains how individuals function. It states that behavior originates from within the individual and is need satisfying. A significant book, easy to read and understand.

_____. "Reality Therapy." In *Current Psychotherapies*, edited by Raymond Corsini. Itasca, Ill.: F. E. Peacock, 1984. In this chapter, Glasser describes in detail the beginnings of reality therapy, his theory of personality, the eight steps of reality therapy, and the processes and mechanisms of psychotherapy. A case example is included to show how the process of reality therapy works.

_____. *Reality Therapy: A New Approach to Psychiatry.* New York: Harper & Row, 1965. Describes Glasser's basic concepts of reality therapy. Glasser also shows how the reality therapist gets involved with the client and how he or she teaches clients more responsible ways to live their lives. This book was a significant contribution to psychotherapy in that it offered an alternative to psychoanalytic therapy.

_____. *Schools Without Failure.* New York: Harper & Row, 1968. Glasser applies the concepts of reality therapy to education, showing that many school practices have promoted a sense of failure in students. He proposes a new program to reduce school failure based on positive involvement, group work, no punishment (but discipline), a different grading system, and individual responsibility.

Ted Eilders

Cross-References

havioral Family Therapy, 394; Cognitive Behavior Therapy, 546; Cognitive Therapy, 586; Existential Analysis and Therapy, 999; Psychoanalysis: Classical versus Modern, 1898; Psychoanalytic Psychology: An Overview, 1905; Rational-Emotive Therapy, 2052.

REFLEXES

Type of psychology: Biological bases of behavior
Field of study: Nervous system

A reflex is one of the most basic types of behavior that can be elicited; over the years, psychologists and physiologists have studied the behavioral and biological processes associated with reflex production in the hope of understanding principles and processes involved in generating both simple behaviors and a variety of more complex behaviors such as learning, memory, and voluntary movement.

Principal terms

CLASSICAL (PAVLOVIAN) CONDITIONING: a simple conditioning procedure, used to study behavioral and biological processes involved in learning, that generally involves pairing two stimuli in time—a neutral stimulus followed by a stimulus that reliably elicits a reflexive response

INFANTILE REFLEXES: a set of innate reflexes that are present for the first few months of life; they disappear as the central nervous system matures

MONOSYNAPTIC REFLEX: a reflex system that consists of only one synapse, the synapse between the sensory input and motor output

POLYSYNAPTIC REFLEX: a reflex system that consists of more than one synapse; these systems typically contain three elements—a sensory element, a motor element, and a central processing element

REFLEX: a highly stereotyped, unlearned response that is elicited by an external stimulus

SPINAL REFLEX: a set of simple reflexes that can be elicited by providing appropriate input to the spinal cord; these reflexes can be generated in the spinal cord even after it has been surgically isolated from the rest of the nervous system

Overview

The reflex is undoubtedly the simplest form of behavior that has been studied widely by psychologists and neuroscientists. Reflexes involve two separate yet highly related events: the occurrence of an eliciting stimulus and the production of a specific response. Most organisms are capable of displaying a variety of complex behaviors; however, because these behaviors are complex, it has been very difficult, if not impossible, to understand biological or psychological processes involved in generating or modifying the variety of complex behaviors that most organisms can display. In attempts to study these complex behaviors, a number of researchers have adopted a strategy of studying simpler behaviors, such as reflexes, that are thought to make up, contribute to, or serve as a model of the more complex behavior.

A number of reflexes can be generated in the mammalian spinal cord even after it has been surgically isolated from the brain. The stretch reflex is an example of a spinal reflex. When a muscle is stretched, such as when a tendon is tapped or when an attempt is made to reach for an object, sensory "detectors" or receptors within the muscle are activated to signal the muscle stretch. These receptors are at the end of very long nerve fibers that travel from the muscle receptor to the spinal cord, where they activate spinal motor neurons. The motor neurons control the same muscle on which the stretch receptor that initiated the stretch signal is located. When activated, the spinal motor neurons signal the muscle, causing it to contract. In this manner, when a muscle stretch is detected, the stretch reflex ensures that a contraction is generated in the muscle to counteract and balance the stretch. This type of reflex is referred to as a "monosynaptic reflex" because it involves only one synapse; the synapse between the sensory receptor neuron and the motor neuron (where a synapse is the junction between two neurons).

Another example of a spinal reflex is the flexion or withdrawal reflex. Anyone who has accidentally touched a hot stove has encountered this reflex. Touching a hot stove or applying any aversive stimulus to the skin activates pain receptors in the skin. These receptors are at the end of long sensory fibers that project to neurons in the spinal cord. The spinal neurons that receive input from the sensory fibers are not motor neurons, as in the stretch reflex, but rather very small neurons called spinal interneurons. The interneurons make synaptic contact on other interneurons as well as on motor neurons that innervate flexor muscles. When activated, the flexor muscles typically cause limb withdrawal. The flexor reflex ensures that a relatively rapid withdrawal of one's hand from a hot stove will occur if it is accidentally touched. The flexor reflex is an example of a "polysynaptic reflex" because there are two or more synapses involved in the reflex (the presence of at least one synapse between a sensory neuron and an interneuron and a second synapse between the interneuron and a motor neuron).

One functional difference between monosynaptic and polysynaptic reflexes is the amount of information processing that can take place in the two reflex systems. The monosynaptic reflex is somewhat limited, because information flow involves only the synapse between the sensory and motor neurons. This type of reflex is ideal for quick adjustments that must be made in muscle tension. Conversely, polysynaptic reflexes typically involve a number of levels of interneurons. Hence, convergence and divergence of information can occur as information flows from sensory to motor elements. In essence, the polysynaptic system, in addition to having afferent and efferent components, has a "processor" of sorts between the sensory and motor elements. In intact organisms, the integration that takes place within the processor allows information to be shared by other regions of the nervous system. For example, some of the interneurons send information upward to the brain. When a hot stove is touched, the brain is informed. This sensory experience is likely to be evaluated and stored by the brain, therefore making it less likely that the hot stove will be touched a second time.

Reflexes are not limited to the spinal cord. Responses involving the musculature of the face and neck can also be reflexive in nature. For example, a puff of air that strikes the cornea of the human eye elicits a brisk, short-latency eyelid closure. Like the polysynaptic spinal reflexes, this eyeblink reflex appears to involve three elements: a sensory nerve, called the trigeminal nerve, that carries information from receptors in the cornea of the eye to the trigeminal nucleus (a cranial nerve nucleus); interneurons that connect the trigeminal nucleus with several other brain-stem neurons; and a motor nerve that originates from brain-stem motor neurons and contacts the muscles surrounding the eye to produce the eyeblink. This reflex is defensive in nature because it ensures that the eyeball is protected from further stimulation if a stimulus strikes the cornea. Not all reflexes involve activation of skeletal muscles. For example, control of the urinary bladder involves a spinal reflex that activates smooth muscles. Also, temperature regulation is partially the product of a reflexive response to changes in external or internal environments. Many of these types of reflexes engage the autonomic nervous system, a division of the nervous system that is involved in regulating and maintaining the function of internal organs.

Not all reflexes involve simple, local, short-latency responses. The maintenance of posture when standing upright is a generally automatic, reflexive system that one does not think about. This system includes neurons in the spinal cord and brain stem. The body's equilibrium system (the vestibular or balance system) involves receptors in the middle ear, brain-stem structures, and spinal motor neurons, while locomotion requires the patterned activation of several reflex systems. Finally, a number of behavioral situations require a rapid response that integrates the motor system with one of the special senses (such as quickly applying the car brakes when a road hazard is seen). These are generally referred to as reaction-time situations and require considerable nervous system processing, including the involvement of the cerebral cortex, when engaged. Nevertheless, these responses are considered reflexive in nature because they involve an eliciting stimulus and a well-defined, consistent response.

Applications

During the late nineteenth century and early twentieth century, Sir Charles Sherrington, a British physiologist, conducted an extensive series of studies concerned with spinal reflexes. He showed that a number of skin stimulations, such as pinching or brushing, produced simple responses even when a spinal transection separated the spinal cord from the rest of the nervous system. From these experiments, he argued that the basic unit of movement was the reflex, which he defined as a highly stereotyped, unlearned response to external stimuli. This work created a flurry of activity among physiologists and psychologists, who tried to trace reflexes throughout the nervous system and assemble them into more complex behaviors.

Reflexes have also been widely studied by psychologists and biologists interested in learning and memory. Russian physiologists Ivan Sechenov and Ivan Pavlov have generally been credited with the first attempts to study systematically how reflexes could be used to examine relationships between behavior and physiology. Pavlov in particular had a huge influence on the study of behavior. Most students are familiar with the story of Pavlov and his successful demonstration of conditioned salivation in dogs produced by pairing a bell with meat powder. Over the years, the Pavlovian conditioning procedure (also known as classical conditioning) has often been used to study the behavioral principles and neural substrates of learning. The conditioning of a variety of reflexes has been observed, including skeletal muscle responses such as forelimb flexion, hindlimb flexion, and eyelid closure, as well as autonomic responses such as respiration, heart rate, and sweat gland activity.

One of the the most widely studied classical conditioning procedures is classical eyelid conditioning. This reflex conditioning procedure has been studied in a variety of species, including rabbits, rats, cats, dogs, and humans. Mostly because of the research efforts of Isadore Gormezano and her colleagues, which began in the early 1960's, much is known about behavioral aspects of classical eyelid conditioning in rabbits. In this paradigm, a mild electric shock or air puff is presented to elicit reliably a reflexive blink from the rabbit. The blink is typically measured by means of devices that are attached to the nictitating membrane, a third eyelid that is present in a variety of species, including the rabbit. During training sessions, a neutral stimulus such as a tone or light is delivered 0.3 to 1.0 second prior to the air puff. After about one hundred of these tone and air-puff pairings, the rabbit learns to blink when the tone or light is presented (the rabbit begins to use the tone to signal the impending air-puff presentation). This preparation has yielded a wealth of data concerning the parameters of behavioral training that produce the fastest or slowest learning rates (such as stimuli intensities, time between stimuli, and number of trials per day). Furthermore, this simple reflexive learning situation has been used to study how the brain codes simple forms of learning and memory. A number of researchers (most notably, Richard F. Thompson) have studied the activity of a variety of brain structures during learning and performance of the classically conditioned eyelid response. These studies have shown that discrete brain regions such as the cerebellum and hippocampus alter their activity to generate or modify the conditioned response. In brief, these researchers have used the conditioning of a very simple reflex to advance the understanding of how the brain might code more complex learning and memory processes.

The study of reflexes has not been limited to learning and memory. Developmental psychologists have studied a variety of innate reflexes that are generated by newborn infants. Sucking is a very prominent reflex that is readily observed in newborns. Also related to feeding is the "rooting reflex," which can be elicited when the cheek of an infant is stroked softly. The skin stimulation causes the infant to open his or her mouth and turn toward the point of stimulation. This reflex has obvious applications in helping the infant locate food. The infant's ability to hold on to objects is, in part, attributable to the presence of the "grasp reflex." When an object touches the palm of a newborn's hand, the newborn's fist will close immediately around the object, thus allowing the infant to hold the object for a short period of time. The infantile reflexes disappear within a few months after birth and are replaced by voluntary responses. Most developmental researchers believe that the infantile reflexes are temporary substitutes for the voluntary responses. Apparently, the voluntary responses are not present during the first few months of life because various parts of the infant nervous system, including the cerebral cortex, have not matured sufficiently to support the behavior. Therefore, the disappearance of the infantile reflexes serves as an important marker of neural and behavioral development.

Context

The study of reflexes has played a prominent role in shaping the field of psychology. Early in the twentieth century, many psychologists and physiologists, among them Sherrington and Pavlov, adopted the reflex as the basic unit of behavior to study, in part because of the relative simplicity of the behavior and in part because of the ease with which the behavior could be reliably elicited by applying external stimuli. Based on his research, Sherrington believed that complex behaviors were produced by chaining together simple reflexes in some temporal order. This basic idea provided the framework for much of the physiological and behavioral work completed early in the twentieth century. Sechenov and Pavlov also believed that the concept of the reflex could explain more complex behaviors. Pavlov, for example, showed that not all reflexes were innate; rather, new reflexes could be established by associating a "neutral" stimulus (a stimulus that did not initially produce a reflex) with a stimulus that reliably elicited a reflex. As a result of this demonstration, Pavlov proposed an elaborate theory of reflex learning that involved forming associations between stimuli in the cerebral cortex.

In the latter half of the twentieth century, many psychologists interested in studying overt behavior and physiologists interested in studying nervous-system function adopted the study of reflexes as a means of simplifying behavior or nervous system activity. Psychologists such as Gormezano, Robert Rescorla, and Allan Wagner, who have studied classical conditioning phenomena, hope to develop a comprehensive understanding of the learning process that occurs when simple paradigms such as classical conditioning are used. Behavioral neuroscientists and neurobiologists (such as Thompson and Eric Kandel) who study nervous-system function have used reflexes as the basic unit of behavior in hope of catching a glimpse of nervous-system function when a fairly simple behavioral response is being generated and modified by learning experiences. In both cases, a major reason for using the reflex as the unit of behavior is to simplify the experimental situation. Indeed, researchers are not likely to understand complex behavioral processes without first understanding how simpler behaviors and nervous-system functions are generated, modified, and maintained. The study of reflexes, from both a behavioral and biological standpoint, has provided and should continue to provide a valuable approach for understanding human behavior as well as understanding how the nervous system generates activity to produce the behavior.

Bibliography

Domjan, Michael, and Barbara Burkhard. *The Principles of Learning and Behavior.* 2d ed. Monterey, Calif.: Brooks/Cole, 1986. This text is widely used by students interested in learning and behavior. The sections on the history of the reflex and its use in the learning research field is particularly applicable to the present discussion.

Fancher, Raymond E. *Pioneers of Psychology.* New York: W. W. Norton, 1979. This book provides biographies of several prominent psychologists who have had an impact on the field. Included is a chapter detailing the experiments and theories of Ivan Pavlov. Valuable for understanding how the study of the reflex fits into the history of psychology.

Gleitman, Henry. *Psychology.* 2d ed. New York: W. W. Norton, 1981. This text provides broad coverage of the field of psychology. The chapters on development, learning, and memory should provide the reader with additional information concerning reflexes and other simple behaviors.

Rosenzweig, Mark R., and Arnold L. Leiman. *Physiological Psychology.* 2d ed. New York: Random House, 1989. This textbook is filled with information concerning a variety of topics within the field of physiological psychology. The sections on motor systems are particularly useful in understanding how reflexes are generated and executed at the neural and muscular level.

Thompson, Richard F. *The Brain: An Introduction to Neuroscience.* New York: W. H. Freeman, 1985. Thompson's book was written to be accessible to individuals who have no background in science. Includes information about spinal reflexes and the neural substrates of learning and memory.

Joseph E. Steinmetz

Cross-References

The Central and Peripheral Nervous Systems, 494; Hindbrain Structures, 1175; Neurons, 1661; Pavlovian Conditioning: Acquisition, Extinction, and Inhibition, 1757; Pavlovian Conditioning: Theoretical Foundations, 1764; Reflexes in Newborns, 2072.

REFLEXES IN NEWBORNS

Type of psychology: Developmental psychology
Field of study: Infancy and childhood

Healthy neonates are born with a repertoire of skills that help them to adapt to their new environment immediately after birth. By exploring the nature and bases of these early abilities, researchers have gained a better understanding of processes that govern development during the earliest periods of the human life cycle.

Principal terms

CORTICAL BRAIN CENTERS: the portions of the brain making up the cerebral cortex and controlling voluntary behavior, higher reasoning, and language skills; the cortical brain centers develop rapidly over the first two years of life

HOMEOSTASIS: the tendency to maintain internal stability by responding in a coordinated fashion to any changes in the external world

PRIMITIVE REFLEX: a reflex controlled by subcortical areas of the brain that gradually disappears over the first year of life

REFLEX: an unlearned and automatic biologically programmed response to a particular stimulus

SUBCORTICAL BRAIN CENTERS: the lower portions of the brain, comprising the brain stem, hindbrain, and midbrain, and controlling the reflex action of simple and uncoordinated behaviors

SUDDEN INFANT DEATH SYNDROME (SIDS): the unexplained death of an infant who suddenly stops breathing during sleep

SURVIVAL REFLEX: inborn responses such as breathing, sucking, and swallowing that enable the newborn to adapt to the extrauterine environment

Overview

For many years, it was thought that newborns were completely helpless, fragile and hardly ready for survival in the relatively unprotected world into which they were born. Extensive research has now shown that the healthy neonate is born with a set of prepared reactions to the environment which aids its survival. These prepared reactions are referred to as reflexes. Reflexes make survival possible by taking charge of new surroundings. The newborn's surroundings were previously controlled and protected by the mother's biological system. Reflexes are inborn responses that help a newborn adapt to his or her new surroundings outside the womb from the moment of birth.

Immediate adjustment to a new environment is essential for the newborn. The extrauterine environment is very different from the environment from which the fetus emerged at birth. The newborn is faced with a variety of changes to which immediate adaption is necessary. Breathing must now be self-sufficient, requiring that the newborn's own lungs be used for the first time. Food must be actively approached, consumed, and digested. During the prenatal period, the fetus received nutrients passively from the mother, and waste was discharged into the mother's bloodstream. For the first time, digestion and waste elimination must now be regulated by the newborn's own lungs, skin, kidneys, and gastrointestinal tract.

Finally, the newborn is much less protected in the extrauterine environment than he or she was when developing within the uterus. The developing fetus experienced a world of constancy because of the insulating effects of life in amniotic fluid. At birth, however, the infant will immediately experience perhaps its first fluctuation in temperature, light, and sound. The neonate will therefore need to be prepared to maintain a relatively constant body temperature and a degree of internal homeostasis immediately after birth. Reflexes assume many of these functions automatically. From the moment of birth, reflexes are elicited by stimuli in the extrauterine environment. Reflex action is controlled largely by subcortical brain centers in the central nervous system.

The human central nervous system (CNS) is organized hierarchically. Simple, uncoordinated actions are controlled by "lower," or subcortical, brain centers; progressively higher-order, coordinated activities are controlled by "higher," or cortical, brain centers. Reflexes are among the simplest patterns of action exhibited by humans and are controlled by lower brain centers. The lower brain centers are the most highly developed at birth, and they control the majority of human behavior until they are supplanted by higher cortical brain centers. As humans mature and their central nervous systems become more developed, the higher brain centers (cortical brain centers) assume control of the previously reflexive behaviors. That is, as humans develop voluntary control over their behavior, reflexes previously elicited automatically by stimulation no longer respond. This occurs rapidly over the first year of life and is evidenced by the disappearance of many reflexive behaviors.

Applications

The most fundamental reflexes exhibited in the newborn involve reactions to unpleasant or life-threatening stimuli. These reflexes protect the infant from further aversion or possible life-threatening situations. For example, several reflexes allow the newborn to maintain a clear airway for normal breathing. This is important because regular breathing rhythms are not firmly established in the newborn; normal, healthy newborns occasionally neglect to breathe for brief periods of time. When this occurs, carbon dioxide builds up in their bloodstream and the breathing reflex is triggered. This causes the neonates reflexively to start breathing again. Should neonates experience a clogged airway because of mucus or some other obstruction, a reflexive sneeze or cough may serve to remove the obstruction.

Similarly, neonates respond reflexively to the presence of food. At birth, a light stroking of the cheek of an infant will result in a rooting reflex. The rooting reflex is characterized as a head turn. This turn positions the baby for nutrient seeking. The sucking and swallowing reflexes enable neonates to consume nutrients, a process that is aided significantly by the activation of other parts of the human digestive tract.

Neonates respond reflexively to changes in temperature and touch. For example, heat causes a neonate's blood vessels to expand so that more heat can be dispersed through the skin. Conversely, cold causes a neonate's blood vessels to contract so that heat can be conserved inside the body. Neonates respond to painful physical stimulation such as a pin prick on the foot by reflexively withdrawing the limb. Similarly, neonates respond to loud noises or bright lights by turning away from the source of the aversive stimulus.

Perhaps one of the most general reflexes is the crying reflex. Crying is an important reflex which alerts care givers that all is not well. Crying is especially important for maintaining homeostasis. Infants cry when they are overstimulated, understimulated, hungry, too cold or hot, in pain, or otherwise uncomfortable. Crying serves to communicate to care givers as well as to release energy, ward off danger, or possibly clear an air passage.

With the exception of the rooting reflex, which is replaced by more voluntarily controlled food-seeking behaviors, the reflexes discussed above remain with humans for their entire lives and are generally referred to as survival reflexes because they play a crucial role in survival across the entire life span.

Newborns also exhibit a variety of reflexive actions that have no clear survival value. These nonadaptive reflexes are referred to as primitive reflexes. Primitive reflexes disappear early in the first year of life. Several of these primitive reflexes are interesting precursors of abilities that will be exhibited later in life. For example, neonates exhibit an early stepping reflex which closely resembles mature walking. This quickly disappears at about eight weeks of life and will reemerge at about twelve to fifteen months as infants take their first true steps. Similarly, newborns will reflexively swim if placed in a prone position on a water surface. Newborns also grasp when the palm is touched. Early versions of both swimming and grasping will disappear in the first three months, and, in the case of grasping, will give way first to slapping movements and then to progressive dexterity of gripping with palm and fingers at about six months.

Evolutionary accounts of the existence of primitive reflexes in humans suggest that they are remnants of survival reflexes present in humans' evolutionary ancestors. For example, the moro reflex is a startle reflex in which an infant, when placed in a supine position on his or her back, raises his or her arms and pulls them toward the center of the chest. The moro reflex serves as a very adaptive clinging response among primates (for example, chimpanzees) that require their infants to hold on to their mother as they travel. Again, this reflex is triggered by perceived loss of balance (falling, contact) with the care giver. For humans, however, it is a primitive reflex with no apparent value. It disappears gradually during the first six months of life.

While having no apparent survival value, the pattern of appearance and disappearance of primitive reflexes is taken as an indication of normal neurological development. The pattern of reflex disappearance follows closely the maturity of the central nervous system. It is suggested that primitive reflexes are controlled primarily by lower subcortical brain centers which are gradually giving way to rapidly developing higher brain centers.

Reflex integrity is an important component of several newborn screening instruments. The Brazelton Neonatal Behavior Assessment Scale (NBAS) explores a newborn's responsiveness to several environmental stimuli as a function of the neurological functioning. The Brazelton scale assesses the strength of twenty reflexes as well as a newborn's ability to respond to twenty-six situations such as orienting to and from a tester's voice. If an infant is extremely unresponsive, a low Brazelton score may indicate the existence of brain damage or other neurological dysfunction.

Lewis Lipsitt, a researcher studying newborn reflexes, has found an important relationship between the integrity of a child's nervous system and the development of reflexes. Lipsitt has conducted research on sudden infant death syndrome (SIDS), a complication in which apparently healthy infants suddenly stop breathing and die in their sleep. The cause of this disorder is unknown. It is most common in infants from two to four months of age. Each year, approximately eight thousand infants in the United States die of this disorder. Lipsitt has posited that infants have a specific learning disability that keeps them from assuming voluntary control of previously involuntary survival reflexes; perhaps some damage to cortical brain centers prevents them from successfully learning the survival reflexes needed. For example, if a four-month-old infant's nasal passage is blocked, the infant may not struggle to clear the breathing passage because his or her survival reflexes have not been sufficiently controlled by cortical brain centers.

Context

The focus on reflexes in newborns has been more generally stimulated by interest in understanding the rapid development of humans during the period of infancy. Infancy is now understood as the period of most rapid development in a human's entire life span. During the first two years of life, an infant's brain will reach 75 percent of its eventual weight. Physical growth will accompany brain growth to enable an infant to display an array of complex motor and cognitive skills that emerge in rapid succession. Developmental psychologists have made considerable progress in understanding this period of development. This progress has been aided by advances in technology and research methods, primarily in the area of brain physiology and function.

Researchers now understand, in contrast to earlier thinking, that humans are born with a variety of skills which aid their survival during this particularly vulnerable developmental period. Previously, researchers, physicians, and parents had assumed that infants were fragile and helpless. Infants are indeed more prepared for life on earth than was reflected in previous attitudes. Today, it is known that all major sense organs are functioning at birth and that newborns are capable of learning and experiencing their world actively very shortly after birth.

Early psychologist William James described infants as born into a blooming, buzzing confusion. This is clearly far from the truth. Reflexes play an important role in the realization of many early developing abilities. Researchers have used them as a window on the developing nervous system, and have understood significant variation in neurological development from the pattern of reflexes. Infants interact with the world reflexively until they have matured enough to engage in more active exploration of their world.

Bibliography

Bower, T. G. R. *Development in Infancy.* 2d ed. New York: W. H. Freeman, 1982. An overview of the developmental milestones during infancy. An excellent introduction to topics in infancy.

Harris, Judith Rich, and Robert M. Liebert. *The Child.* 3d ed. Englewood Cliffs, N.J.: Prentice-Hall, 1991. An excellent review of characteristics of the newborn. Provides a much more thorough view of the baby than other texts in the introductory developmental genre.

Lipsitt, Lewis. "Critical Conditions in Infancy: A Psychological Perspective." *American Psychologist* 34, no. 10 (1979): 973-980. Discusses SIDS in America. Lipsitt describes his model of sudden infant death syndrome.

Maurer, Daphne, and Charles Maurer. *The World of the Newborn.* New York: Basic Books, 1988. A good overview of the entire period of infancy. Describes in very readable detail the emerging competencies of infants as they mature.

Sameroff, Arnold J., ed. *Organization and Stability of Newborn Behavior: A Commentary on the Brazelton Neonatal Behavior Assessment Scale.* Chicago: University of Chicago Press, 1978. This is vol. 43, no. 177 in the series Monographs for Society for Research in Child Development. Provides a critical overview of the assessment of newborn reflexes by the Brazelton neonatal scale and points to research stimulated by the assessment instrument. An excellent overview of the understanding of newborn behavior, neurological functioning, and capacity for interaction.

Shaffer, David Reed. *Developmental Psychology: Childhood and Adolescence.* 2d ed. Pacific Grove, Calif.: Brooks/Cole, 1989. A well-written textbook on developmental psychology. The section on infant physical development provides a good source of extra reading about reflexes.

Richard J. Ricard

Cross-References

Birth: Effects on Physical Development, 429; Infant Perceptual Systems, 1290; Motor Development, 1623; Physical Development: Environmental versus Genetic Determinants, 1823; Prenatal Physical Development, 1861; Sudden Infant Death Syndrome, 2495.

REINFORCEMENT SCHEDULES

Type of psychology: Learning
Fields of study: Behavioral and cognitive models; instrumental conditioning

A schedule of reinforcement is a rule defining the conditions of reinforcer delivery in relation to behavior. Reinforcement schedules influence the development of adaptive and maladaptive behaviors and have profound effects on behavioral persistence and choice behavior.

Principal terms
CONTINUOUS SCHEDULE: a schedule in which each response is followed by a reinforcer
EXTINCTION: a procedure used to eliminate a previously reinforced response by withholding the reinforcer following the response
INTERMITTENT SCHEDULE: a schedule in which some, but not all, responses are followed by a reinforcer
INTERVAL SCHEDULE: a schedule in which reinforcer delivery is contingent upon performance of a response after a specified amount of time has elapsed
PARTIAL REINFORCEMENT EFFECT: behavior trained on an intermittent schedule of reinforcement is more resistant to extinction than behavior trained on a continuous schedule
RATIO SCHEDULE: a schedule in which reinforcer delivery is contingent upon the performance of a specified number of responses
REINFORCEMENT SCHEDULE: a rule specifying the pattern of reinforcer delivery following the performance of a specific response
REINFORCER: a stimulus that strengthens the behavior it follows

Overview

Reinforcement is necessary for the acquisition and maintenance of voluntary behavior. A reinforcer is a stimulus that strengthens the behavior it follows, and the pattern of reinforcer delivery is called the schedule of reinforcement. Reinforcement schedules powerfully influence the rate of response and the pattern with which it occurs.

A continuous schedule is in effect when reinforcers follow every performance of a response; for example, a child is praised every time he brushes his teeth, a salesperson makes a sale every time she calls on a customer, a dolphin receives a fish every time it dives through a hoop. Continuous schedules are very effective when shaping new behavior, and they lead to rapid learning. An extinction schedule, in which responses are never reinforced, results in elimination of the response. If the dolphin no longer receives fish for diving though the hoop, the diving ceases.

Few behaviors are continuously reinforced in real life. People are not rewarded every time they work efficiently or do a kind deed. When a response is reinforced after some, but not all, occurrences, an intermittent reinforcement schedule is in effect. There are two basic types of intermittent schedules: ratio schedules, in which the number of responses is critical; and interval schedules, in which the passage of time determines reinforcement. Each type of schedule can be either fixed or variable.

A fixed-ratio (FR) schedule requires a fixed number of responses per reinforcer delivery. A student who is given a gold star each time she solves two math problems is on an FR-2 schedule. If five problems are required, the schedule would be called FR-5. Factory workers who are paid after finishing a fixed number of pieces or salespeople who are given a bonus after making a fixed number of sales are on fixed-ratio reinforcement.

Fixed-ratio schedules produce high, steady response rates with pauses after reinforcer delivery. The higher the response requirement, the longer the post-reinforcement pause. A factory worker on FR-100 will take longer breaks after reinforcement than a worker on FR-75.

On a variable-ratio (VR) schedule, the number of responses required per reinforcer varies around some average value. A student who is required to complete five math problems for a gold star, then two, then six, then four, then eight, is on a VR-5 schedule. On average, she must complete five problems before receiving a star, but the specific requirement per star varies. Activities such as fishing, selling, and playing a slot machine are reinforced on VR, since the number of casts, sales pitches, or bets needed to produce a reward varies. Compared to fixed-ratio schedules, VR schedules produce faster responses with little or no post-reinforcement pause.

The time taken to complete the responses on ratio schedules is irrelevant. Timing, however, is critical on interval schedules. Fixed-interval (FI) schedules require a fixed amount of time to elapse before a response is reinforced. If a student is rewarded on an "FI-3 minute schedule" for solving math problems, the first problem solved after three minutes has elapsed will produce a star. After reinforcer delivery, another three minutes must elapse before reinforcement is again available.

Like fixed-ratio schedules, FI schedules produce a pause after reinforcement. Longer intervals produce longer pauses. Once responding begins, the response rate increases, at first gradually, then more quickly, as the interval nears its end. The student on FI-3 may not solve any problems for two minutes after being reinforced. She then begins solving, slowly at first, but with increasing rapidity as the time for reinforcement approaches.

On a variable-interval (VI) schedule, the first response after a variable amount of time elapses is reinforced, with the length of the interval varying around some average value. A student solving math problems on a VI-3 minute schedule may get her first star after five minutes, her second after two minutes, her third after three minutes, her fourth after one minute, and her fifth after four minutes. Similarly, a person who refills his birdfeeder at irregular intervals has placed the birds on a VI schedule, and birds will check the empty feeder frequently and steadily to see if it has been refilled. This is a key characteristic of such schedules. Since one never knows how long it will be between reinforcers, one's responding is maintained at a uniform rate.

These simple reinforcement schedules can be combined to produce complex schedules, such as multiple and concurrent schedules. In a multiple schedule, behavior is controlled by two or more simple schedules, each associated with a distinct stimulus. For example, a history teacher who gives a quiz every Friday is reinforcing studying on a FI-7 day schedule, while an English teacher who gives a pop quiz on average once a week is using a VI-7 day schedule. The behavior of a student who is taking both courses will come under control of the multiple FI-VI schedule. Studying for English is likely to be evenly distributed across the week, while studying for history will increase in frequency and intensity as Friday approaches.

Concurrent schedules offer a choice between two or more simple schedules that are available at the same time. Gambling casinos offer several games of chance, each with a different probability of winning. Similarly, at home, a person can choose among watching television, making dinner, reading a book, or cleaning the garage. The choice will be influenced by the frequency, magnitude, and delay of reinforcement scheduled for each activity.

Applications

Knowledge of schedule effects has provided valuable insights into understanding individual differences in behavioral persistence. One child works quickly and steadily, solving dozens of problems, while another gives up after solving one or two. One person gambles away his or her life savings, while another quits after placing a few losing bets. People often attribute these differences to internal personality traits, using terms such as "strong willed" or "weak willed," but behavior analysts argue that these differences are shaped by reinforcement schedules.

The key to behavioral persistence is to increase the schedule requirement gradually. Once a response is trained using continuous reinforcement, the schedule can be changed to an intermittent basis. If a ratio schedule is in effect, an FR-1 schedule can be shifted to FR-2 or FR-3 with little disruption in behavior. Increasing the ratio in small steps, a procedure known as stretching the ratio, produces more and more responding for fewer and fewer reinforcers. Stretching the ratio too rapidly will produce ratio strain, and the individual will stop responding. For example, if a student is reinforced for reading pages in a history book, a change from VR-5 to VR-500 will undoubtedly disrupt the behavior.

This same procedure can be used with interval schedules. In this case, the time interval between reinforcers is gradually increased. Appropriately instituted, the stretching procedure can produce extremely high rates of behavior. Pigeons have been trained to peck disks and rats have been trained to press levers thousands of times for a single, small food reward. Gamblers will feed hundreds of coins into a slot machine, and viewers will watch television for hours for an occasional small monetary or entertainment payoff.

Reinforcement history also influences the rate at which behaviors extinguish when reinforcement is withheld. The partial reinforcement effect refers to the finding that a behavior maintained by continuous reinforcement will extinguish faster than a behavior maintained by intermittent reinforcement. If a vending machine no longer dispenses candy, a person who has received candy every time coins were placed in the machine will stop using the machine after one or two times. A person who has received candy following some, but not all, coin placements will continue using the broken machine longer. Similarly, it is easier to eliminate tantrum behavior in a child whose parents have given him attention after every tantrum than it is in a child whose parents have occasionally, but not always, reinforced tantrums. The continuously reinforced individual can easily detect the change in reinforcement conditions. For the individual who is accustomed to an intermittent schedule, especially one with a high ratio or interval requirement, it will be more difficult to detect the change to extinction. As a result, the behavior of the latter individual is more resistant to extinction.

A sudden change from one reinforcement schedule to another creates behavioral contrast effects. Switching individuals from a schedule that provides a low, or thin, rate of reinforcement to one that provides a high, or rich, rate of reinforcement produces a higher response rate than that shown by individuals who have always been reinforced on the rich schedule. Employees who receive a significant salary increase outperform workers who have been doing the same work for the higher salary. Conversely, a shift from a rich to a thin reinforcement schedule depresses performance below that of individuals who have always worked on the thin schedule. Requiring employees to take a cut in salary without a corresponding adjustment in work load reduces their productivity to a level that is lower than that of employees who have been working for the lower salary all along. Additionally, a change to less favorable reinforcement conditions may create emotional reactions such as anger, aggression, anxiety, and depression. It is noteworthy that during economic recessions there are significant increases in the incidence of physical illnesses, emotional disorders, and domestic violence.

Extensive use of reinforcement schedules is made in educational and therapeutic settings. In addition to using basic ratio and interval schedules to strengthen desirable behaviors, differential schedules are used to modify maladaptive behaviors. The differential reinforcement of low rates of responding (DRL) schedule is useful when a problem behavior occurs at a high rate, such as frequent disruptive behaviors or eating or speaking too rapidly. A DRL schedule provides reinforcer delivery if fewer than a specified number of responses have occurred during a time interval. For a student who asks the teacher for help twenty times per hour on average, a DRL schedule initially might provide a reinforcer if fifteen or fewer help requests are received per hour. The allowable number of responses can be reduced gradually to the final desired level.

The differential reinforcement of other behavior (DRO) schedule is used to extinguish a maladaptive behavior while simultaneously shaping desirable competing activities. The DRO schedule delivers reinforcement if a particular response does not occur during a time interval. Performance of any other response during the interval produces a reinforcer. For an individual who is trying to eliminate snacking during coffee breaks at work, a DRO schedule would deliver a reinforcer contingent upon the performance of alternative behaviors during breaks such as reading or taking a short walk. Many weight-control, smoking, and drug programs incorporate DRO procedures by socially reinforcing clients when they refrain from the problem behavior and show instead an appropriate alternative.

Context

The experimental study of the way in which reinforcement influences the learning of voluntary behavior began with the animal research of Edward Thorndike in the 1890's. For several decades, psychologists worked exclusively with continuous reinforcement schedules. Extensive research was conducted that examined the effects of reinforcement number, magnitude, and timing on the acquisition of a continuously reinforced response and the subsequent extinction of that response.

In the 1930's, B. F. Skinner pioneered the study of intermittent reinforcement and described the different patterns of behavior generated by ratio and interval schedules. In 1957, Charles B. Ferster and Skinner published *Schedules of Reinforcement*, which presented a detailed and systematic analysis of basic and complex schedule effects. The behaviors observed in these early studies were lever pressing in rats and key pecking in pigeons. Other psychologists then examined the impact of schedules on behaviors in different animals and reported similarities of schedule-induced patterns of responding across animal species.

In the late 1950's and early 1960's, researchers demonstrated educational and therapeutic applications of schedules in working with mentally retarded and emotionally disturbed individuals. These applications have since been refined and extended to practically all helping professions.

Research on schedules continues along several avenues. The area of behavioral economics studies human choice behavior on concurrent schedules. Researchers develop mathematical equations to describe how selection of an activity is influenced by the conditions of reinforcement associated with the available choices. This work has important implications for both the prediction and the modification of behaviors in areas such as consumer spending, recyling efforts, and energy conservation.

Most research on schedules has focused on response-dependent reinforcement, which involves the delivery of a reinforcer contingent upon the prior performance of a specific response. In 1948, Skinner described the development of superstitious behavior: a response strengthened by the accidental delivery of a reinforcer following the response. Since the 1970's, considerable attention has been focused on the effects of this accidental or response-independent reinforcement. Research suggests that delivery of noncontingent reinforcers plays a role in the development of maladaptive behavior patterns, including depression, apathy, and passivity.

Reinforcement schedules also provide a tool for evaluating the effects of other variables on behavior. Reinforcing a behavior on a variable schedule, such as VI or VR, generates a steady, uniform rate of response. This can serve as a baseline against which the introduction of another variable, such as a drug, can be examined. This methodology is being used to describe the effects of drugs and punishment, as well as the incentive value of different types of reinforcers on behavior.

Bibliography

Baldwin, John D., and Janice I. Baldwin. *Behavior Principles in Everyday Life.* 2d ed. Englewood Cliffs, N.J.: Prentice-Hall, 1986. Unlike many less-readable introductions to operant behavior theory and reinforcement schedules, this book uses hundreds of examples from ordinary human behavior to illustrate the basic principles. Detailed yet easy to follow, this is one of the best introductions available.

Ferster, Charles B., Stuart Culbertson, and Mary Carol Perrott Boren. *Behavior Principles.* 2d ed. Englewood Cliffs, N.J.: Prentice-Hall, 1975. A book on operant behavior that describes animal experiments and then applies behavior principles to human behavior, including verbal behavior and depression. Much of the book deals with reinforcement schedules. The authors assume no prior knowledge of psychology on the part of the reader.

Ferster, Charles B., and Burrhus Frederic Skinner. *Schedules of Reinforcement.* New York: Appleton-Century-Crofts, 1957. Describes the original animal studies conducted by the authors; still required reading for anyone who desires a complete knowledge of schedules. The amount of detail presented is tremendous, but adequate background is given to make it accessible to the nonspecialist reader.

Miller, L. Keith. *Principles of Everyday Behavior Analysis.* 2d ed. Pacific Grove, Calif.: Brooks/Cole, 1980. An excellent introduction to behavior analysis for the high school or college student. Material is presented in a modified programmed instruction format. Short lessons are accompanied by quizzes and problems demonstrating real-life applications.

Schoenfeld, William N., ed. *The Theory of Reinforcement Schedules.* New York: Appleton-Century-Crofts, 1970. A collection of technical articles that can be understood by a nonspecialist. Particularly interesting are "Schedules as Fundamental Determinants of Behavior" and "Reinforcement Schedules and Stimulus Control."

Skinner, Burrhus Frederic. "A Case History in Scientific Method." *American Psychologist* 11 (1956): 221-233. Reprinted in B. F. Skinner, *Cumulative Record: A Selection of Papers.* 3d ed. New York: Appleton-Century-Crofts, 1972. This often-reprinted article is a Skinner classic. He describes the discovery of and some of the original research on reinforcement schedules in a light, personable style with more than a touch of humor.

Thompson, Travis, and John G. Grabowski. *Reinforcement Schedules and Multi-operant Analysis.* New York: Appleton-Century-Crofts, 1972. An introduction to reinforcement schedules for the lay reader that uses a programmed instruction format. Material is presented in small units, and the student is tested on the material before proceeding to the next unit. The book provides a clear explanation of the way in which schedules exert control over rates and patterns of response.

Linda J. Palm

Cross-References

Behaviorism: An Overview, 401; Instrumental Conditioning: Acquisition and Extinction, 1315; Learning: Generalization and Discrimination, 1437; Learning Defined, 1443; Operant Conditioning Therapies, 1714; Punishment, 2016; Reinforcers and Reinforcement, 2084.

REINFORCERS AND REINFORCEMENT

Type of psychology: Learning
Fields of study: Behavioral and cognitive models; instrumental conditioning

A reinforcer is a stimulus that strengthens the behavior it follows, and reinforcement is the procedure used to establish a contingency between a behavior and a reinforcer. Reinforcement principles are used by educators, employers, parents, and therapists to develop and maintain adaptive human behavior.

Principal terms
AVERSIVE STIMULUS: a painful or unpleasant event
NEGATIVE REINFORCEMENT: a procedure in which a behavior is followed by the termination of an aversive stimulus such that the behavior is strengthened
POSITIVE REINFORCEMENT: a procedure in which a behavior is followed by the presentation of a stimulus such that the behavior is strengthened
REINFORCEMENT CONTINGENCY: a relationship between a specific behavior and a specific reinforcing consequence
REINFORCER: a stimulus that strengthens the behavior it follows

Overview

A basic premise of instrumental conditioning is that voluntary behavior is strengthened when it is followed by a reinforcing consequence. Positive reinforcement occurs when an individual performs a specific behavior and that action is followed by the presentation of a stimulus. The stimulus is called a positive reinforcer if the behavior is more likely to be performed in the future. Consider the example of a student who studies hard for an exam and receives a high grade on the exam. The student then continues to study hard before each exam. For this student, the receipt of a high grade is a rewarding outcome, or a positive reinforcer that maintains study behavior.

Many socially desirable behaviors are developed and maintained by positive reinforcement. A child completes his or her chores in order to watch a television program. A productive employee is rewarded with a paycheck. An athlete practices diligently in order to win a game. A mathematician painstakingly solves a difficult equation to experience a feeling of success.

Positive reinforcers can strengthen inappropriate as well as appropriate behaviors, however; a student who acts like a clown in class and receives smiles and compliments from classmates may continue to show this behavior as long as it produces peer approval. A person who holds up a store and gets away with five hundred dollars may be motivated to commit additional robberies. Even in cases in which a punishing consequence also occurs, the positive reinforcer may be the more potent consequence. An individual may continue selling drugs if the monetary reward far outweighs the discomfort of a short-term incarceration.

While positive reinforcement involves the delivery of favorable or pleasant outcomes following behavior, negative reinforcement occurs when an individual's behavior produces the termination of an aversive stimulus, resulting in an increase in the frequency of that behavior. Suppose that an individual is suffering from a painful headache. The individual takes an aspirin, and the headache goes away. In this example, the headache pain is an aversive stimulus. Termination, or removal of the pain, provides relief and thus serves as a negative reinforcer for the behavior of taking aspirin. Since relief from headache pain is reinforcing, one would expect this individual to take aspirin the next time a headache occurs.

The principle of negative reinforcement underlies the development of many escape and avoidance behaviors. Escape behaviors are actions that allow one to terminate an aversive stimulus that is currently present in the environment. One can escape from an alarm clock buzzer by turning off the alarm, or from a seat belt buzzer by fastening the seat belt. A child might escape from the fists of a bully by crying "uncle" or handing over his lunch money. In time, one may learn avoidance behaviors which prevent the occurrence of an aversive stimulus. One can wake up before the alarm clock buzzer goes off. The child can prevent being hit by avoiding the bully's territory.

A variety of stimuli function as reinforcers. Primary, or unconditioned, reinforcers are stimuli which satisfy biological needs and are inherently rewarding because they promote the survival of the individual and/or species. Primary reinforcers include food, water, oxygen, sleep, sex, and the termination of pain. Secondary, or conditioned, reinforcers are stimuli one has learned to value because they have been associated with other reinforcers in the past. One powerful secondary reinforcer is money. By itself, money cannot satisfy any biological needs. It acquires its reinforcing properties because it can be exchanged for necessary and desirable commodities such as food, housing, clothing, and entertainment.

Two other categories of reinforcers are social reinforcers and activities. Social reinforcers involve attention from others in forms such as glances, nods, praise, smiles, and hugs. The opportunity to engage in a favorite activity, such as going to a party or playing a video game, can serve to strengthen the performance of a less preferred activity, such as washing the dishes or completing a homework assignment.

Material commodities, social attention, and activities are called extrinsic reinforcers because they are provided by the environment that is external to the individual. For many people, intrinsic reinforcers are equally important in maintaining behavior. Intrinsic reinforcers refer to positive thoughts and feelings that one has about one's behavior. A sense of pride and achievement or a feeling of success often maintains the performance of difficult tasks and creative endeavors.

The effectiveness of a reinforcement procedure is influenced by timing, consistency, and frequency of reinforcer delivery. In order to strengthen a new or weak behavior, it is important to reinforce immediately following the performance of the behavior. Each occurrence of the desired behavior should be followed by the reinforcer, while inappropriate behaviors and nonoccurrences of the behavior should not produce the reinforcer. As the behavior becomes more established, longer delays and less frequent reinforcer deliveries can be tolerated.

Another consideration is the magnitude, or size, of the reinforcer. In general, a large reinforcer is more potent than a small reinforcer; however, reinforcer magnitude will depend on the type of reinforcer used and the length of time the individual has been deprived of that reinforcer. Individuals tend to satiate, or get tired of, the same reinforcer after receiving large quantities of it. If a behavior is to be reinforced frequently, it may be best to use smaller amounts of the reinforcer and to use a variety of different reinforcers to reduce the possibility of satiation.

Applications

Reinforcement principles are used to improve human performance in a wide variety of settings. Educators have recognized that academic achievement is typically higher in classrooms in which behavioral management is based on positive reinforcement than on punishment or threat of punishment. In many regular and special education classes, token systems are used, in which students receive secondary reinforcers such as gold stars or check marks contingent upon academic and social achievements. Students can accumulate these token reinforcers and later exchange them for other commodities or activity reinforcers. As appropriate behaviors increase in strength and frequency, gradually the tokens are eliminated.

Another educational application is programmed instruction. The course material is divided into small sections or frames arranged in order of increasing complexity. After completion of each frame, the student is questioned on the material. If the response is incorrect, the student is immediately informed of the error and returns to the preceeding frame for review. A correct reponse produces immediate feedback to that effect. There are a number of advantages of this form of learning over the traditional lecture approach. Each student controls the rate of presentation of the frames and does not have to conform to a single pace set by a lecturer. In addition, students cannot progress to more difficult material until more elementary information has been mastered. Perhaps most important, the student is given immediate feedback about his or her performance. In traditional classrooms, days or weeks may elapse before graded work is returned, thereby delaying reinforcement for academic achievement.

Behavior therapists also use reinforcement procedures to help clients develop adaptive behaviors. Shaping is a technique used to overcome a behavioral deficit and involves teaching a client a new behavior by reinforcing successive approximations to the desired behavior. The desired, or target, behavior is defined along with a starting behavior that is currently part of the client's behavioral repertoire. The client performs the starting behavior and is immediately reinforced. Reinforcement is then withheld until the client performs a behavior that more closely resembles the target behavior. Training continues through a series of steps or approximations until the target behavior is mastered. In shaping a shy child to interact socially with other children, the therapist might use shaping steps including looking in the direction of the children, walking toward the children, listening to the children, talking with the children, and eventually playing with the children. In addition to social skills, shaping has been used to develop language, academic, vocational, and self-help skills. Shaping is also an important component in the training of animals that assist handicapped humans. For example, capuchin monkeys have been shaped to aid paralyzed people with grooming, eating, and household tasks.

In business and industry, the productivity of workers is strongly influenced by reinforcement contingencies. Organizations use tangible reinforcers such as salary, promotions, and retirement benefits to attract new workers and retain employees. Research conducted in business organizations has revealed that employees respond to more than tangible reinforcers. Praise from coworkers and superiors for work well done and frequent feedback about employee performance tend to increase productivity. Encouraging employees to participate in company decision making and acknowledging the value of employee input also produce positive outcomes. These kinds of reinforcers have also been shown to improve morale and social interactions among employees and reduce absenteeism, accidents, and employee theft.

Many Americans are using reinforcement in self-management programs to overcome problems with weight control, physical fitness, and time management. After identifying the problem area and the target behavior, the individual defines a series of subgoals. The achievement of each subgoal is followed by the delivery of a reinforcer. A person who wishes to develop the habit of a daily sixty-minute exercise session might begin by administering a reward for achieving a subgoal of twenty minutes of exercise twice a week. When this behavior is well established, the person moves to the next subgoal, which might involve increasing the length of each session and/or the number of days per week during which exercise occurs. Gradually, exercise behavior is shaped toward the desired level. Many individuals initially use tangible reinforcers for meeting a subgoal, such as going to a motion picture or buying a new item of clothing. Charting one's progress on a graph provides immediate feedback and may motivate continued efforts to reach one's goals. Over time, more natural reinforcers may become part of the program. As physical fitness improves, social reinforcement in the form of compliments from others may be received. The individual may begin to feel better physically and emotionally, thereby elevating self-esteem. These social and intrinsic reinforcers may help maintain positive behavioral changes.

Context

Edward Thorndike conducted the earliest experimental studies of the effects of reinforcement on voluntary behavior in animals. Thorndike placed a hungry animal inside a box and a food reward outside. He then measured the length of time needed for the animal to learn to escape by pulling a string or stepping on a pedal which would release the door latch. Initially, the animal performed only unsuccessful escape behaviors. Eventually, through trial and error, the animal performed the appropriate response. Successive placements in the box resulted in faster escapes. In 1898, Thorndike formulated the law of effect to explain how this learning occurs: Behavior followed by a satisfying state of affairs tends to be repeated, while behavior followed by an annoying state of affairs is less likely to recur. In the early 1900's, Thorndike applied his reinforcement concepts to human learning and made important contributions to the field of educational psychology.

During the 1940's and 1950's, Clark Hull and his colleagues attempted to develop a mathematically precise theory of learning based on the assumption that reduction of a primary drive such as hunger or thirst was the basic mechanism of reinforcement. The Hullians conducted a wealth of experiments examining the effects of drive level and incentive properties of reinforcers on the learning process. Although this approach has largely been abandoned, it is noteworthy in that it dominated experimental research in the fields of learning and motivation for more than twenty years and stimulated development of alternative reinforcement theories.

The most systematic study of reinforcement was conducted by B. F. Skinner and his students. Skinner proposed that voluntary or operant behavior is controlled by its consequences: Reinforcing consequences increase the probability that a behavior will recur, and punishing consequences decrease the probability that a behavior will recur. In the 1930's, Skinner developed the operant conditioning chamber, often called a Skinner box, which contains a simple device that an animal could be trained to manipulate. The chamber was automated to deliver a specific consequence following performance of the desired response. Using this technology, thousands of operant conditioning studies have been conducted describing how variations in reinforcer delivery affect the rate and pattern of responding.

Throughout his career, Skinner never tired of promoting his belief that an understanding of reinforcement principles could be used to improve all aspects of human society. Beginning in the 1960's, application of Skinnerian reinforcement principles appeared in education and clinical psychology. Over succeeding decades, other areas as diverse as economics, sports, and medicine began to incorporate reinforcement concepts.

Since the 1970's, increasing emphasis has been placed on the importance of intrinsic reinforcers, and many cognitive psychologists are examining how internal processes such as expectations about rewards and positive and negative self-evaluations influence the development and maintenance of behaviors. Physiological psychologists continue to search for the biochemical basis of reinforcement in the brain. As knowledge of reinforcement becomes more sophisticated, people's potential for personal development and cooperative social interaction will increase.

Bibliography

Baldwin, John D., and Janice I. Baldwin. *Behavior Principles in Everyday Life.* 2d ed. Englewood Cliffs, N.J.: Prentice-Hall, 1986. Uses hundreds of examples from ordinary human behavior to illustrate the basic principles of operant behavior theory. Detailed yet easy to follow; one of the best introductions available.

Miller, L. Keith. *Principles of Everyday Behavior Analysis.* 2d ed. Pacific Grove, Calif.: Brooks/Cole, 1980. An excellent introduction to behavior analysis for the high school or college student. Material is presented in a modified programmed-instruction format. Short lessons are accompanied by quizzes and problems demonstrating real-life applications.

Skinner, B. F. *About Behaviorism.* New York: Alfred A. Knopf, 1974. Many criticisms of Skinnerian behaviorism have been based on misunderstandings of his position. Skinner addresses these criticisms in this book. Written in a nontechnical style; however, an elementary knowledge of behavior analysis would be helpful to readers of this book.

_____. *Beyond Freedom and Dignity.* New York: Alfred A. Knopf, 1971. A controversial book analyzing the structure and ills of American society. Argues that people have been ineffective in dealing with social problems because they have ignored the causes of human behavior. Nontechnical and highly recommended.

_____. *Science and Human Behavior.* New York: Macmillan, 1953. Principles of reinforcement are applied to a wide variety of topics, including self-control, thinking, government, religion, economics, and education, in this accessible introduction to operant behavior theory.

Watson, David L., and Roland G. Tharp. *Self-Directed Behavior: Self-Modification for Personal Adjustment.* 5th ed. Pacific Grove, Calif.: Brooks/Cole, 1989. A do-it-yourself guide to behavior change. Makes extensive use of principles of reinforcement to help the lay reader improve behaviors in areas such as time management, smoking, overeating, assertiveness, insomnia, budgeting, and social behavior.

Linda J. Palm

Cross-References

Avoidance Learning, 375; Behaviorism: An Overview, 401; Escape Conditioning, 985; Instrumental Conditioning: Acquisition and Extinction, 1315; Learning: Generalization and Discrimination, 1437; Learning Defined, 1443; Operant Conditioning Therapies, 1714; Punishment, 2016; Reinforcement Schedules, 2077.

RELIGION AND PSYCHOLOGY

Type of psychology: Social psychology
Fields of study: Attitudes and behavior; social perception and cognition

The relationship between religion and psychology usually involves the study of religious belief and behavior from a psychological perspective. The psychological study of religion includes a focus on both religious behavior and religious belief, uses various models of human nature, and utilizes many psychological concepts.

Principal terms

EXTRINSIC RELIGION: an immature religious orientation that uses religion for self-serving purposes such as security or a sense of social or economic well-being
INTRINSIC RELIGION: a mature religious orientation that involves religion as a master motive for all aspects of life; a sincere desire to serve the object of devotion
MORAL BEHAVIOR: behavior that conforms to generally accepted ideas of what is right and just in human conduct
QUEST RELIGION: a religious orientation that involves an open-minded approach to existential issues, often involving questioning and doubt
RELIGION: a system of faith or worship that involves a sense of completeness through reconnection and a restraint of errant impulses
RELIGIOUS CONVERSION: a change from one system of faith or worship to another

Overview

Both religion and psychology are broad topics that encompass a vast array of human experience. The study of the psychology of religion is the effort to understand and predict the thoughts, feelings, and actions of persons as they act religiously. (The psychology of religion is different from the idea of psychology itself as a religion, which suggests that the field of psychology, with its own interpretation of the meaning of personal existence, be granted the status of an alternative worldview or a secular religion.) The psychology of religion is also distinct from religious psychology, which usually attempts to integrate the tenets of a faith system (such as Judaism, Islam, or Christianity) with the findings of psychological science.

The word "religion" is rooted in two Latin words: *legare* and *religio*. *Legare* denotes a process of rebinding or reconnecting. *Religio* means to restrain or hold back, which implies that one purpose of religion is to bridle human motives and impulses. Religion can be understood, then, as a force that reconnects human fragmentation to a sense of wholeness and restrains problematic drives and impulses. It should be noted that a supernatural deity is not mentioned or even implied in this definition. Thus, religion may involve a reconnection to God, nature, the self, some cosmic force, or almost anything else as one strives to be complete or whole.

Some research in the psychology of religion considers the function that religion serves for the individual. From this perspective, religion may be seen as a confirmation of hope, a conservation of values, a means by which to establish goals and measure personal development, a source of comfort, or a quest for the ideal relationship. Sigmund Freud, for example, considered religious experience to be a search for an external source of control to supersede the ambivalent feelings that individuals have toward their parents. Thus, Freud viewed God as nothing more, psychologically, than an exalted father. He further maintained that the root of all religion is a longing for a father figure.

Another example of the perceived functional value of religion is in the study of religious conversions. A religious conversion may be understood as simply a transformation or a turning from one belief to another. Conversions may occur within religious contexts that are traditionally accepted by society (such as any major religious tradition) or may occur in cults or sects outside society's mainstream. Psychologists and other social scientists have often focused on the functional value of cultic conversions. One model, for example, suggests that the potential cultic convert must first experience enduring and strongly felt tensions that have not been met by traditional religious institutions. Once the cult movement is encountered, strong emotional bonds are established, and attachments to individuals outside the cult begin to diminish. Eventually, there is an intensive interaction between the new convert and the cult. Through these processes, the individual may believe that his or her needs are being met, while at the same time the control of the cult over the individual becomes substantially stronger. Thus, the religious practices of the cult serve a particular function both for the individual and for the group.

While some psychologists stress the functional aspects of religion, others view the study of religious experience more in terms of its substance by investigating such things as different ways of being religious, whether religiousness is related to social compassion, participation in religious behaviors such as church attendance and prayer, the importance of religion, and openness to doubt. For example, Gordon Allport wanted to investigate the characteristics of mature religion. He distinguished between those with an intrinsic religious orientation that is characterized by an inner, personal, and meaningful faith and those with an extrinsic religious orientation, in which faith is used for some other self-interest. In the mature intrinsic orientation, the person's faith is a "master motive" that will be given priority over other motives, especially those that may conflict (such as a particular economic or sexual motive). In the immature extrinsic religious orientation, religion provides some sort of payoff or gain outside the self, such as the protection of social or economic wellbeing.

Allport's notion of religious orientation has generated considerable interest among psychologists of religion, and his theory has undergone some revision. It appears that intrinsic and extrinsic religiousness are not totally opposite. That is, some people may have both religious orientations, while others may have neither orientation.

Furthermore, some psychologists have questioned whether the intrinsic orientation is really a mature religion. In part, this debate revolves around ways in which religious orientation is measured by means of self-reported responses to questions on a scale. The concern is that some people may respond a certain way to appear "good." An alternative religious orientation that has been proposed as a truly mature religion has been called the "quest" orientation. This orientation is characterized by an active searching for existential truth that may sometimes involve a certain degree of doubt or questioning. Defenders of Allport's notion of mature religion as an intrinsic orientation suggest that a quest orientation may be a necessary step in religious development but should not be understood as mature religion.

Applications

While a psychological study of religion is of interest to many in its own right, others question the value of such research: Why bother with a psychological analysis of religious behavior?

One reason is that religion is apparently an important dimension in the life of many people. Religious conversions, for example, are very prevalent in Western society, and evidence indicates that during the 1980's Africa and many parts of Asia reported large numbers of religious conversions, particularly to Christianity, as well. Conclusions from the 1977-1978 *Gallup Opinion Index* indicate that approximately one-third of all Americans have been "born again." Because religious conversion can also be outside the context of Christianity, and not all Christians may feel comfortable using this term, this percentage may be actually higher. The extent to which these percentages reflect genuine personal conversions is unclear; however, the indications are quite clear that religious conversion of some type, even if it means simply the confirmation of parental upbringing, occurs in the lives of many people.

Religion has other important psychological implications as well. Studies in the 1940's and 1950's showed repeatedly that religious people, as measured by frequency of church attendance, scored higher on measures of racial prejudice than did nonreligious people. This may be a disturbing finding to some, given that most religious teaching, regardless of tradition, stresses compassion, patience, and love for humanity. Yet there were also some notable exceptions to this general pattern. Allport decided to apply the intrinsic-extrinsic religious orientation concept to the study of prejudice. His reasoning was that "extrinsics" may be most likely to demonstrate prejudice, since their religious approach is one in which an individual seeks security and comfort, which are also by-products of prejudice (as when one sees oneself as superior to others). Hence, the person who attends church because it is psychologically comforting or because it increases his or her status in the community is more likely, for similar reasons, to have prejudicial attitudes. Research has generally supported Allport's reasoning. Extrinsically oriented individuals (identified as those with immature religion) demonstrate higher levels of prejudice than either intrinsics or nonreligious individuals. People who score indiscriminately high on both intrinsic and extrinsic measures of religion, however, demonstrate the highest prejudice levels of all. Evidence suggests that these people tend to see things in blanket categories (such as "all religion is good"). Since prejudice is a negative prejudgment based on a stereotype, such people may also tend to see, for example, all minorities as bad.

The relationship between religion and prejudice is actually a part of a much broader question: Does religion have a positive effect on human behavior? Unfortunately, a simple, straightforward answer cannot be provided. One creative study at Princeton Theological Seminary was conducted to see if people with religion on their minds would be more likely to help someone in need. In the study, based upon the New Testament parable of the "Good Samaritan," in which only the Samaritan, not the religiously minded priest or Levite, helped a victim along a roadside, it was discovered that theological students were no more likely to help someone in need if they were about to give a talk on the "Good Samaritan" than if they were to give a talk on the job market for seminary graduates. Rather, the more crucial issue was how much time they had. Those who thought they were late were far less likely to help.

This one study certainly does not determine whether religion is a good predictor of moral behavior. In some cases, research has shown what some may think is intuitively obvious. Most studies indicate that religious individuals are less likely to engage in extramarital sexual behavior or use illicit drugs. Those with an intrinsic religious orientation, compared to extrinsics and the nonreligious, are less likely to cheat on an exam if given an opportunity to do so. Similarly, those who are highly committed to their faith are less likely blindly to obey an authority figure who orders them to hurt someone. It appears that religion can be an important predictor of some significant human behaviors.

Another common question involves religion and mental health. Religious symbolism is frequently found in the speech of those who are seriously disturbed, so this is a legitimate concern. Albert Ellis, an outspoken atheist and the creator of rational-emotive therapy (which suggests that irrational beliefs are at the heart of most psychological problems), considers religion harmful to one's well-being. The idea that one needs some supernatural power on which to rely, insists Ellis, is an irrational belief. Freud, who also saw religion as unhealthy, identified it as a neurosis of the masses. Certainly, the 1978 Jonestown tragedy in Guyana (in which cult members committed mass suicide), as well as a number of other incidents, indicates that people may often engage in bizarre behavior in the name of religion. Yet research on a number of mental health variables, including fear of death, anxiety, loneliness, sense of well-being, dogmatism, and authoritarianism, generally indicates that religious people are neither better nor worse off than other persons.

Context

Psychology and religion have had an intermittent relationship during the twentieth century. William James's classic book *The Varieties of Religious Experience: A Study in Human Nature* (1902) provided the early impetus for the psychology of religion. G. Stanley Hall, the first president of the American Psychological Association, wrote *Jesus, the Christ, in the Light of Psychology* (1917), which dealt with the underlying motivations of religious conversion. From 1920 to 1960, however, there was little interest in the field. Annual reviews on the subject in the *Psychology Bulletin* appeared less regularly from 1904 to 1920 and ceased altogether after 1933. Probably the greatest reason for the demise of the psychology of religion during this period was the idea that psychology should become an established science like the natural sciences. The study of religious experience, reasoned most experts, does not lend itself well to the scientific enterprise. Another reason that psychologists steered away from religion was the rise, during this period, of Freud's psychoanalytic theory, which many believed undermined the legitimacy of religious experience.

During the late 1950's and early 1960's, however, organizations such as the Christian Association for Psychological Studies (with more than two thousand members in 1990) and the Society for the Scientific Study of Religion were founded. The Catholic Psychological Association became division 36 (Psychologists Interested in Religious Issues) of the American Psychological Association. At the same time, professional journals such as the *Journal for the Scientific Study of Religion* were established. In part, this about-face was caused by the changing religious patterns of society. Western culture has become increasingly religious since the 1950's. Also, psychology's infatuation with the prevailing view of science during the 1930's and subsequent decades has waned. No longer do many psychologists believe that psychology should (or can) become a science in the same way that physics, for example, is a science. This means that psychology is open to new methods and new areas of study—including religion.

An even more radical step since the 1970's has been attempts by some psychologists to integrate theology with psychology. Though theology includes Judaism, Islam, Hinduism, and other major world religions, most of the effort at reconciliation has been directed toward Christian theology (particularly evangelical or conservative theology). Journals such as the *Journal of Psychology and Christianity* and the *Journal of Psychology and Theology* have been established as mechanisms of scholarly interchange on the relationship between psychological and theological understandings of the person. Even accredited graduate programs espousing an integrated study have opened and flourished.

Despite these dramatic changes by psychologists with regard to the study of religion, research has indicated that psychologists remain among the least religious of all scientists. Nevertheless, it is of interest to many to see whether these changes will affect the study of religious experience in the decades ahead.

Bibliography

Benner, David G., ed. *Baker Encyclopedia of Psychology.* Grand Rapids, Mich.: Baker Book House, 1985. This encyclopedic reference has a special focus on religious issues and the integration of psychology with the Christian faith, but it includes most other psychological and some theological topics as well. Originally developed for ministers, it is thorough yet very understandable. An excellent 1,200-page resource.

Carter, John D., and Bruce Narramore. *The Integration of Psychology and Theology: An Introduction.* Grand Rapids, Mich.: Zondervan, 1979. This brief paperback successfully accomplishes its mission of presenting a systematic framework by which the relationship between psychology and theology (particularly conservative Christian theology) can be understood. Reasons for the sometimes tense relationship between psychology and religion are also discussed.

Paloutzian, Raymond F. *Invitation to the Psychology of Religion.* Glenview, Ill.: Scott, Foresman, 1983. This two-hundred-page paperback textbook is truly an "invitation" to be introduced to the psychology of religion. The author is reasonably successful at reducing a large amount of material into a compact and readable text. This book is a good place to begin one's study.

Peck, M. Scott. *The Road Less Traveled: A New Psychology of Love, Traditional Values, and Spiritual Growth.* New York: Simon & Schuster, 1978. An application-oriented book that takes the reader on a journey through confrontation and resolution of problems toward a higher level of self-understanding. Borrowing from humanistic psychology, this controversial best-seller is surely thought-provoking.

Stern, E. Mark, ed. *The Other Side of the Couch: What Therapists Believe.* New York: Pilgrim Press, 1981. A fascinating exposé of the private religious beliefs of twenty-four therapists. Each briefly relates his or her own faith, sometimes admitting and other times vehemently denying its influence on his or her psychotherapy. The book can be appreciated by college readers.

Wulff, David M. *Psychology of Religion: Classic and Contemporary Views.* New York: John Wiley & Sons, 1991. A brilliant blend of various strains of thought and research that is destined to become a classic in the psychology of religion. The author deals evenhandedly with all major religious traditions, something not found in most other books in the psychology of religion. Designed for advanced readers at the undergraduate level.

Peter C. Hill

Cross-References

RELIGIOSITY: MEASUREMENT

Type of psychology: Social psychology
Fields of study: Attitudes and behavior; social perception and cognition

The study of religiosity, or religiousness, explores what it means to be religious; psychologists use survey research, including national opinion polls, and psychometric scales to assess types and degrees of religiosity.

Principal terms
ATHEIST: someone who believes that there is no God
ATTITUDE: a learned habit for responding to a stimulus (especially a social one); attitudes have belief, emotional, and action components
DENOMINATION: a specific religious group (sect, cult, or church) such as Reform Judaism, Roman Catholicism, or Methodism
EXTRINSIC: a religious orientation which focuses on the institutional dimension and on the personal and social benefits of participation
I-E SCALE: a psychological test which purports to measure the intrinsic-extrinsic religious orientation of an individual
INTRINSIC: a religious orientation which focuses on the value of religion for its own sake
RELIGIOSITY (RELIGIOUSNESS): a person's attitude toward religion in general; more specifically, the intensity or way in which a person is religious
SECULAR: having no tie to any specific denomination; something not under the influence of religion

Overview

Psychologists regard attitudes as learned habits for responding to social stimuli and attempt to identify the cognitive, affective (emotional), and behavioral components of the attitude. Religiosity (also known as religiousness) is generally understood as a person's essential attitude toward religion in general, as opposed to attitudes toward specific religious denominations or practices. The word "religion" has a Latin root which implies binding and restraining. Religion is therefore a personal and social force which serves to bind people together in a community of worshipers, unite them in reverence with a spiritual dimension of existence, and restrain their inappropriate impulses (via moral commandments).

The form of studying attitudes with which the average American would be most familiar is the national opinion poll as conducted by George Gallup, Louis Harris, a major newspaper or magazine, or a marketing research firm. For example, Gallup has attempted to measure a person's overall religiosity by asking, "How well does the description 'a religious person' apply to you?" The respondent then selects a number from 1 to 10, with 1 indicating that the description is not at all accurate and 10 indicating that it fits perfectly. The median response for Americans is 7 (the mode is 8), with slightly lower averages for those persons who are younger, male, college educated, or living in the West.

Even the pollsters usually break down religion into specific behavioral, cognitive, and affective components. The first behavioral component to be considered would be affiliation: Does the person belong to a specific denomination and, if so, which one? About 90 percent of all Americans claim a religious affiliation (such as Protestant, Catholic, or Jewish), but only about seven in ten say they are actually members of a specific denomination. Again, this figure is slightly lower for men, the young, and people living in the West. Data from denomination records indicate that the largest single denomination in the United States is Roman Catholic (with about a third of the population), with Baptists coming in second, then Methodists. Some denominations (including the United Church of Christ and the Unitarian Universalist Association) appear to be declining in numbers, while others, such as the Church of Jesus Christ of Latter-Day Saints (Mormons), Jehovah's Witnesses, and Pentecostals, are growing because of a combination of birth and conversion rates.

Attendance at worship services is another specific behavior that can be measured. Only 15 percent of Americans claim that they never attend. About four in ten report that they went during the last seven days. Three-fourths, however, express the belief that one can be a good Christian or Jew without frequent church attendance. Three-quarters of Americans claim that their own frequency of church attendance has not changed over the past two years. Interestingly, the four-in-ten attendance figure is virtually identical to that reported in 1937, when Gallup started asking the question; the figure went up a little in the early 1950's and had a low in the late 1960's.

Other measurable religious activities include reading the Bible (that also calculates at about four in ten in the last week) and engaging in prayer (almost half do it "daily"; only one in eight "not at all").

Another approach would be to measure people's level of acceptance or endorsement of specific church policies (or of government laws relating to religion). For example, surveys have found that more than two-thirds of American Catholics disagree with the official teachings of their church of not allowing divorced people to remarry in the church and not permitting couples to use artificial means of birth control. Polls have also discovered that about three-quarters of all Americans would accept teaching about world religions and the Bible (as literature and history) in the public schools.

Cognitive dimensions of religiousness would include anything that people believe about God or spiritual reality as well as what people believe about religion. People have been polled as to whether they believe in God or "a universal spirit." Phrasing the question that way brings about a 95 percent affirmation. About five in six people in the United States agree that Jesus was the Son of God. Four in five believe in some kind of heaven or afterlife, and the same proportion believes in a judgment after death; only a little more than half believe in hell or the devil.

Some of the cognitive components appearing in the polls involve people's beliefs about religion itself. More than half of all Americans believe that religion, rather than being out of date, can answer most of today's problems. More Americans believe that religion is increasing its influence over national life, compared to those who believe that it is losing ground. Despite scandals involving television evangelists, religious institutions still rank toward the top when Americans are asked to express their degree of confidence in institutions, and religious leaders are still high on the list when Americans rate the honesty and ethical standards of individuals.

The affective components of religiosity deal with emotions, priorities, values, and evaluations. For example, in evaluating the overall priority they give to religion in their lives, about half of Americans state that religion is "very important," while only one in eight says it is "not very important." About half of all Americans, in fact, have claimed to have made "a personal commitment" to Christ. In evaluating how well their own church meets their personal and family needs, about six in ten say "good" or "excellent."

Many sociologists and psychologists involved in the scientific study of religion have not been satisfied with the degree of precision possible in the types of one-question measures typically employed by pollsters. These scholars have developed multi-item scales in order to measure some dimension of religiousness. Specific scales have been developed to measure everything from having had a mystical experience to spiritual well-being to adherence to evangelical, fundamentalist Christian doctrine.

Some of the most widely used religiosity scales are based upon Gordon Allport's view of religion as a frame of reference for the meaning of life. This led him, and those investigators who followed in his footsteps, such as Richard Hunt and Morton King, to speculate on intrinsic versus extrinsic orientations to religion. The former type of religiosity is interiorized, private, and devotional, and is based on individual commitment. Some items purporting to measure intrinsic religiosity have dealt with personal piety, church attendance, and subjective rating of the importance of religion. Extrinsic religiosity is more institutional, public, and pragmatic, often using religion as a means to promote other ends. Some of the items on scales designed to measure the extrinsic pole include seeing religion as a vehicle for social relationships, consolation of grief, maintenance of order, and adherence to tradition. Although individuals can lean toward either the intrinsic or the extrinsic pole, it is possible to have an indiscriminately proreligious orientation (both extrinsic and intrinsic) or a purely antireligious orientation (neither intrinsic nor extrinsic).

Applications

Numerous applications of the various measures of religiosity are possible. Researchers can correlate any of these to other attitudes, personality traits, or demographic variables. Questions such as whether religious people are more superstitious, how religiosity differs between Democrats and Republicans, and whether religion helps people cope with marital problems can be addressed. For example, depending upon how one decides to measure religion (and how one measures superstition), there is a slight tendency for more religious people to be a little less superstitious, but there are many people who are neither very religious nor very superstitious—and there are some who are both.

Using data from political polls, it can be verified that Jews, Catholics, and black Baptists tend to vote for Democrats, while most mainline white Protestant groups (Episcopalians, Mormons, and Fundamentalists, in particular) lean toward the Republicans. Much of this correlation can be explained by historical and social-class features, however, in addition to the religious positions of the denominations.

Whether (and how) religion helps people cope with marital or other real-life problems is a difficult question to resolve with mere surveys. True experimentation, with random assignments to experimental and control conditions, would be necessary to confirm a cause-and-effect relationship. What seems to be apparent, however, is that religious people have a lower incidence of divorce and report slightly higher levels of marital satisfaction. This could be attributable to the fact that religious people feel more obligated to report that they have better marital relations, or it could be attributable to the fact that people who have problems in staying with a spouse also have problems in staying with their religion. When parents are asked whether religion has helped strengthen their family relationships, nearly four in five report that it has.

Clinical applications of the measurement of religiosity are also numerous. Very religiously committed individuals may have a problem with entering purely secular psychotherapy. The therapist may be seen as a nonbeliever who will challenge the patient's worldview. Patients' motivation for change may be tempered by the belief that their sufferings are a punishment inflicted by God. There is also the problem of countertransference: Secular therapists can be reluctant to take on such patients; they may also become rapidly frustrated by the religious patient's value system, so alien to their own.

From a more positive perspective, a patient's religion can both serve as a source of impulse control (for example, as a check on suicidal tendencies) and provide a wide range of formal and informal social supports. For all these reasons, it is necessary for clinicians to assess the dimensions of religiosity of their patients. Tolerant therapists can then use the patient's worldview as a reference point. Therapists who cannot tolerate a given patient's religiosity can make an appropriate referral (to another therapist who can) before the therapist is frustrated and the psychotherapeutic relationship has been damaged.

Other applications are possible in social and applied psychology. By understanding the religiosity of their "target segment," for example, advertisers can tailor commercial and political messages in order to synchronize them with the values and worldview of potential customers or voters.

Context

Religion has been the topic of investigation by philosophers since humans had the opportunity to stop and reflect upon the important elements of life. Unfortunately, the line between philosophy and religion often became blurred. Many philosophers (Plato, for example) had an underlying religious agenda implicit in their philosophical speculations, while other thinkers (Saint Augustine of Hippo, Saint Thomas Aquinas) were dedicated advocates of the Church and used philosophy principally to justify and clarify their religious orientation.

Starting in the late nineteenth century, academic psychologists turned to the field of religion and speculated about its origins and importance. William James is one of the foremost examples of this period. His approach was chiefly that of the case study rather than the survey. The positive aspect of this qualitative and narrative approach was that it kept the study of religion within the broader context of human life. The weakness was that two different investigators could look at the same religious person or phenomena and come to drastically different conclusions, for there were no objective data (especially in the form of numbers) to which an opinion could be anchored. Sigmund Freud was only one of several early twentieth century investigators who dismissed religion as a result of repressed sexuality.

A more recent example of the qualitative approach rooted in case studies has been the work of Erik Erikson, who rose beyond his psychoanalytic roots to an empathic appreciation of the uniqueness of the religious experiences of Martin Luther and Mahatma Gandhi. Although Erikson avoided the reductionism so pervasive in Freud, it can be argued that Erikson also had an agenda (his eight-stage epigenetic theory) and read it into the biographies of the men he studied. Other theorists with a positive view of religion would include neo-Freudians such as Carl Jung and Erich Fromm, and humanistic "third force" representatives such as Abraham Maslow. Each of them, however, can be accused of dealing with religion as an afterthought to his model of the human personality. Furthermore, these models are so vague in their treatment of religion that it is arguable that their comments are more philosophical than scientific.

For these reasons, it is understandable why the quantitative approach of the pollsters and test makers has become dominant in academic psychology. Yet doubt may be cast upon the scientific status of that approach as well. One problem is the "lie factor": There may not be sufficient safeguards for the honesty of people's answers. Even though the questions are anonymous, people may (unconsciously) seek to portray themselves in a favorable light (in other words, as more religious than they really are). Another concern is the use of ambiguous terms in questions. Each denomination tends to define terms in its own way. What one denomination calls "services" might be called "worship" or "Mass" by another. The Lord's Supper is also known as Holy Communion and the Eucharist. Terms such as "God" and "personal commitment" may be so vague as to preclude cross-personal quantification.

Some questions may also have several possible reasons underlying a person's response. For example, a person answering "rarely or never" to the question "How often do you ask God to forgive your sins?" may either be an atheist who sees no purpose to the confession or a pious individual who rarely sins. Someone who disagrees with the statement "The word of God is revealed only in the Scriptures" may be either an atheist or someone who believes in the possibility of present-day revelation. Certainly the quest for national polls and standardized tests has ignored the importance of the context that individuals' denominations provide. Religiosity may mean one thing for an Orthodox Jew and another for a Jehovah's Witness.

Many social scientists predicted the demise of religion during the twentieth century. Karl Marx believed that religion was the "opiate" of the people—a social institution used by the ruling classes to control and placate the exploited masses. After a proletarian revolution and the establishment of a just (Communist) social order, reasoned Marx, there would be no need for religion or, for that matter, the other instruments of state repression. Sigmund Freud contended that as science (specifically the theory and treatment offered by psychoanalysis) became more prevalent, people would not need to turn to religion to solve their problems: Society would be composed of self-restrained individuals, and religion would not be needed to control sexual and aggressive drives. B. F. Skinner regarded religious behavior as the result of accidental reinforcement, a superstitious approach to life that would diminish as humanity developed better technology for controlling the contingencies of its own reinforcement.

A safer prediction would be that religion will remain, perhaps in a multitude of reformulations. The trend has been for intellectuals to grow away from the established churches and espouse a secular humanism. This requires those who study religion to rethink certain definitions, such as whether secular humanism can be defined as a religion and whether its religiosity can be measured. The real question is not whether religion will continue to exist, but whether purely qualitative methods of researching religion can attain the precision that science demands and whether purely quantitative methods for measuring religiosity can appreciate the richness of the human religious experience.

Bibliography

Allport, Gordon Willard. *The Individual and His Religion.* New York: Macmillan, 1950. This brief and readable book gives a sympathetic look at how religion can influence the many dimensions of a person's life. Allport lays out the theoretical foundation for his internal-external measurement of religiosity.

Batson, C. Daniel, and W. Larry Ventis. *The Religious Experience in a Social Psychological Perspective.* New York: Oxford University Press, 1982. Focuses on the nature and consequences of the religious experience and the difficulties of studying it with the precision of the scientific experiment. The authors are quite critical of I-E scales.

Erikson, Erik Homburger. *Gandhi's Truth.* New York: W. W. Norton, 1969.

————. *Young Man Luther.* New York: W. W. Norton, 1962. These are sensitive and reverential treatments of great religious leaders, from the perspective of Erikson's eight-stage theory of development.

Gallup, George, and Jim Castelli. *The People's Religion: American Faith in the 1990's.* New York: Macmillan, 1989. This is a comprehensive review of United

States poll data on religion. Most of the poll data discussed in this article can be found in this volume.

Gorsuch, Richard L. "Psychology of Religion." In *Annual Review of Psychology* 39, edited by Mark Rosenweig and Lyman W. Porter. Stanford, Calif.: Annuals Reviews, 1988. This is a good short review of the history of psychology of religion, somewhat sympathetic to Allport.

Hunt, Richard A., and Morton King. "The Intrinsic-Extrinsic Concept: A Review and Evaluation." *Journal for the Scientific Study of Religion* 10, no. 4 (1971): 339-356. Also reprinted in Maloney, below. This is dated, but it is a comprehensive review of the I-E concept, concluding that more precise and valid measures are needed for a truly scientific study of religion.

Maloney, H. Newton, ed. *Current Perspectives in the Psychology of Religion.* Grand Rapids, Mich.: Wm. B. Eerdmans, 1977. This edited volume contains several relevant chapters. The one by Capps applauds the qualitative side of James and Allport. The articles by Flakoll, Warren, and Havens review some of the methodological and measurement approaches used in the scholarly study of religion. The Hunt and King journal article (above) is reprinted in this volume.

Meadow, Mary Jo, and R. D. Kahoe. *Psychology of Religion: Religion in Individual Lives.* New York: Harper & Row, 1984. This is one of the easiest-reading texts in the field. Nevertheless, its topical coverage is quite broad. The authors explore many different ways of measuring specific facets of religion. Next to Hunt and King, their review of the I-E concept is one of the most comprehensive, and it is certainly one of the most balanced.

Spilka, Bernard, Ralph W. Hood, and Richard L. Gorsuch. *The Psychology of Religion: An Empirical Approach.* Englewood Cliffs, N.J.: Prentice-Hall, 1985. Provides a very comprehensive introduction to the quantitative approach in the scientific study of the dimensions of religion. It is written at a higher academic level than the Meadow and Kahoe text.

Wulff, David M. *The Psychology of Religion.* New York: John Wiley & Sons, 1991. A thorough and balanced introduction to the scientific study of religion. Both quantitative and qualitative approaches are introduced.

T. L. Brink

Cross-References

Archetypes: Origins and Nature, 286; Attitude-Behavior Consistency, 320; Attitude Formation and Change, 326; Behavioral Assessment and Personality Rating Scales, 387; The Collective Unconscious, 592; Religion and Psychology, 2090; Survey Research: Questionnaires and Interviews, 2507.

RETICULAR FORMATION

Type of psychology: Biological bases of behavior
Fields of study: Auditory, chemical, cutaneous, and body senses; nervous system;
sleep

*The reticular formation is a system of interneurons in the brain stem that receives
and integrates sensory information from all parts of the body. It influences almost all
functions of the nervous system but is especially known for its effects on attentiveness, waking, and sleeping.*

Principal terms

AFFERENT: a sensory neuron or a dendrite carrying information toward a
structure—for example, sensory stimuli coming into the reticular
formation

AROUSAL: a condition of increased alertness of the cerebral cortex,
produced through cortical stimulation by an activated reticular
formation

BRAIN STEM: the lower, stemlike portion of the brain, including the
medulla oblongata, pons, and midbrain, that connects the spinal cord
to the cerebral hemispheres

EFFERENT: a motor neuron or an axon carrying information away from a
structure, such as in the transmission of stimuli from the reticular
formation to the cerebral cortex

EPILEPSY: a disorder of the nervous system in which the cortex produces
electrical firing that causes convulsions and other forms of seizures;
thought by some to be linked to the reticular formation

INTEGRATION: the process of associating and coordinating incoming
information to influence the mind and behavioral states

INTERNEURON: a neuron that receives information from a sensory neuron
and transmits a message to a motor neuron; very common in the
brain and important in integration

NUCLEUS: a grouping of the cell bodies of neurons that all serve the
same function within a particular region of the brain; not the same as
the nucleus of a cell

RETICULAR ACTIVATING SYSTEM: a cluster of nuclei in the reticular
formation that alert the cerebral cortex about information coming in
from different sensory areas, sometimes producing arousal from sleep

RETICULAR FORMATION: a core of neurons extending through the
medulla, pons, and midbrain that control arousal and sleeping/
waking, as well as motor functions such as muscle tone and posture

SLEEP CIRCUIT: a system of several brain areas, including the reticular
formation, that all produce sleep when stimulated and wakefulness
when stimulation is not present

Overview

The term "reticular formation" is used to refer to one of several so-called reticular structures of the central nervous system. A reticulum is a mesh or network, and reticular formation designates a specific grouping of more than ninety nuclei of interneurons that have common characteristics in the area of the brain stem. The nuclei are clusters of cell bodies of neurons that form a network of their dendritic and axonal cellular processes, those extensions that bring information into the cell and transmit information from the cell.

The mesh reaches throughout the brain stem, as well as to higher and lower regions of the central nervous system as far as the cerebral cortex and spinal cord, serving both sensory and integrative functions. Anatomically, the reticular formation is continuous from the medulla oblongata, the lowest part of the brain stem, through the pons to the midbrain. It connects with the intermediate gray region of the spinal cord and sends processes into the higher brain areas of the thalamus and hypothalamus.

Neurons of the reticular formation contain many dendritic processes, afferent cytoplasmic extensions that carry electrical stimuli toward the cell nucleus, arranged perpendicular to the central axis of the body. Each cell also contains a single long axon with numerous collateral branches that extends along the body's axis, going to the higher or lower regions of the central nervous system. The axon carries impulses away from the nucleus of the neuron toward the synapse, where it passes information on to the next neighboring cell. The axons and dendrites, present in large numbers, make up the mesh, or reticulum, that gives the reticular formation its name. The many aggregated processes make it extremely difficult to identify the clustered groups of neurons (nuclei) to which the individual cells belong.

The reticular formation is a portion of an important informational loop in the brain that allows the modification and adjustment of behavior. This loop extends from the cerebral cortex to subcortical areas (lower brain regions), including the reticular formation, and then back to the cortex. The reticular formation makes connections with all the portions of the loop and plays an important role in exciting or inhibiting the functions of the lower motor neuron centers. This loop is important in practically all functions of the nervous system and behavior, particularly sleep/ wakefulness, emotional stress, depression and distress, the induction of rapid eye movement (REM) sleep, and even sleepwalking.

The process of arousal appears to take place as the reticular formation sends impulses to an area of the thalamus called the midline thalamic nuclei. These nuclei then pass the information on to the cortex, which is stimulated to become more aware that information is coming and more attentive to receiving the information. This is an oversimplification of the process, however, as other areas of the brain also seem to be involved in arousal. The neurotransmitters involved in the reticular formation's connection to the cortex are thought to include both cholinergic and monoamine systems in the arousal process, although these are still not well understood.

Applications

The basic functions of the reticular formation are twofold: to alert the higher centers, especially in the cortex, that sensory information is coming into the processing areas; and to screen incoming information being passed upward on sensory (afferent) pathways toward the higher centers of the brain, blocking the passage of irrelevant information and passing along the information that should be acted upon by the higher brain. All sensory information must be passed through the lower regions of the brain before reaching the associative regions of the cerebral cortex. The cortex is unable to process incoming information unless it has been alerted and aroused and unless the information is channeled through the proper lower brain regions. Besides the reticular formation, the thalamus is also involved in this function, taking information from the reticular formation and passing it on to the cortex, where it is then processed and coordinated to produce motor behavior.

Because the reticular formation has so many pathways from each cell leading to many other cells, it is very quickly inhibited by anesthetics that act by inhibiting the transfer of information between cells at the synapse. This inhibition of activity leads to unconsciousness from a general lack of sensation, and loss of alertness and arousal as polysynaptic pathways are shut down. Under proper medical control, use of anesthesia to turn off the reticular formation can be lifesaving, allowing surgical procedures that could not be tolerated without it.

Lesions of the brain stem may damage the reticular formation, producing the uncontrolled unconsciousness of coma if they occur above the level of the pons on both sides. Coma that results from drug overdose or drug reaction occurs mainly as the result of depression of the reticular formation. Any lesion of the brain stem that affects the reticular formation directly will also have a secondary effect on other structures on the brain stem, causing disappearance of its reflex reactions. Damage to ascending efferent pathways from the reticular formation to the cortex sometimes can also cause coma. Because the reticular formation aids in the brain stem's role in regulating critical visceral vital functions such as breathing and blood circulation, damage to this area may threaten life itself.

The actions of alcohol on behavior also are the result of its effects on the reticular formation. Alcohol blocks the actions of this area, allowing a temporary loss of control over other brain regions. This lack of behavioral inhibition from higher brain centers produces a feeling of excitement and well-being at first. Later effects of continued alcohol intake lead to depression of emotions and behavior, followed by depression of basic body functions that can produce unconsciousness.

The production of unconsciousness through sleep is also associated with the reticular formation, particularly the part that is in the pons and another center in the lower medulla. The lower medullary sleep/waking center seems to work with the basal forebrain to modulate the induction of sleep. Rapid eye movement sleep may be controlled, at least in part, by specific nuclei in the pontine reticular formation.

Stimulation of the reticular formation, as well as other areas (the hippocampus and amygdala), improves memory retention (memory consolidation) if electrical current is applied directly to the reticular cells immediately after a training session. It is difficult to understand how this stimulation operates, however, since in some cases stimulating these same areas instead produces retrograde amnesia, causing the loss of memory retention. It is thought that the level of electrical stimulation may cause these different results. The highest and lowest stimulation levels reduce memory consolidation in some cases, and intermediate stimulation seems to be the most effective. The nature of the training process is also important in the results, as learning seems to be more difficult with high stimulation levels associated with aversive conditioning.

Another aspect of the reticular formation and its possible effects on behavior is the theory that many (or perhaps most) convulsive epileptic seizures may originate there. Since this area can be stimulated by electrical impulses and by convulsive drugs to produce seizures, it is thought that the reticular formation may be the site from which stimulation of the cerebral cortex starts. It is difficult to establish the origins of epilepsy conclusively, since there are no adequate animal models for this disorder, but antiepileptic drugs are shown to depress neuron function in the reticular formation. The actual source of the convulsive behavior is thought to be the nonspecific reticular core of this formation.

Context

The reticular formation influences nearly all aspects of nervous system function, including sensory and motor activities and somatic and visceral functions. It is important in influencing the integrative processes of the central nervous system, acting upon the mind and behavior. Included in this influence are the stimulatory aspects of arousal, awakening, and attentiveness, as well as the inhibitory aspects of drowsiness, sleep induction, and general disruption of the stimulatory functions. To understand how this region of the brain can be so important in such contradictory functions, it is important to consider the integration of excitatory and inhibitory inputs, and the consolidation of their overall influences. Depending upon which type of stimulus has the greatest effect, the net result on behavior can be alertness or drowsiness, active function or the inactivity of sleep.

Research on anesthetized cats in the late 1940's produced an increased understanding of the activities of the reticular formation. It was shown that electrical stimulation of the brain stem caused changes in the cat's electroencephalograph (EEG) readings that were similar to changes occurring in humans when they were aroused from a drowsy state to alertness. From these observations and others, it has been concluded that the ascending reticular system of the brain stem acts as a nonspecific arousal system of the cerebral cortex.

In the 1950's, Donald Lindsley and his colleagues studied the reticular formation as the source of arousal. They showed that two discrete flashes of light shown to a monkey produced discrete electrical responses (evoked potentials) in the visual cortex. If the pulses were very close together, only one potential was evoked, showing that the cortex could not distinguish both within that time. If two electrical stimulations were applied directly to the reticular formation at the short interval, however, two discrete flashes were expressed in the cortex, showing the influence of the reticular formation on the threshold level of the cortex's response to stimuli. J. M. Fuster, one of Lindsley's coworkers, examined the behavioral responses that resulted from electrical stimulation of the reticular formation in monkeys trained to discriminate between two objects. Reducing the time of visual exposure to the objects also reduced the correct responses, but stimulation of the reticular formation at the same time as the visual exposure reduced the error level. This indicated that increased arousal and attentiveness to the visual stimuli were produced by electrical activation of the reticular formation.

J. M. Siegal and D. J. McGinty's work on stimulation of the reticular formation in cats in the 1970's showed that individual neurons seem to have a role in controlling various motor functions of the body. Other studies show that various autonomic responses, such as vomiting, respiration, sneezing, and coughing, may also originate at least in part from the reticular formation.

It is thought that the period of sleep known as rapid eye movement (REM) sleep, or paradoxical sleep, is a time of memory consolidation. During this time, the reticular formation, the hippocampus, and the amygdala are stimulated to activate the higher brain centers, and arousal occurs. REM sleep is considered paradoxical because the brain waves produced during this time are similar to those produced during stimulation of the awake brain. Vincent Bloch and his colleagues have shown that laboratory animals and human subjects deprived of REM sleep display decreased memory consolidation. During this process, short-term memories are converted somehow into long-term memories, which withstand even disruptions of the electrical activities of the brain. The reticular formation is an important part of memory function, but much remains to be discovered about this and other reticular activities.

Bibliography

Carlson, Neil R. *Physiology of Behavior.* 3d ed. Boston: Allyn & Bacon, 1986. This introduction to nervous system physiology, written for college psychology majors, covers the reticular formation in several chapters. Basic anatomy and connections to other parts of the brain are discussed in chapter 4. Chapter 8 touches on the formation's role in control of movement. Chapter 9 covers its role in arousal, sleep, and waking.

Fromm, Gerhard H., Carl L. Faingold, Ronald A. Browning, and W. M. Burnham, eds. *Epilepsy and the Reticular Formation: The Role of the Reticular Core in Convulsive Seizures.* New York: Liss, 1987. This collection of short articles supports the proposal of the first author that all epileptic convulsions are caused by the interaction of areas of the cerebral cortex with the reticular formation. The reticular core is thought to be the activating structure producing the electrical discharges of the cortex. Many references.

Hobson, J. Allan, and Mary A. B. Brazier, eds. *The Reticular Formation Revisited: Specifying Function for a Nonspecific System.* New York: Raven Press, 1980. A compilation of papers presented at an international symposium in 1978. Separate sections cover historical aspects, methods of study, arousal, motor control of the body from the brain stem, chemical regulatory processes and neurotransmitters, and mechanisms of behavioral state control, including sleep. References accompany each paper.

Kaplan, Harold I., and Benjamin J. Sadock, eds. *Comprehensive Textbook of Psychiatry.* 5th ed. Vol. 1. Baltimore: Williams & Wilkins, 1989. The functional neuroanatomy of the brain stem and reticular formation are covered in chapter 1 of this text for medical students. A later portion of the chapter also covers the physiology of sleep.

Klemm, W. R., and Robert P. Vertes, eds. *Brainstem Mechanisms of Behavior.* New York: John Wiley & Sons, 1990. Provides a modern synthesis of the knowledge of this area of psychology, the actions of the medulla, pons, and midbrain. Articles in the first part of the book cover general information on how the brain stem, including the reticular formation, is involved in behavior. The larger second section discusses special research topics. The last article covers brain-stem functions in sleep control. Numerous references.

Romero-Sierra, C. *Neuroanatomy: A Conceptual Approach.* New York: Churchill Livingstone, 1986. This review book for medical students discusses the reticular formation in several sections, with anatomical structure, motor function, and visceral control. Diagrams and lists of functions present the material in an easily understood format. Suggested readings are included.

Schneider, Allen M., and Barry Tarshis. *An Introduction to Physiological Psychology.* 3d ed. New York: Random House, 1986. Several sections of this undergraduate college textbook refer to the reticular formation. Its role in motor control and in sleep and arousal are discussed, as well as its role in producing retrograde amnesia. References are footnoted within the text for ease of identification.

Steriade, Mircea, and Robert W. McCarley. *Brainstem Control of Wakefulness and Sleep.* New York: Plenum Press, 1990. This comprehensive text provides a unity of viewpoint on the topic not found in edited collections. References to the different areas of the reticular formation are found throughout the book, in discussions of the sensory information entering the brain stem and the motor control carrying instructions to muscles, among others. Brain waves in sleep and waking are discussed as originating from the reticular area. Extensive references.

Jean S. Helgeson

Cross-References

Attention, 313; Brain-Stem Structures, 461; The Central and Peripheral Nervous Systems, 494; Functions of Consciousness, 656; Dreams, 836; Insomnia, 1303; Neural Damage and Plasticity, 1655; Sleep: Stages and Functions, 2277; Sleep Apnea Syndromes and Narcolepsy, 2284.

RETIREMENT

Type of psychology: Developmental psychology
Field of study: Aging

Retirement, basically unknown as recently as sixty years ago in the United States, now may take up twenty-five or more years of a person's life. It has achieved a status and acceptance unthought of by past generations. For many people, retirement brings opportunities which add a new richness to life; it also presents problems and pitfalls which require major individual and social effort.

Principal terms

COHORT: a group of people born in the same year or same period of time who share historical experiences in common

DECATHEXIS: the process of withdrawal of libidinal energy from a prized or loved object when it is gone or when its loss is anticipated

DEMENTIA: the loss of mental capacities, usually as a result of illnesses such as Alzheimer's disease

DISENGAGEMENT: the social gerontological theory that as people grow older there is a mutual withdrawal between them and society

LONGITUDINAL: a type of research, used particularly in gerontology, in which the same group of people is studied over a relatively long period of time

ROLE: a set of behaviors expected of a person by him- or herself and by society in given situations or circumstances

SOCIAL SECURITY: the major federal government income program in the United States for retired persons, as well as for disabled persons who are unable to hold a job

VESTING: the rules governing eligibility for pensions, often including working for the same employer for a certain number of years before one is eligible for pension benefits

Overview

It was only with the advent of the industrial society in Western Europe and somewhat later in North America that the possibility that a member of the working class might be able to retire from a regular occupation with some degree of financial security and community support became a viable idea. Until the nineteenth century, only the very rich could voluntarily quit working at an income-producing job.

Agricultural societies needed all able-bodied people to work in order to survive from year to year. From primitive times through the beginnings of the Industrial Revolution, children were involved in the processes of production and remained involved until they became too old or too sick to work any longer. After that, their fate depended on the charity of family and community.

With the rise of industrial, capitalistic nations, surpluses were generated which allowed societies the luxury of supporting children and older persons without requiring them to be involved in the industrial process. In the latter half of the nineteenth century, Germany established a government-sponsored old-age pension plan for workers who reached the somewhat arbitrary age of sixty-five. (The Social Security Act in the United States was not passed until 1935.)

Retirement, then, is a recent phenomenon of industrialized societies. There was no rush to embrace it, however, even though government-sponsored benefit programs made it at least marginally possible from an economic standpoint. Certainly, part of the reason for this reluctance was the so-called Protestant work ethic, which made many people reluctant to quit work while they were still in good enough health to continue.

In *Growing Old in America* (1977), David H. Fischer reports that 50 percent of older Americans were dependent on public welfare in 1935 (the year Social Security was passed) and almost 66 percent by 1940 (before any Social Security benefits had actually been paid). Whether they liked it or not, most older Americans were forced to enter the ranks of the retired.

Since then, the acceptance of retirement by older workers and the general status accorded the retired by society has increased considerably. Sociologist Ernest Burgess, in 1960, called retirement a "roleless role," but many Americans do not see it that way. For many, retirement is a valued time of life in which one is released from the confines of the job (not from work, which for most people is always a part of life), so that activities can be pursued which are deemed to be important and satisfying in their own right. Perhaps one of the most important indications of the change in attitude toward retirement is the number of Americans taking early retirement, defined as retirement before age sixty-five. Reduced Social Security retirement payments are available at age sixty-two, and in 1990 most persons retiring with Social Security benefits were approximately sixty-three years of age or less.

The number of retired individuals increased dramatically in the twentieth century. In 1900, approximately 70 percent of American men age sixty-five or over were employed. By 1960, the figure had decreased to 35 percent. In 1984, about 11 percent of older adult males were in the work force. These figures are for men; the percentage of older women in the work force has increased during this same period of time.

Applications

There are a number of personal factors that people generally take into consideration when they make the decision to retire. One factor is obviously the financial resources available for retirement. Yet the relationship is not as simple as it might seem. Many professionals with adequate income for retirement do not retire at sixty-five, and in fact may never completely retire from their occupation until forced to by serious health problems. On the other hand, middle managers who have reached a plateau in their career advancement often retire before age sixty-two, often with retirement "packages" (in addition to company pensions), which corporations often use to encourage older executives to retire. On the other hand, blue-collar workers, who may wish to retire because of job dissatisfaction, often feel that they must stay on the job as long as possible because of lack of financial resources for retirement.

A number of studies have shown that retirees need about 70 to 80 percent of preretirement income if they are to maintain a life-style similar to that which they enjoyed when they were working at an income-producing job. Many preretirement counselors make use of the image of the three-legged stool when they give advice about financial planning for retirement. The first leg of the stool is Social Security, for which almost all Americans are eligible. The Social Security program was not designed to be the sole support of retired workers and their families. Even though many elderly in the present cohort of retirees do live entirely on their Social Security benefits, these benefits certainly do not provide even a modestly affluent life-style. The second leg of the stool is an employer pension program or a similar program (for example, a Keogh plan). Most employed Americans do not participate in a pension program. For most of those who do, the payments are very modest. When the federal government passed the Employee Retirement Income Security Act (ERISA), it established rules to guarantee pensions that had been promised and to make the requirements for vesting less onerous, but it did not require employers to offer pensions. In fact, since the advent of ERISA, the number of companies offering pension plans has decreased. The third leg of the stool representing adequate financial planning for retirement is private saving and investment. The government attempted to encourage private savings for retirement with the Individual Retirement Account (IRA) program, originally enacted in the early 1980's. The rules of the IRA program were somewhat complex, and they have been changed several times since the original legislation; the program never reached the potential originally hoped for it. Nevertheless, many believe it to be a worthwhile program, particularly for citizens with lower-middle-class incomes. Unfortunately, for those who can only get by with the necessities from payday to payday, there is no realistic opportunity for them to participate in any savings and investment program for retirement.

Another personal factor which plays a major role in retirement decisions is health. Most of the chronic illnesses from which most Americans eventually die—heart disease, cancer, cerebrovascular disease, chronic obstructive pulmonary disease, and others—begin to make themselves felt in an individual's fifties and sixties. Poor health often leads to declines in job competence and satisfaction. Poor health also generally makes for a less than desirable retirement. Contrary to myth, retirement does not lead to poor health and death: Poor health leads to retirement, which sometimes leads to death shortly following retirement. Many retirees, however, actually report feeling better after they have retired. The statistics on the relation of health and retirement may be somewhat biased by the fact that some people indicate that they retired for health reasons even though that was not the primary reason. For some in the retirement-age cohorts, health seems a more socially acceptable reason for retirement than some other reasons.

A final personal factor in a person's retirement decision relates to job satisfaction. It seems self-evident that workers who are dissatisfied with their job would be more inclined to retire (assuming adequate income) than those who find their job satisfying for the many intangibles related to a job—such as workplace friendships, feelings of self-esteem that come from competence, authority, and status, as well as the economic benefits of continuing to work. The latter include not merely income but also, frequently, medical insurance, which is of particular importance to people in the cohorts approaching retirement.

R. M. Cohn reported in the *Journal of Gerontology* (1979) that as people approach retirement, their work satisfaction begins to decrease in its relationship to overall life satisfaction. This may be related to the Freudian idea of decathexis or the social gerontological theory of disengagement. It suggests that the last few years before retirement may be difficult for many employees (and, perhaps, for their employers).

Context

An understanding of adulthood and aging would be impossible in contemporary times without a consideration of the phenomenon of retirement. For many people, the period of retirement will occupy at least one-quarter of their entire life, perhaps considerably more. An understanding of retirement and the role it plays throughout adult life should provide a perspective that will enrich the lives of many. Robert C. Atchley is a pioneer in the study of gerontology in general and retirement in particular. His well-known description of the "phases" of retirement helps to put this significant aspect of life into context.

Atchley's first phase is actually preretirement. This phase may begin a long time before the actual retirement day. It is often filled with fantasies of what retirement will be like. The fantasies may be fairly accurate, or they may be totally unrealistic. If the fantasies do not have a fair degree of realism about them, they may hamper a smooth transition to the actualities of retirement. If the fantasies motivate the individual to make concrete plans about finances, about the location of the retirement home, about provisions for activities, and about many other decisions which need to be made, the fantasies may make a major contribution to a successful retirement.

The second phase is the honeymoon. The honeymoon may involve travel, a hectic social pace, an acting out of some of the preretirement fantasies. The honeymoon may last weeks or years. To a large extent, it depends upon relatively good health, adequate finances, and a positive attitude. The honeymoon cannot last forever, however, and over a period of time, most people settle into a retirement routine. (A classic longitudinal study by James Birren and Robert Butler in the 1960's and 1970's found that one of the most important variables related to successful retirement, and even to length of life, was to have a well-organized daily routine rather than drifting from one chaotic day to the next.)

The next phase, which probably does not apply to all retirees, is disenchantment. This is a period of letdown, even depression. Atchley believes that the more unrealistic the preretirement fantasies were, the more likely a difficult time of disenchantment. The fourth phase is reorientation. People who were disenchanted must "pull themselves together." They begin to develop a more realistic view of this period of their lives. They explore new ways of remaining involved in life and in the community. They may begin to use a senior center for the first time, find a part-time job, develop a hobby, or volunteer for a worthwhile project.

The next phase is that of stability. In most people, this is the longest period in their retirement experience. Atchley describes this as the phase when "people have developed a set of criteria for dealing routinely with change." They recognize their capabilities and limitations. Their pattern of life in retirement is fairly predictable and usually quite satisfying. They have, more or less, adapted to their retirement role.

The final phase is termination. In a sense, this is really no longer part of retirement. What for many is a good retirement, which they have earned and are entitled to, is now replaced by the role of being a sick or dying person. Retirement is no longer a relevant category; the chronic illnesses of old age have taken over. Although many persons go through this phase with great dignity, often the indignities of dementia or institutionalization diminish the individual.

It is important to point out that Atchley's phases are true only in the sense that they refer to an idealized way of looking at the processes related to retirement. There are so many individual differences, so many variations in health and income, so many idiosyncrasies. Spouses may have to act as nurses for their mates. Women who were married at the time of retirement are likely to live five or more years as widows. Incomes which were adequate at retirement may be ravaged by inflation twenty or thirty years later. Retirement may indeed be the best time of life for many, or at least as good as any other time, but no one can ignore the realities. Every period of life has its share of crises, and retirement is no exception.

Bibliography

Atchley, Robert C. *The Social Forces in Later Life.* 3d ed. Belmont, Calif.: Wadsworth, 1980. A basic introduction to many of the issues related to aging. Chapter 8 deals particularly with retirement.

_____. *The Sociology of Retirement.* Cambridge, Mass.: Schenkman, 1976. One of the classic books on retirement, it is based in large part on the author's own research.

Baum, Martha, and Rainer C. Baum. *Growing Old.* Englewood Cliffs, N.J.: Prentice-Hall, 1980. A unique and excellent book on the many issues related to growing old in American society. Chapter 1, "Theoretical Perspectives," and chapter 4, "Retirement: An Emerging Social Institution," are particularly relevant and stimulating.

Hayslip, Bert, Jr., and Paul E. Panek. *Adult Development and Aging.* New York: Harper & Row, 1989. An excellent textbook on the adult period of life. Chapter 11 deals with retirement. Has an extensive list of references; particularly good for finding research journal articles on particular aspects of retirement and other issues.

Palmore, Erdman B., et al. *Retirement: Causes and Consequences.* New York: Springer, 1986. A good general overview of retirement by a number of scholars in the field. Some chapters read well; others require more acquaintance with social-science methodology.

James Taylor Henderson

Cross-References

Ageism, 156; Aging: Cognitive Changes, 180; Aging: Institutional Care, 186; Aging: Physical Changes, 192; Career Selection, Development, and Change, 474; Grandparenthood, 1107; Integrity: Erikson, 1321.

RULE-GOVERNED BEHAVIOR

Type of psychology: Learning
Fields of study: Behavioral and cognitive models; instrumental conditioning

A rule (or instruction) is a verbal stimulus that describes a behavior and its consequences. Rules can establish even complicated behaviors quickly and effectively, but they may produce insensitivity to changing contingencies. The study of rules allows an operant analysis of processes which are often termed "cognitive."

Principal terms
CONTINGENCY: a conditional relation between a response and its consequence or between a discriminative stimulus, a response, and a consequence
DISCRIMINATIVE STIMULUS: a stimulus that signals the availability of a consequence, given that a response occurs
OPERANT BEHAVIOR: behavior that operates on the environment and whose probability is affected by the consequences it produces (sometimes called instrumental behavior)
RULE: a contingency-specifying stimulus, or a verbal statement describing a behavior-outcome relation
RULE-GOVERNED BEHAVIOR: behavior under the control of a dual set of contingencies (the behavior-outcome relation described in the rule and the social consequences for rule-following)
SCHEDULE OF REINFORCEMENT: an arrangement that specifies which responses within an operant class will be reinforced
SHAPING: a procedure based on differential reinforcement for successive approximations of a response to its desired form
STIMULUS CONTROL: behavior occasioned by a stimulus because the stimulus signals some consequence of responding

Overview

Following the tradition of B. F. Skinner, the famous Harvard University psychologist who pioneered the study of operant conditioning, behavior analysts initially examined the behavior of rats and pigeons because nonhuman subjects could be studied under well-controlled conditions in the experimental laboratory. This made it possible for operant psychologists to discover a number of important behavioral principles and to demonstrate that much of the behavior of their experimental subjects was shaped and maintained by contingencies of reinforcement. "Contingencies" can be thought of as cause-effect relations between a context (in operant terms, a "discriminative stimulus"), an action ("response"), and the consequence ("reinforcement") it produces. For example, if pressing a bar is followed by food only when a light is on and never when it is off, a rat's behavior is gradually shaped by these contingencies until the rat only presses the lever when the light is on.

When operant researchers began to bring human subjects into the laboratory, however, the analysis went beyond behavior directly shaped by contingencies to include behavior under the control of instructions or rules. According to Skinner (1966), a rule is a "contingency-specifying stimulus." It functions as a discriminative stimulus (SD), but it differs from other SDs in that it is a *description* of a behavior-outcome relation. Other SDs are stimuli in the environment that acquire control over behavior only through specific training; rules, in contrast, have an immediate effect on behavior because they make use of an already existing language repertoire. For example, through a history of careful shaping, a seeing-eye dog can be trained to stop at red lights and cross the street only when the light is green. A verbal child, however, can be taught the same discrimination simply by being told, "Go when the light is green; don't go when the light is red."

Proverbs, maxims, advice, instructions, commands, and so forth all function as rules when they control behavior. In complete form, rules specify an antecedent condition, an action, and its consequences, and take the form of if-then statements, as in "If you want to get to the other side safely, [then] cross the street only when the light is green." Most rules, however, are only partial statements of contingencies, either specifying exclusively the antecedent (such as a male figure or the word MEN on a door), the behavior (a sign reading DO NOT ENTER), or the consequence ("Lose 25 lbs. in one month!"), and it is left to the individual to fill in the blanks.

Despite an abundance of rules in the human environment, many people are not reliable rule followers. Otherwise, through the mere presence of rules, drivers would respect speed limits, students would study, obese persons would stick to diets, and telling people "Just say no" would solve the drug problem in American society. Control by rules is often deficient because rules only determine the topography, or form, of behavior, but they do not impart the motivation to act. Stated differently, rules tell people what to do (such as "Just say no"), but whether people actually do it depends on other circumstances.

For a rule to be followed, it must be part of an effective contingency: Either the outcome specified in the rule must function as a reinforcer, or the rule giver must be able to mediate aversive consequences for noncompliance. Psychologists Steven C. Hayes and Robert D. Zettle have drawn an important distinction between contingency-shaped and rule-governed behavior. They assert that contingency-shaped behavior is controlled by one set of contingencies, usually consisting of a situation, an action, and a consequence (such as being offered a cigarette, smoking, and feeling relaxed).

In contrast, rule-governed behavior involves two sets of contingencies. One of them is the behavior-outcome relation specified in the rule itself ("If you want to avoid addiction, just say no"). The second involves social consequences for rule following, such as praise or criticism from significant others or social pressure to comply with peer norms. As the following examples will show, at times both sets of contingencies support rule following, but sometimes they compete with each other. Assume that a man is lost and his wife insists that he ask for directions. He is told to "turn left at the light and then follow the signs to the interstate." The man is likely to follow these directions, because both sets of contingencies surrounding rule following are congruent: The natural consequences of finding the highway are indeed reinforcing to him, and the social consequences are reinforcing because following the directions will satisfy his wife and spare him criticism. Now assume that a child is given a box of candy. Her mother says, "You may have only one piece of candy before dinner, or else you will spoil your appetite." The contingency specified in the rule may be ineffective, because eating only one piece of candy if there is more may never have been reinforcing to the child. Hence, if the child obeys, it is not for the contingency specified in the rule but for the parental consequences that would result from noncompliance.

Behavior under the control of a description of contingencies does not involve a new process, but is consistent with an operant framework postulating that the probability of behavior is controlled by its outcome. Rule governance results from an extensive history of reinforcement in which rule following has directly led to contact with the contingencies specified in the rule, to social consequences associated with compliance and noncompliance, or both.

Applications

Teaching people to follow rules is important for a number of reasons, which B. F. Skinner outlined in his book *About Behaviorism* (1974). Most important, many behaviors can be acquired much more quickly through rules than through shaping by the contingencies described in the rules. For example, it is easier to teach a boy the basics of a card game by explaining the rules to him than by playing with him until he gradually (if at all) figures out the rules for himself. Furthermore, there are cases when the contingencies are so complex or vague that most people would never contact them without the help of rules. Learning to type with ten fingers illustrates such a case. Without appropriate instruction, the immediate success accruing from a "hunt-and-peck" method will reinforce typing with two fingers, and the person will never learn to use ten fingers, even though in the long run this would have been much more efficient.

According to Roger L. Poppen (1989), initially people learn rules from a multitude of external sources such as parents, peers, teachers, television, and books, and eventually they learn to extract rules from interacting with and observing environmental contingencies. Parents encourage the rehearsal and internalization of rules so that these self-instructions then help children guide their own behavior in similar circumstances.

The effects of rules on behavior have been extensively studied within a behavior-analytic methodology. A summary of this research can be found in a chapter by Margaret Vaughan in the book *Rule-Governed Behavior: Cognitions, Contingencies, and Instructional Control*, edited by Steven C. Hayes (1989). Most of these human operant studies use a method in which subjects press a button that, according to some schedule of reinforcement, occasionally produces points exchangeable for money. Depending on the preparation, button pressing may be controlled by the contingency between pressing and point delivery; in this case, the behavior would be contingency-shaped. Button pressing may also be controlled by experimenter instructions, in which case the behavior would be rule governed. A number of studies showed that experimenter-provided instructions quickly bring the behavior under stimulus control but also create insensitivity to the scheduled contingencies. For example, telling subjects that "the best way to earn points is to press the button fast" (a fixed-ratio contingency) immediately allows them to respond correctly and earn points. When the contingencies are then surreptitiously changed, however, subjects continue to follow the instructions for long periods of time although they have become obsolete and no longer produce points. In contrast, when subjects receive no instructions and their responses are shaped, sensitivity to changing contingencies develops; that is, when the schedule of reinforcement changes, subjects adjust their behavior to the new schedule and continue to earn points. This observation has led operant researchers to conclude that insensitivity to contingencies may be an inherent property of instructional control.

The insensitivity effect of rules has intriguing implications: Instructing people how to solve problems is immediately effective, but it may be counterproductive in the long run, because individuals may come to act in accordance with outdated rules. Their behavior may come to be guided by what cognitivists call "irrational beliefs" or "unrealistic expectations," which from an operant perspective would be considered inaccurate statements about contingencies resulting from broad overgeneralizations of old rules. The following example illustrates how an "irrational belief" may come to control behavior. A mother might tell her child, "Stop making noise! I don't love you when you are bad." This rule may quiet the child immediately, and because it is effective, the parent may use it in other situations. Over the course of her development, the child learns many instances of what her parent considers "bad" (perhaps disobeying instructions, perhaps asserting herself, showing anger, and so on). Gradually she internalizes a generalized rule, "I am only lovable when others approve of me," and evolves into an adult who is trying to please everybody and feels unworthy at any sign of disapproval, however ineffective this behavior may be.

Humans live in a world in which rules abound, in the form of instructions, advice, warnings, cookbooks, self-help books, laws, and social norms. They are intended to provide guidelines for effective behavior. Even when no external rules are available, most people can formulate their own plans of action. The greatest advantage of rules is that they can be extremely helpful and can establish effective behavior quickly. Their greatest disadvantages are that rules do not produce behavior unless other contingencies support rule following and (as Skinner has pointed out) that they may be troublesome rather than helpful when the contingencies change but the rules do not.

Context

Operant research with human subjects emerged in the 1950's. Originally, behavioral researchers attempted to replicate findings from experimental work with rats and pigeons to demonstrate the generality of the principles of behavior discovered in the animal laboratory. It soon became apparent that people often showed response patterns not comparable to those of animal subjects on the same schedules of reinforcement. For example, a cumulative record of responding on a fixed-interval schedule for animals typically shows "scallops" (a pause after reinforcement, followed by a gradually accelerating response rate until delivery of the next reinforcer). In contrast, human subjects typically time the interval by counting; toward the end, they respond as few times as necessary to obtain the reinforcer.

Behavior analysts suspected that the differences between human and animal responding mainly stemmed from people's prior conditioning history and from instructions, both experimenter-provided and self-generated, with which they approached the experimental tasks. These assumptions began to focus the attention of operant researchers on the role of instructions. By the mid-1970's, instruction following became synonymous with rule-governed behavior and began to evolve into a field of study in its own right.

One importance of rule governance lies in the possibility of a rapprochement between behaviorist and cognitivist positions. Behaviorists have often been accused of disregarding or failing to acknowledge the importance of "higher mental processes." While such accusations are polemic and extremely misleading, it is true that it was not until the mid-1970's that operant psychologists began a systematic empirical analysis of cognitive-verbal processes. The study of rule-governed behavior marked the beginning of the experimental analysis of phenomena that until then pertained to the domain of cognitive psychology.

The analysis of rule-governed behavior is important for another reason. It provides some insights into causal mechanisms that may underlie current cognitive therapies. For example, Roger Poppen (1987) presents an excellent theoretical analysis of a self-efficacy approach and of rational-emotive therapy, while Zettle and Hayes (1982) present a similar analysis of cognitive restructuring and cognitive therapy for depression. The common denominator of these diverse cognitive approaches is their assertion that people's reactions to their environment are mediated by covert verbal statements, which, when dysfunctional, are given labels such as irrational beliefs, low self-efficacy, and negative expectancies. From an operant perspective, such formal categorizations are considered not very useful because formally distinct verbal statements may all have the same function, while statements identical in form may have different functions (one person might say "I can't do it; I'm too dumb" to avoid an unpleasant task, while another person may say the same thing to request assistance).

Within a framework of rule-governed behavior, all these "dysfunctional cognitions" are considered partial statements of contingencies, and the behavior they produce is rule governed. Hence, findings from basic experimental research on rule-governed behavior could conceivably be brought to bear on clinical phenomena, which eventually might lead to a better understanding of psychological dysfunctions and to the development of more effective therapies.

Bibliography

Catania, A. Charles. *Learning.* 2d ed. Englewood Cliffs, N.J.: Prentice-Hall, 1984. Chapter 9 of this book deals with an operant approach to language. On pp. 238-240, Catania presents an excellent brief summary of rule-governed behavior.

Hayes, Steven C., ed. *Rule-Governed Behavior: Cognitions, Contingencies, and Instructional Control.* New York: Plenum Press, 1989. A compendium of ten chapters written by eminent behaviorists who present an in-depth analysis of different aspects of rule-governed behavior. Some of the chapters are very difficult to understand, but others are more accessible. Chapter 2, by B. F. Skinner; chapter 3, by Margaret Vaughan; chapter 9, by Roger L. Poppen; and chapter 10, by Steven C. Hayes et al. are highly recommended.

Poppen, Roger L. "Some Clinical Implications of Rule-Governed Behavior." In *Rule-Governed Behavior: Cognitions, Contingencies, and Instructional Control*, edited by Steven C. Hayes. New York: Plenum Press, 1989. Contains a compelling analysis of clinical phenomena that until recently have been regarded the exclusive domain of cognitive therapists. Poppen shows how rule-governed behavior may account for so-called maladaptive cognitions in terms of ineffective rules. He suggests ways to integrate behavioral and cognitive approaches to therapy.

Skinner, B. F. *About Behaviorism.* New York: Alfred A. Knopf, 1974. This book is highly recommended for anybody not familiar with behaviorism and an operant approach to psychology. It provides an in-depth introduction to behaviorism as a science of behavior and is very readable. A compressed analysis of rule-governed behavior is presented, beginning on p. 123.

_____. "An Operant Analysis of Problem Solving." In *Problem-Solving: Research, Method, and Theory*, edited by Benjamin Kleinmuntz. New York: John Wiley & Sons, 1966. Although Skinner clearly differentiated between two types of operant behavior as early as 1947, when he gave the William James lectures at Harvard University, it was not until 1966 that he published a paper exclusively on this topic. Skinner's paper is recommended to familiarize the student with the original source of the topic.

Vaughan, Margaret. "Rule-Governed Behavior in Behavior Analysis: A Theoretical and Experimental History." In *Rule-Governed Behavior: Cognitions, Contingencies, and Instructional Control*, edited by Steven C. Hayes. New York: Plenum Press, 1989. Vaughan traces the history of rule-governed behavior from the 1950's to 1989 and presents a very accessible summary of relevant experimental research.

Zettle, Robert D., and Steven C. Hayes. "Rule-Governed Behavior: A Potential Theoretical Framework for Cognitive-Behavioral Therapy." In *Advances in Cognitive-Behavioral Research and Therapy*, edited by Philip C. Kendall. Vol. 1. New York: Academic Press, 1982. This chapter presents one of the most widely cited explanations of rule governance. The authors were the first to draw attention to the dual set of contingencies surrounding rules. The chapter also examines the role of self-rules and presents a compelling analysis of various cognitive therapies in terms of rule-governed behavior.

Edelgard Wulfert

Cross-References

SAMPLING

Type of psychology: Psychological methodologies
Fields of study: Experimental methodologies; methodological issues

Probability sampling is a scientific method that uses random selection to generate representative samples from populations. It enables researchers to make relatively few observations and to generalize from those observations to a much wider population. Nonprobability sampling does not ensure the representativeness of selected samples.

Principal terms

ELEMENT: the basic unit about which information is collected and that provides the basis of analysis

OBSERVATION UNIT: the person or persons from whom researchers collect information about a target element; observation units and elements are often identical

PARAMETER: a numerical characteristic of a population

POPULATION: a comprehensive and well-defined group (a universal set) of the elements pertinent to a given research question or hypothesis

SAMPLE: a subset of a population; a group of elements selected from a larger, well-defined pool of elements

SAMPLING ERROR: the extent to which population parameters deviate from sample statistics

SAMPLING FRAME: a list of the sampling units from which a sample is selected; for example, a voter registration roll is the sampling frame for the population of registered voters

SAMPLING UNIT: the element or set of elements considered for selection in some stage of sampling

STATISTIC: a numerical characteristic of a sample; sample statistics are used to make estimates of population parameters

VALIDITY: the condition achieved when conclusions about a sample can be generalized to the population from which the sample was obtained

Overview

A critical part of social research is the decision as to what will be observed and what will not. It is often impractical or even impossible to survey or observe every element of interest. Sampling methodology provides guidelines for choosing from a population some smaller group that represents the population's important characteristics. There are two general approaches to selecting samples: probability and nonprobability sampling.

Probability sampling techniques allow researchers to select relatively few elements and generalize from these sample elements to the much larger population. For example, in the 1984 United States presidential election, George Gallup's final preelection poll correctly predicted that the popular vote would split 59 percent to 41 percent in favor of Ronald Reagan. This accurate prediction was based on the stated voting intentions of a tiny fraction—less than 0.01 percent—of the 92.5 million people who voted in the election. Accuracy was possible because Gallup used probability sampling techniques to choose a sample that was representative of the general population. A sample is representative of the population from which it is chosen if the aggregate characteristics of the sample closely approximate those same aggregate characteristics in the population. Samples, however, need not be representative in all respects; representativeness is limited to those characteristics that are relevant to the substantive interests of the study. The most widely used probability sampling methods are simple random sampling, systematic sampling with a random start, stratified sampling, and multistage cluster sampling.

Nonprobability sampling methods, such as purposive, convenience, and quota sampling, do not ensure a representative sample. These samples are not useful for drawing conclusions about the population because there is no way to measure the sampling error. Purposive and convenience sampling allow the researcher to choose samples that fit his or her particular interest or convenience; quota sampling aims to generate a representative sample by developing a complex sampling frame (a quota matrix) that divides the population into relevant subclasses. Aside from being cumbersome, however, the nonrandom selection of samples from each cell of the quota matrix decreases the likelihood of generating a representative sample.

Probability theory is based on random selection procedures and assumes three things: that each random sample drawn from a population provides an estimate of the true population parameter, that multiple random samples drawn from the same population will yield statistics that cluster around the true population value in a predictable way, and that it is possible to calculate the sampling error associated with any one sample. The magnitude of sampling error associated with any random sample is a function of two variables: the homogeneity of the population from which the random sample is drawn and the sample's size. A more homogeneous parent population will have a smaller sampling error associated with a given random sample. Moreover, sampling error declines as the size of one's random sample increases, since larger samples are more likely than smaller ones to capture a representative portion of the parent population. In fact, when dealing with small populations (less than fifty members), collecting data on the entire population rather than using a sample is recommended because this often improves the reliability and credibility of the data.

When sampling is necessary, it is essential that the researcher first consider the quality of the sampling frame. A sampling frame is the list or quasi list of elements from which a probability sample is selected. Often, sampling frames do not truly include all of the elements that their names might imply. For example, telephone directories are often taken to be a listing of a city's population. There are several defects in this reasoning, but the major one involves a social-class bias. Poor people are less likely to have telephones; therefore, a telephone directory sample is likely to have a middle- and upper-class bias. In order to generalize to the population composing the sampling frame, it is necessary for all of the elements to have equal representation in the frame. Elements that occur more than once will have a greater probability of selection, and the overall sample will overrepresent those elements.

Regardless of how carefully the researcher chooses a sampling frame and a representative sample from it, sample values are only approximations of population parameters. Probability theory enables the researcher to estimate how far the sample statistic is likely to diverge from population values, using two key indices called confidence levels and confidence intervals. Both of these are calculated by mathematical procedures that can be found in any basic statistics book.

A confidence level specifies how confident the researcher can be that the statistics are reliable estimates of population parameters, and a confidence interval stipulates how far the population parameters might be expected to deviate from sample values. For example, in the 1984 presidential election, *The Washington Post* polled a sample of 8,969 registered voters; based on their responses, the newspaper reported that 57 percent of the vote would go to Ronald Reagan and 39 percent would go to Walter Mondale. The poll in *The Washington Post* had a confidence level of 95 percent, and its confidence interval was plus or minus three percentage points. This means that pollsters could be 95 percent confident that Reagan's share of the 92.5 million popular votes would range between 54 percent and 60 percent, while Mondale's vote would vary between 36 percent and 42 percent. When reporting predictions based on probability sampling, the researcher should always report the confidence level and confidence interval associated with the sample.

Applications

A basic principle of probability sampling is that a sample will be representative of the population from which it is selected if all members of the population have an equal chance of being selected in the sample. Flipping a coin is the most frequently cited example: The "selection" of a head or a tail is independent of previous selections of heads or tails. Instead of flipping a coin, however, a table of random numbers is usually used.

A simple random sample may be generated by assigning consecutive numbers to the elements in a sampling frame, generating a list of random numbers equal to one's desired sample size, and selecting from the sampling frame all elements having assigned numbers that correspond to one's list of random numbers. This is the basic sampling method assumed in survey statistical computations, but it is seldom used in practice because it is often cumbersome and inefficient. For that reason, researchers usually prefer systematic sampling with a random start. This approach under appropriate circumstances, can generate equally representative samples with relative ease.

A systematic sample with a random start is generated by selecting every element of a certain number (for example, every fifth element) listed in a sampling frame.

Thus, a systematic sample of one hundred can be derived from a sampling frame containing one thousand elements by selecting every tenth element in the frame. To ensure against any possible human bias, the first element should be chosen at random. Although systematic sampling is relatively uncomplicated, it yields samples that are highly representative of the populations from which they are drawn. The researcher should be alert, however, to the potential systematic sampling problem called sampling frame periodicity, which does not affect simple random methods. If the sampling frame is arranged in a cyclical pattern that coincides with the sampling interval, a grossly biased sample may be drawn.

Earl Babbie has described a study of soldiers that illustrates how sampling frame periodicity can produce seriously unrepresentative systematic samples. He reports that the researchers used unit rosters as sampling frames and selected every tenth soldier for the study. The rosters, however, were arranged by squads containing ten members each, and squad members were listed by rank, with sergeants first, followed by corporals and privates. Because this cyclical arrangement coincided with the ten-element sampling interval, the resulting sample contained only sergeants.

Sampling frame periodicity, although a serious threat to sampling validity, can be avoided if researchers carefully study the sampling frame for evidence of periodicity. Periodicity can be corrected by randomizing the entire list before sampling from it or by drawing a simple random sample from within each cyclical portion of the frame.

The third method of probability sampling, stratified sampling, is not an alternative to systematic sampling or simple random sampling; rather, it represents a modified framework within which the two methods are used. Instead of sampling from a total population as simple and systematic methods do, stratified sampling organizes a population into homogeneous subsets and selects elements from each subset, using either systematic or simple random procedures. To generate a stratified sample, the researcher begins by specifying the population subgroups, or stratification variables, that are to be represented in a sample. After stipulating these variables, the researcher divides all sampling frame elements into homogeneous subsets representing a saturated mix of relevant stratification characteristics. Once the population has been stratified, a researcher uses either simple random sampling or systematic sampling with a random start to generate a representative sample from the elements falling within each subgroup. Stratified sampling methods can generate a highly useful sample of any well-defined population and may have a smaller sampling error than any other sampling method.

Simple random sampling, systematic sampling, and stratified sampling are reasonably simple procedures for sampling from lists of elements. If one wishes to sample from a very large population, however, such as all university students in the United States, a comprehensive sampling frame may not be available. In this case, a modified sampling method, called multistage cluster sampling, is appropriate. It begins with the systematic or simple random selection of subgroups or clusters within a population, followed by a systematic or simple random selection of elements within each selected cluster. For example, if a researcher were interested in the population of all university students in the United States, it would be possible to create a list of all the universities, then sample them using either stratified or systematic sampling procedures. Next, the researcher could obtain lists of students from each of the sample universities; each of those lists would then be sampled to provide the final list of university students for study.

Multistage cluster sampling is an efficient method of sampling a very large population, but the price of that efficiency is a less accurate sample. While a simple random sample drawn from a population list is subject to a single sampling error, a two-stage cluster sample is subject to two sampling errors. The best way to avoid this problem is to maximize the number of clusters selected while decreasing the number of elements within each cluster.

Context

As Raymond Jessen points out, the theory of sampling is probably one of the oldest branches of statistical theory. It has only been since the early twentieth century, however, that there has been much progress in applying that theory to, and developing a new theory for, statistical surveys. One of the earliest applications for sampling was in political polling, perhaps because this area provides researchers with the opportunity to discover the accuracy of their estimates fairly quickly. This area has also been useful in detecting errors in sampling methods. For example, in 1936, the *Literary Digest*, which had been accurate in predicting the winners of the United States presidential elections since 1920, inaccurately predicted that Republican contender Alfred Landon would win 57 percent of the vote over incumbent President Franklin D. Roosevelt's 43 percent. The *Literary Digest*'s mistake was an unrepresentative sampling frame consisting of telephone directories and automobile registration lists. This frame resulted in a disproportionately wealthy sample, excluding poor people who predominantly favored Roosevelt's New Deal recovery programs. This emphasized to researchers that a representative sampling frame was crucial if the sample was to be valid.

In the 1940's, the U.S. Bureau of the Census developed unequal probability sampling theory, and area-probability sampling methods became widely used and sophisticated in both theory and practice. The 1945 census of agriculture in the United States was collected in part on a sample, and the 1950 census of population made extensive use of built-in samples to increase its accuracy and reduce costs.

One of the most important advances for sampling techniques has been increasingly sophisticated computer technology. For example, once the sampling frame is entered into the computer, a simple random sample can be selected automatically. In the future, computer technology, coupled with increasingly efficient and accurate information-gathering technology, will enable researchers to select samples that more accurately represent the population.

Sampling techniques are essential for researchers in psychology. Without relying on sampling as the basis for collecting evaluative data, the risk and cost involved with adopting new methods of treatment would be difficult to justify. Evaluating the effectiveness of new programs would be prohibitive, and some populations are so large and dispersed that observing each element is impossible.

Probability sampling is the most effective method for the selection of study elements in the field of psychology for two reasons. First, it avoids conscious or unconscious biases in element selection on the part of the researcher. If all elements in the population have an equal chance of selection, there is an excellent chance that a sample so selected will closely represent the population of all elements. Secondly, probability sampling permits estimates of sampling error. Although no probability sample will be perfectly representative in all respects, controlled selection methods permit the researcher to estimate the degree of expected error in that regard.

Bibliography

Babbie, Earl R. *The Practice of Social Research.* 4th ed. Belmont, Calif.: Wadsworth, 1986. Written in clear, easy-to-understand language with many illustrations. Babbie discusses both the logic and the skills necessary to understand sampling and randomization. Contains appendices, a bibliography, an index, and an excellent glossary. One of the appendixes contains a table of random numbers.

Blalock, Hubert M., Jr. *Social Statistics.* New York: McGraw-Hill, 1979. Provides an extensive section on sampling that pays particular attention to random sampling, systematic sampling, stratified sampling, and cluster sampling. Although there are some formulas and computations, the majority of the discussion is not technical, and the explanations are clear.

Henry, Gary T. *Practical Sampling.* Newbury Park, Calif.: Sage Publications, 1990. Provides detailed examples of selecting alternatives in actual sampling practice. Not heavily theoretical or mathematical, although the material is based on the theoretical and mathematical sampling work that has preceded it. Provides references for those interested in proceeding deeper into the literature.

Jessen, Raymond James. *Statistical Survey Techniques.* New York: John Wiley & Sons, 1978. Provides a clear introduction to statistical sampling. The examples are clear and relevant, and they illustrate the points made on sampling technique. Although this book is not written for mathematicians, each chapter contains mathematical notes that demonstrate points made in the chapter.

Kish, Leslie. *Survey Sampling.* New York: John Wiley & Sons, 1965. This book is the definitive work on sampling in social research; the coverage ranges from the simplest matters to the most complex and mathematical. Somewhat difficult reading, but Kish manages to be both highly theoretical and extremely practical.

Sudman, Seymour. *Applied Sampling.* New York: Academic Press, 1976. Intended for the majority of survey users who have only limited statistical backgrounds, this book is more readable and less technical than Kish's book. Takes a pragmatic approach to sampling, and provides excellent examples and illustrations.

Karen Anding Fontenot

Cross-References

Data Description: Inferential Statistics, 757; Hypothesis Development and Testing, 1248; Psychological Experimentation: Independent, Dependent, and Control Variables, 1932; The Scientific Method in Psychology, 2148; Statistical Significance Tests, 2375; Survey Research: Questionnaires and Interviews, 2507.

SCHIZOPHRENIA: BACKGROUND, TYPES, AND SYMPTOMS

Type of psychology: Psychopathology
Field of study: Schizophrenias

Schizophrenia is a severe mental illness that interferes with the patient's ability to think and communicate. Researchers have studied the illness for decades, but the causes are still unknown.

Principal terms

ANTIPSYCHOTIC DRUGS: medications, including a group called the
    phenothiazines, that reduce psychotic symptoms
ETIOLOGY: the study of the causes of disease
PROGNOSIS: the expected course and outcome of a disorder
PSYCHOTIC SYMPTOMS: symptoms of major mental disorder that involve
    a loss of contact with reality, such as delusions or hallucinations
SOMATIC TREATMENTS: physical treatments of the body, including drugs
    and surgery

Overview

Schizophrenia affects approximately one out of every hundred individuals. It is considered to be one of the most severe mental illnesses, because its symptoms can have a devastating impact on the life of the patient. The patient's thought processes, communication abilities, and emotional expressions are disturbed. As a result, many patients with schizophrenia are dependent on others for assistance with daily life activities.

Schizophrenia is often confused, by the layperson, with multiple personality disorder. The latter is an illness which is defined as two or more distinct personalities existing within the person. The personalities tend to be intact, and each is associated with its own style of perceiving the world and relating to others. Schizophrenia, in contrast, does not involve the existence of two or more personalities; rather, it is the presence of psychotic symptoms that defines schizophrenia.

The diagnostic criteria for schizophrenia have changed over the years; however, certain key symptoms, including disturbances in thought, perception, and emotional experiences, have remained as defining features. The most widely used criteria for diagnosing schizophrenia are those listed in the *Diagnostic and Statistical Manual of Mental Disorders* (rev. 3d ed., 1987, DSM-III-R). This manual is published by the American Psychiatric Association and is periodically revised to incorporate changes in diagnostic criteria.

The DSM-III-R contains the following symptoms for diagnosing schizophrenia: delusions, hallucinations, flat or inappropriate affect, and incoherence or loosening of associations. No single specific symptom is required for a person to receive a diagnosis of schizophrenia. Further, each of the above symptoms can take a variety of forms. Delusions are defined as false beliefs based on incorrect inference about external reality. Delusions are classified based on the nature of their content. For example, grandiose delusions involve false beliefs about one's importance, power, or knowledge. The patient might express the belief that he or she is the most intelligent person in the world but that these special intellectual powers have gone unrecognized. As another example, persecutory delusions involve beliefs of being persecuted or conspired against by others. The patient might claim, for example, that there is a government plot to poison him or her.

Hallucinations are sensory experiences that occur in the absence of a real stimulus. In the case of auditory hallucinations, the patient may hear voices calling or conversing when there is no one in physical proximity. Visual hallucinations may involve seeing people who are deceased or seeing inanimate objects move on their own accord.

The term "affect" is used to refer to observable behaviors that are the expression of an emotion. Affect is predominantly displayed in facial expressions. When affect is inappropriate, facial expressions are not consistent with the content of a patient's speech or thoughts. For example, the patient might laugh when discussing the death of a loved one. "Flat" affect describes a severe reduction in the intensity of emotional expressions, both positive and negative. Patients with flat affect may show no observable sign of emotion, even when experiencing a very joyful or sad event.

Among the symptoms of schizophrenia, abnormalities in the expression of thoughts are a central feature. When speech is incoherent, it is difficult for the listener to comprehend because it is illogical or incomplete. As an example, in response to the question "Where do you live?," one patient replied, "Yes, live! I haven't had much time in this or that. It is an area. In the same area. Mrs. Smith! If the time comes for a temporary space now or whatever." The term "loose associations" is applied to speech in which ideas shift from one subject to another subject that is completely unrelated. If the loosening of associations is severe, speech may be incoherent. As an illustration of loose associations, in describing her daily schedule at home, one patient said, "It starts out pretty easy, but things always become more complicated. I discussed this with my son, but he doesn't understand. Of course, he is an accountant and his wife recently had a baby. I thought I would enjoy being a grandmother, but now I'm not sure."

With regard to speech, a variety of other abnormalities are sometimes shown by patients. They may use "neologisms," which are new words invented by the patient to convey a special meaning. Some show "clang associations," which involve the use of rhyming words in conversation: "Live and let live, that's my motto. You live and give and live-give." Abnormalities in the intonation and pace of speech are also common.

In addition to these symptoms, some patients manifest bizarre behaviors, such as odd, repetitive movements or unusual postures. Odd or inappropriate styles of dressing, such as wearing winter coats in the summer, may also occur in some patients. More deteriorated patients frequently show poor hygiene. In order to meet the diagnostic criteria for schizophrenia, the individual must show signs of disturbance for at least six months. Further, the presence of other disorders, such as drug reactions or organic brain disorders associated with aging, must be ruled out. Thus, the diagnosis of schizophrenia typically involves a thorough physical and mental assessment.

Applications

Because no one symptom is necessary for a diagnosis of schizophrenia, patients vary in the numbers and intensity of their symptoms. Four subtypes of schizophrenia are recognized; the differentiation among them is based upon the symptom profile, and the criteria are clearly described in DSM-III-R.

Catatonic schizophrenia is predominantly characterized by abnormal motor behavior. The patient may be in a "catatonic stupor," which means that he or she shows a marked reduction in movement and is sometimes mute. Other catatonic schizophrenic patients adopt a rigid posture (catatonic rigidity), which they will maintain despite efforts to move them. In disorganized schizophrenia, the primary symptoms are incoherence, loose associations, and flat or inappropriate affect. In paranoid schizophrenia, the predominant symptom is a preoccupation with a systematized delusion, in the absence of incoherence, loose associations, or abnormal affect. The label undifferentiated schizophrenia is applied to cases that do not meet the specific criteria for catatonic, disorganized, or paranoid schizophrenia, but do show prominent delusions, hallucinations, incoherence, or disorganized behavior.

In his writings, Eugen Bleuler often used the phrase "the group of schizophrenias," because he believed the disorder could be caused by a variety of factors. In other words, he believed that schizophrenia may not be a single disease entity. Today, many researchers and clinicians who work in the field take the same position. They believe that the differences among patients in symptom patterns and the course of the illness are attributable to differences in etiology. Despite the widespread assumption that there are different subtypes of schizophrenia, however, each with its own etiology, there is no definitive evidence to support this. In fact, the four subtypes listed in DSM-III-R show similar courses and receive the same medications and psychotherapeutic treatments. Thus the distinctions among them are purely descriptive at this point.

Because schizophrenic symptoms have such a devastating impact on the individual's ability to function, family members often respond to the onset of symptoms by seeking immediate treatment. Clinicians, in turn, often respond by recommending hospitalization so that tests can be conducted and an appropriate treatment can be determined. Consequently, almost all patients who are diagnosed with schizophrenia are hospitalized at least once in their life. The majority experience several hospitalizations. Typically, the first hospitalization corresponds to the first manifestation of symptoms.

Research on the long-term outcome of schizophrenia indicates that the illness is highly variable in its course. A minority of patients have only one episode of illness, then go into remission and experience no further symptoms. Unfortunately, however, the majority of patients have recurring episodes that require periodic rehospitalizations. The most severely ill never experience remission, but instead show a chronic course of symptomatology. For these reasons, schizophrenia is viewed as having the poorest prognosis of all the major mental illnesses.

Prior to the 1950's, patients with schizophrenia were hospitalized for extended periods of time and frequently became "institutionalized." There were only a few available somatic treatments, and those proved to be of little efficacy. Included among them were insulin coma therapy (the administration of large doses of insulin in order to induce coma), electroconvulsive therapy (the application of electrical current to the temples in order to induce a seizure), and prefrontal lobotomy (a surgical procedure in which the tracts connecting the frontal lobes to other areas of the brain are severed).

In the 1950's, a class of drugs referred to as antipsychotic medications were discovered to be effective in treating schizophrenia. Antipsychotic drugs significantly reduce schizophrenic symptoms in many patients. As a result, the number of hospitalized patients has declined dramatically since the 1950's. Antipsychotic medications have freed many patients from confinement in hospitals and have enhanced their chances for functioning in the community.

Another factor that has contributed to the decline in the number of hospitalized patients with schizophrenia is the nationwide policy of deinstitutionalization. This policy, which has been adopted and promoted by most state governments in the years since 1970, emphasizes short-term hospitalizations, and it has involved the release of some patients who had been in institutions for many years. Unfortunately, the support services that were needed to facilitate the transition from hospital to community living were never put in place. Consequently, the number of homeless schizophrenic patients has increased dramatically. Some of these are patients whose family members have died or have simply lost touch with them. Other patients have withdrawn from contact with their families, despite efforts by concerned relatives to provide assistance. The plight of the homeless mentally ill is of great concern to mental health professionals.

Context

Writing in the late 1800's, an eminent physician named Emil Kraepelin was among the first to document the symptoms and course of this illness, referring to it as "dementia praecox" (dementia of early life). Subsequently, Eugen Bleuler applied the term "schizophrenia," meaning splitting of the mind, to the disorder. Both Kraepelin and Bleuler assumed that organic factors are involved in schizophrenia. Contemporary research, discussed below, has confirmed this assumption; brain scans reveal that a significant proportion of schizophrenia patients do have abnormalities. The precise nature and cause of these abnormalities remain unknown.

In the majority of cases, the onset of schizophrenic symptoms occurs in late adolescence or early adulthood. The major risk period is between twenty and twenty-five years of age. For some patients, there are no readily apparent abnormalities prior to this period. For others, however, the onset of schizophrenia is preceded by impairments in social, academic, or occupational functioning. Some are described by their families as having had adjustment problems in childhood. Childhood schizophrenia is relatively rare. It is estimated to occur in about one out of every ten thousand children. When schizophrenia is diagnosed in childhood, the same diagnostic criteria and treatments are applied. Children who receive the diagnosis are usually placed in special classrooms for the emotionally disturbed.

Schizophrenia shows no clear pattern in terms of its distribution in the population. It occurs in both males and females, although it tends to have a slightly earlier onset in males than in females. The illness strikes individuals of all social, economic, and ethnic backgrounds. Some patients manifest high levels of intelligence and had been excellent students prior to becoming ill; others showed poor academic performance and signs of learning disability.

Schizophrenia is an illness that has been recognized by medicine for more than a hundred years. During this time, only modest progress has been made in research on its etiology. Some significant advances have been achieved in treatment, however, and the prognosis for schizophrenia is better now than ever before. Moreover, there is reason to believe that the availability of new technologies for studying the central nervous system will speed the pace of further discovery.

Bibliography

Bleuler, Eugen. *Dementia Praecox: Or, The Group of Schizophrenias.* Translated by Joseph Zinkin. New York: International Universities Press, 1950. Original German first published in 1911. A classic book in the field, this provides excellent descriptions of the symptoms and very interesting discussions of possible causal factors.

Herz, Marvin I., Samuel J. Keith, and John P. Docherty. *Psychosocial Treatment of Schizophrenia.* New York: Elsevier, 1990. This book, vol. 4 in the Handbook of Schizophrenia series, examines psychosocial causes of schizophrenia and psychosocial treatment approaches. Discusses early intervention. Behavior therapy and supportive living arrangements are covered; results of long-term outcome studies are also reviewed.

Kraepelin, Emil. *Clinical Psychiatry.* Translated by A. Ross Diefendorf. Delmar, N.Y.: Scholars' Facsimiles & Reprints, 1981. A facsimile reprint of the seventh (1907) edition of Kraepelin's classic text. Reveals the origins of contemporary thinking about schizophrenia and other mental disorders.

Neale, John M., and Thomas F. Oltmanns. *Schizophrenia.* New York: John Wiley & Sons, 1980. This book provides a comprehensive overview of the illness and examines many of the research methods for exploring its causes.

Walker, Elaine F., ed. *Schizophrenia: A Life-Span Developmental Perspective.* San

Diego: Academic Press, 1991. The entire life-course of schizophrenic patients is addressed in this book, from early childhood precursors to geriatric outcome.

Elaine F. Walker

Cross-References

Abnormality: Biomedical Models, 39; Abnormality: Family Models, 53; Abnormality: Psychodynamic Models, 74; Madness: Historical Concepts, 1492; Psychoactive Drug Therapy, 1891; Psychological Diagnosis and Classification: DSM-III-R, 1925; Schizophrenia: High-Risk Children, 2135; Schizophrenia: Theoretical Explanations, 2141.

SCHIZOPHRENIA: HIGH-RISK CHILDREN

Type of psychology: Psychopathology
Field of study: Schizophrenias

In order to prevent an illness, it is necessary to have information about specific indicators of risk. Researchers have been conducting studies of children whose parents suffer from schizophrenia in order to identify the indicators of risk for this psychiatric illness; preliminary findings indicate that it may someday be possible to prevent the onset of schizophrenia.

Principal terms
ETIOLOGY: the study of the causes of disease
GENETICS: the biochemical basis of inherited characteristics
LONGITUDINAL: dealing with the growth or change in individuals over a period of time
PREMORBID: the period before the onset of a disease
SCHIZOPHRENIA: a serious mental illness that is characterized by psychotic symptoms, such as delusions, hallucinations, and thought disorders

Overview

The term "high-risk" has been applied to biological offspring of schizophrenic parents, because they are known to be at genetic risk for the same disorder shown by their parents. Numerous researchers are studying high-risk children in order to shed light on the origins of schizophrenia. This approach has many advantages over other research methods and has already yielded some important findings.

The importance of research on children at risk for schizophrenia stems from a need to understand the precursors of the illness. Over the years, researchers have studied schizophrenia from many different perspectives and with a variety of methods. Despite many decades of work, however, investigators have not yet been successful in identifying the causes or developing a cure. Some progress has been made in clarifying the nature and course of schizophrenia, and there have been considerable advances in the pharmacological treatment of symptoms; however, the precursors and the origins still remain a mystery.

Because the onset of schizophrenia usually occurs in late adolescence or early adulthood, patients typically do not come to the attention of investigators until they have been experiencing symptoms for some period of time. At that point, researchers have to rely on the patient and other informants for information about the nature of the individual's adjustment prior to the onset of the illness. These retrospective accounts of the patient's functioning are often sketchy and can be biased in various ways. Yet it is well accepted that progress toward the ultimate goal—the prevention of schizophrenia—will not be achieved until researchers are able to identify individuals who are vulnerable to the disorder.

In response to this concern, several investigators, most notably Sarnoff Mednick and Tom McNeil, emphasized the importance of studying the development of individuals known to be at heightened statistical risk for schizophrenia. Specifically, it was proposed that repeated assessments should be conducted so that data on all aspects of the development of at-risk children would be available by the time they enter the adult risk period for schizophrenia. In this way, it might be possible to identify precursors of the illness in subjects who had not yet received any treatment for the disorder. Another major advantage of studying subjects prior to the provision of treatment is that only then is it possible to differentiate true precursors of the illness from the consequences or side effects of treatment for the illness.

By the late 1950's, it was well established that schizophrenia tends to run in families. The general population rate for the disorder is about one in a hundred. In contrast, it has been estimated that children who have one biological parent with schizophrenia have a 10 to 15 percent chance of developing the disorder. When both biological parents are diagnosed with schizophrenia, the risk rate is thought to be around 40 percent. It is apparent, therefore, that offspring of schizophrenic parents are indeed at heightened risk for developing the same disorder. Thus, Mednick encouraged researchers to conduct longitudinal studies of these "high-risk" children.

The first large-scale prospective longitudinal study of high-risk children was initiated in Denmark in the mid-1960's by Mednick and Fini Schulsinger. They followed a group of one hundred children who had at least one schizophrenic parent and two hundred comparison children whose parents had no psychiatric disorder. Since the Danish study was initiated, a number of other research groups have initiated similar high-risk research programs. These projects are now under way in several United States cities (including New York City; Rochester, New York; Minneapolis, Minnesota; and Atlanta, Georgia) as well as in other countries.

In the sections that follow, the progress of these research programs will be reviewed. In particular, the various areas of abnormality that have been noted in children at high risk for schizophrenia will be discussed. Before reviewing the findings, however, some of the methodological issues involved in high-risk research will be described.

Applications

One of the major challenges in conducting high-risk research is locating the sample. As previously stated, schizophrenia is a relatively rare disorder in that it occurs in about 1 percent of the general population. Moreover, because most schizophrenic patients experience an onset of illness in late adolescence or early adulthood, they are less likely to marry or have children. This is especially true of schizophrenic patients who are men. Consequently, the majority of the subjects of high-risk research are offspring of schizophrenic mothers. Further, of the schizophrenic women who do have children, a substantial portion do not keep their children but instead place them for adoption. This further complicates the task of identifying samples of high-risk children. In order to be assured of identifying a sample of adequate size, researchers in this field establish formal arrangements with local treatment facilities in order to increase their chances of identifying all the high-risk children in their geographic area.

Another important issue confronted by high-risk researchers is the question of when in the child's life span the study should be initiated. Most investigators are interested in identifying the very earliest signs of vulnerability for schizophrenia. Therefore, it is desirable to initiate a high-risk study with subjects who are infants. In this way, investigators will be able to examine the entire premorbid life course of patients. If there are any markers of vulnerability apparent in infancy, they will be able to identify them. The investigator who initiates a study of infant subjects, however, must wait an extended period of time in order to gather any information about their adult psychiatric outcomes. In order to reduce the period between the initiation of the study and the entry of the subjects into the major risk period for schizophrenia, most investigators have initiated high-risk projects on subjects who are in middle or late childhood.

The problem of attrition (loss of subjects) is another one of concern to high-risk researchers. As mentioned, the long-term goal is to compare those high-risk children who succumb to schizophrenia to those who do not. Consequently, the most crucial information will be provided only when the researchers are knowledgeable about the adult psychiatric outcome of the subjects. Because a sample of a hundred high-risk children may eventually yield only ten to fifteen schizophrenic patients, it is of critical importance to investigators that they maintain contact with all subjects so that they can determine their adult psychiatric outcomes.

Finally, the question of how to select an appropriate comparison group is a salient one to high-risk researchers. Again, one of the ultimate goals is to identify specific signs of vulnerability to schizophrenia. An important question is whether the signs identified by researchers are simply manifestations of vulnerability to any adult psychiatric disorder or signs of specific vulnerability to schizophrenia. In order to address this question, many researchers include groups of children whose parents have psychiatric disorders other than schizophrenia.

Reports on the developmental characteristics of high-risk children have been published by eleven high-risk research groups. These studies have revealed some important differences between children of schizophrenic parents and children whose parents have no mental illness. The differences that have been found tend to fall into three general areas: motor functions, cognitive functions, and social adjustment. When compared to children of normal parents, high-risk subjects have been found to show a variety of impairments in motor development and motor abilities. Infant offspring of schizophrenic parents tend to show delays in the development of motor skills, such as crawling and walking. Similarly, studies of high-risk subjects in their middle childhood and early adolescent years reveal deficits in fine and gross motor skills and coordination. It is important to emphasize, however, that these deficiencies are not of such a severe magnitude that the child would be viewed as clinically impaired in motor skills. Yet the deficiencies are apparent when high-risk children, as a group, are compared to children of normal parents.

The occurrence of motor development delays and abnormalities in high-risk children is consistent with the etiologic assumptions made by most researchers in the field. Specifically, such abnormalities would be expected in a disorder that is presumed to be attributable to a central nervous system impairment that is, at least in part, genetically determined.

Numerous studies have found that children at high risk for schizophrenia also show impairments in cognitive functions. Although their scores on standardized tests of intelligence are within the normal range, they tend to be slightly below that of children of normal parents. With regard to specific abilities, investigators have found that high-risk children show deficiencies in their capacity to maintain and focus attention. These deficiencies are apparent as early as the preschool years and involve the processing of both auditory and visual information. Because attentional deficits have been found so consistently in high-risk children, some researchers in the field have suggested that these deficits may be a key marker of risk for schizophrenia.

When compared to children of parents without psychiatric disorder, offspring of schizophrenic parents tend to manifest a higher rate of behavioral problems. These include a higher rate of aggressive behaviors, as well as an increased frequency of social withdrawal. In general, children of schizophrenic parents are perceived as less socially competent than comparison children. It is important to take into consideration, however, that children of parents with other psychiatric disorders are also found to show problems with social adjustment. Consequently, it is unlikely that behavioral adjustment problems are uniquely characteristic of risk for schizophrenia.

Only a subgroup—in fact, a minority—of high-risk children will eventually manifest schizophrenia. The most significant question, therefore, is not what differentiates high-risk children from a comparison group, but rather what differentiates high-risk children who develop schizophrenia from high-risk children who do not. Only a few high-risk research projects have followed their subjects all the way into adulthood. Only limited data are thus available regarding the childhood characteristics that predict adult psychiatric outcome. The findings from these studies confirm the predictions made by the researchers. Specifically, the high-risk children who eventually develop schizophrenia show more evidence of motor abnormalities and attentional dysfunction in childhood than those who do not.

Context

As is the case with all approaches to research, the high-risk method has some limitations. One limitation concerns whether the findings from these studies can be generalized to a wider population. Although it is true that schizophrenia tends to run in families, it is also true that the majority of schizophrenic patients do *not* have a schizophrenic parent. As a result, the subjects of high-risk research may represent a unique subgroup of schizophrenic patients. The fact that they have a parent with the illness may mean that they have a higher genetic loading for the disorder than do schizophrenic patients whose parents have no mental illness. Moreover, there are undoubtedly some environmental stresses associated with being reared by a schizophrenic parent. In sum, high-risk children who become schizophrenic patients may differ from other schizophrenic patients both in terms of genetic factors and in terms of environment. Some other problems with the method, mentioned above, include subject attrition and the extensive waiting period required before adult psychiatric outcome is determined.

Some investigators have attempted to address the issue of identifying markers of vulnerability with alternative methodologies. For example, it has been shown that children with behavioral problems are more likely to develop schizophrenia in adulthood than are children who manifest no significant behavioral difficulties. Thus, some researchers are conducting longitudinal studies of maladjusted children in order to identify precursors of schizophrenia. Taking a novel approach, one study has utilized childhood home movies of adult-onset schizophrenic patients as a database for identifying infant and early childhood precursors. Up to this point, the findings from these studies are consistent with those from high-risk research.

Based on the research findings, there is good reason to believe that individuals who succumb to schizophrenia in adulthood manifested signs of vulnerability long before the onset of the disorder, perhaps as early as infancy. These findings have some important implications. First, they provide some clues to etiology; they suggest that the neuropathological process underlying schizophrenia is one that begins long before the onset of the clinical symptoms that define the illness. Thus, the search for the biological bases of this illness must encompass the entire premorbid life course. Second, the findings suggest that it may eventually be possible to identify individuals who are at risk for schizophrenia so that preventive interventions can be provided. As time goes on, more of the high-risk children who have been the subjects of these investigations will pass through the adult risk period for schizophrenia. One can therefore anticipate that important new findings from high-risk research will be forthcoming.

Bibliography

Gottesman, Irving I. *Schizophrenia Genesis: The Origins of Madness.* New York. W. H. Freeman, 1991. Provides a comprehensive overview of the genetic determinants of schizophrenia, written by the foremost authority in the field. Very readable; explains the theory and methods of behavioral genetics research and presents a detailed description of the findings.

Mednick, Sarnoff A., and Thomas F. McNeil. "Current Methodology in Research on the Etiology of Schizophrenia: Serious Difficulties Which Suggest the Use of the High-Risk Group Method." *Psychological Bulletin* 70, no. 6 (1968): 681-693. This classic paper served to introduce the idea of the high-risk method to researchers in the field of psychopathology. It clearly lays out the rationale behind the approach.

Walker, Elaine F., ed. *Schizophrenia: A Life-Course Developmental Perspective.* San

Diego: Academic Press, 1991. This book provides an overview of knowledge in the life course of schizophrenia. Chapters are written by experts in the field.

Walker, Elaine F., and Richard J. Lewine. "Prediction of Adult-Onset Schizophrenia from Childhood Home Movies of the Patient." *American Journal of Psychiatry* 147, no. 8 (1990): 1052-1056. Preliminary results from a novel study of the precursors of schizophrenia are presented in this paper. This approach complements the high-risk method in that it holds promise for validating the findings of high-risk research.

Watt, Norman F., et al., eds. *Children at Risk for Schizophrenia.* New York: Cambridge University Press, 1984. This edited volume summarizes the major high-risk projects underway throughout the world at the time it was written. It demonstrates the importance of this work in furthering understanding of the origins of schizophrenia.

Elaine F. Walker

Cross-References

Abnormality: Biomedical Models, 39; Abnormality: Family Models, 53; Abnormality: Psychodynamic Models, 74; Madness: Historical Concepts, 1492; Psychoactive Drug Therapy, 1891; Psychological Diagnosis and Classification: DSM-III-R, 1925; Schizophrenia: Background, Types, and Symptoms, 2129; Schizophrenia: Theoretical Explanations, 2141.

SCHIZOPHRENIA: THEORETICAL EXPLANATIONS

Type of psychology: Psychopathology
Fields of study: Models of abnormality; schizophrenias

Schizophrenia is one of the most bizarre and potentially devastating of all psychological disorders. Although it was thoroughly described in the late nineteenth century, the disorder's causes are not yet definitely known. Theoretical explanations, sometimes poorly supported by direct experimental evidence, abound; many of these theories have, however, been abandoned by researchers, most of whom now accept that schizophrenia is primarily an organic disorder.

Principal terms

ANTIPSYCHOTIC DRUGS: drugs that alleviate the symptoms of
schizophrenia; chlorpromazine, haloperidol, clozapine, and
thioridazine are examples

DOPAMINE: a neurotransmitter; a chemical that is released from one
nerve cell and stimulates receptors on another, thus transferring
a message between them

NEGATIVE SYMPTOMS: the absence of normal thoughts, feelings, or
behaviors that should be present but are not; examples are lack of
normal emotional responsiveness, thought blocking, inadequate
social behavior, and inadequate self-care or personal-hygiene
behaviors

POSITIVE SYMPTOMS: abnormal thoughts, feelings, or behaviors that are
present but should not be present; delusions, hallucinations, strange
mannerisms, and inappropriate emotions are examples

POSITRON EMISSION TOMOGRAPHY (PET) SCANNING: a brain-imaging
technique that allows blood flow, energy metabolism, and chemical
activity to be visualized in the living human brain

PSYCHOTOGEN: something that causes, or generates, psychosis; related
adjectives are "psychotogenic" and "schizophrenogenic"

RETICULAR FORMATION: a system in the brain responsible for controlling
arousal and attention, sleeping and waking, perceptual filtering, and
other important functions

Overview

Schizophrenia, an illness that strikes 1 percent of adults, involves changes in all aspects of psychological functioning. Thinking disorders, perceptual distortions and hallucinations, delusions, and emotional changes are the most prominent of such changes. Although some people recover completely, in many others the illness is chronic and deteriorative. The cause of schizophrenia is not known. Theories about schizophrenia can be classified into four types: psychodynamic, family interaction, learning/attention, and organic.

Psychodynamic theories originated with Sigmund Freud, who believed that schizophrenia results when a child fails to develop an attachment to his or her parent of the opposite sex. This causes a powerful conflict (called an Oedipal conflict in males) in which unconscious homosexual desires threaten to overwhelm the conscious self. To prevent these desires from generating thoughts and feelings that cause painful guilt or behaviors that would be punished, the ego defends itself by regressing to a state in which awareness of the self as a distinct entity is lost. Thus, the person's behavior becomes socially inappropriate; the person mistakes fantasies for reality and experiences hallucinations and delusions.

Harry Stack Sullivan, a follower of Freud, believed that failure of maternal attachment creates excessive anxiety and sets the pattern for all future relationships. Unable to cope in a world seen as socially dangerous, the individual retreats into fantasy. Having done so, the individual cannot grow socially or develop a sense of trust in or belonging with others. By late adolescence or early adulthood, the person's situation has become so hopeless that all pretense of normality collapses and he or she withdraws totally and finally into a world of fantasy and delusion.

Family interaction theories dwell even more intensely on parent-child, especially mother-child, relationships. Theodore Lidz and coworkers, after conducting studies on families with a schizophrenic member, concluded that one or both parents of a future schizophrenic are likely to be nearly, if not overtly, psychotic. They proposed that the psychotogenic influence of these parents on a psychologically vulnerable child is most likely to be the cause of schizophrenia.

Gregory Bateson and colleagues proposed a family interaction theory called the double-bind theory. Bateson suggested that schizophrenia results when parents expose a child to a family atmosphere in which they never effectively communicate their expectations, and therefore the child is unable to discover which behaviors will win approval. Scolded for disobeying, for example, the child changes his or her behavior only to be scolded for being "too obedient." Subjected to such no-win situations constantly, the child cannot develop an attachment to the family, and this failure generalizes to all subsequent relationships.

Learning theories propose that failure of operant conditioning causes the bizarre behavior of schizophrenia. In one version, conditioning fails because mechanisms in the brain that support operant learning, such as reinforcement and attention, are faulty, thus preventing the learning of appropriate, adaptive behaviors.

For example, a person who is unable to focus attention on relevant stimuli would be unable to learn the stimulus associations and discriminations necessary for successful day-to-day behavior. Such an individual's behavior would eventually become chaotic. This learning/attention theory proposes a defect in perceptual filtering, a function of the brain's reticular formation. This system filters out the innumerable stimuli that impinge upon one's senses every moment but are unimportant. In schizophrenia, the theory proposes, this filtering system fails, and the individual is overwhelmed by a welter of trivial stimuli. Unable to cope with this confusing overstimulation, the person withdraws, becomes preoccupied with sorting out his or her thoughts, and becomes unable to distinguish internally generated stimuli from external ones.

Organic theories of schizophrenia are influenced by the knowledge that conditions known to have organic causes often produce psychological symptoms that mimic schizophrenia. Among these are vitamin-deficiency diseases, viral encephalitis, temporal-lobe epilepsy, and neurodegenerative diseases such as Huntington's disease and Wilson's disease. Furthermore, evidence suggests that schizophrenia involves a genetic disorder, which presumably manifests itself as some organic brain abnormality. In the stress-diathesis model, such a genetic defect is necessary for the development of chronic schizophrenia but is not sufficient to produce it. Stressful life events must also be present. The genetic abnormality then leaves the person unable to cope with life stresses, the result being psychosis.

Many brain abnormalities have been proposed as causes of schizophrenia. One suggestion is that schizophrenia results from generalized brain pathology. For example, some researchers suggest that widespread brain deterioration caused by either environmental poisoning or infection by a virus causes schizophrenia.

Alternatively, some biochemical abnormality may be at fault. The endogenous psychotogen theory proposes that abnormal production of a chemical substance either inside or outside the brain produces psychotic symptoms by affecting the brain in a druglike fashion. Substances similar to the hallucinogenic drugs lysergic acid diethylamide (LSD) and mescaline are popular candidates for the endogenous psychotogen. The dopamine theory, however, proposes that schizophrenia results when a chemical neurotransmitter system in the brain called the dopamine system becomes abnormally overactive or when dopamine receptors in the brain become abnormally sensitive to normal amounts of dopamine.

Applications

Theories of schizophrenia are instrumental in generating experiments that provide definite knowledge of the condition. Experimental support for psychodynamic theories has not been forthcoming. Therefore, most researchers regard psychodynamic theories of schizophrenia as having little scientific merit. Family interaction theories also have not been supported by subsequent experiments. Although studies have found disturbed family relationships, the evidence suggests that these are the result of, not the cause of, having a schizophrenic individual in the family. Studies consistently fail to find that parent-child interactions are psychotogenic, and the once-popular notion of the schizophrenogenic parent has been discarded. Only learning/attention and organic theories are strongly supported by experimental evidence. The evidence for attentional or learning deficits resulting from a fault in the reticular formation is strong, and it stems from electrophysiological and behavioral studies.

The electroencephalogram (EEG) is often found to be abnormal in schizophrenic patients, showing excessive activation that indicates overarousal. Furthermore, studies of evoked potentials, electrical events recorded from the cortex of the brain in response to specific sensory stimuli, often find abnormalities. Significantly, these occur late in the evoked potential, indicating abnormality in the brain's interpretation of sensory stimuli rather than in initial reception and conduction.

Behavioral studies show that schizophrenic patients often overreact to low-intensity stimuli, which corresponds to their complaints that lights are too bright or sounds are too loud. In addition, patients are often unusually distractible—unable to focus attention on the most relevant stimuli. Orienting responses to novel stimuli are deficient in about half of schizophrenic patients. Patient self-reports also indicate that, subjectively, the individual feels overwhelmed by sensory stimulation.

Thus, considerable evidence suggests that, at least in many patients, there is an abnormality in the sensory/perceptual functioning in the brain, perhaps in the perceptual filtering mechanism of the reticular formation.

Franz J. Kallmann's twin studies of the 1940's provided convincing evidence of a genetic factor in schizophrenia. He found that genetically identical monozygotic twins are much more likely to be concordant for schizophrenia (that is, both twins are much more likely to be psychotic) than are dizygotic twins, who are not genetically identical. Studies using genealogical techniques also showed that schizophrenia runs in families.

The criticism of these studies was that twins not only are genetically similar but also are exposed to the same family environment, and therefore genetic and environmental factors were confounded. Seymour Kety and colleagues, working with adoption records in Denmark, effectively answered this criticism by showing that adopted children are more likely to become schizophrenic when their biological parents suffer from the illness than when their adoptive parents are stricken. These studies showed that schizophrenia is more closely associated with genetic relatedness than with family environment.

Presumably, this genetic predisposition works by producing some organic change. Studies using advanced brain-imaging techniques indicate that, in many patients, there is nonlocalized brain degeneration, which is revealed by the increased size of the ventricles, fluid-filled spaces within the brain. What causes this degeneration is unknown, but some researchers suggest that it is caused by a virus and that a genetic factor increases susceptibility to infection and the subsequent damaging effects of a viral disease. Although direct evidence of a virus has been found in a minority of patients, the viral theory is still considered speculative and unproved. There is no evidence that schizophrenia is contagious.

Experimental evidence of biochemical abnormalities in the brain's dopamine neurotransmitter systems is, however, impressive. Antipsychotic drugs are effective in relieving the symptoms of schizophrenia, especially positive symptoms such as hallucinations and delusions. These drugs block dopamine receptors in the brain. Furthermore, the more powerfully the drugs bind to and block dopamine receptors, the smaller the effective dose that is necessary to produce a therapeutic result.

Further evidence comes from a condition called amphetamine psychosis, which occurs in people who abuse amphetamine and similar stimulants such as cocaine. Amphetamine psychosis so closely mimics some forms of schizophrenia that misdiagnoses have been common. Furthermore, amphetamine psychosis is not an artifact of disturbed personality; experiments show that normal control subjects will develop the condition if they are given high doses of amphetamines every few hours for several days. Amphetamine psychosis, which is believed to result from the overactivation of dopamine systems in the brain, is treated with antipsychotic drugs such as chlorpromazine.

Direct evidence of abnormality in the dopamine systems comes from studies using advanced techniques such as positron emission tomography (PET) scanning. These studies show that the brains of schizophrenic patients, even those who have never been treated with antipsychotic medications, may have abnormally large numbers of dopamine receptors in an area called the limbic system, which is responsible for emotional regulation.

Dopamine-blocking drugs, however, help only a subset of patients. Studies show that those most likely to benefit from medication are patients who display primarily positive symptoms. Patients who show negative symptoms—such as withdrawal, thought blocking, and catatonia—are less likely to be helped by medication. These are precisely the patients, however, who are likely to show nonlocalized brain deterioration. Many researchers believe that there are two types of schizophrenia: one that is characterized by negative symptoms, has a poor prognosis, and is perhaps caused by generalized brain pathology; and a second, which is characterized by positive symptoms, responds well to medication, and is perhaps caused by biochemical abnormality in the dopamine systems of the brain. Attentional deficits may be related to this second type of schizophrenia, since the dopamine pathways originate in the reticular formation of the brain and play a critical role in learning and selective attention.

Context

The disorders that are now called schizophrenia were first characterized in the nineteenth century. Emil Kraepelin first grouped these disorders, referring to them by the collective name dementia praecox in 1893.

Many early neurologists and psychiatrists thought these dementias were organic conditions. This view changed, however, after Swiss psychiatrist Eugen Bleuler published his classic work on the disorder in 1911. Bleuler proposed that the primary characteristic of the condition was a splitting of intellect from emotions. He introduced the term "schizophrenia" (literally, "split mind"). Bleuler, influenced by the psychodynamic theories of Freud, believed that the bizarre content of schizophrenic thoughts and perceptions represented a breaking away from an external reality that was too painful or frightening. His ideas became especially influential in the United States.

Attempts to treat schizophrenia with traditional psychotherapies were, however, unsuccessful. Success rates rarely surpassed the rate of spontaneous recovery, the rate at which patients recover without treatment. Because medical interventions such as lobotomy, insulin shock therapy, and electroconvulsive therapy were also ineffective, psychiatric hospitals were filled with patients for whom little could be done.

The discovery of antipsychotic drugs in the 1950's changed things dramatically. Hospital populations declined. The surprising effectiveness of these medications, in concert with the discovery of amphetamine psychosis in the 1930's and the genetic studies of the 1940's, renewed the belief that schizophrenia is an organic condition.

Two problems impeded further understanding. First, techniques available for investigating the brain were primitive compared with modern techniques. Therefore, reports of organic changes in schizophrenia, although common, were difficult to confirm. Second, since the routinely administered medications powerfully influenced brain functioning, it became a problem to distinguish organic changes that were important in causing the disorder from those that were merely secondary to the action of antipsychotic drugs in the brain.

Indeed, it became "common wisdom" among many psychologists that organic factors identified by researchers were not primary to the disorder but were, rather, side effects of medication. Soft neurological signs such as eye-movement dysfunctions, abnormal orienting responses, and unusual movements were considered drug related even though Kraepelin and others had described them decades before the drugs were discovered. The drugs came to be called "major tranquilizers," implying that medication allowed patients to function more effectively by relieving the overwhelming anxiety that accompanied the disorder but that the drugs did not influence the schizophrenic process itself.

The fact that antipsychotic drugs have little usefulness as antianxiety agents in nonschizophrenics did not shake this opinion. The discovery of more powerful antianxiety agents such as Librium (chlordiazepoxide) and Valium (diazepam) did not either, even after they were shown to be almost useless in treating schizophrenia.

The next dramatic change in understanding schizophrenia came in the 1960's with the discovery of monoamine neurotransmitters, including dopamine, and the discovery that these chemical systems in the brain are strongly affected in opposite ways by psychotogenic drugs, such as cocaine and amphetamine, and antipsychotic drugs, such as chlorpromazine. With the advent of powerful imaging techniques such as PET scanning, research into schizophrenia surged ahead again. Perhaps these techniques will bring about a more complete understanding of, and possibly a cure for, this most devastating of psychological disorders.

Bibliography

Bowers, Malcolm B. *Retreat from Sanity: The Structure of Emerging Psychosis.* New York: Human Sciences Press, 1974. A fascinating description, often in the words of patients, of the experiences many people have in the very early stages of psychosis. Especially interesting are descriptions of "peak" and "psychedelic" experiences resulting from sensory alterations during the onset of the disorder.

Gottesman, Irving I. *Schizophrenia Genesis: The Origins of Madness.* New York: W. H. Freeman, 1991. An excellent, well-written book that is easily accessible to the general reader. Highly recommended.

Gottesman, Irving I., James Shields, and Daniel R. Hanson. *Schizophrenia: The Epigenetic Puzzle.* Cambridge, England: Cambridge University Press, 1982. More technical than *Schizophrenia Genesis* but still accessible to anyone with a solid background in genetics of the type obtained in a good general biology course. Concentrates on genetic studies and gives complete references to original technical articles.

Helmchen, Hanfried, and Fritz A. Henn, eds. *Biological Perspectives of Schizophrenia.* Chichester, England: John Wiley & Sons, 1987. A collection of papers by experts in the field, this is a valuable reference source for readers who are interested in the state of knowledge about schizophrenia in the late 1980's. Many of the papers are quite technical, but the background supplied by other sources in this bibliography should help readers understand them.

Lidz, Theodore, Stephen Fleck, and Alice R. Cornelison. *Schizophrenia and the Family.* New York: International Universities Press, 1965. A collection of papers detailing studies of seventeen families that have a schizophrenic member. Selection of subject families was highly biased, and no appropriate matched control families were studied. Nevertheless, this work was extremely influential among mental health workers. The authors' conclusions are not supported, however, by more recent, more carefully controlled studies.

Snyder, Solomon H. *Madness and the Brain.* New York: McGraw-Hill, 1974. Written in a lively, breezy style, this short volume deals with biomedical factors in many psychological disorders, including schizophrenia. Especially interesting is Snyder's discussion of drug effects, neurotransmitters, and schizophrenia.

Sullivan, Harry Stack. *Schizophrenia as a Human Process.* New York: W. W. Norton, 1962. Perhaps the most available of Sullivan's writings, this book is actually a collection of articles written by him between 1924 and 1935. Once widely popular, Sullivan's theories have not been supported experimentally and are no longer accepted by most psychologists.

Torrey, Edwin Fuller. *Surviving Schizophrenia: A Family Manual.* Rev. ed. New York: Perennial Library, 1988. One of the best books available for the general reader on schizophrenia. Intended primarily for members of families that have a schizophrenic family member, this book should be read by everyone who is interested in the disorder, including every mental health worker. Torrey writes wonderfully and pulls no punches when dealing with outmoded theories and poorly done experiments. Many libraries have only the first edition; read the revised edition if possible.

William B. King

Cross-References

THE SCIENTIFIC METHOD IN PSYCHOLOGY

Type of psychology: Psychological methodologies
Fields of study: Descriptive methodologies; experimental methodologies;
  methodological issues

The scientific method in psychology involves the careful and direct observation of behavior, using the physical senses, followed by the application of logical reasoning to determine the laws underlying the behavior. Direct observation of the mind is impossible, but psychologists can scientifically study human behavior to make educated guesses about what goes on in the mind.

Principal terms

CONSTRUCT: an unobservable phenomenon that is understood to exist but difficult to define scientifically; examples include love, intelligence, attractiveness, honesty, stress

CORRELATION: a statistical but not necessarily causal relationship between two variables

DEDUCTION: a type of logic by which one draws a specific conclusion from one or more known truths or premises; often formed as an "if/then" statement

EMPIRICAL EVIDENCE: data or information derived objectively from the physical senses, without reliance on personal faith, intuition, or introspection

EXPERIMENT: a study in which one or more factors (independent variables) are manipulated by the experimenter to observe the effect(s) on another factor (dependent variable)

EXTERNAL VALIDITY: a property of a research study (not necessarily an experiment) that is relevant and applicable to the real world

FALSIFICATION: the disproving of a hypothesis by testing a prediction generated from it

HYPOTHESIS: an educated guess about the relationship between two or more variables, derived from inductive reasoning; often tested by an experiment

INDUCTION: a type of logic by which one arrives at a general premise or conclusion based on generalization from a large number of known, specific cases

INTERNAL VALIDITY: a property of an experiment that is designed well enough so that there is only one straightforward interpretation of the results

THEORY: a model explaining the relationship between several phenomena; derived from several related hypotheses which have survived many tests

Overview

Scientific research in psychology has four goals: the description, prediction, explanation, and control of behavior. When the goal is description, scientists use descriptive, or observational, research; for prediction, they use correlational research; for explanation, they use experiments; and for control, they use application.

Description is fundamental to the scientific method, and observational research is the foundation upon which all other research is built. The initial observations, like a blueprint, must be accurate and unbiased. Science requires that all observations be verifiable and repeatable: checked and double-checked.

Verifiability and repeatability are sometimes difficult, since many psychologists study phenomena that are not directly observable. Psychologists who study the mind—thoughts, feelings, mental illness, altered states of consciousness—must be able to report some observable behavior(s) related to the underlying mental process. Since they cannot directly observe dreams, for example, they may study verbal reports about dreams; though they cannot directly observe anger, they can measure blood pressure or calculate a score on a questionnaire about anger.

When psychologists use indirect measures such as these, they are using what is called an "operational definition" of an underlying "construct." The construct is what the psychologist really wants to study (an unobservable phenomenon such as love, intelligence, or anger), and the operational definition is the specific behavior that is observed and measured (for example, the score on the questionnaire). By using an operational definition, other scientists can then try to replicate the study and verify the results. Later, other scientists will study the same construct using different operational definitions. Collecting all these observations is like collecting all the pieces before beginning work on a big puzzle.

Correlational research is the next step, analogous to sorting the puzzle pieces into piles by color. Scientists try to find out what phenomena are correlated to one another; that is, they look for patterns between two or more phenomena. Positive correlations are those in which two phenomena covary in the same direction: For example, the more religious a woman is, the more religious her husband is likely to be. Negative correlations are those in which two phenomena covary in opposite directions: For example, the longer an institutionalized child remains unadopted, the less mentally stable the child is likely to be later. Patterns of this kind allow scientists to predict one phenomenon when they know something about the second. Most people do this in everyday life: When preparing to meet the husband of a religious coworker, one probably expects him to be religious also; and one might be concerned if one were told that the child one was about to adopt had already been waiting for three years.

Correlations do not allow perfect prediction. Some religious women marry nonreligious men, and some late-adopted children thrive. Correlations also do not explain why a pattern exists in the relation of two variables. In some instances, one phenomenon may directly cause the second: Religious individuals may specifically seek out other religious people as partners, and living in an institution for a long time may make a child unstable. On the other hand, the cause of the correlation may not be direct: Perhaps religious people are simply more likely to meet one another because they go to the same places. Children who are not adopted right away may be those who were previously abused or ill, and it is this prior experience which makes them unstable, not the institutionalization.

To explain why a correlation exists, scientists turn to experimentation. Based on the correlations they see (also on common sense and prior knowledge), they make an educated guess about which phenomenon might be a cause and which might be an effect. This process of looking at patterns and trying to figure out the underlying law explaining them is called induction; the educated guess about the law is called a hypothesis. The experimenter can then test the hypothesis with an experiment.

To test the hypothesis, the experimenter formulates a prediction that assumes the hypothesis is true. If the hypothesis is that A causes the positive correlation between A and B, then the prediction is that when the experimenter increases A, B should increase too. (This kind of reasoning is called deduction.) For the actual experiment, then, the experimenter manipulates the factor thought to be the cause of a correlation and observes what happens to the factor thought to be the effect. (These factors are called, respectively, the independent and the dependent variables.)

The experimenter must also consider other factors which might influence the dependent variable; these are called control variables. When these other variables are accounted for, the experimenter will know that any change in the dependent variable must result from the manipulation of the independent variable. Then the experiment has what is called internal validity, and the experimenter can be confident about interpreting the cause of the correlation. In the puzzle analogy, one can now feel confident that the same-colored pieces really go together and are not the same color simply by chance.

To control behavior in the real world, people must apply the results of scientific experiments to nonlaboratory settings. To do this, it is necessary to have many puzzle pieces already interconnected. A set of interconnected hypotheses which have withstood experimental testing is called a theory. Using this knowledge, someone can manipulate a variable known to have a particular effect in order to make a change in the real world.

Since real-world settings are always more complicated than controlled laboratory settings, application of scientific knowledge is difficult. Experiments that do not apply well to real-world settings are said to have poor external validity. Scientists can increase the external validity of their research by doing experiments in nonlaboratory settings (such as schools, prisons, and hospitals), but this usually reduces their ability to control the situation. Thus, experiments in real-life settings must constantly be refined.

Scientific research in psychology is an extension of the kind of thinking people do every day. To some extent, everyone is a psychologist, and everyone is a scientist. Using the scientific method, however, requires that one be much more careful than one normally is. Thus, progress in scientific research is slow, but it is more reliable than simply using common sense.

Applications

In their everyday thinking, people often rely on common sense, "folk wisdom," and opinion for information. These methods may seem reasonable, but the information they yield is not as reliable as that obtained using the scientific method.

For example, when one sees a couple who look and act alike, one may smile and think, "Well, birds of a feather flock together." When a friend becomes infatuated with someone whose life seems totally different from the friend's, one thinks, "Of course: Opposites attract." Folk wisdom may seem to explain everything, but, according to the tenets of science, both these "laws" of behavior cannot be correct at the same time. How can birds of a feather flock together if opposites attract?

Each of these sayings is actually a hypothesis: an educated guess based on generalizing from repeated observations (the process of induction). Using the scientific method, one applies deduction to each hypothesis to come up with testable predictions. For example, one can predict that *if* birds of a feather flock together, *then*, when one observes hundreds of couples, one will find that partners are more alike than are randomly chosen pairs. On the other hand, one can also predict that *if* opposites attract, *then* partners will seem less alike than will randomly chosen pairs. Both these predictions cannot be true; either one will be wrong or both will be wrong (it could be that partners are neither more alike nor less alike than random pairs). By testing the predictions, one will be able to rule out at least one of the two hypotheses, a process called falsification.

Actual research on this topic has shown that there are positive correlations between partners; that is, partners are indeed more alike than are randomly chosen individuals. In fact, in terms of hundreds of different attributes, from height to arm length, introversion to religiosity, intelligence to attractiveness, the correlations between partners are always positive. Not only has science falsified (or, colloquially, "disproved") the hypothesis that opposites attract; it has verified repeatedly that birds of a feather flock together. A hypothesis that has withstood many tests is eventually considered to be a fact, and assortative mating, the process of choosing a partner similar to oneself, is now considered to be a scientific fact.

Falsification of folk-wisdom hypotheses can also have important social consequences. Eyewitness testimony has held an important role in the judicial system for centuries. Jurors put great weight on such testimony and are more likely to believe witnesses who appear confident than those who are less confident about what they saw. Are these assumptions valid? How accurate is eyewitness testimony? Are more confident witnesses really more accurate than less confident ones?

Investigations into the psychology of perception, memory, and recall suggest that commonsense notions about eyewitnesses are not valid at all. When people witness an event, they do not actually record all of it like a video camera. Selected pieces of information get stored in the memory, and when the witness tries to remember the event, other elements are filled in by the brain. This filling-in process, called memory reconstruction, is totally subconscious; most memories are reconstructed this way, but people are unaware of it. They are equally likely to swear to the truth of a "fact" that was actually reconstructed as they are to swear to the validity of an actual event. In the courtroom, confident people will be perceived by a jury as more accurate than those with a less confident demeanor, but science has shown that the confident witnesses are actually no more accurate than less confident witnesses. A witness' confidence about identification of a suspect, for example, is unrelated to his or her accuracy.

Interestingly, although science has discredited this commonsense assumption about the relationship between confidence and accuracy of memory, it has upheld another piece of relevant folklore. The phrase "They all look alike to me" has sometimes been heard in a negative context, implying the lack of individuality of people of a different racial or ethnic descent from the speaker. Scientific testing has shown that people do, in fact, have more difficulty recognizing individuals of other races than of their own. This means that recognition of suspects in a lineup is especially inaccurate when the witness is of a different race from that of the suspect.

The law has been slow to incorporate the findings of scientific psychology. Common sense seems so valid, and judges and lawyers traditionally have relied more on other methods of reasoning than on scientific method. Scientific findings are making their way into the courtroom, however; many jurisdictions now allow lawyers to call psychologists as experts to testify about the low reliability of eyewitness recall and suspect identification. Also, most courts have acted on the basis of scientific studies and ruled out the admissibility of hypnosis as a memory enhancer. Psychological science is also being used increasingly in civil law, for example, to demonstrate statistically whether broad-based discrimination is occurring at a particular workplace or to describe to a jury the consequences of victimization.

Context

The scientific method is one of many methods of acquiring knowledge. It is based on the seventeenth century philosophy of empiricism, which holds that truth can be reached only by direct observation of the world using the physical senses. This approach to knowledge rules out the use of intuition, faith, or introspection. Scientific, or empirical, data are thought to be objective and verifiable.

Empiricists also believe in the principle of uniformitarianism, the belief that there is only one set of laws that governs the universe and that these laws are the same (or uniform) throughout time and space. Scientific, or empirical, phenomena are therefore thought to be repeatable by different observers at different times and places. Scientists generally will not accept the results of a study until it is shown that the study is repeatable, or replicable.

Parapsychology (the discipline concerned with extrasensory perception, telepathy, and clairvoyance) is not considered to be scientific because it is not uniform or replicable. Similarly, some of the methods of understanding used in clinical psychology (such as empathy) are not considered scientific because they are not empirical. Most of psychology, however, is scientific, and most psychologists are empiricists.

Sometimes it is difficult for psychologists to be empirical, because the topic they study, the mind, is not directly observable. Most psychologists therefore study behavior, which is directly observable. Sometimes, observing behavior makes possible educated guesses about what is going on in the mind; still, most psychologists prefer to stick only to the study of behavior.

To psychologists, behavior can include everything from individual actions to group dynamics to the activity of specific cells. Different psychologists specialize their study at different levels of behavior. Reductionists believe that, to understand how something works, one should try to figure out what all the parts are and how they fit together. Psychologists who are reductionists tend to be physiological psychologists: They study the brain, sense organs, hormones, and nervous system. Holists, on the other hand, believe in the phrase "The whole is greater than the sum of its parts"; social psychologists try to understand people by studying the context in which they behave.

Science in general tends to be more reductionist than holistic, and as psychology has become more empirical and more reductionist, people have begun to change their perception that psychology is a "soft" science. As the scientific method is increasingly utilized by psychologists, psychological research will be applied more often to law and social policy, lending its expertise to solve real-world problems the way biology does for medicine and physics does for technology.

Bibliography

Campbell, Donald Thomas, and Julian C. Stanley. *Experimental and Quasi-Experimental Designs for Research.* Chicago: Rand McNally, 1963. This short book is a classic upon which many social science research methods texts are based. Focus is on internal and external validity, and the pros and cons of a variety of research designs. Accessible but somewhat technical, the book addresses methodology alone, without psychological content.

Goldstein, Martin, and Inge F. Goldstein. *How We Know: An Exploration of the Scientific Process.* New York: Plenum Press, 1978. A book on the philosophy of science, intended for the reader who is neither scientist nor philosopher. Explains the scientific approach using historical examples in the fields of medicine, physics, and clinical psychology. Compares scientific to nonscientific approaches to knowing. Easy to browse through if so desired.

Platt, John R. "Strong Inference." *Science* 146 (October, 1964): 347-353. This classic article presents the philosophy of scientific falsification, whereby scientists rule out different hypotheses one by one, leaving the strongest, presumably correct hypothesis as the sole survivor of rigorous attempts at disproof. Platt, along with many others, believes that psychology will remain a "soft" science until this approach is used on a more regular basis.

Plutchik, Robert. *Foundations of Experimental Research.* 3d ed. New York: Harper & Row, 1983. This standard psychology research methods text includes many examples in historical context, and thus might be more interesting for the generalist than most other methods texts. Focus is on definitional issues, scientific reasoning, and problem solving rather than research design.

Siegel, Michael H., and H. Philip Zeigler, eds. *Psychological Research: The Inside Story.* New York: Harper & Row, 1976. A collection of articles by famous psychologists, each describing not only their research results but also the process, problems, accidents, and insights that occurred along the way. A wide diversity of research topics and a very personal approach make this book a good read for professionals and psychology newcomers alike.

Linda Mealey

Cross-References

Animal Experimentation, 252; Case-Study Methodologies, 481; Complex Experimental Designs: Interactions, 625; Data Description: Descriptive Statistics, 751; Data Description: Inferential Statistics, 757; Developmental Methodologies, 817; Sources of Experimental Bias, 1006; Field Experimentation, 1031; Hypothesis Development and Testing, 1248; Observational Measures in Psychology, 1700; Psychological Experimentation: Independent, Dependent, and Control Variables, 1932; Quasi-Experimental Designs, 2024; Sampling, 2122; Survey Research: Questionnaires and Interviews, 2507; Within-Subject Experimental Designs, 2647.

SEASONAL AFFECTIVE DISORDER

Type of psychology: Psychopathology
Field of study: Depression

Seasonal affective disorder is a variant of depression which has received significant research attention since the early 1980's. It may be related to premenstrual syndrome, carbohydrate-craving obesity, and bulimia. Seasonal affective disorder responds to a form of treatment known as phototherapy.

Principal terms
DOUBLE-BLIND STUDY: an experimental design in which neither the experimenter nor the subjects know which subjects are receiving the active treatment
HYPERSOMNIA: sleeping more than ten hours per day
LIBIDO: a person's sex drive
LUX: the amount of light emitted by one candle one meter away; 2,500 lux equals the light from 2,500 candles one meter away
PLACEBO: a treatment that is therapeutically inert

Overview

Seasonal affective disorder (SAD) became the focus of systematic scientific research in the early 1980's. Research originally focused on seasonal changes in mood that coincided with the onset of winter and became known as winter depression. Symptoms consistently identified by Norman Rosenthal and others as indicative of winter depression included hypersomnia, overeating, carbohydrate craving, and weight gain. Michael Garvey and others found the same primary symptoms and the following secondary ones: decreased libido, irritability, fatigue, anxiety, problems concentrating, and premenstrual sadness. Several researchers have found that winter depression is more of a problem at higher latitudes. Thomas Wehr and Norman Rosenthal report on a description of winter depression by Frederick Cook during an expedition to Antarctica in 1898. While winter depression is the form of seasonal affective disorder receiving the most initial attention, there is another variation that changes with the seasons.

Summer depression affects some people in the same way that winter depression affects others. Both are examples of seasonal affective disorder. According to Wehr and Rosenthal, symptoms of summer depression included agitation, loss of appetite, insomnia, and loss of weight. Many people with summer depressions also have histories of chronic anxiety. As can be seen, the person with a summer depression experiences symptoms which are almost the opposite of the primary symptoms of winter depression.

In order to diagnose a seasonal affective disorder, there must be evidence that the symptoms vary according to a seasonal pattern. If seasonality is not present, the diagnosis of SAD cannot be made. The seasonal pattern for winter depression is for it to begin in November and continue unabated through March. Summer depression usually begins in May and continues through September. Siegfried Kasper and others reported that people suffering from winter depression outnumber those suffering from summer depression by 4.5 to 1. Wehr and Rosenthal reported that as people come out of their seasonal depression they experience feelings of euphoria, increased energy, less depression, hypomania, and possibly mania.

Philip Boyce and Gordon Parker investigated seasonal affective disorder in Australia. Their interest was in determining whether seasonal affective disorder occurs in the Southern Hemisphere and, if so, whether it manifests the same symptoms and temporal relationships with seasons as noted in the Northern Hemisphere. Their results confirmed the existence of seasonal affective disorder with an onset coinciding with winter and remission coinciding with summer. Their study also provided evidence that seasonal affective disorder occurs independently of important holidays and celebrations, such as Christmas. There is also a subsyndromal form of seasonal affective disorder. This is usually seen in winter depression and represents a milder form of the disorder. It interferes with the person's life, although to a lesser degree than the full syndrome, and it is responsive to the primary treatment of seasonal affective disorder.

Three hypotheses are being tested to explain seasonal affective disorder. The first is the melatonin hypothesis; the second is the circadian rhythm phase shift hypothesis; and the third is the circadian rhythm amplitude hypothesis.

The melatonin hypothesis is based upon animal studies and focuses on a chemical signal for darkness. Studies show that during darkness, the hormone melatonin is produced in greater quantities; during periods of light, it is produced in lesser quantities. Increases in melatonin level occur at the onset of seasonal affective disorder (winter depression) and are thought to be causally related to the development of the depression.

A second hypothesis is the circadian rhythm phase shift hypothesis. This hypothesis contends that the delay in the arrival of dawn disrupts the person's circadian rhythm by postponing it for a few hours. This disruption of the circadian rhythm is thought to be integral in the development of winter depression. Disruptions in the circadian rhythm are also related to secretion of melatonin.

The third hypothesis receiving much interest is the circadian rhythm amplitude hypothesis. A major tenet of this hypothesis is that the amplitude of the circadian rhythm is directly related to winter depression. Lower amplitudes are associated with depression, and higher ones with normal mood states. The presence or absence of light has been an important determinant in the amplitude of circadian rhythms.

While each of these hypotheses has data to support it, the melatonin hypothesis is falling out of favor. Rosenthal and others administered to volunteers in a double-blind study a drug known to suppress melatonin secretion and a placebo. Despite melatonin suppression, there was no difference in the degree of depression experienced by the two groups (drug and placebo). Both the circadian rhythm phase shift hypothesis and the circadian rhythm amplitude hypothesis continue to have significant research interest and support.

Applications

Seasonal affective disorder was officially recognized in 1987 in the American Psychiatric Association's *Diagnostic and Statistical Manual of Mental Disorders*, (rev. 3d ed., DSM-III-R). It was included in the manual as a variant of major depression. In order to diagnose the seasonal variant, the depressed person must experience the beginning and ending of the depression during sixty-day windows of time at the beginning and ending of the season and must meet the criteria for the diagnosis of major depression. Additionally, that person must have had more than three episodes of seasonal affective disorder, and two episodes must have occurred consecutively. Finally, the ratio of 3 to 1 seasonal to nonseasonal episodes must exist in the absence of any seasonally related psychosocial stressors (such as Christmas). Including the diagnosis in the DSM-III-R not only validates individuals who report feeling better or worse at different times of year but also encourages researchers to study the causes, variations, and treatments of this form of depression.

Philip Boyce and Gordon Parker, two Australian scientists, studied seasonal affective disorder in the Southern Hemisphere. Since the Southern Hemisphere has weather patterns reversed from those in the Northern Hemisphere, and since holidays occurring during the winter in the Northern Hemisphere occur during the summer in the Southern Hemisphere, these researchers were able to reproduce Northern Hemisphere studies systematically while eliminating the possible influence of holidays, such as Christmas. Their findings support those of their colleagues in the Northern Hemisphere. There is a dependable pattern of depression beginning during autumn and early winter and ending in the late spring and early summer.

It is important to study the prevalence of seasonal affective disorder in order to understand how many people are affected by it. Siegfried Kasper and others investigated the prevalence of seasonal affective disorder in Montgomery County, Maryland, a suburb of Washington, D.C. The results of their study suggested that between 4.3 percent and 10 percent of the general population is affected to some extent by seasonal affective disorder. Mary Blehar and Norman Rosenthal report data from research in New York City that between 4 percent and 6 percent of a clinical sample met the criteria for seasonal affective disorder. More significantly, between 31 percent and 50 percent of people responding to a survey reported changes to their life which were similar to those reported by seasonal affective disorder patients. There are strong indications that the overall prevalence rate for seasonal affective disorder is between 5 percent and 10 percent of the general population. As much as 50 percent of the population may experience symptoms similar to but less intense than seasonal affective disorder patients.

Prevalence studies have found that the female-male ratio for seasonal affective disorder is approximately 4 to 1. The age of onset is about twenty-two. The primary symptoms of seasonal affective disorder overlap with other diagnoses which have a relatively high female-to-male ratio. For example, people diagnosed with winter depression frequently crave carbohydrate-loaded foods. In addition to carbohydrate-craving obesity, there is another serious disorder, bulimia nervosa, which involves binging on high-carbohydrate foods and has a depressive component. Bulimia nervosa is much more common in females than it is in males.

While most of the research has focused on seasonal affective disorder in adults, it has also been found in children. Children affected with seasonal affective disorder seem to experience a significant decrease in their energy level as their primary symptom rather than the symptoms seen in adults. This is not unusual; in many disorders, children and adults experience different symptoms.

The winter variant of seasonal affective disorder is much more common than the summer variant. It appears that winter depression is precipitated by the reduction in light that accompanies the onset of winter. As a result, it is also quite responsive to phototherapy. Summer depression, the summer variant of seasonal affective disorder, is precipitated by increases in humidity and temperature associated with the summer months. This suggests a different (and currently unknown) mechanism of action for the two variations of seasonal affective disorder.

The importance of light in the development and treatment of the winter variant of seasonal affective disorder has been demonstrated in a variety of studies worldwide. The general finding is that people living in the higher latitudes are increasingly susceptible to seasonal affective disorder in the winter.

While the mechanism of seasonal affective disorder is still unknown, an important rediscovery has been the use of light to treat it. Phototherapy has been found to be a very important and effective nonpharmacological treatment of the winter form of seasonal affective disorder. Studies have repeatedly shown that bright light, at least 2,500 lux, is more effective than dim light (300 lux). While most studies have compared 2,500-lux light to 300-lux light or other treatments, some researchers have investigated the effect of 10,000-lux light on seasonal affective disorder. Phototherapy treatments using 2,500-lux sources require between two and four hours per day of exposure to reap antidepressant benefits. When 10,000-lux sources of light are employed, the exposure time decreases to approximately thirty minutes a day. Certainly, most people suffering from seasonal affective disorder would prefer to take thirty minutes for their phototherapy treatments than the two to four hours required for 2,500-lux treatments.

Thomas Wehr and others investigated the differences in treatment efficacy when light was applied to the eyes rather than to the skin. They found that the antidepressant benefits were greater when the light was applied to the eyes. This suggests that the eye plays an important role in the effectiveness of phototherapy.

A study by Frederick Jacobsen and others investigated the timing of the phototherapy. This is important because if extending the duration of daylight were necessary for phototherapy to serve as an antidepressant, then the phototherapy must occur in the morning. Also, if phototherapy serves to change the timing of circadian rhythm, it must occur in the morning. The results of this study suggest that the antidepressant effect of phototherapy does not depend upon the timing of the treatment: Both morning and midday treatments were effective in lifting the depression of seasonal affective disorder.

One of the major advantages of phototherapy is that it is a nonpharmacologic approach to treating depression. The fact that no medications are involved allows the patient to avoid the unpleasant and potentially dangerous side effects of medications. Unfortunately, however, phototherapy also has a potentially dangerous side effect. Many researchers are concerned about the possible effect of ultraviolet light on the health of the patient.

Context

The observation that seasons affect people's moods is not new. Hippocrates, writing in 400 B.C., noted in section 3 of his "Aphorisms" that, "Of natures (*temperaments?*), some are well- or ill-adapted for summer, and some for winter." What Hippocrates noticed (and many others since him have noticed) is that there are differences in the way people experience the various seasons. Summer and winter are the most extreme seasons in terms of both light and temperature and, not surprisingly, are the seasons in which most people have problems coping.

As noted above, a physician, Frederick Cook, on an expedition to Antarctica in 1898, noted that the crew experienced symptoms of depression as the days grew shorter. This same report (mentioned by Wehr and Rosenthal) revealed that "bright artificial lights relieve this to some extent." Emil Kraepelin reported in 1921 that approximately 5 percent of his patients with manic-depressive illness also had a seasonal pattern to their depressions. The data from antiquity to the present strongly favor the existence of a form of mood disturbance associated with seasonal variation. Just as the observation of seasonal variations in mood and behavior dates back to antiquity, so does the use of light as a treatment. Wehr and Rosenthal report that light was used as a treatment nearly two thousand years ago. Not only was light used but also it was specified that the light was to be directed to the eyes.

Seasonal affective disorder is a variant of major depressive disorder in the DSM-III-R. It seems to have some degree of relationship to carbohydrate-craving obesity, bulimia nervosa, bipolar disorder (formerly known as manic-depressive illness), and premenstrual syndrome. It affects women more often than men and is more frequently seen covarying with winter than with summer. The winter variant is probably caused by changes in light; it is more severe in the higher latitudes. The summer variant seems to be attributable to intolerance of heat and humidity and would be more prevalent in the lower latitudes. Most of the research both in the United States and internationally has focused on the winter variant and its relationship with light and latitude; there is much less research into the summer variant.

Bibliography

Blehar, Mary C., and Norman E. Rosenthal. "Seasonal Affective Disorders and Phototherapy." *Archives of General Psychiatry* 45, no. 5 (1989): 469-474. Summarizes a National Institute of Mental Health workshop on seasonal affective disorder. The authors discuss issues related to the diagnosis and prevalence of the syndrome. In addition, they present possible mechanisms of action for phototherapy as a treatment and the use of animal models to study seasonal affective disorder. A good summary that avoids being overly technical.

Boyce, Philip, and Gordon Parker. "Seasonal Affective Disorder in the Southern Hemisphere." *American Journal of Psychiatry* 145, no. 1 (1988): 96-99. This study surveyed an Australian sample to determine the extent to which the people experienced symptoms of seasonal affective disorder and to see if the pattern was similar to that of people in the Northern Hemisphere. The results are presented as percentages and are easily understood. Addresses the issue of separating holidays from climatic changes and presents a table of symptoms for seasonal affective disorder.

Garvey, Michael J., Robert Wesner, and Michael Godes. "Comparison of Seasonal and Nonseasonal Affective Disorders." *American Journal of Psychiatry* 145, no. 1 (1988): 100-102. These authors present similarities and differences between affective disorders that covary with seasons and those that do not. Despite the inclusion of statistical analyses, the article is understandable to those without a background in statistics.

Jacobsen, Frederick M., Thomas A. Wehr, Robert A. Skwerer, David A. Sack, and Norman E. Rosenthal. "Morning Versus Midday Phototherapy of Seasonal Affective Disorder." *American Journal of Psychiatry* 144, no. 10 (1987): 1301-1305. Tests the difference in therapeutic effectiveness as a function of when phototherapy is administered. Some statistics are presented, but understanding statistics is not essential, as the accompanying text and figures communicate the findings quite clearly.

Kasper, Siegfried, Susan L. Rogers, Angela Yancey, Patricia M. Schulz, Robert A. Skwerer, and Norman E. Rosenthal. "Phototherapy in Individuals with and Without Subsyndromal Seasonal Affective Disorder." *Archives of General Psychiatry* 46, no. 9 (1989): 837-844. This study extends research into seasonal variants of affective disorder to people who have less intense forms. Addresses issues of the difficulty of establishing adequate experimental control and practical implications for people with these disorders.

Kasper, Siegfried, Thomas A. Wehr, John J. Bartko, Paul A. Gaist, and Norman E. Rosenthal. "Epidemiological Findings of Seasonal Changes in Mood and Behavior." *Archives of General Psychiatry* 46, no. 9 (1989): 823-833. A thorough description of the major prevalence study on seasonal affective disorder. The statistics are fairly advanced, but the authors' use of figures and tables makes the results understandable. An extensive reference list is provided.

Rosenthal, Norman E. *Seasons of the Mind.* New York: Bantam Books, 1989. An exceptionally clear and well-written presentation of what is known about seasonal affective disorder by one of the pioneering investigators in the field. The disorder is placed within a historical context and includes a description of symptoms and a self-test. Discusses the risks and benefits of various treatments, including psychotherapy, antidepressant medication, and light therapy. Numerous anecdotes are used to illustrate major points. Includes literary allusions to SAD, suggestions for helping oneself, guidelines for determining when one needs professional help, and a list of resources for more information and help. An excellent book for nonprofessional readers.

Wurtman, Richard J., and Judith J. Wurtman. "Carbohydrates and Depression." *Scientific American* 260 (January, 1989): 68-75. The authors provide a good review of seasonal affective disorder and the relationships that may exist between it and maladaptive behaviors. They also review the more important theories about the cause and treatment of seasonal affective disorder.

James T. Trent

Cross-References

Abnormality: Biomedical Models, 39; Bipolar Disorder, 422; Circadian Rhythms, 514; Clinical Depression, 527; Depression: Theoretical Explanations, 789.

SELF: DEFINITION AND ASSESSMENT

Type of psychology: Social psychology
Fields of study: Personality assessment; personality theory; social perception and cognition

The self is a complex and multifaceted entity that is a combination of what an individual would like to be, what an individual is currently like, and what others would like the individual to be; because the self is created through, and has implications for, an individual's interactions with others, it is critical that its social nature be studied.

Principal terms
ACTUAL SELF: the self as the person sees himself or herself at the present time; large discrepancies between the actual and ideal selves can lower self-esteem
CONDITIONAL LOVE: love and praise that is given to another person with the expectation that the person will do something for the individual giving the love
IDEAL SELF: the self as the individual would like to be if the individual could be perfect in his or her own eyes
LOOKING-GLASS SELF: a sense of self that is created by imagining how others see the individual in comparison with how the individual would like to be seen
SELF-CONCEPT: the sum total of the attributes, abilities, attitudes, and values that an individual believes defines who he or she is
SELF-ESTEEM: a relatively permanent positive or negative feeling about self that may become more positive or negative as the individual encounters successes and failures in daily life
SELF-IMAGE: a specific attribute, ability, attitude, or value that a person believes makes up part of his or her self; self-image combines to create the self-concept
SPONTANEOUS SELF-CONCEPT: how individuals would automatically describe themselves at a particular moment; situations and other people influence how an individual views his or her self at a given time
TRAITS: relatively enduring tendencies that make people behave in particular ways
UNCONDITIONAL LOVE: love that is given with no expectations attached; when a baby cries, for example, a parent gives him or her food without asking for anything in return

Overview
The concept of self has been researched in depth since psychologist William James

first discussed it in 1892. James believed that the self involves two basic factors that blend to determine the person. First, there is the "I," which represents the simple fact that a person realizes that he or she is separate and different from others. Second, there is the "me," which represents all that the person associates with his or her self. James believed that there are three aspects to the "me" that determine how an individual describes and feels about his or her self: the "material me," the "social me," and the "spiritual me."

The material me represents all the worldly goods and possessions that a person uses to define who he or she is. The social me represents all the interactions and relationships with others that are an important part of how a person views himself or herself. The spiritual me involves the more metaphysical nature of self that centers on one's quest for knowledge and growth. It represents one's sensations, emotions, thoughts, and inner states.

To avoid some of the confusion caused by James's use of the terms "I" and "me," current theorists of the self tend to distinguish between the total self, called the self-concept; a particular aspect of self, called the self-image; and the feelings one has about the self, called self-esteem. Numerous theorists, most notably Harry Stack Sullivan and Charles Horton Cooley, discussed the implications that other people have for an individual's conception of his or her own self.

Sullivan believed that a child comes to develop a sense of self when the mother figure begins to give conditional love. When babies are very young, parents unconditionally love them and meet their needs. As children grow older, they are taught that parents expect certain things from their children and that their love and praise may depend on the child's ability to do what they want. In this way, the child sees that the mother can be good ("she gives me what I want") or bad ("she does not give me what I want"). Along with this realization comes the knowledge that how the child acts often influences whether it is good mother or bad mother who responds. This teaches the child that his or her self includes both the good me (things that I do well) and the bad me (things that I do wrong).

Cooley agrees that the way others respond to the individual has a profound impact on how he or she views his or her self; Cooley refers to what he calls the "looking-glass self." According to this concept, the way people believe that others perceive them determines how they feel about themselves. People "reflect" on how they appear to others, and then try to modify their selves in a direction that they believe will make others see them as they want to be seen.

By using reflections in this way, the individual tries to project a particular self-image, then interprets how he or she thinks others are responding to that image. If the person thinks others are responding the way he or she had intended ("I wanted to be seen as honest and they agree"), then that image is likely to become part of the self-concept. If the person believes that others are responding negatively ("I wanted to be seen as suave, but she thinks I'm a jerk"), then the person is likely to question his or her ability to maintain that particular self-image.

Each person is born with, or quickly develops, a particular temperament (he or she likes certain things more than others, tends to be in a certain mood more than others, and gets upset by certain things more than others). Each person is also born with obvious characteristics that will determine, to some degree, how others will act toward him or her. Unchangeable characteristics, such as race and gender, are often used by others to categorize what people will be like. The way one is treated by these other individuals helps one to negotiate a sense of self. A person tries to convince others of what he or she is like, watches to see how others react to that, and then tries to fine-tune the image of self he or she is creating by using that feedback. Over time, these factors create a self-concept.

Once a person has a fairly stable idea of who he or she is and what he or she can do, that idea influences the situations in which that person finds him- or herself. For example, if a woman believes she is a good tennis player, then she is likely to put herself into a situation in which playing good tennis is important. Then, after she behaves, she asks, "Is my behavior consistent with the image of self I have?" If the answer to that question is "yes," then it feeds the self-concept, and the woman becomes even more certain of who she is. If, however, the answer is "no," then it loops back and causes the woman to question who she is. In this manner, a self-concept is created and continually tested in everyday life.

Applications

There are many life experiences that can be explained by understanding the concept of self. To develop a sense of self fully, an individual must go through a lengthy and complicated negotiation process in which he or she tries on different selves and observes how others react. Adolescence is probably the most striking example of this negotiation process. Individuals such as parents, teachers, and other authority figures tell the child what is right or wrong or what he or she can and cannot do. Suddenly, peers become an important part of this negotiation process: The adolescent tries to balance the desires of the parents and authority figures with the demands being put on him or her by friends and peers while trying to show the world what kind of self he or she would like to have.

The health of the self-concept depends on the adolescent's ability to complete the balancing act successfully and create a sense of self that blends societal demands with what the individual most wants to be. The teenager is experiencing a storm of bodily changes, an increase in expected responsibilities, pressure from peers to do the "in" thing, and an internal need to know "Who am I?" and "What am I meant to do in this world?" What career a person seeks, what schools a person attends, and what friends a person chooses to be with all depend on how a person comes to view his or her self and who the person thinks he or she is as a person at the end of this negotiation process.

For years psychologists have tried to create questionnaires to measure the self-concept. Answering prewritten questions is an imperfect method, at best, for measuring an individual's self-concept. When someone answers on a scale that he or she is "very aggressive," it does not necessarily mean that he or she is an aggressive person. Perhaps he or she just hurt someone accidentally before walking into the room and is feeling bad about it. Besides the survey, then, how can psychologists measure self-concept?

The answer lies with a less structured technique made popular by psychologist William McGuire. This technique, called the "spontaneous self-concept measure," asks subjects to write down the first twenty words or phrases they think of when they are asked, "Who are you?" This is a particularly useful method because the test does not suggest which characteristics are important. The subjects decide for themselves whether to mention "aggressive" as a word that describes them. Psychologists can then look at the kinds of descriptors individuals are using and gain some insight as to what characteristics make up their self-concept, how they feel about themselves, and how certain they are of themselves. If an individual mentions on line 4 that he or she is "shy" and then mentions on line 13 that he or she is "outgoing," this may signal to professionals that the person is uncertain of his or her self-image on the shy-outgoing dimension.

More often than not, the cause of an uncertain self lies in the negotiation process. If an individual hears from one group of people that he or she is "great" and "really smart" but constantly hears from others that he or she is "worthless" and "stupid," developing a stable sense of self will be very difficult. If an individual has continuously received conflicting messages about who he or she is, how can the process be turned around to stabilize the person's sense of self?

The answer, unfortunately, is not an easy one. It would be helpful to discover exactly what the individual considers to be important and unimportant about his or her self. It is often the case that a person has unrealistic standards because of the conflicting messages the person has received about his or her worth and abilities. It is entirely possible that the person has decided that the most important thing about his or her self is the ability to please everyone. Then the person will go through life constantly putting on a different face and acting like a different person.

A person may act intelligent around people who think being smart is important, and unintelligent around people who think it is not important. It is even possible that the individual will experiment with drugs and alcohol even if he or she does not like them or disapproves of their use, solely because someone who is important to him or her thinks that doing such things is important. In this manner, the individual may be overly influenced by the important people in his or her life and may never come to have a sense of self that is stable, secure, and positive.

To stabilize his or her sense of self, such a person must be convinced that it is perfectly all right not to be everything to everyone. The person will have to be convinced that true friends will accept the person for who he or she is rather than for who he or she can pretend to be. When a person projects a secure and satisfied sense of self to others, then others are more likely to accept that person.

Context

The study of the "self" grew out of early attempts by the Greek philosophers to understand what makes each human being different from, yet similar to, all other human beings. There was a need to understand how the environment in which one is reared, the challenges one is presented, and the people one encounters all work together to create a self that will influence one for the rest of one's life. Only when one understands how the development of self occurs normally can one do anything to help those individuals whose self-concepts are unstable or negative.

Intense attempts to study the self did not come about until the late 1800's and the early 1900's. Study of the self has played a large role in the history of psychological inquiry, and twentieth century views on self suggest that the influence of this topic will not diminish. As the world becomes increasingly complex, the multitude of factors that will influence a child's development of self-concept will continue to increase. Many demands are placed on individuals to be different people at different times. A tug-of-war such as this is bound to have a dramatic impact on how people view and feel about their selves.

Studying the self has been important in psychology because what people do in a social setting touches others. Kurt Lewin's research in the late 1940's provided the first empirical support to suggest to the science of psychology that the other individuals with whom a person comes in contact will have a profound impact on who the person becomes. Lewin argued that "behavior is a function of the person and the environment." Whenever someone behaves, to understand that behavior one must understand something about his or her personality or his or her self and something about the environment in which the person has interacted. Lewin did not believe that the term "environment" meant solely the physical environment. Other individuals are a significant part of one's environment. If the argument is carried to its logical conclusion, one's self-concept is a construction of one's own attributes, abilities, attitudes, and the values of the significant others with whom one has interacted and continues to interact.

In the late 1970's, research began to address the developmental nature of self. Perhaps the most comprehensive attempt to systematize the developmental processes that create the self has been made by Mark Snyder. Snyder attempts to describe how an individual develops an identity that focuses on internal characteristics of self versus external characteristics. If an individual is constantly concerned with how he or she is doing in a situation—asking him- or herself, "Do I fit in?" or "Do my clothes look good?"—then he or she may be considered a "high self-monitor." An individual, however, called a "low self-monitor" is more concerned with whether he or she is behaving according to his or her internal standards, asking him- or herself, "Am I doing this because someone else wants me to or because I want to?" The aspect of self the person monitors (the inside or the outside) in a social situation will have a profound impact on how others will view, and act toward, the person. Given the importance of other persons in the development of one's self-concepts, clearly internal/external difference can drastically influence self-concept development.

The aspect of self that a person is monitoring or controlling (the internal or the external) indicates how that person will behave, what other people this person will choose to be with, what kinds of things this person will want to do, and even which products this person may want to buy. Psychology has as its goal a concern with trying to predict how different people will behave in different situations. Study of the nature and development of self has moved professionals a long way toward being able to predict such behavior. In this sense, the study of the self, in general, and the development of particular kinds of selves, more specifically, has been of great importance to the field of psychology.

Bibliography

Buss, Arnold. *Self-consciousness and Social Anxiety.* San Francisco: W. H. Freeman, 1980. Very clearly written, this book tracks the development of internal and external awareness of self as well as some of the developmental causes of shyness and social anxiety.

Cooley, Charles H. *Human Nature and the Social Order.* New York: Charles Scribner's Sons, 1902. This is an early, but thorough, account of self-concept development. This was the first work to stress clearly that other individuals have a profound impact on the development of the self-concept.

Goffman, Erving. *The Presentation of Self in Everyday Life.* Garden City, N.Y.: Doubleday, 1959. A short book that is extremely fun to read and easy to understand, this is a contemporary look at the way people alter themselves to get by in everyday life.

Snyder, Mark. *Public Appearances, Private Realities: The Psychology of Self-Monitoring.* New York: W. H. Freeman, 1987. Snyder tracks the development of the self-monitoring construct and systematically tells the reader how an internal or external monitoring of self affects people's behavior. It is easy to understand, clearly written, and thoroughly enjoyable.

Williams, Robert, and James D. Long. *Manage Your Life.* Boston: Houghton Mifflin, 1991. This book is intended to serve as a guide for personal growth in a variety of areas. The most significant chapters deal with changing the aspects of the self-concept with which a person is dissatisfied. It is a very readable book that uses real-life examples to help convey the main points.

Randall E. Osborne

Cross-References

Attitude-Behavior Consistency, 320; Identity Crises: Erikson, 1255; Midlife Crises, 1575; Self-Actualization, 2168; Self-Concept Origins, 2175; Self-Disclosure, 2182; Self-Esteem, 2188; Self-Perception Theory, 2193; Self-Presentation, 2200; Social Identity Theory, 2297.

SELF-ACTUALIZATION

Type of psychology: Personality
Fields of study: Humanistic-phenomenological models; personality theory

Self-actualization, a constructive process of functioning optimally and fulfilling one's potentials, is perhaps the central concept and most influential model within humanistic psychology. The self-actualization theory and model have had important applications in the fields of counseling, education, and business, and hold significant implications for basic conceptions of humankind and for society.

Principal terms

ACTUALIZING TENDENCY: the innate, directional, positive force toward maintaining and enhancing the organism, achieving congruence between experience and awareness, and realizing potentials

EXISTENTIALISM: a viewpoint emphasizing concern with human existence and situation in the world; it gives meaning to life through the free choice of mature values and commitment to responsible goals

HUMANISTIC PSYCHOLOGY: a branch of psychology that emphasizes growth and fulfillment, autonomy, choice and responsibility, and ultimate values such as truth, love, and justice

ORGANISMIC THEORY: an approach that extends the holistic view to the entire organism, emphasizing unity, coherence, integrity, and consistency

PHENOMENOLOGY: an approach that stresses openness to direct experience in introspective or unsophisticated ways, without using analysis, theory, expectations, or interpretation

SELF: the unified and integrated center of one's experience and awareness, experienced both subjectively, as actor, and objectively, as recipient of actions

SYNERGY: the degree to which a society's institutions are structured so that one's activities yield benefit both to oneself and to the larger group

Overview

Self-actualization is often defined as a process of growing and fulfilling one's potential, of being self-directed and integrated, of moving toward full humanness. The most complete description of the self-actualizing person has been provided by the psychologist Abraham Maslow, who devoted much of his professional life to the study of exceptional and significantly growing individuals. Maslow abstracted several ways in which self-actualizing people could be characterized.

Compared to ordinary or average persons, self-actualizing persons, as Maslow describes them, may be characterized as follows. They show a more efficient and accurate perception of reality, seeing things as they really are rather than as distortions based on wishes or neurotic needs. They accept themselves, others, and nature as they are. They are spontaneous both in behavior and in thinking, and focus on problems outside themselves rather than being self-centered. Self-actualizing persons enjoy and need solitude and privacy; are autonomous, with the ability to transcend culture and environment; have a freshness of appreciation, taking pleasure and finding wonder in the everyday world; and have peak experiences or ecstatic, mystic feelings that provide special meaning to everyday life. They show social interest, which is a deep feeling of empathy, sympathy, identification, and compassionate affection for humankind in general, and have deep interpersonal relationships with others. They carry a democratic character structure that includes humility, respect for everyone, and emphasis on common bonds rather than differences; they distinguish between means and ends, and possess a clear sense of ethics. Self-actualizers have a philosophical and unhostile sense of humor, and are creative and inventive in an everyday sense. They are resistant to enculturation, with a degree of detachment and autonomy greater than that found in people who are motivated simply to adjust to and go along with their own in-groups or society. Their value system results from their great acceptance of self and others, and easily resolves or transcends many dichotomies (such as work/pleasure, selfish/unselfish, good versus bad) that others view as absolute opposites.

Carl Rogers, another influential humanistic psychologist, characterized the fully functioning person in ways that parallel Maslow's description. Rogers' theory holds that people have an actualizing tendency, which is an inherent striving to actualize, maintain, and enhance the organism. When people function according to valuing processes based within them and are therefore following their actualizing tendency, experiences can be accurately symbolized into awareness and efficiently communicated. Thus, according to Rogers, full humanness involves openness to experiences of all kinds without distorting them. People thus open to experience will show a flexible, existential kind of living that allows change, adaptability, and a sense of flowing. These people trust their own internal feelings of what is right, and they use the self as their basis for and guide to behavior. Rogers, like Maslow, holds that such people do not necessarily adjust or conform to cultural prescriptions, but nevertheless they do live constructively.

Rogers, Maslow, and most self-actualization theorists present an optimistic and favorable view of human nature. Unlike Sigmund Freud and classical psychoanalysts, who believed humans to be basically irrational and human impulses to require control through socialization and other societal constraints, self-actualization theorists regard human nature as constructive, trustworthy, positive, forward moving, rational, and possessing an inherent capacity to realize or actualize itself.

Although Maslow approached his study of growing individuals from a somewhat more absolute, rational, theoretical perspective than Rogers, who came from a more relativistic, phenomenological, and clinical direction, the theorizing and empirical observations of both psychologists converge upon a similar description of a self-actualizing or fully functioning person who makes full use of capacities and potentialities. Such descriptions have aroused much positive as well as negative reaction. One reason is the implicit suggestion that humankind can or should be self-actualizing. The values of actualizing one's self, of fulfilling one's potentials and possessing the characteristics described by Maslow and Rogers, are always implied; thus, self-actualization is more than a psychological construct. It becomes a possible ethic. Many humanistic proponents have viewed values as necessary in their theorizing; Maslow made an impassioned plea that values, crucial to the development of humanistic psychology, be integrated into science.

Critics of self-actualization theory have argued that it reflects the theorists' own values and individualist ideology; that it neglects sociohistorical and cultural changes by being rooted in unchanging biology; that there may be social-class or cultural bias in the descriptions; that the concept may be misused, and encourage the creation of a cultural aristocracy of "superior" people; and that many people may well choose an ideal self that does not match Maslow's characterization. In addition, critics have misunderstood the concept by erroneously thinking that self-actualizing is synonymous with selfishness and self-indulgence, or is consistent with asocial or antisocial behavior. In fact, Maslow and Rogers described self-actualizers as not being overly concerned with themselves, but as typically engaged in larger issues and problems such as poverty, bigotry, warfare, and environmental concerns; as having a highly ethical nature; and as having relationships with others that have a positive and even therapeutic quality.

The various criticisms and arguments surrounding self-actualization have led to clarifications and improvements in understanding the concept, and attest the vitality of this major, provocative, and influential psychological construct.

Applications

Self-actualization presents a growth model that can be and has been used in diverse areas such as counseling, education, and business. In addition, there are implications for people's way of conceptualizing humankind and for structuring institutions and organizing society.

As a model for therapists and counselors and their clients, it is an alternative to the medical or illness model, which implies that the person coming to the therapist is beset by disease and requires a cure, often from some external source or authority. The self-actualization model represents a positive process, a fostering of strengths; it is concerned with growth choices, self-knowledge, being fully human, and realizing one's potential; yet it also encompasses an understanding of anxiety, defenses, and obstacles to growth. Psychological education, growth facilitation, self-help and self-learning, and counseling to deal with problems of living and with dysfunctional defenses all are implied in the self-actualization model for human fulfillment and actualization of potentials. This model also avoids problems associated with an adjustment model, in which therapists may socialize conformity or adjustment to a particular status quo or societal mainstream.

Carl Rogers employed the model in his nondirective, client-centered counseling, later called the person-centered approach. Grounded in trust and emphasizing the therapist's unconditional positive regard, empathy, and genuineness, this therapy system allows the client's natural and healthy growth tendencies and organismic valuing processes to determine choices and behaviors. Much research has supported the importance of these therapist characteristics and has documented the increased congruence and process of growth of clients, beginning with Rogers' own empirical research explorations. Rogers' approach to counseling has become one of the most influential in the psychotherapy field.

Maslow's application of self-actualization theory to management represents another very influential contribution. Douglas McGregor described a humanistic theory of management (theory Y) that respects human rights and treats workers as individuals. This theory was contrasted with theory X, a managerial view that holds that people dislike work and must therefore be controlled, coerced, conditioned, or externally reinforced to get high work productivity. Maslow's own book on management assumes the existence of higher needs in all workers that, if met in the world of work, would demonstrate the inherent creativity and responsibility of workers and result in greater satisfaction, increased self-direction, and also greater work productivity. Many influential management theorists, including McGregor, Rensis Likert, and Chris Argyris, have acknowledged Maslow's influence on them. Many field and research studies have supported the value of the self-actualization model as applied to management. Maslow contended that such enlightened management policies are necessary for interacting with a growing, actualizing population; in the world of work, as elsewhere, the highest levels of efficiency can be obtained only by taking full account of the need for self-actualization that is present in everyone.

One of the major conclusions and implications stemming from the self-actualization model is that a synergic society can evolve naturally from the present social system; such a society would be one in which every person may reach a high level of fulfillment.

Ruth Benedict tried to account for differences in societies that related to the overall human fulfillment they could afford their citizens. She prepared brief descriptions of four pairs of cultures. One of each pair was an insecure society, described as nasty, surly, and anxious, with low levels of moral behavior and high levels of hatred and aggression. The contrasting culture was a secure one, described as comfortable, showing affection and niceness. The concept of synergy differentiated these two groups. In high-synergy societies, social arrangements allowed for mutually reinforcing acts that would benefit both individual people and the group; these societies were characterized by nonaggression and cooperation. In low-synergy societies, the social structure provided for mutually opposed and counteractive acts, whereby one individual could or must benefit at the expense of others; these were the cultures in which aggression, insecurity, and rivalry were conspicuous.

Roderic Gorney described how the absolute amount of wealth in a society did not determine the degree of synergy or quality of life in that society. More crucial, he found, were the economic arrangements within the society—whether the resources were concentrated among a "have" group (low synergy) or were dispersed widely to all (high synergy). Gorney argued that low-synergy arrangements in societies promoted higher levels of aggression and mental disorder. Thus, to minimize aggression and mental disorder and to promote self-development and zestful investment in living and learning, Gorney specified that a society should increase the degree of synergy fostered by its institutions.

Thus, the self-actualization model and theory have clear implications for societies and their political and economic structures. The model suggests action and implies consequences. It stresses a particular type of relationship between the society and the individual as a social being. The commingling of individual and social concerns and involvements translates self-actualization theory into practical consequences, and is precisely what Maslow described as characterizing his self-actualizers. Self-actualizing people easily resolve superficial dichotomies, and choices are not inevitably seen as either/or. Work and play, lust and love, self-love and love for others need not be opposites. Maslow described the individual-societal holism by noting that self-actualizing people were not only the best experiencers but also the most compassionate people, the great reformers of society, and the most effective workers against injustice, inequality, and other social ills.

Thus, what self-actualization theory suggests is an integration of self-improvement and social zeal; Maslow held that both can occur simultaneously.

Context

The development of the self-actualization concept was influenced by many sources. Carl G. Jung, Otto Rank, and Alfred Adler, departing from Freud's classical psychoanalytic formulations, emphasized the importance of individuality and social dimensions. Jung, credited with being the first to use the term self-actualization, developed the concept of the self as a goal of life; self-actualization meant a complete differentiation and harmonious blending of the many aspects of personality. Rank emphasized the necessity of expressing one's individuality to be creative. Adler described self-actualization motives with the concept of striving for superiority or perfection; this innate striving, or great upward drive, was a prepotent dynamic principle of human development. Adler also believed that a constructive working toward perfection (of self and society) would result from a loving, trustworthy early social environment.

Kurt Goldstein, the first psychologist who explicitly used self-actualization as the master motive or most basic sovereign drive, was a leading exponent of organismic theory; this approach emphasized unity, consistency, coherence, and integrity of normal personality. Goldstein held self-actualization to be a universal phenomenon; all organisms tend to actualize their individual capacities and inner natures as much as possible. Prescott Lecky also propounded the achievement of a unified and self-consistent organization as the one developmental goal; his concepts of self-consistency and unified personality have much in common with organismic theory. Later, Gordon Allport stressed methods for studying the unique and undivided personality; he described motivation for normal adults as functionally autonomous, and in the individual's conscious awareness. Fritz Perls's Gestalt therapy emphasized here-and-now awareness and integrated personality.

Sociology and cultural anthropology influenced other theorists. Karen Horney spoke of the real self and its realization; Erich Fromm wrote of the "productive orientation," combining productive work and productive love; and David Riesman described the autonomous person and theorized about inner- and other-directed personalities. Arthur Combs and Donald Snygg, influenced by the phenomenological approach, emphasized the maintenance and enhancement of the self as the inclusive human need motivating all behavior. Their description of the adequate self is quite similar to the contemporary description of self-actualization.

Existentialist views, emphasizing the present, free will, values and ultimate concerns, and subjective experience as a sufficient criterion of truth, influenced conceptualizing about self-actualization. Rollo May's description of existential being is important in this respect.

From all these sources came the backdrop for the modern description of self-actualization—the emphasis on the uniqueness of the individual; a holistic, organismic, and phenomenological approach to human experience and conduct; and the need to discover a real self and to express, develop, and actualize that self.

Self-actualization, as a concept, a theory, and a model, has extended the domain and impact of psychology. Humanistic psychology has become an important paradigm for understanding personality, psychopathology, and therapy. Applications have been extensive in education, counseling, religion, and business. Suggesting action and implying consequences, self-actualization holds clear and significant implications regarding the dimensions of psychology, the basic conception of humankind, and the functions and organization of society.

Bibliography

Goble, Frank G. *The Third Force: The Psychology of Abraham Maslow.* New York: Grossman, 1970. An accessible, highly readable book. Summarizes in brief, succinct chapters the major concepts and ideas of Maslow, such as basic needs, human potential, psychological growth, values, and synergy. Concludes with a survey of applications in education, mental health, and business and industry.

Jones, Alvin, and Rick Crandall, eds. "Handbook of Self-Actualization." Special issue. *Journal of Social Behavior and Personality*, no. 5 (1991). A collection of papers on self-actualization and optimal functioning, including theoretical and analytical papers, empirical studies, and examination of issues in assessing self-actualization. The papers, variable in quality and sophistication, cover the field broadly, present interesting implications, and point to future directions.

Maslow, Abraham Harold. *Motivation and Personality.* 3d ed. New York: Harper & Row, 1987. Presents Maslow's classic paper describing self-actualizing people and includes major sections on his motivation theory, on normality and abnormality, and on methodology in psychology. Slightly revised by editors, this third edition is more readable than earlier ones. Two additional chapters succinctly describe Maslow's tremendous influence and impact. Includes chronological bibliography of his writings.

_____. *Toward a Psychology of Being.* 2d ed. Princeton, N.J.: Van Nostrand Reinhold, 1968. A second major book of Maslow's psychological writings, with significant sections on growth and motivation, self-actualizing cognition, creativeness, and values. The style is rather pedantic.

Rogers, Carl Ransom. *On Becoming a Person.* Boston: Houghton Mifflin, 1961. A highly readable book and an excellent introduction to Rogers' warm, personal, direct style of communicating his ideas. Covers the fully functioning person, Rogers' views on dimensions of the helping relationship and ways people grow in therapy, and applications of his approach in education, the family, and other areas.

_____. *A Way of Being.* Boston: Houghton Mifflin, 1980. A clear presentation of experiences and ideas personally and professionally important to Rogers. Personal chapters deal with experiences in communication, origins of his philosophy, views on reality and his career, and feelings on aging. Other chapters describe foundations, applications, and implications of his person-centered approach, including education, community building, and empathy as a way of life. Includes chronological bibliography of Rogers' works.

Edward R. Whitson

Cross-References

Abnormality: Humanistic-Existential Models, 60; Existential Analysis and Therapy, 999; Gestalt Therapy, 1088; Humanism: An Overview, 1203; Humanistic Trait Models: Gordon Allport, 1210; Person-Centered Therapy, 1777; Self-Esteem, 2188.

SELF-CONCEPT ORIGINS

Type of psychology: Social psychology
Field of study: Social perception and cognition

Social psychologists posit that the origins of the self-concept are rooted in a lifelong process of social interaction; individuals develop self-awareness and self-knowledge through familial and cultural socialization and the assumption of social roles.

Principal terms

ATTRIBUTION: an explanation about the underlying causes of social behavior, which may be either dispositional or situational

LONGITUDINAL STUDY: a research methodology that requires psychologists to test the same subjects repeatedly over a specified period of time

REFERENCE GROUP: the individuals who are meaningful to a person and often are the focus of social comparison processes

REFLECTED APPRAISAL: a psychological process whereby a person infers the nature of the perceptions and evaluations that other people hold about him or her

SELF-CONCEPT: all the thoughts that a person holds about himself or herself

SELF-ENHANCEMENT: a psychological process whereby an individual bolsters his or her self-concept and self-esteem

SELF-ESTEEM: the result of a person's evaluation of his or her self-concept; a favorable evaluation is associated with high self-esteem, a negative evaluation with low self-esteem

SELF-PERCEPTION: a psychological process whereby individuals infer the nature of their attitudes and beliefs by observing their own behavior

SOCIAL COMPARISON: a psychological process that involves comparing one's abilities and opinions with those of one's reference group

SOCIAL REALITY: the shared opinions, beliefs, and values of one's reference group

Overview

Social psychologists generally consider the self-concept to consist of the beliefs that people hold about their abilities, interests, aptitudes, and psychological characteristics. The origins of the self-concept are rooted in human social interaction. The social psychological perspective maintains that individuals develop self-awareness and self-knowledge through the process of socialization and the assumption of social roles. Psychologists posit that a positive self-concept, high self-esteem, and other measures of good psychological adjustment are the result of a self-enhancing pattern of psychological processes that are commonly engaged in during human social interaction. Three of these psychological processes that are particularly relevant to the development of the self-concept are self-perception, reflected appraisal, and social comparison.

Self-perception theory describes a process whereby individuals make judgments about their attitudes, beliefs, and other psychological characteristics. Self-perception theory, which was first described by Daryl Bem in 1972, posits that individual self-awareness is somewhat limited and that people have no innate understanding of the content of their self-concepts. Rather, people infer the nature of their attitudes and beliefs through an ongoing process of social observation. That is, individuals observe their habitual patterns of behavior and the situations in which they occur and learn about themselves by making attributions about the causes underlying their behavior.

Behaviors that are attributed to one's personal attitudes, beliefs, or personality characteristics may have a profound impact on the self-concept. On the other hand, Bem argued that behaviors which are attributed to situational factors are discounted; hence, they are unlikely to influence the self-concept. Suppose, for example, a young boy finds that he tends to spend his after-school hours at athletic practice. He may very likely attribute his behavior to the fact that he enjoys athletics and describe himself as "athletic" or a "jock." Thus, his after-school behavior is attributed to personal preference and has an impact on his definition of himself. On the other hand, if a corporate intern finds that she is working harder and becoming more productive as the date of her annual salary review approaches, she may not attribute her behavior to the fact that she is "hard-working" or a "workaholic," but rather to the situation (the annual salary review). People who attribute their behavior to situational factors such as coercion or obligations are unlikely to internalize their behavior; thus, the self-concept is relatively unaffected.

The second process implicated in self-concept formation, reflected appraisal, was described by sociologist Charles Horton Cooley in 1902. Reflected appraisal refers to a process by which individuals develop a sense of themselves as reflected in others' eyes. Cooley used a metaphor, the "looking-glass self," to describe the active, social nature of this process. He theorized that people attend to the manner in which other people respond to them. People infer the nature of others' judgments of their behavior by observing reactions, such as praise or blame, to their actions. These judgments, in turn, can become incorporated into a person's self-concept. For example, a child may be scolded by his parent for accidentally breaking a vase while playing in the house. If the parent repeatedly berates the child for being clumsy on this and other occasions, the child may begin to perceive himself as awkward and ungainly, and thus become self-conscious about his clumsiness. That is, when individuals repeatedly experience acceptance or rejection in social encounters, they may alter their self-concepts in order to become consistent with these responses.

Another psychological process that has an important influence on self-concept formation is social comparison. Social comparison theory, which was introduced by Leon Festinger in 1954, describes a process of self-evaluation in relation to one's reference group. A reference group is made up of the individuals that are meaning-ful in a person's life, which might include parents, close friends, role models, and so on. Festinger argued that people are not content to take their opinions and abilities for granted. He proposed that personal opinions or abilities are not determined by reference to objective reality. Rather, people are motivated to evaluate their opinions and abilities subjectively, in terms of social reality, which consists of the shared beliefs, opinions, and values of one's salient reference group.

The use of selective social comparisons plays an important role in the manage-ment of a positive self-concept. People may compare themselves with a role model who provides them with a goal or standard for achievement. A young trainee, for example, might compare her professional advancement in a corporation with the career of a fast-track female executive whom she admires. Alternatively, people may compare themselves with someone less fortunate in order to enhance their self-concept. Students who receive a mediocre exam score, for example, may feel better about their academic ability if they consider the hapless students who failed the exam. Thus, social comparisons have important motivational and self-enhancing functions in self-concept formation.

Applications

Social psychologists have investigated the relationship of self-perception, reflected appraisal, and social comparison to the formation of the self-concept and the en-hancement of self-esteem. Many researchers are interested in identifying the manner in which these psychological processes are related to individual differences in the nature of the self-concept. This line of research generally focuses on the content of beliefs that individuals hold about themselves. Other researchers are interested in identifying how the selective use of these processes is related to individual differ-ences in self-esteem. This line of research is concerned with how individuals evalu-ate their self-concepts.

Psychologists Frances Haemmerlie and Robert Montgomery conducted a series of studies in the early 1980's that were designed to investigate the effects of self-perception on the self-concept. These researchers were interested in studying the effects of structured social behavior upon shyness and social anxiety. They recruited a sample of college men who seldom dated and had high scores on a social anxiety scale. Haemmerlie and Montgomery hypothesized that shyness had an important effect on the self-concept because shy people are likely to avoid social encounters. In turn, people who avoid social situations and date infrequently are likely to label themselves as socially inept, hence internalizing this negative trait into their self-concept. Negative self-perceptions of this type are particularly resistant to change because people may become increasingly reclusive.

Haemmerlie and Montgomery's studies were designed to provide several positive social experiences for these shy subjects who came to the laboratory for a number of experimental sessions over the course of a few weeks. Female college-age confeder-ates had been employed by the researchers to chat pleasantly with the shy subjects while they were waiting for the experimenters. The shy men were told that the confederates were fellow subjects; they did not know that these women had been paid to initiate conversations with them. Haemmerlie and Montgomery found that after their series of chats with the female confederates, most of their shy subjects reported increased self-confidence, less anxiety, and greater feelings of competence in mixed-sex interactions. In support of self-perception theory, Haemmerlie and Montgomery concluded that shy subjects had attributed their pleasant conversations with these women to factors about themselves rather than the situation. Thus, by observing themselves chatting with pleasant women, they began to see themselves as less anxious and more socially competent, thus changing their self-concept in a positive fashion.

Another important social influence on self-concept formation is the perceived evaluations of the people who are close to oneself. A longitudinal study conducted by Richard Felson in the late 1980's investigated the influence of parental reflected appraisal on the self-concept of elementary- and middle-school-age children. He asked parents to provide appraisals of their children. This measure was considered to be an actual appraisal. Then, he asked the children to describe their parents' perceptions of them. This measure was considered to be a reflected appraisal. He compared actual to reflected appraisals in order to ascertain the accuracy of the reflected appraisals. The relationship of actual and reflected appraisals to the child's self-concept was then measured.

First, Felson found that children's self-concepts were indeed influenced by both the actual and perceived appraisals of their parents. This suggests that the opinion of significant others does in fact influence the self-concept. He also found, however, that while children were basing part of their self-concept on reflected parental appraisal, the children's reflected appraisals were not very accurate. Felson hypothesized that reflected appraisals from people other than parents with whom children interact augment parental reflected appraisals. These findings suggest that parents are not the only important socializing agents in a child's social environment, and the self-concept may be influenced by significant persons outside the child's family.

Much of the self-concept research has been conducted with children, adolescents, or college-age subjects. This emphasis may reflect, to some degree, cultural assumptions that the self-concept is formed fairly early in life and that it remains relatively stable throughout adulthood. Some psychologists, however, have been interested in documenting the selective use of psychological processes to enhance one's self-esteem and maintain a positive self-image in other population samples. In the mid-1980's, social psychologists Joanne Wood, Shelley Taylor, and Rosemary Lichtman investigated the impact of breast cancer upon women's self-concept. They hypothesized that adults respond to a life-threatening event such as cancer through an ongoing process of adjustment. An important part of the adjustment process, they argued, is the selective use of social comparisons to maintain a positive self-concept and to enhance self-esteem.

Wood and her colleagues found that women who were adjusting well, both psychologically and physically, to their illnesses tended to report selective social comparisons when discussing their illness, surgery, physical recovery, and subsequent adjustment. For the most part, these women tended to make social comparisons with other breast cancer patients who were relatively disadvantaged. For example, one patient who was recovering from a mastectomy might compare herself with another cancer patient who had died. Another, married patient might say that she was adjusting well to her treatment but that she pitied the unmarried cancer patients who did not have the support of a husband. Thus, women who were adjusting well tended to make social comparisons by selecting dimensions upon which they were relatively advantaged. Wood and her colleagues argued that these findings suggested that selective, self-enhancing social comparisons play an important role in adjustment to stress and negative life events.

The results of these studies suggest that social interaction does indeed play an important role in the formation of the self-concept and the maintenance of self-esteem. Self-perception, reflected appraisal, and social comparison are important factors in the lifelong process of developing self-knowledge and self-awareness. Further, it appears that most people are motivated to maintain a positive self-concept and strive to enhance their self-esteem. Thus, the social psychological conception of mental health and well-being focuses upon this selective use of psychological processes in the development of the self-concept.

Context

Selfhood, identity, and individuality are common recurring themes in Western thought. For centuries, philosophers have held debates about human nature and the soul. These themes recur in the history of psychological theory and research, as evidenced by social and personality psychologists' long-standing interest in the social origins of the self-concept. William James's *The Principles of Psychology* (1890) contains a chapter on the development of the self that is considered to be a classic. This chapter introduced the social psychological concept of the self and self-esteem. Many of the more recent psychological theories of self-concept formation and self-esteem enhancement trace their origins to this work. For example, Cooley's conception of the "looking-glass self" is based upon James's notion of the social self. Cooley's writings, in turn, influenced the work of another sociologist, George Herbert Mead. Mead's work, which was published in the early 1930's, was influential in promoting the view of the reciprocal relationship of the individual to society. Both Cooley and Mead are important figures in the symbolic interactionist perspective in sociological social psychology.

In the late 1920's and early 1930's, there was little mention of the self-concept in American psychology. During that time, the science of behaviorism, popularized by John B. Watson and B. F. Skinner, was the prevailing model in psychology. This model focused on observable behavior, not internal psychological processes, and research into the origin and nature of the self-concept was neglected in favor of learning and behavior change. This shift was reversed in the 1940's, when Gordon

Allport published his influential essay on the self-concept in psychology.

Since the 1940's, research on the self-concept, self-esteem, and social interaction has increased dramatically. Social psychologists, in particular, have been active contributors to the field. The roles of seemingly disparate theoretical concepts such as social comparison, self-perception, and reflected appraisal have been acknowledged as contributing to a single psychological process. Since the late 1960's, research into these processes has continued, and many theorists have turned their energies to outlining comprehensive theories of the self. These theories attempt to integrate research findings in attitude change, value formation, attribution theory, and other social cognitive theories. In addition to contributing to basic research, self-concept studies have made contributions to many other applied fields, such as mental health, scholastic achievement, educational psychology, and stress management.

Bibliography

Gergen, Kenneth J. *The Concept of Self.* New York: Holt, Rinehart and Winston, 1971. An excellent summary of the self-concept written by an important contributor to the field. Presents a historical overview of the study of the self and includes chapters summarizing theoretical issues in conceptualizing the self-concept, psychological processes in self-concept formation and maintenance, and the influence of the self-concept on interpersonal behavior (for example, level of aspiration, self-presentation).

Rosenberg, Morris. *Conceiving the Self.* New York: Basic Books, 1979. A thorough review of the principles of self-concept formation and self-esteem maintenance for the general reader. Identifies important motivational factors that influence the self-concept and self-esteem. Summarizes research findings on the relationship of social class, minority status, and group membership to self-esteem.

Schlenker, Barry R., ed. *The Self and Social Life.* New York: McGraw-Hill, 1985. Introduces and summarizes a number of different research perspectives on the self-concept for the college-level reader. The focus is the reciprocal relationship of the individual and the social environment. Specific topics include self-presentation, self-regulation of behavior, and an attributional model of excuses.

Taylor, Shelley E. *Positive Illusions: Creative Self-Deception and the Healthy Mind.* New York: Basic Books, 1989. Summarizes a large number of research studies that investigate the relationship of self-enhancing biases in social psychological processes to mental health and psychological adjustment. Discusses the effects of social psychological processes on the self-concept, coping, and physical health. Accessible to the general reader. Contains a number of everyday examples of important concepts and principles.

Wegner, Daniel M., and Robin R. Vallacher, eds. *The Self in Social Psychology.* New York: Oxford University Press, 1980. Eleven chapters written by eminent social psychologists working within self theory. Provides an introduction to the field for the college-level reader. Specific topics include the self-perception of motivation and emotion, self-presentation, self-disclosure, and prosocial behavior.

Yardley, Krysia, and Terry Honess, eds. *Self and Identity: Psychosocial Perspectives.* New York: John Wiley & Sons, 1987. Introduces the college-level reader to the social psychological view of self, from both historical and theoretical perspectives, and its relationship to the social environment. Includes separate sections on the cognitive and affective nature of the self-concept and its formation. Another series of chapters discusses the development of psychological disorders (for example, self-awareness and shyness) and their treatment.

Cheryl A. Rickabaugh

Cross-References

Attachment and Bonding in Infancy and Childhood, 307; Cognitive Dissonance Theory, 560; Gender-Identity Formation, 1062; Parenting Styles, 1740; Racism, 2037; Self: Definition and Assessment, 2162; Self-Esteem, 2188; Self-Perception Theory, 2193; Self-Presentation, 2200; Sexism, 2240; Social Identity Theory, 2297; Social Schemata, 2329.

SELF-DISCLOSURE

Type of psychology: Social psychology
Field of study: Interpersonal relations

Self-disclosure is the process of revealing personal information during communication with others. Progress in self-disclosure depends on personal skills and interpersonal intimacy; appropriate self-disclosure is important in communicating effectively and maintaining healthy close relationships.

Principal terms
INTERDEPENDENCE: a type of relationship in which both parties' outcomes are jointly determined; interdependent relationships are stronger and more enduring than simple exchanges
INTIMACY: closeness or depth of communication; intimate self-disclosure reveals information and feelings that are important to one's self-concept
LONELINESS: the experience of insufficient or inadequate relationships; inappropriate or inexpressive self-disclosures can lead to loneliness
RECIPROCITY: the even exchange of intimacy levels in personal communication; responding "in kind" can build trust in a relationship
SOCIAL PENETRATION: the process of increasing breadth and depth of communication as a relationship develops over time

Overview

Self-disclosure is the process of communicating personal information to another individual. It involves a willingness to reveal intimate thoughts and feelings rather than superficial or obvious characteristics. Scientists studying personal relationships have found that, as two people become acquainted and interact over time, they reveal more of themselves to each other. For example, when two people first know each other, their conversation may be limited to the weather, mutual interests, and similarly "safe" topics. The topics they discuss are neutral, and the feelings they express are matters of public knowledge. As their relationship develops, they feel comfortable disclosing more intimate feelings and experiences. Later in their friendship, their conversation may be entirely about their feelings, personal problems, and other experiences that are not public knowledge. Self-disclosure is the process by which communication in a relationship becomes more private and intimate.

The term self-disclosure was introduced by psychologist Sidney Jourard in his 1964 book *The Transparent Self: Self-Disclosure and Well-Being.* Early work by therapists and researchers speculated that self-disclosure is essential for the health and growth of personal relationships; however, not all self-disclosures serve to promote relationships. Disclosures can be distinguished as either appropriate or inappropriate. Healthy intimacy is promoted when one's self-disclosure suits the time and place as well as the relationship. When two people are close friends, for example, it is appropriate for them to reveal personal information or feelings to each other.

In contrast, confessing intimate feelings or confiding personal experiences to a stranger or mild acquaintance is inappropriate. Personal revelations are too intimate for those interactions. Such inappropriate self-disclosure elicits withdrawal or rejection by others. Self-disclosure can also be inappropriate because it is not intimate enough. For example, if two long-time friends converse about their lives, and one refuses to tell the other about a problem because it is somewhat personal, the other will feel rejected or slighted. Because of their history as friends, personal confidences are appropriate, while non-disclosure is not.

The quality of self-disclosure was considered in the 1973 book *Social Penetration: The Development of Interpersonal Relationships* by Irwin Altman and Dalmas Taylor. Altman and Taylor argue that, as a relationship develops, communication between partners increases in two qualities or dimensions: breadth and depth. Breadth increases before depth. Communication becomes broader as partners add more topic areas to their conversation. Eventually the two people's communication also deepens: Their interaction becomes less superficial and more intimate. For example, two people whose early friendship is based on a common interest in music will discover other things in common (greater breadth) as they communicate. Eventually, they not only talk about what they mutually enjoy but also confide in each other and help each other solve problems (greater depth).

Altman and Taylor argue that most relationships develop in a more satisfactory way when self-disclosure proceeds (breadth before depth) over time; however, not all individuals conform to this ideal. For example, some persons are "low revealers," unable to proceed to more personal levels of communication over time. Others are "high revealers," indiscriminately disclosing too much to others, irrespective of the exact relationships or interactions between them. Disclosing too little prevents a relationship from becoming more intimate, and may result in its termination. Disclosing too much signals intrusiveness rather than intimacy, and it usually causes others to withdraw rather than to respond with equal intimacy.

Healthy self-disclosure adheres to a "norm of reciprocity"—the expectation that partners will exchange disclosures, taking turns revealing similar levels of intimacy. For example, if one partner confides to the other, "I am worried that I might not succeed in reaching this goal," the other can reciprocate by admitting similar feelings or understanding the fear of failure. It would not be reciprocal to change the subject or offer superficial reassurance such as, "I know you will do just fine." Self-disclosure is risky, because it makes the revealer more vulnerable to the confidant's rejection or ridicule. Reciprocal self-disclosure establishes trust, since partners are confiding on similar levels and their knowledge of each other is balanced.

As relationships develop, Altman has argued, immediate reciprocity is unnecessary, because trust has already been established. Thus, long-time friends can have nonreciprocal conversations without threatening their level of intimacy. In a particular interaction, one partner may confide while the other listens without reciprocating. They both know that their roles can be reversed in some future conversation. Disclosure depends on the style as well as the content of communication. An individual may wish to discuss a personal problem or concern with a friend, but not know how to express himself or herself effectively. The complaint, "Sometimes things can be very hard for a person to deal with," is more vague and less disclosing than the statement, "I feel very frustrated and need help solving a problem." In this example, the former disclosure is closed and impersonal while the latter is more open and personal. To be open and personal, self-disclosing statements should be relevant to the immediate situation, expressed in personal terms ("I feel . . ." rather than "People say . . ."), specifically addressed to the listener, clearly explanatory rather than vague or hinting, and specific rather than general.

Applications

Differences in patterns of self-disclosure can account for differences in relationship development, conflict, personal distress, and loneliness. Individual differences in self-disclosure—the fact that some people are high revealers and others low revealers—help explain why some relationships become more intimate while others never progress. For example, a low revealer may feel unable to reciprocate when a new friend confides a secret or problem. The nondiscloser may be unsure of the other's response to a personal revelation, fearful of rejection, or unable to express himself or herself. The friend who has confided in the nondiscloser is left feeling unsatisfied or mistrustful by the lack of response, and may discourage future interactions.

In contrast, a high revealer's indiscriminate disclosures can offend others. Overdisclosing to a stranger can cause him or her to withdraw and terminate any further interaction. Even friends can be disturbed by a high revealer's willingness to confide inappropriately to others besides themselves. Their own confidences in the overdiscloser may also seem to be at risk. Differences in people's willingness and ability to engage in self-disclosure can affect the success and development of their relationships.

Two kinds of interactions may appear to violate the rules of developing self-disclosure: brief intimate encounters and "love at first sight." In the first case, a brief interaction with a stranger involves unusually deep self-disclosure. Psychologist Zick Rubin has dubbed this the "Fort Lauderdale phenomenon," for the Florida city that is a popular destination for spring vacation travel. A college student on vacation may feel less inhibited about self-disclosure with others encountered there, because he or she will not see any of these people again. Thus, high levels of self-disclosure are possible because no future relationship is anticipated.

In "love at first sight," two people may become quickly and mutually attracted and communicate intimately with each other with the intention of maintaining their relationship in the future. Altman and Taylor warn, however, that the two individuals have no history of communication, so no trust has been established between them. The risk of conflict is high, and conflict is likely to be more destructive than if the relationship had been established more gradually. Thus, disclosing too much, too fast, can doom a relationship even when disclosure is reciprocal and when both partners have similar motives.

The relationship between psychological adjustment and quantity or amount of self-disclosure has been explored by Valerian Derlega and Alan Chaikin in their 1975 book *Sharing Intimacy: What We Reveal to Others and Why*. Derlega and Chaikin suggest that adjustment is a curvilinear (changing) function of self-disclosure, rather than a linear (constant) one. That is, a person's adjustment does not continually increase as the amount that he or she self-discloses increases. Initially, as self-disclosure increases from low to medium levels, adjustment also improves—up to a point. Beyond that optimal point, increasing from medium to high self-disclosure actually reduces psychological adjustment. In other words, disclosing too much can interfere with a person's well-being and relationship success.

Self-disclosure is important to psychological well-being. Friends value being able to talk to and "be themselves" with each other. Intimacy involves more than being honest and revealing secrets, however; it is possible to express oneself about personal concerns without participating in an intimate relationship. For example, one may keep a diary or "confide" in a pet. There are also some relationships that have no expectation of reciprocity. A patient or client must describe personal experiences and feelings to a physician or psychotherapist without expecting him or her to respond in kind. In these contexts, it is helpful to be able to express oneself honestly without fear of rejection or criticism. Research evidence confirms that the process of articulating and confiding one's concerns significantly helps in coping with stress and trauma. Diaries and professional relationships are not a substitute for real intimacy, however; genuine intimacy is an outcome of communication within relationships, not of one-sided expression. Confiding in others who are willing to listen is essential to gaining the benefits of social support.

Personal relationships are based on interdependence—the reliance of both parties on joint outcomes. Reciprocity in self-disclosure represents a mutual investment that builds such interdependence. Withholding a confidence at one extreme and over-disclosing at the other are both hindrances to satisfactory intimacy. People who fail to establish and maintain intimacy with others experience loneliness. Loneliness is defined as the experience of inadequate or insufficient relationships. A person feels lonely when he or she has fewer relationships than are wanted or when existing relationships fail to meet his or her needs. A pattern of inappropriate or inexpressive self-disclosure can ultimately lead one to experience chronic loneliness.

Training in social skills may help those who suffer the consequences of unsatisfactory relationships or loneliness. Individuals could be taught, in psychotherapy or support groups, to modify their self-disclosure. Overdisclosers could become selective in choosing their confidants, and low revealers could learn how to express themselves more openly and personally. Like other relationship skills, self-disclosure requires motivation and competence, but contributes to better communication and higher self-esteem.

Context

Research on self-disclosure was influenced by the human potential movement of the 1960's and 1970's. Early theorists such as Jourard argued that it is important to be able to reveal aspects of oneself to a few significant others. Work by Altman and Taylor and by Derlega and Chaikin extended the concept of self-disclosure into the context of personal relationships and communication. Work conducted in the 1970's and 1980's explored the ways people choose topics and levels in disclosing to others. Self-disclosure has come to be regarded more as an aspect of interpersonal communication than of self-development. Whether a disclosure is appropriate depends on the relationship of the discloser to the listener and on the expectations of both individuals.

Altman and Taylor's theory of social penetration recognizes that self-disclosure involves changes in both the quantity and quality of intimate communication. Later research has concentrated on identifying the qualities of appropriate and healthy communication. An understanding of how self-disclosure is developed and how it contributes to communication is important in the study of close relationships; identifying problems in self-disclosure can lead to solving those problems. Research on loneliness has led to the development of social-skills training programs. Lonely people can be taught to listen better, ask open-ended questions, and show their attention to those with whom they interact. Similarly, self-disclosure skills can be improved with education based on an understanding of intimate communication.

Research and theory on self-disclosure contribute to a larger body of work on communication in close relationships. The study of relationships combines the observations and perspectives of social psychology, sociology, counseling, and communication studies. Early work in this multidisciplinary field focused on how relationships begin, including motivations for affiliation and factors in interpersonal attraction. Researchers have since turned their attention to relationship development and maintenance, processes dependent on the quality and quantity of partners' communication. Self-disclosure is a central goal of intimate communication. An understanding of self-disclosure and its role in developing and maintaining intimacy is essential to improving and stabilizing the significant relationships in people's lives.

Bibliography

Adler, Ronald B., Lawrence B. Rosenfeld, and Neil Towne. *Interplay: The Process of Interpersonal Communication.* New York: Holt, Rinehart and Winston, 1980. Focuses on the skills and processes at work in effective communication; offers examples and suggestions for improving listening, expressing, and verbal and nonverbal language. The text also reviews the risks and advantages involved in self-disclosure. Very readable and practical.

Altman, Irwin, and Dalmas A. Taylor. *Social Penetration: The Development of Interpersonal Relationships.* New York: Holt, Rinehart and Winston, 1973. This short, very readable book presents the theory of social penetration, describing how self-disclosure varies in breadth and depth over time. Includes helpful illustrations and numerous examples.

Brehm, Sharon S. *Intimate Relationships.* 2d ed. New York: Random House, 1991. Brehm's text reviews the major issues and processes in close relationships: attraction, love, sexuality, social exchange, fairness, commitment, power, jealousy, communication, conflict and dissolution, loneliness, the social network, and therapeutic intervention. Aimed at college students, the book is rich with examples and helpful aids to learning.

Duck, Steve. *Relating to Others.* Chicago, Ill.: Dorsey Press, 1988. Duck, an important influence in the field of close relationships, discusses the stages in the life cycle of a relationship, from first meeting to maintenance to dissolution. Includes research findings and theoretical context, and suggests additional sources. Extremely readable for the college or high school student.

Knapp, Mark L. *Interpersonal Communication and Human Relationships.* Boston: Allyn & Bacon, 1984. Knapp, a leading communication researcher, explains the nature of interpersonal communication and describes its form in dialogue, ritual, and intimacy. Discusses the important elements in personal communication and how these can be evaluated and developed.

Rubin, Zick. *Liking and Loving: An Invitation to Social Psychology.* New York: Holt, Rinehart and Winston, 1973. Rubin's book presents research and theory on interpersonal attraction and communication in the context of social psychology. Discusses examples of self-disclosure and exceptions to reciprocity and social penetration in the chapter "Becoming Committed."

Ann L. Weber

Cross-References

Affiliation and Friendship, 142; Coping: Social Support, 700; Emotional Expression, 954; Intimacy in Adulthood: Erikson, 1363; Psychotherapeutic Goals and Techniques, 1996; Rational-Emotive Therapy, 2052; Self: Definition and Assessment, 2162; Self-Concept Origins, 2175; Self-Presentation, 2200.

SELF-ESTEEM

Type of psychology: Social psychology
Fields of study: Childhood and adolescent disorders; cognitive development; social perception and cognition

Self-esteem research examines how individuals come to feel as they do about themselves. Psychologists seek to understand how self-esteem develops and what can be done to change negative views of the self once they have been established.

Principal terms
ATTRIBUTIONS: assumptions about the causes for behavior, made on three levels: internal/external, stable/temporary, and specific/global
IDENTITY NEGOTIATION: the attempt to create the type of self one would like to have; conflicts arise if people view themselves differently from the way others see them
IMMUTABLE CHARACTERISTICS: physical attributes (such as gender) that are present at birth and that others assume give them information as to the kind of person they are seeing
INHERITABLE TRAITS: personality characteristics (such as aggressiveness) that may be inherited from parents and are presumed to influence the kind of person an individual becomes
SELF-CONCEPT: the sum total of the attributes, abilities, attitudes, and values that an individual believes define who he or she is
SELF-EFFICACY: the beginning realization experienced by the individual during infancy that he or she is a self capable of actions and that these actions have consequences
SELF-ESTEEM: a relatively permanent positive or negative feeling about the self that may become more positive or negative as a person encounters success and failure in daily life

Overview

Self-esteem is a term with which almost everyone is familiar, yet it is not necessarily easily understood. Psychologist William James gave the first clear definition in 1892 when he said that self-esteem equals success divided by pretensions. In other words, feelings of self-worth come from the successes an individual achieves tempered by what the person had expected to achieve. If the person expected to do extremely well on an exam (his or her pretensions are quite high) and scores an A, then his or her self-esteem should be high. If, however, the person expected to do well and then scored a D, his or her self-esteem should be low.

This important but simplistic view of self-esteem started a movement toward a better understanding of the complex series of factors that come together to create the positive or negative feelings individuals have about who they are. Once a person has developed a self-concept (a global idea of all the things that define who and what a person is), that person is likely to exhibit behaviors that are consistent with that self-concept. If a young woman believes that she is a good tennis player, then she is likely to put herself in situations in which that factor is important. Once she behaves (in this case, plays her game of tennis), she is likely to receive feedback from others as to how she did. This feedback determines how she will feel about her tennis-playing ability. Over time, these specific instances of positive or negative feedback about tennis-playing ability will come together to create the more global feelings of positivity or negativity a person has about the self in general.

Even though an individual may believe that she is good at tennis, her ability may not live up to those expectations, and she may receive feedback telling her so (for example, losing in the early rounds of a tournament). In this case, the individual may come to feel somewhat negative about her tennis ability. If this continues to happen, she will adjust her view of her ability and come to believe that she is not a good tennis player after all. To the extent that the person truly wanted to be good, this realization can cause her to feel quite negative about all aspects of her self. When this happens, the person is said to have developed low self-esteem.

The reality of how self-esteem develops, however, is more complicated than this example demonstrates. People do not always accept the feedback that others offer, and they may believe that their failure means nothing more than having an off day. In order to understand the impact that success and failure will have on self-esteem, it is important to understand the kinds of attributions people make for their successes and failures. When a person succeeds or fails, there are three levels of attributions that can be made for explaining the occurrence. First, the individual must decide if the event occurred because of something internal (something inside caused it to happen) or something external (something in the environment caused it to happen). Second, it must be decided whether the event occurred because of a stable factor (since it happened this time, it will happen again) or a temporary circumstance (it probably will not happen again). Finally, it must be decided whether the event occurred because of something specific (this failure resulted because of poor tennis ability) or something global (failure resulted at this undertaking because of lack of ability to do anything).

It is easy to see that the kinds of attributions individuals make for their successes and failures will have a profound impact on how a particular event influences their self-esteem. If a decision is made that a failure at tennis occurred because of something internal (lack of ability), stable (the ability will never be present), and global (lack of *any* ability), then a failure is going to damage self-esteem severely. Self-esteem is created through the blending of expectations for success, actual levels of success, and the kinds of attributions made for why success or failure occurred.

Once positive or negative self-esteem has developed, it will perpetuate itself in a cycle. If a person believes that he is a failure, he may put himself into situations in which he is destined to fail. If he does not think he can succeed, he may not put forth the amount of effort that success would require. Similarly, if a person believes that he is a success, he will not let one little failure cause him to change his entire opinion of his self. Self-esteem, once it is created, is very difficult to change. If a person dislikes who she is, yet someone else tries to tell her that she is wonderful, she probably will not believe that person. More likely, she will wonder what this person could possibly want from her that he or she is willing to lie and be so nice to get it. On the other hand, if the person feels positive about herself, a single instance of failure will be written off as bad luck, poor effort, or a simple fluke. A negative self-esteem cycle, once it gets started, is very difficult to change, and learning how to break this cycle is the single greatest challenge to self-esteem therapists.

Applications

Understanding self-esteem has considerable practical importance in daily life. If it is believed that all successes come from external sources (luck or someone's pity), then good things coming from others can be seen as an attempt to degrade the individual or offer a bribe. People feeling this way relate to others in a judgmental way and cause them to turn away. When others turn away, the person takes it as a signal that he or she was correct about his or her unworthiness, and the negative self-esteem level is perpetuated.

If this negative self-esteem cycle is to be broken, it is important to convince the person of the critical point made by George Herbert Mead. According to Mead, self-esteem is a product of people's interpretation of the feedback that they receive from others. A person with low self-esteem often misinterprets that feedback. If someone with low self-esteem is told, "You look really nice today," he or she is likely to misinterpret that to mean, "You usually look terrible; what did you do different today?"

Ralph Turner has said that the self is not fixed and that the person with low self-esteem must be convinced that he or she is not at the mercy of a self: He or she can be, and is, the creator of a self. It helps to put the person into a situation in which he or she can succeed with no possibility for the wrong attributions to be made. If a person cannot read, this failure will generalize to other situations and is likely to be considered a stable and global deficiency. If this person is taught to read, however, even a person with low self-esteem would find it difficult to argue that the success was situational. In this way, the person begins to see that he or she can take control and that failures need not be catastrophic for the other self-conceptions he or she might hold.

A person with negative self-esteem is extremely difficult to help. It takes more than the providing of positive feedback to assist such a person. Imagine a series of circles, one inside the other, each one getting smaller. Take that smallest, innermost circle and assign it a negative value. This represents an overall negative self-esteem. Then assign negative values to all the outer circles as well. These represent how the person feels about his or her specific attributes.

If positive messages are directed toward a person with negative values assigned to all these layers of self-esteem, they will not easily penetrate the negative layers; they will be much more likely to bounce off. Negative messages, on the other hand, will easily enter the circles and will strengthen the negativity. Penetration of all the negative layers can, however, sometimes be achieved by a long-term direction of positive and loving messages toward the person with low self-esteem. In effect, the innermost circle, that of global self-esteem, will eventually be exposed. Self-esteem can then be improved if enough positive, loving messages can be directed at the level of the person's global self-esteem. This is a difficult process, partly because as soon as the person's negative self-image comes into serious question, confusion about his or her identity results; living in self-hate, although often painful, is still more secure than suddenly living in doubt.

Once the negative signs have been replaced with positive ones, the new self-esteem level will be as impervious to change as the negative one was. Now, when the person enters a situation, he or she will have more realistic expectations as to what he or she can and cannot do. The person has been taught to make realistic attributions about success and failure. Most important, the individual has been taught that one need not succeed at everything to be a worthy person. William James suggested in 1892 that striving does as much to alleviate self-esteem problems as actual success. Once the individual is convinced that setting a goal and striving rather than not trying at all is all it takes to feel good about him- or herself, the person is truly on the way to having high self-esteem.

Context

An interest in self-esteem developed along with interest in psychological questions in general. Early psychologists such as Sigmund Freud, Carl G. Jung, William James, and others all realized that an important part of what makes individuals think and act the way they do is determined by the early experiences that create their sense of self and self-esteem. A very important aspect of psychological inquiry has been asking how and why people perceive and interpret the same event so differently. Self-esteem and self-concept play a big role in these interpretations. Knowing an individual's self-esteem level helps one to predict how others will be perceived, what kind of other individuals will be chosen for interaction, and the kinds of attitudes and beliefs the person may hold.

An understanding of childhood development and adolescence would be impossible without an understanding of the forces that combine to create a person's sense of self-esteem. Adolescence has often been described as a time of "storm and stress" because the teenager is trying to negotiate an identity (create a sense of self and self-esteem that he or she would like to have). Teenagers' own wishes and desires, however, are not the only things they must consider. They are receiving pressure from parents, peers, and society as a whole to be a certain kind of person and do certain kinds of things. Only when self-esteem development is fully understood will it be known how to alleviate some of the trials and tribulations of adolescence and ensure that teenagers develop a healthy and productive view of their worth.

The role of self-esteem will probably be even greater as psychological inquiry moves ahead. Contemporary society continues to tell people that if they want to succeed, they have to achieve more. Yet economic downturns and increasing competition to enter colleges and careers make it even more difficult for young people to live up to those expectations and feel good about who they are. The role that psychologists with experience in self-esteem enhancement training will play in the future cannot be overemphasized. In order for adults to lead healthy, productive, and satisfied lives, they must feel good about who they are and where they are going. This requires an intimate understanding of the factors that combine to create people's expectations for success and the likelihood that they will be able to achieve that level of success. Self-esteem development must be kept in mind in helping young people create for themselves a realistic set of expectations for success and an ability to make realistic attributions for why their successes and failures occur.

Bibliography

Coopersmith, Stanley. *The Antecedents of Self-Esteem.* Palo Alto, Calif.: Consulting Psychologists Press, 1981. A very well-written and informative look at the background factors that influence the development of self-esteem. Includes statistics and figures but is fairly nontechnical, and the comprehensiveness of the book is well worth the effort.

Girodo, Michel. *Shy?* New York: Pocket Books, 1978. A delightful self-help book that is designed to help individuals overcome shyness. Helps the reader understand the connection between shyness and self-esteem. Appropriate for all age-groups, from junior high school on up.

Jones, Warren H., Jonathan M. Cheek, and Stephen R. Briggs. *Shyness: Perspectives on Research and Treatment.* New York: Plenum Press, 1986. Presents a thorough view of the development of shyness and the impact it has on social relationships. Many individuals with low self-esteem suffer from shyness, and it is difficult to understand one without the other. The writing is technical; appropriate for a college audience.

Mussen, Paul Henry, and Nancy Eisenberg-Berg. *Roots of Caring, Sharing, and Helping.* San Francisco: W. H. Freeman, 1977. Although this book is only partially related to self-esteem, it has a thorough discussion of how situations and other people influence children—influences which certainly cannot be ignored for their impact on self-esteem. Appropriate for most high school and college students.

Rosenberg, Morris. *Society and the Adolescent Self-Image.* Princeton, N.J.: Princeton University Press, 1972. Although written in the mid-1960's, this is still one of the best books available on self-esteem. Rosenberg's influence remains strong, and the self-esteem scale he included in this book is still widely used to measure self-esteem. Appropriate for both college and high school students.

Randall E. Osborne

Cross-References

Affiliation and Friendship, 142; Attitude Formation and Change, 326; Child Abuse, 507; Identity Crises: Erikson, 1255; Self: Definition and Assessment, 2162; Self-Perception Theory, 2193; Social Perception: Others, 2311.

SELF-PERCEPTION THEORY

Type of psychology: Social psychology
Fields of study: Attitudes and behavior; social perception and cognition

Self-perception theory examines how behavior can affect attitudes. It has provided insights into techniques for changing attitudes and gaining compliance. It has also provided insights into the effects of rewarding a behavior on intrinsic interest in that behavior.

Principal terms

ATTITUDE: evaluation of someone or something that can be either positive or negative and can vary in level of intensity

ATTRIBUTION PROCESS: the process of inferring a causal explanation for an observed behavior

COUNTERATTITUDINAL BEHAVIOR: behavior engaged in by an individual that is inconsistent with an attitude held by that individual

FOOT-IN-THE-DOOR EFFECT: the tendency of compliance with a large request to be greater if it is preceded by compliance with a much smaller request

INDUCED-COMPLIANCE PARADIGM: an experimental technique in which individuals are coaxed into engaging in a behavior that is different from what would be expected based on their prior attitudes

INTRINSIC MOTIVATION: an individual's level of interest in engaging in a particular form of behavior for its own sake

OVERJUSTIFICATION EFFECT: the tendency of external factors that are perceived to be controlling an individual's behavior to undermine the individual's intrinsic motivation to engage in that behavior

SELF-PERCEPTION: the observation of one's own behavior

Overview

Self-perception theory, which was proposed by psychologist Daryl Bem in 1965, consists of two postulates. The first is that individuals learn about their own attitudes, emotions, and other internal states partially by inferring them from observations of their own behavior and the circumstances in which their behavior occurs. The second is that, to the extent that individuals' internal cues regarding their internal states are weak or ambiguous, they must infer those internal states in the same way that an observer would—based on external cues. Thus, the theory proposes that people's knowledge of their own feelings often comes from inferences based on external information rather than from direct internal access to their feelings.

To understand the self-perception process, one must first consider how an individual generally learns about another person's feelings. The person's behavior is observed, and possible external factors that might account for the behavior are considered. If powerful external inducements for the behavior are observed, the person's behavior is likely to be attributed to those external inducements. If, however, compelling external causes of the behavior are not observed, the person's behavior is likely to be attributed to some internal factor in the individual, such as an attitude or an emotion.

For example, if an observer watches a person give a speech supporting a certain political candidate, the observer may infer that the person likes that candidate. If, however, the observer knows that the person was forced to give the speech or was offered a large sum of money to give the speech, the observer is likely to attribute the speech to the external inducement rather than to the person's attitude toward the candidate. This process of determining the causal explanation for a behavior is called the attribution process.

Self-perception theory posits that when internal cues are not particularly informative, people act like observers of their own behavior and engage in this same attribution process. Thus, when people engage in a new behavior and perceive no external factors controlling their behavior, they are likely to infer an attitude that provides an explanation for that behavior. Through this process, an individual's behavior can affect his or her attitude. For example, if an individual eats pistachio ice cream for the first time with no external inducement and is then asked if he likes pistachio ice cream, he is likely to infer his attitude based on how much of the ice cream he ate and how fast he ate it.

The theory specifies two factors, however, that limit the extent to which an observed behavior will affect an attitude. First, if the individual has clear prior internal information regarding his or her attitude toward the behavior, a given instance of the behavior is not likely to affect that attitude. If a person has eaten and expressed a liking for pistachio ice cream many times before, a new instance of eating that ice cream is not likely to affect that person's attitude toward it. Second, if there is a strong external inducement for the behavior, the behavior will be attributed to that external factor rather than to an attitude. If a person was ordered at gunpoint to eat the ice cream or was offered a large sum of money to eat the ice cream, she would not infer from the behavior that she likes pistachio ice cream, but rather that she ate the ice cream because of the external inducement (the threat of punishment or the promise of reward).

Self-perception theory has been supported by various lines of research. The critical assumption underlying the theory is that individuals sometimes do not have internal access to the causes of their own behavior. This notion has been supported by a variety of findings summarized by psychologists Richard Nisbett and Timothy Wilson. These studies have shown that people often do not have accurate knowledge of why they behave as they do. For example, female subjects were asked to choose a favorite from among four pairs of virtually identical stockings hanging on a rack. The position of each pair of stockings was varied, and the researchers found that the rightmost pair (usually the last pair examined) was chosen 80 percent of the time. When the subjects were asked to explain their choices, they had no trouble generating reasons; however, none of the subjects mentioned that the position of the pair of stockings affected the choice, even though it was clearly a major factor. Similar deficits in causal self-knowledge have been shown in connection with a wide variety of phenomena, including why people feel the way they do about books and films, and what factors affect their moods.

The primary hypothesis derived from self-perception theory is that, when individuals engage in a new behavior that differs from their past behavior and there appears to be little or no external inducement, they will infer an attitude that is consistent with that behavior. Many studies using the induced-compliance paradigm have supported this hypothesis. In the typical study, individuals are led to write an essay expressing an attitude on an issue that is different from their own initial attitude. If the subjects perceive that they can choose whether to write an essay and they are not offered a substantial external inducement (for example, a large amount of money) for doing so, their attitudes become more consistent with the attitudes expressed in their essays. If, however, the subjects are not given a choice or are offered a substantial external inducement to write an essay, they do not change their attitudes. Thus, the subjects in these studies infer their attitudes from their behavior unless their behavior appears to be controlled by a lack of choice or a large external inducement.

Applications

Self-perception theory has implications for the development of attitudes and emotions, persuasion, compliance, and intrinsic motivation. According to Bem, the self-perception process begins in early childhood, when children are taught how to describe their internal states in much the same way that they learn to describe external objects and events. For example, if a child consumes large quantities of grape juice, the parent may tell the child, "You really like grape juice." Similarly, if a child has a temper tantrum, the parent may say, "You're really angry, aren't you?" In this way, children learn how to infer their own attitudes and emotions. The socialization process can thus be viewed as training in how to infer one's attitudes and emotions in a culturally appropriate manner.

Self-perception processes can continue to affect an individual's attitude throughout his or her life span. Induced-compliance research indicates that, whenever people are induced to behave in a way that is somehow different from their past behavior and do not perceive a strong external inducement for doing so, their attitudes will become more favorable toward that behavior. Thus, by subtly encouraging a change in a person's behavior, one can effect a change in that person's attitude (persuasion).

One application of this notion is to psychotherapy. Various techniques used in psychotherapy encourage the client to behave in new, more beneficial ways; it is hoped that such techniques also lead the client to develop new, more beneficial attitudes. Consistent with this idea, a number of studies have shown that, when subjects are induced to write favorable statements about themselves or present themselves to an interviewer in self-enhancing ways and they perceive that they freely chose to do so, they experience an increase in self-esteem.

Self-perception theory has implications for compliance as well as persuasion. Compliance is acceding to a request from another. Research has shown that one way to increase compliance with a particular request is to first gain compliance with a smaller request. This phenomenon is known as the foot-in-the-door effect, a name derived from the door-to-door sales strategy of first getting one's foot in the door. In the first demonstration of this phenomenon, some subjects were asked to comply with a small request: to sign a safe-driving petition. All of them agreed to do so. Two weeks later, all the subjects were asked to comply with a larger request: to place "Drive Carefully" signs in their front yards. Subjects who had been asked to sign the petition were three times more likely to comply with the larger request than those subjects who had not been asked to sign the petition. Many subsequent studies have confirmed this effect.

Self-perception theory provides the most widely accepted explanation of the foot-in-the-door effect. Compliance with the initial request is posited to lead individuals to infer either that they like to be helpful or that they like the requester or the type of request with which they have complied. The newly formed attitudes resulting from the initial compliance make the subject more receptive to the second, larger request. This technique is commonly used by salespeople, and it is also employed to increase compliance with requests made by charitable organizations, such as the Red Cross. More generally, the foot-in-the-door effect suggests that each small commitment people make to a personal, organizational, or career goal will lead to a larger commitment to that goal.

All the above applications of self-perception theory are based on the notion that, when behavior is not sufficiently justified by external inducements, an individual will infer that he or she is intrinsically motivated to engage in that behavior. Research on the overjustification effect has revealed a complementary tendency of people to infer that they are not intrinsically motivated to engage in an activity if there appears to be too much external justification for the behavior. From the perspective of self-perception theory, if an individual is initially intrinsically motivated to engage in a behavior but is offered a large external inducement for performing the behavior, the person may infer that he or she is performing the behavior for the external inducement; this attribution will lead the individual to conclude that he or she is not interested in the activity for its own sake. Thus, large external inducements for engaging in a previously enjoyable activity may overjustify the activity, thereby undermining intrinsic interest in that activity.

The classic demonstration of the overjustification effect was conducted by psychologists Mark Lepper, David Greene, and Richard Nisbett. Nursery school children were first given a chance to play with colorful felt-tip markers. The researchers measured the amount of time each child played with the markers, taking it as an indication of intrinsic motivation. Two weeks later, the children were divided into three groups that were approximately equal in their initial levels of intrinsic motivation. Each child in the first group was simply asked to play with the markers. The children in the second group were told that, if they played with the markers, they would receive a "good player award," a gold star, and a ribbon when they were done. The third group of children was not offered rewards for playing with the markers; after they were done, however, the children were given the awards, stars, and ribbons anyway.

Approximately one week later, each child was observed in a free-play period in which he or she could play with the markers or engage in other activities. The group of children that had previously been offered and had received rewards for playing with the markers spent less free time engaged in that activity than the group that received no rewards and the group that unexpectedly received the rewards. Thus, intrinsic motivation to perform the activity was undermined in children who had previously been offered a substantial external inducement to engage in it. Probably because of their reduced intrinsic interest, these same children drew lower-quality pictures with the markers than the children in the other groups. Similar effects have been shown for both children and adults across a wide range of activities. In addition, overjustification effects have been shown to result from external inducements such as deadlines and competition as well as from various types of rewards.

Behaviorists such as B. F. Skinner have popularized the strategy of using rewards to reinforce behavior. Based on the overjustification research, the wisdom of this strategy has been challenged. Rewards are commonly used in child-rearing, education, and work settings, yet in all three settings it is harmful to undermine the individual's intrinsic motivation to engage in the desired behaviors. For example, if a child has some intrinsic interest in doing homework, offering a reward for doing the homework is likely to motivate the behavior but is also likely to undermine the child's intrinsic interest in the activity; thus, when the reward is no longer offered, the child may be less likely to engage in the activity than before he or she was ever offered a reward for doing it.

If the individual has no intrinsic interest in the behavior, there is no problem with using rewards, because there is no intrinsic motivation to undermine. In addition, research has shown that rewards do not necessarily undermine intrinsic motivation; they do so only to the extent that the reward is perceived to be a factor controlling the behavior. Thus, if a behavior is subtly rewarded or the rewards are viewed as indicators of the quality of one's performance, they may actually increase rather than decrease intrinsic motivation. The key to the effective use of rewards is therefore to present them in such a way that they are perceived to be rewards for competence rather than efforts to coerce the individual into engaging in the task.

Context

Self-perception theory first gained prominence in 1967, when Daryl Bem argued that the theory could provide an alternative explanation for the large body of evidence supporting Leon Festinger's influential cognitive dissonance theory. From its inception in 1957, cognitive dissonance theory generated considerable supportive research. The theory proposed that, when an individual holds to cognitions such that one cognition logically implies the opposite of the other, the individual experiences a negative tension state, known as dissonance, and becomes motivated to reduce the dissonance; this can be done by changing one of the cognitions or by adding consonant cognitions, which reduces the overall level of inconsistency.

Most of the research on the theory utilized the induced-compliance paradigm. In these studies, subjects would be induced to engage in a behavior contrary to their prior attitudes; if the subjects engaged in such counterattitudinal behavior while perceiving that they had a choice and had no sufficient external justification for doing so, they were assumed to be experiencing dissonance. Study after study supported the prediction that these subjects would change their attitudes so that they would be more consistent with their behavior, presumably to reduce dissonance.

Bem argued that self-perception theory could account for these findings more simply than dissonance theory by positing that, when subjects in these studies observed themselves engaging in a behavior with little external inducement, they logically inferred an attitude consistent with that behavior. Thus, Bem offered a cognitive explanation for the most popular motivational theory of the time. Since then, it has virtually become a tradition in social psychology for cognitive theories to be pitted against motivational theories in attempting to account for social attitudes and behavior.

This challenge to dissonance theory was viewed as a major controversy in the field, and it generated much research that attempted to support one theory or the other. Finally, in the mid-1970's, research emerged that resolved the controversy. Evidence was obtained that supported dissonance theory by showing that, when people engage in counterattitudinal behavior with little external inducement, they do experience a negative psychological state, and this negative state does motivate the attitude change following counterattitudinal behavior. It was also found, however, that, when individuals engage in behavior that is different from behavior that would be implied by their prior attitudes but not so different that it is really inconsistent with prior attitudes, an attitude change may still occur; this attitude change is best accounted for by self-perception theory. Self-perception theory is also still considered to be the best explanation for the foot-in-the-door and overjustification effects, effects that do not involve counterattitudinal behavior and therefore cannot be explained by cognitive dissonance theory.

Bibliography

Bem, Daryl J. "Self-Perception Theory." In *Advances in Experimental Social Psychology*. Vol. 6, edited by Leonard Berkowitz. New York: Academic Press, 1972. This chapter is the definitive summation of self-perception theory. Includes discussions of the roots of the theory, research relevant to it, and the theory's place within the field of social psychology.

Cialdini, Robert B. *Influence: Science and Practice*. Glenview, Ill.: Scott, Foresman, 1988. Summarizes what has been learned about techniques intended to influence another's attitudes and behavior and how these techniques work. Includes a discussion of the foot-in-the-door technique and other strategies that capitalize on self-perception processes.

Deci, E. L., and R. M. Ryan. *Intrinsic Motivation and Self-Determination in Human Behavior.* New York: Plenum Press, 1985. Reviews evidence concerning the over-justification effect and other processes that affect intrinsic motivation. Places this research within the broader context of a general theory concerning internal and external sources of motivation. Offers a compelling account of how people develop or fail to develop a sense of autonomy and discusses the ways in which people who function autonomously differ from people who do not.

Fazio, R. H. "Self-Perception Theory: A Current Perspective." In *Social Influence: The Ontario Symposium.* Vol. 5, edited by M. P. Zanna, J. M. Olson, and C. P. Herman. Hillsdale, N.J.: Lawrence Erlbaum, 1987. An overview of self-perception theory that places the theory within the context of recent advances in theory and research in social psychology.

Lepper, M. R., and David Greene, eds. *The Hidden Costs of Reward.* Hillsdale, N.J.: Lawrence Erlbaum, 1978. A collection of chapters detailing theoretical perspectives and research on the overjustification effect. Also discusses the practical implications of the findings.

Wilson, T. D., and J. I. Stone. "Limitations of Self-Knowledge: More on Telling More Than We Can Know." In *Self, Situations, and Social Behavior.* Vol. 6 in *Review of Personality and Social Psychology.* Beverly Hills, Calif.: Sage, 1985. Reviews the evidence suggesting that people have limited access to their internal states and the causes of their own behavior. Discusses factors that influence accuracy of self-knowledge.

Jeff Greenberg

Cross-References

Attitude-Behavior Consistency, 320; Attitude Formation and Change, 326; Causal Attribution, 487; Cognitive Dissonance Theory, 560; Emotion: Cognitive and Physiological Interaction, 881; Emotion and Attribution Theory, 921; Motivation: Cognitive Theories, 1606; Radical Behaviorism: B. F. Skinner, 2045; Self-Concept Origins, 2175; Work Motivation, 2654.

SELF-PRESENTATION

Type of psychology: Social psychology
Field of study: Social perception and cognition

Self-presentation is behavior with which people try to affect how they are perceived and judged by others; much social behavior is influenced by self-presentational motives and goals.

Principal terms
IMPRESSION MANAGEMENT: the attempt to control the impressions of oneself that others form; synonymous with "self-presentation"
INGRATIATION: a strategy of self-presentation in which one seeks to elicit liking and affection from others
INTIMIDATION: a self-presentational strategy in which one tries to appear dangerous or fearsome to others
POWER: the ability to influence others' behavior; whether legitimately or fraudulently, successful self-presentation increases one's power
SELF-MONITORING: a personality trait that describes how readily and flexibly one adjusts one's self-presentations to fit different social situations
SELF-PROMOTION: a strategy of self-presentation in which one seeks respect for one's competence and skill
SOCIAL ANXIETY: an uneasy apprehension caused by the threat of real or imagined evaluation from others
SUPPLICATION: the self-presentational strategy of appearing to be hapless and helpless; when successful, it may elicit nurturance and support from others

Overview

Although they may or may not be consciously thinking about it, people often try to control the information that others receive about them. When they are deliberately trying to make a certain impression on others, people may carefully choose their dress, think about what to say, monitor their behavior, pick their friends, and even decide what to eat. Self-presentation refers to the various behaviors with which people attempt to manage and influence the impressions they make on others. Nearly any public behavior may be strategically regulated in the service of impression management, and people may behave quite differently in the presence of others from the way they behave when they are alone. Moreover, self-presentation is not always a conscious activity; without planning to, people may fall into familiar patterns of behavior that represent personal habits of self-presentation.

The impressions of someone that others form substantially determine how they treat that person. Obviously, if others like and respect someone, they behave differently toward him or her from the way they would if the person were disliked or mistrusted. Thus, it is usually personally advantageous for a person to have some control over what others think of him or her. To the extent that one can regulate one's image in others' eyes, one gains influence over their behavior toward one and increases one's interpersonal power. Self-presentational perspectives on social interaction assume that people manage their impressions to augment their power and maximize their social outcomes.

Self-presentation, however, is usually not deceitful. Although people do occasionally misrepresent themselves through lying and pretense, most self-presentation communicates one's authentic attributes to others. Because frauds and cheats are rejected by others, dishonest self-presentation is risky. Instead, impression management usually involves the attempt to reveal, in a selective fashion, those aspects of one's true character that will allow one to attain one's current goals. By announcing some of their attitudes but not mentioning others, for example, people may appear to have something in common with almost anyone they meet; this simple tactic of impression management facilitates graceful and rewarding social interaction and does not involve untruthfulness at all. Over time, genuine, realistic presentations of self in which people accurately reveal portions of themselves to others are likely to be more successful than those in which people pretend to be things they are not.

Nevertheless, because most people have diverse interests and talents, there may be many distinct impressions they can honestly attempt to create, and people may seek different images in different situations. Edward Jones and Thane Pittman identified four discrete strategies of self-presentation that produce disparate results. When people seek acceptance and liking, they typically ingratiate themselves with others by doing favors, paying compliments, mentioning areas of agreement, and describing themselves in attractive, desirable ways. On other occasions, when they wish their abilities to be recognized and respected by others, people may engage in self-promotion, recounting their accomplishments or strategically arranging public demonstrations of their skills. Both ingratiation and self-promotion create socially desirable impressions and thus are very common strategies of self-presentation.

In contrast, other strategies create undesirable impressions. Through intimidation, people portray themselves as ruthless, dangerous, and menacing so that others will do their bidding. Such behavior is obnoxious and tends to drive others away, but if those others cannot easily escape, intimidation often works. Drill sergeants who threaten recalcitrant recruits usually are not interested in being liked; they want compliance, and the more fierce they seem, the more likely they may be to get it. Finally, using the strategy of supplication, people sometimes present themselves as inept or infirm in order to avoid obligations and elicit help and support from others. A person who plays sick in order to stay home from work or school is engaging in supplication.

People's choices of strategies and desired images depend on several factors, such as the values and preferences of the target audience. People often tailor their self-presentations to fit the interests of the others they are trying to impress. In one study

of this phenomenon, college women were given job interviews with a male interviewer who, they were told, was either quite traditional or "liberated" in his views
toward women. With this information in hand, the women dressed, acted, and spoke
differently for the different targets. They wore more makeup and jewelry, behaved
less assertively, and expressed a greater interest in childen to the traditional interviewer than they did to the liberated interviewer.

Individuals' own self-concepts also influence their self-presentations. People typically prefer to manage impressions that are personally palatable, both because they
are easier to maintain and because they help bolster self-esteem; however, self-
presentations also shape self-concepts. When people do occasionally claim images
they personally feel they do not deserve, their audiences may either see through the
fraudulent claim and dispute the image or accept it as legitimate. In the latter case,
the audience's approving reactions may gradually convince people that they really do
deserve the images they are projecting. Because a person's self-concept is determined, in part, by feedback received from others, self-presentations that were once
inaccurate can become truthful over time as people are gradually persuaded by others that they really are the people they were pretending to be.

Applications

Studies of self-presentation demonstrate that people are capable of enormous sub-
tlety as they fine-tune their public images. For example, Robert Cialdini and his
colleagues have identified several ingenious, specific tactics of ingratiation. Observations of students at famous football colleges (such as Notre Dame, Ohio State,
the University of Southern California, Arizona, Pittsburgh, and Louisiana State) revealed that after a weekend football victory, students were especially likely to come
to class on Monday wearing school colors and insignia. If their team had lost, however, such identifying apparel was conspicuously absent. Further laboratory studies
suggested that the students were strategically choosing their apparel to publicize
their association with a winning team, a tendency Cialdini called "basking in reflected glory." By contrast, they were careful not to mention their connection to a
loser. In general, people who seek acceptance and liking will advertise their association with other desirable images, while trying to distance themselves from failure
and other disreputable images.

Furthermore, they may do this with precise sophistication. In another study by
Cialdini, people privately learned that they had a trivial connection—a shared birth-
date—with another person who was said to have either high or low social or intellectual ability. The participants then encountered a public, personal success or failure
when they were informed that they had either high or low social ability themselves.
Armed with this information, people cleverly selected the specific self-descriptions
that would make the best possible impression on the researchers. If they had failed
their social ability test, they typically mentioned their similarity with another person
who had high intellect but did not bring up their connection to another person with
higher social ability than themselves. They thus publicized a flattering link between

themselves and others while steering clear of comparisons that would make them look bad. In contrast, if they had passed the social ability test and the researchers already thought highly of them, people brought up their connection to another person who had poorer social ability. By mentioning their resemblance to less talented others, people not only reminded their audiences of their superior talent, but seemed humble and modest as well.

Self-presentation can be ingenious, indeed. In general, if they wish to ingratiate themselves with others, people with deficient images try to find something good to communicate about themselves that does not contradict the negative information the audience already has. If they are already held in high esteem, however, people typically select modest, self-effacing presentations that demonstrate that they are humble as well as talented.

People do not go to such trouble for everyone, however; if people do not care what a particular audience thinks, they may not be motivated to create any impression at all. One experiment that illustrated this point invited women to "get acquainted" with men who were either desirable or undesirable partners. Snacks were provided; the women who were paired with attractive men ate much less than the women stuck with unappealing partners. Because women who eat lightly are often considered more feminine than those who eat heartily, women who wanted to create a favorable impression strategically limited their snack consumption; in contrast, those who were less eager to impress their partners ate as much as they liked.

On occasion, people care too much what an audience thinks. One reason that people suffer from social anxieties such as shyness or stage fright is that their desire to make a particular impression on a certain audience is too high. According to theorists Mark Leary and Barry Schlenker, people suffer from social anxiety when they are motivated to create a certain impression but doubt their ability to do so. Any influence that increases one's motivation (such as the attractiveness, prestige, or power of an audience) or causes one to doubt one's ability (such as unfamiliar situations or inadequate personal social skills) can cause social anxiety. This self-presentation perspective suggests that, if excessive social anxiety is a problem, different therapies will be needed for different people. Some sufferers will benefit most from behavioral social skills training, whereas others who have passable skills simply need to worry less what others are thinking of them; cognitive therapies will be best for them.

Finally, people differ in their self-presentational proclivities. Those high in the trait of "self-monitoring" tend to be sensitive to social cues that suggest how one should act in a particular situation and are adept at adjusting their self-presentations to fit in. By comparison, low self-monitors seem less attentive and flexible, and tend to display more stable images regardless of their situational appropriateness. High self-monitors are more changeable and energetic self-presenters, and as a result, they create social worlds that are different from those of low self-monitors. Because they can deftly switch images from one audience to the next, high self-monitors tend to have wider circles of friends with whom they have less in common than do low self-monitors. Compared to high self-monitors, lows must search harder for partners with whom they share broader compatibilities. Over time, however, lows are likely to develop longer-lasting, more committed relationships with others; they invest more in the partners they have. High self-monitors are more influenced by social image than lows are, a self-presentational difference with important consequences for interaction.

Context

The roots of self-presentation theory date back to the very beginnings of American psychology and the writings of William James in 1890. James recognized that the human self is multifaceted, and that it is not surprising for different audiences to have very different impressions of the same individual. After James, in the early twentieth century, sociologists Charles Horton Cooley and George Herbert Mead stressed that others' impressions of an individual are especially important, shaping that person's social life and personal self-concept. The most influential parent of this perspective, however, was Erving Goffman, who was the first to insist that people actively, consciously, and deliberately construct social images for public consumption. Goffman's book *The Presentation of Self in Everyday Life* (1959) eloquently compared social behavior to a theatrical performance staged for credulous audiences, complete with scripts, props, and backstage areas where the actors drop their roles.

As it emerged thereafter, self-presentation theory seemed to be a heretical alternative to established explanations for some social phenomena. For example, whereas cognitive dissonance theory suggested that people sometimes change attitudes which are inconsistent with their behavior in order to gain peace of mind, self-presentation theory argued that people merely report different attitudes that make them look consistent, without changing their real attitudes at all. Nevertheless, despite theoretical controversy, Goffman's provocative dramaturgical analogy gradually became more widely accepted as researchers demonstrated that a wide variety of social behavior was affected by self-presentational concerns. With the publication in 1980 of a work by Barry Schlenker, the first book-length review of self-presentation research, impression management theory finally entered the mainstream of social psychology.

The lasting importance of self-presentation theory lies in its reminders that people are cognizant of the images they present to others and often thoughtfully attempt to shape those images to accomplish their objectives. As a result, much social behavior has a self-presentational component. An angry boss may have real problems controlling his temper, for example, but he may also occasionally exaggerate his anger to intimidate his employees. Even people suffering from severe mental illness may engage in impression management; research has revealed that institutionalized schizophrenics sometimes adjust the apparent severity of their symptoms so that they seem well enough to be granted special privileges without seeming so healthy that they are released back into the threatening free world. In this case, self-presentation theory does not suggest that schizophrenics are merely pretending to be disturbed; obviously, most psychotic people are burdened by real psychological or biological problems. Impression management, however, may contribute in part to their apparent illness, just as it does to many other social behaviors. In general, self-presentation theory does not claim to replace other explanations for behavior, but it does assert that much of what people do is influenced by self-presentational motives and concerns.

Bibliography

Baumeister, Roy F., ed. *Public Self and Private Self.* New York: Springer-Verlag, 1986. Extends and refines self-presentation theory with individual chapters written by experts in the field. Difficult reading for a layperson, but essential reading for an advanced student of impression management. Its erudite discussion persuasively demonstrates the fundamental importance of self-presentation in social life.

Brissett, Dennis, and Charles Edgley, eds. *Life as Theater: A Dramaturgical Sourcebook.* 2d ed. New York: Aldine de Gruyter, 1990. A collection of many short papers that illustrate the uses of self-presentation concepts in sociology, political science, anthropology, and communication studies. Meant as a college text; contains a very useful bibliography.

Goffman, Erving. *The Presentation of Self in Everyday Life.* Garden City, N.Y.: Doubleday, 1959. This classic work coined the term "self-presentation" and almost single-handedly created this field of study. Goffman suggested that people stage dramatic performances for their audiences, carefully selecting their lines and props. The book can be easily read by undergraduates and is still full of fresh insights.

Jones, E. E., and Thane Pittman. "Toward a General Theory of Strategic Self-Presentation." In *Psychological Perspectives on the Self,* edited by Jerry Suls. Hillsdale, N.J.: Lawrence Erlbaum, 1982. Describes and differentiates the strategies of ingratiation, intimidation, self-promotion, and supplication. Although written for a college audience, its clever analysis will intrigue most readers.

Leary, Mark R., and Rowland S. Miller. *Social Psychology and Dysfunctional Behavior: Origins, Diagnosis, and Treatment.* New York: Springer-Verlag, 1986. Three chapters of this book use self-presentational concepts to help explain maladaptive behavior ranging from schizophrenia to shyness and stage fright. Accessible to a lay reader. Demonstrates the utility of the self-presentation perspective on problematic behavior.

Schlenker, Barry R. *Impression Management: The Self-Concept, Social Identity, and Interpersonal Relations.* Monterey, Calif.: Brooks/Cole, 1980. A complete and readable introduction to the study of impression management. An excellent, comprehensive source that collects relevant research and theory; it devotes individual chapters to specific self-presentational behaviors such as self-descriptions, expressed beliefs, and personal appearance.

_____, ed. *The Self and Social Life.* New York: McGraw-Hill, 1985. Contains chapters contributed by eminent researchers who explore various applications of the self-presentation perspective. Topics such as excuse making, self-control, detection of deceit, and social power are covered in a scholarly smorgasbord that shows how pervasive impression management is. College audiences will have no difficulty with this collection.

Snyder, Mark. *Public Appearances, Private Realities: The Psychology of Self-Monitoring.* New York: W. H. Freeman, 1987. A very readable, entertaining study of important individual differences in self-presentation. The differences between the social worlds of high and low self-monitors will fascinate most readers.

Rowland Miller

Cross-References

Attitude-Behavior Consistency, 320; Self: Definition and Assessment, 2162; Self-Concept Origins, 2175; Self-Disclosure, 2182; Self-Esteem, 2188; Self-Perception Theory, 2193.

SENSATION AND PERCEPTION DEFINED

Type of psychology: Sensation and perception
Fields of study: Auditory, chemical, cutaneous, and body senses; vision

The study of sensation and perception examines the relationship between input from the world and the manner in which people react to it. Through the process of sensation, the body receives various stimuli that are transformed into neural messages and transmitted to the brain. Perception is the meaning and interpretation given to these messages.

Principal terms
ABSOLUTE THRESHOLD: the smallest amount of stimulus that can be
detected by the senses 50 percent of the time
ACUITY: the ability to detect minute details
ATTENTION: the ability to focus mentally
PERCEPTION: the organization and interpretation of sensory information,
thus allowing people to recognize events and meaningful objects
SENSATION: the process by which the nervous system and sensory
receptors receive and represent stimuli received from the
environment
SENSORY DEPRIVATION: a condition in which an organism is deprived
of sensory stimulation
SENSORY RECEPTORS: specialized body cells that convert physical energy,
such as sound or light, into neural impulses

Overview

Although the distinction between sensation and perception is not always clear, psychologists attempt to distinguish between the two concepts. Sensation is generally viewed as the initial contact between organisms and their physical environment. It focuses on the interaction between various forms of sensory stimulation and how these sensations are registered by the senses (by the nose, skin, eyes, ears, and tongue). The process by which an individual then interprets and organizes this information to produce conscious experiences is known as perception.

The warmth of the sun, the distinctive sound of a jet airplane rumbling down the runway, the smell of freshly baked bread, and the taste of an ice-cream sundae all impact the body's sensory receptors. The signals received are transmitted to the brain via the nervous system; there, interpretation of the information is performed. The body's sensory receptors are capable of detecting very low levels of stimulation. Eugene Galanter's studies indicated that on a clear night, the eye is capable of viewing a candle at a distance of 30 miles (48 kilometers), while the ears can detect the ticking of a watch 20 feet (6 meters) away in a quiet room. He also demonstrated that the tongue can taste a teaspoon of sugar dissolved in 2 gallons (about 7.5 liters) of water, while people can feel a bee wing falling on the cheek and can smell a single drop of perfume in a three-bedroom apartment. Awareness of these faint stimuli demonstrates the absolute thresholds, defined as the minimum amount of stimulus that can be detected 50 percent of the time.

A person's ability to detect a weak stimulus, often called a signal, depends not only on the strength of the signal or stimulus but also on the person's psychological state. For example, a child remaining at home alone for the first time may be startled by an almost imperceptible noise. In a normal setting, with his or her parents at home, the same noise or signal would probably go unnoticed. Scientists who study signal detention seek to explain why people respond differently to a similar signal and why the same person's reactions vary as circumstances change. Studies have shown that people's reactions to signals depend on many factors, including the time of day and the type of signal.

Much controversy has arisen over the subject of subliminal signals—signals that one's body receives without one's conscious awareness. It has long been thought that these subliminal signals could influence a person's behaviors through persuasion. Many researchers believe that individuals do sense subliminal sensations; however, the chances that this information will somehow change an individual's behaviors is highly unlikely. Researchers Anthony Pratkanis and Anthony Greenwald suggest that in the area of advertising, subliminal procedures offer little or nothing of value to the marketing practitioner.

An individual's initial response to a stimulus may change over time. For example, when a swimmer first enters the cold ocean, the initial response may be to complain about the water's frigidity; however, after a few minutes, the water feels comfortable. This is an example of sensory adaptation—the body's ability to diminish sensitivity to stimuli that are unchanging. Sensory receptors are initially alert to the coldness of the water, but prolonged exposure reduces sensitivity. This is an important benefit to humans in that it allows an individual not to be distracted by constant stimuli that are uninformative. It would be very difficult to function daily if one's body were constantly aware of the fit of shoes and garments, the rumble of a heating system, or constant street noises.

The reception of sensory information by the senses, and the transmission of this information to the brain, is included under the term "sensation." Of equal importance is the process of perception: the way an individual selects information, organizes it, and makes an interpretation. In this manner, one achieves a grasp of one's surroundings. People cannot absorb and understand all the available sensory information received from the environment. Thus, they must selectively attend to certain information and disregard other material. Through the process of selective attention, people are able to maximize information gained from the object of focus, while at the same time ignoring irrelevant material. To some degree, people are capable of controlling the focus of their attention; in many instances, however, focus can be shifted undesirably. For example, while one is watching a television show, extraneous stimuli such as a car horn blaring may change one's focus.

The fundamental focus of the study of perception is how people come to comprehend the world around them through its objects and events. People are constantly giving meaning to a host of stimuli being received from all their senses. While research suggests that people prize visual stimuli above other forms, information from all other senses must also be processed. More difficult to understand is the concept of extrasensory perception (ESP). More researchers are becoming interested in the possible existence of extrasensory perception—perceptions that are not based on information from the sensory receptors. Often included under the heading of ESP are such questionable abilities as clairvoyance and telepathy. While psychologists generally remain skeptical as to the existence of ESP, some do not deny that evidence may someday be available supporting its existence.

Applications

Knowledge of the fields of sensation and perception assists people in understanding their environment. By understanding how and why people respond to various stimuli, scientists have been able to identify important factors which have proved useful in such fields as advertising, industry, and education.

Max Wertheimer discussed five laws of grouping that describe why certain elements seem to go together rather than remain independent. The laws include the law of similarity, which states that similar objects tend to be seen as a unit; the law of nearness, which indicates that objects near one another tend to be seen as a unit; the law of closure, which states that when a figure has a gap, the figure still tends to be seen as closed; the law of common fate, which states that when objects move in the same direction, they tend to be seen as a unit; and the law of good continuation, which states that objects organized in a straight line or a smooth curve tend to be seen as a unit. These laws are illustrated in the figure on the following page.

The laws of grouping are frequently utilized in the field of advertising. Advertisers attempt to associate their products with various stimuli. For example, Loudon and Della Bitta, after studying advertising dealing with menthol cigarettes, noted that the advertisers often show mentholated cigarettes in green, springlike settings to suggest freshness and taste. Similarly, summertime soft-drink advertisements include refreshing outdoor scenes depicting cool, fresh, clean running water, which is meant to be associated with the beverage. Also, advertisements for rugged four-wheel-drive vehicles utilize the laws of grouping by placing their vehicles in harsh, rugged climates. The viewer develops a perception of toughness and ruggedness.

The overall goal of the advertisers is to provide consumers with appropriate sensations that will cause them to perceive the products in a manner that the advertisers desire. By structuring the stimuli that reach the senses, advertisers can build a foundation for perceptions of products, making them seem durable, sensuous, refreshing, or desirable. By utilizing the results of numerous research studies pertaining to perception, subtle yet effective manipulation of the consumer is achieved.

Another area that has been researched extensively by industry deals with color. If one were in a restaurant ordering dinner and received an orange steak with purple

Law of Nearness

Law of Similarity

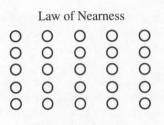

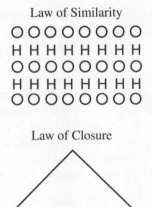

Law of Common Fate

Law of Closure

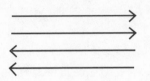

Law of Good Continuation

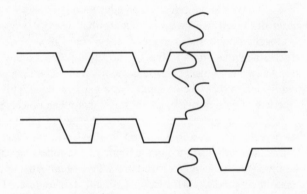

French fries and a blue salad, the meal would be difficult to consume. People's individual perceptions of color are extremely important. Variations from these expectations can be very difficult to overcome. Researchers have found that people's perceptions of color also influence their beliefs about products. When reactions to laundry detergents were examined, detergent in a blue box was found to be too weak, while detergent in a yellow box was thought to be too strong. Consumers believed, based on coloration, that the ideal detergent came in a blue box with yellow accentuation. Similarly, when individuals were asked to judge the capsule color of drugs, findings suggested that orange capsules were frequently seen as stimulants, white capsules as having an analgesic action, and lavender capsules as having a hallucinogenic effect.

Studies have shown that various colors have proved more satisfactory than others for industrial application. Red has been shown typically to be perceived as a sign of danger and is used to warn individuals of hazardous situations. Yellow is also a sign of warning. It is frequently used on highway signs as a warning indicator because of its high degree of visibility in adverse weather conditions. Instrument panels in both automobiles and airplanes are frequently equipped with orange- and yellow-tipped instrument indicators, because research has demonstrated that these colors are easily distinguished from the dark background of the gauges. Finally, industry has not overlooked the fact that many colors have a calming and relaxing effect on people. Thus, soft pastels are often used in the workplace.

The field of education has also benefited from research in the areas of sensation and perception. Knowing how young children perceive educational materials is important in developing ways to increase their skills and motivation. Textbook publishers have found that materials need to be visually attractive to children in order to help them focus on activities. Graphics and illustrations help the young learner to understand written materials. Size of printed text is also important to accommodate the developmental level of the student. For example, primers and primary-level reading series typically have larger print to assist the student in focusing on the text. As the child's abilities to discriminate letters and numbers become more efficient with age, the print size diminishes to that of the size of characters in adult books. Similar techniques continue into high school and college; especially in introductory courses, texts are designed utilizing extensive amounts of color, along with variation in page design. The reader's eyes are attracted by numerous stimuli to pictures, figures, definitions, and charts strategically placed on each page. This technique allows the author to highlight and accent essential points of information.

Context

The study of sensation and perception began more than two thousand years ago with the Greek philosophers and is one of the oldest fields in psychology. There are numerous theories, hypotheses, and facts dealing with how people obtain information about their world, what type of information they obtain, and what they do with this information once it has been obtained. None of this information has been sufficient to account for human perceptual experiences and perceptual behavior, so research in the area of sensation and perception continues.

The philosopher Thomas Reed made the original distinction between sensations and perceptions. He proposed that the crucial difference between them is that perceptions always refer to external objects, whereas sensations refer to the experiences within a person that are not linked to external objects. Many psychologists of the nineteenth century proposed that sensations are elementary building blocks of perceptions. According to their ideas, perceptions arise from the addition of numerous sensations. The sum of these sensations thus creates a perception. Other psychologists believed that making a distinction between sensations and perceptions was not useful.

The first psychologists saw the importance of perception when they realized that information from the senses was necessary in order to learn, think, and memorize. Thus, research pertaining to the senses was a central research component of all the psychological laboratories established in Europe and the United States during the late nineteenth and early twentieth centuries. By studying perceptions, researchers can identify potential environmental hazards that threaten the senses. Studying perception has also enabled people to develop devices that ensure optimal performance of the senses. For example, on a daily basis, one's senses rely on such manufactured objects as telephones, clocks, televisions, and computers. To be effective, these devices must be tailored to the human sensory systems.

The study of sensations and perceptions has also made it possible to build and develop prosthetic devices to aid individuals with impaired sensory function. For example, hearing aids amplify sound for hard-of-hearing individuals; however, when all sounds are amplified to the same degree it is often difficult for people to discriminate between sounds. From the work of Richard Gregory, a British psychologist, an instrument was developed that would only amplify speech sounds, thus allowing a person to attend more adequately to conversations and tune out background noise.

Another important application of research in the area of sensation and perception is consumer marketing. Companies carefully test the perceptual appeal of their products before marketing them. Taste, smell, and appearance have been modified to meet the appeal of the broadest possible population. Advertising also capitalizes on perception research by packaging and marketing products in a manner designed to draw the broadest possible consumer appeal. Finally, understanding perception is important for comprehending and appreciating the perceptual experience called art. When knowledge of perception is combined with the process of perceiving artistic works, this understanding adds an additional dimension to one's ability to view a work of art.

Bibliography

Goldstein, E. Bruce. *Sensation and Perception*. 3d ed. Belmont, Calif.: Wadsworth, 1989. An excellent overview of the field of sensation and perception. Chapters focus on typical subjects dealing with vision, hearing, and touch, but Goldstein also adds interesting chapters on perceived speech and the chemical senses.

Gregory, R. L. *Eye and Brain: The Psychology of Seeing*. 3d ed. New York: World University Library, 1978. A broad book on vision for the general reader. Beneficial for students in the areas of psychology, biology, and physiology. Includes many illustrations that help to explain complex matters in an understandable fashion.

Matlin, M. W. *Sensation and Perception*. 2d ed. Boston: Allyn & Bacon, 1988. Matlin's book is an introductory text covering all general areas of sensation and perception. Themes carried throughout the text are intended to provide additional structure for the material; these themes reflect the author's eclectic, theoretical orientation.

Rock, Irvin. *Perception*. New York: Scientific American Library, 1984. Rock deals particularly with perception and pays little attention to sensation other than vision. The text is designed to be an introductory work to motivate the reader to future studies. The book essentially explores the perception of the properties, distance, and motion of objects.

Schiff, William. *Perception: An Applied Approach.* Boston: Houghton Mifflin, 1980. Schiff's book is concerned with how people can, and do, use their senses to comprehend their world and their relation to it. Interesting chapters cover such topics as social-event perception, personal perception, and individual differences in perception.

Sekuler, Robert, and Robert R. Blake. *Perception.* New York: Alfred A. Knopf, 1985. Sekuler and Blake attempt to explain seeing, hearing, smelling, and tasting to students of perception. Extensive use of illustrations allows the reader to understand materials more fully. A series of short illustrations is also utilized by the authors to depict additional concepts.

Eugene R. Johnson

Cross-References

Attention, 313; The Auditory System, 344; Depth Perception, 796; Gestalt Laws of Organization, 1082; Hearing and Sound Waves, 1151; Kinesthesis and Vestibular Sensitivity, 1381; Psychophysical Scaling, 1963; Sensory Modalities and Stimuli, 2214; Signal Detection Theory, 2271; Smell and Taste, 2290; Visual Neural Processing, 2629.

SENSORY MODALITIES AND STIMULI

Type of psychology: Sensation and perception
Fields of study: Auditory, chemical, cutaneous, and body senses; vision

Humans process information using at least five sensory modalities: sight, sound, taste, smell, and the body senses, which include touch, temperature, balance, and pain. Because people's sensation and perception of external stimuli define their world, knowledge of these processes is relevant to every aspect of daily life.

Principal terms
CUTANEOUS: relating to the skin
GUSTATION: the sense of taste
OLFACTION: the sense of smell
PERCEPTION: the processes by which the brain interprets neural messages sent from the sense organs
PROXIMATE: a term applied to questions and answers regarding the immediate, physical explanation for existence of a behavior, structure, or function; used as the opposite of "ultimate"
RECEPTOR: a cell inside a sense organ that transduces (converts) captured environmental energy into neural signals
SENSATION: a two-step process by which a sense organ intercepts environmental energy and converts it into neural signals
ULTIMATE: a term applied to historical or evolutionary questions and answers about the existence of a behavior, structure, or function; used as the opposite of "proximate"
UMWELT: the individual sensory experience of reality as determined by the particular combination of sense organs that an organism has

Overview
Humans have five sense organs: the eyes, ears, taste buds, nasal mucosa, and skin. Each sense organ is specialized to intercept a particular kind of environmental energy and then to convert that energy into a message the brain can interpret. Together, these two processes are called sensation.

The first step of sensation, the interception of external energy, is done by the part of the sense organ that is in direct contact with the environment. Each sense organ has a specialized shape and structure designed to intercept a particular form of energy. The second step, conversion of the captured energy into signals the brain can understand, is done by cells inside the sense organ called receptors. Receptors are structures to which physicists and engineers refer as transducers: They convert one form of energy into another. Artificial transducers are common. Hydroelectric plants, for example, intercept flowing water and convert it to electricity; then appliances convert the electricity into heat, moving parts, sound, or light displays. Receptors are biological transducers which convert environmental energy intercepted by the sense organ into neural signals. These signals are then sent to the brain, where they are interpreted through a process called perception.

The eye, the best understood of all the sense organs, consists of a lens which focuses light (a kind of electromagnetic energy) through a small hole (the pupil) onto a sheet of cells called the retina. The retina contains the eye's receptor cells: the rods, which are sensitive to all wavelengths of light in the visible spectrum, and three kinds of cones, which are sensitive to those wavelengths that the brain perceives as blue, green, and yellow.

The ear funnels air pressure waves onto the tympanic membrane (more commonly known as the eardrum), where vibrations are transmitted to the inner ear. In the inner ear, receptors called hair cells are stimulated by different frequency vibrations; they then send signals to the brain which are interpreted as different pitches and harmonics.

Taste buds are small bumps on the tongue and parts of the throat which are continuously bathed in liquid. Receptors in the taste buds intercept any chemicals which have been dissolved in the liquid. Molecules of different shapes trigger messages from different receptors. Humans have several kinds of taste receptors which send signals the brain interprets as bitter, at least two kinds of receptors which send signals interpreted as sweet, and one kind of receptor each that sends messages interpreted as salty and sour.

The nasal mucosa, the sense organ for smell, is a layer of cells lining parts of the nasal passageways and throat; it intercepts chemicals directly from inhaled air. Apparently, cells in the nasal mucosa can produce receptor cells (called olfactory receptors) throughout life. This way, people can develop the capacity to smell "new" chemicals which they could not smell before. New olfactory receptors seem to be created in response to exposure to novel chemicals, analogous to the production of antibodies when the immune system is exposed to foreign material. Because of this ability constantly to create new olfactory receptors, it is not possible to list and categorize all the different types of smells.

The skin is the largest sense organ in the human body; its sense, touch, actually consists of several different senses, collectively referred to as the cutaneous senses. Receptors called mechanoreceptors are triggered by mechanical movements of the skin and send signals that the brain interprets as vibration, light or deep pressure, and stretching. Thermoreceptors intercept heat passing in or out of the body through the skin; their signals are interpreted by the brain as warmth and cold, respectively. Receptors which are triggered when skin cells are damaged are called nociceptors; their signals to the brain are interpreted as pain.

Some animals have sense organs that humans do not and can thereby sense and perceive stimuli that humans cannot. Many birds, and probably a variety of marine creatures, for example, can detect variations in the earth's magnetic field; some fish and invertebrates can detect electrical fields. Other animals have sense organs similar to, but more sensitive than, humans'; they can intercept a broader range of energy or detect it at lower levels. Insects, for example, can see ultraviolet light, while pit vipers can see infrared. Elephants can hear infrasound, and mice can hear ultrasound. The olfactory sensitivity of most animals far surpasses that of humans. Because of differences in sensory apparatus, each animal experiences a different sensory reality; this is termed each animal's *Umwelt*.

Applications

One application of the knowledge of sensory modalities is in the field of bioengineering. Knowing that sense organs are biological transducers allows the possibility of replacing damaged or nonfunctional sense organs with artificial transducers, the same way artificial limbs replace missing ones. Today's most advanced artificial limbs can be connected directly to nerves that send information from the motor (movement) areas of the brain; thus, a person can direct movement of the artificial limb with neural messages via thoughts. Similarly, bioengineers are researching the use of small sensors that can be set up to send electrical signals directly to a person's sensory nerves or the sensory cortex of the brain. Researchers have already developed the first version of a hearing aid to help people who have "nerve deafness" in the inner ear but whose auditory processing centers in the brain are still intact.

Another field which applies the findings of experimental sensory psychologists is called human factors engineering. People who design complicated instrument panels (for example, in jet cockpits or nuclear reactors) must have an understanding of what kinds of stimuli will elicit attention, what will be irritating, and what will fade unnoticed into the background. Using knowledge of how sound is transmitted, and how the human brain perceives sound, human factors engineers have designed police and ambulance sirens which make one type of sound while the vehicle is moving quickly (the air-raid-type wailing sound), and another while the vehicle is moving slowly, as through a crowded intersection (alternating pulses of different pitches). These two types of sounds maximize the likelihood that the siren will be noticed in the different environmental settings. Research by human factors engineers has also prompted many communities to change the color of fire engines from red to yellow; since red is difficult to see in twilight and darkness, and bright yellow can be seen well at all times of day, yellow makes a better warning color.

Research by human factors engineers and environmental psychologists is also used to improve commercial products and other aspects of day-to-day living, answering questions such as, How loud should the music be in a dentist's waiting office? What color packaging will attract the most buyers to a product? How much salt does a potato chip need? How much light is necessary to maximize production in a factory? Will noise in a domed stadium cause hearing damage in the fans? Research on sensation and perception is applied in almost every setting imaginable.

Knowledge of sensation and perception can also be used to influence the behavior of other animals. Since people visit zoos during the daytime, nocturnal animals are often housed in areas bathed in only red light. Most nocturnal animals are color-blind, and since red light by itself is so difficult to see, the animals are tricked into perceiving that it is nighttime, and they become active for the viewers. Knowing that vultures have an exceptionally good sense of smell and that they are attracted to the scent of rotting meat allowed scientists to find an invisible but dangerous leak in a long, geographically isolated pipeline; after adding the aroma of rotting meat into the pipeline fuel, they simply waited to see where the vultures started circling—and knew where they would find the leak.

The knowledge that sensation and perception differ across species has also influenced the biggest and perhaps most important field in all of psychology: learning theory. The so-called laws of learning were derived from observations of animals during the acquisition of associations between two previously unassociated stimuli, between a stimulus and a response, or between a behavior and a consequent change in the environment. These laws were originally thought to generalize equally to all species and all stimuli. This belief, along with the prevailing Zeitgeist which held that learning was the basis of all behavior, led to the assumption that studies of any animal could serve as a sufficient model for discovering the principles guiding human learning and behavior. It is now known that such is not the case.

Although laws of learning do generalize nicely in the acquisition of associations between biologically neutral stimuli, each animal's sensory apparatus is designed specifically to sense those stimuli that are relevant for its life-style, and how it perceives those stimuli will also be related to its life-style. Therefore, the meaning of a particular stimulus may be different for different species, so results from studies on one animal cannot be generalized to another; neither can results from studies using one stimulus or stimulus modality be generalized to another.

Finally, it is important to note that scientific inquiry itself is dependent upon human understanding of the human senses. Scientific method is based on the philosophy of empiricism, which states that knowledge must be obtained by direct experience using the physical senses (or extensions of them). In short, all scientific data are collected through the physical senses; thus, the entirety of scientific knowledge is ultimately based upon, and limited by, human understanding of, and the limitations of, the human senses.

Context

In the late nineteenth and early twentieth centuries, Wilhelm Wundt, often considered the "father" of scientific psychology, aspired to study the most fundamental units (or structures) of the mind. Wundt and other European psychologists (called structuralists) focused much of their attention on the description of mental responses to external stimuli—in other words, on sensation and perception. Around the same time, educational philosopher William James developed functionalism in the United States. Functionalists avoided questions about what was happening in the mind and brain and focused on questions about why people respond the way they do to different stimuli.

Today, both the structuralist and the functionalist methodologies have been replaced, but the fundamental questions they addressed remain. Psychologists who study sensation and perception still research both how sense organs and the brain work together to produce perceptions (these are referred to as proximate studies) and why people and other animals have their own particular *Umwelts* (these are referred to as ultimate studies). Results from proximate and ultimate studies typically lead to different kinds of insights about the human condition. Proximate studies lead to solutions for real-world problems, while studies of ultimate functions provide enlightenment about the evolution of human nature and humans' place in the world; they help identify what stimuli were important throughout human evolutionary history.

For example, the human ear is fine-tuned so that its greatest sensitivity is in the frequency range that matches sounds produced by the human voice. Clearly, this reflects the importance of communication—and, in turn, cooperation—throughout human evolution. More specifically, hearing sensitivity peaks nearer to the frequencies produced by female voices than male voices. This suggests that human language capacity may have evolved out of mother-infant interactions rather than from the need for communication in some other activity, such as hunting.

Knowing what kinds and intensities of stimuli the human sense organs can detect suggests what stimuli have been important for human survival; furthermore, the way the brain perceives those stimuli says something about their role. Most stimuli that are perceived positively are, in fact, good for people; food tastes and smells "good" because without some kind of psychological inducement to eat, people would not survive. Stimuli that are perceived negatively are those that people need to avoid; the fact that rotting foods smell "bad" is the brain's way of keeping one from eating something that might make one sick. To give an example from another sensory modality, most adults find the sound of a crying baby bothersome; in order to stop the sound, they address the needs of the infant. Cooing and laughing are rewards that reinforce good parenting.

Bibliography

Brown, Evan L., and Kenneth Deffenbacher. *Perception and the Senses.* New York: Oxford University Press, 1979. This text differs from most textbooks on sensation in that it integrates ethological, cross-species information with the traditional coverage of human sensory physiology and psychophysics. Although technical, the book is user-friendly. Each chapter has its own outline, glossary, and set of suggested readings.

Buddenbrock, Wolfgang von. *The Senses.* Ann Arbor: University of Michigan Press, 1958. Easy-to-read descriptions of different *Umwelts*, with many fascinating examples. Since the focus is almost entirely on ultimate explanations rather than sensory mechanisms, new technologies have not made this book outdated. (See Lowenstein, below.)

Burkhardt, Dietrich, Wolfgang Schleidt, and Helmut Altner. *Signals in the Animal World.* New York: McGraw-Hill, 1967. Thirty-two very readable essays on the sensory systems of a wide variety of animals, including senses not shared by humans. Each essay is accompanied by at least one high-quality photograph and several drawings. Text provides a delightful combination of proximate and ultimate descriptions of different sensory *Umwelts*.

Hall, Edward Twitchell. *The Hidden Dimension.* Garden City, N.Y.: Anchor Books, 1969. Written by an anthropologist, this book on cross-cultural differences in use of space includes three chapters (4, 5, and 6) on the perception of space as influenced by each sensory modality. These provide good examples of using human factors and environmental psychology to address real-world problems, particularly problems in architecture and interpersonal communication.

Lowenstein, Otto. *The Senses.* Baltimore: Penguin Books, 1966. Similar in style and ease of reading to Buddenbrock's book of the same name (see above), this book differs by focusing on proximate, rather than ultimate, explanations of sensation. Approximately half of the book is devoted to electromagnetic senses, with most of the rest devoted to mechanoreception, especially the skin senses; includes only a small portion on chemical sensation.

Scharf, Bertram, ed. *Experimental Sensory Psychology.* Glenview, Ill.: Scott, Foresman, 1975. Includes an introduction, a chapter on psychophysics, chapters on each sensory modality, and a postscript on the direction of modern studies. Provides excellent detailed descriptions of sensory mechanisms and psychophysical laws. Includes many diagrams, formulas, and technical terms but is still very readable.

Seligman, Martin E. P. "On the Generality of the Laws of Learning." *Psychological Review* 77, no. 5 (1970): 406-418. The article that triggered the ongoing debate over the generalizability of the results of learning studies across different species and different types of stimuli. Although written for a professional audience, the paper describes the basic assumptions of learning studies, so previous familiarity with learning theory is not necessary.

Stone, Herbert, and Joel L. Sidel. *Sensory Evaluation Practices.* Orlando, Fla.: Academic Press, 1985. Although written for professionals, this text can provide the layperson with insight into the world of product research. Mostly describes techniques for designing studies of the sensory evaluation of food products, but most of the principles are generalizable to other products and industries.

Linda Mealey

Cross-References

The Auditory System, 344; Color Vision, 611; Hearing: Loudness, Pitch, and Frequency, 1146; Hearing and Sound Waves, 1151; Pain, 1727; Sensation and Perception Defined, 2207; Smell and Taste, 2290; Touch and Pressure, 2578; The Visual Spectrum, 2635.

SEPARATION, DIVORCE, AND FAMILY LIFE:
ADULT ISSUES

Type of psychology: Developmental psychology
Fields of study: Adulthood; coping; interpersonal relations

Divorce results in serious psychological and economic consequences for parents and children; adults must confront feelings of anger, loss, and alienation. They need to create new lives, with different social and economic realities, and must often approach relationships with their children in new ways.

Principal terms
BEST INTERESTS OF THE CHILD: the legal tests for deciding who gets custody and, when necessary, for deciding about a termination of parental rights
CUSTODIAL PARENT: the parent with physical custody—the parent with whom the child normally lives
DIVORCE MEDIATION: mediation of the terms of divorce by a mental health professional or a team composed of such a professional and an attorney
INVOLUNTARY CHILD-ABSENCE SYNDROME: a pattern of depression and anger shown by fathers who are out of touch with their children
JOINT LEGAL CUSTODY: an arrangement in which each parent has the right to provide input on major decisions affecting the child but only one has physical custody
JOINT PHYSICAL CUSTODY: an arrangement in which each parent has significant time living with the child, who usually moves between homes; the time with each parent does not have to be exactly equal
NONCUSTODIAL PARENT: the parent who has only visitation rights to see the child and the obligation to pay child support
PARENTAL ALIENATION SYNDROME: the alienation of children from one parent, usually the noncustodial parent
POST-TRAUMATIC STRESS DISORDER (PTSD): a pathological condition caused by severe stress such as an earthquake or a divorce; it has an acute stage and a chronic stage
SOLE CUSTODY: all rights to make decisions, to have physical custody of a child, and to receive support on the behalf of the child; the noncustodial parent may get visitation rights and owes support

Overview
Once it was believed that traumatic events, such as earthquakes or divorce, would cause shock followed by quick and complete recovery. Studies of people exposed to natural disasters, however, have shown that recovery is a process with acute followed by chronic stages. The sequence is called post-traumatic stress disorder (PTSD). The

acute stage is marked by denial, defensive reactions, and passivity. Cognitive integration, realism, and active adjustment mark the chronic stage. Reactions to divorce follow this pattern. Divorce is not one event, but a continuum beginning in an unhappy marriage and continuing for many years. Divorce is a catalyst for change, but many factors influence which choices will be available. Rage is almost inevitable, and it can serve as a defense against depression. Divorce is the only major interpersonal crisis with a high probability of violence.

Judith Wallerstein and Sandra Blakeslee in 1989 proposed a stage model for divorce in their book *Second Chances*. Their three stages are an acute stage, a transitional stage, and a stage of renewed stability. Escalating unhappiness ends with the divorce decision and ejection of one parent from the home. In the acute stage, divorce unleashes primitive impulses, sometimes including violence, often in front of the children. People act in odd ways, and parental affairs frighten children.

Females are almost twice as likely to have initiated the divorce, are more likely to believe it is justified, and adjust better initially. Many experience euphoria at escaping and defensively deny real problems, anxieties, inadequate skills, and the chaos in their homes. Women first tend to be more independent, and men more likely to attempt reconciliation. More women feel that they control the divorce; males feel controlled by their external situations.

During the transitional stage, the divorced persons make efforts to solve problems and develop new life-styles through trial and error. Families are unstable; there are new lovers and friends. In the renewed-stability stage, cognitive restructuring that reflects post-divorce reality occurs, allowing major changes in parenting, social, and occupational behaviors. Self-esteem often drops. The differences in adjustment favoring women decrease. Ten years after divorce, almost half of females and about one-third of males remain very angry and feel exploited and rejected.

Adjustment during this stage depends on the resources available compared with the needs that must be met. Females tend to have more social resources, but males tend to have more financial resources. Women who are divorced by their early thirties are often energized, and 70 percent remarry. Assertive women tend to do well; maintaining a low-conflict relationship with the former husband predicts physical and emotional health.

According to Wallerstein and Blakeslee's research, females have a difficult job maintaining both parenting and economic support. Child support is a constant source of tension and conflict. Women in their late thirties and older are often immobilized by anger, depression, and helplessness. Many work hard at low-paying jobs and gain little; many women believe that eligible men are too hard to find and give up. Few older women studied by Wallerstein and Blakeslee explored new second chances. They involved themselves in clubs, friends, and churches but remained lonely and missed their marriage roles. They tended to become dependent on their children, and they had more physical complaints.

Many men who are divorced in their twenties stop maturing; most fail in second marriages. Of those studied by Wallerstein and Blakeslee, half had no stable careers five years after the divorce. Fewer than a third paid full child support, and most saw their children rarely, if at all. Most of their social contacts were with dates or male friends. Most took the blame for their failed marriages; older men more than older women had regrets, accepted responsibility, and did not remarry. Having visitation rights was experienced as being far inferior to watching their children grow up day by day, and many men had little life except their work.

More than half of divorced fathers eventually lose close contact with their children. When a custodial parent uses the children against the noncustodial parent, the children may become hostile toward the "out" parent. The majority of divorced fathers show the involuntary child-absence syndrome characterized by depression, anxiety, physical symptoms, and anger.

Joint physical custody, usually simply called joint custody, means that both parents share significant time with the children. This solves some problems but produces new ones. Most states reduce child-support payments with joint custody, although some of a parent's costs continue even when the child is with the other parent. Joint custody requires the continuation of stressful adjustments. More joint physical custody fathers stay involved with their children, pay more support, and talk with the mothers, yet the communication is too often hostile, and some fathers do become violent. Joint legal custody means that both parents can share important decisions. The child lives with one parent, and the other has visitation rights. Joint legal custody can ease a father's feelings of powerlessness about his children. This is beneficial both emotionally and economically, because fathers will be more likely to stop disapproving of the divorce and more likely to pay child support. More joint legal custody fathers continue parenting; they also start fewer court battles.

Many adults, especially women, ultimately grow in competence and self-esteem after a divorce. People with histories of talent, marketable skills, and social networks do best; the person filing the divorce petition is more likely to be happy and more social. The most consistent winners are well-established men in their thirties and forties. All the men in Wallerstein and Blakeslee's studies who initiated divorce had another, usually younger, woman waiting. The best predictor of good adjustment was a successful second marriage. These men knew they wanted, and found, women they believed to be less critical, sexier, or more responsive. Once remarried, they developed community ties and more friendships than unmarried men. Many did well as parents of a new set of children.

Lenore Weitzman has critiqued joint custody and no-fault divorce as impoverishing mothers. Many women experience a sharp drop in their standard of living immediately after divorce, but do better with a few years. Unmarried mothers with custody have, on average, about half the earnings of single-father households. The average child-support payments made (by those men who do pay) represent about half the cost of rearing each child. Fewer than half of divorced women receive full payments. Fathers are unlikely to pay for college, and most focus on legal duties—not on the children's needs.

Remarriage often improves a divorced woman's economic condition, and it may increase the happiness and economic status of a single parent of either sex. Remarriages tend to be fragile, however, and the divorce rates higher. The failure of a second marriage produces more trauma than a first failure. Fathers who marry mothers with children encounter financial burdens. Unless parents bringing children to a remarriage make a special effort to create a significant legitimate role for a stepparent, the stepparent often feels like an outsider.

Applications

Research on the effects of divorce shows that the effects are often harmful and may last a lifetime. Sometimes they may even last over generations; the children of divorce who witnessed physical abuse at home are much more likely to be abusive or to be abused. Problems are created that need to be addressed by family therapy and other interventions.

Stage models of divorce adjustment have important implications for family therapy. Clinicians must evaluate the amount of time elapsed since the beginning of the divorce process when judging the appropriateness of a divorcing or divorced client's reactions. Because early reactions to divorce are so different from long-term reactions, therapists should be careful about assuming that a happy client will continue doing well. Women surveyed soon after divorce may have good emotional health, unless they are victims of violence, despite problems with social support and finances. This good adjustment, however, can gradually deteriorate in the face of unpleasant realities.

Single-parent families make the poorest transition; they are more vulnerable, and have few economic and social resources. Female self-esteem drops as stress and fear of being alone continue. Males may cope with feelings of helplessness by having distorted and abnormally negative perceptions of their former wives. The need for counseling services may be even greater after a divorce than before or during the divorce. Fifty-five percent of divorced adults and 60 percent of adults divorced after a second marriage seek counseling. There is no significant difference between male and female readiness to seek professional help.

Father dropout is infrequent for fathers who have joint custody (and who were involved with the children before the separation), but joint custody is not a magic solution to the problems of the children or parents of divorce. High levels of conflict between former spouses correlate with poor adjustment of parents and children. Since the legal adversary system often promotes conflict, more use should be made of nonadversary procedures such as mediation of disputes to reduce continuing conflict between parents. Mediators help resolve disputes by acting as referees and information sources. The variables that determine whether mediation will be successful must be explored. When divorcing parents are each uncritically supported by an attorney of their own sex, a voluntary settlement is less likely. Interventions with divorcing families and their children need to address distorted attributions and perceptions that result from a flawed cognitive restructuring process as well as personal and environmental factors.

There needs to be greater understanding about the psychological issues that underlie the inadequate parenting provided by noncustodial parents, mainly fathers. The quality of parenting by a father before divorce does not accurately predict post-divorce parenting. The present system of forcing fathers to pay support without receiving some compensating right or benefit has resulted in withdrawn fathers. Visitation needs to be designed to meet the needs of both children and fathers or it fails in its essential purpose. The legal system's response to the feminization of poverty—using more force to make males pay more—motivates more fathers to contest custody and creates lasting bad feelings. Even those fathers who do pay support rarely pay for college once the court order expires. The children of divorce underachieve relative to their parents and their peers from intact homes.

Divorce makes females feel powerless because of the financial and emotional costs of rearing children. It makes males feel powerless because they face the loss of power in their relationships with their children. Moreover, many men face the prospect of having a large part of their salary support not only their children but also the woman who has made it difficult to continue to be a parent. Custodial mothers need more money; noncustodial fathers need easier and more rewarding access to their children. Children need to be in real relationships with both parents.

Research on divorce and its effects suggests many changes that could be made in how divorce is handled and in how families can best approach life after divorce. Among the things that are needed are reasonable support orders, with strict enforcement as well as a sharing of parental power. Moderately priced and high-quality day care services are needed; more mental health professionals are needed to work in mediation, family services, and private practice to help divorced parents reduce conflict and avoid focusing on blame and power.

About 12 percent of parents become or remain friends after divorce. An additional 38 percent manage to cooperate by considering the child or children first instead of attempting to win a power struggle with the other parent. Few "friends after divorce" remain friends after one partner enters a new stable relationship, but they usually continue to cooperate. New female partners are more likely to be threatened by a former spouse and create problems in the coparenting arrangement. The new partners in the process should be recognized and involved. Further study is needed on how to encourage cooperation between former spouses to create healthier "binuclear" families for the estimated one in three children who will grow up with stepparents.

Context

Longitudinal research on the process of divorce is a relatively recent area of psychology. The historical impetus was the adoption by all states of some form of no-fault divorce, beginning in California in 1970. No-fault divorce contributed to a great increase in divorces—to a level of one divorce for every two marriages, a rate double that of most countries. The explosion in the number of people undergoing divorce made their experiences a desirable area for large-scale research. Divorce research has origins in sociology, social psychology, clinical psychology, and developmental psychology. The results have been surprising and disturbing, with implications for cognitive psychology, stress theory, and personality theories.

The traditional view of divorce was that it was a one-time traumatic event with a few aftereffects. Both the public and psychologists believed that ties between the parents of children should be cut to allow stepfathers to replace former husbands more easily. It is now known that the effects of separation and divorce act much like other severe traumas and produce a prolonged post-traumatic stress disorder. Stage models of divorce, and Wallerstein and others' research results, have shown that recovery is often very slow, if indeed it occurs at all. Children have a continued need for close contacts with biological fathers, and fathers suffer from the loss of parenting experiences. Clinical problems persist in a very large percentage of the divorced, and these problems relate to the lack of critical resources.

Psychologists once thought that human development ended after adolescence. Now it is known that people continue to grow and change throughout their lives. Maturation can be stunted by the absence of healthy family structures; full social maturation of men requires parenting experiences. Theories of child development are mainly based on observations of intact two-parent families. Finally, the psychology of personality variables and cognitive learning may be altered by recent research on the long-term effects of divorce. Perceptions of the locus of control in the divorced person shifts as real power to control events changes. Cognitive restructuring in stressful situations may be adaptive and protective, but the tendency of divorced males to devalue their former mates severely can be mean-spirited and harmful. Understanding the cognitive mechanisms operating in this behavior will help in coping with severe stress.

The implications of divorce are important and pervasive. About 15 million children are growing up in single-parent homes, and 10 million in homes with a stepparent. Predictions from early research are that about a third of them will be seriously disturbed, depressed, poorly motivated, or easily defeated by rejections and losses. Large numbers of older divorced women are living alone in poverty. Millions of young men remain fixated at an immature level of development, preoccupied with dating and working but disconnected from future generations.

Bibliography

Gray, J. D., and R. C. Silver. "Opposite Sides of the Same Coin: Former Spouses' Divergent Perspectives in Coping with Their Divorce." *Journal of Personality and Social Psychology* 59, no. 6 (1990): 1180-1191. Canadians rated their former spouses; both agreed that the former wife was more likely to have wanted the divorce. Both saw the other as more desirous of a reconciliation, and the men devalued their former partners to an extent not found in most normal groups of people. Gray and Silver interpret these results in terms of cognitive mechanisms for coping with severe chronic stresses.

Knox, David. *Choices in Relationships: An Introduction to Marriage and the Family.*

2d ed. St. Paul.: West, 1988. An excellent source for information about the American family, from its formation through dating and marriage to separation, divorce, and postdivorce adjustment. There is a wealth of relevant statistical information as well as comprehensive reviews of psychological research on the effects of separation, divorce, custody arrangements, and remarriage.

Stark, Elizabeth. "Friends Through It All." *Psychology Today* 20 (May, 1986): 54-60. A study of the long-term adjustment of couples who stayed in contact either because of shared parenting or personal reasons. Stark finds that many divorced people develop positive and mutually satisfying relationships but that these often become more distant when one former spouse develops a new romantic involvement. Stark identifies several factors that predict a positive continuing relationship.

Wallerstein, Judith S., and Sandra Blakeslee. *Second Chances: Men, Women, and Children a Decade After Divorce.* New York: Ticknor & Fields, 1989. A very important source of information about the long-term effects of separation, divorce, and remarriage. Wallerstein followed a sample of sixty couples and their 131 children for more than fifteen years and produced comprehensive data on changes within the individuals' lives. She identifies factors related to doing well and poorly for both adults and the children of divorce.

Weitzman, Lenore J. *The Divorce Revolution.* New York: Free Press, 1985. The author makes a strong case that changes in divorce laws have caused the feminization of poverty. The work is not without methodological flaws, and the author is a determined advocate of her thesis that no-fault divorce and joint or father custody harm women; however, there is much important information here about an escalating social problem.

Leland C. Swenson

Cross-References

Couples Therapy, 718; Dissolution, 824; Intimacy in Adulthood: Erikson, 1363; Love, 1486; Separation, Divorce, and Family Life: Children's Issues, 2227; Stressors, 2471.

SEPARATION, DIVORCE, AND FAMILY LIFE: CHILDREN'S ISSUES

Type of psychology: Developmental psychology
Fields of study: Coping; infancy and childhood; psychodynamic and neoanalytic models

Research on divorce and separation has provided insight into how this event affects family life and child development. Understanding the consequences of divorce-related issues for children has permitted the refinement of methods to prevent or relieve the emotional distress associated with family breakup.

Principal terms

CUSTODIAL PARENT: as decided by the court, the parent with whom a child lives after a divorce

DISPLACEMENT COMMUNICATION: a method of indirect communication that uses an object or fictional character to represent the action and thoughts of the person to whom one is talking

EGO DEFENSE MECHANISMS: unconscious and irrational ways in which people distort reality in order to reduce anxiety

EGOCENTRIC THINKING: an intellectual tendency to attribute the cause of events to oneself

ENMESHMENT: an excessively close relationship between parent and child in which adult concerns and needs are communicated and in which overdependence on the child is apparent

REGRESSION: an ego defense mechanism that a person uses to return to an earlier stage of development when experiencing stress

STAGE THEORY OF DEVELOPMENT: the belief that development moves through a set sequence of stages; the quality of behavior at each stage is unique but is dependent upon movement through earlier stages

Overview

Separation and divorce terminate the social and legal contract of marriage and result in the breakup of a family. Divorce can represent the end of emotional suffering and an escape from an abusive environment, and it can provide the potential for personal growth. Conversely, the adult experience of divorce and separation can be devastating. Strong feelings of loss, anxiety, and damage to self-esteem often accompany divorce. Anger, depression, and guilt are also commonly reported. Divorced men are more likely than married men to experience psychiatric problems, serious accidents, and poor health; divorced women frequently experience depression and economic impoverishment.

The trouble that children have in adjusting to divorce has long been acknowledged. Between 30 and 50 percent of children of divorced parents experience long-lasting problems related to the divorce. Primary symptoms include anger and aggressive behavior, sadness, low self-esteem, depression, and impaired academic performance. Children of divorced parents are also more likely to experience trouble with intimate relationships in adulthood.

Contemporary workers no longer view divorce as a discrete event, but as a process. Neil Kalter takes this view in his book *Growing Up with Divorce: Helping Your Child Avoid Immediate and Later Emotional Problems* (1989). He describes divorce as a three-stage process: the immediate-crisis stage, the short-term aftermath stage, and the long-range period. The help children will require hinges upon which stage the divorce is in, their level of emotional and intellectual development, and their gender.

During the immediate-crisis stage, parents are often enraged. Wounded pride and self-esteem provoke responses ranging from verbal insult to physical violence. Frequently during this initial stage, little regard for the children is apparent, and children react with shock and disbelief. They are frightened, surprised, and saddened by the news that their parents are divorcing. They see that their parents are often short-tempered and occasionally show extreme anger. Conversely, they may see a parent crying, oversleeping, and anxious. During this stage, parents are often inattentive to the needs of their children. When parents show these behaviors, it creates stress for children. There are additional sources of stress for children as well. The rupture of a safe and predictable home environment and the loss of father-presence troubles them. If the parent with whom a child is living is having emotional trouble, enmeshment can represent another source of stress. Enmeshment refers to an excessively close and overdependent relationship between a parent and a child.

As parents and children move into the short-term aftermath stage, the realities of the divorce are better understood. Issues of economic support, custody, and visitation schedules become routine, and with effort, life becomes more predictable. Warfare between parents, however, often proceeds. Children are frequently enlisted as allies, weapons, and messengers in this battle. It is also possible for parents to develop an enmeshed relationship with a child during this stage. Sometimes parents do this unconsciously in an attempt to ward off feelings of loneliness and rejection. The children are counted on for adultlike emotional support as well as help with child-rearing and household chores.

Another source of stress to children is the sense that they have lost their parents. The noncustodial parent is often absent in both the psychological and the physical sense. By this time, most children have little or no contact with the noncustodial parent. Since this is likely to be their father, children often lose access to the father-child relationship. This is unfortunate, because the father represents a model of masculine behavior that is important for both genders. The children may also see their mother less frequently. She may be working longer hours, engaging in acquiring additional training, or investing more time in her social life. Dating on the part of the single parent represents a particularly salient source of stress for children, especially older elementary school children and adolescents. Young children fear abandonment, while older children harbor competitive feelings and resentment toward their parents' dating partners. Older children must also face the reality of their parents' sexuality.

Between two and three years after the divorce, the long-range period begins. A major source of stress for children during this period occurs when parents continue to show open anger toward each other. This happens primarily because one parent is having trouble accepting the divorce. This parent may feel a desperate need for emotional support and entertain a fantasy of reuniting with the former spouse. Alternatively, one parent may feel the need to heap punishment on the other for deciding upon the divorce. This particular source of stress has been found to increase the likelihood that children will develop severe emotional and/or behavioral disorders. Serious—and, if necessary, legal—efforts to put an end to warring between parents must now be made. A second important source of stress to children during the long-range period is remarriage.

The remarriage of a parent is stressful to children of all ages, with the possible exception of infants. Children often view a stepparent as a rival for the time and love of the custodial parent. Younger children may fear abandonment. Loyalty conflicts between the stepparent and the noncustodial parent may exist. Children often become angry because the fantasy that their parents may reunite is shattered. Finally, children frequently become furious when a stepparent takes on the role of a parent. This is particularly true if the stepparent assigns chores and takes on a disciplinary role too quickly. The situation will be especially stressful if new siblings are brought to the marriage, thereby increasing feelings of competition for the time and affection of the custodial parent.

Divorce presents children with myriad external stressors. Older children, because of their expanding intellectual abilities, often create debilitating internal stressors for themselves as well.

Applications

Knowledge gained through study of the divorce process can be used to help children adapt. Examining some of the issues involved in helping children between three and five years of age adjust to divorce will help to illustrate this point. One must understand, however, that reactions to divorce are largely tied to the developmental level of the child.

During the immediate-crisis stage, stressors for preschool children include unpredictable daily routines, warfare between parents, distraught parents, and loss of the father-child relationship. During the short-term aftermath stage, key stressors are fighting between parents, enmeshed relationships, and the loss of the father-child relationship. Stressors in the long-range period include parental warfare, relocations, a distant father-child relationship, and remarriage.

A common symptom indicating a reaction of preschool children to stress is called regression. Regression is an ego defense mechanism. Ego defense mechanisms are ways in which people distort reality in order to reduce stress; regression is evident when a child returns to an earlier stage of development. Regression in sleeping patterns, eating habits, motor achievements, language, toilet training, and emotional independence all signal trouble. For example, a child who was consistently using the toilet may begin to soil and wet himself or herself again. Children may also show a failure to develop psychologically; for example, a child of four may continue to panic when her mother leaves her sight.

In addition to regression, preschool children display the ego defenses of displacement and denial. Displacement is apparent when children show their anger at parents indirectly by becoming uncooperative or by fighting more frequently with other children. Denial is apparent when they simply do not admit that the divorce has taken place, or deny the divorce in fantasy. Preschool children also show a phenomenon known as emotional resonance. They resonate to the anger of their parents, and this results in diffuse feelings of distress. If warring between parents is not controlled, it produces chronic fear and a reluctance to engage in new activities and begin new social relationships.

An intellectual characteristic of preschool children is their tendency to have trouble separating fact from fantasy. They also show egocentric thinking—the tendency to attribute the cause of events to themselves. Consequently, they can create their own stress. For example, they are likely to blame themselves for the divorce, believing that their father left because they were bad. Leaving a child at a day-care center may lead her to fear that she is being abandoned because she is no longer loved. In a similar way, relocations and remarriage can spawn egocentric fantasies. Once such fantasies are developed, children believe them.

Preschool children have a more advanced striving for independence from their mothers than younger children. The absence of a father will hamper this progress. Both genders are expanding their social worlds; however, their sense of social and emotional independence is still shaky. They need a safe home-base in order to consolidate their independence. Since children are attempting to establish their independence from their mothers, their fathers provide a good alternative relationship. Further, boys need access to their fathers to nurture their emerging sense of masculine identity. Girls look to their fathers for acceptance of their feminine identity. In males, long-term father absence may produce a reluctance to interact with other boys; in females, it increases the probability of an enmeshed relationship with their mothers. Further, as children become more psychologically distant from their father, they may become angry at being forced to visit him. In addition, they may misunderstand why they must visit. For example, they may believe they are forced to visit because their mother does not care about them or does not want them around. This can produce symptoms of displaced anger, sadness, and withdrawal.

The thrust in helping these children cope is to reduce or eliminate their stress. Several steps are recommended in order to reduce external stress. Efforts should be made to ensure that the child's daily schedule is routine and predictable. Anger between parents should be reduced or eliminated. Professional help should be obtained for a distraught parent. Finally, establishing an effective coparenting relationship is critically important. In this way, the child's divorce environment can be brought in line with his or her needs. Children between the ages of three and five need a predictable, safe, and tranquil environment. Although alleviating sources of external stress is enormously helpful, the stress that children create themselves must also be addressed.

Research shows that discussing the divorce with preschool children before it occurs is helpful. The content of the discussion should be concrete and make clear what the divorce will mean. For example, the child should be told which parent will be moving out, where this parent will be living, and when he or she will see the noncustodial parent. Any changes in daily routine should also be explained. Reasons for the divorce should be explained in age-appropriate terms. The child's role in the divorce should be made clear, and it should be explained that divorce is adult business and that the child had no part in the decision. It should be emphasized that the divorce does not mean that parents will stop loving the child or will love the child any less.

If stress is minimized and the divorce has been clearly explained, chances are much better that post-divorce adjustment will go smoothly. It is, however, still possible, and perhaps likely, that the child will display divorce-related symptoms. If signals of distress occur, they are probably a result of egocentric fantasies. A technique known as displacement communication has been found to be an extremely effective way to reduce or eliminate sources of internal stress; Kalter's book provides several excellent examples of how to apply this approach.

Context

The study of divorce as it affects family life and child development has long been of concern to psychology. Many works on the subject began to appear in the 1970's, reflecting an increased need for knowledge that corresponded to a rising divorce rate (the rate of divorce tripled between 1960 and 1980). In 1977, the *Journal of Divorce* was founded as a vehicle for the publication of data relating to divorce. This journal publishes interdisciplinary findings on all aspects of divorce—from clinical practice to theory and research. It will be important to persist in accumulating data on divorce-related effects on child development, since projections indicate that divorce rates are expected to continue increasing.

Beginning in the late 1970's, systematic studies of how divorce affects child development began to appear. During this time, the emphasis in research shifted from describing case studies and reporting descriptive statistics to refining existing knowledge of how children perceive and react to divorce. The focus was on understanding specific divorce-related effects on psychological development, and the way in which long-range effects are mediated as a function of developmental level and family relations became a popular area of research. Further, significant gains have been made in understanding how to mediate in the divorce process in order to minimize negative consequences on children.

Contemporary understanding of how divorce affects child development may be viewed as growing out of Erik Erikson's theory of personality development and Jean Piaget's theory of intellectual development. Although some disagreement exists in the details of their perspectives, in general, agreements outweigh disagreements. Both are stage theorists who adhere to the notion that development is not a continuous process. This means that characteristics of personality and intelligence differ in quality as a function of age. These characteristics are so different that they are better described as new features of the person—features that did not exist before. As stage theorists, Erikson and Piaget adhere to the notion that development unfolds in an invariant sequence of stages. Consequently, success at earlier stages in development is viewed as crucial for success at later stages. Both theorists agree that achievements of emotional and intellectual development depend on biological maturity; that is, biological maturity is necessary to permit a child to benefit, or suffer, from experience. Both theorists would predict that the impact of divorce on a child will depend on the child's developmental level and gender and on the types of experiences to which he or she is exposed.

Data gathered since the 1960's on how divorce affects children lend validity to these perspectives. The notion that development occurs in a stagelike manner and unfolds in an invariant sequence has generally been supported. The notion that early success or failure affects later development has become clear. The tenet that experience interacts with biological maturity to determine outcome has also found strong support in the divorce literature. Furthermore, the stress-related symptoms that children display in attempting to cope with divorce clearly support Erikson's notions about the function of ego defense mechanisms.

Bibliography

Hetherington, E. M., M. Cox, and R. Cox. "The Aftermath of Divorce." In *Mother-Child, Father-Child Relationships*, edited by Joseph H. Stevens, Jr., and Marilyn Mathews. Washington, D.C.: National Association for the Education of Young Children, 1978. This chapter represents pioneering work that documents how divorce affects children. Reactions of children to the news of divorce and to its aftermath are vividly described.

Johnston, Janet R., and Linda E. Cambell. *Impasses of Divorce: The Dynamics and Resolution of Family Conflict.* New York: Free Press, 1988. The authors' project focused on helping parents mediate differences in hostile divorce situations. Issues sustaining conflict and preventing the development of a coparenting relationship are discussed, and methods to achieve a resolution are presented. An excellent source for family counselors.

Kalter, Neil. *Growing Up with Divorce: Helping Your Child Avoid Immediate and Later Emotional Problems.* New York: Free Press, 1989. Presents comprehensive advice on the emotional pitfalls of divorce, warning signs of distress, and methods of preventing and alleviating distress in children from infancy through adolescence. Provides a chapter on communicating with children that parents will find very useful.

Wallerstein, Judith S., and Joan Berlin Kelly. *Surviving the Breakup: How Parents and Children Cope with Divorce.* New York: Basic Books, 1980. The results of a five-year study investigating how parents and children adjust to divorce. The authors present data on how parents reacted to divorce and how these parental reactions affected their children's adjustment. They also report how children interpreted and reacted to the divorce and how their views solidified or changed over the period of the study.

Wallerstein, Judith S., and Sandra Blakeslee. *Second Chances: Men, Women, and Children a Decade After Divorce.* New York: Ticknor & Fields, 1989. This is a follow-up of Wallerstein's original study, cited above. Wallerstein's work presents data on the long-term effects of divorce on both parents and children, and for this reason it is extremely valuable. Useful for those who are anticipating divorce, attempting to cope with divorce, or interested in the long-term consequences of divorce.

Alan J. Beauchamp

Cross-References

Attachment and Bonding in Infancy and Childhood, 307; Behavioral Family Therapy, 394; Gender-Identity Formation, 1062; Psychotherapy with Children, 2009; Separation, Divorce, and Family Life: Adult Issues, 2220; Strategic Family Therapy, 2382.

SEX HORMONES AND MOTIVATION

Type of psychology: Motivation
Fields of study: Endocrine system; physical motives; sexual disorders

Sex hormones control sexual maturation and exert an important influence on sexual motivation. The role of the sex hormones varies across species; they play only a limited role in humans.

Principal terms
ANDROGENS: a class of male sex hormone; testosterone is the major androgen in mammals
ANTIANDROGEN DRUGS: drugs which suppress the production of testosterone and lower sex drive
ESTRADIOL: a female sex hormone produced by the ovaries; often referred to as estrogen
HORMONES: chemical substances produced in the body which travel in the bloodstream to various organs, where they exert an influence
PHEROMONE: a chemical released by one animal which affects the behavior of another; usually a smell
PROGESTERONE: a female sex hormone which has an important function in the menstrual cycle
TESTOSTERONE: the principal male sex hormone produced by the testes

Overview

Sex hormones exert an important influence on behavior. These hormones control sexual maturation at puberty, and they have an impact on the sex drive and sexual activity throughout the life span. In most animal species, sex hormones completely control sexual behavior. In humans, their role is more limited. Human sexual motivation is the result of the complex interplay of hormones, psychological factors, and social factors.

At puberty, the brain releases several hormones which travel through the bloodstream to target organs. In males, the targets are the testes; in females, the ovaries. In response to the hormones released from the brain, these targets begin to produce the sex hormones. The principal male sex hormone is testosterone (the name refers to the fact that it is produced by the testes). With the production of testosterone at puberty, human males experience the growth of facial and body hair, bones and muscles develop more fully, the voice deepens, and the genitals grow. In females, two sex hormones are produced by the ovaries at puberty: estradiol (often called estrogen) and progesterone. Estradiol is responsible for breast development, changes in female appearance (for example, wider hips), and maturation of the genitals and uterus. Progesterone plays a major role in preparing the female body for menstruation and pregnancy. It should be noted that although testosterone is called the "male sex hormone," it is also found in females, though in much smaller quantities. The same applies to the female sex hormones which are found in males.

After puberty is completed, the sex hormones continue to play a role in sexual motivation. In most animal species, the female goes through a regular cycle, the estrous cycle, during which sex hormones are released, causing an increase in sex drive. During this phase of the cycle, she will seek a male partner with the goal of reproduction (she is said to be "in heat"). In the presence of a female in estrus, the male experiences an increase in the sex hormone testosterone, and he will be sexually attracted to the female. For example, male rats will ignore a female whose ovaries have been removed and thus cannot produce estradiol; however, an injection of estradiol will make the female interested in sex, and males will approach her for sexual activity. In these animals, sexual behavior is largely determined by the females' sexual readiness, which depends on the phase of estrus.

In most animal species, the male learns of a female's sexual readiness by the presence of a chemical she emits, called a pheromone. Pheromones are usually derived from vaginal secretions during estrus. If pheromones are collected from an animal in estrus and applied to another that is not in estrus, males will approach the nonreceptive female and attempt sexual intercourse. In humans, pheromones do not appear to play a significant role in sexual attraction.

Humans are quite different from other animals in other respects. While the sex hormones do have an important influence, they do not control sexual motivation and behavior. Research has shown that males who have abnormally low levels of testosterone have problems achieving erection and often have a very low sex drive. Injections of testosterone restore the ability to obtain normal erection in these cases. Abnormally high levels of testosterone, however, do not cause an unusually high sex drive. Apparently, there is a minimum level of testosterone necessary for normal sexual behavior, but higher levels do not seem to have any significant effect.

Like females of other animal species, the human female goes through a cycle during which levels of sex hormones are increased. This cycle in humans and primates is called the menstrual cycle. Although human females experience cyclic increases in the sex hormones estradiol and progesterone, there is no clear indication of change in sexual motivation during this phase. For most women, sex drive does not vary with sex hormone levels. For example, women who have had their ovaries removed continue to experience a normal sex drive. The same usually applies to women who have undergone menopause, the stage of the life in the late forties during which the ovaries cease producing sex hormones. Most postmenopausal women continue to enjoy a normal sex life in spite of their reduced sex hormone levels.

Though the role of the sex hormones in sexual motivation in human females is limited, it appears that testosterone plays a role. In women, small amounts of testosterone are produced by the adrenal glands (small glands which secrete several hormones and are located atop the kidneys). Removal of the adrenal glands often abolishes the sex drive in women. In adult female monkeys whose adrenal glands and ovaries have been removed, injections of testosterone restore sex drive and sexual activity. In human females, while testosterone appears to play a role, many psychological factors such as attitudes and religious beliefs seem to be more important in understanding sexual motivation.

Applications

Knowledge about sex hormones and their role in sexual motivation has been used in several ways. With the discovery that castration, or removal of the testes, drastically lowers sex drive, it was concluded that some cases of impaired sex drive in males may be caused by low levels of testosterone. For example, a soldier was castrated by an explosive during World War I. As a result, he lost interest in sex, was unable to obtain an erection, and lost significant muscle mass; his hips also expanded. After receiving five injections of high doses of testosterone, he was experiencing normal erections, his sex drive returned, and he began to gain weight and muscle mass. For males whose sexual difficulties are caused by abnormally low levels of testosterone, regular injections tend to restore a normal sex drive and the ability to achieve erections. Studies reveal, however, that not all individuals who are castrated experience changes in sexual behavior. For reasons which are unclear, some males appear capable of sexual behavior in spite of the removal of the testes.

Giving doses of estradiol or progesterone to human males has several effects. First, excesses of these hormones cause a sharp decline in the production of testosterone, which may interfere with sex drive, erection, and ejaculation. Administering estradiol also causes breast enlargement in men. When given to men, progesterone causes a decrease in sex drive and erection ability. It does not tend to make males develop a female appearance, as estradiol does. This knowledge has been applied to treating sex offenders. Compulsive sex offenders, especially child molesters, are sometimes given injections of progesterone to help them control their sexual urges. When combined with counseling, this treatment may be useful in helping these persons gain some control over their sexual activity. While receiving the injections, the sex offenders often lose their sex drive and have trouble achieving erections. These effects are only temporary and disappear when progesterone is no longer given.

Women with unusually low levels of estradiol do not appear to suffer from direct sexual problems. They do experience difficulties with vaginal lubrication. Vaginal dryness makes sexual intercourse difficult and painful as a result of friction. The remedy for this problem is the use of a lubricant, or estradiol replacement therapy (taking regular doses of estradiol).

One early theory of homosexuality proposed that an imbalance in the sex hormones was responsible for sexual attraction to members of the same sex. According to the theory, male homosexuality was caused by a deficiency in testosterone or an excess of estradiol. This would explain why some men display the behavior expected of women: attraction to men and, according to popular stereotypes, effeminate mannerisms. Female homosexuality was thought to be caused by excess testosterone and, possibly, insufficient estradiol. Scientific tests of the theory have consistently failed to support it. Homosexuals, both male and female, do not differ from heterosexuals in their circulating sex hormone levels. Therefore, the hormone imbalance theory of homosexuality is no longer accepted. In fact, abnormally low levels of testosterone in men do not make them sexually attracted to men; the typical result is a decrease in sexual interest for any type of sexual partner. In women, excessively elevated levels of testosterone do not cause lesbianism; if anything, they tend to increase women's sexual interest in men. Factors other than levels of sex hormones are important in understanding homosexuality.

Another application involves the treatment of transsexuals. Transsexualism is a rare but interesting condition in which the person feels that nature made a mistake and placed him or her in the body of the wrong sex. A transsexual man is an anatomical male who firmly believes that he is a woman in a man's body. A transsexual woman believes that she is a male in the wrong body. Transsexuals who strongly desire to change their sex will sometimes receive hormone treatments. For a transsexual male, this consists of taking regular doses of estrogens. As a result, the male will experience breast growth, smoother skin, loss of muscle mass, and decreases in erection and sperm production. The treatment does not change facial and body hair or raise the pitch of the voice, but physical appearance will become femalelike. For transsexual women, testosterone is administered, which leads to growth of facial and body hair, deepening of the voice, and the end of menstruation. After living with these changes for two years, those who are seeking a sex-change operation may do so at one of several specialized centers. The sex-change surgery for males involves the removal of male genitals and creation of an artificial vagina. For females, the opposite procedure is undertaken. The results of these procedures are still controversial, as there are many possible problems, and not all transsexuals are satisfied with the outcome.

Context

The term "hormone" is derived from the Greek *hormaein*, which means "to set in motion." It was first used in 1904 to refer to those bodily substances which can have a profound influence on human development and behavior. All knowledge about the sex hormones is relatively new. Undoubtedly, much more will be discovered in the next decade as medical technology continues to develop rapidly.

Knowledge about the effects of castration dates back to ancient China and Arabic countries. In these countries castration was practiced to provide safe guardians of the royal harem. The castrated guardians, or eunuchs, were considered safe since their sexual motivation was impaired as a result of testosterone deficiency. In Europe, at the beginning of the nineteenth century, boys in church choirs were sometimes castrated to ensure their continued ability to sing soprano.

Thus, a general understanding about the importance of the testes in affecting human development and behavior is not new. Information about the exact nature and role of sex hormones, however, is relatively new. For example, the eighteenth century physician Simon Tissot believed that the results of castration were caused by impairments in semen production. According to his view, the loss of semen caused a decrease in strength, passivity, and a variety of other complications. It was not until the twentieth century that the loss of testosterone was identified as the mechanism underlying the effects of castration.

Although sexual motivation in lower animals is readily understood in terms of sex hormones and instincts, human sexual behavior is much more complex. A number of cultural and psychological factors, in combination with sex hormones, interact to determine human sexual motivation and behavior. The range of sexual activities in lower animals is limited and rigidly controlled by the phase of the female's estrous cycle. In humans, there is tremendous variability in types of sexual behavior, timing and frequency of sex, choice of partners, number of partners, and context of sexual activity. These variables are influenced by cultural standards regarding sexual activity. In permissive cultures, such as Polynesia, sexual experimentation is encouraged and expected. Other cultures are more restrictive and discourage sex before marriage.

Within each culture, other factors such as peer group influence, familial and religious beliefs and values toward sexuality, and individual fears (such as pregnancy and sexually transmitted diseases) can also have an impact on human sexual behavior. For example, the threat of acquired immune deficiency syndrome (AIDS) has led some individuals to change their sexual behavior. Abstinence and monogamy are advocated by some, while others, including many adolescents, have adopted few changes.

Thus, although sex hormones play an important role in human sexual behavior, especially with respect to sexual maturity and sex drive, several cultural and psychological influences are more important. In order to address the problems of teenage pregnancy and sexually transmitted disease, including AIDS, all of these factors which determine human sexual motivation and behavior must be explored in depth.

Bibliography

Carlson, Neil R. *Foundations of Physiological Psychology.* Boston: Allyn & Bacon, 1988. One of the standard texts on the physiological basis of human and animal behavior. The importance of sex hormones in development and motivation is emphasized throughout the chapter on reproductive behavior (chapter 9).

Katchadourian, Herant A. *Fundamentals of Human Sexuality.* 5th ed. Fort Worth, Tex.: Holt, Rinehart and Winston, 1989. One of the best and most readable books on human sexuality. The discussion of sex hormones in chapter 4 is thorough and clear; psychological and cultural influences on sexual motivation are covered in chapters 8, 9, 20, and 21. The presentation is accessible to high school and college students.

Masters, William H., Virginia E. Johnson, and Robert C. Kolodny. 3d ed. *Human Sexuality.* Glenview, Ill.: Scott, Foresman, 1988. An overview of human sexuality by some of the world's foremost sex researchers. Although the coverage of sex hormones is limited, the material on the other determinants of human sexual motivation is thorough, detailed, and understandable.

Pinel, John P. J. *Biopsychology.* Boston: Allyn & Bacon, 1990. Another good introductory text to the physiology of human and animal behavior. The chapter "Hormones and Sex" is detailed and clearly presented; several good case studies are offered to illustrate how hormonal problems can affect human sexual development.

Richard D. McAnulty

Cross-References

Gonads, 1094; Homosexuality, 1182; Hormones and Behavior, 1189; Sexual Behavior Patterns, 2246; Sexual Dysfunction, 2253; Sexual Variants and Paraphilias, 2259.

SEXISM

Type of psychology: Social psychology
Field of study: Prejudice and discrimination

Sexism is prejudice against persons on the basis of their gender. Sexism may exist at the interpersonal level, where it is expressed in individual beliefs and behaviors; alternatively, it may become institutionalized when social institutions and practices encourage gender bias.

Principal terms

DISCRIMINATION: differential behavior directed toward a person that is a result of prejudice toward the person's social group
EXPRESSIVENESS: a cluster of psychological traits associated with emotional warmth and nurturance
INSTRUMENTALITY: a cluster of psychological traits associated with assertiveness and competence
MALE-AS-NORMATIVE PRINCIPLE: the use of male-gendered linguistic constructions as a standard or generic form—that is, to refer to both males and females
PREJUDICE: a negative attitude toward a social group
PSYCHOLOGICAL TRAIT: a stable personality characteristic that directs a person's thoughts, emotions, and behavior; traits are stable and consistent over time and across situations
ROLE: a social position that is associated with a set of behavioral expectations
STEREOTYPE: a set of generalized beliefs and expectations about a social group

Overview

The psychological basis for sexism, as for other forms of prejudice, is the human tendency to form stereotypes about persons who are members of certain social groups. Stereotypes may be either positive or negative; they consist of sets of interrelated beliefs and expectations that a person holds about a particular social group. When these stereotypes affect people's interpersonal behavior, sexism can result, leading to prejudice and discrimination.

Gender stereotypes are reflected in beliefs and attitudes about the general nature of men and women as members of distinct social groups. In addition, gender stereotypes are related to the development of expectations about men's and women's psychological characteristics, interests, aptitudes, and behaviors. For example, if a person believes that women are more nurturant than men, then he or she might expect that women are more likely than men to be employed as child care workers. In turn, these expectations may affect how people behave in social situations. The presence of different expectations for male and female performance may lead to differential treatment on the basis of gender. For example, if the director of a child-care center expects women to be superior nursery school teachers, then he or she may be likely to discriminate against males who apply for an available teaching position.

Psychological research has established that gender stereotypes are quite pervasive in American culture. Considerable attention has been directed toward identifying the content of gender stereotypes. That is, psychologists are interested in the particular nature of beliefs that individuals hold about men and women in American culture. In a classic study, Paul Rosenkrantz, Inge Broverman, and their colleagues asked Americans to describe characteristics of the typical American man and woman. Their findings, which were first reported in the late 1960's, have been supported by subsequent research. Thus, their research appears to provide an accurate portrayal of the gender stereotypes commonly held by American adults.

These researchers found that subjects tended to describe men and women in terms of two different clusters of psychological traits, or personality characteristics. Women were more likely to be characterized by a group of traits which could be summarized as representing an expressiveness cluster. That is, men and women agreed that, as a group, women were caring, warm, and emotionally expressive. In contrast, men were characterized by a group of traits that could be described as an instrumentality cluster. In this instance, the typical man was perceived to be assertive, dominant, and competent. Thus, perceptions of men and women, as members of social groups, were conceived in terms of opposing psychological characteristics.

In the early 1980's, Kay Deaux and Laurie Lewis conducted a series of studies that elaborated upon this pioneering research. They hypothesized that instrumentality and expressiveness are only two possible distinctions between men and women. Deaux and Lewis believed that additional factors were likely to play an important role in gender stereotyping. In their research program, male and female subjects were given a list of gender-relevant characteristics. Subjects then were asked to estimate the likelihood that a man or woman possessed each characteristic. The results of these studies indicated that gender stereotypes do in fact consist of a number of related components. Subjects reliably associated certain psychological traits, role behaviors, occupations, and physical characteristics with gender.

The male stereotype consisted of the instrumentality cluster coupled with masculine psychological and physical characteristics. Subjects perceived the typical male to be strong and masculine, likely to hide his feelings, sexy, and muscular. Men typically were described as breadwinners and as being likely to take the initiative in encounters with the opposite sex. The typical male roles included blue-collar worker, businessman, athlete, and "macho man." In contrast, the female stereotype consisted of the expressiveness personality cluster coupled with feminine psychological and physical characteristics. Subjects described the typical woman as being smart and attractive, but also feminine, sensitive, and emotional. Women often were stereotyped as housewives and were perceived to be likely to be engaged in domestic chores such as child rearing and cooking. On the other hand, female stereotypes were not simply relegated to the domestic role. Subjects also held stereotypes that were representative of female athletes, businesswomen, and "sexy women."

Although there appears to be some overlap between male and female categories, it is clear that gender stereotypes do parallel the common roles that men and women typically assume in society. In addition, males and females are perceived to be members of distinctly different social groups. For the most part, people expect men and women to display opposing psychological characteristics and role behaviors. Finally, it should be noted that psychologists have found remarkable cross-cultural similarity in the content of gender stereotypes.

Applications

There is a large body of psychological research that has investigated the effects of sexism. Some psychologists have investigated how gender stereotypes may influence people's perceptions of women in certain social roles (for example, as leaders). Others have studied how the use of sexist language might be related to the formation and maintenance of gender stereotypes.

The effects of gender stereotypes are particularly pronounced when people must form first impressions and make social judgments about others on the basis of little information. Natalie Porter and her colleagues have studied the factors that persons consider when they are asked to identify the leader of a small group. They asked subjects to view a photograph of an all-male group, an all-female group, or a mixed-sex group. Subjects were then asked to guess which person in the photograph held the position of group leader.

First, Porter and her colleagues found that subjects were likely to rely upon spatial configuration as an important cue in determining which person was the leader of the group. In the cases of all-male and all-female groups, the majority of subjects identified the person at the head of the table as the group leader. When the group consisted of both male and female members, and a male was seated at the head of the table, this person also was designated as leader by a majority of subjects. When a female occupied the head position in a mixed-sex group, however, her position at the table was disregarded. In this situation, any of the other males in the group was selected. It is clear from these results that women are less likely than men to be seen as leaders of mixed-sex groups. The results of this study are consistent with the content of gender stereotypes described by Deaux and Lewis.

Gender stereotypes are also apparent in the everyday use of language. For example, many linguists have pointed out that the English language traditionally has regarded the male linguistic forms as normative. The male-as-normative principle refers to the tendency for "man" to be used to refer to all human beings. Thus, the male is considered to be the representative, or prototype, of the human species. An example of the male-as-normative principle is the use of the pronoun "he" as a generic pronoun that is intended to refer to both males and females. An example of the use of he as a generic pronoun is, "While stress is a normal concomitant of our daily lives, man's ever-increasing pace of life may in fact shorten his life span."

The use of the male-as-normative principle has been subjected to two primary criticisms. First, the use of a male-gendered pronoun is often ambiguous. When a writer asserts that "man's ever-increasing pace of life may in fact shorten his life span," the reader may assume that men are more susceptible to the negative effects of stress than women. An alternative interpretation is that humans, regardless of sex, are negatively affected by stress. The second criticism focuses on issues of gender equality. The use of the male-as-normative principle implies that women are exceptions to the general rule. Critics argue that the use of the male generic encourages people to think exclusively of males, rather than including females. Further, they claim that language and thought are closely related and that sexist language may foster gender stereotypes.

In the early 1980's, psychologist Janet Shibley Hyde investigated the effects of sexist language on children's thought processes. She was particularly interested in discovering whether children understood the male-as-normative principle. She asked elementary-school-age children to complete a story about another child. Each of the children was given a sentence with which to begin his or her story (for example, "When a kid goes to school, _____ often feels excited on the first day"). One-third of the sentences provided "he" in place of the blank, one-third included "they," and one-third included "he or she." Hyde found that children's stories indeed were influenced by the use of gender pronouns. When "he" or "they" was provided to the child, fewer than 20 percent of the stories were about females. This effect was especially pronounced when boys were tested. Not one boy who was provided with the pronoun "he" wrote a story about a girl. In contrast, when the pronouns "he or she" were supplied, 42 percent of the stories were about females. Hyde concluded that when children hear the word "he," even when used as a generic pronoun, they tend to think of males.

A number of practical suggestions have been made to avoid the use of sexist language. One simple change is to use the pronoun "they" in place of "he." The results of Hyde's study, however, would suggest that the use of "he or she" would be a better alternative. Others have argued that the single pronouns "he" and "she" might be used with equal frequency throughout written text. Such suggestions are not trivial. Since the 1970's, many textbook publishers have issued guidelines that forbid the use of sexist language. The American Psychological Association (APA) has provided similar guidelines for manuscripts that are submitted for publication in journals published by the APA.

Context

Psychological research investigating the causes and effects of sexism is rooted in the specialized field of differential psychology, which investigated ethnic and gender differences in psychological variables such as intelligence and mental abilities. As early as 1879, Gustave LeBon provided a description of gender differences in which he noted women's innate inferiority to men, an observation echoed by many other differential psychologists of that period. Hence, the tendency to observe differences between social groups was reflected in both the attitudes and research efforts of early psychological researchers, and continues today.

Historically, social psychologists have studied people's beliefs about differences between social groups and their attitudes toward members of other social groups. The first study of stereotypes was conducted in 1922 by Walter Lippmann, a public opinion researcher. His identification of the stereotype concept provided a means for the scientific study of ethnocentrism. The rise of Fascism and its thesis of group superiority and inferiority in pre-World War II Europe concerned many social scientists and provided an impetus for the development of systematic studies of intergroup relations. While perceptions of different ethnic groups was the focus of social psychological studies of stereotypes conducted before the 1940's, the study of gender stereotypes was initiated by the publication of a study conducted by Samuel Fernberger in 1948.

Social psychologists continued to study stereotypes and their relation to prejudice in the post-World War II era. Gordon Allport's *The Nature of Prejudice* (1954) provided a theoretical model that explained the process of stereotyping and the development and maintenance of prejudice. In Allport's view, stereotypes are negative attitudes toward the members of other groups that are accompanied by rigid, inflexible thought processes. His conceptualization of stereotypes and prejudice remained unchallenged until the late 1960's, when social psychological research demonstrated that categorization and stereotyping were normal consequences of human thought processes.

The political unrest that characterized American society during the Vietnam War era was reflected in an explosion of social psychological studies of racism and sexism. In addition, the prevailing societal concerns about political and social inequality coincided with demands among feminist scholars for the conduct of nonsexist psychological research. This resulted in the emergence of a new field in the early 1970's, the psychology of women. Nonsexist, gender-fair psychological research has been promoted as a legitimate field of study by the establishment of a specialized section within the APA (Division 35) that is dedicated to the psychology of women. Scholarship in this field is dedicated to the study of sexism, gender differences and similarities, and other aspects of gender-role socialization.

Bibliography

Deaux, Kay, and M. E. Kite. "Thinking About Gender." In *Analyzing Gender*, edited by Beth B. Hess and Myra Marx Ferree. Newbury Park, Calif.: Sage Publications, 1987. This easy-to-read review article reports research on sex differences, the nature of and attitudes toward men and women, gender stereotypes, and conceptions of masculinity and femininity. Deaux and colleague Laurie Lewis' research on gender stereotypes is reviewed and discussed in terms of gender belief systems held by men and women.

Janssen-Jurreit, Marielouise. *Sexism: The Male Monopoly on History and Thought.* New York: Farrar, Straus & Giroux, 1982. A cultural history of sexism for the sophisticated reader. Describes how sexist attitudes have shaped thought and scientific endeavors in Western culture, and discusses a theory of sexism.

Tavris, Carol, and Carole Wade. *The Longest War: Sex Differences in Perspective.* 2d ed. New York: Harcourt Brace Jovanovich, 1984. An entertaining and easy-to-read introduction to the psychology of women. Gender differences and similarities are discussed, in addition to the biological and social factors relevant to gender-role socialization.

Thorne, Barrie, Cheris Kramarae, and Nancy Henley. *Language, Gender, and Society.* Rowley, Mass.: Newbury House, 1983. Contains an excellent collection of papers that address the nature of sexist language and research findings on gender differences in language use. Draws parallels among gender, power, and social class and their relationship to language and its use. An accessible and valuable source of information.

Walsh, Mary Roth, ed. *The Psychology of Women: Ongoing Debates.* New Haven, Conn.: Yale University Press, 1987. Using a debate format, noted authorities on the psychology of women present their arguments about controversial issues. Topical issues include mental health, psychological characteristics, differences, and social issues. A very accessible yet informative introduction for the general reader.

Williams, John E., and Deborah L. Best. *Sex and Psyche: Gender and Self Viewed Cross-Culturally.* Newbury Park, Calif.: Sage Publications, 1990. The authors have conducted one of the best global studies of stereotypes. Here they present the results of a cross-cultural study of sex-role stereotypes, ideologies, and values in thirty countries. A wealth of statistical data is summarized in a format suitable for the college-level reader.

Cheryl A. Rickabaugh

Cross-References

Causal Attribution, 487; Cognitive Ability: Gender Differences, 540; Feminist Psychotherapy, 1025; Gender-Identity Formation, 1062; Effects of Prejudice, 1848; Psychology of Women: Karen Horney, 1950; Psychology of Women: Sigmund Freud, 1956; Racism, 2037; Self-Concept Origins, 2175; Social Schemata, 2329.

SEXUAL BEHAVIOR PATTERNS

Type of psychology: Motivation
Fields of study: Endocrine system; nervous system; physical motives

Sexual behavior patterns help to ensure the survival of virtually all species. There is a rich diversity of patterns in the animal kingdom, each shaped by evolutionary, ecological, and environmental factors on the one hand and hormonal and neural factors on the other.

Principal terms
MONOGAMY: the sexual relationship between one male and one female
PHEROMONES: chemical substances released by an animal to communicate sexual status, ownership of territory, or danger
POLYANDRY: the sexual relationship between one female and more than one male
POLYGYNY: the sexual relationship between one male and more than one female
PROXIMATE CAUSE: the internal physiological reason for a behavior to occur or change; usually involves the nervous or endocrine system
SEX HORMONES: androgens secreted by the testes in males, and estrogens and progesterone secreted by the ovaries in females; each sex also produces a smaller quantity of the other sex's hormones
SEXUAL SELECTION: anatomical or behavioral traits that allow an animal to compete with members of its own sex (intrasexual selection) for the opportunity to mate with a member of the other sex (intersexual selection)
ULTIMATE CAUSE: the evolutionary reason for a behavior to occur or change; based on increasing the probability of successfully producing more offspring

Overview

Sexual behavior patterns represent one of the most important aspects of an organism's life. These patterns not only provide for the successful perpetuation of the species but also allow the individual to contribute genetically to future generations. Sexual behavior is unlike other physical motives, such as feeding and drinking, which are required for the individual's survival and which are initiated to some extent by measurable changes in blood sugar and cellular hydration. Engaging in sexual behavior is neither necessary to live nor stimulated by the depletion of a bodily fluid or chemical substance.

Two types of questions, relating to ultimate and proximate causality, must be addressed when sexual behavior patterns are examined. The first question asks why the pattern developed; the second asks how it occurs. For example, many species breed only during particular seasons, and the onset of these periods is often associated with changes in plumage or coloration, or the growth of anatomical structures such as antlers. Why do these changes take place? This question of ultimate causality is really asking about purpose or function; in these examples, one answer could be that the alteration makes the animal more attractive to a potential mate.

The second question, concerning proximate causation, asks how these changes come about or what the more immediate cause is. In this case, the answer could be related to a change in the animal's hormonal secretions. Thus, the sexual behavior pattern of a given species is determined by many factors, each with ultimate and proximate causes.

One of these factors is sexual selection, a concept originated by Charles Darwin in *The Descent of Man and Selection in Relation to Sex* (1871) and related to the example mentioned above. There are two kinds of selection, intersexual and intrasexual. In the first, one sex's ability to secure a mate is related to its anatomical and behavioral traits. Examples that pertain to males include antlers, the peacock's feathers—and the way he displays the fully fanned-out feathers for the female—and the song of some bird species which is used to "advertise" the male's availability for mating as well as the fact that he has obtained a territory relatively free of intruders.

Intrasexual selection involves those anatomical and behavioral traits that are used to compete with members of the same sex for access to a member of the other sex. The battle between males to establish dominance that for the winner often leads to the opportunity to mate is a common example. A well-known phenomenon in mice, the Bruce effect, provides a different sort of intrasexual selection example. The presence of an unknown male during the early stages of pregnancy can cause a female to abort, which results in her becoming sexually receptive and hence a potential mate for the strange male. In this case, the ultimate cause is that this enables the male to sire more offspring, while the proximate cause is that his odor alters the female's hormone secretions in such a way as to terminate pregnancy.

Various mating systems have evolved that also determine the type of sexual behavior pattern. Monogamy represents a sexual relationship between one female and one male, sometimes for life. One advantage is that it precludes the effort necessary to search for a mate during each breeding cycle or season. It may, however, sometimes be more advantageous for a female to enter a good territory already inhabited by a male and one or more other females than to form a monogamous relationship with a male who lives in a dangerous territory or one with fewer resources. These systems are called polygynous, as opposed to those that are polyandrous, in which one female has a sexual relationship with more than one male. Although polyandrous systems are uncommon, polyandry does occur in situations in which the female can lay many eggs in various nests while the different males do most or all of the incubating.

Unlike some species, such as humans, who reproduce throughout the year, most species breed only during one or more restricted times of the year. The ultimate cause could be that hatching or birth occurs at a time when the environmental features are more optimal in terms of temperature, predators, or food availability. Proximate factors have been well studied, and it is known that changes in the amount of light per day or temperature can cause an animal's endocrine system to become reproductively active. In female mammals, these periods are called estrous cycles; it is only during these cycles that pregnancy can occur. Animals kept in laboratories and maintained with constant and optimal amounts of light and other environmental factors will breed all year long.

The changes in hormonal secretions that precede the onset of a breeding period are critical for several reasons. Physiological processes such as maturation of the egg or ovum, the formation of the hard shell of the egg in birds and reptiles, ovulation, preparation of the uterus for implantation of the ovum in mammals, and development of sperm depend upon particular hormones. Hormones are also important because they act directly on regions of the brain to increase an organism's motivation to reproduce. In addition, by affecting sensory processes, hormones directly or indirectly enable an animal to communicate its reproductive readiness over distances. Examples include pheromones, which are odors that are emitted by many species to attract a sexual partner, some types of singing in birds and croaking in frogs, and the increased swelling and reddening of the genital region in monkeys.

Applications

Sexual behavior patterns are extremely varied; only by studying them in detail have scientists uncovered some general principles that apply to various groupings of species. Appreciating the differences between even closely related species prevents oversimplified generalizations from one species to another.

Many species of birds have relatively prolonged and intricate courtship and mating patterns. The ring dove was extensively studied in the laboratory by Daniel Lehrman and his colleagues in the 1950's and 1960's and by a number of other scientists since then. Although the dove has breeding cycles in nature, it reproduces almost the entire year if kept in the laboratory under constant conditions of fourteen hours of light and ten hours of dark per day and 22 degrees centigrade.

The male dove's courtship begins with cooing sounds while in a bowing posture. This continues for a period of time until he selects a nest site and then coos from that location. When sufficiently aroused, the female also "nest-coos," which tells the male that it is time to gather material for the nest. Eventually the female ovulates, and the birds mate. She lays two eggs; both parents incubate the eggs, and both participate in feeding the young squabs by regurgitation.

Experiments have shown that androgens, the male sex hormones secreted from the testes, stimulate the male dove's courtship behavior, which in turn stimulates the female's ovaries to release the female sex hormones estrogen and progesterone. Hearing her own nest coos affects the female's physiology by playing a major role in the development of the follicles, the ovarian structures that contain her gametes, or eggs, which will be fertilized by the sperm. These hormones are important for ovulation and for mating behavior. Behavioral participation in the building of the nest produces further hormonal changes, which increase each partner's motivation to sit on the eggs. Visual and tactile sensory input from the eggs stimulates prolactin from the pituitary gland in both sexes, which functions to keep the parents incubating until the eggs hatch; it also causes the production of "crop milk," the partially digested food that is regurgitated for the hatchlings. These behavioral-hormonal interrelationships have been shown to exist in other species, and they point out the importance of particular sexual behavior patterns for successful reproduction.

Another example of the role of behavior patterns in the survival of the species comes from experiments on rats by Norman Adler. A female rat comes into "heat" or "estrus" on only one day during the latter portion of her four-day estrous cycle. Her period of heat begins several hours before ovulation and ends several hours afterward. It is only during this time that she will mate and can become pregnant. During the first few days of the estrous cycle, the female secretes hormones that cause growth of the follicles, ovulation, and sexual behavior. If her eggs or ova are fertilized, her estrous cycling stops until after delivery of the litter. As in the case of the dove, a female rat will continue to have estrous cycles all year long under constant environmental conditions in the laboratory, unless she becomes pregnant.

Under those constant conditions, the male continues to secrete androgens and is almost always ready to mate. Placing a sexually receptive female and sexually active male together in a cage results in a predictable sequence of behaviors. The male will investigate the female and, on the basis of certain odors attributable to her estrogen and progesterone, will find her "attractive." In response to the male's interest in her and her attraction to him, she engages in proceptive behaviors—sexually stimulating activities that maintain the pair's interaction. In the rat, these behaviors include a "hopping and darting" form of locomotion and ear quivering. The male will mount the female, and if sufficiently motivated, she will show receptivity by adopting the "lordosis" posture (characterized by immobility, arched back, and raised genital region). On many of these mounts, the male will be able to intromit his penis into her vagina; after an average of ten to fifteen intromissions, he will ejaculate. A number of minutes will elapse and the sequence will begin again; it will be repeated several times in a single sexual session.

In one experiment, males were allowed to intromit a varying number of times with a first female; then, before ejaculating, they were each placed with a second female. In this way, various females received different numbers of intromissions prior to an ejaculation. The significant finding was that the female needs a number of intromissions plus an ejaculation to become pregnant. If she receives only one or two intromissions prior to an ejaculation, her likelihood of becoming pregnant is greatly reduced. The stimulation she receives from these intromissions is necessary to alter her hormonal secretions in preparation for pregnancy. Additionally, males who intromit fewer than six times prior to an ejaculation release fewer sperm, hence reducing the probability that their partners will become pregnant. This result is related to the fact that subdominant male rats have fewer intromissions and reduced fertility, but only when a more dominant male is nearby.

Scientists study primate species both because they are interesting in their own right and because the researchers wish to gain some understanding of human behavior. The rhesus monkey, a commonly studied primate, is polygynous and native to India; it has a breeding season that begins in the fall and lasts about five months. Instead of an estrous cycle, it has a menstrual cycle that is almost identical to that of human females.

Mating behavior is not controlled as exclusively by hormones as it is in lower species, but the frequency of copulation is greatest around the time of ovulation. Attractivity of the female is enhanced by estrogen, but (as is not the case in the rat) it is reduced by progesterone, the hormone that is at its highest level after ovulation in the second half of the menstrual cycle. Experiments have shown that for optimal mating behavior to occur, androgen is necessary for the male, and both estrogen and androgen are required in the female. Female monkeys, like female humans, normally secrete androgen, although at much lower levels than males do (just as male monkeys and humans secrete female sex hormones). Studies on human females have shown that levels of androgen during the menstrual cycle correlate with increased sexual motivation and gratification.

Context

Charles Darwin was influential in convincing scientists and nonscientists alike that humans and other animals are products of evolution and that they share common ancestors. Further, Darwin and his successors have argued that behavior, like anatomy, has changed as a result of natural selection, the process whereby traits that allow an organism to produce more offspring will be inherited by subsequent generations.

In part because of Darwin's emphasis on the similarity between animals and humans, William James in the late nineteenth century and William McDougall in the early twentieth century proposed that much of human behavior is based on instincts. Instincts are behaviors that are characterized by their lack of dependence on learning, fairly rigid performance, and presence in all members of at least one sex of a species.

The question of instincts is a key issue in the long-standing controversy in psychology between "nature" and "nurture," or the relative role of inborn versus environmental or learned factors in behavior. Over the years, some behaviors that were thought to be pure instincts have been shown to be affected by learning or experience, and other behaviors have been shown to be more inborn than originally thought. Furthermore simply calling a behavior an instinct does little to shed light on either its ultimate or its proximate causes.

Partly as a result of the debate over instincts, the study of animal and human behavior has taken two somewhat separate paths. On the one side are primarily psychologists, psychobiologists, and neuroscientists who investigate the more proximate causes of sexual behavior patterns in the laboratory under controlled conditions. Their progress has helped to gather information on the nervous system, the endocrine system, the interaction between the two, and their relationship to environmental factors such as light, temperature, and the presence of potential mates.

Evolutionary biologists, animal behaviorists, sociobiologists, and ethologists tend to study sexual and other behaviors under natural conditions. Ethologists Konrad Lorenz and Nikolaas Tinbergen focused on more instinctive, "species-specific" behaviors emphasizing ultimate causation.

It is often difficult for a laboratory scientist to devote much attention to evolutionary concerns, and it is equally difficult for the animal behaviorist to focus on the nervous and endocrine systems. Information from one approach often complements the other, however, and a complete understanding of the effect of all relevant factors is necessary for the study of sexual behavior patterns.

Bibliography

Austin, Colin Russell, and Roger Valentine Short, eds. *Reproductive Patterns.* Cambridge, England: Cambridge University Press, 1972. This is a delightful and relatively short book covering a variety of species, including detailed descriptions of sexual patterns in marsupials and elephants. In addition, it provides information on the immunological issues of reproduction and on the effects of aging.

Crews, David, ed. *Psychobiology of Reproductive Behavior: An Evolutionary Perspective.* Englewood Cliffs, N.J.: Prentice-Hall, 1987. Twelve articles cover a wide range of species, including humans. The emphasis in this book is on ultimate and proximate causation of reproductive behavior, and the articles are written by experts in their fields.

Hutchison, John Bower, ed. *Biological Determinants of Sexual Behaviour.* New York: John Wiley & Sons, 1978. A collection of twenty-four articles covering the role of development and experience, physiological mechanisms, sensory stimulation, evolutionary concerns, and reproductive strategies in the sexual behavior of animals. Included are several readings pertaining to humans and other primates.

Komisaruk, Barry R., et al., eds. *Reproduction: A Behavioral and Neuroendocrine Perspective.* New York: New York Academy of Sciences, 1986. More than forty articles, all written by individuals who were or are associated with the Institute of Animal Behavior at Rutgers University, a program that emphasizes evolutionary physiological issues in the study of reproduction.

Lehrman, Daniel S. "The Reproductive Behavior of Ring Doves." *Scientific American* 211 (November, 1964): 48-54. This article presents a classic example of the relationships between and among the mating partners, internal physiological mechanisms, and the environment.

Harold I. Siegel

Cross-References

SEXUAL DYSFUNCTION

Type of psychology: Psychopathology
Field of study: Sexual disorders

Sexual dysfunction can occur in the desire, excitement, or orgasm phase of sexual responding: Desire disorders include hypoactive (inhibited) desire, sexual aversion, and excessive desire; problems related to excitement are female sexual arousal disorder and male erectile disorder; problems with orgasm include premature ejaculation and inhibited orgasm; dyspareunia and vaginismus are pain disorders.

Principal terms
DYSPAREUNIA: painful intercourse
EJACULATION: expulsion of semen from the urethra during orgasm
ERECTILE DYSFUNCTION: recurrent and persistent inability to attain or maintain a firm erection of the penis despite adequate stimulation
FEMALE SEXUAL AROUSAL DISORDER: failure to obtain or maintain vaginal lubrication despite adequate stimulation
HYPOACTIVE SEXUAL DESIRE: lack of interest in sexual expression with anyone
PREMATURE EJACULATION: unintentional ejaculation before or shortly following insertion of the penis in the vagina
SENSATE FOCUS: a therapeutic exercise involving concentration on sensations produced by touching
SEXUAL AVERSION DISORDER: a dysfunction characterized by extreme fear and avoidance of genital contact with a partner
SQUEEZE TECHNIQUE: a treatment for premature ejaculation in which a man signals his partner to apply manual pressure to his penis to avoid ejaculation
VAGINISMUS: involuntary spasms of the muscles of the outer third of the vagina

Overview

In order to understand sexual dysfunction, it is necessary to examine the process of sexual response. William Masters and Virginia Johnson found that the basic sexual response cycle is the same in both men and women, including the excitement, plateau, orgasmic, and resolution phases. Excitement begins when the individual becomes aroused. Increased levels of sexual tension lead to the plateau phase and to orgasm. During resolution, there is a decrease in sexual tension and a return to an unstimulated state. In both genders, there are two basic physiological responses to sexual stimulation: myotonia (muscle tension) and vasocongestion (filling of blood vessels with blood).

Based on the physiological research of Masters and Johnson, Helen Kaplan proposed a framework that puts more emphasis on the subjective experience of sexual response, dividing it into the phases of desire, excitement, and orgasm. The categories of sexual dysfunction are described in the American Psychiatric Association's *Diagnostic and Statistical Manual of Mental Disorders* (rev. 3d ed., 1987, DSM-III-R) using these frameworks.

Problems with sexual desire include hypoactive sexual desire, sexual aversion, and excessive sexual desire. In cases of hypoactive sexual desire disorder, found in both genders, interest in sex and sexual fantasy are deficient or absent. The problem typically lasts for a given time period, rather than over a lifetime, and sometimes people experience it situationally—such as with a partner but not during masturbation. The second type of desire disorder, sexual aversion, occurs when there is a strong fear of sexual relations and a desire to avoid genital contact with a partner. An individual with sexual aversion may still engage in fantasy and masturbation. The sources of sexual desire disorders are not clear, but people who experience sexual aversion sometimes have been the victims of incest or rape. Also, low sexual desire has been associated with depression, fear of loss of control, fear of pregnancy, marital conflict, and lack of attraction to one's partner. Excessive sexual desire involves a preoccupation with sexuality and the use of sexual activity to reduce tension resulting from pervasive thoughts about sex.

A second category of dysfunction involves the excitement phase. Some people feel sexual desire but are unable to participate in intercourse because of a lack of physiological arousal. It is often situational and in women is characterized by a lack of vaginal lubrication, which can result from biological factors such as low estrogen levels or from psychological factors, including apathy or fear. Equivalent to vaginal lubrication in women is the engorgement and erection of the penis in men. Commonly used terms to describe sexual arousal disorders are "frigidity" in women and "impotence" in men, although researchers now consider them to be derogatory. Instead, the preferred term for women is "female sexual arousal disorder," and the preferred term for men is "erectile dysfunction."

Lifelong erectile dysfunction is characterized by the inability to maintain penetration with a partner at any point throughout life, although the person may experience nighttime erections and erections during masturbation. In comparison, nonlifelong erectile inhibition is applied to the man who previously had erections with a partner but is presently unable to experience them. Masters and Johnson think that the label of nonlifelong erectile dysfunction is appropriate when a man is unable to experience an erection in at least one-quarter of his sexual encounters. Erectile problems are frequently caused by a combination of biological and psychological factors. Low levels of testosterone, the use of certain drugs, and disorders that restrict penile blood flow are biological causes. Fatigue, worry, and relationship difficulties are typical psychological problems. Erectile dysfunction is the most common complaint of men who seek sex therapy.

Difficulties of orgasmic response occur in both genders. Women with inhibited orgasm may look forward to sex, experience excitement and lubrication, and enjoy sexual contacts, but they do not reach orgasm. There is an involuntary inhibition of the orgasmic reflex. Difficulty with orgasm is one of the most common sexual complaints among women. Inhibited orgasm is rarely the result of physiological causes. Relatively nonorgasmic women tend to have more negative attitudes toward masturbation, greater guilt feelings about sex, and problems communicating with a partner about the need for stimulation of the clitoris. In comparison, inhibited male orgasm refers to the inability of a man to have an orgasm by ejaculating during intercourse. It is seldom encountered by therapists; it may result from sex guilt, fear of impregnating someone, or dislike for a partner. Another orgasm-related problem for males is premature ejaculation. The preferred definition of premature ejaculation is consistently reaching orgasm so quickly that it greatly reduces a man's own enjoyment of the experience, impairs a partner's satisfaction, or both.

Finally, although men and women both can experience pain involving intercourse, pain is more commonly found in women. Dyspareunia is the technical term. Pain is commonly a result of lack of lubrication because of insufficient arousal or hormone levels. Vaginal infections can also lead to pain; contraceptive substances can also irritate the vagina. Pain at the opening may result from an intact hymen, whereas pain deep in the pelvis during thrusting may be caused by jarring of the ovaries. Another source of deep pain is endometriosis, a condition in which uterine tissue implants on various places in the abdominal cavity. An uncommon type of pain in women is vaginismus, characterized by strong, involuntary contractions of the outer third of the vagina.

Applications

There are several commonly used techniques for treating sexual dysfunction. As necessary, some address the issue of marital conflict and attempt to resolve it. Other techniques focus on individual psychological difficulties in one partner or the other. Sometimes it is necessary to help a couple develop communication skills. Other times, sexual difficulties are rooted in a lack of knowledge, so information and instruction are provided.

One popular technique is systematic desensitization. It involves learning muscle-relaxation exercises. A set of scenes that produce anxiety are constructed by the therapist together with the client. The scenes are arranged from least to most anxiety-producing. The goal is to replace the response of anxiety with the response of relaxation. Therapy begins with the client imagining the least anxiety-producing scenes. If anxiety occurs, the client is told to give up the image of the scene and to use the relaxation exercises. The exercise is repeated until the client no longer feels anxiety associated with that scene. Then the next scene is imagined by the client, and so on. The process generally takes from five to fifteen sessions.

Another technique is that of nondemand pleasuring together with sensate focus. To use the exercises of nondemand pleasuring and sensate focus, the couple would be asked to refrain from sexual contacts of any kind until instructed to do so by the therapist. During treatment, the couple would get take-home assignments that gradually increase sexual contact from the point of hugging and kissing to being able eventually to have sexual intercourse. The partners would be assigned to alternate in the roles of giver and receiver. Playing the role of giver would be to explore and touch the receiver's body. The giver would not attempt to arouse the receiver in a sexual manner. To use the sensate focus exercise, the receiver would concentrate on the feelings that come about as a result of the touch of the giver. The receiver would be instructed to prevent or end any kind of stimulation that was uncomfortable or unpleasant by informing the partner to that effect. The next step involves a progression to breast and genital touching while continuing to avoid stimulation that is orgasm-oriented. After the couple attains a satisfactory level of arousal by means of nondemand pleasuring and sensate focus, they engage in nondemand sexual intercourse.

The most effective type of therapy for women who have inhibited orgasm is that of masturbation training. Research indicates that masturbation is the technique that is most likely to produce orgasm in women. If there are negative attitudes toward masturbation, the therapist must first work on those feelings. During the systematic course of masturbation training, the woman is instructed to explore her genitals by touch while in the privacy of her home. Once she becomes comfortable with the exploration, she tries to find the most pleasurable, sensitive area. At another time, she increases the intensity and duration of her self-stimulation and includes fantasy. If the woman has still not had an orgasm, she is often instructed to use a vibrator. Once the woman begins having orgasms, her partner is integrated into her sexual experience.

A common approach for premature ejaculation that was developed by Masters and Johnson is the squeeze technique. During stimulation, when the man signals that he is about to ejaculate, the partner applies a strong pressure directly below the head of the penis, or at the base of the penis, with her hand. The pressure is applied for three to five seconds and ends with a sudden release of the hand. After the sensation of ejaculation goes away, in about twenty to thirty seconds, she begins to stimulate her partner once again. The process is done three or four times per session. Then ejaculation is allowed. Initially, the process is conducted outside the vagina. With increasing practice and greater control, the couple proceeds to have intercourse, but they employ the squeeze technique with the hand as often as needed.

Whatever the source of a person's inability to respond sexually as he or she wishes, the problem can worsen if a fear of failure develops. The fear can lead to self-fulfilling behavior. One element of therapy is the need to identify and eliminate the fear of failure and sexual inadequacy, along with reducing maladaptive thoughts that have a tendency to occur during sexual intimacy. Other useful suggestions for people with problems are to refrain from setting goals of sexual performance and to avoid behaving as a spectator, or monitor, during sex. While involved in monitoring one's own performance, it is difficult to enjoy sexual experiences. It is also useful to understand that failures will occur in any sexual relationship. What is important is the way that an individual or a couple deals with the failures, rather than letting occasional failures ruin a relationship.

Context

Scientific explanations became the dominant interpretations of human behavior as religious explanations of behavior declined prior to 1900. By the beginning of the twentieth century, scientists were still unable to accept the scientific study of sexual behavior, however; there were many myths concerning sexuality, and the prevalent attitude was that all sexual acts that did not have reproduction as their goal were deviant. For example, the act of masturbation absurdly was seen, even by some scientists, as the cause for a variety of human ailments, including insanity, poor eyesight, and digestive problems.

Most of the early knowledge of sexual behavior was based on observations of animals or people in non-Western cultures. The person who was central in the emergence of the modern study of sexuality was Havelock Ellis. He published a number of influential volumes on sexual issues in the early 1900's. Also influential in the study of sexuality was Sigmund Freud, who devised a broad theory of behavior that emphasized sex as the central part of human development. In the mid-1930's, Alfred Kinsey and his colleagues began interviewing thousands of volunteers about their sexual behavior. The findings provided beneficial information and paved the way for other researchers, including Masters and Johnson. Instead of interviewing people about their sexuality, Masters and Johnson directly observed volunteers in the laboratory through one-way glass as the volunteers masturbated and had intercourse. They were the first scientists to study sexual behavior through systematic observation in the laboratory, resulting in a model of the human sexual-response cycle. Before the work of Masters and Johnson, it was believed that men and women were different in their sexual responses. Instead, it was found that men and women have very similar responses.

Once therapists became aware of the sexual functioning of the body, they were able to treat sexual dysfunction by new behavioral means, rather than relying on time-consuming, expensive psychotherapy. Psychotherapy involves a restructuring of the entire personality and is based on the Freudian theory that sexual difficulties are symptoms of emotional conflict originating in childhood. Instead, the therapeutic approaches that grew out of the scientific knowledge about the sexual response cycle were more direct, more effective, and less time-consuming. In conclusion, the scientific study of sex provided information that has helped reduce the amount of ignorance about sexuality. Ignorance is a common underlying cause of sexual dysfunction in general.

Bibliography

Allgeier, Elizabeth Rice, and Albert Richard Allgeier. "Sexual Dysfunctions and Therapy." In *Sexual Interactions.* 3d ed. Lexington, Mass.: D. C. Heath, 1991. The chapter is a highly readable description of sexual problems. The book itself is an excellent and thorough textbook used in colleges and universities across the country.
American Psychiatric Association. *Diagnostic and Statistical Manual of Mental Disorders* Rev. 3d ed. Washington, D.C.: Author, 1987. In the United States this is

the authoritative scheme for classifying psychological disorders. It groups about 230 psychological disorders and conditions into seventeen major categories of mental disorder, including diagnoses for almost every complaint a person could imagine.

Belliveau, Fred, and Lin Richter. *Understanding Human Sexual Inadequacy.* New York: Bantam Books, 1980. A paperback for the lay person that has been officially endorsed by Masters and Johnson. It summarizes the key work of Masters and Johnson on sexual dysfunction and is written in nontechnical language, supplying information that is based on established facts.

Haslam, Michael Trevor. *Psychosexual Disorders: A Review.* Springfield, Ill.: Charles C Thomas, 1979. Written by a psychiatrist, the book provides a perspective from the medical profession. It offers considerable detail and includes anatomical diagrams.

Heiman, Julia R., Joseph LoPiccolo, and Leslie LoPiccolo. *Becoming Orgasmic: A Sexual and Personal Growth Program for Women* Rev. ed. New York: Prentice-Hall, 1988. The book gives step-by-step suggestions to try to help women increase their ability to respond sexually in a variety of positive, growth-promoting ways. The suggestions are practical, creative, and interesting. Although the book is specifically written for women, men will also find it useful. The authors are well-respected sex researchers.

Masters, William H., and Virginia E. Johnson. *Human Sexual Inadequacy.* Boston, Mass.: Little, Brown, 1970. A classic book that is technical and directed toward the professional audience. It is an extremely important book, because Masters and Johnson were the first researchers to use the direct-observation methods that provided a foundation for treating sexual problems.

Szasz, Thomas Stephen. *Sex by Prescription.* Syracuse, N.Y.: Syracuse University Press, 1990. A short book that criticizes a variety of assumptions that guide the practices of some sex therapists. Also examined are the relationships among cultural beliefs about sexuality during several historical periods. Reactions of the medical community to sexual problems and problems in interpersonal relationships are discussed.

Deborah R. McDonald

Cross-References

Abnormality: Psychodynamic Models, 74; Adolescence: Sexuality, 130; Aging: Physical Changes, 192; Separation, Divorce, and Family Life: Adult Issues, 2220; Sex Hormones and Motivation, 2234; Sexual Variants and Paraphilias, 2259.

SEXUAL VARIANTS AND PARAPHILIAS

Type of psychology: Psychopathology
Field of study: Sexual disorders

Sexual variations, or paraphilias, are unusual sexual activities, in that they deviate from what is considered normal at a particular time in a particular society; paraphilias include behaviors such as exhibitionism, voyeurism, and sadomasochism. It is when they become the prime means of gratification, displacing direct sexual contact with a consenting adult partner, that paraphilias are technically present.

Principal terms
> EXHIBITIONISM: a behavior in which a person, who is usually a male, exposes the genitals to an involuntary observer
> FETISHISM: a sexual behavior in which a person becomes aroused by focusing on an inanimate object or a part of the human body
> FROTTEURISM: pressing or rubbing against a stranger in a public place for sexual gratification
> SEXUAL MASOCHISM: the experiencing of sexual arousal by suffering physical or psychological pain
> SEXUAL SADISM: the intentional infliction of pain on another person for sexual excitement
> TRANSVESTISM: a behavior in which a person obtains sexual excitement from wearing clothing of the opposite gender
> VOYEURISM: the derivation of sexual pleasure from looking at the naked bodies or sexual activities of others without their consent
> ZOOPHILIA: sexual contact between humans and animals

Overview

Paraphilias are sexual behaviors that are considered a problem for the person who performs them and/or a problem for society because they differ from the society's norms. Psychologist John Money, who has studied sexual attitudes and behaviors extensively, claims to have identified about forty such behaviors.

Exhibitionism is commonly called "indecent exposure." The term refers to behavior in which an individual, usually a male, exposes the genitals to an involuntary observer, who is usually a female. The key point is that exhibitionistic behavior involves observers who are unwilling. After exposing, the exhibitionist often masturbates while fantasizing about the observer's reaction. Exhibitionists tend to be most aroused by shock and typically flee if the observer responds by laughing or attempts to approach the exhibitionist. Most people who exhibit themselves are males in their twenties or thirties. They tend to be shy, unassertive people who feel inadequate and afraid of being rejected by another person. People who make obscene telephone calls have similar characteristics to the people who engage in exhibitionism. Typically, they are sexually aroused when their victims react in a shocked manner. Many masturbate during or immediately after placing an obscene call.

Voyeurism is the derivation of sexual pleasure through the repetitive seeking of situations in which to look, or "peep," at unsuspecting people who are naked, undressing, or engaged in sexual intercourse. Most masturbate during the voyeuristic activity or immediately afterward in response to what they have seen. Further sexual contact with the unsuspecting stranger is rarely sought. Like exhibitionists, voyeurs are usually not physically dangerous. To a degree, voyeurism is socially acceptable, but it becomes atypical when the voyeuristic behavior is preferred to sexual relations with another person or when there is a high degree of risk. Most voyeurs are not attracted to nude beaches or other places where it is acceptable to look because they are most aroused when the risk of being discovered is high. Voyeurs tend to be men in their twenties with strong feelings of inadequacy.

Sadomasochistic behavior encompasses both sadism and masochism; it is often abbreviated "SM." The dynamics of the two behaviors are similar. It is thought that sadists are less common than masochists. Sadomasochistic behaviors have the potential to be physically dangerous, but most people involved in these behaviors participate in mild or symbolic acts with a partner they can trust. Most people who engage in SM activities are motivated by a desire for dominance or submission rather than pain. Interestingly, many nonhuman animals participate in pain-inflicting behavior before coitus. Some researchers think that the activity heightens the biological components of sexual arousal, such as blood pressure and muscle tension. It has been suggested that any resistance between partners enhances sex, and SM is a more extreme version of this behavior. It is also thought that SM offers people the temporary opportunity to take on roles that are the opposite of the controlled, restrictive roles they play in everyday life. The term "sadism" is derived from the Marquis de Sade, a French writer and army officer who was horribly cruel to people for his own erotic purposes. In masochism, sexual excitement is produced in a person by his or her own suffering. Preferred means of achieving gratification include verbal humiliation and being bound or whipped.

Fetishism is a type of sexual behavior in which a person becomes sexually aroused by focusing on an inanimate object or part of the human body. Many people are aroused by looking at undergarments, legs, or breasts, and it is often difficult to distinguish between normal activities and fetishistic ones. It is when a person becomes focused on the objects or body parts ("fetishes") to the exclusion of everything else that the term is most applicable. Fetishists are usually males. Common fetish objects include women's lingerie, high-heeled shoes, boots, stockings, leather, silk, and rubber goods. Common body parts involved in fetishism are hair, buttocks, breasts, and feet.

The term "pedophilia" is from the Greek language and means "love of children." It is characterized by a preference for sexual activity with children and is engaged in primarily by men. The activity varies in intensity and ranges from stroking the child's hair to holding the child while secretly masturbating, manipulating the child's genitals, encouraging the child to manipulate his/her own genitals, or, sometimes, engaging in sexual intercourse. Generally, the pedophile, or sexual abuser of children, is related to, or an acquaintance of, the child, rather than a stranger. Studies of imprisoned pedophiles have found that the men typically had poor relationships with their parents, drink heavily, show poor sexual adjustment, and were themselves sexually abused as children. Pedophiles tend to be older than people convicted of other sex offenses. The average age at first conviction is thirty-five.

Transvestism refers to dressing in clothing of the opposite sex to obtain sexual excitement. In the majority of cases, it is men who are attracted to transvestism. Several studies show that cross-dressing occurs primarily among married heterosexuals. The man usually achieves sexual satisfaction simply by putting on the clothing, but sometimes masturbation and intercourse are engaged in while the clothing is being worn.

Zoophilia involves sexual contact between humans and animals as the repeatedly preferred method of achieving sexual excitement. In this disorder, the animal is preferred despite other available sexual outlets. Necrophilia is a rare dysfunction in which a person obtains sexual gratification by looking at or having intercourse with a corpse. Frotteurism is a fairly common behavior involving a person, usually a male, who obtains sexual pleasure by pressing or rubbing against a fully clothed female in a crowded public place. Often it involves the clothed penis rubbing against the woman's buttocks or legs and appears accidental.

Applications

A problem in the definition and diagnosis of sexual variations is that it is difficult to draw the line between normal and abnormal behavior. Patterns of sexual behavior differ widely across history and within different cultures and communities. It is impossible to lay down the rules of normality; however, attempts are made in order to understand behavior that differs from the majority and in order to help people who find their own atypical behavior to be problematic, or to be problematic in the eyes of the law.

Unlike most therapeutic techniques in use by psychologists, many of the treatments for paraphilias are painful, and the degree of their effectiveness is questionable. Supposedly, the methods are not aimed at punishing the individual, but perhaps society's lack of tolerance toward sexual deviations can be seen in the nature of the available treatments. In general, all attempts to treat the paraphilias have been hindered by the lack of information available about them and their causes.

Traditional counseling and psychotherapy alone have not been very effective in the treatment of modifying the behavior of paraphiliacs, and it is unclear why the clients are resistant to treatment. Some researchers believe that the behavior might be important for the mental stability of paraphiliacs. If they did not have the paraphilia, they would experience mental deterioration. Another idea is that, although people are punished by society for being sexually deviant, they are also rewarded for it. For the paraphilias that put the person at risk for arrest, the danger of arrest often becomes as arousing and rewarding as the sexual activity itself. Difficulties in treating paraphiliacs may also be related to the emotionally impoverished environments that many of them experienced throughout childhood and adolescence. Convicted sex offenders report more physical and sexual abuse as children than do the people convicted of nonsexual crimes. It is difficult to undo the years of learning involved.

Surgical castration for therapeutic purposes involves removal of the testicles. Surgical castration for sexual offenders in North America is very uncommon, but the procedure is sometimes used in northern European countries. The reason castration is used as a treatment for sex offenders is the inaccurate belief that testosterone is necessary for sexual behavior. The hormone testosterone is produced by the testicles. Unfortunately, reducing the amount of testosterone in the blood system does not always change sexual behavior. Furthermore, contrary to the myth that a sex offender has an abnormally high sex drive, many sex offenders have a low sex drive or are sexually dysfunctional.

In the same vein as surgical castration, other treatments use the administration of chemicals to decrease desire in sex offenders without the removal of genitalia. Estrogens have been fairly effective in reducing the sex drive, but they sometimes make the male appear feminine by increasing breast size and stimulating other female characteristics. There are also drugs that block the action of testosterone and other androgens but do not feminize the body; these drugs are called antiandrogens. Used together with counseling, antiandrogens do benefit some sex offenders, especially those who are highly motivated to overcome the problem. More research on the effects of chemicals on sexual behavior is needed; the extent of the possible side effects, for example, needs further study.

Aversion therapy is another technique that has been used to eliminate inappropriate sexual arousal. In aversion therapy, the behavior that is to be decreased or eliminated is paired with an aversive, or unpleasant, experience. Most approaches use pictures of the object or situation that is problematic. Then the pictures are paired with something extremely unpleasant, such as an electric shock or a putrid smell, thereby reducing arousal to the problematic object or situation in the future. Aversion therapy has been found to be fairly effective but is under ethical questioning because of its drastic nature. For example, chemical aversion therapy involves the administration of a nausea- or vomit-inducing drug. Electrical aversion therapy involves the use of electric shock. An example of the use of electric shock would be to show a pedophile pictures of young children whom he finds sexually arousing and to give an electric shock immediately after showing the pictures, in an attempt to reverse the pedophile's tendency to be sexually aroused by children.

Other techniques have been developed to help clients learn more socially approved patterns of sexual interaction skills. In general, there has not been a rigorous testing of any of the techniques mentioned. Furthermore, most therapy is conducted while the offenders are imprisoned, providing a less than ideal setting.

Context
Beliefs regularly change with respect to what sexual activities are considered nor-

mal, so most therapists prefer to avoid terms such as "perversion," instead using "paraphilia." Basically, "paraphilia" means "love of the unusual." Aspects of paraphilias are commonly found within the scope of normal behavior; it is when they become the prime means of gratification, replacing direct sexual contact with a consenting adult partner, that paraphilias are technically said to exist. People who show atypical sexual patterns might also have emotional problems, but it is thought that most people who participate in paraphilias also participate in normal sexual behavior with adult partners, without complete reliance on paraphilic behaviors to produce sexual excitement. Many people who are arrested for paraphilic behaviors do not resort to the paraphilia because they lack a socially acceptable sex partner. Instead, they have an unusual opportunity, a desire to experiment, or perhaps an underlying psychological problem.

According to the approach of Kurt Freund and his colleagues, some paraphilias are better understood as disturbances in the sequence of courtship behaviors. Freund has described courtship as a sequence of four steps: location and appraisal of a potential partner; interaction that does not involve touch; interaction that does involve touch; and genital contact. Most people engage in behavior that is appropriate for each of these steps, but some do not. The ones who do not can be seen as having exaggerations or distortions in one or more of the steps. For example, Freund says that voyeurism is a disorder in the first step of courtship. The voyeur does not use an acceptable means to locate a potential partner. An exhibitionist and an obscene phone caller would have a problem with the second step: They have interaction with people that occurs before the stage of touch, but the talking and showing of exhibitionistic behaviors are not the normal courtship procedures. Frotteurism would be a disruption at the third step, because there is physical touching that is inappropriate. Finally, rape would be a deviation from the appropriate fourth step.

As a result of social and legal restrictions, reliable data on the frequency of paraphilic behaviors are limited. Most information about paraphilias comes from people who have been arrested or are in therapy. Because the majority of people who participate in paraphilias do not fall into these two categories, it is not possible to talk about the majority of paraphiliacs in the real world. It is known, however, that males are much more likely to engage in paraphilias than are females.

Bibliography

Allgeier, E. R., and A. R. Allgeier. "Atypical Sexual Activity." In *Sexual Interactions*. 3d ed. Lexington, Mass.: D. C. Heath, 1991. A highly readable description of sexual variations. Contains photographs, charts, and tables which help make the material understandable. Provides a multitude of references. The book itself is an excellent, thorough textbook.

Gebhard, P. H., W. B. Pomeroy, B. Wardell, J. H. Gagnon, and C. V. Christenson. *Sex Offenders: An Analysis of Types*. New York: Harper & Row, 1965. Also available in paperback from Bantam Books, 1967, this book provides a detailed analysis of many types of atypical sexual behaviors that are against the law, with excellent information about the psychological and social factors that are involved in the development of these behaviors. The authors are well-respected researchers on other aspects of sexuality, in addition to paraphilias.

Rosen, Michael A. *Sexual Magic: The S/M Photographs.* San Francisco: Shaynew Press, 1986. Contains essays written by people who engage in sadomasochistic activities. Includes photographs of the people. In general, provides a personal, honest look into the lives of real people, using a case-study approach.

Stoller, Robert J. "Sexual Deviations." In *Human Sexuality in Four Perspectives,* edited by Frank A. Beach and Milton Diamond. Baltimore: The Johns Hopkins University Press, 1977. Provides a review of several common atypical sexual behaviors, along with several case studies. Concise and readable. Part of an interesting, well-rounded book on sexuality in general.

Weinberg, Thomas S., and G. W. Levi Kamel, eds. *S and M: Studies in Sadomasochism.* Buffalo, N.Y.: Prometheus Books, 1983. Composed of eighteen articles that provide thought-provoking information on a variety of issues relating to sadism and masochism.

Deborah R. McDonald

Cross-References

Abnormality: Behavioral Models, 33; Abnormality: Legal Models, 67; Abnormality: Psychodynamic Models, 74; Adolescence: Sexuality, 130; Homosexuality, 1182; Sex Hormones and Motivation, 2234; Sexual Behavior Patterns, 2246; Sexual Dysfunction, 2253.

SHORT-TERM MEMORY

Type of psychology: Memory
Field of study: Cognitive processes

Short-term (or working) memory refers to the mental process of temporarily retaining and manipulating information for the production of a wide range of cognitive tasks, including comprehension, problem solving, and learning.

Principal terms

ANTEROGRADE AMNESIA: an inability to recall information that occurs after the event that creates the amnesia

CODING: the process of transforming external information into a form that can be stored in the memory system

ELABORATIVE REHEARSAL: giving meaning to information to enable encoding processes

ENCODING: the process of transforming information into a form that can be stored in the memory system

INTERFERENCE: the loss or displacement of a memory trace because of different information being presented

MAINTENANCE REHEARSAL: retaining information in short-term memory by repeating it over and over again

PHONOLOGICAL LOOP: a concept describing the coding of speech-based information in short-term (working) memory

TRACE LIFE: the amount of time information can be retained in working memory without further processing

VISUO-SPATIAL SKETCHPAD: a concept describing the coding and manipulation of visual and spatial images in short-term (working) memory

Overview

Imagine that a woman needs to make a telephone call and that a friend has just told her the number to call; she does not have pencil and paper to write down the number. Two options are immediately available to help her remember the number. She could repeat the number over and over until she makes the call (a technique known as maintenance rehearsal), or she could give the number some kind of meaning that would help her recall it (elaborative rehearsal). The mental process that allows a person to perform those operations is commonly called short-term, or working, memory.

William James, in 1890, used the term "primary memory" to describe the information under conscious awareness (immediate memory) and the term "secondary memory" to describe inactive information (indirect memory). This type of dualism evolved into the terms "short-term memory" and "long-term memory," a distinction that was based upon the idea that each memory type was independent and was the result of different underlying mental processes.

Richard Atkinson and Richard Shiffrin, in 1968, further developed this approach by proposing a stage model, or modal model, of memory that included the sensory register, the short-term store, and the long-term store. Subsequently, extensive research programs focused on the short-term store. These experimental findings resulted in the view, postulated by Alan Baddeley in 1986, that emphasizes the mental processes involved in the memory function rather than describing a static (inactive or passive) storage bin where information is saved. With this approach came the label working memory and the metaphor of a mental workbench performing a wide range of cognitive operations. As Henry Ellis and Reed Hunt (1991) explained, "Memory is determined by what is done to the information, not by where the information is stored." This is the view of an active, mental process characterized by specific functions and limitations.

Three basic characteristics define short-term (working) memory: trace life, storage capacity, and nature of the code. With respect to trace life, Lloyd and Margaret-Intons Peterson (1959) demonstrated that current, active information in the working memory bank is subject to rapid forgetting (in about twelve seconds) if the information does not receive further processing. They showed that if people are not allowed to rehearse or elaborate information they have just encountered, that information is lost. For example, they asked people to recall a series of letters, but immediately after they indicated the letters to be recalled, the people in the experiment were required to count backward by threes. The activity of counting backward interfered with remembering the letters. Similarly, if one is trying to recall a telephone number one has just heard, but is interrupted on the way to the telephone to call it, the telephone number is usually lost.

George Miller wrote a paper entitled "The Magic Number Seven, Plus or Minus Two," in 1956, that made the strong and influential case regarding the storage capacity of short-term memory. This notion has been tested in a variety of settings, using a variety of information units. Regardless of whether people are asked to remember a list of letters, numbers, or words, or even a group of objects, most people remember about seven items. This finding has produced a wide range of applications. Telephone numbers, one may note, are composed of seven numbers.

Further study of the capacity of short-term memory revealed the ability to "chunk" information and, in so doing, remember more information than merely seven individual, independent bits of information. This process involves reorganizing single bits of information (with the assistance of information previously encoded in long-term storage) into larger units of information. For example, one could remember each individual letter of the word "chunk" and recall five letters, c h u n k (hence, five units). One might also form the letters into one unit and, instead, recall the word chunk (one unit). Chunking dramatically increases the amount of information that can be retained in short-term (or working) memory.

To account for the nature of the code (the form used to understand and store information), Alan Baddeley designed a model of working memory that includes the phonological loop and the visuo-spatial sketchpad. A wide range of experimental evidence indicates that a phonetic (or acoustic or sound) code is used in short-term memory. For example, if a person is asked to retain a list of words or letters and the items sound alike, fewer items are recalled and more errors are found. On the other hand, if the items sound different, recall is better and fewer errors are found. Baddeley refers to this as the phonological similarity effect and explains that this effect occurs because the short-term memory store is based on a phonological code. Accordingly, items that sound similar will have similar codes.

Also related to the phonological code is the word-length effect. In essence, this refers to the finding that words with more syllables take more time to read, and are less likely to be recalled from short-term memory than are monosyllabic words. On the other hand, if a word takes longer to read and to pronounce (either aloud or to oneself), the opportunity for a strong memory trace is greater.

The visuo-spatial sketchpad in Baddeley's model refers to the use of an imagery code in short-term memory. For example, one might imagine one's kitchen and focus on the location of the sink. To do this, one most likely generates a mental image of the kitchen. Another example of the visuo-spatial sketchpad involves recognizing words or patterns when a person is reading. Still another example of this function is the process in which people engage when comparing two shapes. Imagine a test in which people are asked to indicate whether geometric clusters are similar or different when they are presented in different orientations. How do they perform this task? Experimental evidence indicates that most people engage in mental rotation to make their decisions about the figures. In other words, they imagine the particular geometric cluster turned in different directions and compare it to each of the other figures.

Applications

The essential role of short-term (or working) memory is usually taken for granted—until some event disrupts the memory process. In a hypothetical example of the consequences of not having a properly functioning short-term memory system, imagine a man named Bill waking up one morning without one. First, he gets out of bed (he can still walk, because he has the benefit of long-term memory) and trips over his cat. He finds himself on the floor, but cannot remember how he got there. He walks to the bathroom to brush his teeth, but when he gets there he does not remember why he is there. He wanders into the kitchen to make coffee; he puts water into the coffee maker and bends down to pet the cat. Then he rises and fills the coffee maker with water again, because he does not remember the event that happened only a few seconds before.

The telephone rings and Bill answers it. His friend Jane asks him to meet her in fifteen minutes; he agrees and hangs up. In the meantime, the water from the coffee maker is spilling over the kitchen counter, and Bill has no idea why that is happening. The doorbell rings, and his next-door neighbor asks to borrow some milk. Being a good neighbor, Bill agrees to get some milk and goes into the kitchen. Once there, Bill realizes that he must turn off the coffee maker. He steps in the spilled coffee, then goes into the bedroom to change his socks. Meanwhile, the neighbor Bill has forgotten leaves; eventually Jane calls, asking why Bill did not meet her.

One's very existence and quality of life depend on the functioning of short-term (working) memory. The preceding example may seem preposterous, yet there are a large number of cases of people who have impaired short-term memory. Several types of events can result in memory deficits and disorders, including head injuries, strokes, and disease-related dementia.

The term "amnesia" refers to a class of disorders that involve various types of memory dysfunction. Some types of amnesia are associated with loss of long-term memory functioning. In these cases, a person may be able to learn new information, but has difficulty recalling previous information. Other types of amnesia are associated with impaired short-term (working) memory. These people have difficulty learning new information but can recall previously learned information. There are amnesiacs who have memory deficits relating to both short-term and long-term memory.

In general, when short-term memory is impaired, people are unable to process and retain new information effectively. The case of William Scoville's patient H. M., described in the 1950's, provides an interesting example of short-term memory impairment. H. M. suffered from a severe form of epilepsy that could not be controlled by medication. Scoville surgically removed portions of H. M.'s brain (the temporal lobes) in an attempt to remedy the epilepsy problem.

After the surgery, H. M. experienced striking short-term memory impairment, called anterograde amnesia. H. M.'s memory disorder was studied in depth, and many of the characteristics that define short-term memory functions were illuminated. H. M. was able to remember information from his past, but he was unable to remember new information. For example, H. M.'s mother reported that he could still mow the lawn, because he remembered how to do so, but he was unable to find the lawn mower when he left it parked somewhere.

H. M. was unable to remember or recognize anyone he met or any place he visited after the surgical procedure. He engaged in intense conversations with people, but subsequently could recall neither the conversation nor the person with whom he had the conversation. Moreover, H. M. was taught procedures for accomplishing tasks, and his performance of those tasks revealed that he had learned the task; however, H. M. consistently claimed that he had never before performed the tasks. In other words, he did not remember the event of learning the task, but his performance revealed that he had retained some of the skills associated with the learning event.

Clearly, the short-term memory process, though often taken for granted, is an essential and integral part of mental functioning. This process also plays a major role in the study of psychology.

Context

With the first humans came the first speculations about mental processes. Inherent in studies of mental activities are studies of memory, since memory is necessary for learning. The role of memory was a central element of philosophies of the mind. This point is exhibited in historical accounts of the mind that referenced memory processes. These accounts reveal the underlying theories of mental processes postulated at the time of the philosophies.

For example, both Aristotle and Plato used the analogy of a wax tablet to describe the memory process. According to this perspective, experience was merely stamped into the brain. These views are consistent with the idea of memory being a static store or receptacle rather than a dynamic process. These static views assume a passive organism rather than an active, dynamic information processor.

This concept of memory continued through the ages, changing very little until the science of psychology began in the late nineteenth century. As psychology evolved, so did the field of memory. This evolution is reflected in a change from the static, storage view of memory to the idea of memory as an active process. This change parallels the evolution of the image of humans as passive experience-storage units to seeing humans as active information processors; this "evolution" is often called the "cognitive revolution." Whether the change is called evolution or revolution, it happened largely as a result of the foundation provided by innovative research such as that conducted by Hermann Ebbinghaus.

In the early 1880's, Ebbinghaus moved the study of memory from the domain of philosophy to the domain of science when he embarked on an intensive investigation of the memory process. Ebbinghaus used himself as an experimental subject and spent two years memorizing nonsense syllables to see whether simple repetition would facilitate the recall process. Keeping copious notes in a strict scientific environment, he found that rote rehearsal improved the memory retrieval process.

Ebbinghaus' work was particularly important because it showed that mental processes could be simplified and studied using a rigorous, scientific method. In addition, he provided data that are fundamental for understanding memory processes and that paved the way for the vast program of memory research that is flourishing today.

Studies associated with short-term or working memory focus on dynamic, immediate, cognitive activities. In general, these mental processes are involved in understanding the world; specifically, these investigations advance knowledge about learning, comprehension, problem solving, thought construction, and expression. Trends include mapping regions of the brain and discovering neurotransmitters (brain chemicals) that are affiliated with working memory activities. The working memory process provides a rich domain for investigations of mental activities. Many researchers believe that future investigations of the process will reveal the keys to discovering the essence of mental activity.

Bibliography

Baddeley, Alan D. *Human Memory: Theory and Practice.* Boston: Allyn & Bacon, 1990. Provides a comprehensive review of the memory process, by drawing from a wide range of literature domains, including cognitive psychology, psychobiology, neurology, cognitive science, and early historical accounts. In addition, Baddeley offers a thorough account of the working memory hypothesis.

_____. *Working Memory*. Oxford, England: Oxford University Press, 1986. Provides a scholarly report of working memory that has been very influential in the memory field. The writing may be too technical for readers who desire only an overview of general concepts, but it is essential for those interested in a deeper understanding of working memory.

Deutsch, Diana, and J. Anthony Deutsch, eds. *Short-Term Memory*. New York: Academic Press, 1975. This text consists of fifteen papers written by short-term memory researchers. Both the topics and the writing style are rather technical; however, this edition is very useful for anyone needing classical, comprehensive, detailed information about the intricacies of the short-term memory process.

Ellis, Henry C., and R. Reed Hunt. *Fundamentals of Human Memory and Cognition*. 5th ed. Dubuque, Iowa: Wm. C. Brown, 1991. A very readable text composed of numerous examples and illustrations of empirical evidence and practical applications that bring the information to life. Ellis and Hunt employ their expertise in effective, efficient encoding strategies to produce a text that describes complex cognitive processes in a manner that facilitates understanding and recall. They include both historical and current theoretical accounts of short-term memory.

Solso, Robert L. *Cognitive Psychology*. 3d ed. Boston: Allyn & Bacon, 1991. An undergraduate text for courses in cognitive psychology. Solso provides an account of memory that is written on a level appropriate for most high school and college students. Can be used not only to learn more about short-term memory but also to learn about memory processes in general.

Wyer, Robert S., and Thomas K. Srull. *Memory and Cognition in Its Social Context*. Hillsdale, N.J.: Lawrence Erlbaum, 1989. Wyer and Srull take a social cognition approach to the discussion of short-term memory, using the label "work space" to describe this process. They argue that the social context in which mental processes occur must be considered to provide an accurate and useful model of cognitive processes.

Zechmeister, Eugene B., and Stanley E. Nyberg. *Human Memory: An Introduction to Research and Theory*. Monterey, Calif.: Brooks/Cole, 1981. This text uses the term "primary memory," usually associated with William James, to discuss short-term memory. A particularly interesting feature is the book's carefully and simply planned experiments that can be conducted by the reader to illustrate the core issues.

Pennie S. Seibert

Cross-References

Cognitive Maps, 566; Encoding Strategies and Encoding Specificity, 960; Forgetting and Forgetfulness, 1049; Long-Term Memory, 1479; Memory: Long-Term versus Short-Term, 1517; Theories of Memory, 1537.

SIGNAL DETECTION THEORY

Type of psychology: Sensation and perception
Fields of study: Cognitive processes; methodological issues

Signal detection theory is a mathematical model for understanding how sounds or other stimuli are detected in the presence of background noise. It replaces classical threshold theory in psychophysics and provides a method for separating a person's sensitivity to a stimulus from any bias or response criterion.

Principal terms
BIAS: a consistent tendency to respond positively or negatively in a situation
CATCH TRIAL: in a study measuring sensitivity to certain stimuli, a trial in which no stimulus is presented
CORRECT REJECTION: responding, "No, I do not detect a stimulus" on a trial in which the stimulus is not presented; it is a correct response
FALSE ALARM: responding, "Yes, I detect a stimulus" on a trial in which the stimulus is not presented; it is an incorrect response
HIT: responding, "Yes, I detect a stimulus" on a trial in which the stimulus is present; it is a correct response
MISS: responding, "No, I do not detect a stimulus" on a trial in which the stimulus is actually present; it is an incorrect response
NOISE: any stimulus (not necessarily sound) in the environment that is not the signal but may cause a person to think that a stimulus has been presented
PSYCHOPHYSICS: the study of the relationship between the physical properties of a stimulus and the way in which they are perceived
SENSITIVITY: in signal detection theory, a measure of an individual's ability to detect a stimulus independent of other factors such as criteria for guessing
THRESHOLD: the minimum stimulus intensity necessary for an individual to detect a stimulus; usually defined as that intensity detected 50 percent of the time it is presented

Overview
Signal detection theory is not a "theory" in the traditional sense as much as a term used to describe certain types of measurement procedures. Developed by mathematicians and engineers at the University of Michigan, Harvard University, and the Massachusetts Institute of Technology in the 1950's, signal detection theory is based on a method of statistical hypothesis testing and on findings in electronic communication. It provides a method to measure two factors independently: a person's sensitivity to sound or other stimulation, and any bias or decision criterion the person

might adopt that affects the person's performance during a sensitivity test.

A typical measurement procedure might involve detection of sound in a quiet room. Invited into the acoustically insulated chamber, an individual puts on earphones and is told to pay attention to a small warning light that comes on periodically. The instructions are to report, for each occurrence of the warning light, whether a sound is heard through the earphones at that time. The sounds coming through the earphones vary in intensity, though not in frequency; they may initially be of very low amplitude, or they may be readily audible. Indeed, the warning light may come on with no sound at all; this is a "catch" trial—a situation designed to catch someone who simply pretends to hear a sound every time the light comes on. No matter what the sound, the individual being tested must respond with either "Yes, I heard a sound" or "No, I heard nothing."

Much of the time the response is "yes" when a sound is present; this is called a hit, because it is a correct recognition of the stimulus. Often, when no sound is presented, the individual says "no," giving a correct rejection. Sometimes, however, the response is "yes" when no sound is present, a false alarm, and sometimes the individual says "no" when the sound is in fact present, a miss. Thus the experimenter collects data showing the number of hits, false alarms, misses, and correct rejections for each individual participant.

Individuals are told exactly what proportion of the trials will be catch trials. This gives them some idea of what to expect. If the experiment were set up with 90 percent catch trials and participants in the study were given no knowledge of this, they might think, hearing so little, that something was wrong with the earphones. These same people would expect a session with 20 percent catch trials, for example, to sound very different. When there is a lower proportion of catch trials, individuals tend to respond "yes" more than when the proportion is higher; thus, they maximize hits and (since there are few catch trials) cannot make many false alarms. If there is a high proportion of catch trials, individuals tend to say "no" more, thus making fewer false alarms, but also making fewer hits. Thus, both hits and false alarms vary depending on the number of catch trials even though the sound intensities are exactly the same in each of these conditions.

Imagine taking part in this without putting on the earphones. With no way to know whether a sound is present, one could only guess. In guessing, however, one might guess "yes" more frequently if told there would be few, rather than many, catch trials. This educated guessing is what a normal participant does. When unsure as to the presence of a sound, people guess; the probability of guessing "yes" is given by the proportion of catch trials. The psychologist collecting these data determines the number of hits and false alarms for each individual and compares them with a "guessing line," the percentage of hits and false alarms for one who merely guesses. The degree of difference between these two modes of response is a pure measure of sensitivity; bias has been eliminated with the guessing baseline. Sensitivity is high when the individual hears most of the sounds presented and has to guess on few of them, and it is low when many of the responses are guesses.

There is another measurement: The experimenter also determines each person's bias, or decision criterion in responding. The decision criterion, which changes whenever the number of catch trials changes, may also be influenced by other factors. For example, there is always some noise going on when a stimulus is received. Even in an acoustically quiet chamber, there are sounds from one's own heart, blood rushing through vessels, and breathing. These vary from moment to moment, and they do influence perception of sound, particularly those that may seem very weak. Outside a quiet chamber there are other noisy backgrounds, hums of air conditioners, computers, street traffic, and so on.

In addition, people who participate in these measurement studies bring different decision criteria that are characteristic of their own personalities. For example, a participant may not respond with a "yes" unless absolutely certain that a sound is present, saying "no" otherwise and thus failing to make all the hits—but also making few false alarms. Another might respond with a "yes" whenever it seems as though a sound could conceivably be present and say "no" only when absolutely certain there is no sound. These two people might have the same sensitivity; that is, they could perceive the sounds equally well, but the number of sounds presented that they identify correctly would be different. They would therefore achieve equal measures of sensitivity but very different measures of bias. Signal detection theory, then, provides an ingenious method for the measurement of an individual's sensitivity to sounds or other stimuli independent of factors that impinge on that individual's decision.

Applications

Signal detection methods are applied in studies in which a stimulus or event is to be detected. Used to separate sensation from motivational bias, these methods are most successful with simple stimuli.

One of the earliest and simplest of these studies involves perceptual vigilance. The basic task is to detect a few signals against a background pattern of noise similar to the signal. The best known of these displays is the Mackworth clock, which presents clockwise jumps of a black pointer across a white field. The signal jumps are twice as large as the repetitive background jumps, and they occur at irregular time intervals ranging, for example, from forty-five seconds to ten minutes. The noise here occurs at a high rate and is constant, regular and monotonous.

An observer sits in a small cubicle for half-hour periods watching this moving pointer, monitoring it and responding only when the pointer makes a long jump. At the beginning, attention is high and the observer makes few errors. After all, it is an easy task. As time goes on, however, the observer tires, loses concentration, and begins missing signals. The jumps all begin to look alike; after an hour or so, one in every four or five long jumps may be missed. There are few, if any, false alarms.

This vigilance decrement occurs with listening tasks as well. In fact, it is a common observance in nearly all tests of attention and is applicable to many everyday situations: factory workers monitoring displays on shift, inspectors in industry examining merchandise for flaws, even students sitting in classrooms listening for important points in lectures. Although psychologists were aware of these declines before the theory of signal detection was formulated, their study of this changed with the new method. They began to address new questions. What difference does the nature of the noise make? How might the observer shift the bias, or criterion of response, over time or over situations?

It is perhaps not surprising to find that sensitivity is higher when the signal is most different from the background noise. More interesting is the finding that if there are very few signals, there often is no measurable decline in sensitivity even if the observers miss more signals over time. This occurs because they also make fewer false alarms over the same time; that is, they become more cautious in their response—a shift in bias. One sees shifts of bias of this sort in many situations. For example, a physician may diagnose a disease on the basis of insufficient data in cases where failure to detect it would be disastrous and making a false alarm would be relatively insignificant. On the other hand, military personnel would not want to begin sending out retaliatory nuclear weapons against an enemy unless absolutely certain the attack to which they are responding is actually occurring. A false alarm here is unthinkable, so they exhibit extreme caution—a very high bias against a response.

Signal detection theory has been helpful in applied human research, in perceptual studies, and in studies of memory. Measures of sensitivity in memory parallel those in perception. Effects of variables such as aging, epilepsy and other brain dysfunction, brain insults such as concussions, or periods of oxygen deprivation have been examined more recently for their effects on sensitivity. In a 1977 signal detection study of head-injured patients, Diane McCarthy found that patients recovering from concussions show, during the acute stages of head injury, sensitivity scores similar to an elderly population and considerably lower than normal control subjects. They also show some residual deficit six weeks later, even when the head injury is not severe. Interestingly, this shows a period of reduced sensitivity to stimulation, not merely confusion.

Signal detection theory has provided a routine method in experimental psychology. It is applied in situations where a pure measure of sensitivity, unaffected by changing criteria, is desired. Additionally, it may be used when the target of interest is the criterion or bias itself—for example, in studies of personality factors in response decisions.

Context

In the late nineteenth century, experimenters in psychophysics questioned how accurately people's perceptions correspond to the physical stimulation they receive. They asked to what extent a person's reported perception actually reflects the physical changes going on in the real world.

One way of answering this was to try to discover how strong a stimulus needed to be before people noticed or detected that stimulus. There are sounds, for example, so soft that they cannot be heard, or can be heard only by a few individuals, and there are sounds so intense that all hearing individuals detect them. At what point in increasingly intense levels is a sound just barely detectable? Psychophysicists called this level the threshold. They assumed that this level of intensity, this limen, was like the threshold of a door in which one was either inside or outside, never in between. They assumed that all sounds less intense than the threshold, all stimulation that is subliminal or below the limen, would never be detected, and that all sounds more intense than the threshold would always be detected.

With this theory in hand, experimental psychologists began measuring thresholds. They determined empirically, for example, how much sugar must go into a certain amount of distilled water at a given temperature before it can be tasted, how intensely a 440 hertz sound has to be played under certain acoustical conditions before it is heard, and how intense a spot of white light has to be in a darkened room for a dark adapted subject to detect it in peripheral vision. They made measurements and ran into difficulties.

Measured thresholds were always imprecise, as the only measurement taken was the occurrence of hits. They were unlike the threshold of a door, a line with no breadth. Sometimes an individual would report hearing a sound that was very weak, then report not hearing a sound that was quite a bit more intense. Most of the time, however, intense sounds were heard and weak ones were not, so that researchers calculated an average, an intensity of sound that a subject reported hearing 50 percent of the time. This they defined empirically as the threshold, assuming that their inability to measure a point perfectly was attributable simply to procedural error or imprecise measurement.

Increasingly, however, researchers began to recognize that threshold measures were contaminated, or confounded, by other factors. These were experimental factors such as how important it seemed to a person not to let a sound go unnoticed or not to appear foolish saying a sound was heard when it might not even have been there at all. Signal detection theory provided an alternative, a method for determining a person's sensitivity to a stimulus independent of any bias in response. These methods are now a standard part of experimental psychology, providing another way to determine how perceptions correspond to physical changes in the real world.

Bibliography

Commons, Michael L., John A. Nevin, and Michael C. Davison, eds. *Signal Detection: Mechanisms, Models, and Applications.* Hillsdale, N.J.: Lawrence Erlbaum, 1991. A collection of scholarly papers based on the tenth annual Harvard Symposium for the Quantitative Analysis of Behavior. The chapters, quantitative and theoretical in approach, illustrate sensitivity and bias as independent parameters in signal detection theory. The final three chapters give clear articulation to major applications and are of interest in themselves.

Green, David Martin, and John A. Swets. *Signal Detection Theory and Psychophysics.* Huntington, N.Y.: R. E. Krieger, 1974. An quantitative presentation of the general theory of signal detection and early experiments applying the theory to sensory and to decision processes for the serious reader. The final chapter contains applications of signal detection theory to ongoing problems in psychology: vigilance, attention, psychophysics, reaction time, and memory.

Levine, Michael W., and Jeremy M. Shefner. *Fundamentals of Sensation and Perception.* 2d ed. Pacific Grove, Calif.: Brooks/Cole, 1991. A college textbook for students of sensation and perception, this proceeds from an introductory chapter to a clear and well-illustrated discussion of psychophysics. The pages on signal detection theory are replete with figures and diagrams, and the theory is described in historical and theoretical context. A short, enjoyable, and highly readable introduction.

Ludel, Jacqueline. *Introduction to Sensory Processes.* San Francisco: W. H. Freeman, 1978. Requires no prior study of sensory processes, anatomy, physiology, or perception. More than an introduction, Ludel gradually and clearly explores topics in depth. Her description of signal detection theory unfolds in the chapter on auditory perception. Conversational in tone, the book also contains mnemonics and pronunciation guides.

Mackworth, Jane F. *Vigilance and Attention: A Signal Detection Approach.* Harmondsworth, Middlesex, England: Penguin Books, 1970. Mackworth demonstrates how signal detection methods may contribute to understanding attention, vigilance, and other cognitive processes. The focus is on monitoring displays and on situations demanding continuous attention rather than on theory. Clearly shows how method contributes to research in a particular area. This is not introductory, but is well written and accessible.

Bonnie S. Sherman

Cross-References

Attention, 313; Decision Making as a Cognitive Process, 769; Pattern Recognition as a Cognitive Process, 1747; Psychophysical Scaling, 1963; Sensory Modalities and Stimuli, 2214.

SLEEP: STAGES AND FUNCTIONS

Type of psychology: Consciousness
Field of study: Sleep

The study of sleep stages and functions involves descriptions of the electrophysiological, cognitive, motor, and behavioral components of various sleep stages as well as the potential functions served by each. The sleep-wake cycle is one of several human circadian rhythms that regulate human attention, alertness, and performance.

Principal terms

CIRCADIAN RHYTHMS: human biological cycles that fluctuate on a daily basis, for example, the sleep-wake cycle, body temperature

DESYNCHRONIZED ELECTROENCEPHALOGRAM (EEG): an irregular brain-wave pattern that is caused by large groups of neurons firing at different times and rates in a given brain region

HYPNAGOGIC IMAGERY: dreamlike, fantasy images that occur in the borderline state between waking and sleeping

MYOCLONIA: brief, jerking movements of the skeletal muscles of the legs and arms

NONRAPID EYE MOVEMENT (NREM) SLEEP: four stages of sleep as measured by electrical changes in the brain, level of muscular activity, and eye movement patterns

PARADOXICAL SLEEP: another term for REM sleep, so named because it is paradoxical that elements of a waking electroencephalogram (EEG) are present in a sleeping state

RAPID EYE MOVEMENT (REM) SLEEP: a special stage of sleep that involves desynchronized electrical brain activity, muscle paralysis, rapid eye movements, and narrative dream recall

SYNCHRONIZED ELECTROENCEPHALOGRAM (EEG): a regular, repetitive brain-wave pattern that is caused by multitudes of neurons firing at the same time and same rate in a given brain region

Overview

Sleep, one of the most mysterious of human circadian rhythms, can be characterized as a naturally induced alteration in consciousness. Although the sleeper may appear to be unconscious, many complex cognitive, physiological, and behavioral processes occur during sleep. For example, parents may sleep through a nearby police siren yet easily awaken to their crying infant.

Efforts to understand sleep have focused on behavioral and electrical changes that occur each night. During every moment of a person's life, the brain, eyes, and muscles are generating electrical potentials that can be recorded by a polygraph. Minute electrical signals are conveyed through tiny disk electrodes attached to the scalp and face, which are recorded by the polygraph as wave patterns that can be described in terms of frequency, amplitude, and synchronization. Frequency is measured by the number of cycles that occur per second (cps), amplitude by the distance between the peaks and troughs of waves, and synchronization by the regular, repetitive nature of the waves.

Use of the polygraph has resulted in the identification of four stages of nonrapid eye movement (NREM) sleep, as well as a special stage referred to as rapid eye movement (REM) sleep. Each stage is described in terms of electrical changes in brain-wave patterns, speed and pattern of eye movements, and muscular activity in the body. Brain-wave activity is measured by the electroencephalogram (EEG), eye movement patterns with the electrooculogram (EOG), and muscle activity by the electromyogram (EMG).

Three EEG patterns can be described for NREM sleep. First, as a sleeper progresses from stages one through four, the waves increase in amplitude or voltage from approximately 50 to 100 microvolts in stage one to about 100 to 200 microvolts in stage four. Second, the frequency of the waves decreases gradually from 4 to 8 cps in stages one and two to 1 to 4 cps in stages three and four. Last, the waves become progressively more synchronized from stages one to four, so that by stage four, the waves assume a slow, regular pattern sometimes called S sleep, for slow-wave sleep or synchronized sleep. Each of these patterns is reflected in the type of brain-wave activity present, with stages one and two consisting predominantly of theta waves and stages three and four of delta waves.

In addition to the changes in brain electrical activity, the EMG records a gradual diminution of muscular activity as the sleeper progresses through each stage of NREM sleep. By the onset of stage four, the EMG is relatively flat, revealing a deep state of muscular relaxation. In fact, virtually all physiological activity is at its lowest during stage four, including respiration, heart rate, blood pressure, digestion, and so on. In this sense, stage four is considered to be the deepest stage of sleep.

As stated previously, the sleeper is not in an unconscious state, but is in a different level of consciousness. Cognitive activity is present in all stages of NREM sleep. Hypnagogic imagery, consisting of dreamlike images sometimes indistinguishable from REM dreams, is present in stage one. Subjects are easily awakened during this sleep stage, and regressions to a waking state are quite common. Often, these regressions occur because of myoclonias, which are brief jerking movements of the muscles. Since stage one is sometimes viewed as a transitional state between sleeping and waking, it should not be too surprising that sleep talking occurs primarily in this stage. Stage one sleep lasts for approximately fifteen minutes.

The sleeper is somewhat more difficult to arouse during stage two, and the cognitive activity present is more thoughtlike and fragmentary than in stage one. If the subject recalls any mental activity, it is rather sparse. Stage two also lasts for approximately fifteen minutes.

It was once assumed that dreams only occur in REM sleep, but it is now common knowledge that dreams of a different variety occur in stages three and four. These dreams are not of the narrative or storylike variety found in REM sleep; rather, they resemble nonsequential thoughts, images, sensations, or emotions. As might be expected in the deepest sleep stage, it is quite difficult to awaken the sleeper who is in stage four. Paradoxically, a subject awakened in stage four will often claim not to be sleeping. Finally, sleepwalking, night terrors, and bed-wetting, all of which are developmental disorders, occur predominantly in stage four. Stage three lasts approximately ten minutes, while the first episode of stage four usually lasts about fifty minutes.

Suddenly, about ninety minutes after falling asleep, the subject rapidly regresses back through the stages of NREM sleep to a special stage usually called stage one-REM sleep, or sometimes simply REM sleep. Three major changes occur in the electrical activity measured in this stage. First, the EEG pattern becomes highly desynchronized, resembling a combination of waking and stage one-NREM brainwave activity. For this reason, REM sleep is sometimes called paradoxical sleep, because it is paradoxical that elements of a waking EEG should be present in a sleeping condition. Second, the EMG recordings become almost completely flat for most skeletal muscles, resembling paralysis. Finally, there is an onset of rapid eye movements, as measured by the EOG.

Cognitive activity, in the form of narrative or storylike dreams, is rich and varied in REM sleep—hence the term D sleep, for dreaming or desynchronized sleep. It is interesting to note that the rapid eye movements correspond closely with dream content. For example, if a person dreams of something running from left to right, the direction of rapid eye movements will also be left to right.

Throughout the remainder of the evening, a cycle of approximately ninety minutes will be established from one REM episode to the next. All together, the sleeper will experience four to five REM episodes in a typical eight-hour sleep period, with each one lasting for a longer interval than the previous one. The first REM episode may last only five to ten minutes, while the final one may be thirty to forty minutes or longer in duration. In contrast, S sleep episodes decrease in length throughout the evening, and will disappear completely after two to three episodes.

Applications

Although a description of sleep stages can be provided with relative ease, identifying a clear function for sleep is a more difficult proposition. Yet applications of sleep research are inextricably linked with the functions of sleep. For the typical layperson, the seemingly obvious function of sleep is to repair and restore the body after daily mental and physical exertion. This commonsense approach has been formalized by science as the repair and restoration theory. One of the most frequently used methods to assess this theory is to examine the mental and physical effects of sleep deprivation. If the primary function of sleep is to repair the body, then loss of sleep should disrupt cognitive, motor, and behavioral processes. Early laboratory research with animals seemed to support this position. If sleep deprivation persisted for a sufficient time, usually between three and twenty days, death ensued in laboratory animals. Unfortunately, to maintain sleep deprivation in animals, it is necessary to keep them active. Perhaps the continuous activity, rather than the sleep deprivation, killed the animals.

If it were possible to allow animals to rest and relax, but not sleep, would the sleep deprivation still prove fatal? This question was addressed by anecdotal accounts of human sleep deprivation during the Korean War. As a means of extracting confessions from American soldiers, Korean military intelligence operatives commonly subjected prisoners of war to sustained bouts of sleep deprivation. In the face of overwhelming exhaustion and clear signs of personality disintegration, American soldiers were often induced to sign confessions of their alleged war crimes. Yet Randy Gardner, a seventeen-year-old high school student, experienced sleep deprivation for 264 hours to get his name in the *Guinness Book of World Records* with no apparent permanent effects and no profound temporary deficits. Why would people respond in such radically different ways to sleep deprivation? One hypothesis proposes that severe adverse effects arise as a function of stress and inability to rest and relax, rather than from the loss of sleep. Furthermore, laboratory investigations with volunteer subjects suggest that those individuals who exhibit severe reactions to sleep deprivation almost always have some predisposition to abnormal behavior. Sleep researchers would not deny that sleep serves to restore the body; however, rest and relaxation may serve the same restorative functions in the absence of sleep, which would suggest that repair and restoration is not the sole or even primary function of sleep.

To redress the shortcomings of the repair and restoration theory, an alternative theory of a need to sleep has been proposed. The adaptive or evolutionary theory postulates that the need to sleep arose in the course of biological evolution as an adaptive mechanism to conserve energy during the evening hours, when it would be inefficient to search for food and other resources. Sleep, according to this view, serves a function similar to the hibernation observed in several species of mammals. These animals reduce their metabolic processes to barely detectable levels during winter to conserve energy when food resources are scarce. To do otherwise would threaten the survival of these animals. It is important to note that the adaptive theory still considers sleep to be a real need; in essence, sleep is a remnant of the human evolutionary past when human forebears did not have the convenience of twenty-four-hour supermarkets to acquire their sustenance. Humans deprived of sleep will become just as irritable and ill-tempered as a groundhog prevented from hibernating.

Several predictions have been generated from the adaptive theory, most of which have been supported by scientific observations. First, the theory predicts that predators such as large cats and bears, which obtain most of their nutrients in one large meal per day, would sleep much more than grazing animals such as cattle and horses, who must eat frequently to survive. A second prediction of the theory is that predators such as wolves and mountain lions, which have few natural enemies, would sleep more than prey such as rabbits and guinea pigs, which are at risk if they fail to maintain constant vigilance. Finally, animals such as bats, which are well protected by the environment in which they live, would sleep for relatively long periods of time. These predictions are documented by scientific observations, which provide support for the adaptive or evolutionary theory of sleep.

The functions of sleep are extremely important in clinical applications. If the repair and restoration theory lacks strong scientific support, attempting to recover lost sleep time may serve no functional purpose. Indeed, most subjects expect to sleep for several hours longer than normal after staying awake for twenty-four hours, presumably because they believe sleep is required for repair and restoration of the body. In practice, however, most subjects report only four to six total hours of poor-quality sleep following such deprivation. Even after 264 hours of sleep deprivation, Randy Gardner slept for only fourteen hours and forty minutes the first evening, then resumed a normal nocturnal sleep pattern of eight hours per evening.

Knowledge of sleep stages may be especially valuable in diagnosing and treating sleep disorders, since the frequency, patterns, and symptoms of these disorders may be associated with specific stages of sleep. For example, knowledge of the muscular paralysis that accompanies REM sleep has been instrumental in diagnosing the cause of male impotence. Partial or total erections are present in about 95 percent of REM periods. Therefore, men who complain of impotence yet demonstrate normal REM erections can be diagnosed as suffering from psychologically based impotence. These patients may benefit from psychotherapy or sexual counseling. In contrast, men who do not achieve REM erections are diagnosed as suffering from organically based impotence and require hormone therapy or surgical implantations.

Nocturnal enuresis, or bed-wetting, is a stage four developmental disorder present in about four to five million children annually in the United States. The exact cause of this disorder is undetermined, although the extreme muscular relaxation during stage four sleep likely contributes to its occurrence. To prevent nocturnal enuresis, the patient must learn to associate a full bladder with waking up. Typically, a special apparatus is placed under the child, which sounds a loud buzzer when urine completes the circuit. Eventually, the child will learn to associate the feeling of a full bladder with waking up in the absence of the buzzer.

Context

Since sleep is a universal human experience, it is probably safe to conclude that it has interested people since the dawn of humanity; however, scientific inquiry into sleep is a relatively recent phenomenon. Early interest in sleep arose during the late nineteenth century from a need to isolate the brain structure responsible for lethargy syndromes. Similarly, the electrophysiological study of sleep originated with a discovery in 1875 by the English physiologist Richard Caton that the brain continually produces low-voltage waves. This discovery was largely ignored until 1929, when a German psychiatrist, Hans Berger, found that he could record from large groups of neurons by attaching electrodes to the scalp and the forehead. Berger's discovery marked the beginning of modern electroencephalography. With the advent of EEG recordings, it was not long before A. L. Loomis, E. N. Harvey, and G. A. Hobart found, in 1937, that EEG recordings could be used to differentiate stages of sleep. In 1952, Nathaniel Kleitman at the University of Chicago gave Eugene Aserinsky, one of his new graduate students, the assignment of watching the eye movements of sleeping subjects. Aserinsky quickly noted the rapid, darting nature of eye movements during certain times of the night, which differed from the usual slow, rolling eye movements observed at other times. William Dement later coined the term REM sleep; sleep in which slow, rolling eye movements predominate later came to be known as NREM sleep (for nonrapid eye movement sleep). Finally, in 1957, Dement and Kleitman presented the current system of four NREM sleep stages and stage REM.

As a naturally induced alteration in consciousness that can be studied objectively with electrophysiological recording equipment, sleep has assumed a prominent role in the psychology of consciousness. Electrophysiological recording techniques that were originally developed in sleep research are now widely used to study other aspects of consciousness, such as hemispheric asymmetries, meditation, sensory isolation, biofeedback, dreams, and drug effects on the brain and behavior. In addition, sleep is one of the few alterations in consciousness that plays a central role in several areas of psychological inquiry. For example, physiological psychologists are concerned with the neurobiological mechanisms underlying sleep, as well as the functions of sleep. From their perspective, sleep is simply one of many human behaviors and cognitive processes whose biological basis must be ascertained. Developmental psychologists are interested in age-related changes that occur in sleep, and attempt to develop applications of those findings for concerned parents of young children. Finally, physicians and clinical psychologists are often presented with patients who suffer from physical and/or psychological stress as a function of sleep disorders. These professionals are interested in developing effective drug and psychological therapies that can be used to treat sleep-disordered patients. Sleep is a concern in many areas of psychology.

Because sleep is universal in humans, it will continue to play a major role in consciousness studies and throughout the discipline of psychology. Future research will likely focus on applications of sleep research to industrial settings that employ shift workers. The emphasis will be on reducing fatigue and improving performance among employees by gradually adjusting them to shift work and by changing employee work schedules infrequently. In addition, research will seek ways to improve diagnostic procedures and treatments for a variety of sleep disorders, including insomnia, hypersomnia, sleep apnea, narcolepsy, and enuresis. The focus will be on developing effective drug and psychological therapies. Finally, pure research will continue to examine the functions of sleep, and to delineate more clearly the adverse effects of sleep, even those of a temporary nature.

Bibliography

Cohen, David B. *Sleep and Dreaming: Origins, Nature, and Functions.* New York: Pergamon Press, 1979. A comprehensive review of sleep and dreaming research, including sleep stages, functions, development, and disorders. Also includes findings on sex differences in the effects of REM sleep deprivation. Somewhat technical; recommended for advanced college students only.

Coleman, Richard M. *Wide Awake at 3:00 A.M.: By Choice or by Chance?* New York: W. H. Freeman, 1986. Reveals how a person's biological clock (or sleep-wake cycle) works and how it controls periods of sleep, alertness, mood, and performance. Also examines sleep stages, functions, and sleep disorders. Highly readable; recommended for high school and college students, as well as other interested adults.

Dement, William C. *Some Must Watch While Some Must Sleep.* San Francisco: San Francisco Book Company, 1976. William Dement, founder of the sleep disorders clinic at Stanford University, provides a nontechnical, personal report of sleep stages, dreams, and sleep disorders. Immensely readable and often humorous. Highly recommended for junior high school, high school, and college students, as well as other interested adults.

Hobson, J. Allan. *Sleep.* New York: Scientific American Library, 1989. A broad and interdisciplinary view of sleep research, combining knowledge drawn from neurology, psychology, and animal behavior studies. The nontechnical language and lavish illustrations are two major advantages of this book. Highly recommended for high school and college students.

Webb, Wilse B. *Sleep: The Gentle Tyrant.* Englewood Cliffs, N.J.: Prentice-Hall, 1975. A nontechnical overview of sleep research, focusing particularly on behavioral components of sleep and sleep disorders. Somewhat dated, but perhaps the most comprehensive introductory book available on sleep that can be easily understood by most high school and college students.

Richard P. Atkinson

Cross-References

Altered States of Consciousness, 220; Brain-Stem Structures, 461; Circadian Rhythms, 514; Dreams, 836; Hindbrain Structures, 1175; Insomnia, 1303; Reticular Formation, 2103; Sleep Apnea Syndromes and Narcolepsy, 2284.

SLEEP APNEA SYNDROMES AND NARCOLEPSY

Type of psychology: Consciousness
Field of study: Sleep

Sleep apnea syndromes are a class of sleep disorders which result in repeated pauses in breathing during the night and cause repeated interruptions of the sleep cycle. Sleep apnea may be caused by physical obstruction of the upper airway or by neurological difficulties. Narcolepsy, another sleep disorder, is characterized by excessive daytime sleepiness, cataplexy, sleep paralysis, hypnagogic hallucinations, and irregular manifestations of REM sleep. The disorder is lifelong, and its origin is unknown.

Principal terms

APNEA: the cessation of breathing

CATAPLEXY: a brief, sudden episode of muscle weakness or paralysis; in narcoleptic patients, usually triggered by emotion

ELECTROENCEPHALOGRAPHY: a technique used to measure electrical (brain-wave) activity through the scalp

HYPNAGOGIC HALLUCINATIONS: vivid auditory or visual hallucinations which occur at the transition from wakefulness to sleep, or from sleep to wakefulness

INSOMNIA: a complaint of poor, insufficient, or nonrefreshing sleep

RAPID EYE MOVEMENT (REM) SLEEP: a type or stage of sleep characterized by rapid eye movements, vivid dreaming, and lack of skeletal muscle tone

Overview

Sleep apnea syndromes include a variety of conditions, all of which result in the temporary cessation of breathing during sleep. Sleep apnea may affect people of all ages, but it is more common among elderly patients. Individuals with sleep apnea do not necessarily have breathing difficulty while awake, and while many people who do not have apnea experience pauses in breathing during sleep, sleep apnea patients experience much longer pauses (typically fifteen to sixty seconds), and these may occur one hundred to six hundred times per night. Three basic types of apnea exist: obstructive, central, and mixed.

Obstructive sleep apnea (OSA) is caused by an obstruction of the upper airway during sleep and is the most common type of apnea. Breathing effort continues with OSA, but it is ineffective because of the patient's blocked airway. Individuals with OSA will commonly report that they experience excessive daytime sleepiness (EDS). Also, loud snoring occurs at night, which is a result of the vibration of tissues in the upper airway and is caused by the passage of air through a narrow airway. Another feature which is common in OSA patients is excessive body weight. OSA occurs more often in males than in females.

Children are also affected by this disorder; the most common cause is swelling of the tonsils. Therefore, all children are at risk of developing OSA, though some groups of children, such as those with Down syndrome, facial malformation, or muscular disorders, are more at risk than others. Children with OSA are typically underweight, because they usually have difficulty swallowing; they may even enjoy eating less because they are not able to smell or taste food as well as others.

Patients with obstructive sleep apnea frequently report falling asleep while driving, watching television, or reading, but some patients report little or no EDS. OSA patients may also experience intellectual or personality changes, which are probably usually related to EDS, but in severe cases may be attributable to lowered levels of oxygen reaching the brain. Another symptom associated with OSA is erectile impotence.

Central sleep apnea (CSA) is caused by a temporary absence of the effort to breathe while sleeping, and it is considered to be a rare disorder; fewer than 10 percent of all apnea patients experience CSA. CSA differs from OSA in that there is no obstruction of the upper airway, and breathing effort does not continue as it does in OSA. Patients rarely have CSA alone; the majority have both CSA and OSA episodes during the night. CSA is usually diagnosed when more than 55 percent of the episodes are central. Many authors point out that the mechanisms responsible for the two types of apnea may overlap; CSA may be attributable to a failure of the systems which monitor oxygen levels in the blood, resulting in the periodic loss of the breathing effort. CSA patients may experience between one hundred and three hundred episodes per night.

Central sleep apnea patients commonly complain of insomnia, which is poor, insufficient, or nonrefreshing sleep. Other symptoms associated with CSA are depression and decreased sexual drive. Patients with neurological disorders such as encephalitis, brain-stem tumor, and Shy-Drager syndrome may also have CSA. The range of disorders associated with CSA makes it difficult to make absolute statements about the cause of this form of apnea.

The third type of apnea is mixed sleep apnea (MSA). MSA is a pause in breathing which has both obstructive and central components. Most patients with MSA are generally considered to be similar to OSA patients in terms of symptoms, physical causes, and treatment options; however, there are also those MSA patients whose apneic episodes are characterized by long central components, and these individuals are more similar to CSA patients in terms of symptoms, cause, and treatment.

Narcolepsy is a sleep disorder which includes symptoms such as EDS, overwhelming episodes of daytime sleep, disturbed nocturnal sleep, cataplexy (sudden, brief episodes of muscle weakness or paralysis which are emotionally triggered), hypnagogic hallucinations, sleep-onset rapid eye movement (REM) periods (or SOREMPs, the occurrence of REM sleep within fifteen minutes of sleep onset as indicated by electroencephalographic, or EEG, analysis), and sleep paralysis. Four symptoms— EDS, cataplexy, sleep paralysis, and hypnagogic hallucinations—are often referred to as the "narcoleptic tetrad," although all four symptoms are rarely seen in the same patient. Narcoleptics rarely have problems falling asleep at night, but they do awaken more frequently and exhibit more body movements during sleep than normal subjects. Narcoleptics are also frequently disturbed by vivid dreams.

The EDS associated with narcolepsy is most often experienced during boring, sedentary situations, but it may also occur when the person is highly involved with a task. Though narcoleptics may awaken from a "sleep attack" feeling refreshed, narcoleptic sleepiness is persistent and cannot be alleviated by any amount of sleep. For years, many believed that the sleep attacks associated with narcolepsy could be attributable to a sudden "urge" to sleep, but more recent thought suggests that these sleep episodes may result from a sudden failure to resist the ever-present sleepiness that narcoleptics experience.

Not all patients with narcolepsy experience cataplexy. In a study to determine the differences between narcoleptics with cataplexy and those without cataplexy, it was determined that patients who experienced cataplexy had a higher prevalence of hallucinations, sleep paralysis, and nocturnal sleep disturbance. Thus, cataplectics generally seem to be more impaired during sleep and while awake. For this reason, some have suggested that two groups of narcoleptic patients may exist: those with cataplexy and those without cataplexy. During a cataplectic episode, the narcoleptic patient maintains consciousness; however, if the episode is particularly long, the patient may enter REM sleep. Patients with severe cataplexy may experience complete paralysis in all but the respiratory muscles; these episodes can result in injury, although the most common episodes could be characterized by the patient dropping objects, losing posture, or halting motions.

Sleep paralysis in narcolepsy is experienced as the inability to move during the onset of sleep or upon awakening. These episodes may last from a few seconds to ten minutes and can be reversed by external stimuli such as another person touching the patient or calling his or her name. Sleep paralysis can be particularly frightening, although many patients learn that these episodes are usually brief and will end spontaneously. Adding to this fright, however, are the visual, auditory, or tactile hallucinations which may accompany sleep paralysis. Sleep paralysis and hypnagogic hallucinations occur in about 60 percent of narcoleptic patients. Much like patients with sleep apnea, narcoleptics may exhibit psychopathology, but it is most likely related to effects of their disturbed sleep rather than to the sleep disorder itself.

Applications

Individuals with apnea may repeatedly experience dangerously low levels of oxygen in their blood while sleeping. Oxygen is essential to the body's proper functioning, and if one does not receive the amount of oxygen the body needs, health may be affected in some way; heart disease and stroke are strongly associated with the occurrence of apnea. While it is not known if apnea actually causes these complications, the association is important nevertheless. Exposure to such low levels of oxygen in the blood over a prolonged period may result in increased blood pressure and poor circulation, as well as disturbance of heart rhythms.

Since both narcolepsy and apnea patients often experience nocturnal sleep difficulties, their quality and quantity of sleep is lowered. As a result, many patients with both disorders experience excessive daytime sleepiness. This may present itself as a problem during such activities as work or driving. Studies indicate that narcolepsy and apnea patients are more likely to have automobile accidents, poor job performance, and less job satisfaction than those without a sleep disorder, in part because of the fact that these patients often fall asleep during such activities. Diagnosis of sleep apnea and narcolepsy in a sleep disorders clinic involves a number of measurements. The Multiple Sleep Latency Test measures the tendency of a patient to fall asleep during the day. This test, in addition to polysomnographic recording and the patient's medical history, aids in determining the proper treatment for these disorders.

Treatment of sleep apnea depends on a number of factors, which include frequency and type of apnea, quality of nighttime sleep, amount of oxygen in the blood during sleep, frequency and type of heart rhythm disturbance, and the tendency to sleep during waking hours. CSA patients may be treated using oxygen administration during sleep, which reduces the number of central apnea events, drug therapy, or mechanical ventilation, but all treatments for CSA have the potential to increase the occurrence of OSA in these patients. Various treatments available to patients with obstructive or mixed apnea include weight loss, drug therapy, surgery, and medical management.

Weight loss can be an important part of treatment for patients with OSA. In many cases, weight loss alone results in a reduction of the frequency and severity of apnea. Since adequate weight loss may take months, however, this option alone is not likely to be feasible for serious cases of apnea. Drug therapy has met with limited success in treating apnea patients, but there are many drugs which are being studied, and these may prove effective in treating the disorder. Surgical treatment for severe cases of apnea was, in the past, limited to tracheostomy. More recently, however, removal of unnecessary tissue in the area of obstruction has been found to reduce apnea events significantly in certain patients. Facial reconstruction is also an option in more severe cases.

Treatments for apnea which involve medical management are constantly being developed. These include the insertion of a tube which bypasses the point of obstruction, allowing normal breathing to occur, and continuous positive airway pressure (CPAP). CPAP is a technique that uses air pressure to eliminate the closure of the airway in the nasal passages. In effect, CPAP provides a "splint" for the area that causes the obstruction; it also increases lung volume. This treatment is comfortable and easy to use for most patients, and is thus very promising.

Treatments for narcolepsy all center on managing its symptoms, as there is no cure for narcolepsy itself. Fortunately, cataplexy, sleep paralysis, and hypnagogic hallucinations improve or disappear over time in approximately one-third of all narcoleptic patients. Medication may be prescribed to decrease the severity of daytime sleepiness, nocturnal sleep disturbance, and cataplexy. Regularly scheduled naps throughout the day may be used as an effective supplement to medication. Such naps may also reduce the need for medications by relieving the effects of insufficient sleep. Many doctors employ this method of treatment, because it is important for patients to adjust their life-style in order to deal with the effects of narcolepsy.

Context

The scientific study of sleep began in the nineteenth century, although there was certainly interest in sleep prior to that time. Technological advances during the 1930's and 1940's allowed scientists to investigate the processes of sleep with more precision than before. In 1929, Hans Berger first recorded the EEG activity of humans. This development led to the discovery of patterns of brain-wave activity during sleep and the later description of REM sleep. This period of technological growth began the modern era of sleep studies; since that time, much has been learned about sleep and how it relates to other physiological processes.

Recognition of sleep apnea as a distinct sleep disorder began in 1966, and it is estimated today that as many as one in every thirty to fifty adults has sleep apnea to the extent that their quality of life is affected in some manner. Since its description, sleep apnea has received intensive investigation by a variety of medical specialists; in sleep apnea studies, it is not uncommon to see a heart surgeon working with a psychologist and a child specialist. This is attributable to the fact that sleep apnea can be the result of a number of physical or neurological problems, and it affects patients in a number of different ways.

Between one in a thousand and one in ten thousand women and men experience narcolepsy, and the usual age of onset is between fifteen and thirty-five. In half the cases, the onset of narcoleptic symptoms is preceded by severe psychological stress, an abrupt change in the sleep-wake schedule, or some other special circumstance. Scientists suspect a genetic factor in the occurrence of narcolepsy that may involve the immune system, but data also suggest that a strong environmental factor may play a role in the development of the disorder.

In an essay in *Principles and Practice of Sleep Medicine* (1989), Christian Guillemenault writes that the word "narcolepsy" was first used in 1880 to describe a pathological condition characterized by recurring, irresistible episodes of sleep which were of short duration. Interest in the disorder grew, and in 1960 it was discovered that a narcoleptic patient exhibited sleep-onset REM periods. This phenomenon became one of the cornerstone symptoms in the diagnosis of narcolepsy, and narcolepsy has since been described as primarily a disorder of REM sleep.

Investigation of sleep is showing how important sleep is to human physical and psychological health. Many theories exist which attempt to account for why people sleep; studies indicate that tissue restoration is enhanced during sleep, the ability to concentrate suffers if one is deprived of sleep for a significant period of time, and one may experience distinct mood changes without proper sleep. As stated earlier, cardiovascular complications are frequently associated with sleep apnea, as are work-related accidents and changes in intellectual ability. Sudden infant death syndrome (SIDS) is thought by some to be associated with sleep apnea. For these reasons, the study of sleep apnea, narcolepsy, and sleep in general is crucial to the health of many people. As psychologists and physicians further understand the processes involved in human and animal sleep, they will come closer to providing more effective treatment for patients with sleep apnea and narcolepsy.

Bibliography

Anch, A. Michael, C. P. Browman, M. M. Mitler, and James K. Walsh. *Sleep: A Scientific Perspective.* Englewood Cliffs, N.J.: Prentice-Hall, 1988. The authors cover the entire spectrum of sleep study in this work, integrating the history of sleep studies with more recent knowledge of the field. The book addresses physiological as well as psychological issues and gives sufficient definitions, information, and references for those who wish to study sleep in a more in-depth manner.

Dement, William C. *Some Must Watch While Some Must Sleep.* San Francisco: W. H. Freeman, 1974. A book by a scientist who many consider to be the leading authority in the field of sleep studies. Easily read by high school or college students. Very informative; provides an excellent starting point for further study.

Issa, Faiq G., Paul M. Surrat, and John E. Remmers, eds. *Sleep and Respiration.* New York: John Wiley & Sons, 1990. A compilation of articles and discussions by many of the leading scientists of the field. Especially helpful are the sections after each chapter in which the topic is discussed among specialists. Somewhat advanced, but a basic knowledge of sleep disorders is sufficient for understanding most of the material in this book.

Kryger, Meir H., Thomas Roth, and William C. Dement, eds. *Principles and Practice of Sleep Medicine.* Philadelphia: W. B. Saunders, 1989. A very comprehensive work on the subject of sleep disorders. The entire spectrum of sleep and its disorders is covered, with extensive material on treatment practices. A large glossary and numerous references make this book an ideal tool.

Mendelson, Wallace B. *Human Sleep: Research and Clinical Care.* New York: Plenum Medical Book Company, 1987. Provides an overview of research and treatment practices for a number of sleep disorders.

Alan K. Gibson
Shirley A. Albertson Owens

Cross-References

Attention, 313; Brain Injuries: Concussions, Contusions, and Strokes, 448; Insomnia, 1303; Neurons, 1661; Sexual Dysfunction, 2253; Sleep: Stages and Functions, 2277; Sudden Infant Death Syndrome, 2495.

SMELL AND TASTE

Type of psychology: Sensation and perception
Field of study: Auditory, chemical, cutaneous, and body senses

The senses of taste and smell, which are closely related, depend on sensory receptors known as chemoreceptors. These receptors detect molecules of various kinds and respond by generating nerve impulses. Chemoreception is believed to depend on proteins in receptor cell membranes that can recognize and combine with molecules from the environment.

Principal terms

ADAPTATION: a reduction in the number of nerve impulses generated by a receptor while a stimulus is held constant

ALKALOIDS: a group of organic substances, many of them toxic plant products, that have a strongly bitter taste

CHEMORECEPTORS: sensory receptor cells that generate nerve impulses on coming in contact with chemicals from the environment

OLFACTORY BULBS: two narrow extensions at the base of the brain to which extensions of olfactory cells make connections

OLFACTORY CELL: the chemoreceptor for the sense of smell

PAPILLA (pl. PAPILLAE): a moundlike outgrowth containing taste buds

TASTE BUD: a small bundle of taste receptor cells surrounded by supportive cells and communicating with the exterior through a small pore

Overview

The senses of taste and smell, which are closely related, depend on a type of sensory receptor cell known as a chemoreceptor. This receptor detects molecules of various kinds and responds on contact with them by generating nerve impulses. Although the basis for the detection is incompletely understood, chemoreceptor cells are believed to contain proteins in their surface membranes that are able to recognize and combine with various kinds of molecules. Combination with a recognized molecule causes the protein to open an ion channel in the surface membrane. The resulting ion flow creates an electrical change in the membrane that triggers generation of a nerve impulse by the chemoreceptor cell.

Chemoreceptors for taste occur primarily on the upper surface of the tongue. A comparatively few taste receptors are also located on the roof of the mouth, particularly on the soft palate, and in the throat. The taste receptors in these locations are parts of taste buds, which are small, pear-shaped bundles of cells. Molecules from the exterior environment reach the taste receptor cells through a small pore at the top of a taste bud. All together, there are about ten thousand taste buds on the tongue and throat. The taste buds of the tongue, which are only 30 to 40 micrometers in diameter and thus microscopic, are embedded in the surfaces of small, mound-like outgrowths called papillae. The papillae give the surface of the tongue its rough or furry texture.

Taste receptor cells occur in taste buds along with other cells that play a purely supportive structural role. Individual taste receptor cells are elongated and bear thin, fingerlike extensions at their tips that protrude through the pore of a taste bud. Combination with chemicals from the environment, which must dissolve in the saliva of the mouth to reach the taste buds, probably occurs in the membranes of the fingerlike processes at the tips of the taste receptor cells. The opposite end of the taste receptor cells makes connections with sensory nerves serving the taste buds.

Each taste receptor cell probably has membrane proteins that can combine with a variety of molecules from the environment; however, individual taste cells, depending on their location on the tongue, typically combine more readily with some molecular types than with others. Taste cells with a preponderance of membrane proteins recognizing and combining with organic molecules, such as carbohydrates, alcohols, and amino acids, are crowded near the tip of the tongue. Combination of these taste receptors with organic molecules gives rise to nerve impulses that are interpreted in the brain as a sweet taste. Just behind the tip of the tongue is a region containing taste receptor cells that combine most readily with inorganic salts; combination with these substances gives rise to nerve impulses that are interpreted in the brain as a salty taste.

Farther to the rear of the tongue, particularly along the sides, are taste receptor cells that combine most readily with the hydrogen (H^+) ions released by acids; this combination is perceived as a sour taste. The rear of the tongue contains taste receptor cells that combine most readily with a wide variety of organic and inorganic molecules, particularly long-chain organic molecules containing nitrogen and a group of organic substances called alkaloids. All the alkaloids, including molecules such as quinine, caffeine, morphine, and strychnine, give rise to a bitter taste. People tend to reject substances stimulating the bitter taste receptors at the rear of the tongue. This may have a survival value, because many bitter substances, including alkaloids produced by a variety of plants, are strongly poisonous. Many of the organic molecules with a bitter taste differ from those with a sweet taste by only minor chemical groups. A few substances, such as pepper, primarily stimulate pain rather than taste receptors when present in foods.

The distribution on the tongue of regions of strongest taste does not mean that the taste receptor cells in these areas are limited to detecting only sweet, salty, sour, or bitter substances; all regions of the tongue can detect molecules of each type to at least some extent.

Traditionally, the wide range of different flavors that humans can differentiate, which easily amounts to thousands, has been considered to be the result of subtle combinations of the four primary flavors: sweet, salty, sour, and bitter. There are indications, however, that the picture may be considerably more complex than this. Persons can be "taste-blind" for certain very specific, single molecules, such as the chemical phenylthiocarbamide (PTC). The ability to taste this substance, which has a bitter flavor, is hereditary; some persons can taste PTC, and some cannot. The pattern of inheritance suggests that a membrane protein able to combine with PTC is present in some persons and not in others. Persons taste-blind for PTC do not have the specific membrane protein and cannot respond to the presence of the chemical even though other bitter flavors can be detected. It is possible that there are a wide variety of specific membrane proteins like the one responsible for detecting PTC distributed in the surface membranes of the taste receptor cells of the tongue.

The chemoreceptors responsible for the other chemical sense, the sense of smell, are located within the head at the roof of the nasal cavity. The receptor cells detecting odors, called olfactory cells, are distributed among supportive cells in a double patch of tissue totaling about 5 square centimeters in area. Although limited to this area, the olfactory region contains between 10 and 100 million olfactory cells in the average person.

Each olfactory cell bears between ten and twenty fine, fibrous extensions that protrude into a layer of mucus that covers the olfactory area. The membranes of the extensions contain the protein molecules that recognize and combine with chemicals to trigger a nerve impulse by an olfactory cell. In order to reach the fibrous extensions, molecules detected as odors must dissolve in the mucous solution covering the olfactory region.

The opposite ends of the olfactory cells penetrate directly into the cranial cavity through microscopic channels in the shelf of bone separating the top of the nasal cavity from the base of the brain. On the brain side of the bony shelf, the extensions of the olfactory cells make connections with nerve cells of the brain. The region of the brain connecting with the olfactory cells consists of two narrow swellings, the olfactory bulbs, which extend along the lower surface of the brain. Olfactory cells are the only receptor cells known to make direct connections in this way with nerve cells of the brain. All other sensory receptors make indirect connections to the brain via sensory nerves and, in most cases, other nerve cells that make interconnections in the spinal cord. The extensions of olfactory cells making connections with the olfactory bulbs are known collectively as the olfactory or first cranial nerve.

Efforts to identify primary odors equivalent to the primary sweet, salty, sour, and bitter flavors have been largely unsuccessful. Humans can detect and identify thousands or even tens of thousands of different substances by smell, some in concentrations of only a few molecules per olfactory cell. There are thousands of different substances that individuals may be unable to recognize. These observations indicate that, as with the receptors for taste, many different kinds of specific receptor molecules in the olfactory cell membranes recognize and combine with molecules of odorous substances to trigger nerve impulses. There seems to be little rhyme or reason to the types and classes of molecules registering as different odors: Molecules of widely different sizes and structure may smell the same, and closely related molecules that differ only in minor chemical groups, or in the folding arrangement of the same chemical groups, may smell quite different.

Applications

The chemoreceptors responsible for the senses of taste and smell typically adapt rapidly to continued stimulation by the same molecules. In adaptation, a receptor cell generates nerve impulses most rapidly when first stimulated; with continued stimulation at the same intensity, the frequency of nerve impulses drops steadily until a baseline of a relatively few impulses per second is reached. Adaptation for the senses of taste and smell also involves complex interactions in the brain, because discernment of tastes and smells continues to diminish even after chemoreceptors reach their baselines.

For the sense of taste, adaptation is reflected in the fact that the first bite of food, for example, has the most intensely perceived taste. As stimulation by the same food continues, the intensity of the taste and a person's perception of the flavor steadily decrease. If a second food is tasted, the initial intensity of its taste is high, but again intensity drops off with continued stimulation. If the first food is retasted, however, its flavor will again seem stronger. This effect occurs because adaptation of the receptors detecting the initial taste lessens during the period during which the second food is tasted. If sufficient time passes before the first food is retasted, the flavor will appear to be almost as strong as its first taste. For this reason, one gains greater appreciation of a meal if foods are alternated rather than eaten and finished separately.

Taste receptor cells have a life expectancy of about ten days. As they degenerate, they are constantly replaced by new taste cells that continually differentiate from tissue at the sides of taste buds. As humans reach middle age, the rate of replacement drops off, so that the total number of taste receptor cells declines steadily after the age of about forty-five. This may account for the fact that, as people get older, nothing ever tastes as good as it did in childhood. Smoking also decreases the sensitivity of taste receptor cells, and thereby decreases a person's appreciation and appetite for foods.

Olfactory cells also adapt rapidly to the continued presence of the same molecules and slow or stop generating nerve impulses if the concentration of the odoriferous substances is maintained. This response is also reflected in common experience. When engaged in an odor-generating activity such as cooking or interior painting, a person is strongly aware of the odors generated by the activity only initially. After exposure for more than a few minutes, the person's perception of the odor lessens and eventually disappears almost completely. If the person leaves the odoriferous room for a few minutes, however, allowing the olfactory receptors and brain centers to lose their adaptation, the person is usually surprised at the strength of the odor if he or she returns to the room.

The region at the top of the nasal cavity containing the olfactory cells lies outside the main stream of air entering the lungs through the mouth and nose. As a result, the molecules dissolving in the mucous layer covering the olfactory cells are carried to this region only by side eddies of the airflow through the nose. Flow to the olfactory region is greatly improved by sniffing, a response used by all air-breathing vertebrates as a way to increase the turbulence in the nasal passages and thereby to intensify odors from the environment. Head colds interfere with people's sense of smell through congestion and blockage of the nasal cavity, which impedes airflow to the olfactory region.

Although humans are not nearly as sensitive to odors as are many other animals, their ability to detect some substances by smell is still remarkable, particularly in the case of smells generated by putrefaction. Some of the mercaptans, for example, which are generated in decaying flesh, can be detected in concentrations in air as small as 0.0000000002 milligram per milliliter. One of these substances, methyl mercaptan, is mixed in low concentration in natural gas. The presence of this mercaptan allows people to detect natural gas, which otherwise would be odorless, by smell.

Context

The idea that taste and smell receptors operate by recognizing specific molecular types is an old one, dating back to the first century B.C., when Titus Lucretius Carus proposed that the sense of smell depends on recognition of atomic shapes. Definitive experimental demonstration of this mechanism for the sense of smell, however, was not obtained until 1991, when Linda Buck and Richard Axel finally isolated members of a large family of membrane proteins that can actually do what Lucretius proposed: They recognize and bind specific molecular types and trigger responses by olfactory cells. Axel and Buck have obtained indications that there are hundreds of different proteins in the family responsible for molecular recognition in the sense of smell.

One of the many interesting features of the family is that, as with the sense of taste, many people inherit a deficiency in one or more of the membrane proteins so that they are congenitally unable to detect a particular odor. There are in fact many thousands of different odors to which persons may be insensitive, which directly supports the idea that the family of membrane proteins responsible for detecting individual molecular types is very large indeed. Another interesting feature of the mechanism is that there are many odors for which people must be "educated." People cannot recognize them on first encounter, but later learn to discern them. This indicates that membrane proteins recognizing previously unknown molecules may be induced; that is, they may be newly synthesized and placed in olfactory cell membranes in response to encountering a new chemical in the environment. People can also smell, and often taste, totally new artificial substances never before encountered by humans or indeed any other animal. Thus, the chemoreceptors have membrane proteins capable of recognizing molecules never encountered in animal evolution.

Both taste and smell receptors are linked through nerve connections to regions of the brain stem that control visceral responses, as well as to the areas of the cerebral cortex registering conscious sensations. As a result, different odors and tastes may give rise to a host of involuntary responses, such as salivation, appetite, thirst, pleasure, excitement, sexual arousal, nausea, or even vomiting, as well as to consciously perceived sensations. The odor of a once-enjoyed food may make someone ill in the future if the person became sick after eating the food; previously unobjectionable or even pleasant odors and tastes may become unpleasant and nauseating to women during pregnancy. The odor of other foods, such as some of the ranker cheeses, may be repulsive at first experience but later appetizing as a person learns to enjoy them. The degree to which many substances are perceived as pleasant or unpleasant is also related to their concentration. Many substances perceived as pleasantly sweet in low concentration, for example, taste bitter and unpleasant at higher concentrations.

A part of the perception of pleasantness or unpleasantness in taste or smell is related to the body's nutritional needs. Persons who are deficient in the insulin hormone, for example, so that their cells cannot metabolize glucose, develop a craving for sweets. Several studies have shown that children, if left to themselves, will select a combination of foods that generally satisfies their nutritional needs.

Bibliography

Berne, Robert M., and Matthew Levy, eds. *Physiology.* 2d ed. St. Louis: C. V. Mosby, 1988. Chapter 12, "Chemical Senses," in this standard college physiology text outlines the anatomy and physiology of the systems integrated in the senses of taste and smell. Includes a discussion of the neural connections and regions of the brain involved in the perception of taste and smell. Intended for students at the college level, but clearly written; should be accessible to readers at the high school level.

Coren, Stanley. *Sensation and Perception.* New York: Academic Press, 1979. A simply written, easily understood discussion of the senses, sensory cells, and routes traveled by sensory information through the spinal cord to the brain. Provides a clear and interesting description of the basics of perception in the cerebral cortex.

Guyton, Arthur C. *Textbook of Medical Physiology.* 7th ed. Philadelphia: W. B. Saunders, 1986. Chapter 48, "Sensory Receptors and Their Basic Mechanisms of Action," in this readable and clearly written text outlines the fundamental activities of sensory receptors. Chapter 62, "The Chemical Senses—Taste and Smell," presents more detailed information on the chemoreceptors active in detection of taste and smell, and the connections between these receptors and the brain. Intended for college and medical students, but easily understood by readers at the high school level.

Milne, Lorus Johnson, and Margery Milne. *The Senses of Animals and Men.* New York: Atheneum, 1962. A simple and entertaining survey of the senses and their importance in humans and other animals, written for a popular audience. Provides interesting and thought-provoking comparisons between the sensory systems of humans and of other animals.

Schmidt-Nielsen, Knut. *Animal Physiology, Adaptation, and Environment.* 4th ed. New York: Cambridge University Press, 1990. A standard college text by one of the greatest animal physiologists. Provides a deeply perceptive comparison of sensory systems in humans and other animals. Chapter 8 describes the senses. The text is remarkable for its lucid and entertaining description of animal physiology.

Stephen L. Wolfe

Cross-References

The Central and Peripheral Nervous Systems, 494; Psychophysical Scaling, 1963; Sensation and Perception Defined, 2207; Sensory Modalities and Stimuli, 2214; Signal Detection Theory, 2271; Taste Aversion and Learning Theory, 2520; Touch and Pressure, 2578.

SOCIAL IDENTITY THEORY

Type of psychology: Social psychology
Field of study: Prejudice and discrimination

Social identity theory examines the relationship between group membership and self-esteem. It has provided insights into intergroup conflict, ethnocentrism, cultural affirmation, and self-hatred, predicting both individual and group responses to an unfavorable self-concept.

Principal terms

DISTINCTIVENESS: the basis for group identification; positive distinctiveness fosters strong ties to one's group, and negative distinctiveness motivates individuals to find ways to establish a positive self-image

IN-GROUP BIAS: the tendency to discriminate in favor of one's own group

MINIMAL GROUP PARADIGM: an experimental technique in which individuals are grouped according to an arbitrary criterion such as a coin toss

PERSONAL IDENTITY: aspects of one's self-image that are based on one's own qualities and achievements

SELF-IMAGE: the self as one pictures or imagines it

SOCIAL CATEGORIZATION: the classification of people and groups according to attributes that are personally meaningful

SOCIAL CHANGE: a group-based strategy for image enhancement; superiority is achieved by creatively recasting negative attributes or engaging in direct competition with favorable groups

SOCIAL COMPARISON: contrasting oneself with others to evaluate the acceptability of one's attitudes, opinions, and behaviors

SOCIAL MOBILITY: an individual-based strategy for image enhancement whereby a person "exits" an inferior group or "passes" as a member of a more prestigious group

Overview

Social identity theory maintains that all individuals are motivated to achieve and maintain a positive self-concept. A person's self-concept derives from two principal sources: personal identity and social identity. Personal identity includes one's individual traits, achievements, and qualities. Social identity includes the group affiliations that are recognized as being part of the self, such as one's image of oneself as a Protestant, a blue-collar worker, or a conservative. Some individuals emphasize the personal aspects in their quest for a favorable self-image, while others emphasize their social identities. Social identity theory focuses on the latter. It attempts to explain when and how individuals transform their group affiliations to secure a favorable self-concept.

Psychologist Henri Tajfel introduced social identity theory in 1978. The theory maintains that a person's social identity emerges from the natural process of social categorization. People categorize, or classify, themselves and other people by many criteria, including occupation, religious affiliation, political orientation, ethnicity, economic class, and gender. An individual automatically identifies with some categories and rejects others. This creates a distinction between "in-groups," with which one identifies, and "out-groups," with which one does not identify. A person who identifies himself or herself as a Democrat, for example, would consider other Democrats members of the in-group and would view Republicans as members of the out-group. Individuals inevitably compare their groups with other groups; the goal of the comparisons is to establish the superiority of one's own group, or the group's "positive distinctiveness," on some level, such as affluence, cultural heritage, or spirituality. If the comparison shows that the individual's group memberships are positive and valuable, the social identities become an important part of the self. If, however, one's group appears inferior, one's self-image acquires "negative distinctiveness." The individual is then motivated to acquire a more satisfactory self-concept.

Tajfel and John Turner proposed three strategies that can be used to enhance one's self-concept: "exit," "pass," and "voice." The first two strategies represent attempts to validate the self. Both involve rejecting or distancing oneself from the devalued group to improve identity; both presume that social mobility exists. Exit involves simply leaving the group. This response is possible only within flexible social systems that permit individual mobility. Although individuals cannot usually shed affiliations such as race or gender, they can openly discard other affiliations, such as "Buick owner" or "public school advocate." If dissatisfied with an automobile, one trades it in for another; if unhappy with the public school system, one may exit and move one's children into a private school. Pass, a more private response, occurs when individuals with unfavorable group memberships are not recognized as belonging to that group. A Jew may pass as a Gentile, for example, or a fair-skinned black person may pass as a Caucasian. Typically in such cases, the objective features that link the individual to the devalued group are absent or unnoticeable.

Voice, the final strategy for identity improvement, is a collective response: Group members act together to alter the group's image and elevate its social value. Also called the "social change" approach, it is common in rigid social systems in which individual movement away from the disparaged group is impossible. It also occurs when psychological forces such as cultural and personal values bind the individual to the group. Members of such physically identifiable groups as women, blacks, or Asians might adopt the social change strategy, for example, as might such cultural or religious group members as Irish Catholics or Orthodox Jews.

Voice is a complex response. Simply recognizing that social mobility is blocked for members of one's own group is insufficient to prompt social change activity. Two additional perceptions of the overall social structure are important: its stability and its legitimacy. Stability is concerned with how fixed or secure the social hierarchy seems. Theoretically, no group is completely secure in its relative superiority; even groups that historically have been considered superior must work to maintain their favored position. If members of a denigrated group believe that alternatives to the current social hierarchy are possible, they are encouraged to reassess their own value. Legitimacy, in contrast, involves the bases for a group's negative distinctiveness. If a group believes that its social inferiority is attributable to illegitimate causes—such as discrimination in hiring practices or educational opportunities—group members will be more likely to challenge their inferior position.

Voice challenges to negative distinctiveness take two general forms: social creativity and direct competition. Social creativity involves altering or redefining the elements of comparison. The group's social positions and resources, however, need not be altered. In one approach, a group may simply limit the groups with which it compares itself, focusing on groups that are similar. A group of factory workers may choose to compare itself with warehouse workers or postal employees rather than with a group of advertising executives. This approach increases the chances that the outcome of the comparison will be favorable to one's own group. The group might also identify a new area of comparison, such as bilingual fluency, in its effort to enhance group distinctiveness.

Finally, the group might recast some of its denigrated attributes so that its value is reassessed. A new appreciation for group history and culture often emerges from this process. The Civil Rights movement, an important force for social change in the 1960's, caused this to occur. In the context of that movement, the label "Negro" was replaced by "black," which was recast by African Americans to symbolize group pride. Under the slogan "Black is beautiful," the natural look became more valued than the traditional Euro-American model. African Americans were less likely to lighten or straighten their hair or use makeup to make their skin appear lighter.

Direct competition, in contrast, involves altering the group's social position. It is often an institutional response; consequently, it encourages competition among groups. Displaced groups target institutions and policies, demanding resources in an effort to empower the group politically and economically. In the 1960's, for example, black students demonstrated for curricular changes at colleges and universities. They demanded greater relevance in existing courses and the development of Black Studies programs to highlight the group's social and political contributions. In the 1970's, the women's movement demanded economic and political changes, including equal pay for equal work, and greater individual rights for women, such as abortion rights and institutionalized child care.

Applications

Social identity theory has been used to explain several intergroup processes. Among these are the phenomenon known as in-group bias (observed in laboratory experiments) and the actions of some subordinate groups to challenge their relative inferiority through collective (voice) approaches. The response of African Americans in the 1950's and 1960's to negative perceptions of their group illustrates the latter process.

In-group bias is the tendency to favor one's own group over other groups. In laboratory experiments, young subjects have been put in groups according to simple and fairly arbitrary criteria, such as the type of artwork they preferred. The goal was to establish a "minimal group situation": an artificial social order in which subjects could be easily differentiated but which was free of any already existing conflicts. Once categorized, subjects were asked to perform one of several tasks, such as distributing money, assigning points, evaluating the different groups, or interpreting group members' behavior. In all the tasks, subjects repeatedly showed a preference for their own groups. They gave to in-group members significantly more points and money than they gave to out-group members—despite a lack of previous interaction among the subjects. When describing in-group members, they attributed altruistic behavior to the person's innate virtuous and admirable qualities rather than to outside causes. When describing out-group members, however, they reversed the pattern, attributing altruistic behavior to situational factors and hostile behavior to personal character. Thus, even without any history of competition, ideological differences, or hostility over scarce resources, subjects consistently demonstrate a preference for their in-group.

Social identity theory predicts this pattern. The powerful need to achieve a positive self-image motivates a person to establish the value of his or her group memberships. Since groups strongly contribute to an individual's self-image, the individual works to enhance the group's image. Group successes are, by extension, the individual's successes. Daily life offers many examples of group allegiance, ranging from identification with one's country to support of one's hometown baseball team. Experiments in social identity suggest that ethnocentrism—the belief in the superiority of one's own ethnic group—serves important psychological needs.

Social identity theory also explains why some subordinate groups challenge their relative inferiority through rebellion or social change while others do not. The theory predicts that individuals who are objectively bound to negatively distinct groups—by gender or skin color, for example—will have fewer options for self-enhancement. Because they are driven by the powerful need to obtain a worthy self-image, however, they are unlikely to engage in self-hatred by accepting the denigrated image imposed on them by others. Instead, they will engage in some form of voice—the collective approach to image improvement.

Psychologists studying social identity do not directly explore the historical background of a group's negative self-image. Rather, they perform laboratory experiments and field studies designed to determine individuals' actual perceptions of groups—how individuals identify groups and whether they see them as having a positive or negative image. Social psychologists also attempt to measure the changes that occur in group self-image over time; they can then infer that social or political movements have affected that image. Studies involving African-American children—

for whom the essential identifying element is a physical one, race—provide an example.

In the landmark 1954 Supreme Court decision *Brown v. Board of Education*, which mandated school desegregation, social scientists presented evidence that educational segregation produced feelings of inferiority in black children. Support was drawn in part from a 1947 study by Kenneth and Mamie Clark, in which they compared the preferences of black and white children between the ages of three and seven for dolls with either dark or fair skin tones. Approximately 60 percent of the black children said that the fair-skinned doll was the "nicer" doll, the "nicer color" doll, or the doll they "preferred to play with." The dark-skinned doll, by contrast, "looked bad." Based on a combination of this negative self-image and the fact that African Americans are objectively bound to their group by their race, social identity theory would predict collective action for social change.

The Civil Rights movement embodied that collective, or voice, activity, and it offered blacks a new context within which to evaluate black identity. Results from studies performed in the 1970's suggest that, indeed, there was a significant rise in black self-esteem during that period. A replication of the Clarks' study by other researchers showed a clear preference for the dark-skinned doll among black children. Later analyses of comparable doll studies showed that such preferences for one's own group were most common among young subjects from areas with large black populations and active black pride movements.

A positive self-image may also emerge when social and cultural themes and historical events are reinterpreted within a group. A group's cultural image may be emphasized; its music, art, and language then become valued. To continue using the African-American example, in the twentieth century, black music, which once had been the music of the oppressed—work songs and spirituals—evolved into a music that communicated ethnic identity in a new way. Blues and jazz became a focus of group pride; jazz, in particular, become renowned worldwide. The acceptance of jazz as a valuable art form by people of many races and nationalities illustrates another frequent outcome of activity for generating a positive self-concept: It often initiates a response from the larger society that improves the group's relative position in that society.

Context

Social identity theory evolved from a series of experiments conducted in England at the University of Bristol in the 1970's. Originated by social psychologist Henri Tajfel, the theory represents the collaborative efforts of Michael Billig, John Turner, and several other European associates over a decade-long period.

Like many social science theories, social identity theory has both personal and intellectual origins. Tajfel's own identity as a European Jew who survived World War II contributed significantly to his desire to understand conflicts between groups. His early work in the psychology of prejudice and his personal distrust of reductionist or oversimplified models of psychological processes laid the foundation for the theory. Other concepts, including stereotypes, values, ethnocentrism, and the social psychology of minorities, became incorporated into the theory; these themes contributed to the attractiveness of the theory in Europe, a region recognized for its religious, linguistic, and social diversity and for the conflicts this diversity has caused.

Group processes have long been emphasized in American social psychology, but the main thrusts have varied over the years. Kurt Lewin's work in the late 1940's, for example, focused on leadership in small groups; research in the mid-1950's examined the relationship of intergroup contact to prejudice and discrimination. In the late 1950's, Muzafer Sherif studied intergroup relations in socially created groups that he and his colleagues observed in real-life settings for extended periods of time. In the 1960's, however, internal conflicts in the field of social psychology led to the development of two distinct subdisciplines: sociological social psychology and psychological social psychology. Intergroup relations began to seem too sociological a topic for psychologists to study. This split, coupled with a renewed emphasis on studying individual cognitive processes, resulted in the displacement of intergroup studies in American social psychology in the 1970's.

Social identity theory revived American research on intergroup relations in the early to mid-1980's. Following more than a decade of political and social turmoil in the United States, social psychologists were looking for better ways to understand conflict between groups. They began to ask new questions and to adopt a wider variety of methodologies, including surveys and field studies. Race, class, and gender were recognized as critical psychological variables. The "group member"—an individual with a sociocultural history that affected social behavior—became accepted as a respectable research subject. Social identity theory provided both theorists and researchers with a broad paradigm from which to investigate intergroup conflict, group identification, ethnocentrism, hostility, and social change strategies.

The three central psychological processes—motivation, emotion, and cognition— are incorporated into social identity theory in a logical and sophisticated manner. Earlier social psychological theories usually emphasized one or two of those processes. Both comprehensive and complex, the theory offers a way of understanding a wide range of psychological topics.

Bibliography

Brown, R. "Intergroup Relations." In *Introduction to Social Psychology*, edited by Miles Hewstone, Wolfgang Stroebe, Jean-Paul Codol, and G. Stephenson. New York: Basil Blackwell, 1988. Brown summarizes intergroup relations literature in this accessible chapter in a social psychology textbook. Locates social identity theory in the broader context of intergroup relations and explains important terms clearly, providing excellent examples; can be understood by the college or high school student.

Messick, David M., and Diane M. Mackie. "Intergroup Relations." In *Annual Review of Psychology* 40. Stanford, Calif.: Annual Reviews, 1989. Reviews intergroup relations theory and research from a cognitive perspective. Categorization, in-group and out-group effects, and intergroup bias are emphasized. Tajfel's social identity theory dominates the section on intergroup bias; his work is examined and critiqued. Variants of social identity theory are discussed.

Tajfel, Henri, ed. *Differentiation Between Social Groups: Studies in the Social Psychology of Intergroup Relations.* London: Academic Press, 1978. Presents the work of the team of European social psychologists that conceptualized and formalized social identity theory. Thorough and detailed, it is important to those who wish to replicate key experiments or to understand the empirical and theoretical foundations of the theory.

_____. *Human Groups and Social Categories.* Cambridge, England: Cambridge University Press, 1981. An easy-to-read account of Tajfel's conceptualization of intergroup conflict, accessible to college students. This book incorporates his early work on prejudice, essays on social perception and categorization, stereotypes, children's images of insiders and outsiders, and social identity theory. Includes both theory and research, emphasizing descriptions of the former. Tajfel provides an extensive bibliography.

Tajfel, Henri, and John Turner. "The Social Identity Theory of Intergroup Behavior." In *Social Psychology of Intergroup Relations*, edited by Stephen Worchel and William G. Austin. 2d ed. Chicago: Nelson-Hall, 1986. An excellent summary of social identity theory. This chapter focuses on the origin and importance of the theory, including intergroup competition and conflict. It offers examples of the concepts and attempts to answer practical questions.

Turner, John C. *Rediscovering the Social Group: A Self-Categorization Theory.* New York: Basil Blackwell, 1987. Turner's book argues for the group as an important social phenomenon and articulates assumptions made about the relationship between the individual and the group in social identity theory. Provides the reader with a valuable backdrop for understanding many of Tajfel's predictions in a readable blend of theoretical and empirical work.

Jaclyn Rodriguez

Cross-References

Aggression: Definitions and Theoretical Explanations, 162; Attributional Biases, 338; Causal Attribution, 487; Groups: Nature and Function, 1125; Theories of Intergroup Relations, 1356; Effects of Prejudice, 1848; Racism, 2037; Self-Esteem, 2188; Social Perception: Others, 2311; Social Schemata, 2329.

SOCIAL LEARNING: ALBERT BANDURA

Type of psychology: Personality
Fields of study: Behavioral and cognitive models; cognitive learning

Albert Bandura's social learning theory, later called social cognitive theory, provides a theoretical framework for understanding and explaining human behavior; the theory embraces an interactional model of causation and accords central roles to cognitive, vicarious, and self-regulatory processes.

Principal terms
DETERMINISM: the doctrine that behavior is caused by events independent of one's will
MODEL: a person whose behavior is imitated by another person
MODELING: giving verbal or written instructions and/or demonstrating a behavior for teaching purposes
OBSERVATIONAL LEARNING: the acquisition of a behavior by imitating someone else's performance (also called vicarious learning)
OUTCOME EXPECTANCIES: the consequences expected to result from an action
RECIPROCAL DETERMINISM: an interactional model proposing that environment, personal factors, and behavior all operate as interacting determinants of one another
REINFORCEMENT: a contingency by which a response produces a desirable consequence, which increases the future probability of that response
SELF-EFFICACY: the perception or judgment of one's ability to perform a certain action successfully

Overview

Social learning theory, later amplified as social cognitive theory by its founder, social psychologist Albert Bandura, provides a unified theoretical framework for analyzing the psychological processes that govern human behavior. Its goal is to explain how behavior develops, how it is maintained, and through what processes it can be modified. It seeks to accomplish this task by identifying the determinants of human action and the mechanisms through which they operate.

Bandura lays out the conceptual framework of his approach in his book *Social Learning Theory* (1977). His theory is based on a model of reciprocal determinism. This means that Bandura rejects both the humanist/existentialist position viewing people as free agents and the behaviorist position viewing behavior as controlled by the environment. Rather, external determinants of behavior (such as rewards and punishments) and internal determinants (such as thoughts, expectations, and beliefs) are considered part of a system of interlocking determinants that influence not only behavior but also the various other parts of the system. In other words, each part of the system—behavior, cognition, and environmental influences—affects each of the other parts. People are neither free agents nor passive reactors to external pressures. Instead, through self-regulatory processes, they have the ability to exercise some measure of control over their own actions. They can affect their behavior by setting goals, arranging environmental inducements, generating cognitive strategies, evaluating goal attainment, and mediating consequences for their actions. Bandura accepts that these self-regulatory functions initially are learned as the result of external rewards and punishments. Their external origin, however, does not invalidate the fact that, once internalized, they in part determine behavior.

As self-regulation results from symbolic processing of information, Bandura in his theorizing has assigned an increasingly prominent role to cognition. This is reflected in his book *Social Foundations of Thought and Action: A Social Cognitive Theory* (1986), in which he no longer refers to his approach as social learning but as social cognitive theory. People, unlike lower animals, use verbal and nonverbal symbols (language and images) to process information and preserve experiences in the form of cognitive representations. This encoded information serves as a guide for future behavior. Without the ability to use symbols, people would have to solve problems by enacting various alternative solutions until, by trial and error, they learned which ones resulted in rewards or punishments. Through their cognitive abilities, however, people can think through different options, imagine possible outcomes, and guide their behavior by anticipated consequences. Symbolic capabilities provide people with a powerful tool to regulate their own behavior in the absence of external reinforcements and punishments.

According to Bandura, the most central of all mechanisms of self-regulation is self-efficacy, defined as the belief that one has the ability, with one's actions, to bring about a certain outcome. Self-efficacy beliefs function as determinants of behavior by influencing motivation, thought processes, and emotions in ways that may be self-aiding or self-hindering. Specifically, self-efficacy appraisals determine the goals people set for themselves, whether they anticipate and visualize scenarios of success or failure, whether they embark on a course of action, how much effort they expend, and how long they persist in the face of obstacles. Self-efficacy expectations are different from outcome expectations. While outcome expectancies are beliefs that a given behavior will result in a certain outcome, self-efficacy refers to the belief in one's ability to bring about this outcome. To put it simply, people may believe that something can happen, but whether they embark on a course of action depends on their perceived ability to make it happen.

Perhaps the most important contribution of social learning theory to the understanding of human behavior is the concept of vicarious, or observational, learning, also termed learning through modeling. Before the advent of social learning theory, many psychologists assigned a crucial role to the process of reinforcement in learning. They postulated that without performing responses that are followed by reinforcement or punishment, a person cannot learn. In contrast, Bandura asserted that much of social behavior is not learned from the consequences of trial and error but is acquired through symbolic modeling. People watch what other people do and what happens to them as a result of their actions. From such observations, they form ideas of how to perform new behaviors, and later this information guides their actions.

Symbolic modeling is of great significance for human learning because of its enormous efficiency in transmitting information. Whereas trial-and-error learning requires the gradual shaping of the behavior of individuals through repetition and reinforcement, in observational learning, a single model can teach complex behaviors simultaneously to any number of people. According to Bandura, some elaborate and specifically human behavior patterns, such as language, might even be impossible to learn if it were not for symbolic modeling. For example, it seems unlikely that children learn to talk as a result of their parents' reinforcing each correct utterance they emit. Rather, children probably hear and watch other members of their verbal community talk and then imitate their behavior. In a similar vein, complex behaviors such as driving a car or flying a plane are not acquired by trial and error. Instead, prospective drivers or pilots follow the verbal rules of an instructor until they master the task.

In summary, Bandura's social learning theory explains human action in terms of the interplay among behavior, cognition, and environmental influences. The theory places particular emphasis on cognitive mediating factors such as self-efficacy beliefs and outcome expectancies. Its greatest contribution to a general theory of human learning has been its emphasis on learning by observation or modeling. Observational learning has achieved the status of a third learning principle, next to classical and operant conditioning.

Applications

From its inception, social learning theory has served as a useful framework for the understanding of both normal and abnormal human behavior. A major contribution that has important implications for the modification of human behavior is the theory's distinction between learning and performance. In a now-classic series of experiments, Bandura and his associates teased apart the roles of observation and reinforcement in learning and were able to demonstrate that people learn through mere observation.

In a study on aggression, an adult model hit and kicked a life-size inflated clown doll (a "Bobo" doll), with children watching the attack in person or on a television screen. Other children watched the model perform some innocuous behavior. Later, the children were allowed to play in the room with the Bobo doll. All children who had witnessed the aggression, either in person or on television, viciously attacked the doll, while those who had observed the model's innocuous behavior did not display aggression toward the doll. Moreover, it was clearly shown that the children modeled their aggressive behaviors after the adult. Those who had observed the adult sit on the doll and hit its face, or kick the doll, or use a hammer to pound it, imitated exactly these behaviors. Thus, the study accomplished its purpose by demonstrating that observational learning occurs in the absence of direct reinforcement.

In a related experiment, Bandura showed that expected consequences, while not relevant for learning, play a role in performance. A group of children watched a film of an adult model behaving aggressively toward a Bobo doll and being punished, while another group observed the same behavior with the person being rewarded. When the children subsequently were allowed to play with the Bobo doll, those who had watched the model being punished displayed fewer aggressive behaviors toward the doll than those who had seen the model being rewarded. When the experimenter then offered a reward to the children for imitating the model, however, all children, regardless of the consequences they had observed, attacked the Bobo doll. This showed that all children had learned the aggressive behavior from the model but that observing the model being punished served as an inhibiting factor, which was removed by the promise of a reward. Again, this study showed that children learn without reinforcement, simply by observing how others behave. Whether they then engage in the behavior, however, depends on the consequences they expect will result from their actions.

Models not only teach people novel ways of thinking and behaving but also can strengthen or weaken inhibitions. Seeing models punished may inhibit similar behavior in observers, while seeing models carry out feared or forbidden actions without negative consequences may reduce their inhibitions.

The most striking demonstrations of the disinhibitory effects of observational learning come from therapeutic interventions based on modeling principles. Bandura, in his book *Principles of Behavior Modification* (1969), shows how social learning theory can provide a conceptual framework for the modification of a wide range of maladaptive behaviors. For example, a large number of laboratory studies of subjects with a severe phobia of snakes showed that phobic individuals can overcome their fear of reptiles when fearless adult models demonstrate how to handle a snake and directly assist subjects in coping successfully with whatever they dread.

In later elaborations, the scope of social learning theory was amplified to include self-efficacy theory. Self-efficacy is now considered the principal mechanism of behavior change, in that all successful interventions are assumed to operate by strengthening a person's self-perceived efficacy to cope with difficulties.

How can self-efficacy be strengthened? Research indicates that it is influenced by four sources of information. The most important influence comes from performance attainments, with successes heightening and failures lowering perceived self-efficacy. Thus, having people enact and master a difficult task most powerfully increases their efficacy percepts. A second influence comes from vicarious experiences. Exposing people to models works because seeing people similar to oneself successfully perform a difficult task raises one's own efficacy expectations. Verbal persuasion is a third way of influencing self-efficacy. Convincing people that they have the ability to perform a task can encourage them to try harder, which indeed may lead to successful performance. Finally, teaching people coping strategies to lower emotional arousal can also increase self-efficacy. If subsequently they approach a task more calmly, the likelihood of succeeding at it may increase.

Bandura and his associates conducted a series of studies to test the idea that vastly different modes of influence all improve coping behavior by strengthening self-perceived efficacy. Severe snake phobics received interventions based on enactive, vicarious, cognitive, or emotive treatment modalities. The results confirmed that the degree to which people changed their behavior toward the reptiles was closely associated with increases in self-judged efficacy, regardless of the method of intervention. It is now widely accepted among social learning theorists that all effective therapies ultimately work by strengthening people's self-percepts of efficacy.

Context

Social learning theory was born into a climate in which two competing and diametrically opposed schools of thought dominated psychology. On the one hand, psychologists who advocated psychodynamic theories postulated that human behavior is governed by motivational forces operating in the form of largely unconscious needs, drives, and impulses. These impulse theories tended to give circular explanations, attributing behavior to inner causes that were inferred from the very behavior they were supposed to cause. They also tended to provide explanations after the fact, rather than predicting events, and had very limited empirical support.

On the other hand, there were various types of behavior theory that shifted the focus of the causal analysis from hypothetical internal determinants of behavior to external, publicly observable causes. Behaviorists were able to show that actions commonly attributed to inner causes could be produced, eliminated, and reinstated by manipulating the antecedent (stimulus) and consequent (reinforcing) conditions of the person's external environment. This led to the proposition that people's behavior is caused by factors residing in the environment.

Social learning theory presents a theory of human behavior that to some extent incorporates both viewpoints. According to Bandura, people are neither driven by inner forces nor buffeted by environmental stimuli; instead, psychological functioning is best explained in terms of a continuous reciprocal interaction of internal and external causes. This assumption, termed reciprocal determinism, became one of the dominant viewpoints in psychology.

An initial exposition of social learning theory was presented in Albert Bandura and Richard H. Walters' text *Social Learning and Personality Development* (1963). This formulation drew heavily on the procedures and principles of operant and classical conditioning. In his book *Principles of Behavior Modification*, Bandura placed much greater emphasis on symbolic events and self-regulatory processes. He argued that complex human behavior could not be satisfactorily explained by the narrow set of learning principles behaviorists had derived from animal studies. He incorporated principles derived from developmental, social, and cognitive psychology into social learning theory.

During the 1970's, psychology had grown increasingly cognitive. This development was reflected in Bandura's 1977 book, *Social Learning Theory*, which presented self-efficacy theory as the central mechanism through which people control their own behavior. Over the following decade, the influence of cognitive psychology on Bandura's work grew stronger. In his book *Social Foundations of Thought and Action: A Social Cognitive Theory*, he finally disavowed his roots in learning theory and renamed his approach "social cognitive theory." This theory accorded central roles to cognitive, vicarious, self-reflective, and self-regulatory processes.

Social learning/social cognitive theory became the dominant conceptual approach within the field of behavior therapy. It has provided the conceptual framework for numerous interventions for a wide variety of psychological disorders and probably will remain popular for a long time. Its founder, Albert Bandura, was honored with the Award for Distinguished Scientific Contributions to Psychology from the American Psychological Foundation in 1980 in recognition of his work.

Bibliography

Bandura, Albert. *Principles of Behavior Modification.* New York: Holt, Rinehart and Winston, 1969. Presents an overview of basic psychological principles governing human behavior within the conceptual framework of social learning. Reviews theoretical and empirical advances in the field of social learning, placing special emphasis on self-regulation and on symbolic and vicarious processes. Applies these principles to the conceptualization and modification of a number of common behavior disorders such as alcoholism, phobias, and sexual deviancy.

_____. *Social Foundations of Thought and Action: A Social Cognitive Theory.* Englewood Cliffs, N.J.: Prentice-Hall, 1986. Presents a comprehensive coverage of the tenets of current social cognitive theory. Besides addressing general issues of human nature and causality, provides an impressive in-depth analysis of all important aspects of human functioning, including motivational, cognitive, and self-regulatory processes.

_____. *Social Learning Theory.* Englewood Cliffs, N.J.: Prentice-Hall, 1977. Lays out Bandura's theory and presents a concise overview of its theoretical and experimental contributions to the field of social learning. Redefines many of the traditional concepts of learning theory and emphasizes the importance of cognitive processes in human learning.

Evans, Richard I. *Albert Bandura, the Man and His Ideas: A Dialogue.* New York: Praeger, 1989. An edited version of an interview with Bandura. Easy to read, presenting Bandura's thoughts on the major aspects of his work in a very accessible form. The spontaneity of the discussion between Evans and Bandura gives a glimpse of Bandura as a person.

Rotgers, Frederick. "Social-Learning Theory, Philosophy of Science, and the Identity of Behavior Therapy." In *Paradigms in Behavior Therapy: Present and Promise*, edited by Daniel B. Fishman, Frederick Rotgers, and Cyril M. Franks. New York: Springer-Verlag, 1988. Places Bandura's social learning theory in the context of contemporary behavior theory and examines its philosophical roots. Difficult because it requires some basic understanding of the philosophy of science, but provides an excellent analysis of the philosophical underpinnings of Bandura's theory.

Schultz, Duane. *Theories of Personality.* 4th ed. Pacific Grove, Calif.: Brooks/Cole, 1990. Chapter 15 of this book contains an excellent summary of Bandura's work. Gives an easy-to-read overview of his philosophical position (reciprocal determinism), discusses his theory (including observational learning and self-regulatory processes), and presents a summary of relevant research conducted within the framework of social cognitive theory. An ideal starting point for anyone who would like to become familiar with Bandura's work.

Edelgard Wulfert

Cross-References

SOCIAL PERCEPTION: OTHERS

Type of psychology: Social psychology
Fields of study: Interpersonal relations; social perception and cognition

Social perception deals with how people think about and make sense of other people—how they form impressions, draw conclusions, and try to explain other people's behavior. Sometimes called social cognition or the study of "naïve psychology," social perception focuses on factors that influence the way in which people understand other people and on how people process, organize, and recall information about others.

Principal terms

ACTOR-OBSERVER BIAS: the tendency to infer that other people's behavior is caused by dispositional factors but that one's own behavior is the product of situational causes

CAUSAL ATTRIBUTION: an inference or conclusion about what caused another person's behavior

CORRESPONDENCE BIAS or FUNDAMENTAL ATTRIBUTION ERROR: the tendency to underestimate the role of situational factors and to overestimate the role of dispositions in explaining behavior that is actually caused by situational factors

DISCOUNTING: reducing the role of a particular cause in producing a behavior because of the presence of other plausible causes

DISPOSITION: a quality, attribute, or trait that distinguishes one person from another

PRIMACY EFFECT: the tendency for things that are seen or received first to be more influential than things that come later

PRIMING: the process (usually indirect) of bringing something to mind

SCHEMA (pl. SCHEMATA): a mental structure that organizes information and expectations about people, objects, and events

SELF-FULFILLING PROPHECY: the tendency to behave in ways that make one's initially incorrect beliefs about others come true

Overview

Social perception deals with two general classes of cognitive-perceptual processes through which people process, organize, and recall information about others. Those that deal with how people form impressions of other people's personalities (called person perception) form the first class. The second class includes those processes that deal with how people use this information to draw conclusions about other people's motivations, intentions, and emotions in order to explain and predict their behavior (called attribution processes). This importance of social perception in social psychology is revealed in the fact that one's impressions and judgments about others, whether accurate or not, can have profound effects on one's own and others' behavior.

People are naturally motivated to understand and predict the behavior of those around them. Being able to predict and understand the social world gives people a sense of mastery and control over their environment. Psychologists who study social perception have shown that people try to make sense of their social worlds by determining whether other people's behavior is produced by a disposition—some internal quality or trait unique to a person—or by something in the situation or environment. The process of making such determinations, which is called causal attribution, was developed by social psychologists Fritz Heider, Edward Jones and Keith Davis, and Harold Kelley in the late 1950's and early 1960's.

According to these attribution theorists, when one decides that a person's behavior reflects a disposition (when, for example, one decides that a person is friendly because he acted friendly), one has made an internal or dispositional attribution. In contrast, when one decides that a person's behavior was caused by something in the situation—he acted in a friendly way to make someone like him—one has made an external or situational attribution. The attributions one makes for others' behaviors carry considerable influence in the impressions one forms of them and in how one will behave toward them in the future.

Unfortunately, people's impressions and attributions are not always accurate. For example, in many situations, people seem to be inclined to believe that other people's behavior is caused by dispositional factors. At the same time, they believe that their own behavior is the product of situational causes. This tendency has been called the actor-observer bias. Moreover, when people try to explain the causes of other people's behavior, especially behavior that is clearly and obviously caused by situational factors (factors such as a coin flip, a dice roll, or some other situational inducement), they tend to underestimate situational influences and overestimate the role of dispositional causes. This tendency is referred to as correspondence bias or the fundamental attribution error. In other words, people prefer to explain other people's behavior in terms of their traits or personalities rather than in terms of situational factors, even when situational factors actually caused the behavior.

In addition to these biases, social psychologists have examined other ways in which people's impressions of others and inferences about the causes of their behavior can be inaccurate or biased. In their work, for example, psychologists Daniel Kahneman and Amos Tversky have described a number of simple but efficient thinking strategies, or "rules of thumb," called heuristics. The availability heuristic is the tendency to explain behaviors on the basis of causes that are easily or quickly brought to mind. Similarly, the representativeness heuristic is the tendency to believe that a person who possesses characteristics that are associated with a social group probably belongs to that group. Although heuristics make social thinking more efficient and yield reasonable results most of the time, they can sometimes lead to significant judgment errors.

Bias can also arise in social perception in a number of other ways. Because of the enormous amount of social information that they must process at any given moment, people have developed various ways of organizing, categorizing, and simplifying this information and the expectations they have about various people, objects, and events. These organizational structures are called schemata. For example, schemata that organize information about people's membership in different categories or groups are called stereotypes or prototypes. Schemata that organize information about how traits go together in forming a person's personality are called implicit personality theories (IPTs). Although schemata, like heuristics, help make social thinking more efficient and yield reasonable results most of the time, they can also sometimes lead to significant judgment errors, such as prejudice and discrimination.

Finally, social perception can be influenced by a variety of factors of which people are unaware but which can exert tremendous influence on their thinking. Social psychologist Solomon Asch was the first to describe the primacy effect in impression formation. The primacy effect is the tendency for things that are seen or received first to have a greater impact on one's thinking than things that come later. Many other things in the environment can prime one, or make one "ready," to see, interpret, or remember things that one might not otherwise have seen, thought about, or remembered. Priming occurs when something in the environment makes certain things easier to bring to mind.

During the 1970's and 1980's, social psychologists made numerous alterations and extensions of the existing theories of attribution and impression formation to keep pace with the field's growing emphasis on mental (cognitive) and emotional (affective) processes. These changes focused primarily on incorporating work from cognitive psychology on memory processes, the use of schemata, and the interplay of emotion, motivation, and cognition.

Applications

Social psychologists have argued that many social problems have their roots in social perception processes. Because social perception biases can sometimes result in inaccurate perceptions, misunderstandings, conflict between people and groups, and other negative consequences, social psychologists have spent much time and effort trying to understand them. Their hope is that by understanding such biases they will be able to suggest solutions for them. For example, in a number of experiments, social psychologists have attempted to understand the social perception processes that may lead to stereotyping, which can result in prejudice and discrimination.

For example, one explanation for why stereotypes are so hard to change once they have been formed is the self-fulfilling prophecy. Self-fulfilling prophecies occur when one has possibly inaccurate beliefs about others (such as stereotypes) and acts on those beliefs, bringing about the conditions necessary to make those beliefs come true. In other words, when one expects something to be true about another person (especially negative things), one frequently looks for and finds what one expects to see. At other times, one actually brings out the negative (or positive) qualities one expects to be present. In a classic 1968 study by social psychologists Robert Rosenthal and Lenore Jacobsen, for example, children whose teachers expected them to show a delayed but substantial increase in their intelligence (on the basis of a fictitious intelligence test) actually scored higher on a legitimate intelligence quotient (IQ) test administered at the end of the school year. Presumably, the teachers' expectations of those students caused them to treat those students in ways that actually helped them perform better. Similarly, social psychologists Rebecca Curtis and Kim Miller have shown that when people think someone they meet likes them, they act in ways that lead that person to like them. If, however, people think a person dislikes them, they act in ways that actually make that person dislike them.

The behaviors that produce self-fulfilling prophecies can be subtle. For example, in 1974, social psychologists Carl Word, Mark Zanna, and Joel Cooper demonstrated that the subtle behaviors of interviewers during job interviews can make applicants believe that they performed either poorly or very well. These feelings, in turn, can lead to actual good or poor performance on the part of the applicants. What was most striking about this study, however, was that the factor that led to the subtle negative or positive behaviors was the interviewers' stereotypes of the applicants' racial group membership. Black applicants received little eye contact from interviewers and were not engaged in conversation; the behaviors displayed by interviewers in the presence of white applicants were exactly the opposite. Not surprisingly, black applicants were seen as less qualified and were less likely to be hired. Clearly, subtle behaviors produced by racial stereotypes can have major consequences for the targets of those stereotypes.

The relevance of social perception processes to everyday life is not restricted to stereotyping, although stereotyping is indeed an important concern. In academic settings, for example, situational factors can lead teachers to form impressions of students that have little bearing on their actual abilities. Social psychologist Edward Jones and his colleagues have examined the way in which primacy effects operate in academic settings. Two groups of subjects saw a student perform on a test. One group saw the student start out strong and then begin to do poorly. The other group saw the student start out poorly and then begin to improve. For both groups, the student's performance on the test was identical, and the student received the same score. The group that saw the student start out strong and then falter thought the student was brighter than the student who started out poorly and then improved. Clearly, first impressions matter.

Finally, research on the correspondence bias makes it clear that one must be very careful when trying to understand what people are like. In many situations, the demands of people's occupations or their family roles force them to do things with which they may not actually agree. Substantial research has shown that observers will probably think these persons have personalities that are consistent with their behaviors. Lawyers, who must defend people who may have broken the law, debaters, who must argue convincingly for or against a particular point of view, and actors, who must play parts that they did not write, are all vulnerable to being judged on the basis of their behavior. Lawyers may not actually believe that their clients are innocent, but must defend them as though they do. Debaters often argue for positions with which they do not agree. Actors play roles that do not match their personalities. Unless one is particularly sensitive to the fact that, when they are doing their jobs, these persons' behaviors do not reveal anything about their true personalities, one may actually (and incorrectly) believe that they do.

Context

The study of social perception has multiple origins that can be traced back to a number of influential researchers and theorists. It was one of the first topics to be emphasized when the modern study of social psychology began during World War II. Current perspectives on social perception processes can be traced to the early work of Solomon Asch, a social psychologist who emigrated to the United States before the war. His work yielded important demonstrations of primacy effects in impression formation.

Also important to the development of an understanding of social perception was the work of Fritz Heider, another German émigré, who came to the United States as World War II was ending in Europe. Heider's influential book *The Psychology of Interpersonal Relations* (1958) arguably started the cognitive approach to social perception processes. In many circles, it is still regarded as a watershed of ideas and insights on person perception and attribution.

Perhaps the most important historical development leading up to the modern study of social perception, however, was the work of Jerome Bruner and other "new look" cognitive psychologists. Following World War II, a number of psychologists broke with the then traditional behaviorist/learning theory perspective and applied a Gestalt perspective to human perception. They emphasized the subjective nature of perception and interpretation and argued that both cognition (thinking) and situational context are important in determining "what" it is that a person perceives. Using ambiguous figures, for example, they demonstrated that the same object can be described in many different ways depending on the context in which it is seen. One of Bruner's students, Edward Jones, has made significant contributions to the understanding of attribution and interpersonal perception during his career.

The perspectives offered by all these theorists share some common themes. First, they all acknowledged that social perception is inherently subjective; the most important aspect of understanding people is not what is "true" in an objective sense, but rather what is believed to be true. Second, they acknowledged that people think about other people and want to understand why people do the things they do. Finally, they believed that some general principles govern the ways in which people approach social perception and judgment, and they set out to demonstrate these principles scientifically.

During the 1960's and 1970's, social perception research experienced unprecedented attention and enthusiasm. Attribution theories were developed and refined, and in the 1970's cognitive psychology's influence on the field began to grow. In the future, social perception research and theory will continue to focus on basic theoretical problems (such as cognitive processes and the role of emotion in perception and cognition) that have substantial social applications (such as finding solutions to the problems posed by prejudice and misperception). Understanding the broader scope of human social perception—the interplay of complex thinking "systems"— will no doubt become a priority as the field attempts to deal more comprehensively with the enduring mystery of how to understand what makes people tick.

Bibliography

Eiser, J. Richard. *Social Judgment.* Pacific Grove, Calif.: Brooks/Cole, 1991. Presents a detailed and broad overview of topics in social judgment, including categorization, the effects of emotion on judgment, causal attribution, and other issues. Describes major theories and research in detail, and provides useful context within which to understand social perception's importance in everyday life.

Heider, Fritz. *The Psychology of Interpersonal Relations.* New York: John Wiley & Sons, 1958. This classic text presents Heider's attribution and balance theories as well as a number of ideas that were to influence the field for more than twenty years; intended for advanced college students and graduate students.

Jones, Edward Ellsworth. *Interpersonal Perception.* New York: W. H. Freeman, 1990. Presents a detailed overview and review of topics including impression formation, emotion perception, causal attribution, and attributional biases. Describes major theories and research in detail, and provides useful context within which to understand social perception's importance in everyday life. Available in paperback; engagingly written.

Jones, Edward Ellsworth, et al. *Social Stigma: The Psychology of Marked Relationships.* New York: W. H. Freeman, 1984. A collection of notable social psychologists collaborated on this book while they were all Fellows at the Center for Advanced Study in the Behavioral Sciences at Stanford University. It presents a broad selection of work (both empirical and theoretical) on stigma and its effects on social perception and judgment.

Kahneman, Daniel, et al. *Judgment Under Uncertainty: Heuristics and Biases.* Cambridge, England: Cambridge University Press, 1982. A volume that presents a broad selection of work (both empirical and theoretical) on heuristics and biases in social perception and judgment. It is an advanced book and quite dense, but it is probably the best collection of articles on the topic. Available in paperback.

Schneider, David J., Albert H. Hastorf, and Phoebe C. Ellsworth. *Person Perception.* 2d ed. Reading, Mass.: Addison-Wesley, 1979. Provides a detailed description of person perception research and theory. Available in paperback, this book will appeal to college students and to others with a serious interest in the topic.

Shaver, Kelly G. *An Introduction to Attribution Processes.* Cambridge, Mass.: Winthrop, 1975. Reprint. Hillsdale, N.J.: Lawrence Erlbaum, 1983. Provides a thorough description and analysis of attribution theory and research up to 1975. Unfortunately, the book has not been updated to include more recent developments and advances, but it is a good primer of basic theoretical and conceptual issues.

Zebrowitz, L. A. *Social Perception.* Pacific Grove, Calif.: Brooks/Cole, 1990. Presents a detailed and broad overview of topics in social perception, including impression formation, emotion perception, causal attribution, and attributional biases. Describes major theories and research in detail, and provides useful context within which to understand social perception's importance in everyday life. Available in paperback, this book will appeal to college students and those who have a serious interest in the topic.

John H. Fleming

Cross-References

SOCIAL PSYCHOLOGICAL MODELS: ERICH FROMM

Type of psychology: Personality
Fields of study: Humanistic-phenomenological models; psychodynamic and
neoanalytic models

*Erich Fromm studied the effects of political, economic, and religious institutions
on human personality. Fromm's work provides powerful insights into the causes of
human unhappiness and psychopathology as well as ideas about how individuals
and social institutions could change to maximize mental health and happiness.*

Principal terms
DYNAMIC ADAPTATION: changes in thoughts, feelings, and/or behaviors
that have enduring consequences for an individual's personality
ESCAPE FROM FREEDOM: the unconscious adoption of personality traits
that reduce anxiety at the expense of one's individuality
FREEDOM FROM: freedom from external constraints such as prison,
hunger, and homelessness
FREEDOM TO: freedom to maximize individual potential through
productive love and productive work
MENTAL HEALTH: to Fromm, this means maximizing individual potential
PERSONALITY: the manner in which individuals dynamically adapt to
physical and social circumstances in order to survive and reduce
anxiety
PRODUCTIVE LOVE: interpersonal relationships based on mutual trust,
respect, and cooperation
PRODUCTIVE WORK: daily activities that allow creative expression and
engender self-esteem

Overview

The approach of Erich Fromm (1900-1980) to the study of human personality
starts from an evolutionary perspective. Specifically, Fromm maintained that humans, like all other living creatures, are motivated to survive and that survival requires adaptation to their physical surroundings. Humans are, however, unique in
that they substantially alter their physical surroundings through the creation and maintenance of cultural institutions. Consequently, Fromm believed that human adaptation is primarily in response to the demands of political, economic, and religious
institutions.

Fromm made a distinction between adaptations to physical and social surroundings that have no enduring impact on personality (static adaptation—for example,
an American learning to drive on the left side of the road in England) and adaptation
that does have an enduring impact on personality (dynamic adaptation—for example, a child who becomes humble and submissive in response to a brutally domineer-
ing, egomaniacal parent). Fromm consequently defines personality as the manner in

which individuals dynamically adapt to their physical and social surroundings in order to survive and reduce anxiety.

Human adaptation includes the reduction of anxiety for two reasons. First, because humans are born in a profoundly immature and helplessly dependent state, they are especially prone to anxiety, which, although unpleasant, is useful to the extent that it results in signs of distress (such as crying) which alert others and elicit their assistance. Second, infants eventually mature into fully self-conscious human beings who, although no longer helpless and dependent, recognize their ultimate mortality and essential isolation from all other living creatures.

Fromm believed that humans have five basic inorganic needs (as opposed to organic needs associated with physical survival) resulting from the anxiety associated with human immaturity at birth and eventual self-consciousness. The need for relatedness refers to the innate desire to acquire and maintain social relationships. The need for transcendence suggests that human beings have an inherent drive to become creative individuals. The need for rootedness consists of a sense of belonging to a social group. The need for identity is the need to be a unique individual. The need for a frame of orientation refers to a stable and consistent way of perceiving the world.

Mental health for Fromm consists of realizing one's own unique individual potential, and it requires two kinds of freedom that are primarily dependent on the structure of a society's political, economic, and religious institutions. Freedom from external constraints refers to practical concerns such as freedom from imprisonment, hunger, and homelessness. This is how many people commonly conceive of the notion of freedom. For Fromm, freedom from external constraints is necessary, but not sufficient, for optimal mental health, which also requires the freedom to maximize one's individual potential.

Freedom to maximize individual potential entails productive love and productive work. Productive love consists of interpersonal relationships based on mutual trust, respect, and cooperation. Productive work refers to daily activities that allow for creative expression and provide self-esteem. Fromm hypothesized that people become anxious and insecure if their need for transcendence is thwarted by a lack of productive work and love. Many people, he believed, respond to anxiety and insecurity by an "escape from freedom": the unconscious adoption of personality traits that reduce anxiety and insecurity at the expense of individual identity.

Fromm described five personality types representing an escape from freedom. The authoritarian type reduces anxiety and insecurity by fusing himself or herself with another person or a religious, political, or economic institution. Fromm distinguished between sadistic and masochistic authoritarians: The sadistic type needs to dominate (and often hurt and humiliate) others, while the masochistic type needs to submit to the authority of others. The sadist and the masochist are similar in that they share a pathetic dependence on each other. Fromm used the people in Nazi Germany (masochists) under Adolf Hitler (a sadist) to illustrate the authoritarian personality type.

Destructive individuals reduce anxiety and insecurity by destroying other persons or things. Fromm suggested that ideally people derive satisfaction and security through constructive endeavors, but noted that some people lack the skill and motivation to create, and therefore engage in destructive behavior as an impoverished substitute for constructive activities.

Withdrawn individuals reduce anxiety and insecurity by willingly or unwillingly refusing to participate in a socially prescribed conception of reality; instead, they withdraw into their own idiosyncratic versions of reality. In one social conception, for example, many devout Christians believe that God created the earth in six days, that Christ was born approximately two thousand years ago, and that He has not yet returned to earth. The withdrawn individual might singularly believe that the earth was hatched from the egg of a giant bird a few years ago and that Christ had been seen eating a hamburger yesterday. Psychiatrists and clinicians today would generally characterize the withdrawn individual as psychotic or schizophrenic.

Self-inflated people reduce anxiety and insecurity by unconsciously adopting glorified images of themselves as superhuman individuals who are vastly superior to others. They are arrogant, strive to succeed at the expense of others, are unable to accept constructive criticism, and avoid experiences that might disconfirm their false conceptions of themselves.

Finally, Fromm characterized American society in the 1940's as peopled by automaton conformists, who reduce anxiety and insecurity by unconsciously adopting the thoughts and feelings demanded of them by their culture. They are then no longer anxious and insecure, because they are like everyone else around them. According to Fromm, automaton conformists are taught to distrust and repress their own thoughts and feelings during childhood through impoverished and demoralizing educational and socializing experiences. The result is the acquisition of pseudo-thoughts and pseudo-feelings, which people believe to be their own but which are actually socially infused. For example, Fromm contended that most Americans vote the same way that their parents do, although very few would claim that parental preference was the cause of their political preferences. Rather, most American voters would claim that their decisions are the result of a thorough and rational consideration of genuine issues (a pseudo-thought) instead of a mindless conformity to parental influence (a genuine thought—or, in this case, a nonthought).

Applications

In *Escape from Freedom* (1941), Fromm applied his theory of personality to a historical account of personality types by a consideration of how political, economic, and religious changes in Western Europe from the Middle Ages to the twentieth century affected "freedom from" and "freedom to." Fromm argued that the feudal political system of the Middle Ages engendered very little freedom from external constraints. Specifically, there was limited physical mobility; the average person died in the same place that he or she was born, and many people were indentured servants who could not leave their feudal lord even if they had somewhere to go. Additionally, there was no choice of occupation: One's job was generally inherited from one's father.

Despite the lack of freedom from external constraints, however, economic and religious institutions provided circumstances that fostered freedom to maximize individual potential through productive work and productive love. Economically, individual craftsmanship was the primary means by which goods were produced. Although this was time-consuming and inefficient by modern standards, craftsmen were responsible for the design and production of entire products. A shoemaker would choose the design and materials, make the shoes, and sell the shoes. A finished pair of shoes thus represented a tangible manifestation of the creative energies of the producer, thus providing productive work.

Additionally, the crafts were regulated by the guild system, which controlled access to apprenticeships and materials and set wages and prices in order to guarantee maximum employment and a fair profit to the craftsmen. The guilds encouraged relatively cooperative behavior between craftsmen and consequently engendered productive love. Productive love was also sustained by the moral precepts of the then-dominant Catholic church, which stressed the essential goodness of humankind, the idea that human beings had free will to choose their behavior on Earth and hence influence their ultimate fate after death, the need to be responsible for the welfare of others, and the sinfulness of extracting excessive profits from commerce and accumulating money beyond that which is necessary to exist comfortably.

The dissolution of the feudal system and the consequent transition to parliamentary democracy and capitalism provided the average individual with a historically unprecedented amount of freedom from external constraints. Physical mobility increased dramatically as the descendants of serfs were able to migrate freely to cities to seek employment of their choosing; however, according to Fromm, increased freedom from external constraints was acquired at the expense of the circumstances necessary for freedom to maximize individual potential through productive work and productive love.

Capitalism shifted the focus of commerce from small towns to large cities and stimulated the development of fast and efficient means of production, but assembly-line production methods divested the worker of opportunities for creative expression. The assembly-line worker has no control over the design of a product, does not engage in the entire production of the product, and has nothing to do with the sale and distribution of the product. Workers in a modern automobile factory might put on hub caps or install radios for eight hours each day as cars roll by on the assembly line. They have no control over the process of production and no opportunity for creative expression, given the monotonous and repetitive activities to which their job confines them.

In addition to the loss of opportunities to engage in productive work, the inherent competitiveness of capitalism undermined the relatively cooperative interpersonal relationships engendered by the guild system, transforming the stable small-town economic order into a frenzied free-for-all in which people compete with their neighbors for the resources necessary to survive, hence dramatically reducing opportunities for people to acquire and maintain productive love. Additionally, these economic changes were supported by the newly dominant Protestant churches (represented by the teachings of John Calvin and Martin Luther), which stressed the inherent evilness of humankind, the lack of free will, and the notion of predetermination—the idea that God had already decided prior to one's birth if one is to be consigned to heaven or hell after death. Despite the absence of free will and the idea that an individual's fate was predetermined, Protestant theologians claimed that people could get a sense of God's intentions by their material success on Earth, thus encouraging people to work very hard to accumulate as much as possible (the so-called Protestant work ethic) as an indication that God's countenance is shining upon them.

In summary, Fromm argued that the average person in Western industrial democracies has freedom from external constraints but lacks opportunities to maximize individual potential through productive love and productive work; the result is pervasive feelings of anxiety and insecurity. Most people respond to this anxiety and insecurity by unconsciously adopting personality traits that reduce anxiety and insecurity, but at the expense of their individuality, which Fromm referred to as an escape from freedom. For Fromm, psychopathology is the general result of the loss of individuality associated with an escape from freedom. The specific manifestation of psychopathology depends on the innate characteristics of the individual in conjunction with the demands of the person's social environment.

Fromm argued that while escaping from freedom is a typical response to anxiety and insecurity, it is not an inevitable one. Instead, he urged people to embrace positive freedom through the pursuit of productive love and work, which he claimed would require both individual and social change. Individually, Fromm advocated a life of spontaneous exuberance made possible by love and being loved. He described the play of children and the behavior of artists as illustrations of this kind of lifestyle. Socially, Fromm believed strongly that the fundamental tenets of democracy should be retained but that capitalism in its present form must be modified to ensure every person's right to live, to distribute resources more equitably, and to provide opportunities to engage in productive work.

Context

Fromm's ideas reflect the scientific traditions of his time as well as his extensive training in history and philosophy, in addition to his psychological background. Fromm is considered a neo-Freudian (along with Karen Horney, Harry Stack Sullivan, and others) because of his acceptance of some of Freud's basic ideas (specifically, the role of unconsciously motivated behaviors in human affairs and the notion that anxiety-producing inclinations are repressed or prevented from entering conscious awareness) while rejecting Freud's reliance on the role of biological instincts (sex and aggression) for understanding human behavior. Instead, the neo-Freudians were explicitly concerned with the influence of the social environment on personality development.

Additionally, Fromm was very much influenced by Charles Darwin's theory of evolution, by existential philosophy, and by the economic and social psychological ideas of Karl Marx. Fromm's use of adaptation in the service of survival to define personality is derived from basic evolutionary theory. His analysis of the sources of human anxiety, especially the awareness of death and perception of isolation and aloneness, is extracted from existential philosophy. The notion that human happiness requires productive love and work and that capitalism is antithetical to mental health was originally proposed by Marx. Fromm's work has never received the attention that it deserves in America because of his open affinity for some of Marx's ideas and his insistence that economic change is utterly necessary to ameliorate the unhappiness and mental illness that pervade American society. Nevertheless, his ideas are vitally important from both a theoretical and practical perspective.

Bibliography

Becker, Ernest. *The Birth and Death of Meaning.* 2d ed. New York: Free Press, 1971. Becker presents a general description of Fromm's ideas embedded in a broad interdisciplinary consideration of human social psychological behavior.

Fromm, Erich. *Anatomy of Human Destructiveness.* New York: Holt, Rinehart and Winston, 1973. An in-depth examination of the destructive personality type.

_____. *The Art of Loving.* New York: Harper, 1956. A detailed analysis of how to love and be loved. Distinguishes between genuine love and morbid dependency.

_____. *Escape from Freedom.* New York: Farrar & Rinehart, 1941. Fromm's early seminal work, in which his basic theory about the relationship between political, economic, and religious institutions and personality development was originally articulated. All of Fromm's later books are extensions of ideas expressed here.

_____. *Marx's Concept of Man.* New York: Frederick Ungar, 1961. An introduction to Marx's ideas, including a translation of Marx's economic and philosophical manuscripts of 1844.

_____. *The Revolution of Hope: Toward a Humanized Technology.* New York: Harper & Row, 1968. A detailed discussion of how capital-based economies can be transformed to provide opportunities for productive work without sacrificing productive efficiency, technological advances, or democratic political ideals.

Sheldon Solomon

Cross-References

SOCIAL PSYCHOLOGICAL MODELS: KAREN HORNEY

Type of psychology: Personality
Fields of study: Personality theory; psychodynamic and neoanalytic models;
  psychodynamic therapies

*Karen Horney's social psychoanalytic theory focuses on how human relationships
and cultural conditions influence personality formation; the theory describes how
basic anxiety, resulting from childhood experiences, contributes to the development
of three neurotic, compulsive, rigid personality styles: moving toward others, moving
away from others, and moving against others. Normal personality is characterized
by flexibility and balance among interpersonal styles.*

Principal terms

BASIC ANXIETY: a feeling of insignificance, helplessness, and being
  threatened in a world that is perceived as hostile because of one's
  childhood experiences

EXTERNALIZATION: experiencing unresolved, repressed inner turmoil as
  occurring outside oneself; holding external factors responsible for
  one's problems

IDEALIZED SELF: alienation from the real self that is characterized by
  grandiose, unrealistic conceptions of the self and unattainable
  standards

NEUROSIS: inflexible behaviors and reactions, or discrepancies between
  one's potential and one's achievements

NEUROTIC TRENDS: unconscious, compulsive patterns of neurotic
  behavior that are exhibited through the three patterns of moving
  toward, moving away from, and moving against people

SEARCH FOR GLORY: compulsive and insatiable efforts to fulfill the
  demands of the idealized self

SELF-REALIZATION: development of one's inherent capacities and real self

TYRANNY OF THE SHOULD: rigid or overly difficult inner dictates or
  commands that emerge out of the idealized image

Overview

Karen Horney (1885-1952) spent the major part of her career explaining how personality patterns, especially neurotic patterns, are formed, how they operate, and how they can be changed in order to increase individual potential. In contrast to Sigmund Freud's view that people are guided by instincts and the pleasure principle, Horney proposed that people act out desires to achieve safety and satisfaction in social relationships. She was optimistic about the possibility for human growth and believed that, under conditions of acceptance and care, people move toward self-realization, or the development of their full potential. She wrote almost exclusively, however, about personality problems and methods for solving them.

Horney believed that it is impossible to understand individuals or the mechanisms of neurosis apart from the cultural context in which they exist. Neurosis varies across cultures, as well as within the same culture, and it is influenced by socioeconomic class, gender, and historical period. For example, in *The Neurotic Personality of Our Time* (1937), Horney noted that a person who refuses to accept a salary increase in a Western culture might be seen as neurotic, whereas in a Pueblo Indian culture, this person might be seen as entirely normal.

The neurotic person experiences culturally determined problems in an exaggerated form. In Western culture, competitiveness shapes many neurotic problems because it decreases opportunities for cooperation, fosters a climate of mistrust and hostility, undermines self-esteem, increases isolation, and encourages people to be more concerned with how they appear to others than with fulfilling personal possibilities. It fosters the overvaluing of external success, encourages people to develop grandiose images of superiority, and leads to intensified needs for approval and affection as well as to the distortion of love. Moreover, the ideal of external success is contradicted by the ideal of humility, which leads to further internal conflict and, in many cases, neurosis.

Cultural patterns are replicated and transmitted primarily in family environments. Ideally, a family provides the warmth and nurturance that prepares children to face the world with confidence. When parents have struggled unsuccessfully with the culture, however, they create the conditions that lead to inadequate parenting. In its most extreme form, the competitiveness of the larger culture leads to child abuse, but it can also lead to parents' preoccupation with their own needs, an inability to love and nurture effectively, or a tendency to treat children as extensions of themselves. Rivalry, overprotectiveness, irritability, partiality, and erratic behavior are other manifestations of parental problems.

Within this negative environment, children experience fear and anger, but they also feel weak and helpless beside more powerful adults. They recognize that expressing hostility directly might be dangerous and result in parental reprisals or loss of love. As a result, children repress legitimate anger, banishing it to the unconscious. By using the defense mechanism of reaction formation, they develop emotions toward parents that are the opposite of anger, and they experience feared parents as objects of admiration. Children unconsciously turn their inner fears and anger against themselves and lose touch with their real selves. As a result, they develop basic anxiety, or the feeling of being alone and defenseless in a world that seems hostile.

In order to cope with basic anxiety, individuals use additional defensive strategies or neurotic trends to cope with the world. These involve three primary patterns of behavior: moving away from others, moving toward others, and moving against others. In addition, neurotic individuals develop an idealized self, an unrealistic, flattering distortion of the self-image that encourages people to set unattainable standards, shrink from reality, and compulsively search for glory rather than accept themselves as they are.

Applications

One of Karen Horney's most significant contributions revolved around her practical discussion of three frequently observed constricting behavior patterns that represent neurotic trends. She wrote about these in rich detail in *Our Inner Conflicts: A Constructive Theory of Neurosis* (1945), a highly readable book. The person who moves toward others believes: "If I love you or give in, you will not hurt me." The person who moves against others believes: "If I have power, you will not hurt me." The person who moves away from others thinks: "If I am independent or withdraw from others, they will not hurt me."

The person who moves toward others has chosen a dependent or compliant pattern of coping. The person experiences strong needs for approval, belonging, and affection, and strives to live up to the expectations of others through behavior that is overconsiderate and submissive. This person sees love as the only worthwhile goal in life and represses all competitive, hostile, angry aspects of the self. The moving-against type, who has adopted an aggressive, tough, exploitive style, believes that others are hostile, that life is a struggle, and that the only way to survive is to win and to control others. This person sees herself or himself as strong and determined, and represses all feelings of affection for fear of losing power over others. Finally, the moving-away type, who has adopted a style of detachment and isolation, sees himself or herself as self-sufficient, private, and superior to others. This person represses all emotion and avoids any desire or activity that would result in dependency on others.

The interpersonal patterns that Horney discussed are no longer known as neurotic styles, but as personality disorders. Many of the behaviors that she described can be seen in descriptions of current diagnostic categories that appear in the American Psychiatric Association's *Diagnostic and Statistical Manual of Mental Disorders* (rev. 3d ed., 1987, DSM-III-R), such as dependent personality disorder, narcissistic personality disorder, and obsessive-compulsive personality disorder. Like Horney's original criteria, these categories describe inflexible and maladaptive patterns of behavior and thinking that are displayed in various environments and result in emotional distress and/or impaired functioning.

In her practice of psychoanalysis, Karen Horney used free association and dream analysis to bring unconscious material to light. In contrast to Freud's more passive involvement with patients, she believed that the psychoanalyst should play an active role not only in interpreting behavior but also in inquiring about current behaviors that maintain unproductive patterns, suggesting alternatives, and helping persons mobilize energy to change.

Horney also made psychoanalysis more accessible to the general population. She suggested that, by examining oneself according to the principles outlined in her book *Self-Analysis* (1942), one could increase self-understanding and gain freedom from internal issues that limit one's potential. Her suggestions indicate that a person should choose a problem that one could clearly identify, engage in informal free association about the issue, reflect upon and tentatively interpret the experience, and make specific, simple choices about altering problematic behavior patterns. Complex, long-standing issues, however, should be dealt with in formal psychoanalysis.

Context

Karen Horney was one of the first individuals to criticize Freud's psychology of women. In contrast to Freudian instinct theory, she proposed a version of psychoanalysis that emphasized the role that social relationships and culture play in human development. She questioned the usefulness of Freud's division of the personality into the regions of the id, ego, and superego, and viewed the ego as a more constructive, forward-moving force within the person.

Horney's work was enriched by her contact with psychoanalysts Harry Stack Sullivan, Clara Thompson, and Erich Fromm, who also emphasized the role of interpersonal relationships and sociocultural factors and were members at Horney's American Institute of Psychoanalysis when it was first established. Horney's work also resembled Alfred Adler's personality theory. Her concepts of the search for glory and idealized self are similar to Adler's concepts of superiority striving and the superiority complex. Furthermore, Adler's ruling type resembles the moving-against personality, his getting type is similar to the moving-toward personality, and his avoiding type is closely related to the moving-away personality.

Horney anticipated many later developments within cognitive, humanistic, and feminist personality theory and psychotherapy. Abraham Maslow, who was inspired by Horney, built his concept of self-actualization on Horney's optimistic belief that individuals can move toward self-realization. Carl Rogers' assumptions that problems are based on distortions of real experience and discrepancies between the ideal and real selves are related to Horney's beliefs that unhealthy behavior results from denial of the real self as well as from conflict between the idealized and real selves. In the field of cognitive psychotherapy, Albert Ellis' descriptions of the mechanisms of neurosis resemble Horney's statements. He borrowed the phrase "tyranny of the should" from Horney and placed strong emphasis on how "shoulds" influence irrational, distorted thinking patterns. Finally, Horney's notion that problems are shaped by cultural patterns is echoed in the work of feminist psychotherapists, who believe that individual problems are often the consequence of external, social problems.

Bibliography

Horney, Karen. *Neurosis and Human Growth: The Struggle Toward Self-Realization.* New York: W. W. Norton, 1950. Presents Horney's theory in its final form. Describes the ways in which various neurotic processes operate, including the tyranny of the should, neurotic claims, self-alienation, and self-contempt. Discusses faulty, neurotic solutions that are developed as a way to relieve internal tensions through domination, dependency, resignation, or self-effacement.

_____. *The Neurotic Personality of Our Time.* New York: W. W. Norton, 1937. Outlines the manner in which culture influences personality difficulties and describes typical behavior problems that result from the exaggeration of cultural difficulties in one's life.

_____. *New Ways in Psychoanalysis.* New York: W. W. Norton, 1939. Describes major areas of agreement and disagreement with Freud, as well as important elements of her own theory; highly controversial when first published.

_____. *Our Inner Conflicts: A Constructive Theory of Neurosis.* New York: W. W. Norton, 1945. Identifies and describes, through rich detail and examples, the three neurotic trends of moving toward others, moving away from others, and moving against others; highly readable and a good introduction to Horney's main ideas.

_____. *Self-Analysis.* New York: W. W. Norton, 1942. Provides guidance for readers who may wish to engage in informal free association, self-discovery, and personal problem solving.

Quinn, Susan. *A Mind of Her Own: The Life of Karen Horney.* New York: Summit Books, 1987. Readable, honest, fascinating biography of Horney's life; provides insights into personal factors that influenced Horney's theoretical and clinical work.

Westkott, Marcia. *The Feminist Legacy of Karen Horney.* New Haven, Conn.: Yale University Press, 1986. This book integrates Karen Horney's earlier papers on the psychology of women with the more complete personality theory that emerged over time.

Carolyn Zerbe Enns

Cross-References

Antisocial Personality, 265; Borderline, Histrionic, and Narcissistic Personalities, 441; Ego Defense Mechanisms, 860; Individual Psychology: Alfred Adler, 1275; Psychoanalysis: Classical versus Modern, 1898; Psychoanalytic Psychology and Personality: Sigmund Freud, 1912; Psychology of Women: Karen Horney, 1950; Psychology of Women: Sigmund Freud, 1956; Self-Actualization, 2168; Social Psychological Models: Erich Fromm, 2318.

ALPHABETICAL LIST

CATEGORY LIST